PURE

JavaScript

Second Edition

R. Allen Wyke
Jason D. Gilliam
Charlton Ting
Sean Michaels

SAMS

201 West 103rd Street, Indianapolis, Indiana 46290

Pure JavaScript, Second Edition

Copyright © 2002 by Sams Publishing

International Standard Book Number: 0-672-32141-6

Library of Congress Catalog Card Number: 00-111512

Printed in the United States of America

First Printing: August 2001

04   03   02   01   4   3   2   1

Trademarks

All terms mentioned in this book that are known to be trademarks or service marks have been appropriately capitalized. Sams Publishing cannot attest to the accuracy of this information. Use of a term in this book should not be regarded as affecting the validity of any trademark or service mark.

Warning and Disclaimer

Every effort has been made to make this book as complete and as accurate as possible, but no warranty or fitness is implied. The information provided is on an "as is" basis. The author(s) and the publisher shall have neither liability nor responsibility to any person or entity with respect to any loss or damages arising from the information contained in this book or from the use of the CD or programs accompanying it.

ACQUISITIONS EDITOR
Shelley Johnston Markanday

DEVELOPMENT EDITOR
Jonathan Steever

MANAGING EDITOR
Charlotte Clapp

PROJECT EDITOR
Elizabeth Finney

COPY EDITOR
Rhonda Tinch-Mize

INDEXER
Sandra Henselmeier

PROOFREADERS
Antonio Reitz
Rebecca Martin
Debra Sexton

TECHNICAL EDITOR
Andrew Watt

TEAM COORDINATOR
Amy Patton

MEDIA DEVELOPER
Dan Scherf

INTERIOR DESIGNER
Karen Ruggles

COVER DESIGNER
Aren Howell

PAGE LAYOUT
Ayanna Lacey

Overview

Contents

PART II   PROGRAMMING IN JAVASCRIPT

CD-ROM ONLY CHAPTERS

10   DOM CORE   (CD-ROM) 1401

11 DOM HTML   (CD-ROM) 1477

12 DOM Events   (CD-ROM) 1729

14 JScript RunTime   (CD-ROM) 1821

About the Authors

R. Allen Wyke, of Durham, North Carolina is vice president of Research and Development at the eMarketing solutions company Engage, where he works with product managers, product marketing, and engineering to help ensure that their products have the proper vision and direction in both online and offline worlds. He has also developed intranet Web pages for a leading telecommunications and networking company, as well as worked on several Internet sites.

Wyke is the author of seven books on various Internet technologies including Perl, JavaScript, and PHP. In the past, he has also written the monthly *Webmaster* column for SunWorld, and a weekly article, "Integrating Windows and Unix," for ITworld.com.

Jason D. Gilliam is a software developer at ichat, Inc. At ichat, he develops Web-based chat and discussion group software using C++, JavaScript, HTML, and various other Internet technologies. In addition to his work at ichat, he has developed intranet Web pages and numerous C++ applications for a leading telecommunications company and has worked on several Internet sites for other organizations. Gilliam is also a contributing author to *JavaScript Unleashed, Third Edition*. He holds a bachelor's degree in Computer Engineering from North Carolina State University. Jason and his wife live in Cary, North Carolina.

Charlton Ting, of Vienna, Virginia is a software engineer for KOZ Inc who began programming in JavaScript with its first beta release. He has worked extensively with many Internet technologies while developing Internet telephony solutions at Lucent Technologies. His programming experience includes a variety of languages such as Java, C++, Smalltalk, Perl, HTML, XML, and Pascal. Ting holds degrees in Computer Engineering and Electrical Engineering from North Carolina State University.

Sean Michaels is a software engineer at Avesair, Inc. where he designs and implements next generation mobile commerce applications. He has been in the Internet space since 1994 and has a depth of experience in developing highly distributed fault tolerant applications. He has used Java, C++, and XML extensively over the years. Previously, he coauthored the *Official Netscape ONE* book and the *Official Netscape Technologies Developer Guide* from Netscape Press. Michaels holds a degree in Latin from Millsaps College in Jackson, MS and a degree in Computer Science from Mississippi College.

Dedications

This one is for my sisters: Sandra, Valerie, and Evelyn. They truly are inspirations in my life and have broadened my visions and provided support well beyond anything I would have ever imagined. I love each of you very much.

—R. Allen Wyke

I dedicate this book to my wonderful wife, Deena, who is the greatest! Your constant encouragement, love, and support has carried me through the writing of this book. I love you!

—Jason D. Gilliam

This book is dedicated to my family: John, Alice, Angela, Melissa, Olivia, and Tilly. Thank you for all your love and support for everything I've done in my life. I love you all very much.

—Charlton Ting

I would like to dedicate this book to my wife April and my two children Noah, and Anna, and to the memory of my father Alan Michaels without whose influence I would not be here today.

—Sean Michaels

Acknowledgments

R. Allen Wyke

On the publishing side, I would like to thank Bob Kern of TIPS Publishing and my coauthors, Jason and Chuck, for their professionalism, hard work, and overall support in the proposing and writing of this book. I would also like to thank Shelley Johnston-Markanday, who has been nothing short of an absolutely fabulous acquisitions editor, and Jon Steever, who developed the book and kept us focused. Additionally, I would like to thank everyone at Sams who worked on the book and helped make sure that was the best it could be.

I would also like to thank Dan Jaye for the professional opportunities he has allowed me to pursue at Engage, as well as the pressure to push the envelope a little more. And finally, I would like to thank the wonderful woman in my life, J, and the rest of the "Raccoons." It's never a dull moment around any of you.

Jason D. Gilliam

I would like to thank Bob Kern of TIPS Publishing and my coauthors, Allen and Chuck, for their efforts in developing and writing this book. I would also like to thank our acquisitions editor, Shelley Johnston-Markanday, and development editor, Jon Steever, for all their hard work as well as everyone at Sams who helped make this book a success.

I would also like to thank the "lunch guys" for their open ears and words of encouragement.

Charlton Ting

I would like to thank Bob Kern of TIPS Publishing for all his hard work in making this book possible. I also want to thank my coauthors, Allen and Jason, for all their hard work, dedication, and encouragement to bring this book together and make it such a great success. It's truly an honor to work with you guys. Additionally I would like to thank Shelley Johnston-Markanday, Scott Meyers, Jon Steever, and everyone at Sams who worked so hard at making this book so successful.

I also want to thank all my friends who have been there when I needed them: Mike, Carolyn, Monty, Theresa, Mitch, Sabrina, John O, Sunil "the Z Doc" Cherukuri, Blanke, Cosima, Nairn, Airmer Roberts, and anyone I may have forgotten to mention. You guys are the greatest friends anyone could have.

Sean Michaels

I would like to thank Bob Kern at TIPS Publishing for putting up with my antics during the authoring process. Also, the coauthors: Allen, Chuck, and Jason for giving me a solid foundation to work with and making the first edition of this book successful. I would also like to thank the folks at Sams Publishing: Shelley Johnston-Markanday, Scott Meyers, and Jon Steever for guiding the book through the process.

Tell Us What You Think!

As the reader of this book, *you* are our most important critic and commentator. We value your opinion and want to know what we're doing right, what we could do better, what areas you'd like to see us publish in, and any other words of wisdom you're willing to pass our way.

You can e-mail or write me directly to let me know what you did or didn't like about this book—as well as what we can do to make our books stronger.

Please note that I cannot help you with technical problems related to the topic of this book, and that due to the high volume of mail I receive, I might not be able to reply to every message.

When you write, please be sure to include this book's title and author as well as your name and phone or fax number. I will carefully review your comments and share them with the author and editors who worked on the book.

Fax: 317-581-4770

Email: webdev@samspublishing.com

Mail: Mark Taber
              Associate Publisher
              Sams Publishing
              201 West 103rd Street
              Indianapolis, IN 46290 USA

Introduction

Welcome to *Pure JavaScript, 2nd Edition*! This book has been written by JavaScript programmers for JavaScript programmers, and has been updated to cover the most current version of the language. It is your complete reference for developing, testing, and deploying JavaScript solutions in pages and on Web sites.

Pure JavaScript was not written to teach a person how to program, but rather to provide the details and semantics of the JavaScript language so programmers can exploit it as they see fit. JavaScript has evolved over the past few years and is reaching into new areas, especially in the most current browsers and server-side environments, most of which are addressed in this book. The book itself is broken into three main parts, including references on concepts, techniques, and syntax. Each represents a valuable step in learning and using the language.

Part I, "A Programmer's Overview of JavaScript," acts as a bridge for programmers who are currently programming in another language. It covers some programming techniques, such as the use of regular expressions, event handlers, exceptions, and even debugging. Many times programmers don't want to buy a beginners book on JavaScript because they do not need to know how to program, but rather they need specifics about the language. When they know these specifics and semantics, the syntax is easy. This section provides the necessary information for such a programming migration.

Part II, "Programming in JavaScript," shows you the advantages and strengths of JavaScript. It discusses some of the pros and cons of using the language on the client-side, server-side, and even within the Windows Script Host environment. Programmers will learn how to use JavaScript in real-world instances. They will be introduced to some of the browser issues as well as how to process Web information. In addition, programmers will be shown how to access Java functions within an applet and to use server-side JavaScript for Internet, intranet, or extranet development. After you have completed this section, you will be ready to move forward and start programming. This leads you into the last section of the book.

Part III, "JavaScript Reference," makes up the majority of the book and contains some of the most useful information for current JavaScript programmers—reference material organized by object. Each property, method, and event is discussed in detail under its associated object; and you'll see an example of its use. Each entry also shows the appropriate language version and environment (browser, server, and so on) support.

The section itself is broken into nine chapters. The first chapter covers the core JavaScript objects and syntax. The next chapter covers objects specific to the client-side, which is where JavaScript really has its roots. The third, fourth, fifth, and sixth chapter in this section outlines the various support for the Document Object Model (DOM) within JavaScript. The seventh chapter covers server-side JavaScript objects for the Netscape and iPlanet Enterprise servers, and the Active Server pages (ASP) environment present in Microsoft's IIS Web Servers. The second to last chapter in the section covers the JScript RunTime objects, and the final chapter covers Windows Script Host.

And that covers it! For new JavaScript programmers, welcome to the world of JavaScript. For those of you wanting a good, solid reference for your programming needs, we hope you find this book to be the most resourceful and current title on the shelves today!

R. Allen Wyke
Jason Gilliam
Charlton Ting
Sean Michaels

PART I

A PROGRAMMER'S OVERVIEW OF JAVASCRIPT

CHAPTER 1

What Is JavaScript to a Programmer?

In the beginning, there were Assembly and compiled languages. Later came scripting languages such as sed, awk, and Perl, which many programmers used to perform a variety of tasks. Followed by, in the late 80s and early 90s, the Internet, which exploded into a technological revolution that allowed anyone with a modem to communicate and retrieve information from around the world. As the Internet grew in number of users, it was obvious that an increase in functionality was needed in the browsers and the data they were rendering.

HTML, even with its advantages, was falling short of providing the control many developers wanted when creating Web pages and applications. This prompted the use of server-side programs, or scripts as they were often called, to handle some of the page dynamics developers needed from their sites.

These programs helped Web developers by allowing them to increase a site's functionality as well as process user-submitted information. However, *CGI*, or *common gateway interface*, scripts had to generate and return a response when the user sent incorrect or incomplete information. This led to the unnecessary back-and-forth transmission of data between browser and server. But, overall, it was a minor price to pay for the functionality it provided.

With time, and an increase in traffic, it became increasingly obvious that client-side intelligence was needed to offload some of the CGI functionality. Something was needed to perform this error checking and to decrease the amount of time a user spent connecting to a server to validate data. This would also enable the Web site to offload some of its processing load to the browser machine, which meant an increase in the overall performance of a site.

It was partially this lack of client-side functionality and efficiency that helped spawn a new scripting language—one that could be executed within a browser's environment and not on the server. This language could be used to perform client-side tasks such as form validation and dynamic page content creation—one that would put the programming into HTML publishing. Welcome to the birth of JavaScript.

Welcome to JavaScript

On December 4, 1995, Netscape and Sun jointly introduced JavaScript 1.0, originally called LiveScript, to the world. This language, unlike its server-based predecessors, could be interpreted within the then new Netscape Navigator 2 browsers. As an interpreted language, JavaScript was positioned as a complement to Java and would allow Web developers to create and deploy custom applications across the enterprise and Internet alike. JavaScript gave Web developers the power to truly program—not just format data with HTML.

In addition to the client-side control developers desired, Netscape implemented server-side JavaScript. This allowed developers to use the same programming language on the server as they did in their pages for browsers. Database connection enhancements were added to the language (called LiveWire), allowing the developer to pull information directly from a database and maintain user sessions for common functionality such as shopping carts. JavaScript had truly bridged the gap between the simple world of HTML and the more complex CGI programs on the server. It provided a common language for Web developers to design, implement, and deploy solutions across their networks and distributed the overall processing load of their applications.

The next level of acceptance in the world of JavaScript was Microsoft's implementation of the language in its Internet Explorer 3 browser—the implementation was called JScript. Similar to Netscape, Microsoft also implemented the language on the server-side (JScript 2.0) within its ASP (Active Server Pages) environment. It also allowed developers the flexibility of using a common language on both the client and server-side, while providing many of the robust features, such as object invocation and usage, in compiled languages.

JAVASCRIPT VERSUS JSCRIPT, AND WHAT IS ECMASCRIPT?

JScript 1.0 was based on the published documentation from Netscape, so essentially it is the same thing as JavaScript 1.0. However, there were a few "features" that Netscape did not publish, as well as some functionality that was not re-created by Microsoft correctly. The result of this is that there are some discrepancies between JScript 1.0 and JavaScript 1.0.

Since the release of these initial browsers, JavaScript and JScript were both submitted to the ECMA (European Computer Manufacturers Association) standardization body and have become the standard known as ECMAScript (ECMA-262). Because of this standardization, it is now considered that JavaScript is Netscape's implementation of ECMAScript while JScript is Microsoft's implementation.

The adoption of the first edition of ECMAScript occurred in June 1997 followed by its adoption by the International Organization for Standardization and International Electrotechnical Commission in April 1998 (ISO/IEC 16262). A second edition of the standard was approved by ECMA in June 1998, and a third edition was adopted in December 1999.

NOTE

Because Netscape's JavaScript was the foundation of all this, the book will refer to JavaScript, JScript, and ECMAScript simply as JavaScript except where a differentiation is needed.

So, what is JavaScript to the programmer? Well, in its purest form, it is an object-based, cross-platform, loosely-typed, multi-use language that allows a programmer to deploy many types of solutions to many clients. It not only involves adding functionality to Web pages as rendered within a browser, it also allows server-side processing for Netscape and Microsoft Web servers.

JScript has also been included in Microsoft's Windows Script Host (WSH), to allow programmers to write scripts to be executed on the operating system itself, and most recently as a major language under their .NET strategy (more on that later). When operating within the WSH environment, JScript is similar to the old DOS batch files, but gives programmers more functionality and versatility in what they can accomplish. This type of advancement has allowed the language to take hold in the computer world and continue to progress.

In addition to the benefits of these environments in which JavaScript can be executed, security measures are in place to protect end users against malicious code. Even though it is still young in terms of age, JavaScript is very mature and powerful. This functionality, ability, and versatility positions JavaScript as the best solution for many programmers.

Now that you've learned about what JavaScript is, you should dive a little deeper into what it means to a programmer. Being programmers ourselves, we know that a few strategically placed words do not make a language useful; so first, we'll look at the object-based characteristics of JavaScript.

Object-Based Technology

The fact that you are reading this reference somewhat implies that you have programmed in JavaScript or at least one other language before, even if only for one semester in college. Going one step further, I bet the language you programmed in was either C++, Java, or Perl—with each having various levels of object orientation (OO). Java specifically is OO by virtue of having all programmer created objects extend from core Java language classes or their own.

Object-Oriented Programming

For those of you unfamiliar with object-oriented programming (OOP), it is a concept that allows you to create reusable objects or classes in code. An object or class has associated with it various characteristics and functionality that defines what kind of properties and states it can take on. After these are created and defined, it is possible to create new instances—sometimes referred to as *children*—that inherit the capability to have the same characteristics of their *parent* object.

To give you an example of how this might work, let's create a vehicle object. Some of the characteristics assigned to this vehicle object are the number of doors, the color, and the type (such as sports car or truck). In addition to these characteristics, let's define the ability to move or stop the vehicle. The pseudo-code for this type of object might look something similar to the following:

```
object vehicle(){
  // Characteristics of the vehicle
  num_doors;
  color;
  type;

  // Methods used to move and stop the truck. Note that the move()
  // method takes a direction as an argument. This direction could
  // be something like forward, backward, left, or right.
  move(direction);
  stop();
}
```

Now that this vehicle object is defined, it is easy to create new instances of it. A vehicle that is a car with four doors and is red can be easily created. You could also create a vehicle that is a truck with two doors and is black. The possibilities are endless.

In addition to creating these instances of the vehicle object, you have also made it possible to program in the ability to change the state of your instance. This is accomplished by specifying whether it is stopped or moving. Again, this method of programming can make the possibilities endless and certainly reusable.

Here is another example in pseudo-code to illustrate this concept. The sample creates a black, two-door truck that is moving forward:

```
// Create the new instance of the vehicle
myTruck = new vehicle();

// Define the type, number of doors and color
myTruck.doors = 2;
myTruck.color = "black";
myTruck.type = "truck";

// Define the "state" of the truck
myTruck.move(forward);
```

The basic process here is to create an instance of the vehicle object and then to assign characteristic values to it. It is these values that make it a unique instance of this object, which we have specified as a truck.

The existence of the vehicle object itself allows us to easily create more vehicles with different characteristics. When programming, this "ease" translates into less code—something all programmers like to hear.

Now that this object is defined, it is possible to create new instances that inherit its characteristics without having to redefine them. You are able to capitalize on any over-laps in characteristics within objects by doing this. The idea is to create a general, mas-ter object that gives you the ability to then derive child instances that provide all the functionality and characteristics you need.

We can take this a step further by creating new objects—not instances—that inherit the parent objects' characteristics. Doing so allows us to derive child instances from the child object that we have decided will inherit only certain characteristics. We could define a child object to only pass on the parent object's color characteristic to any child instances of its own. It is the concept of this object orientation that allows you to per-form this modular type of programming.

The following pseudo-code example shows how we could create an `airplane` object based on the previous `vehicle` object:

```
// Create the new object that inherits the vehicle
object airplane(){

  // Inherit the vehicle object
  this = new vehicle();

  // Define the doors property, then assign it to the size
  // property of the plane object, which makes the most sense
  this.doors = "747";
  this.size = this.doors;

  // Assign the color and type of plane
  this.color = "silver";
  this.type = "American Airlines";

  // Define the "state" of the plane
  this.move(up);

  // Now that the object is created with the values, return the
  // object.
  return this;
}
```

Not all languages support this concept, and there are other languages only based on its concepts. This concept definitely supplies advantages to the language, but it is not required to write good, effective, modular code. JavaScript is a perfect example of how a language has applied some of these concepts, but is not completely OO. It does this by being *object based*.

> **NOTE**
>
> Talking about OOP in further detail is beyond the focus of a JavaScript book, but it is worth some investigation if you are a real programming enthusiast. Check out your local bookstore for a selection of titles on this subject. You can also visit Object Central (`http://www.objectcentral.com`) on the Web for reference and links to OOP information.

So how does object-based programming fit into the equation? It is very similar to OO except that it does not have all the functionality or characteristics. There are limited amounts of inheritance, scope, and functionality that you can perform with an object-based language. This should not be taken as mark against JavaScript, because it makes the language easier to learn and maintain for the developer. OOP is no easy beast to tackle and will provide many headaches before it is implemented correctly.

JavaScript also makes up for many of its OO limitations by allowing you to create your own object-like elements, as well as extend the core objects in the language by proto-typing new properties. To get an idea of how this is done, take a look at JavaScript object orientation.

Object Orientation of JavaScript

Before we go into a lot of detail on the object orientation of JavaScript, let's outline the details of the core components as well as between server-side and client-side objects. Both sets of objects are specific to their runtime environment, so default object initialization and creation occur at different times. Because of this characteristic, you will look at the language in several parts:

- Core
- Client-side
- Server-side
- JScript-specific
- Windows Script Host

Core

First and foremost, it is important for you to know and understand the core objects in the JavaScript language. These objects are generally found across all implementations and are defined in the ECMAScript standard. These objects lay the foundation for the shared functionality, such as mathematical, array, or date related, which are used in most all scripts. Figure 1.1 shows a list of these core objects.

As you can see, the core objects are Array, Boolean, Date, Function, Global, Math, Number, Object, RegExp, Error, and String. In addition to these objects, both Netscape and Microsoft have created objects specific to their core implementations. These are not specific to any environment, and are therefore core objects in the sense of their consistency. Figure 1.2 shows these objects.

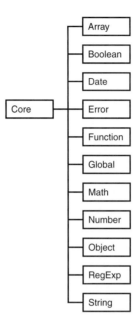

Figure 1.1

Core ECMAScript object hierarchy.

Client-Side

Client-side JavaScript is, at its lowest level, a set of objects created when a page is loaded in the browser. In addition, there are also objects that revolve around the browser loading the page and other derived objects that are created when certain tags are contained on a page. These derived objects inherit some of the various characteristics of their parent object and also allow scripting access to the HTML tag's properties.

Understanding the hierarchy of the JavaScript objects is essential if you plan on doing any in-depth programming. You will get a better understanding of how parent and child objects interact as well as how they are referenced. To help with this understanding, Figure 1.3 gives a graphical representation of the basic client-side JavaScript hierarchy.

As depicted in this diagram, all client-side objects are derived from either the `Window` or `navigator` objects. Considering that this is an object-based language, this structure makes complete sense. All objects on a given page are constructed within the browser's displaying window, hence all these objects are descendants of the `Window` object. By using the `Window` object, a programmer is allowed to access the various frames, documents, layers, and forms on a page, as well as many other objects and properties.

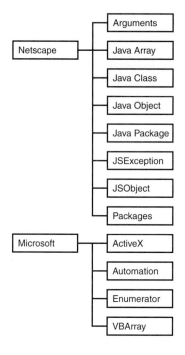

Figure 1.2

Core object hierarchy for Microsoft and Netscape environments.

The `navigator` object pertains to elements that are part of the browser itself. This specifically refers to the plug-ins installed and the *MIME (Multipart Internet Mail Extension)* types with which the browser is associated. Using the `navigator` object allows checking of the browser version, determining the plug-ins installed, and what programs are associated with the various MIME types registered on the system. There is also the ability to access other properties of the browser.

In addition to these client-side objects, browsers starting with Internet Explorer 5 and Netscape 6 have implemented features to support the *Document Object Model (DOM)*. The DOM is a method in which documents can be referenced. We talk more about the DOM in Chapter 4, "Client-Side Scripting," but wanted to include Figure 1.4 to show you the objects that make up this model.

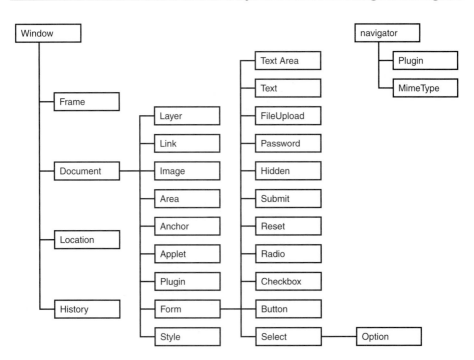

Figure 1.3

Client-side JavaScript object hierarchy.

Server-Side

Similar to client-side, server-side JavaScript has several objects from which all other objects are derived. The root objects are the `DbPool` and `database` objects, for the Netscape and iPlanet implementations, from which you can create connections to a database, as well as access cursors, stored procedures, and the resultsets you generate. Within the Microsoft ASP environment, you have access to several other objects, such as `Response`, `Session`, and `Request`. Figure 1.5 shows the server-side objecthierarchy.

> **NOTE**
>
> Programmers familiar with Java will find this very similar to the Java language. There are not as many objects/classes in the JavaScript language, but the structure and manner in which you access them are similar.

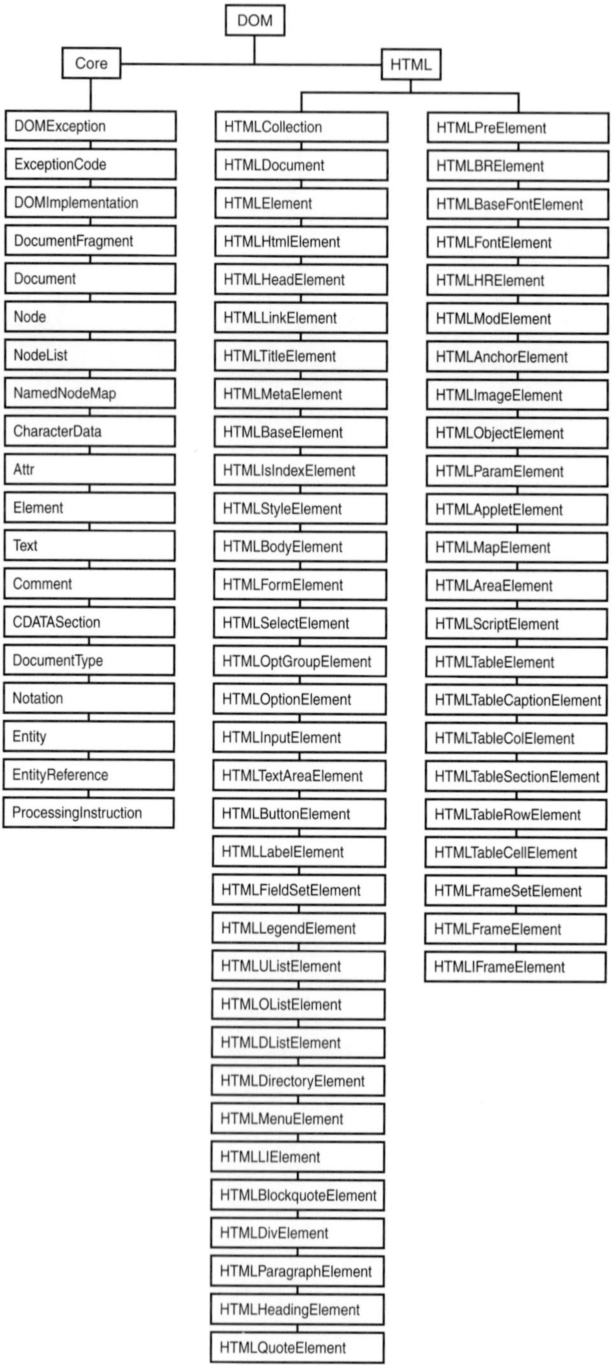

```
                                    ┌───────┐
                                    │  DOM  │
                                    └───┬───┘
              ┌─────────┐          ┌────┴────┐
              │  Core   │          │  HTML   │
              └────┬────┘          └────┬────┘
```

Core	HTML	
DOMException	HTMLCollection	HTMLPreElement
ExceptionCode	HTMLDocument	HTMLBRElement
DOMImplementation	HTMLElement	HTMLBaseFontElement
DocumentFragment	HTMLHtmlElement	HTMLFontElement
Document	HTMLHeadElement	HTMLHRElement
Node	HTMLLinkElement	HTMLModElement
NodeList	HTMLTitleElement	HTMLAnchorElement
NamedNodeMap	HTMLMetaElement	HTMLImageElement
CharacterData	HTMLBaseElement	HTMLObjectElement
Attr	HTMLIsIndexElement	HTMLParamElement
Element	HTMLStyleElement	HTMLAppletElement
Text	HTMLBodyElement	HTMLMapElement
Comment	HTMLFormElement	HTMLAreaElement
CDATASection	HTMLSelectElement	HTMLScriptElement
DocumentType	HTMLOptGroupElement	HTMLTableElement
Notation	HTMLOptionElement	HTMLTableCaptionElement
Entity	HTMLInputElement	HTMLTableColElement
EntityReference	HTMLTextAreaElement	HTMLTableSectionElement
ProcessingInstruction	HTMLButtonElement	HTMLTableRowElement
	HTMLLabelElement	HTMLTableCellElement
	HTMLFieldSetElement	HTMLFrameSetElement
	HTMLLegendElement	HTMLFrameElement
	HTMLUListElement	HTMLIFrameElement
	HTMLOListElement	
	HTMLDListElement	
	HTMLDirectoryElement	
	HTMLMenuElement	
	HTMLLIElement	
	HTMLBlockquoteElement	
	HTMLDivElement	
	HTMLParagraphElement	
	HTMLHeadingElement	
	HTMLQuoteElement	

Figure 1.4

DOM object hierarchy.

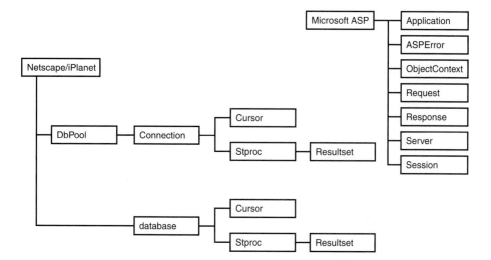

Figure 1.5

Server-side object hierarchy.

JScript Runtime

As with about every other language that Microsoft has put its hands on, its JScript implementation contains objects that are specific to their runtime environment. Because their JScript engine is used within several of their applications and is a very important part of their .NET initiative, you will notice that many of the additional objects are familiar if you have ever worked with COM. Figure 1.6 illustrates the objects that are specific to the JScript implementation.

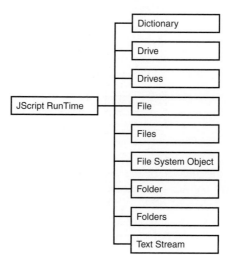

Figure 1.6

JScript RunTime object hierarchy.

Windows Script Host

In addition to the JScript-specific objects, Microsoft has also implemented objects that are part of its Windows Script Host environment. These objects, and associated code, are often used by administrators to perform everyday tasks previously done with batch files. The Windows Script Host, however, is much more powerful than the batch files of yesterday, and should be seriously considered for your administrative tasks. Figure 1.7 outlines the object hierarchy of the Windows Script Hostobjects.

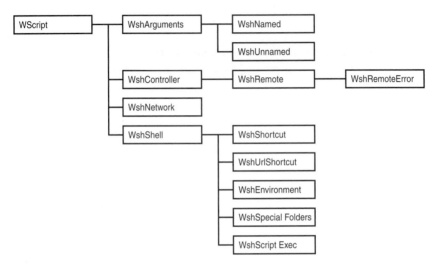

Figure 1.7

Windows Script Host object hierarchy.

Object Access

Because of this object hierarchy, accessing the various objects and elements on a page is accomplished by using the hierarchy itself. If you wanted to access a specific text field in a form on a page, you would do so using the following syntax:

```
window.document.formName.textboxName.value
```

TIP

With JavaScript, programmers have the ability to create their own objects or extend the core ones defined by the language. The explanation of how to create your own objects—and some examples—is covered in the section on functions in Chapter 2, "Details of the Language." If you want to learn more about extending the functionality of the existing objects, look up objects with the *prototype* property in the reference section of this book.

Because JavaScript is object based, it automatically provides many advantages to using a modular approach to your programming. By creating your own objects and methods, you are able to better maintain the code with which you are working. You will be creating code that can be reused in other programs, locations, and instances. Why write virtually the same code twice (or many times), when you can create it once and pass the characteristics that differentiate it from other, similar objects?

Modular Programming

To program in a modular fashion in JavaScript really involves three key things. Using these items in your programming will allow you to create code that can be reused from project to project. These are

- Creating your own objects
- Defining general functions to handle common tasks
- Placing reusable code in external JavaScript source files (commonly `*.js` files)

NOTE

As with any other language, remember that good comments within your code and documentation are often the most beneficial aspects of programming.

Because creating your own objects is discussed in Chapter 2, let's take a look at defining functions to handle common tasks. As with other programming languages, there are instances in which you have to perform certain processes over and over. Many times this might involve a different value of parameters passed, but the processes you go through are the same.

As an example, think of verifying a date entered by a user. This user is supposed to enter the month, date, and year in a form that will be submitted to your Web server for further processing. One of the concerns of the programmer is that he needs to have the date in a MM/DD/YYYY format, where the month and date need to be two characters and the year should be four.

To accomplish this task, you can create a single function that prepends a 0 in front of any single digit passed. This function could simply check to see if the value passed was less than the number 10, and, if so, it would perform the prepend. By defining this process in a function, a programmer will be able to use the same function for both the month and date verification. This avoids the trouble of writing a function for each. Even though this is a simple example, it illustrates the benefits of function and code reuse.

Programmers can also modularize their programming techniques by including their code in external JavaScript source files. This allows them to write code once, store it in a single location, and include it on many pages by simply referencing the location of the source file. If the function needs to change, they only have to change it in a single file and not every file that uses it. It is simple things such as these that save Web programmers hours or days of work time.

TIP

> Do you serve ads on your Web site? If so, you might want to consider placing your ad tags in an external JavaScript source file. This will allow you to change the tags across your entire site if need be. There might be some browser issues with older versions, so if you make this decision, be sure you at least cover the browsers you wish to support.

Security

One of the biggest issues facing Internet development today is security. It is not possible to successfully develop any kind of application, whether it's Web based or based on the Web, and not have to implement some kind of security features. A program's security measures can ultimately determine how valuable the overall application is to a user. If the code can be tampered with or is subject to destruction from another program, the program will be subject to scrutiny and denial of use.

Because JavaScript is interpreted most often within a browser's environment, a user can be subject to malicious code. Browser's run off the operating system itself, meaning that it has access to a user's file system. This makes it feasible that a JavaScript program could take advantage of a hole in the browser's security measures to access the file system. After a programmer has accomplished this, many things are possible—even access to private documents or the ability to delete them altogether. This leaves a user at the mercy of a hacker.

Providing security for JavaScript scripts is actually twofold. One is that of responsibility, which lies with the programmer. A programmer must ensure that the script the user executes is not malicious. The second responsibility falls to the users themselves. Users should make the ultimate decision whether to run a script on their systems—this is something that must be implemented in the browser's functionality.

Because of these potentially destructive situations, there are various levels of security that users and programmers can rely on when programming in JavaScript. As discussed, some are the responsibility of the programmer, whereas others involve measures put in place by the browser that allow the user to control what is executed on his system.

What Security Measures Are in Place?

When JavaScript 1.0 was released in the Navigator 2.0, Internet Explorer 3.0 (JScript 1.0), and Opera 3.0 browsers, the only real security layer was that of a user having the ability to turn JavaScript on or off. The browser itself controlled the runtime environment for the language and any security measures it had in place.

In this model, when JavaScript was enabled, it was up to the browser to protect the user from any harmful code. Originally, this seemed like a thorough plan for implementing security. *Leave it to the experts to protect the users.* However, where there is a will there is a way, and the first misuses of JavaScript began to surface.

One of the first items that seemed to be a potential problem occurred when frames were used on a Web site. Because frames load separate documents in each of the predefined areas, it is possible to load documents from several different domains and servers to make up the content displayed to the user. The problem arose when a document's JavaScript variables from one server were available for examination and modification on another. But this was only the start of the potential security holes that would follow.

To help protect users from the frame problem, Navigator 2, Internet Explorer 3, and Opera 3 implemented the *Same Origin Policy*. This policy prevented JavaScript code sent from one server from accessing properties of a document sent from another server, port, or protocol and returning that information to its original server.

Obviously, this policy does not affect all the elements of a given document, but it does include a core set. At the time of this printing, the document properties that must pass this origin check are in Table 1.1.

Table 1.1   **Document Objects That Must Pass Origin Verification**

Object	Property/Method
`document`	Read/Write: `anchors`, `applets`, `cookie`, `domain`, `elements`, `embeds`, `forms`, `lastModified`, `length`, `links`, `referrer`, `title`, `URL`, each form instance, each Java class available to JavaScript via LiveConnect Write: all other
`image`	`lowsrc`, `src`
`layer`	`src`
`location`	all except `location.X` and `location.Y`
`window`	`find`

Because it might be desirable for a script to access variables located on a page served from another server within the same domain, there is an exception to this security model. By definition, it would not be possible to access and upload document properties in a frame served from `http://myscripts.purejavascript.com` from another frame that was delivered from `http://mydocs.purejavascript.com`. Even though the domain is the same, the complete URL is not.

To get around this minor situation, programmers can set the `document.domain` property to the suffix of the current domain. This will allow them to access JavaScript properties on pages served from other servers within their domain. Following the example in the last paragraph, using the following line in the code can enable this feature:

```
document.domain = "purejavascript.com";
```

Setting this property will allow you to access the other *sub-domains* within your domain.

Data Tainting

When JavaScript 1.1 was released in Navigator 3.0, Netscape furthered its security implementation by using what is referred to as *data tainting*. In addition to the security model in the first generation JavaScript browsers, data tainting allowed the user and programmer to specify if they wanted scripts to access properties in other documents from other servers. When data tainting is not enabled, which is the default, the user will get a message saying that accessing document properties from other servers is not allowed.

NOTE

Data tainting was only implemented in JavaScript 1.1, and because the majority of users are now using browsers that support language versions higher than this, it is recommended not to use this security approach. However, this section is relative to understand some of the history of security within JavaScript, as well as answer some questions for anyone having to create code for Navigator 3 browsers.

Users can enable tainting if they want scripts on a page to have global access to other scripts and document properties. This is a security risk, but might be necessary within an enterprise environment in which other security measures are in place. To enable data tainting, environment variables must be set for the browser running the scripts. Table 1.2 shows how this can be accomplished on the various operating systems.

Table 1.2   How to Enable Data Tainting for Your Navigator Browser

Operating System	Environment Variable	Notes
Windows	`NS_ENABLE_TAINT=1`	Set this in the `autoexec.bat` for all Windows systems.
UNIX	`NS_ENABLE_TAINT=1`	Depending on which shell you are in, you will use some form of `set` `env` or `env` to set this variable.
Macintosh	Remove the two ASCII slash (`//`) comments before the `NS_ENABLE_TAINT`	This can be found by editing the resource with type `Envi` and number `128` in the Navigator application itself. It should be near the end.
OS/2	`NS_ENABLE_TAINT=1`	Set this in the `config.sys`.

After this variable is set, a number of document properties are affected. Table 1.3 shows a list of the document objects that are tainted by default.

Table 1.3   Document Objects That Are Tainted by Default

Object	Tainted Property
document	cookie, domain, forms, lastModified, links, referrer, title, URL
Form	action, name
each Form instance	checked, defaultChecked, defaultValue, name, selected, selectedIndex, text, toString, value
history	current, next, previous, toString
image	name
Link	hash, host, hostname, href, pathname, port, protocol, search, toString
location	hash, host, hostname, href, pathname, port, protocol, search, toString
Option	defaultSelected, selected, text, value
Plugin	name
window	defaultStatus, > name, status

TIP

As a programmer, you can test to see if the Navigator 3 user has tainting enabled by using the `navigator.taintEnabled()` method. See this entry in Chapter 8, "Client-Side" for an example of using this method.

In addition to the user having the ability to specify how he wants to handle tainting, a programmer can specify, or *taint*, objects or information that cannot be passed from one script to the next without the user's permission. When this occurs, the browser will pop up a dialog box that allows the user to decide whether the information can be passed.

NOTE

For more information on data tainting, see the Client-Side JavaScript Guide on Netscape's DevEdge (`http://developer.netscape.com`) site. There is an entire section ("Using Data Tainting in JavaScript 1.1") in the "JavaScript Security" chapter devoted to security and the concepts of data tainting.

Because data tainting did not provide the true security model JavaScript needed, Netscape deprecated its functionality in JavaScript 1.2 and replaced it with Signed Scripts. This is the current and most complete model that has been implemented, and should be used by JavaScript developer's moving forward.

Signed Scripts

Signed scripts allow a programmer the ability to gain access, after user authorization, to restricted information. This model, which was based on the signed objects model in

Java, uses LiveConnect and the Java Capabilities API to execute its functionality. Using this model gives programmers very defined control over what they can and cannot do on a user's machine.

TIP

> More information on the Java Capabilities API can be found on Netscape's DevEdge site at `http://developer.netscape.com/docs/manuals/ signedobj/capabilities`.

When using this model, you have the ability to sign external JavaScript source files (called through the `src` attribute of the `<script>` tag), event handlers, and code that is included inline on the page. The actual signing of these scripts is implemented by using Netscape's Page Signer tool, which is available at `http://developer.netscape.com`.

This Page Signer tool allows you to build a JAR (Java Archive) file that includes the programmer's security certificate and code. When the browser encounters a `<script>` tag that has an `archive` attribute set, it will go through the proper verification process before the script is executed. This process involves popping up a Java Security dialog box that gives the user the ability to grant or deny the rights to the script. The following is an example of syntax used on a page that includes a signed script:

```
<script src="myScripts.js" archive="sample.jar"></script>
```

If the code is inline, the JAR file will contain only the programmer's certificate. Calling the appropriate JAR file would then resemble the following, which does not have the `src` attribute, and it would have the code between the beginning and ending `<script>` tags.

```
<script archive="sample.jar" id="purejs">
// Your code here
</script>
```

Even though signed scripts are based on a Java model, there are enough differences in the languages that make it a bit harder to secure JavaScript code. Unlike JavaScript, a Java programmer can protect, make private, or make final variables and methods in their code. This inherently protects them from hackers because these elements cannot be accessed or changed—the Java language defines them as such.

Some expanded privileges can be accessed through the `netscape.security.PrivilegeManager.enablePrivilege()` method, which gives more control in scripting. This Java method allows a programmer to try to enable one of a set of privileges by asking the user to accept or reject his access. As with other signed scripts, this will prompt the user to grant or deny a programmer's request. The following list shows the privileges that a programmer can attempt to access for these purposes:

- `UniversalBrowserAccess`—Allows both reading and writing of privileged data in browser.

- `UniversalBrowserRead`—Allows the reading of privileged data in browser. This is required when using an `about:` (but not `about:blank`), getting any property of the `history` object, or getting the value of the data property of a `DragDrop` event within your scripts.
- `UniversalBrowserWrite`—Allows the writing of privileged data in browser. This is required when setting any property of an `event` object, adding or removing any of the browser's bars (location, menu, status, and so on), as well as using several of the methods and setting some of the properties of the `Window` object within your scripts.
- `UniversalFileRead`—Allows the script to read files on the file system of the machine on which it is running. This is required when using a file upload within your scripts.
- `UniversalPreferencesRead`—Allows the script to read browser preference settings.
- `UniversalPreferencesWrite`—Allows the script to write browser preference settings.
- `UniversalSendMail`—Allows the script to send mail under the user's name. This is required when using a `news:` or `mailto:` within your scripts.

JavaScript has quite an extensive list of security measures in place that can be used by the programmer. However, a programmer should use the security measures in a manner that maximizes his effectiveness. If this is not done, the scripts are subject to hacking.

Now that you have an understanding of the security measures in place for JavaScript, take a look at some of the overall advantages of using the language as a means of deploying solutions on the Internet or within an enterprise.

Advantages of JavaScript

Up to this point, you might not have seen any big reasons where and why JavaScript can help you. It is object based, can be interpreted within a browser, and there are security measures in place—but the same can be said for Java. Now that browsers support plug-ins and ActiveX controls, it is possible to design client-side functionality with more common languages such as C++ or Visual Basic. So what does JavaScript really give you?

For starters, it is platform independent. This is a major advantage over ActiveX controls and plug-ins because they have to be recompiled and potentially rewritten for the various platforms out there today. Previous versions of Navigator and the new Netscape 6, for example, run on many different platforms, and even though most of these are various flavors of Unix, at its core, you would still have to build a control or plug-in for Windows 16- and 32-bit systems, MacOS, Unix, BeOS, OS/2, and the list goes on. Also note that flavors of Unix and Linux can run on several types of processors (MIPS, Intel, PowerPC, and so on), and Windows NT runs on Intel and Alpha machines. This becomes quite an extensive list of components to maintain if you develop in a platform-dependant language.

Another advantage of JavaScript is that both Netscape and Microsoft Web servers have built-in interpreters. Both of these companies have implemented this in a different fashion, but, as a Web developer, you still have the ability to use the same language on the server-side that you do on the client-side. The only real competitor to JavaScript in this aspect is Java with its Java applet and servlet technology.

Platform Independence

Platform independence is probably the number one reason to use JavaScript within your applications. True, some environments interpret JavaScript a bit differently, but the majority of the language is processed the same. The code is interpreted so that you can write it once and let the execution environment interpret it.

This is a simple concept, but can be a big factor in deciding how to implement an application solution. As a programmer, you do not want to have to modify code to work on different operating systems or recompile for different microprocessors. You want to write the code once and be done with it. You want to be able to make changes easily and quickly without having to recompile 10 or 15 times. Let's face it; you want and need JavaScript.

Client-Side and Server-Side Versatility

The majority of the discussion so far has focused on using JavaScript on the client-side. Even with its initial release, JavaScript has also been implemented on the server-side within the Netscape/iPlanet and Microsoft Web servers. This server-side code contains many of the same objects and methods as the client-side, but it also has objects specific to the server environment—objects that allow you to connect to, query, and get results from a database. All this information is collected and processed before the server sends the page back to the requesting browser.

By providing this scripting capability on the server, a programmer can now use the language to dynamically build pages based on the execution of the server-side scripts it contains. Server-side JavaScript also can be used to maintain state for users as they move through a site. This maintaining of state is often implemented as a shopping cart on commercial sites. As users shop on a given site, server-side JavaScript can be used to track them and keep selected items in their carts.

Microsoft has also implemented a type of server-side JScript within its *Internet Information Server (IIS)*. Its implementation is used in *Active Server Pages (ASP)*, where the ASP filter parses a site's pages before they are sent back to the requesting browser. JScript is also a very important language within Microsoft's .NET initiative, where developers can use the language to create Web services that operate much the same as COM objects, but across the Internet. As with Netscape's implementation, this allows a Web developer to dynamically build the content of a page before it is sent back to the browser.

NOTE

Remember that JScript is Microsoft's equivalent to JavaScript.

Because of the functionality of these pages, ASP has given developers the ability to use JScript to call server-side components (such as ActiveX controls), pass the necessary parameters, and write the results to the screen. This allows a Web site to modularize all the functionality of building pages with individual components that are responsible for their specific tasks. JScript is used to handle the requests and results to and from these modules, and then write the results to the page.

When to Use JavaScript

One of the most important things to know about JavaScript is when to use it. Even though it provides much needed functionality in many scenarios, often it is simply not needed. One reason is the fact that JavaScript is not always interpreted the same or correctly—an important point to remember.

As a programmer, you should be able to write code, no matter how simple or complex, that will be executed correctly. However, there are browsers that have bugs that prevent JavaScript from working the way it was programmed. Before programming in JavaScript, you should first try to understand any documented bugs that exist. Doing so can save you hours of debugging in the long run. You can often find these bug lists on the Web, so check out our resource section toward the end of this chapter to get started.

Try to determine if you really need to use JavaScript on a given page as well. Ask yourself whether you are using it to add functionality to the page or just to make its appearance better. JavaScript can do a lot of neat things to a Web page, but, if it causes your page to break in certain browsers, you should avoid using it. A fine line exists between what you gain in functionality and what you expose as problems, so be sure to test your code with as many browsers and platforms as possible.

Depending on programmers' objectives when using JavaScript, they might be able to impose browser requirements. If they have stated that their pages only work in browsers later than Netscape 6 and Internet Explorer 5, it is safe for them to use JavaScript 1.3 or lower for their scripting needs. This immediately eliminates them from having to support older browsers, which can save many lines of code. Developers might not be able to impose these restrictions on a Web site, but it is likely that they can on Web-based applications.

Overall, programmers should be smart about using the language. They need to evaluate what their objectives are and who their audience is. When these requirements are defined, they can reverse engineer the project to determine what code they need to write. This is often a much easier approach than starting with an idea and trying to make it work in all circumstances.

Now that you've taken a quick look at some of the general issues to analyze before using JavaScript, take a look at what you can do with it. The following sections contain some of the common uses of the language, as as some more complex and specific uses.

Web Page Enhancements

Web page enhancements were the first real use of JavaScript. Any of you who have been working with the Internet since the release of Netscape Navigator 2 probably remember those annoying scrolling messages in the status bar of the browser window. This was one of the first enhancements done using JavaScript. Even though it became annoying, it definitely caught the eye of users.

Another popular item JavaScript is used for is writing the current date and time to a page. Some sites write the date and time the document was last modified, whereas others write the current date and time. This is widely used on sites that are news related in which the date of the document is very important to readers.

TIP

> Writing the date and time to a page is a perfect item to modularize. If the code is written as a function, it can be included easily on all your pages and called when needed. If you are using some kind of browser intelligence on the server side, it is possible to include this function based on the browser that is requesting the page. If it can interpret JavaScript, make it part of the page. If it cannot, do not include it.

A final example of using JavaScript to enhance Web pages is to produce rollover buttons. This usually occurs on pages in which the linked images change when a user rolls over them. It is also possible to program in a down state when a user clicks and holds their mouse button down on the image. Even though this is a simple enhancement, it makes a page look and feel more professional. This effect allows a Web site to give the user the same experience as using his favorite application, be it a Web browser, a word processor, or a money manager.

These three implementations of JavaScript to enhance Web pages are pretty simple, but are by no means the limit of what can be done. Many sites have used JavaScript for advertisements, pop-up navigation windows, page redirects, and validating forms. Because the language is executed within the browser's environment and is often used to complement HTML publishing, there is virtually no limit to what can be done.

TIP

> If you want to use JavaScript to enhance your Web pages, don't make the mistake of trying to think of something cool you can do with the language. You should try to reverse engineer it. Think of something cool for your site, and then figure out how to implement it in JavaScript.

Interactive E-Mail

Interactive e-mail is something that has come about within e-mail applications. It wasn't long ago that many of these programs were only able to read text e-mails. These programs now have the capability to render HTML e-mail within their interface, which extends the formatting options a user can exploit. This not only improves the look and feel of the e-mail, but it also improves the readability of it. If a user wants something in italic, you can put it in italic.

Because HTML e-mail has become widely used in the Internet community, more and more e-mail applications are supporting it. In addition to HTML, Netscape and Microsoft's most recent e-mail applications support JavaScript within the body of an e-mail message (assuming that the user has it enabled). This makes it possible for a user to send HTML e-mails containing JavaScript that is interpreted when the recipient reads the message.

As a programmer, you need to keep in mind that an e-mail application is not a browser. Users are very particular about what they experience in their messages, and overuse of JavaScript could lead to annoying your recipients. JavaScript should be used sparingly in e-mails. It should be reserved for simple page enhancements such as image and link rollovers or calling ads within your message. Anything beyond this could cause problems when the application interprets your scripts.

Web-Based Applications

Web-based applications are probably the most useful instances of JavaScript. They allow a programmer to set user browser requirements, which in turn gives them a head start on the version of JavaScript they have at their disposal. This also results in limited exposure to browser bugs because programmers can define which browsers they support.

One of the most common uses of JavaScript within Web-based applications seems to be in controlling forms on a page. This can be anything from checking a user's values before submission to dynamically adjusting the values based on user-selected data. By implementing JavaScript at this level, a programmer is able to reduce the amount of user error when submitting forms. No more invalid credit card numbers because one digit too many was entered. No more usernames and passwords submitted as e-mail addresses, and no more incomplete forms.

JavaScript is also used in more full-blown Web-based applications. These applications are not necessarily for the common Internet user to experience, but rather are interfaces to enterprise level applications a company might have purchased. Some of the more common applications are used for reporting or ad delivery and management. Because the content on the application's pages is dynamic and always changing, a developer usually interfaces the application with a database or system process to build the pages on-the-fly. Using JavaScript allows developers to verify items before requests are made, as well as add an appealing look and feel to the application.

Windows Scripting

Microsoft's Windows Script Host comes with Windows 98, including Windows 2000, and can be installed in Windows 95 and NT 4 systems. This scripting host is language independent for ActiveX scripting on Windows 32-bit systems. *Language independent* means that a variety of programming languages can be used in conjunction with the host. The reason it's mentioned in this book is that it natively supports JScript—Microsoft's implementation of ECMAScript.

NOTE

In addition to the JScript language, this scripting host also supports Visual Basic Script (VBScript) as well as other third-party languages such as Perl, REXX, TCL, and Python.

Using JScript in the scripting host allows an administrator or user to create scripts that perform various tasks on the operating system. These can be as simple as logon scripts or can be used to call ActiveX controls to perform more complex tasks. If you work in the Microsoft Windows environment, you will find this implementation of JScript can be very helpful.

TIP

For more information on the Windows Script Host, check out Microsoft's Developer Network site at `http://msdn.microsoft.com/scripting` and click the link to Windows Script Host.

JavaScript Resources

When you program a lot in a particular language, especially one that's Internet related, you come across many resources. Additionally, when you program a lot in a particular language, especially one that's Internet related, you need many resources. So to conclude this introductory chapter, we have included some resources for you. There's everything from general information to core documentation and references to newsgroups—all on the JavaScript language and all online.

General Information

One of the most important types of resources in any given language is the general resource. Even if a book carries comprehensive coverage of a topic, it might not have conveyed the subject matter in a form that you understood. For this reason, you might want to study the same topic from a different person's perspective. Table 1.4 lists some resources that will allow you to do this.

Table 1.4   *General Resources*

Resource	URL
About.com Focus on JavaScript	`http://javascript.about.com/compute/javascript/mbody.htm`
DevEdge Online	`http://developer.netscape.com/tech/javascript/index.html`
Danny Goodman's JavaScript Pages	`http://www.dannyg.com/javascript`

Resource	URL
JavaScript.com	`http://www.javascript.com`
Developer.com	`http://developer.earthweb.com/dlink.`
	`index-jhtml.72.1313.-.0.jhtml`
Doc JavaScript	`http://www.webreference.com/js`
The JavaScript	`http://www.starlingtech.com/books/`
Workshop	`javascript`
JavaScript World	`http://www.jsworld.com`
Java/JavaScript	`http://www.dezines.com/dezines/`
Resources on the	`javalinks.html`
Internet	
Microsoft Developer's	`http://msdn.microsoft.com/scripting`
Network	
Timothy's JavaScript	`http://www.essex1.com/people/timothy/`
Examples	`js-index.htm`
Using JavaScript and	`http://www.javaworld.com/javaworld/`
Graphics	`jw-08-1996/jw-08-javascript.html`
Using JavaScript's	`http://www.javaworld.com/javaworld/`
Built-In Objects	`jw-05-1996/jw-05-javascript.html`
Voodoo's Introduction	`http://rummelplatz.uni-mannheim.de/`
to JavaScript	`~skoch/js/script.htm`
WebCoder.COM	`http://webcoder.com`
Yahoo! Computers and	`http://dir.yahoo.com/computers_and_`
Internet, Programming	`internet/programming_languages/`
Languages, JavaScript	`javascript`
Open Directory Top,	`http://dmoz.org/Computers/`
Computers, Programming,	`Programming/Languages/JavaScript`
Languages, JavaScript	

Reference

Another important resource for any programmer is true reference documentation. This documentation represents information about that language as defined by standards or by companies who have built or implemented the language. Table 1.5 includes a list of online resources for the various reference documents out there today.

Table 1.5   Reference Resources

Resource	URL
Ecma-262 (ECMAScript)	`http://www.ecma.ch/ecma1/STAND/ECMA-262.HTM`
Microsoft Scripting	`http://msdn.microsoft.com/scripting/`
Technologies (JScript)	`default.htm?/scripting/jscript/`
	`techinfo/jsdocs.htm`

Resource	URL
Mozilla.org	`http://www.mozilla.org/js`
Netscape's Core JavaScript 1.4 Reference	`http://developer.netscape.com/docs/ manuals/js/core/jsref/index.htm`
Netscape's Server-Side JavaScript 1.2 Reference	`http://developer.netscape.com/docs/ manuals/js/server/jsref/index.htm`
Netscape's Client-Side JavaScript 1.3 Reference	`http://developer. netscape.com/docs/ manuals/js/client/jsref/index.htm`

Newsgroups

The final resource that we are going to discuss is the old standby—Usenet, or Newsgroups. Newsgroups are often a very good forum to post questions about problems and see responses to issues that others are having. It's global collaboration at its best and often is an overlooked resource. Table 1.6 lists some of our favorites, so be sure to check them out before giving up on any project.

Table 1.6   Newsgroup Resources

Server	Newsgroup
secnews.netscape.com	`netscape.public.mozilla.jseng`
secnews.netscape.com (Secure)	`netscape.dev.js-debugger`
	`netscape.dev.jsref`
	`netscape.dev.livewire`
	`netscape.dev.livewire.dbconfig`
	`netscape.dev.livewire.programming`
	`netscape.dev.visual-javascript`
	`netscape.devs-livescript`
Public Newsgroups	`comp.lang. javascript`

Moving On

This chapter covers the overview of the JavaScript language. As you can see, JavaScript is actually a very powerful scripting language that has many advantages. Security features are in place, and other implementations of the language make it worth any programmer's time to learn.

In the next chapter, you will take a look at the details of the language. Details that will give you, the programmer, an understanding of how the language deals with operators, data types, variables, functions, loops, conditionals, as well as how to correctly implement JavaScript within the body of an HTML document.

CHAPTER 2

Details of the Language

For experienced programmers to pick up a new language quickly, they look for similarities at the core of the new language and other languages they have used. These similarities generally include operators that enable programs to function, variables that provide memory, and the ability to apply the same operation to various items. Understanding how to use these core pieces of the language is essential if you want to begin programming in JavaScript.

If you have been programming for a long time, you might be tempted to skip over this chapter. Because JavaScript is still a young scripting language with some wrinkles to be ironed out, it is a good idea to understand these instances for backward compatibility reasons. Taking a little time to make sure that the core elements perform as you are expecting will save a lot of programming time in the future.

Things to Know about JavaScript Syntax

Before getting too deep into the core elements of the language, there are a few things a programmer should know about JavaScript syntax. Understanding these points will get you up and programming in a more timely fashion.

The Semicolon

If you have done any programming in C, C++, or Java, even as simple as a *Hello World* program, you already know 75% of all there is to know about the JavaScript semicolon (;). Just the same as C and C++, the semicolon is placed at the end of a JavaScript statement to signify that the code between the beginning of the line and the semicolon should be executed before moving to the next portion of code. If you forget a semicolon at the end of a line in C++, you get compile errors, but JavaScript doesn't complain. Because JavaScript is a loosely typed language, forgetting a semicolon tells JavaScript to assume that you intended for one to appear at the end of the line, and it executes your code accordingly. This does not mean that you should not use semicolons! It is good programming practice to always include semicolons at the end of a line of code except when dealing with statements such as for, while, and if.

Although it is good programming practice to have only one functional piece of code per line, there are times when it is advantageous to put two independent pieces of code on one line. When this case arises, you must use a semicolon to separate the two pieces of code. In Listing 2.1, a semicolon is used to separate two independent pieces of variable declaration code that are placed on one line. Notice that semicolons were placed at the end of each line although JavaScript would do it for you. The result of executing the code is the phrase, "The sales tax on $5 is $.3", being displayed in the browser.

Listing 2.1   Using Semicolons

```
<html>
<script type="text/javascript" language="JavaScript">
<!--

// Declare 2 numeric variables on the same line
var fiveDollars = 5; var salesTax = 0.06;

// Compute the sales tax on 5 dollars and use the
// document.write() function to display the result.
document.write("The sales tax on $");
document.write(fiveDollars);
document.write(" is $");
document.write(fiveDollars*salesTax);

//-->
</script>
</html>
```

Using the <script> Tag

The first time a programmer works with a new language, he'll want to know the key pieces of syntax needed to start programming. In JavaScript, the HTML <script> tag is that key piece. <script> tags tell the browser that everything between <script> and </script> should be interpreted by the interpreter specified in the type attribute. There is no limit to the number of <script> tags that can be used, as long as they are used in pairs.

Notice that the browser interprets the code between the <script> tags based on the type attribute. Because the *type* attribute has no default value it is important that the type attribute be set any time the `<script>` tag is used. To set the content type to the most current version of JavaScript supported by the browser, use the format `<script type="text/javascript">`. It is also possible to force the interpreter to use older versions of JavaScript (`<script type="text/javascript1.2">`, for example) as well as other languages such as Microsoft's JScript (`type="text/jscript"`).

NOTE

> Before HTML 4, the *language* attribute of the `<script>` tag was the only way to set the scripting language. But as of HTML 4, the *language* attribute was deprecated in favor of the content *type* attribute discussed above. In order to ensure backward compatibility, both attributes are specified in the `<script>` tags throughout all the code examples in this book.

Comments

JavaScript is very generous with its commenting options by providing the `/* */` comment tags from C, the `//` comment tag from C++, and the `<!-- -->` tags from HTML. Just as in C and C++, the `/* */` enables comments to span multiple lines by just placing comments between the two tags. The `//` comment tag enables comments to be placed between the `//` and the end of the line. As mentioned earlier, JavaScript provides one other comment tag that might not be familiar to you, the HTML `<!--` comment. JavaScript interprets this comment the same way it interprets the `//` characters. You are probably asking yourself, "Why use two different comment tags that do the same thing?" Some older browsers that did not understand the `<script>` tags would display all the code between the `<script>` tags as standard HTML text. To prevent this with non-JavaScript–enabled browsers, `<!--` is placed on the line directly below the `<script>` tag, and `//-->` is placed on the line directly above the closing `</script>` tag. This causes non-JavaScript–enabled browsers to treat the code between the tags as HTML comments, but allows browsers with JavaScript interpreters to execute the code. Examples of this style of commenting can be seen in the examples throughout the book.

NOTE

> The `//` comment characters have to be placed in front of the HTML `-->` comment closer because JavaScript will misinterpret `-->` as a pre-decrement operator.

Data Types and Variables

Before discussing JavaScript operators, conditionals, and loops, one should understand JavaScript data types and variables. These are building blocks that will be important going forward. Fortunately, JavaScript kept its implementation of data types simple and easy to use, unlike other programming languages. In addition to simple data types, variables are much easier to work with because there are no restrictions on the types of values they can hold.

Numbers

JavaScript's approach to numbers is different from other languages because every number is treated as a floating-point number. JavaScript does support integers, octals, and hexadecimals from a formatting perspective, but, at the lowest level, JavaScript sees numbers as floating-point numbers. The following sections discuss different formats that numbers can have at the higher level.

Integers

Integers are numbers that contain no fractional parts, can be positive or negative, and can be formatted as a decimal, octal, or hexadecimal in JavaScript. Because integers are actually floating-point numbers in JavaScript, it is possible for the numbers to be very large.

- Decimal integers, also referred to as base 10, are probably the most common numerical values programmers use in their code. This type of integer is made up of numbers from 0 to 9 and cannot begin with leading zeros.
- Octal integers, also referred to as base 8, are a little different from decimal integers in that they must begin with a leading zero. Each digit following the leading zero can be 0 to 7.
- Hexadecimal integers, also referred to as base 16, must begin with 0x or 0X. Each digit following the leading zero can be 0 through 15, but 10 through 15 are represented by the letters a (or A) through f (or F).

Floating-Point Numbers

Unlike the integer, floating-point numbers can contain fractional parts and can use exponential notation for added precision. Floating-point numbers are made up of a decimal integer followed by a period (.) and the fractional portion of the number.

Exponential notation can be used by adding an e or E to the end of a floating-point number followed by a decimal integer that does not exceed three digits. This tells JavaScript to multiply the floating-point number by 10 to the exponent of the number following the e.

Built-in Values

Because computer programs are often used to solve scientific problems, the programs must know many of the numerical constants that are used in math and science. To make programming easier for you, JavaScript has included some of the more commonly used numerical constants in the Math object, which are shown in Table 2.1.

Table 2.1   Numerical Constants Provided by JavaScript

Math Constant	Description
Math.E	Base of natural logarithms
Math.LN2	Natural log of 2
Math.LN10	Natural log of 10
Math.LOG2E	Base 2 log of e

Math Constant	Description
Math.LOG10E	Base 10 log of e
Math.PI	Pi
Math.SQRT1_2	Square root of 1/2
Math.SQRT2	Square root of 2

Special Values

JavaScript also provides some special values that are common in the mathematical world but not so common in the computer world. These special values are available through the Number object, as shown in Table 2.2.

Table 2.2   Special Numerical Values

Number Constant	Description
Number.MAX_VALUE	Largest representable number
Number.MIN_VALUE	Smallest representable number
Number.NaN	Not a number
Number.POSITIVE_INFINITY	Positive infinity
Number.NEGATIVE_INFINITY	Negative infinity

Strings

Strings provide programs a voice with which to communicate. It would be inconceivable to create a programming language today that did not use strings because they are so important.

JavaScript Strings

In the world of C and C++, dealing with strings is like having to go to the dentist—dreaded! Dealing with strings in JavaScript is like going to a big candy store. A string is made up of any number of characters or a lack of characters. Strings are declared by placing the characters that make up the string between a pair of double quotes (" ") or single quotes (' '). What if a string contains double quotes or single quotes? No problem. JavaScript interprets single quotes as part of the string if the single quotes are inside a pair of double quotes. Likewise, double quotes are considered part of the string if they appear between a pair of single quotes. If single quotes are your only option for declaring a string that contains single quotes, or if double quotes must be used to declare a string that contains double quotes, you will you need to use escape sequences (see the next section, "Special Characters").

Special Characters

Just as in C and C++, escape sequences, which are noted by a backslash character (\), allow special characters that cannot normally be stored in a string to be declared. Table 2.3 lists all the possible escape characters.

Table 2.3   Escape Sequences and Their Associated Characters

Escape Sequence	Character
\b	Backspace
\f	Form feed
\n	New line
\r	Carriage return
\t	Tab
\'	Single quote
\"	Double quote
\\	Backslash
xxx	Character represented by three octal digits *xxx* (000 to 377)
xx	Character represented by two hexadecimal digits *xx* (00 to FF)
\uXXXX	Unicode character represented by four hexadecimal digits XX (0000 to FFFF).

Other Data Types

Outside of the world of computers, there are uncertainties and indefinable values that we come in contact with daily. When computer programs are written to simulate the world we live in, they must handle uncertainties and values that have no definition. JavaScript provides some special data types to handle these situations.

Boolean

The Boolean data type is much simpler than any of the other data types because it has only two possible values: true and false. Sometimes it is easier to think of true as on or yes and false as off or no when working with some expressions that use the Boolean data type. In JavaScript, true and false are often represented by 1 (true) and 0 (false).

null

JavaScript provides the keyword null for representing a condition in which there is no value. In some languages, null and 0 are considered the same value, but JavaScript sees null and 0 as two completely different values.

Undefined Values

At this point, you might be thinking that undefined and null are essentially the same, but this is not true. In fact, undefined is a concept rather than a keyword like the null data type. Undefined is equivalent to NaN for numbers, the string undefined for strings, and false when dealing with Boolean values.

What to Know About Variables

Computer programs would not do much if they did not have some type of temporary memory. Variables provide a way for data to be stored during the execution of a program. Some languages, such as C and C++, impose many restrictions on how variables are used, but JavaScript keeps variables simple and easy to use.

Naming Variables

One of the keys to writing great code is to use variable names that help you, and programmers that modify your code, remember what data is stored in the variable. Before beginning to think of great variable names, remember the following guidelines imposed on variable names by JavaScript:

- The first character of the name must be a letter or an underscore (_).
- All characters following the first character can be letters, underscore, or digits.
- Letters can be either upper- or lowercase. JavaScript does distinguish between the two cases. For example, a variable called jobTitle is different from a variable called JOBtitle.

Assigning Values

When the perfect variable name has been derived, it is time to declare that variable and assign it a value. To declare a variable, use the keyword var followed by the variable name. Some programmers prefer to keep their code compact by declaring multiple variables using the same var statement. When this is the case, the variable names are separated by commas. At this point, the variable is undefined because no value has been assigned to it. Keep in mind that undefined is a special JavaScript value.

Now that the variable is declared, a value can be assigned to it using the assignment operator (=). In many cases, the declaration and assignment steps are performed in one step. If a value is assigned to a variable that has not been declared using the var keyword, JavaScript will automatically create a global variable. Listing 2.2 demonstrates the ways variable declaration and assignment can be performed. The code displays the sentence "James is 49 and 6 feet tall." in the browser window.

Listing 2.2   Variable Declaration and Assignment

```
<html>
<script type="text/javascript" language="JavaScript">
<!--

//Variable declaration without assignment
var firstName;

//Variable assignment without declaration
firstName = "James";

//Variable declaration and assignment
var age = 49, height = 6;

//Display the results
document.write(firstName," is ",age," and ",height," feet tall.");
```

Listing 2.2   Continued

```
//-->
</script>
</html>
```

TIP

Always use the var keyword to declare all variables to prevent variable scope problems.

Scope

A variable can be either global or local in JavaScript. All variables are global unless
they are declared in a function; in which case the variable is local to that function. It is
possible for two variables with the same name to exist if one is global and the other is
local to a function. When accessing the variable from within the function, you are
accessing the local variable. If the variable is accessed outside the function, the global
variable is used (see Listing 2.3).

CAUTION

Always use the var keyword to declare local variables in functions. Without var,
JavaScript will create a global variable.

Listing 2.3   Variable Scope Example

```
<html>
<h2><u>Computer monitor specifications</u></h2>

<script type="text/javascript" language="JavaScript">
<!--

//Initialize global variables
color = "green";
var size = 15;

//Declare a monitor specification function
function monitorSpecs()
{
  //Declare and set variables inside function
  color = "purple";
  price = "$300.00";
  var size = 17;
  document.write("The ",size," inch ",color);
  document.write(" monitor is ",price);
}

//Display results of monitorSpecs() function
monitorSpecs();
```

```
//Display variable values outside of function
document.write("<br>The ",size," inch ",color);
document.write(" monitor is ",price);

//-->
</script>
</html>
```

The results of running this script within the body of an HTML document can be seen in Figure 2.1. The code begins by declaring two global variables, `color` and `size`. The `monitorSpecs()` function creates a new variable called `size` that only exists within the scope of the function. Because the function did not specify `var`, the global variable `color` was changed from `green` to `purple`. In addition, a new global variable, `price`, was declared within the function because the word `var` was not used.

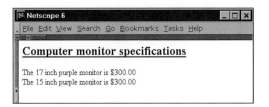

Figure 2.1

The 17-inch monitor has the same color price due to the use of global variables.

Type Conversion

In languages such as C and C++, type conversion is very important and complicated, but, in JavaScript, type conversion is effortless. Unlike other languages, JavaScript allows a variable to hold any data type at any time. This means that a variable can be assigned a string initially, but then could later contain a integer. JavaScript also attempts to perform all necessary type conversions for you, such as strings to numbers and numbers to strings.

Arrays

Arrays enable programmers to store multiple data, based on a numbered position called an index, into one storage structure. The numbering of the index always starts at 0 and goes up. Also, JavaScript supports having arrays within arrays, called *multidimensional* arrays.

The implementation of arrays in JavaScript has been changing ever since JavaScript was introduced. The original implementation of arrays in JavaScript 1.0 was not really an array at all but rather JavaScript objects with multiple property settings. A true `Array` object was added in JavaScript 1.1, and additional features added in following versions. Today, arrays are very robust and full featured, but, because of their changing past, you should spend some time digging into the history of arrays as they apply to JavaScript versions. You will begin by understanding how arrays work in the latest versions of JavaScript and then go back and learn how arrays were created in. JavaScript 1.1

One-Dimensional

To create an instance of an array, you must use the new operator along with the Array object. There are four ways to declare an array. First, an empty array that contains no elements can be created by leaving the constructor parameters empty as shown in the following JavaScript statement:

```
var x = new Array();
```

The second way to create an array is to fill in the constructor parameters with the array elements. One of the nice things about JavaScript arrays is that an array can contain elements of various types. For example, the following JavaScript statement creates an array that contains three strings, "red", "yellow", and "green", as well as the integers 1, 5, and 8:

```
var x = new Array("red","yellow","green",1,5,8);
```

The third way to create an array is to fill in the constructor parameter with just the size of the array. This causes the array to be initialized to hold the number of elements specified, but does not specify the actual elements. For example, the following JavaScript statement creates an array that can hold 6 elements.

```
var x = new Array(6);
```

NOTE

> The var x = new Array(*n*); format, described previously, is not recognized by JavaScript 1.2, so the number specified in the constructor parameter is stored as an element in position 0.

The fourth, and quickest, way to create an array is to use the standard array square brackets to fill in the array elements directly:

```
var x = ["red","yellow","green",1,5,8];
```

After an array has been created, it can be written to and read from using the [] operator. By placing a position number in this operator, the data stored at this index can be accessed and even overwritten.

String Indexes

So far, you have only accessed elements in arrays via the numerical index, but it is possible to index arrays using strings. To access an element, a string index value is placed into the [] operator. Listing 2.4 demonstrates the use of strings as indexes for a clothing store's product quantity array. Figure 2.2 displays the clothing store's current inventory of products.

Listing 2.4   Using Strings for Array Indexes

```html
<html>
<h2><u>Clothing Store Inventory</u></h2>

<script type="text/javascript" language="JavaScript">
<!--

//Populate an array with product quantities
function populateArray(products)
{
  products["shirts"]=46;
  products["pants"]=23;
  products["hats"]=14;
  products["socks"]=153;
}

//Display product quantities
function displayArray(products)
{
  document.write(products['shirts']," shirts.<br>");
  document.write(products['pants']," pants.<br>");
  document.write(products['hats']," hats.<br>");
  document.write(products['socks']," pairs of socks.");
}

//Create a product quantity array
var productQty = new Array();

//Set product quantities
populateArray(productQty);

//Display the product quantities
displayArray(productQty);

//-->
</script>
</html>
```

Figure 2.2

The clothing store's current inventory of products is displayed using string indexes to access arrays.

Length

Unlike arrays in C and C++, JavaScript allows the size of an array to change dynamically at any time. For example, it is possible to write directly to a position that was not even declared using the [] operator. The length of the array can also be changed by altering the length attribute of the Array object. If the length of an array is originally 10 and is reduced to 5 by changing the value stored in the length attribute, the elements in position 5 through 9 are lost.

One of the advantages to using the Array object is the methods it provides to manipulate and access itself. Table 2.4 lists some of the methods that are currently available in the Array object. Details of these methods can be found in Chapter 7, "Core Language," in the "Array" section.

Table 2.4 **Methods Available in the Array Object**

Method	Description
join()	Concatenates all elements into one string
reverse()	Reverses the order of the elements in the array
sort()	Sorts elements in array
concat()	Concatenates an array on to an array
slice()	Returns a subsection of the array
splice()	Inserts and removes elements from an array
push()	Adds elements to the end of an array
pop()	Deletes the last element from an array
unshift()	Adds elements to the front of an array
shift()	Deletes elements from the front of an array
toString()	Converts elements to a string

Multidimensional

To create multidimensional arrays in JavaScript, the element of an array must be another array. The inner array can be accessed by putting two [] operators back to back. Listing 2.5 uses a multidimensional array to hold an inventory list of brake parts. As seen in Figure 2.3, the brake parts list is accessed by using double [] operators and displayed in a table.

Listing 2.5 **Using a Multidimensional Array**

```
<html>
<h2><u>Brake Parts Inventory List</u></h2>

<script type="text/javascript" language="JavaScript">
<!--

//Display brake part inventory in a table
function displayInventory(table)
{
  document.write("<table border=on>");
```

```
document.write("<th>Item Number</th><th>Item Name</th>");
document.write("<th>Model Number</th><th>Quantity</th>");
//Display each part
for(x=1; x<=3; x++)
{
  document.write("<tr><td>",x,"</td>");
  //Display all information for each part
  for(y=0; y<=2; y++)
  {
    document.write("<td>",table[x][y],"</td>");
  }
  document.write("</tr>");
}
document.write("</table>");
}

//Create a brake parts inventory list using a
//multidimensional array
part1 = new Array("Brake Pads","39D48G",78);
part2 = new Array("Brake Shoes","7D9UK3",45);
part3 = new Array("Rotors","97WOST","14");
brakeParts = new Array("",part1,part2,part3);

//Display the inventory of brake parts
displayInventory(brakeParts);

//-->
</script>
</html>
```

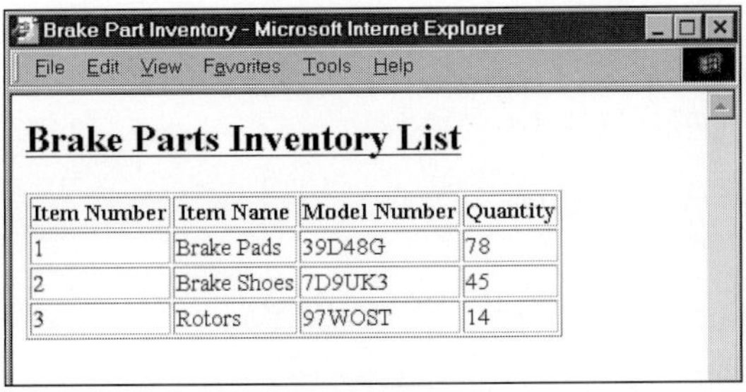

Figure 2.3

Using a multidimensional array to display the inventory list of brake parts.

Arrays as Objects

Because arrays are essentially JavaScript objects, it is possible to access the elements of arrays as properties if a string index is used. Dot notation is used, rather than the [ ] operators. For example, the clothing store example, in Listing 2.4, could have been created using properties as shown in Listing 2.6. Notice how the [] operators and dot notation are used interchangeably when accessing the contents of the array. The result of executing the code is the same as previously shown in Figure 2.2.

Listing 2.6   Accessing Array Properties

```
<html>
<h2><u>Clothing Store Inventory</u></h2>

<script type="text/javascript" language="JavaScript">
<!--

//Populate an array with product quantities
function populateArray(products)
{
  products.shirts=46;
  products.pants=23;
  products["hats"]=14;
  products["socks"]=153;
}

//Display product quantities
function displayArray(products)
{
  document.write(products['shirts']," shirts.<br>");
  document.write(products['pants']," pants.<br>");
  document.write(products.hats," hats.<br>");
  document.write(products.socks," pairs of socks.");
}

//Create a product quantity array
var productQty = new Array();

//Set product quantities
populateArray(productQty);

//Display the product quantities
displayArray(productQty);

//-->
</script>
</html>
```

JavaScript 1.0 Arrays

As mentioned earlier, JavaScript originally used the Object() constructor to create arrays in JavaScript 1.0. Because the properties of an Object() could be accessed by using the [] operator, it was possible to give the illusion of an array.

To create an array using this concept, a new object is created using the Object() constructor. Once created, elements can be assigned to the object using the [] operators.

Because this is just a basic object, the programmer is responsible for keeping track of the length of the array. The easiest way to remember the length is to create a property called length. Unfortunately, properties use the same positions that are accessed by the [ ] operator, so the length property would actually be array position 0.

Listing 2.7 demonstrates how to create an array representing a toolbox using the Object() constructor. The code displays the sentence "The toolbox holds: hammer wrench nails" in the browser window.

Listing 2.7 Creating Arrays in JavaScript 1.0

```
<html>
<script type="text/javascript" language="JavaScript">
<!--

//Create a toolbox array using the Object() constructor
var toolbox = Object();
toolbox.length=3;    //array position zero
toolbox[1]="hammer";
toolbox[2]="wrench";
toolbox[3]="nails";

//Display the items in the toolbox.
document.write("The toolbox holds:  ");
for(x=1; x<=toolbox.length; x++)
{
  document.write(toolbox[x]," ");
}

//-->
</script>
</html>
```

Operators

JavaScript provides most of the common operators that can be found in other programming languages. Because of JavaScript's way of handling strings, some of these operators are a bit easier to use than in other languages.

Arithmetic

Just the same as other programming languages, JavaScript allows many arithmetic operations. These operations include the common addition and subtraction that all programmers use as well as the less common modulus and incremental.

NOTE

All the common arithmetic operators will attempt to convert strings to numbers when applicable. If a string cannot beconverted to a number, NaN (*Not A Number*) will be returned.

Those who have programmed in other languages will find that JavaScript is very robust in its support of operators and mathematical functions. This is not only because of the built-in operators, but also because of the access to advanced mathematical operations that are provided through the Math object. The functions of this object are shown in Table 2.5 and are covered in Chapter 7.

Table 2.5   Advanced Mathematical Methods

Method	Description
Math.abs()	Absolute value
Math.acos()	Arc cosine
Math.asin()	Arc sine
Math.atan()	Arc tangent
Math.atan2()	Arc tangent
Math.ceil()	The smallest integer that is greater than or equal to a number (ceiling).
Math.cos()	Cosine
Math.exp()	Natural exponent
Math.floor()	The largest integer that is equal or less than a number (floor).
Math.log()	Natural logarithm
Math.max()	The larger of two numbers
Math.min()	The smaller of two numbers
Math.pow()	Power of
Math.random()	Random number
Math.round()	Round
Math.sin()	Sine
Math.sqrt()	Square root
Math.tan()	Tangent

Addition

The addition operator (+) is, of course, one of the most widely used and common operators. If the values on either side are numerical values, the values are added together. When the values are strings, they are concatenated together. The following line of code

```
var resultOfAdd = 34 + 12;
```

would set the variable *resultOfAdd* equal to 46, whereas this line of code

```
var resultOfAdd = "a" + "corn";
```

would set the variable *resultOfAdd* equal to the string "acorn".

Subtraction

The subtraction operator (-) subtracts the number to the right of the operator from the number on the left. When either of the operands are strings, an attempt is made to convert the strings to numbers. For example, the following lines of code

```
var aNum = String("102");
var resultOfSub = 25 - aNum;
```

convert the string stored in *aNum* to a number before performing the subtraction operation. The result of the subtraction (-77) is then stored in the variable `resultOfSub`.

Multiplication

The multiplication operator (*) works the same as it would in any other language by multiplying the left operand by the right operand. The multiplication operator is no different from subtraction in its efforts to handle strings. If either of the values is a string, an attempt is made to convert the string to a number. For example, the following lines of code

```
var aNum = String("7");
var resultOfMult = 5 * aNum;
```

convert the string stored in *aNum* to a number before performing the multiplication operation. The result of the multiplication (35) is then stored in the variable `resultOfMult`.

Division

The division operator (/) is the operator that, although simple, can be confusing when you have been writing code all day and your senses are dulled. You ask yourself, "Which number divides into the other?" Reading the expression from left to right, the left value is divided by the right value. As before, if either of the operands is a string, an attempt is made to convert the string to a number. For example, the following lines of code

```
var aNum = String("7");
var resultOfDiv = 42 / aNum;
```

convert the string stored in *aNum* to a number before performing the division operation. The result of the division (6) is then stored in the variable `resultOfDiv`.

Modulus

Although the modulus operator (%) is not used as often as some of the other operators, I am always excited when I do get to use it because it usually means I am performing a neat math trick. This operator starts similar to the division operator, by dividing the left value by the right, but, instead of returning the normal result of division, only the remainder is returned by the operation. Once again, if either value is a string, an attempt is made to convert the string to a number. For example, the following lines of code

```
var aNum = String("3");
var resultOfMod = 26 % 3;
```

convert the string stored in *aNum* to a number before performing the modulus operation. The remainder of 2 is then stored in the variable `resultOfMod`.

Pre-Increment

The pre-increment operator (++) combines two very common steps that programmers use over and over again into one, thus making code more concise and readable. This operator is especially handy when working with for loops. In your code, the pre-increment operator is placed directly before the variable to be incremented. The operation begins by incrementing the variable by 1. The new incremented value is returned by the operation to be used in another expression. If the variable is a string, it is converted to a number. For example, the following segment of code

```
//The price is $5.00 dollars
var price = String("5");

//Add the shipping rate ($3.00 dollars) to the price after incrementing price
var pricePlusShipping = (++price) + 3;
```

converts the string stored in *price* to a number before performing the pre-increment operation. The pre-increment operation results in the variable *price* being changed from 5 to 6 dollars, and the value of 9 dollars is stored in the variable *pricePlusShipping*.

Post-Increment

The post-increment operator (++) has the same operator as the pre-increment operator but it behaves differently based on its position. First, the post-increment operator appears directly after the variable that is to be incremented. Unlike the pre-increment operator, the post-increment operator returns the original value before it is incremented by 1. If either of the values is a string, an attempt is made to convert the string to a number. For example, the following segment of code

```
//The price is $5.00 dollars
var price = String("5");

//Add the shipping rate ($3.00 dollars) to the price before incrementing price
var pricePlusShipping = (price++) + 3;
```

converts the string stored in *price* to a number before performing the post-increment operation. The post-increment operation causes the variable *price* to be changed from 5 to 6 dollars but the original price of 5 dollars is added to the shipping rate resulting in the value of 8 dollars being stored in the variable *pricePlusShipping*.

Pre-Decrement

The pre-decrement operator (- -) is very similar to the pre-increment operator in its placement to the left of a variable and its order of execution. But there is one key difference between the operators: the pre-decrement operator decrements the value by 1. Once again, if the variable is a string, it is converted to a number. For example, the following segment of code

```
//The price is $20.00 dollars
var price = String("20");
```

```
//Subtracted discount ($6.00 dollars) from the price after decrementing price
var priceMinusDiscount = (--price) - 6;
```

converts the string stored in *price* to a number before performing the pre-decrement operation. The pre-decrement operation would result in the variable *price* being changed from 20 to 19 dollars, and the value of 13 dollars being stored in the variable *priceMinusDiscount.*

Post-Decrement

The post-decrement operator (--) is very similar to the post-increment operator in its placement to the right of a variable and its order of execution. But, as the name implies, the post-decrement operator decrements the value by 1. If the variable is a string, it is converted to a number. The following segment of code

```
//The price is $20.00 dollars
var price = 20

//Subtract the discount ($6.00 dollars) from the price before decrementing
price
var priceMinusDiscount = (price--) - 6;
```

converts the string stored in *price* to a number before performing the post-decrement operation. The post-decrement operation causes the variable *price* to be changed from 20 to 19 dollars but the original price of 20 dollars is used to calculate the value of 14 dollars that is stored in the variable *priceMinusDiscount.*

Unary Negation

The unary negation operator (-) is usually used when performing a mathematical equation in which a number needs to be changed from positive to negative or vice versa. When negating a variable, keep in mind that the contents of the variable do not change, only the value returned is negated. As with all the other operators, if the value is a string, an attempt is made to convert the string to a number. For example, the following segment of code

```
var aNumber = String("67");
var resultOfNeg = -aNumber;
```

converts the string stored in *aNumber* to a number before performing the negation operation. The result of negation on the number results in the value of -67 being stored in the variable *resultOfNeg.*

String

The addition operator (+) has a special purpose when dealing with strings. If the values on either side of the addition operator are strings, the strings are concatenated together. If only one of the values is a string, the other value is converted to a string and concatenated with the first value. To help understand these various combinations of applying the addition operator to numeric and string values, see Listing 2.8.

Listing 2.8   Using the Addition Operator on Numeric and String Values

```
<html>
<script type="text/javascript" language="JavaScript">
<!--

// Declare 2 numeric variables and 2 string variables
var sStringVar1 = "Hello";
var sStringVar2 = "World";
var nNumVar1 = 5;
var nNumVar2 = 10;

// Apply the addition operator to create 3 totals
var sStringTotal = sStringVar1 + sStringVar2;
var nNumTotal = nNumVar1 + nNumVar2;
var sStringNumTotal = sStringTotal + nNumTotal;

// Use the document.write() function to write the totals to the page
// Notice that we even use the addition operator in place of a comma
// to concatenate the results with some text on the page.
document.write("<b>The string total is: </b>"+sStringTotal+"<br>");
document.write("<b>The numeric total is: </b>",nNumTotal,"<br>");
document.write("<b>The string + numeric total is: </b>",sStringNumTotal);

//-->
</script>
</html>
```

The results of running this script within the body of an HTML document can be seen in Figure 2.4. As the figure shows, when the addition operator is applied to two strings or a string and a numeric value, a string concatenation occurs. As expected, when applying this operator to the two numeric values, the numbers are added.

Figure 2.4

Using the addition operator to add numbers and concatenate strings.

Assignment

What good are variables if data cannot be assigned to them? Similar to all languages, JavaScript provides assignment operators to allow data to be stored in variables. The basic format of the assignment operator is shown in the following example, where a value of 6 is assigned to the variable x:

```
x = 6;
```

In addition to this one-to-one assignment, this operator can also be stacked to create simultaneous assignments. Simultaneous means that several variables can be assigned at once. This is demonstrated in the following example, where variables x, y, and z all contain the value of 6:

```
x = y = z = 6;
```

Anytime multiple assignment operators occur in the same expression, they are evaluated from right to left. So in the previous example, z would be assigned the value 6 first. After the assignment has been made, y would be assigned the value stored in z and, finally, x would be assigned the value stored in y. The overall effect is that all three variables would be assigned a value of 6.

Because the assignment operator is an operator, similar to addition (+) or subtraction (-), it can be used within an expression. This enables a programmer to perform an assignment and evaluate a mathematical expression all in one step.

```
y = (x = 3) + 4;
```

In the preceding example, the value 3 is assigned to the variable x, which is then added to the value 4 and assigned to the variable y. After the expression is fully evaluated, y will contain the value 7. This enables programmers to accomplish three operations at once. They are able to assign a value to the x variable, perform addition, and assign the result to the y variable. Features such as this help make JavaScript very versatile and easy to use.

Now that you have looked at how the assignment operator works, look at a more detailed example—one that performs each of the assignments discussed, as well as some more complex ones. Listing 2.9 contains such an example, and Figure 2.5 shows the result.

Listing 2.9   Use of the Assignment Operators in JavaScript

```
<html>
<script type="text/javascript" language="JavaScript">
<!--

// Declare variables using single assignment
x = 3;
y = 7;
z = 9;

//Display the values stored in the variables after single assignment
document.write("<u>After single assignment</u><br>");
document.write("x=",x,"<br>y=",y,"<br>z=",z,"<br>");

//Perform multiple assignment on variables
x = y = z = 14;
```

Listing 2.9 *Continued*

```
//Display the values stored in the variables after multiple assignment
document.write("<u>After multiple assignment</u><br>");
document.write("x=",x,"<br>y=",y,"<br>z=",z,"<br>");

//Perform multiple assignment in one expression
x = (y = 17) + (2 * (z = 2));

//Display the values stored in the variables after multiple assignment
//in one expression.
document.write("<u>After multiple assignment in one expression</u><br>");
document.write("x=",x,"<br>y=",y,"<br>z=",z,"<br>");

//-->
</script>
</html>
```

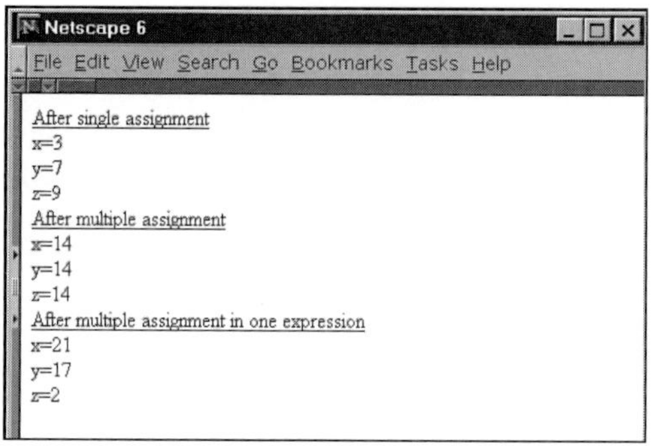

Figure 2.5

The result of various assignment operations.

In addition to the basic assignment operator, JavaScript also offers a number of advanced assignment operators that extend assignment functionality. These operators combine the functionality of basic assignment and other operators into one functional operator. Table 2.6 shows these advanced assignment operators along with their equivalent operations. Details of these assignment operators can be found in Chapter 7.

Table 2.6 *Advanced Assignment Operators*

Operator	Example	Description
+=	x+=y	x = x + y;
-=	x-=y	x = x - y;
*=	x*=y	x = x * y;
/=	x/=y	x = x / y;

Operator	Example	Description
%=	x%=y	x = x % y;
<<=	x<<=y	x = x << y;
>>=	x>>=y	x = x >> y;
>>>=	x>>>=y	x = x >>> y;
&=	x&=y	x = x & y;
|=	x|=y	x = x | y;
^=	x^=y	x = x ^ y;

All the advanced assignment operators, except for +=, will attempt to convert strings to numbers before performing the operation. If strings are used with the += operator, the left operand is concatenated to the end of the right operand. For example, in Listing 2.10, the string "lighthouse" would be assigned to the variable y and the phrase "y= lighthouse" is written to the browser.

Listing 2.10   Using the Addition Operator to Perform String Concatenation

```
<html>
<script type="text/javascript" language="JavaScript">
<!--

// Declare a string
y = "light";

//Concatenate the string "house" to the
//end of string stored in the variable y
y += "house";

// Print the output to the screen
document.write("y= ",y);

//-->
</script>
</html>
```

So far, you have only considered assignment of values to variables, but what about assigning a reference to a variable? When the assignment operator works on primitive values (numbers, strings, Boolean, null, and undefined), a copy of the value is made. When the assignment operator works on JavaScript objects, references to the objects are copied. To demonstrate this difference, Listing 2.11 creates a variable and an array to hold numbers. The variable is then copied by value to another variable, and the array is copied by reference to another array. To show the difference, the value stored in one of the variables and one of the arrays is changed, and then all the values are displayed in the browser as seen in Figure 2.6.

Listing 2.11   Assignment by Value Versus by Reference

```
<html>
<script type="text/javascript" language="JavaScript">
<!--

//Declare a variable and an array object
var number1 = 94;
var arrayOfNum1 = new Array(23,86);

//Assign by value
var number2 = number1;

//Assign by reference
var arrayOfNum2 = arrayOfNum1;

//Modify value stored in copied variable and array.
number2 = 29;
arrayOfNum2[1] = 47;

//Display the values stored in each variable and array
document.write("number1=",number1,"<br>");
document.write("number2=",number2,"<br>");
document.write("arrayOfNum1[0]=",arrayOfNum1[0],"<br>");
document.write("arrayOfNum1[1]=",arrayOfNum1[1],"<br>");
document.write("arrayOfNum2[0]=",arrayOfNum2[0],"<br>");
document.write("arrayOfNum2[1]=",arrayOfNum2[1],"<br>");

//-->
</script>
</html>
```

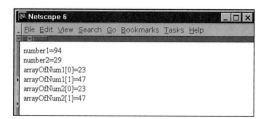

Figure 2.6

The variables `number1` and `number2` are assigned values by value, whereas the arrays `arrayOfNum1` and `arrayOfNum2` are assigned values by reference.

Logical

JavaScript provides three logical operators. Without these operators, programs would be very long and complex. At first glance, most programmers might think that they already know how these operators work, but it is important to dig a little deeper. Not knowing how the logical operators work can lead to what would appear to be random errors that are impossible to locate and correct. So take the time to read the description of each of the logical operators.

> **NOTE**
>
> JavaScript defines `true` as anything other than `0` (zero), `""` (empty string), `null`, `undefined`, or, of course, `false`.

Logical AND

The logical AND operator (`&&`) returns `true` if the expression to the left and the expression to the right of the operator evaluate to `true`. If either the left, right, or both expressions evaluate to `false`, the result of the operation is `false`.

Unfortunately, the implementation of the logical AND operator in JavaScript is more complex than what was just mentioned. The AND operation begins by evaluating the left operand. If the left operand evaluates `false`, the basic logic of the AND operator is complete, so the right operand is never evaluated. But if the left operand evaluates `true`, the right operand must be evaluated to determine the final result of the AND operation. In either case, the final result returned by the AND operation is actually the result of the last operand to be evaluated.

Logical OR

The logical OR operator (`||`) returns `true` if the expression to the left or the expression to the right of the operator evaluates to `true`. If both the left and the right expressions evaluate to `false`, the result of the operation is `false`.

Similar to the logical AND operator, it is important that you understand how JavaScript actually evaluates the logical OR operator. The OR operation begins by evaluating the left operand. If the left operand evaluates `true`, the basic logic of the OR operator is complete, so the right operand is never evaluated. But if the left operand evaluates `false`, the right operand must be evaluated to determine the final result of the OR operation. In either case, the final result returned by the OR operation is actually the result of the last operand to be evaluated.

Logical NOT

The logical NOT operator (`!`) is not as complex as the comparison operators. The result of the expression following the operator is inverted. If the expression evaluates to `true`, the result of the operation is `false`. If the expression evaluates to `false`, the result is `true`. When the expression evaluates to a non-Boolean value, it is converted to `true` or `false` before performing the inversion.

Comparison

JavaScript provides the usual comparison operators found in most languages plus a couple of more unusual ones. JavaScript had some inconsistencies in the operator department during its early years, which resulted in the addition of some unconventional comparison operators. For this reason, it is important to understand how these operators work.

Equal

The equal operator (==) compares the value on the left of the operator to the value on the right of the operator. If the values are equal, true is returned from the operation. If the values are not equal, false is returned from the operation.

Originally, JavaScript attempted to convert the operands of the equality operator to the same type before performing a comparison. For example, if the left operand of an equal operator is a number and the right operand is a string, JavaScript would attempt to convert the string to a number so that two numbers are compared. In an attempt to guess what would be in the then unreleased ECMAScript standard, the decision was made not to do type conversion on the operands of the equality operator in JavaScript 1.2. When the ECMAScript standard was released, it supported type conversion, so JavaScript 1.3 came full circle by once again attempting to convert the operands of the equality operator to the same type before performing a comparison.

JavaScript determines which behavior should be used by the <script> tag. By setting the language attribute of the <script> tag equal to JavaScript, type conversion will be used. If the language attribute is set to "JavaScript1.2", no type conversion will be used. An example of this behavior is demonstrated in the Listing 2.12.

Listing 2.12   Type Conversion and the Equal Operator

```
<html>
<script type="text/javascript" language="JavaScript">
<!--
// Type-conversion turned on
document.write("The == operator with type-conversion turned on returns: ");
document.write(3=="3");
// -->
</script>

<script type="text/javascript1.2" language="JavaScript1.2">
<!--
// Type-conversion turned off
document.write("<br>The == operator with type- ");
document.write("conversion turned off returns: ");
document.write(3=="3");
// -->
</script>
</html>
```

TIP

> Avoid setting the `language` attribute to `"JavaScript1.2"` in your code because the industry standard is for type conversion to be used on the operands of the equality operator.

So far you've seen when type conversion is used with the equality operator, but you haven't seen how the type conversion operates. Understanding how type conversions work for the equality operators will again save time when trying to find bugs. Type conversion adheres to the following rules:

- True is converted to the number 1, and `false` is converted to zero before being compared.
- If either of the operands are NaN, the equality operator returns `false`.
- `null` and `undefined` are equal.
- `null` and `undefined` are not equal to 0 (zero), `" "`, or `false`.
- If a string and a number are compared, attempt to convert the string to a number and then check for equality.
- If an object and a string are compared, attempt to convert the object to a string and then check for equality.
- If an object and a number are compared, attempt to convert the object to a number and then check for equality.
- If both operands of an equality operation are objects, the addresses of the two objects are checked for equality.

Not Equal

The not equal operator (`!=`) compares the value on the left of the operator to the value on the right. If the values are not equal, `true` is returned from operation. If they are equal, `false` is returned. The `!=` operator is victim to the same type-conversion bug as the `==` operator. As with the `==` operator, use the `language` attribute of the `<script>` tag to force the desired behavior.

Greater Than

The greater than operator (`>`) compares the value on the left of the operator to the value on the right. If the value on the left is greater than the value on the right, `true` is returned from operation. If the value on the left of the operator is less than or equal to the value on the right, `false` is returned. If either of the values is a string, it is converted to a number before the comparison takes place.

Less Than

The less than operator (`<`) compares the value on the left of the operator to the value on the right. If the value on the left is less than the value on the right, `true` is returned from operation. If the value on the left of the operator is greater than or equal to the value on the right, `false` is returned. If either of the values is a string, it is converted to a number before the comparison takes place.

Greater Than or Equal

The greater than or equal operator (`>=`) compares the value on the left of the operator to the value on the right. If the value on the left is greater than or equal to the value to the right of the operator, `true` is returned from operation. If the value on the left of the operator is less than the value on the right, `false` is returned. If either of the values is a string, it is converted to a number before the comparison takes place.

Less Than or Equal

The less than or equal operator (`<=`) compares the value on the left of the operator to the value on the right. If the value on the left is less than or equal to the value on the right, `true` is returned from the operation. If the value on the left of the operator is greater than the value on the right, `false` is returned. If either of the values is a string, it is converted to a number before the comparison takes place.

Identity

The identity operator (`===`), also referred to as strict equal, compares the value on the left of the operator to the value on the right. If the value on the left is equal to the value on the right side of the operator, `true` is returned from operation. If the values are not equal, `false` is returned. No type conversion is performed on the operands before the comparison.

Non-Identity

The non-identity operator (`!==`), also referred to as strict does-not-equal, compares the value on the left of the operator to the value on the right. If the value on the left is not equal to the value on the right side of the operator, `true` is returned from operation. If the values are equal, `false` is returned. No type conversion is performed on the operands before the comparison is made.

NOTE

The identity and non-identity operators are only available in JavaScript 1.3 and later.

Conditional

Many programmers are not familiar with the conditional operator (`?:`), even though it exists in numerous languages. Most individuals will use the standard `if` statement rather than the conditional operator, even though they do the same thing. The conditional operator is a little harder to read than the standard `if` statement, but it is much more compact, which is important when download time is a consideration.

The format of the conditional operator can be a bit confusing. An expression that evaluates to a Boolean is always placed to the left of the question mark (`?`). If the expression evaluates to `true`, the value between the question mark and the colon (`:`) is returned from the operation. If the expression evaluates to `false`, the value following the colon is returned. In Listing 2.13, a standard `if` statement is shown, along with same functionality produced by using the conditional operator. Figure 2.7 shows that the same functionality is produced from both the `if` statement and the conditional operator.

Listing 2.13   The Conditional Operator and `if` Statement Are Compared

```
<html>
<script type="text/javascript" language="JavaScript">
<!--

// Set the mail flag to "YES"
mailFlag = "YES"
var message1;
var message2;

//Standard if statement
if (mailFlag == "YES")
message1 = "You have email!";
else
message1 = "No email.";

//Same statement using conditional operator
message2 = (mailFlag == "YES") ? "You have email!" : "No email.";

// Print the message to the screen
document.write("The if statement returns: ",message1,"<br>");
document.write("The conditional operator returns: ",message2);

//-->
</script>
</html>
```

Figure 2.7

The result of using the `if` statement is the same as using the conditional operator.

Bitwise

The bitwise operators look similar to the comparison operators, but their functionality is very different. If you have ever worked with truth tables, you might recognize the operators in this section. Bitwise operators in JavaScript only work with integers that are 32 bits in length. If an integer is not 32 bits, it is turned into a one because the bitwise operators evaluate numbers at the binary level where everything is ones and zeros. Bitwise operations are not used often in programming, but there are times when the operators are indispensable.

Bitwise AND

The bitwise AND operator (&) looks at the integer numbers on both sides of the operator as 32-bit binary numbers. Then the logical AND (&&) operator, discussed earlier in the chapter, individually evaluates each of the 32 bits representing the number to the left of the operator to the corresponding bit of the number to the right of the operator. The 32-bit binary result of logical AND operation is converted to an integer value and returned from the bitwise AND operation.

Bitwise OR

The bitwise OR operator (|) looks at the integer numbers on both sides of the operator as 32-bit binary numbers. Then the logical OR (||) operator, discussed earlier in the chapter, individually evaluates each of the 32 bits representing the number to the left of the operator to the corresponding bit of the number to the right of the operator. The 32-bit binary result of logical OR operation is converted to an integer value and returned from the bitwise OR operation.

Bitwise XOR (exclusive OR)

The bitwise XOR operator (^) looks at the integer numbers on both sides of the operator as 32-bit binary numbers. Unlike the bitwise OR operator, bitwise XOR uses a special version of the logical OR operator, called exclusive OR, to evaluate each bit of a binary number.

NOTE

An exclusive OR operation returns true if either the value to the left or the value to the right of the operator is true, but not both. If both values are false or both values are true, the result of the operation is false.

The exclusive OR individually evaluates each of the 32 bits representing the number to the left of the bitwise XOR operator to the corresponding bit of the number to the right of the operator. The 32-bit binary result of exclusive OR operation is converted to an integer value and returned from the bitwise XOR operation.

Bitwise NOT

The bitwise NOT operator (~) is simpler than the bitwise AND, OR, and XOR operators. The bitwise NOT operator begins by looking at the number to the right of the operator as a 32-bit binary number. Each bit of the given number is reversed so that all ones become zeros and all zeros become ones. The 32-bit binary result is converted to an integer value and returned from the bitwise NOT operation.

Shift Left

The shift left operator (<<) looks at the integer to the left of the operator as a 32-bit binary number. All the bits in this number are shifted to the left by the number of positions specified by the integer to the right of the operator. As the bits are shifted to the left, zeros are filled in on the right. Because the number can only be 32 bits long, the extra bits on the left are lost. The 32-bit binary result of shifting operation is converted to an integer value and returned from the shift left operation.

Shift Right with Sign

The shift right with sign operator (>>) is similar to the shift left operator. The shift right with sign operator looks at the integer to the left of the operator as a 32-bit binary number. All the bits in this number are shifted to the right by the number of positions specified by the integer to the right of the operator. As the bits are shifted to the right, either ones or zeros are filled in on the left. If the original number is positive, ones are added to the left side of the binary number. On the other hand, if the original number is negative, zeros are used. Because the result can only be 32 bits long, the extra bits on the right are lost. The 32-bit binary result of the shifting operation is converted to an integer value and returned from the shift right with sign operation.

Shift Right Zero Fill

The shift right zero fill operator (>>>) operates the same as the shift right with sign operator, except that the binary number is always padded on the left with zeros, regardless of the sign of the original integer.

Precedence

JavaScript, similar to other languages, enables numerous operators to be used in one expression. Because operators can appear just about anywhere within an expression, JavaScript follows guidelines that determine which operator is evaluated first, second, third, and so on. Table 2.7 shows the precedence of all the JavaScript operators. The **Read From...** column tells what order (left-to-right or right-to-left) operators of equal precedence are evaluated. It is possible to override the precedence of operators by using parentheses.

TIP

Use parentheses to ensure that your code operates like you expect and to make your code more readable.

Table 2.7   Operator Precedence

Precedence	Read From...	Operator	Operator Type
Highest	L to R	., []	Member access
	L to R	(), new	Call/ create instance
	R to L	++, --, +,	Pre/Post
		-, !, ~,	Increment/Decrement,

Table 2.7 Continued

Precedence	Read From...	Operator	Operator Type
			void, and so on.
			delete, typeof
	L to R	`*, /, %`	Multiplication, division, modulus
	L to R	`+, -`	Addition, Subtraction
	L to R	`<<, >>, >>>`	Bitwise shift
	L to R	`<, <=, >, >=`	Relational operations
	L to R	`==, !=,` `===, !==`	Equality operations
	L to R	`&`	Bitwise AND
	L to R	`^`	Bitwise XOR
	L to R	`|`	Bitwise OR
	L to R	`&&`	Logical AND
	L to R	`||`	Logical OR
	R to L	`?:`	Conditional
	R to L	`=, *=, /=,` `%=, +=, -=,` `<<=, >>=,` `>>>=, &=,` `^=, |=`	Assignment operation
Lowest	L to R	`,`	Multiple evaluation

Loops and Conditionals

Loops and conditionals give programs the power to make decisions and perform tasks multiple times. JavaScript provides the standard conditionals and looping structures that are available in many computer languages. In fact, these structures were patterned after those found in C, C++, and Java, so if you have written code in any of these languages, you will find this section very straightforward.

Conditionals

Conditional statements enable programs to make decisions based on preset conditions that use the operators discussed earlier in the chapter.

if

The `if` statement is by far the most common conditional statement simply because it is simple and easy to use. The format of a simple `if` statement looks as follows:

```
if (expression)
  statement;
```

If the expression in parentheses evaluates to `true`, the statement is executed; otherwise, the statement is skipped. The statement to be executed can appear on the same line as the if expression, but the code is usually easier to read if the statement appears on the next line as shown in the preceding pseudo code. If two or more lines of code are to be executed, curly braces {} must be used to designate what code belongs in the if statement.

Use the keyword else to extend the functionality of the basic if statement to provide other alternatives if the initial statement should fail. The format of an if...else combination resembles the following:

```
if (expression)
  statement1;
else
  statement2;
```

Now, if the expression evaluates to true, statement1 is executed; otherwise, statement2 is executed. Listing 2.14 demonstrates the use of if and else with a hotel occupancy example. When executed, the code returns the message "There are not enough rooms for 5 guests.".

Listing 2.14 Basic if...else Structures

```
<html>
<script type="text/javascript" language="JavaScript">
<!--

//Declare variables
var emptyRooms = 2;  //Two people per room
var numberOfGuests = 5;

if (emptyRooms == 0)
  document.write("There are no rooms available.");
else
{
  if ((emptyRooms*2) >= numberOfGuests)
    document.write("There are enough rooms for ",numberOfGuests," guests.");
  else
    document.write("There are not enough rooms for ");
    document.write(numberOfGuests," guests.");
  }
}

//-->
</script>
</html>
```

Notice how Listing 2.14 used curly brackets {} to nest an if...else structure inside another if...else structure. Nesting gives programs more decision-making power, but this power comes at the cost of readability.

else...if

The else...if phrase is used in place of nested if...else structures to make code more readable. Each else...if phrase is followed by an expression enclosed in parentheses. Use as many else...if statements as needed. Use a final else statement to execute code when all other conditionals evaluate to false. Listing 2.15 has the same functionality as the code in Listing 2.14, but it uses the else...if structure. This code displays the phrase, "There are not enough rooms for 5 guests.".

Listing 2.15   Making Nested if...else Statements More Readable with the else...if Phrase

```
<html>
<script type="text/javascript" language="JavaScript">
<!--

//Declare variables
var emptyRooms = 2;   //Two people per room
var numberOfGuests = 5;

if (emptyRooms == 0)
  document.write("There are no rooms available.");
else if ((emptyRooms*2) >= numberOfGuests)
  document.write("There are enough rooms for ",numberOfGuests," guests.");
else
  document.write("There are not enough rooms for ",numberOfGuests," guests.");

//-->
</script>
</html>
```

switch

JavaScript offers the switch statement as an alternative to using the if...else structure. The switch statement is especially useful when testing all the possible results of an expression. The format of a switch structure resembles the following:

```
switch (expression)
{
  case label1:
    statement1;
    break;
  case label2:
    statement2;
    break;
  default:
    statement3;
}
```

The switch statement begins by evaluating an expression placed between parentheses, very similar to the if statement. The result is compared to labels associated with case structures that follow the switch statement. If the result is equal to a label, the statement(s) in the corresponding case structure are executed. A default structure can be used at the end of a switch structure to catch results that do not match any of the case labels. Listing 2.16 gives an example of the switch structure.

Listing 2.16   Using the switch **Structure**

```
<html>
<script type="text/javascript" language="JavaScript">
<!--

//Declare variables
var color = "green";

//Display the color of the car based on the variable "color"
switch (color)
{
  case "red":
    document.write("The car is red.");
    break;
  case "blue":
    document.write("The car is blue.");
    break;
  case "green":
    document.write("The car is green.");
    break;
  default:
    document.write("The car is purple.");
}

//-->
switch
</script>
</html>
```

There are a few key points to note about the format of the switch structure in Listing 2.16. First, notice that a colon (:) always follows a label. Second, curly brackets {} are used to hold all the case structures together, but they are not used within a case structure, even when multiple statements are to be executed. Finally, the keyword break is used to break out of the entire switch statement after a match is found, thus preventing the default structure from being executed accidentally. The result of executing the code in Listing 2.16 is the string "The car is green." being displayed.

Loops

There are times when the same portion of code needs to be executed many times with slightly different values. Use loops that run until a condition is met to create this functionality.

for

The for loop is a structure that loops for a preset number of times. JavaScript uses the C and C++ for loop structure. This particular structure is flexible, which makes this type of loop very useful.

From a very high level, the for loop is made up of two parts: condition and statement. The condition portion of the structure determines how many times the loop repeats, whereas the statement executes every time the loop occurs.

The condition structure is contained within parentheses and is made up of three parts, each separated by a semicolon (;). The first part of the condition structure initializes a variable to a starting value. In most cases, the variable is declared within this section as well as initialized. The second part is the actual conditional statement that determines how many times the loop will be iterated. The third and final part determines how the variable, which was initialized in the first part, should be changed each time the loop is iterated. This third part gives the for loop its flexibility by causing the variable to be incremented, decremented, factored, or any other adjustment trick you can devise. The format of the for loop appears as follows:

```
for (initialize; condition; adjust)
{
statement;
}
```

It is important to take time to think about how to implement for loops because it is easy to accidentally create an infinite loop. Specifically, make sure that the conditional will catch the adjusted variable at some point. In many cases, it is advantageous to use the variable in the statement portion of the for loop, but take care not to adjust the variable in such a way that an infinite loop is created. Listing 2.17 makes use of the for loop to create a multiplication table as shown in Figure 2.8.

Listing 2.17 Multiplication Table Using for Loop

```
<html>
<script type="text/javascript" language="JavaScript">
<!--

document.write("<h2>Multiplication table for 4</h2>");
for (var aNum = 0; aNum <= 10; aNum++)
{
  document.write("4 X ",aNum," = ",4*aNum,"<br>");
}

//-->
</script>
</html>
```

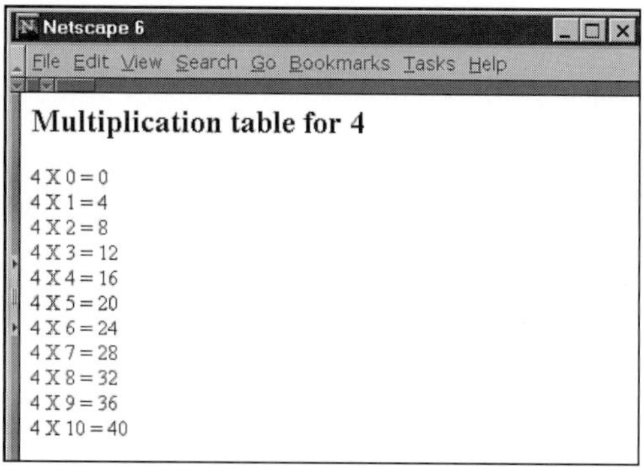

Figure 2.8

The multiplication table is created using a `for` loop.

while

When the `for` loop is too restrictive for a particular piece of code, consider using the `while` loop. The `while` loop can do everything that the `for` loop can do, but not as cleanly. So why even use the `while` loop? The `while` loop goes beyond the `for` loop's capabilities by not restricting the number of times the loop will execute.

The `while` loop is easy to understand if the phrase "While true, loop" is remembered. This phrase means that while the expression in parentheses evaluates to `true`, execute the statements in the loop. After the last statement in the loop is executed, go back to the top of the loop and evaluate the expression again. When the expression evaluates to `false`, the next line of code following the `while` loop structure is executed. To keep the loop from executing indefinitely, a statement must be included in the loop that modifies a variable in the expression. The format of the `while` loop resembles the following:

```
while (expression)
{
   statement;
}
```

Because the expression is evaluated before the loop, it is possible the loop will never be executed if the expression should evaluate to `false` the first time. Listing 2.18 simulates an automated traffic light using the `while` loop.

Listing 2.18   Automated Traffic Light Using *while* Loop

```
<html>
<script type="text/javascript" language="JavaScript">
<!--

//Declare variables
var light = "red";                //traffic light
```

```
var counter = 1;                    //create car traffic
var carsInLine = new Array();  //cars in line
//Make 5 cars go through intersection
while (counter <= 5)
{
  document.write("Car ",counter," approaches intersection.<br>");
  carsInLine[carsInLine.length++] = counter;

  //When 2 cars are in line light turns green
  if (carsInLine.length == 2)
  {
    light = "green";
    document.write("Traffic light turns ",light,"<br>");
  }

  //while light is green cars pass through intersection
  while (light == "green")
  {
    document.write("Car ",carsInLine[carsInLine.length-1]);
    carsInLine.length--;
    document.write(" goes through intersection.<br>");

    //When no cars are in line light turns red
    if (carsInLine.length == 0)
    {
      light = "red";
      document.write("Traffic light turns ",light,"<br>");
    }
  }
  counter++;    //Next car
}

//-->
</script>
</html>
```

Listing 2.18 uses two while loops to simulate an automated traffic light. The first while loop could have just as easily been created using a for loop, but the second while loop would have been nearly impossible to implement using a for loop. The while loop handles this type of conditional loop with ease. In Figure 2.9, you see that the traffic light automatically turns green when two cars are in line at the intersection. After the two cars go through the intersection, the light turns red.

do...while

The do...while loop is simply a variation of the basic while loop that was just discussed. Other than syntax, the only difference between the do...while loop and the while loop is that the do...while loop always executes the loop once before evaluating the expression for the first time. This difference is seen in the following format:

```
do
{
  statement;
}
while (expression);
```

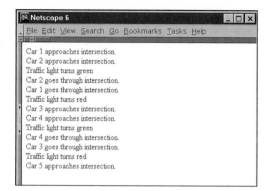

Figure 2.9

Simulating a traffic light using two while loops.

After the loop has executed for the first time, the expression in parentheses is evaluated. If true, the loop is executed again. When the expression evaluates to false, the next line of code following the while structure is executed. As was the case with the while loop, a statement must be included in the loop that modifies a variable in the expression to prevent an infinite loop. Also, notice that a semicolon (;) must be placed after the rightmost parenthesis. Listing 2.19 is the same automated traffic light simulator as shown in Listing 2.18, except do...while loops are used instead of while loops.

Listing 2.19   Automated Traffic Light Using do...while Loop

```
<html>
<script type="text/javascript" language="JavaScript">
<!--

//Declare variables
var light = "red";           //traffic light
var counter = 1;             //create car traffic
var carsInLine = new Array();  //cars in line
//Make 5 cars go through intersection
while (counter <= 5)
{
  document.write("Car ",counter," approaches intersection.<br>");
  carsInLine[carsInLine.length++] = counter;
```

Listing 2.19   Continued

```
//If light green then execute loop more than once
do
{
  //When 2 cars are in line light turns green
  if (carsInLine.length == 2)
  {
    light = "green";
    document.write("Traffic light turns ",light,"<br>");
  }

  //When no cars are in line light turns red
  if (carsInLine.length == 0)
  {
    light = "red";
    document.write("Traffic light turns ",light,"<br>");
  }

  //Cars pass through intersection while light is green
  if (light == "green")
  {
    document.write("Car ",carsInLine[carsInLine.length-1]);
    carsInLine.length--;
    document.write(" goes through intersection.<br>");
  }
}
while (light == "green");

counter++;   //Next car
}

//-->
</script>
</html>
```

The output generated from running Listing 2.19 is exactly the same as executing Listing 2.18.

for...in

The for...in loop should not be confused with the for loop because they are quite different. The only similarity is that both iterate through the loop a set number of times, but this is as far as the similarity goes. The for...in loop is a special looping construct found only in JavaScript to provide access to all the enumerated properties of a JavaScript object. This includes elements of the Array object because they are stored the same way that property names are stored in JavaScript object. The statement(s) in the loop are executed for each property of an object until every property has been accessed. Any parts of an object—such as methods and some properties—that are not enumerated are not accessed by this looping structure. The format of the `for...in` loop appears as follows:

```
for (variable in object)
{
  statement;
}
```

Before the statements in the loop are executed, a property name of the object specified to the right of the keyword `in` is assigned to the variable on the left side of the keyword `in`. The variable would then be used within the loop code. This process will continue until all the properties have been accessed. Unfortunately, the order in which the properties are accessed can vary, so do not assume a particular order. Listing 2.20 shows the properties of a simple HTML button.

Listing 2.20 Accessing Property Names of the `Button` Object Using a `for...in` Loop

```
<html>
<form name="aForm">
  <input type="button"
         name="Big_Button"
         value="Big Button"
         onClick="alert('The Big Button was pressed!')";
  >
</form>
<script type="text/javascript" language="JavaScript">
<!--

var aProperty;
for (aProperty in document.aForm.Big_Button)
{
  document.write(aProperty,"<br>");
}

//-->
</script>
</html>
```

Notice that in Figure 2.10, the name of the properties in the `Big Button` object, rather than the values stored in those properties, was returned.

break

The keyword `break` provides a way for JavaScript to exit out of loop structures and `switch` conditionals prematurely. Most of the time, the word `break` appears on a line by itself, but there are times when a label will follow the keyword. When a label is used, JavaScript completely breaks out of the area designated by `label` and proceeds to the code that follows the area.

Figure 2.10

The properties of the Big Button object.

JavaScript labels can be thought of as placeholders. To label a statement, simply place the label name followed by a colon (:) in front of the code that needs to be broken out of during code execution. Labels are useful when working with nested loops, as shown in Listing 2.21.

Listing 2.21   Using Breaks and Labels

```
<html>
<script type="text/javascript" language="JavaScript">
<!--

//Create outerloop
forLoop1:
for (var counter1 = 1; counter1 <= 5; counter1++)
{
  //Create innerloop
  for (var counter2 = 1; counter2 <= 5; counter2++)
  {
    //Display values in counters for both loops
    document.write("Counter1=",counter1);
    document.write(" Counter2=",counter2,"<br>");

    //Determine when to break out of loop
    if (counter2 == 3)
      break;
    if (counter1 == 3)
      break forLoop1;
  }
}
```

```
document.write("All done!");

//-->
</script>
</html>
```

Notice how the break statement with no label (see Figure 2.11) breaks out of just the inner loop. When the break statement is used with a label, JavaScript knows at which level to break.

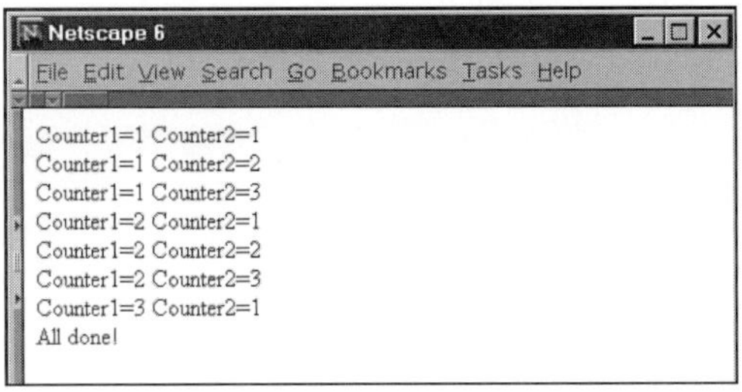

Figure 2.11

Result of using labels and nested loops.

continue

Unlike the JavaScript break structure, the continue statement forces the execution of the code to continue at the beginning of the loop. Similar to the keyword break, the continue keyword usually appears on a line by itself, but there are times when a label will follow the keyword. When a label is used, JavaScript immediately jumps to the beginning of the loop designated by a label and begins executing code.

The beginning of a loop varies depending on the type of loop structure. Table 2.8 shows where each looping structure jumps when a continue structure is encountered.

Table 2.8   Where the continue Statement Jumps

Looping Structure	Continue Jumps To
for	Expression in parentheses following the for keyword
while	Expression in parentheses following the while keyword
do...while	Expression in parentheses following the while keyword
for...in	Next property name in the object

CAUTION

A bug in Navigator 4 causes the expression in parentheses following the while keyword to not get executed when jumped to using a continue statement. Instead, execution of code starts at the top of the loop after the continue statement.

As discussed in the break section, JavaScript labels can be thought of as placeholders. To label a statement, simply place the label name followed by a colon (:) in front of the code where code execution should continue. Listing 2.22 demonstrates the use of label and continue.

Listing 2.22   Using the continue **Statement and Labels**

```
<html>
<script type="text/javascript" language="JavaScript">
<!--

//Create outerloop
outerLoop:
  for (var counter1 = 1; counter1 <= 2; counter1++)
  {
    document.write("Top of outerLoop.<br>");
    //Create innerloop
    innerLoop:
      for (var counter2 = 1; counter2 <= 2; counter2++)
      {
        //Display values stored in counters of both loops
        document.write("Top of innerLoop.<br>");
        document.write("Counter1=",counter1,"<br>");
        document.write("Counter2=",counter2,"<br>");

        //Determine where to continue looping
        if (counter2 == 2)
        {
          document.write("Continue at top of innerLoop.<br>");
          continue;
        }
        if (counter1 == 2)
        {
          document.write("Continue at top of outerLoop.<br>");
          continue outerLoop;
        }
        document.write("Bottom of innerLoop.<br>");
      }
    document.write("Bottom of outerLoop.<br>");
  }

document.write("All done!");

//-->
</script>
</html>
```

This example is a bit complicated, so take time to compare Listing 2.22 to the output in Figure 2.12. Notice how the phrase "Bottom of innerLoop" was not printed after the "Continue at top of innerLoop" because code execution jumped back to beginning of the innermost loop. When a label was attached to the continue keyword, code execution jumped back to the beginning of the loop labeled outerLoop.

CAUTION

Even though JavaScript provides labels, continue statements, and break statements, be careful when using these constructs because they can lead to errors that are hard to trace if they are used improperly.

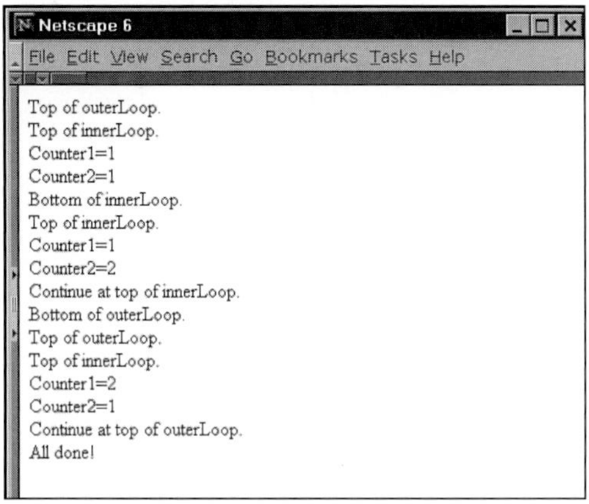

Figure 2.12

Result of using the continue statement in nested loops.

with

The object-oriented design of JavaScript quite often requires long lines of code to access properties and methods of objects. JavaScript provides a special with statement to help reduce the length of code needed to access these properties and methods. The with statement works by placing the repetitive portion of the object's path in parentheses after the with keyword. Now, any properties or methods used within the with statement will automatically have the repetitive portion of the object's path (located in parentheses) added to the front of the string. Listing 2.23 shows how the with statement can save time when resetting text fields to their default values.

Listing 2.23   The with Statement Reduces Repetitive Code

```
<html>
<!--Create a form that has 3 text fields and a reset button-->
<form name="personalInfoForm">
Name<input type="text" name="nameBox"><br>
Occupation<input type="text" name="occupationBox"><br>
```

Listing 2.23   Continued

```
Age<input type="text" name="ageBox"><br>
<input type="button" name="ResetButton"
value="Reset" onClick="ResetFields()">
</form>

<script type="text/javascript" language="JavaScript">
<!--

//Set text field values initially
ResetFields();
//Reset text fields to default values
function ResetFields()
{
  with(document.personalInfoForm)
  {
    nameBox.value="[Enter your name]";
    occupationBox.value="Student";
    ageBox.value="";
  }
}

//-->
</script>
</html>
```

In Figure 2.13, you see that the text fields contain default data that appear initially as well as any time the Reset button is clicked. To achieve this functionality, the Reset button is connected to a function, called `ResetFields()`, that assigns default values to the text fields. To reduce repetitive code, the `with` statement was used in setting the default values, as seen in Listing 2.23.

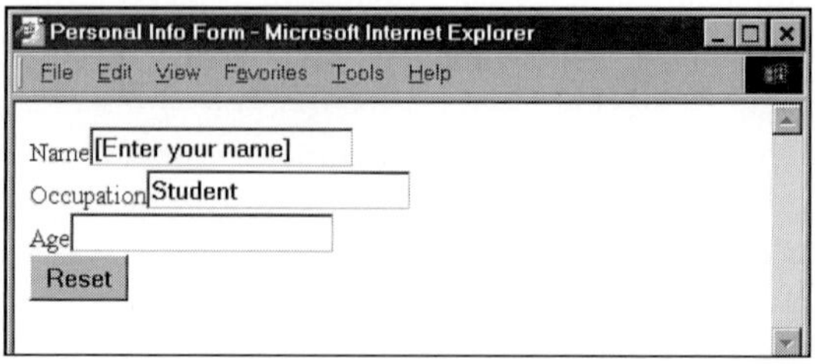

Figure 2.13

Using the `with` statement reduces the amount of code needed to set the default text box values.

Functions

One of the strengths of JavaScript is that it provides support for functions, which is uncommon among scripting languages. On the other hand, JavaScript functions are not as fully developed as those found in languages such as C and C++. The functionality that JavaScript does provide through its functions is more than enough to make Web pages come alive.

Syntax

The syntax of JavaScript functions is very straightforward. All function declarations must begin with the keyword `function` followed by the name of the function. The name of the function is the name that will be used to call on the function within code. Parentheses are placed after the function name to hold arguments that are to be passed into the function. If more than one argument is to be passed into the function, use commas to separate the arguments. On the other hand, if no arguments need to be passed into the function, leave the space between the parentheses empty. Finally, curly brackets are used to contain the code related to the function. Curly brackets are not optional: They are required in JavaScript, even if the function is only made up of one line of code.

Call By Value Versus Call By Reference

If you have done programming in C or C++, you are probably familiar with the phrases call by value and call by reference as related to function arguments. In very basic terms, *call by reference* passes the location of the actual argument to the function, whereas *call by value* makes a copy of the argument to be used just within the function. JavaScript keeps the functionality of passing arguments simple by just using call by value. Using call by value gives the freedom to manipulate the arguments within the function without fear of changing the argument's values outside the function. Listing 2.24 shows an example of JavaScript call by value.

Listing 2.24   Call By Value

```
<html>
<script type="text/javascript" language="JavaScript">
<!--

//Declare variables
var aString = "banana"
var aNumber = 15;

//Function declaration
function test(aString, aNumber)
{
  aString = "orange";
  aNumber = 124;

  //Display values stored in function variables.
  document.write("During function call:<br>");
  document.write("aStringCopy=",aString,"<br>");
  document.write("aNumberCopy=",aNumber,"<br>");
}
```

Listing 2.24   *Continued*

```
//Display variables before function call
document.write("Before function call:<br>");
document.write("aString=",aString,"<br>");
document.write("aNumber=",aNumber,"<br>");

//Call on function
test(aString,aNumber);

//Display variables after function call
document.write("After function call:<br>");
document.write("aString=",aString,"<br>");
document.write("aNumber=",aNumber,"<br>");

//-->
</script>
</html>
```

In Figure 2.14, you see that the values stored in `aString` and `aNumber` appeared to be changed while in the function `test`. But after exiting the function, the values reverted back to their initial value. What actually happened was that a local copy of the variables was made for use within the function. These new variables even have the same name as the ones that were passed into the function. After execution of the function was completed, the local variables no longer existed, so final values displayed were of the original variables.

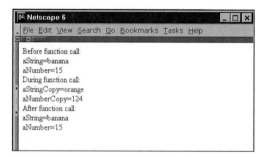

Figure 2.14

Result of using call by value.

If you need to pass in a large number of arguments but do not want to assign each one to a variable, it is possible to access the arguments as an array. To do this, leave the area in parentheses blank and use the `arguments` object and the array operator `[]` to access each argument. Listing 2.25 displays the arguments passed into the function using the `arguments` array as shown in Figure 2.15.

Listing 2.25   ***Accessing Function Arguments with the*** arguments ***Array***

```
<html>
<script type="text/javascript1.2" language="JavaScript1.2">
<!--

//Create a function that displays the arguments it receives.
function displayArguments()
{
  document.write("The following arguments were passed:<br>");
  for(i=0; i<arguments.length; i++)
  {
    document.write(i," = ",arguments[i],"<br>");
  }
}

//Pass some arguments into function
displayArguments(34,"hat",-7945,"shoes");

//-->
</script>
</html>
```

Figure 2.15

The arguments passed into the displayArguments() *function using the* arguments *array.*

Returning Values

What if a value needs to be passed back from a function to be used later in the code? JavaScript provides a return statement that can be used in a function to return a value back to the statement that called the function. The value to be returned is simply placed after the keyword return. The undefined value is returned from a function if no value is specified after the keyword return or if the return statement is not used at all.

A value returned from a function can be assigned to a variable or used within an expression. In Listing 2.26, the value returned from the function is used in an expression to write the phrase "3*5=15" to the browser window.

Listing 2.26   *Returning a Value from a Function*

```
<html>
<script type="text/javascript" language="JavaScript">
<!--

//Function declaration
function multiplyByFive(aNumber)
{
  return aNumber*5;
}

//Display variables before function call
document.write("3*5=",multiplyByFive(3));

//-->
</script>
</html>
```

Functions as Objects

The functions that have been described so far are created statically when the Web page is loaded, but there is also a dynamic function that is not created until it is called, which enables functions to be objects. The syntax for this type of function is very similar to the declaration of a variable.

```
var varName = new Function(argument1,...,lastArgument);
```

The keyword Function is used to create a new function dynamically from the arguments. All the arguments must be strings, and the last argument should always contain the functionality of the function. Listing 2.27 shows a simple example of using the Function object. Once again the phrase "3*5=15" is written to the browser window.

Listing 2.27   *Returning a Value from a Function*

```
<html>
<script type="text/javascript" language="JavaScript">
<!--

//Create the dynamic Function
var multiplyByFive = new Function("y","return y*5");

document.write("3*5=",multiplyByFive(3));

//-->
</script>
</html>
```

Moving On

In this chapter, you were introduced to the details of the JavaScript language that are common across many computer languages. Armed with an understanding of JavaScript data types, variables, operators, loops, conditionals, functions, and basic syntax, which were covered in this chapter, you could start constructing JavaScript programs right now. But don't you want to learn some JavaScript specific programming techniques that will help you tap into JavaScript's full potential? In the next chapter, we will do just that by diving into some JavaScript programming techniques that take JavaScript beyond just a plain computer scripting language.

PART II

PROGRAMMING IN JAVASCRIPT

CHAPTER 3

Programming Techniques

In Chapter 2, "Details of the Language," you were given a quick overview of the core JavaScript language to show you differences and similarities to other computer languages. Now it is time to go to the next level by examining some of the features of the JavaScript language and programming techniques that will make your JavaScript programs more powerful and more resilient to errors and maybe even make you say, "Wow, I didn't know JavaScript could do that!"

In this chapter we will look at pattern matching and event handling and show you how to use these two pieces of JavaScript functionality to make your JavaScript programs more powerful. This chapter will also examine two programming techniques that will make your JavaScript programs less error prone. You will be introduced to the try...catch block and shown how to use it. You will also be introduced to some free JavaScript debugging programs and techniques.

Pattern Matching

Two of the most common uses of Web pages today are for gathering and distributing data. These two areas, by nature, use data manipulation to understand what the user needs and then return information tailored to the user's specifications. One of the key tools for processing data is pattern matching. Some scripting languages, such as Perl, are well suited to handle pattern matching, whereas others provide very little pattern matching capabilities. If you are familiar with Perl, you will probably recognize JavaScript pattern matching because it was based on Perl's implementation of pattern matching. The implementation of pattern matching into JavaScript greatly aids in the processing of data for the Internet.

JavaScript uses the `RegExp` (short for Regular Expression) object to handle pattern matching. This object holds the pattern definition, as well as provides methods for performing matching. You'll begin by learning how to define patterns and then by learning how to use the `RegExp` objects to test for pattern matches.

Defining the RegExp Object

The `RegExp` object can be created in two different ways, which are similar to defining strings. The first way is to use the `RegExp` constructor and the keyword `new`:

```
var lastName = new RegExp("Jones");
```

This notation creates a new `RegExp` object called `lastName` and assigns the pattern *Jones*. The same functionality could have been accomplished by using a direct assignment:

```
var lastName = /Jones/;
```

To differentiate this notation from that used to define strings, the forward slash character (`/`) is used to designate the beginning and end of the pattern. Notice that forward slashes were not needed in the `RegExp()` constructor because this could be distinguished from the `String()` constructor.

Defining Patterns

The syntax used to define patterns in JavaScript could be considered a scripting language in itself because it is so extensive. There are special characters for creating almost any pattern one could imagine, including characters for handling groups, repetition, position, and so on. Table 3.1 shows the special pattern matching characters available in JavaScript.

Table 3.1 Special Pattern Matching Characters

Character	Description
\w	Matches any word character (alphanumeric).
\W	Matches any non-word character.
\s	Matches any whitespace character (tab, newline, carriage return, form feed, vertical tab).
\S	Matches any non-whitespace character.
\d	Matches any numerical digit.
\D	Matches any character that is not a number.
[\b]	Matches a backspace.
.	Matches any character except a newline.
[...]	Matches any one character within the brackets.
[^...]	Matches any one character not within the brackets.
[x-y]	Matches any character in the range of x to y.
[^x-y]	Matches any character not in the range of x to y.
{x,y}	Matches the previous item at least x times but not to exceed y times.

Character	Description
{x,}	Matches the previous item at least x times.
{x}	Matches the previous item exactly x times.
?	Matches the previous item once or not at all.
+	Matches the previous item at least once.
*	Matches the previous item any number of times or not at all.
|	Matches the expression to the left or the right of the | character.
(...)	Groups everything inside parentheses into a subpattern.
\x	Matches the same characters that resulted from the sub-pattern in group number x. Groups, which are designated with parentheses, are numbered from left to right.
^	Matches the beginning of the string or beginning of a line, in multiline matches.
$	Matches the end of the string or end of a line, in multiline matches.
\b	Matches the position between a word character and a non-word character.
\B	Matches the position that is not between a word character and a non-word character.

These special pattern matching characters are used within the pattern to aid in defining complex patterns. Looking at Table 3.1, you might notice that characters such as the asterisk (*), plus sign (+), and backslash (\) hold special meanings that would keep them from being used as a literal. For example, what if you wanted to find all the plus signs (+) in a string? To use a literal plus sign, a backslash (\) must precede the sign. Table 3.2 shows all the characters that require a backslash character to be taken literally within a pattern.

Table 3.2   Literal Characters

Character	Description
\f	Form feed
\n	Newline
\r	Carriage return
\t	Tab
\v	Vertical tab
\/	Forward slash (/)
\\	Backward slash (\)
\.	Period (.)
*	Asterisk (*)
\+	Plus (+)
\?	Question Mark (?)
|	Horizontal bar (|)

Table 3.2   Continued

Character	Description
\(	Left parenthesis (
\)	Right parenthesis)
\[	Left bracket ([)
\]	Right bracket (])
\{	Left curly brace ({)
\}	Right curly brace (})
\xxx	ASCII character represented by the octal number *xxx*
\xHH	ASCII character represented by the hexadecimal number *HH*
\cX	The control character represented by *x*

There is one final piece of syntax that JavaScript provides for creating patterns. Unlike the syntax covered so far, these pieces of syntax appear outside the forward slashes that define the pattern. These attributes are shown in Table 3.3.

Table 3.3   Pattern Attributes

Character	Description
g	Global match. Finds all possible matches.
i	Makes matching not case sensitive.

Testing for Pattern Matches

When a pattern has been defined, it can be applied to a string by using special methods that exist in the RegExp and String objects. The pattern matching methods in the String object require RegExp objects, as shown in Table 3.4.

Table 3.4   Pattern Matching Methods in the String Object

Method	Description
match(*regExpObj*)	Searches for *regExpObj* pattern in string and returns result.
replace(*reqExpObj*,*str*)	Replaces all occurrences of the *regExpObj* pattern with *str*.
search(*reqExpObj*)	Returns the position of matching *regExpObj* pattern within the string.
split(regExpObj,max)	The string is split everywhere there is a matching *regExpObj* pattern up to *max* splits. The substrings are returned in an array.

The pattern matching methods in the RegExp object require String objects, as shown in Table 3.5.

Table 3.5 **Pattern Matching Methods in the** `RegExp` **Object**

Method	Description
`exec(str)`	Searches for pattern in `str` and returns result
`test(str)`	Searches for pattern in `str` and returns `true` if match found, otherwise `false` is returned
`(str)`	Same as `exec(str)` method

Listing 3.1 uses the `RegExp` constructor, special pattern syntax, and the String `replace()` method to replace digits 3 to 5 that exist in the string with nines as seen in Figure 3.1.

Listing 3.1   Using Regular Expressions

```
<html>
<script type="text/javascript" language="JavaScript">
<!--

//Create a text string
var str = "John traded 5 oranges for 135 grapes.<br>";

//Create RegExp object
var span3to5 = new RegExp("[3-5]","g");

document.write(str);
document.write("Replace digits 3 to 5 with nines.<br>");
document.write(str.replace(span3to5,"9"));

//-->
</script>
</html>
```

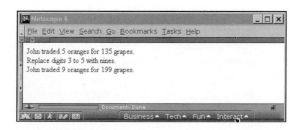

Figure 3.1

The digits 3 to 5 are replaced with nines.

Events and Event Handlers

If you have ever done any graphical user interface programming, you are already familiar with the concept of events. *Events* are actions that take place outside of your program yet might or might not directly impact your program. Many events take place within your browser that you never see and never need to worry about. But there are times when you really want to do something in your code when an event takes place.

For example, consider a Web page that provides users with an interface to change their password on some computer system. The Web page has a text box for the username and a text box for the new password as well as a button to submit the new password information. Before the username and password get submitted to some other system, you want to intercept the event that occurs when the user clicks the Submit button and verify that the password adheres to some specific password rules. A password rule might state that passwords must be greater than three characters in length but less than 15 characters. By having access to events that take place behind the scenes of the browser, you can cancel the submit action and alert the user to the problem with the password she entered.

In this section you will see the types of browser events that JavaScript will let you intercept and how to capture and take action based on those events.

Events

Many different types of events take place in browsers. JavaScript provides access to a number of events that would be useful to you, such as the `click` event, which occurs when the left mouse button is pressed once. Most of the events correspond to an HTML element that a user can see and manipulate such as a button or a check box. Table 3.6 contains a list of events that can be captured by JavaScript and the JavaScript object with which the event is associated.

Table 3.6 **Browser Events**

Event	Object	Occurs When...
Abort	Image	images do not finish loading
Blur	Button, Checkbox, FileUpload, Frame, Layer, Password, Radio, Reset, Select, Submit, Text, Textarea, Window	input focus is removed from the element
Change	FileUpload, Select, Text, Textarea	value of the element ischanged
Click	Area, Button Checkbox, Document, Link, Radio, Reset, Submit	element is clicked
DblClick	Area, Document, Link	mouse button is double-clicked

Event	Object	Occurs When...
DragDrop	Window	object is dropped onto browser Window
Error	Image, Window	there is an error in the page or image
Focus	Button, Checkbox, FileUpload, Frame, Layer, Password, Radio, Reset, Select, Submit, Text, Textarea, Window	input focus is given to element
KeyDown	Document, Image, Link, Textarea	key is depressed
KeyPress	Document, Image Link, Textarea	key pressed and held down
KeyUp	Document, Image Link, Textarea	key is released
Load	Document, Image, Layer, Window	page is loaded into browser
MouseDown	Button, Document, Link	left mouse button is depressed
MouseMove	Window	mouse cursor is moved
MouseOut	Area, Layer, Link	mouse cursor is moved out of the element's bounds
MouseOver	Area, Layer, Link	mouse is moved over element
MouseUp	Button, Document, Link	mouse button is released
Move	Frame	element is moved
Reset	Form	form is reset
Resize	Frame, Window	browser window is resized
Select	Text, Textarea	input field is selected
Submit	Form	form is submitted
Unload	Window	current page is unloaded

Of the events covered in the previous table, the Error and Abort events deserve a little more explanation because they are not as straightforward as the rest.

The Error event is used by the Window and Image objects to indicate that an error occurred while either loading an HTML page or loading an image. This type of error will result in the browser issuing a JavaScript syntax error or a runtime error.

The Abort event is used by the Image object to indicate that the loading of an image was aborted. This type of event occurs often because users become impatient waiting for a large image to load, so they stop the image load before it completes by clicking the browser's Stop button or clicking a link to another page.

Event Handlers

Now that you know the types of events that JavaScript provides, access to them is just a matter of capturing those events. Events are captured using event handlers. By assigning a function or a single line of JavaScript code to an object's event handler, you can capture an event and take action. Table 3.7 shows all the event handlers and the events they are associated with.

Table 3.7   Event Handlers

Event	Event Handler
Abort	onAbort
Blur	onBlur
Change	onChange
Click	onClick
DblClick	onDblClick
DragDrop	onDragDrop
Error	onError
Focus	onFocus
KeyDown	onKeyDown
KeyPress	onKeyPress
KeyUp	onKeyUp
Load	onLoad
MouseDown	onMouseDown
MouseMove	onMouseMove
MouseOut	onMouseOut
MouseOver	onMouseOver
MouseUp	onMouseUp
Move	onMove
Reset	onReset
Resize	onResize
Select	onSelect
Submit	onSubmit
Unload	onUnload

Capturing Events

Event handlers can be defined in one of two ways. The first and most common way is to define the handler inside HTML tags much in the same way HTML tag properties are assigned. For example, to display an alert box when a button is clicked, simply assign a JavaScript alert box to the onClick event handler inside the button's HTML tag as follows:

```
<form name="myForm">
<input
  type="button"
  name="myButton"
```

```
  value="Press Me"
  onClick="alert('myButton was pressed')">
</form>
```

Anytime `myButton` is clicked an alert box will be displayed that tells the user that "`myButton was pressed`". Remember that not all events are associated with every object. To see what events and event handlers are available to a particular object, look for the object in Chapter 8, "Client-Side."

The second way to define event handlers is to define the handler inside JavaScript code using dot notation. Listing 3.2 demonstrates how to assign a JavaScript alert box to the `onClick` event handler using dot notation.

Listing 3.2   Defining Event Handlers Using Dot Notation

```
<html>
<form name="myForm">
<input type="button" name="myButton" value="Press Me">
</form>

<script type="text/javascript" language="JavaScript">
<!--
document.myForm.myButton.onclick="alert('myButton was pressed')";
//-->
</script>
</html>
```

In listing 3.2 `myButton` was initially created using standard HTML tags. Directly after creating the button JavaScript dot notation is used to access the button object and assign an alert box to the `onclick` handler.

NOTE

Notice that in Listing 3.2 the `onclick` property was written using a lowercase c rather than an uppercase C as was used when accessing the `onClick` property via the HTML input tag. This is not a typo! When defining event handlers inside HTML, use the uppercase characters as shown in Table 3.7. When defining event handlers inside JavaScript code using dot notation, the event handlers must not contain any uppercase characters.

Canceling Events

One of the most common uses of event handlers is validation of data entered through an HTML form. For example you might want to verify that a password entered by a user in a password change form is valid before submitting the form to the server. If the password entered by the user is not valid, the user should be notified of the problem and the form should not be submitted. Utilizing the material covered so far, it is easy to capture the `Click` event of the form's submit button and alert the user of the problems with the password entered. But how do you prevent the event from continuing and the form from being submitted to the server? The Submit event can be canceled by simply returning false in the event handling routine. Listing 3.3 demonstrates how to cancel the form submission.

Listing 3.3   Canceling the Submit Event

```
<html>
<script type="text/javascript" language="JavaScript">
<!--

function validatePassword()
{
  passwd = document.passwordForm.password.value;

  //Password must be between 3 and 15 characters
  if((passwd.length < 3) || (passwd.length > 15))
  {
    alert("Password must be less than 15 characters but greater than 3!");
    return(false);
  }
}

//-->
</script>

<center>
<h1>Password Change Page</h1>
Please enter your user name and new password.<br>
(Password must be between 3 and 15 characters.)<br><br>

<form name="passwordForm"
      action="success.html"
      onSubmit="return validatePassword()">
Username: <input type="text" name="username"><br>
Password: <input type="password" name="password"><br>
<input type="submit">
</form>
</html>
```

Not all the event handlers allow you to stop an event from taking place, but some do. Of the events that can be stopped, the value used to stop the event varies. Table 3.8 shows the events that acknowledge return codes and what values to return to cancel the event.

Table 3.8   Event Handler Return Values

Event	Value to Return to Cancel Event
OnClick	false
OnKeyDown	false

Event	Value to Return to Cancel Event
OnKeyPress	false
OnMouseDown	false
OnMouseOver	true (prevents URL from appearing in status bar)
onMouseUp	false
onReset	false
onSubmit	false

Invoking Event Handlers

There are times when you might want to explicitly invoke a particular event handler even though no event took place. This is easy to accomplish because the event handlers are essentially pointers to functions stored as a property of an object that should be executed when a particular event occurs. To invoke an event handler, simply use dot notation to execute the event handler as if it were a function. For example, in the following piece of code, we want to alert the user about a sweepstakes when he moves his cursor over the Lamborghini link. We also want to remind him of the sweepstakes when he goes back to the previous page. To do this, the event handler for the Lamborghini link is executed when the user clicks the Previous Page link.

```
<a href="sweepstakes.html"
    onMouseOver="alert('Enter our sweepstakes for a chance to win a brand new
➥sports car!')">Lamborghini</a><br>
<a href="intro.html"
    onClick="document.links[0].onmouseover()">Previous Page</a>
```

Timers

Even though JavaScript does not directly provide an event-driven timer, we will discuss timers in this section because timers should generally be thought of in terms of events. Because JavaScript does not directly provide a timer, it is possible to use the Window object's setInterval() method to serve the same purpose.

NOTE

The setInterval() method is supported in JavaScript 1.2 and higher.

The setInterval() method repeatedly calls a function or evaluates an expression each time a time interval (in milliseconds) has expired. This method continues to execute until the window is destroyed or the clearInterval() method is called.

For example, in Listing 3.4 the setInterval() method is executed when the document opens and begins to call the dailyTask() function every 20,000 milliseconds. The dailyTask() function evaluates the time each time it is called, and when it is 8:00 a.m., the code within the if statement is called, alerting the user and then clearing the interval. When the clearInterval() method is called, setInterval() halts execution.

Listing 3.4 Creating a Timed Event with the `setInterval()` Method

```
<html>
<script type="text/javascript" language="JavaSCript">
<!--
  function dailyTask()
  {
    var today = new Date();
    if ((today.getHours() == 8) && (today.getMinutes() == 0))
    {
      alert("It is 8:00 a.m.");
      clearInterval(timerID);
    }
  }
  //Set interval to 20,000 milliseconds
  timerID = setInterval("dailyTask()",20000);

//-->
</script>
</html>
```

As mentioned earlier the `setInterval()` method is only available in JavaScript 1.2 and higher. If you need to support an earlier version of JavaScript, you will have to use the `setTimeout()` method.

The `setTimeout()` method is usually used to evaluate an expression after a specific amount of time. Unlike the `setInterval()` method, the `setTimeout()` method is a one-time process that is not repeated an infinite number of times. Listing 3.5 produces the same result as Listing 3.4, using the `setTimeout()` method instead of the `setInterval()` method.

Listing 3.5 Creating a Timed Event with the `setTimeout()` Method

```
<html>
<script type="text/javascript" language="JavaScript">
<!--
  function dailyTask()
  {
    var today = new Date();
    if ((today.getHours() == 8) && (today.getMinutes() == 0))
    {
      alert("It is 8:00 a.m.");
    }
  }
  //Set delayed execution of function to 20,000 milliseconds
  setTimeout("dailyTask()",20000);

//-->
</script>
</html>
```

Exceptions

As of JavaScript 1.4 exception handling has been added to allow you to capture and handle exceptions that occur in your JavaScript programs. The syntax that was chosen was the typical `try...catch`, `throw`, and `finally` statements that are found in other languages such as Java and C++. With these statements you can now throw your own errors, cleanly capture errors, and take the appropriate action based on the error thrown.

throw

The `throw` statement allows you to throw your own errors to be captured by the `try...catch` statement. The actual error that you throw can be any type of object so long as the `try...catch` statement knows how to handle the object. For example an error could be a number, string, or even a user-defined object that contains a number and an array of strings. The format of the `throw` statement resembles the following:

```
throw error
```

try...catch

The `try...catch` statement marks a block of code to try and a block of code to catch errors if an exception should be thrown. The format of the `try...catch` statement resembles the following:

```
try
{
   code
}
catch (error)
{
   code
}
```

The `try` block consists of one or more lines of code enclosed by brackets just below the `try` statement, whereas the `catch` block consists of one or more lines of code enclosed by brackets just below the `catch` statement. The `catch` block can also be passed the actual error that was thrown by specifying an object to hold the error in parentheses. This error object can then be used within the `catch` block. The error object and parentheses are optional and are only needed if you intended to access the actual error thrown from the `catch` block.

If an exception is thrown in the `try` block or within a function called by a statement in the `try` block using the `throw` statement, the code in the `catch` block is executed immediately to handle the error exception that was just thrown. If no exception is thrown while the `try` block is executed, the `catch` block is skipped.

NOTE

The `try...catch` statement can be nested to provide even more error handling.

In Listing 3.6, the `try...catch` and `throw` statements are used to help validate passwords in a simple password validation program. If a password is less than 5 characters in length or greater than 10, the user is presented with an error message thanks to the `try...catch` block.

Listing 3.6 *Password Validation Using the `try...catch` **Block***

```
<html>
<script type="text/javascript" language="JavaScript">
<!-- hide

function ValidatePassword(password)
{
  try
  {
    //Make sure password has at least 5 characters
    if(password.length < 5 )
    {
      throw "SHORT";
    }

    //Make sure password has no more than 10 characters
    if(password.length > 10 )
    {
      throw "LONG";   //too many characters
    }

    //Password ok
    alert("Password Validated!");
  }
  catch(e)
  {
    if(e == "SHORT")
    {
      alert("Not enough characters in password!");
    }
    if(e == "LONG")
    {
      alert("Password contains too many characters!");
    }
  }
}
//-->
</script>

<h2>Password Validator</h2>

<form name="myform">
Please enter password: <input type="password" name="password"><br><br>
```

```
<input type=button name="validate"
       value="Validate!"
       onClick="ValidatePassword(myform.password.value)">
</form>

</html>
```

Runtime Errors

In addition to capturing user-defined errors, the `try...catch` block can also capture runtime errors that JavaScript throws without the assistance of the `throw` statement. You can capture these errors using the `try...catch` block much as you would capture your own user-created errors. The ECMA-262 (Third edition) standard defines six types of error objects that can be thrown by JavaScript. These errors are shown in Table 3.9 with a short description of the type of error they represent.

Table 3.9   Runtime Errors

Error Name	Description
EvalError	The `eval` function was used in a way that is not defined.
RangeError	A numerical value exceeded the allowable range.
ReferenceError	An invalid reference value was detected.
SyntaxError	A parsing error occurred.
TypeError	An operand was a type that was not expected.
URIError	One of the URI handling functions was used in a way that is not defined.

When a runtime error occurs, an Error object is returned. To determine the type of error, simply access the `name` property. Listing 3.7 purposely creates a runtime error by trying to use an undefined variable. The catch block determines the type error and displays an error message to the user.

Listing 3.7   Catching a Runtime Error

```
<html>
<script type="text/javascript" language="'JavaScript"'>
<!-- hide
try
{
  //The following line will create a type error
  //because the variable aNum is undefined.
  sum = 5 + aNum;
  document.write("sum=",sum);
}
catch(e)
{
  if(e.name == "TypeError")
  {
```

Listing 3.7   Continued

```
    alert("A type error occurred.");
  }
}
//-->
</script>
</html>
```

finally

The `finally` block is an optional block of code that is executed each time an exception is thrown. This is especially useful in languages that work with files in which a file handle must be properly closed whether or not an error occurred. In the event that no error occurs, the code in the `finally` block is executed after the `try...catch` block but before the code following the `try...catch` block is executed. When an error is thrown, the `finally` block executes after the `try...catch` block. The format of the `try...catch` block plus the `finally` block looks as follows:

```
try
{
  code
}
catch (error)
{
  code
}
finally
{
  code
}
```

In Listing 3.8, the `finally` statement ensures that the password field is cleared whether or not the password is valid. If the password field had been cleared below the `finally` box, the field would only get cleared if the password was valid because there is a `return` statement in the `catch` block. If the password field had been cleared inside the `catch` box, the field would only get cleared if an error was thrown. Because the password field needed to be cleared regardless of errors, the `finally` block was used.

Listing 3.8   Password Validation Using the `finally` Block

```
<html>
<script type="text/javascript" language="JavaScript">
<!-- hide

function ValidatePassword(password)
{
  try
  {
    //Make sure password has at least 5 characters
    if(password.length < 5 )
```

```
  {
    throw "SHORT";
  }

  //Make sure password has no more than 10 characters
  if(password.length > 10 )
  {
    throw "LONG";  //too many characters
  }
}
catch(e)
{
  if(e == "SHORT")
  {
    alert("Not enough characters in password!");
  }
  if(e == "LONG")
  {
    alert("Password contains too many characters!");
  }
  return(1);
}
finally
{
  document.myform.password.value="";
}

//Password ok
alert("Password Ok!");
}
//-->
</script>

<h2>Password Validator</h2>

<form name="myform">
Please enter password: <input type="password" name="password"><br><br>
<input type=button
       name="validate"
       value="Validate!"
       onClick="ValidatePassword(myform.password.value)">
</form>

</html>
```

Debugging

If you are used to doing programming in languages such as C++ and Java, you are probably accustomed to using some type of debugging tool to help you locate and fix problems in your code. Now that JavaScript is finding its place in the coding community, we are finally seeing support of a native and comprehensive third-party scripting and debugging environment that is similar to those found in mature programming languages (such as C++, Visual Basic, and Java).

JavaScript scripting and debugging tools help the developers take advantage of more automated preventive and, to a lesser extent, corrective controls. If you do not have access to JavaScript debugging tools, or the debugging job is very small, a simple JavaScript alert box can work as a debugging tool. In this chapter, you will examine two free JavaScript debugging options that are at your disposal.

Microsoft Script Debugger

The *Microsoft Script Debugger (MSSD)* is a free downloadable script debugging tool that works as an integrated part of Internet Explorer (version 3.01 and later). MSSD also comes with Windows 2000 and Microsoft's Personal Web Server. You can use MSSD to write and, most importantly, debug your JavaScript (known as JScript with the Microsoft implementation) or Visual Basic Script (VBScript) code. MSSD has the advantage of being able to handle the debugging demands of ActiveX, Java, JScript, and VBScript. (The MSSD can be downloaded from `http://msdn.microsoft.com/scripting/`.)

Features

The following are the main features of the Microsoft Script Debugger:

- Dynamic view of HTML structure
- JavaScript, VBScript, and Java can be debugged seamlessly within the same document.
- Code is color coded
- Ability to set breakpoints
- Can step over, through, and out of each line of code
- Call stack
- Immediate expression window

Tips

The MSSD is easy to use, but there are a few things to know that will have you debugging your code quicker in MSSD.

Starting the Debugger

The only way to start MSSD is to first open Internet Explorer and load the desired HTML source file. Then you can activate MSSD by choosing View, Source.

NOTE

If MSSD isn't installed, viewing the source will open the source file in the Notepad editor.

To start the debugging process, choose Edit, Break at Next Statement from Internet Explorer, or choose Debug, Break at Next Statement from MSSD, and execute the script. This starts the debugger and stops it at the first statement in the current script.

The Break at Next Command

The Break at Next Statement command (which appears on the Script Debugger option of the View menu of Internet Explorer and the Debug menu of MSSD) is similar to a step command, in that the debugger executes the next statement in the script and then breaks, except that you can also use it when you are not currently running the script.

This is an important debugging feature of MSSD because a lot of JavaScript code is commonly declared in the header (or <head> tag) section of an HTML file, and this command is the only way to debug that code. This is because the code in the header of the file has already been executed by the time the HTML file is loaded. Also, any breakpoints set after the HTML file has been loaded are lost if you reload the page.

Evaluating Expressions

An expression can be evaluated with the aid of MSSD's immediate window and the following two methods:

- `Debug.write(string)`—This method writes a specified string, which is often the value of a variable, to the immediate window with no intervening spaces or characters between each string.
- `Debug.writeln([string])`—This method is identical to the preceding method, except that a newline character is inserted after each string. Also, the string argument is optional. If it's omitted, only a newline character is written to the immediate window.

A Final Word on the Microsoft Script Debugger

The Microsoft Script Debugger provides a very helpful environment for you to kick-start your JavaScript debugging and testing. The tools provided in MSSD are similar to tools usually found in full-blown programming language environments such as Visual Basic and C++. Also, MSSD's interface, setup, and installation are all very user friendly and intuitive.

However, MSSD has some limitations in that you need to switch frequently between Internet Explorer and MSSD to conduct debugging, and that you can't print source code. If you want more functionality than what MSSD offers, you might want to consider Microsoft's Visual InterDev 6.0. This product offers all the script-debugging features listed here, plus a full-blown Web developing environment.

At the least, MSSD is certainly a good tool to have in your arsenal, and it's a great value to boot because it's free. However, it can't take the place of writing solid code and systematically testing your code.

The `alert()` Method

If you have coded in any language for any length of time, you know that one of the simplest and quickest ways to debug functionality problems is to display the content of important variables at various stages of your program's execution. By doing so, you can determine if your code is executing as you intended. This technique is especially useful when you cannot get your hands on a full-featured JavaScript debugger, or you are short on time and don't want to fire up a JavaScript debugger to solve a simple functionality problem. JavaScript has a handy method called alert() that lends itself well to stopping the execution of your script to see a value of a variable. With a little thought and proper placement of this method, you can quickly track down functionality problems in scripts.

Listing 3.9 contains some JavaScript code that is supposed to set the color and type of a car. One look at the result, as seen in Figure 3.2, and you can see something went wrong. The script was supposed to set the vehicle type to "car" with the setType() function and the vehicle color to "red" with the setColor() function. If these two functions had worked properly, a string would be written to the screen; otherwise, an alert message would be displayed to let you know that one of the assignment operations failed. No alert message was displayed, but the variable representing the vehicle's color was never set to "red".

Listing 3.9   Problem Code

```
<html>
<script type="text/javascript" language="JavaScript">

//Create two global variables used to describe the vehicles
var vehicleColor;
var vehicleType;

//Set the type of vehicle
function setType()
{
  return(vehicleType="car");
}

//Set the color of the vehicle
function setColor()
{
  return(vehicleColor="red");
}

//If the vehicle type and color were not properly set alert the user.
if(setType() || setColor())
{
  document.write("The " + vehicleType + " is " + vehicleColor);
}
else
  alert("The vehicle type and color could not be set");

</script>
</html>
```

Figure 3.2

There is a problem associated with setting the color of the car.

In Listing 3.10, `alert()` methods are used to debug the code. An `alert()` method is placed in each of the variable-setting functions to determine if each function is being executed. More `alert()` methods are placed before and after the `if` statement to show how the conditional evaluates.

Listing 3.10 Debugging Using the `alert()` Method

```
<html>
<script type="text/javascript" language="JavaScript">

//Create two global variables used to describe the vehicles
var vehicleColor;
var vehicleType;

//Set the type of vehicle
function setType()
{
  alert("Inside the setType function.");  //Debug statement
  return(vehicleType="car");
}

//Set the color of the vehicle
function setColor()
{
  alert("Inside the setColor function.");  //Debug statement
  return(vehicleColor="red");
}

//Debug statement
alert("Before if statement: type="+vehicleType+" color="+vehicleColor);

//If the vehicle type and color were not properly set alert the user.
if(setType() || setColor())
{
  //Debug statement
  alert("After if statement: type="+vehicleType+" color="+vehicleColor);

  document.write("The " + vehicleType + " is " + vehicleColor);
}
```

Listing 3.10   Continued

```
else
  alert("The vehicle type and color could not be set");

</script>
</html>
```

When Listing 3.10 is executed, the first alert box displayed shows that both variables are undefined before the execution of the `if` statement. The next alert box shows that the `setType()` function was executed. The final alert box shows the vehicle type set to `"car"`, but the color is still undefined after the `if` statement, as you can see in Figure 3.3. What happened to the `setColor()` function? The `alert()` method in the `setColor()` function was never executed, which lets us know that the `setColor()` function was never called from within the `if` statement.

Figure 3.3

Debugging using the `alert()` method.

If the first argument in a logical OR operation evaluates to `true`, the second argument is never evaluated. Because the `setType()` function returned `true`, the `setColor()` function was never executed. The problem is easily corrected by simply changing the logical OR operator to a logical AND operator.

CAUTION

After your code checks out, don't forget to remove the `alert()` methods that you added for debugging or else your program will display these alerts to those who use your scripts.

Moving On

In this chapter, you were introduced to some programming techniques that will make your JavaScript programs more powerful and more resilient through the use of JavaScript pattern matching, event handling, exception handling, and debugging. Part II, "Programming in JavaScript," provides a look at the environments in which JavaScript can be interpreted and into the actual use of the language.

CHAPTER 4

Client-Side Scripting

The first three chapters of this book introduced you to JavaScript, exposed you to its semantics, and covered several programming techniques to help you get started. In Part II, "Programming in JavaScript," we are going to cover the environments in which JavaScript is interpreted, including the client-side, server-side, and in the Windows Script Host environment.

In this chapter specifically, you will look at several aspects of the language. We'll look at how the browsers interpret JavaScript, how to deal with some of the issues that surround browsers, and how they handle the scripts—issues such as bugs and differences in functionality.

Later, you will look at how JavaScript can extend a browser's functionality. This is accomplished with some of its object arrays and through the use of LiveConnect—the Java to JavaScript bridge. We will also cover tasks that will allow you to process form data and without having to send pages back and forth to the server. Cookies, another key component, will also be covered in this chapter.

The next topic we will discuss is Window manipulation. Windows appear to be very basic on the outside, but the underlying JavaScript provides a lot of power for configuring and manipulating windows to meet your design needs.

This chapter will also include coverage of the dynamic positioning of HTML and XHTML elements and their manipulation using JavaScript. Finally, the chapter will take a look into XUL—the XML-Based User Interface Language, which is a new language created by our friends at Mozilla.org and used to build the user interface for the Netscape 6 and Mozilla browsers.

This chapter has a lot of material in it, so lets get started by talking about which browsers support JavaScript and some of their issues.

Supporting Browsers and Their Issues

Even though JavaScript seems to have been a foundation building block in today's Internet technology, it wasn't always there. It wasn't until Netscape Navigator 2.0 and Internet Explorer 3.0, that its functionality was included. Currently, only four major browsers interpret JavaScript: Netscape Navigator, Internet Explorer, Opera, and HotJava. However, just because they interpret the language does not mean that they do so in the same manner, which is something you will be looking into shortly.

NOTE

Because many users use AOL's online service to connect to the Internet, you should know that the AOL browser is actually an Internet Explorer browser with different "chrome."

For those of you familiar with Java, you know that various *JVMs*, or *Java Virtual Machines*, can interpret the language differently. JavaScript is similar, except that the market can often be considered more fragmented. For the most part, browsers do interpret JavaScript the same—at least the core language semantics. The big distinction is that they all have different version support as well as diverse bugs.

To give you an idea of the versions and support among these browsers, take a look at Table 4.1. It breaks down these runtime environments by browser version and language version.

Table 4.1   Language Support by Browser Version

Browser	Version	Language
Netscape Navigator	2.0	JavaScript 1.0
	2.02 for OS/2	JavaScript 1.1
	3.0	JavaScript 1.1
	4.0–4.05	JavaScript 1.2
	4.06–4.5	JavaScript 1.3
	6.0	JavaScript 1.5
Microsoft Internet	3.0	JScript 1.0
Explorer	4.0–4.5	JScript 3.0
	5.0	JScript 5.0
	5.5	JScript 5.5
	6.0	JScript 6.0
HotJava	3.0	JavaScript 1.4
Opera	3.0–3.5	JavaScript 1.1
	4.0–5.0	JavaScript 1.3
		JavaScript 1.4

NOTE

Opera has done an excellent job of keeping up with standards in its browsers; however, understanding what it supports exactly can be a bit confusing. Table 4.1 is a rough idea of their support, but for more information we recommend that you visit `http://www.opera.com/opera4/specs.html#ecmascript` for version 4 information and `http://www.opera.com/opera5/specs.html#ecmascript` for version 5.

JAVASCRIPT 1.1 IN NAVIGATOR 2.02 FOR OS/2?

If you take a second look at Table 4.1, you will notice that the 2.02 version of Navigator for OS/2 is JavaScript 1.1–compliant. This is because the OS/2 versions of the Navigator browsers were co-developed by engineers from both Netscape and IBM.

The OS/2 version of Navigator was not announced or in beta until the 3.0 version of the browser was already released. Those of you who used the 3.0 browsers heavily might have noticed that they seemed more buggy than the 2.0 versions. Added enhancements seemed to make the code more unstable, which prompted the OS/2 version using the more stable 2.0 interface to be built, but included the 3.0 backend.

Because browser versions are often determined using JavaScript, an OS/2 user with Navigator 2.02 can start the browser with the "-3" option that will tell its user agent string to report that it is a 3.0 browser rather than a 2.02. Because it has the capability to interpret all the JavaScript on the page, this option allows the user to experience all the enhancements for the 3.0 browsers.

These facts are important for programmers to properly implement features in their scripts. You can now check the Navigator 2.02 for OS/2 browser and know that it is JavaScript 1.1–compliant—with or without the -3 option. All of this, of course, was remedied with the release of Netscape Communicator 4.61 for OS/2, which has support for JavaScript 1.3.

New browsers are released a couple of times a year, which forces the market to become fragmented in terms of the JavaScript runtime environment with which users will be accessing a site. Extra care needs to be taken in writing scripts so browsers will interpret them correctly. As discussed in Chapter 2, "Details of the Language," most of the version control can be accomplished using the `language` or `type` attribute of the `<script>` element, but not all browsers correctly implement this. As a programmer, you will have to write in code to accommodate these browsers.

The first browser you are going to look at is Netscape's Navigator browser. It was the pioneering browser that first interpreted the language co-developed by Sun and Netscape. We will also look at Internet Explorer, Opera, and HotJava as well.

Netscape Navigator

Netscape Navigator (see Netscape 6.0 in Figure 4.1) first included its support for JavaScript in its version 2 browsers. This was a major step for JavaScript because Navigator was by far the most widely used browser in the world. Web developers could add scripts to their pages and feel very confident that the majority of their visitors would be able to experience their enhancements. And things have not stopped there.

Recently, Netscape released version 6 of its browser, which was a complete rewrite and is shown in Figure 4.1, from the ground up. This time, its support for official standards has been relatively unmatched. It has even gone so far as to not support old elements and tags that were implemented in Navigator 4, which provides its own problems, but reflects Netscape's dedication to standardization.

Figure 4.1

Netscape 6 browser.

Similar to anything else Netscape has implemented in its browsers, it has continued to expand the language and add to it. With each major release, new functionality through standards support have been added that keep it ahead of other browsers. Table 4.2 outlines the JavaScript support in these browsers and gives you some additional information.

Table 4.2   JavaScript Language Support by Browser

Browser Version	Language Version	Notes
2.0	JavaScript 1.0	First browser to interpret JavaScript.

Browser Version	Language Version	Notes
2.02 for OS/2	JavaScript 1.1	As discussed in previous sidebar, this browser has the 2.0 interface, and it has the 3.0 back-end for rendering HTML and interpreting JavaScript.
3.0	JavaScript 1.1	First version to support the src attribute of the <script> tag, which can be used to include external JavaScript source.
4.0–4.05	JavaScript 1.2	Enhancements for Dynamic HTML and added signed scripts as a model of security.
4.06–4.7	JavaScript 1.3	Completes Navigator's support for ECMAScript 1st Edition, as well as other enhancements expected in the 2nd Edition.
6.0	JavaScript 1.5	Adds support for the DOM Level 1 and some Level 2 as well as ECMAScript 3rd Edition.

TIP

Netscape's DevEdge site has more information on JavaScript bugs. It can be accessed at `http://developer.netscape.com/tech/javascript/index.html`, and then follow the link for `Known Bugs`.

Internet Explorer

Even though Internet Explorer (see version 5.5 in Figure 4.2) was the second browser to follow suit in its support of JavaScript, it seems to have avoided the Navigator problems just discussed. However, JScript does have issues that inhibit its performance and functionality as well.

Because Microsoft did not want to purchase the licensing to JavaScript from Netscape to implement in its Internet Explorer browser, it had to reverse-engineer the scripting language and give it a new name. This led to the birth of JScript.

In the short run, this seemed like a bad thing for JavaScript programmers. Now that two versions of the language were on the market, how could programmers be assured that their scripts would work in both browsers? Luckily, this version incompatibility only lasted for version 3 of Internet Explorer. By the time version 4 of the browser came out, the first edition of the ECMAScript standard was well on its way to adoption, and Microsoft based its JScript 3.0 on the standard. This refocused and aligned both JavaScript and JScript and reduced the problems of incompatibility between them. There are, however, a few quick things to watch for in the older versions of the browser:

- Microsoft provides the ability for users to update their scripting engines without updating the browser. It also distributes different engines with minor updates to the browser.
- No support for the `Image` object on the Windows platform in version 3 of the browser.
- Support for the `src` attribute of the `<script>` tag was implemented in the 3.02 maintenance release of Internet Explorer and did not fully work.

Figure 4.2

Internet Explorer 5.5 browser.

NOTE

Microsoft refers to its interpreter as a *JScript Scripting Engine*. This terminology will be used in this section.

Table 4.3 breaks down the browsers that have been released by Microsoft and its JScript support by version. The table also includes some notes that give more information about what the release added to the language.

Table 4.3   JScript Language Support by Browser

Browser Version	Language Version	Notes
3.0	JScript 1.0	First Internet Explorer browser to interpret JScript.
4.0–4.5	JScript 3.0	Added enhancements for Dynamic HTML and support for

Browser Version	Language Version	Notes
		the first edition of ECMAScript. This is the first version to fully support the src attribute of the <script> tag, which can be used to include external JavaScript source.
5.0	JScript 5.0	Supports the third edition of ECMAScript.
5.5	JScript 5.5	Supports ECMAScript 3rd Edition and DOM Level 1 and some Level 2 items.

There is another topic that we want to discuss here, which is the user's ability to update his scripting engine without having to update his browser. This makes it very possible for a user to implement an Internet Explorer 5.0 browser that has the 5.5. JScript engine.

One good thing is that the more recent versions of the engines have functions to allow developers to determine what version of the engine users are running. Watch out because using some of these functions on version 3.0 engines causes errors. Luckily, version 3 is few and far between at this point, so it puts developers at less of an impossible situation.

Listing 4.1 includes the Microsoft-specific elements that a developer can use to determine the version of the scripting engine the user has.

Listing 4.1   JScript's Elements for Determining Scripting Engine Version Information

```
<script language="JScript" type="text/javascript">
<!--
// Create a variable to hold all the engine information in a single string.
var jscriptVer = ScriptEngine() + " " + ScriptEngineMajorVersion() + "." +
                 ScriptEngineMinorVersion() + " Build " +
                 ScriptEngineBuildVersion();

// Write the string to the user's browser.
document.write('<b>You are running:</b> ' + jscriptVer);

// Write each of the individual elements of the engine's version to the
// browser.
document.write('<br><br><b>ScriptEngine:</b> ' + ScriptEngine());
document.write('<br><b>ScriptEngineMajorVersion:</b> ');
document.write(ScriptEngineMajorVersion());
document.write('<br><b>ScriptEngineMinorVersion:</b> ');
document.write(ScriptEngineMinorVersion());
```

Listing 4.1   Continued

```
document.write('<br><b>ScriptEngineBuildVersion:</b> ');
document.write(ScriptEngineBuildVersion());
// -->
</script>
```

TIP

In case you are wondering, the scripting engine for JScript is contained in the jscript.dll. You can check the properties in this DLL file to see what version you have on your machine.

The result of opening Listing 4.1 in Internet Explorer 5.5 on Windows is shown in Figure 4.3. As you can see, this can be very helpful if developers need to know the specific build the user implements when executing his scripts. However, you should be careful to avoid versions that do not support these elements.

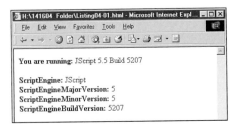

Figure 4.3

Internet Explorer 5.5 displaying its scripting engine information.

Opera

The Opera browser (see version 5.0 in Figure 4.4) has received a lot of press because of its support for standards, such as *cascading style sheets (CSS)*. The developers at Opera Software have taken on the responsibility of providing a lot of functionality to their users without a lot of unneeded flash. Opera is mostly a pure rendering engine, but it does have support for Navigator plug-ins and Java. This allows its users to gain the needed support to position it as a real alternative.

The main thing you will want to watch out for in Opera browsers is the user agent string—it has the ability for users to select the string sent. This was included to allow the Opera browser to access pages built for Navigator 4, or perhaps Internet Explorer 5, which can make it tricky for JavaScript programmers to accurately detect the browser version.

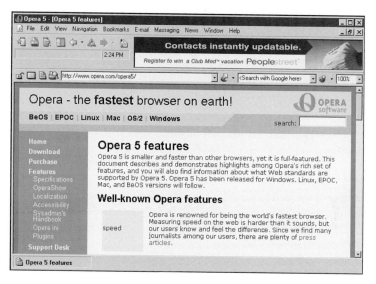

Figure 4.4

The Opera 5.0 browser is available at http://www.opera.com.

HotJava

The final browser that we are going to mention is Sun's HotJava browser, which included support for JavaScript in version 3.0. It uses the Rhino implementation (JavaScript engine written in Java) from Mozilla.org for its interpretation and is the only browser that was officially released that supported JavaScript 1.4. To be honest, this browser is rarely used and has not been updated in over a year, but we did want to mention it.

Extended Browser Functionality

In addition to the scripting functionality you can add to Web pages, JavaScript can also be used to extend your browser's functionality. Today's most functional browsers support plug-ins or ActiveX controls. These plug-ins are loaded by the browser when it starts and are accessed when called via HTML tags on a page. Because plug-in instances run as objects within the browser's environment, some core JavaScript objects can be used to access, modify, and control their functionality.

JavaScript also supports interaction with Java applets embedded in a page. This type of interaction can occur in both directions—from the applet to scripts on a page, and from scripts to the applet. The technology behind this is referred to as LiveConnect and will be discussed in more detail later in the chapter.

Built-In Functions for Control

Not all browsers have the same methods for their extended functionality, but some common language elements allow developers to access these various items. These are considered *built-in* control elements in the JavaScript language itself, and access to this functionality is through two included arrays.

These two items are arrays containing references to all the applets the browser has loaded on a given page and all the plug-ins the browser has installed. Through these arrays, a developer is able to access and interact with these components.

Applet Array

The applet array stores references to all the Java applets loaded on a page. This allows a developer to retrieve the total number of applets on a page and to directly interact with them. If the developer is using LiveConnect to interact with the applet, the applet itself can be referenced by its indexed location. The second applet, for instance, could have its information accessed by the following JavaScript code:

```
var myAppletInfo = document.applets[1];
```

This allows developers to store information about this applet in a variable, where they can then parse it and process the information about the applet. The information stored in the myAppletInfo example would contain the applet's name, dimensions, and the layout package used to create the applet.

With the increased use of Web-based, enterprise-level applications, it is not uncommon for a developer not to know how many applets are on a page. Pages are built dynamically depending on the type of request by the user, and the resulting page might depend completely on the number of items the user selected to view. Because this number can vary, a developer might have to include JavaScript code that analyzes the page to see how many applets are on it. Listing 4.2 shows an example of this.

Listing 4.2   Checking for Java Applets with the `length` *Property of the Applet Array*

```
<html>
<head>
<title>Checking for Java Applets</title>
<script language="JavaScript1.1" type="text/javascript">
<!--
function checkApplets(){

  // Store the number of applets on the page in a variable
  var numApplets = document.applets.length;

  // If there are no applets on the page, then go to the "noapplets"
  // page.
  if(numApplets == 0){
    window.location.href = "http://www.purejavascript.com/noapplets.html";
```

```
    // If there is only one applet on the page, go to the
    // "oneapplet" page.
    } else if (numApplets == 1){
      window.location.href = "http://www.purejavascript.com/oneapplet.html";

    // If there are more than two applets on the page, go to the
    // "manyapplets" page.
    } else if (numApplets > 2){
      window.location.href = "http://www.purejavascript.com/manyapplets.html";
    }
}
// -->
</script>
</head>

<body onLoad='checkApplets()'>
<center>
<table border="1">
  <tr>
    <td>
      <applet code="TestApplet"
        codebase="."
        width="200"
        height="35"
        name="AppletOne"
        mayscript>
        This browser is not able to run Java applets
        <param name="clickurl"
              value="http://www.purejavascript.com/cgi-bin/redirect.cgi">
      </applet>
    </td>
  </tr>
    <tr>
      <td>
        <applet code="TestApplet"
          codebase="."
          width="200"
          height="35"
          name="AppletTwo">
          This browser is not able to run Java applets
          <param name="clickurl"
                value="http://www.purejavascript.com/cgi-bin/redirect2.cgi">
        </applet>
      </td>
  </tr>
</table>
</center>
</body>
</html>
```

As you can see in Listing 4.2, after the page has fully loaded, an onLoad event handler is called by the <body> tag. This event triggers a function that checks to see how many applets were loaded on the page. Depending on the number of applets loaded, the browser might be redirected to another location. If the number of applets on the page is two, the page does not redirect to another location.

NOTE

You are only able to access properties and the results of applet methods after the applet is fully loaded and running. To ensure this, use the onLoad event handler in the <body> tag. Note that there are bugs in certain platforms of Navigator browsers that incorrectly fire this event. Be sure to account for these instances.

As you can see, the applet array can be a very helpful resource in accessing the applets on your pages. You should use it with caution, however, because not all browsers that support JavaScript support the ability to run applets.

Plug-In Array

The plug-in array is the second array that can be used to control elements loaded by an HTML page. Developers commonly determine whether a particular plug-in is installed on the user's machine by using this array. When this has been determined, the developer can then make the appropriate decisions about whether to try and load the plug-in.

The actual plug-in array has several properties that can be used to retrieve this information. These include items such as the name of the plug-in, the actual filename, and a description. Listing 4.3 demonstrates the use of the plug-in array by writing the information it can retrieve to the page. Figure 4.5 shows the result of running this in a browser with several plug-ins installed.

NOTE

The following example only works in Netscape browsers, but Internet Explorer does in fact support this array (or as Microsoft calls it, "collection"). For more information on what properties and methods are supported under this collection, visit http://msdn.microsoft.com/workshop/author/dhtml/reference/collections/plugins_0.asp.

Listing 4.3   Checking the Plug-Ins Array

```
<html>
<head>
<title>Checking the plug-ins Array</title>
</head>
<body>
<script language="JavaScript" type="text/javascript">
<!--
```

```
// Store the number of plug-ins in a variable.
var numPlugins = navigator.plugins.length;

// Write the title of the page.
if (numPlugins > 0){
  document.write('<h3>The Plug-ins You Have Installed</h3><hr>');
}else{
  document.write('<h3>You have No Plug-ins Installed.</h3>');
}

// Write the various installed plug-in information to the page.
for (i = 0; i < numPlugins; i++){
  currPlugin = navigator.plugins[i];
  document.write('<p><b>Name:</b> ' + currPlugin.name + '<br>');
  document.write('<b>Filename:</b> ' + currPlugin.filename + '<br>');
  document.write('<b>Description:</b> ' + currPlugin.description + '<br>');
}
// -->
</script>
</body>
</html>
```

Figure 4.5

The result of running Listing 4.3 in a browser with several plug-ins installed.

In the script, you access the total number of plug-ins installed by using the `length` property of the plug-ins array. After this has been done, determine the appropriate header to write to the page and run through a `for` loop writing the plug-ins information as well. This is a fairly simple example, but accessing these properties can be very useful when determining what elements you want your pages to use when loaded by a browser.

LiveConnect

LiveConnect is a Netscape-specific technology, starting with Netscape Navigator 3, that provides a communication link among JavaScript scripts, Java, and plug-ins. It allows JavaScript to access certain Java core functionality through the `Packages` object. It can also access specific Java applets through the `Applet` array and plug-ins through the `Plugin` array.

In this section, you'll take a closer look at LiveConnect as it pertains to Java applets. You'll also step through some examples of using LiveConnect to extend the browser's interpretation of scripts and Java.

Why LiveConnect?

LiveConnect plays a very important role in linking JavaScript and Java together so that each can rely and expand on the functionality the other has to offer. The ability to dynamically change and interact with a Java applet on a page after it is loaded makes it easy for a Web developer to harness the power of Java. This can be done in modular fashion because it is completely possible that another developer wrote the applet.

On the flip side, LiveConnect enables an applet to access information contained in scripts. Because information can be passed to and from the applets, developers are able to maximize the functionality of their pages when using it. Using LiveConnect within an enterprise gives the developer the ability to exploit these features. Netscape has developed LiveConnect so that it fits nicely within its vision and adds to the mix of technologies that support the "write once, run anywhere" theories.

LiveConnect Examples

The following two examples will give you a better understanding of how LiveConnect works within Netscape's browsers. The first example shows you how JavaScript can access some of the Java language functionality natively (through the `Packages` object). The second example shows how you can use JavaScript to interact with an applet.

Listing 4.4 uses some of Java's native methods available via the `Packages` object. In this example, a user can type some information in a form text box, and then click the Print button to print his text to the Java Console. The `onClick` event is used to pass the text information to a JavaScript function, where it then writes the information. The result of running this example in a browser is shown in Figure 4.6.

NOTE

For this to work in Netscape 6, you must have selected the option to install the Java runtime during your initial installation.

Listing 4.4 Accessing Java Methods Through JavaScript's Packages *Object*

```
<html>
<head>
<title>LiveConnect Example #1</title>
<script language="JavaScript1.2" type="text/javascript">
<!--

//This function takes the text entered in by the user and prints
//it to the Java Console.
function writeToConsole(inText){
  Packages.java.lang.System.out.println(inText);
}
// -->
</script>
</head>

<body>
<form>
  <input type="text" name="entered" width="10">
  <input type="button" value="Print"
          onClick='writeToConsole(form.entered.value)'>
</form>
</body>
</html>
```

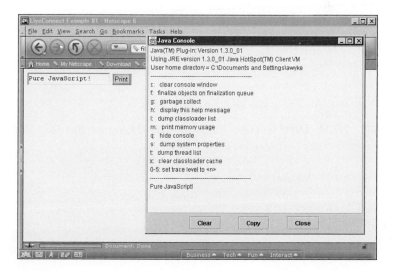

Figure 4.6

Using the Packages *object to access the* System.out.println() *method in Java.*

The second example is a little more complex. It takes text entered by the user and passes it to a method within an applet to change the text the applet is displaying. To help you get a full understanding of this example, this listing includes both the applet code and the JavaScript code needed to perform this task. Listing 4.5 shows the Java code necessary, whereas Listing 4.6 shows the JavaScript.

Listing 4.5 Java Code Used in the Example

```java
// Imported classes
import java.applet.*;
import java.awt.Graphics;

public class PSLiveConnectExample extends Applet {

  // Initialize an instance of a public string variable
  public String sText;

  // Initial the string itself with a value
  public void init() {
    sText = new String("Pure JavaScript");
  }

  // Draw the string in the applet at this location
  public void paint(Graphics gArea) {
    gArea.drawString(sText, 20, 20);
  }

  // Method used to change the string when passed to the applet
  // from JavaScript.
  public void changeString(String aString) {
    sText = aString;
    repaint();
  }
} }
```

Listing 4.6 HTML Used to Load the Applet and Change the Text Within It

```html
<html>
<head>
<title>LiveConnect Example #2</title>
</head>

<body>
<center>
<table border="1">
  <tr>
    <td align="center">
      <applet
        code="PSLiveConnectExample.class"
```

```
            codebase="."
            name="TextChanger"
            width="150"
            height="25"
            mayscript>
      </applet>

      <form name="inputForm">
        <input type="button" value="Change Text"
               onclick="document.TextChanger.changeString(document.inputForm.
                        ➥inputText.value)">
        <input type="text" size="20" name="inputText">
      </form>
    </td>
  </tr>
</table>
</center>
</body>
</html>
```

As you can see in Listing 4.6, the applet that displays the initial `"Pure JavaScript"` text is loaded. After the page has finished loading, the user can enter text into the text box and click the Change Text button to modify the text displayed by the applet. This button directly accesses the `changeString()` method in the applet to change the text from the default to that entered by the user. Figure 4.7 shows the result of changing this text.

Figure 4.7

Using JavaScript to change the text in a Java applet.

Form Processing

Before JavaScript was developed, most developers used server-side programs to send information from the Web server back to a user's browser after a form was submitted. When using a form, the user would enter his information and submit the form to the server. This usually was slow, due to transmission delay back and forth to the server and the fact that the Web server did most of the work with the form, such as parsing information and validation.

JavaScript helps speed up this process by interacting with the form data, similar to these server-side programs, before it is sent to the server. This saves the Web server work and reduces the amount of time spent transmitting information. Using JavaScript for form processing can be very useful to the developer and time-saving to the user.

NOTE

Form processing refers to the ability of Web developers to pass fields of information from the browser to be processed by a server. When this information is passed to the server, developers can use it as their application sees fit.

Many forms collect user information such as names, addresses, or interests. By collecting this information, developers open up a whole new level of possibility in their sites' functionality. They are no longer placing static information out on their site for the world to see; rather, it is a means of communication—communication between users and their sites.

Communication between users and sites is mostly done through forms. When a user fills out an online form and submits it, the information needs to be validated and processed. Without client-side scripting languages, these actions can only be done on the server-side. The validation and processing work can be broken out by using JavaScript, which is where the language's use of form processing really benefits developers.

Accurate processing of forms is dependent on the validity of the information given. It is very easy to input incorrect data into a form and then submit it. When this is done, you generally let the server handle any problems that might occur. These problems can be avoided if JavaScript is used on the client-side to validate the data before it is submitted. JavaScript can check the data content and format before transmitting the data, which, in turn, frees the server from encountering and dealing with these types of problems. The server's only job now is to process the information being sent.

FORM SUBMISSION 101: GET VERSUS POST

When creating a form, one of the attributes you must specify within the <form> tag is method. This attribute can be set to either GET or POST, both of which can be used as the type of submission for the form. However, their uses differ slightly.

GET, which is the default setting, passes the form values on to the URL. This is sent in a single transmission to the URL specified in the action attribute. The following simple form can be used as an example:

```
<form action="http://www.purejavascript.com/cgi-bin/sampleform.cgi"
    ➥method="get">
  <select name="state">
    <option value="NC">North Carolina</option>
    <option value="SC">South Carolina</option>
    <option value="CA">California</option>
  </select>
  <input type="button" value="Submit">
</form>
```

When the user selects one of the items from the pull-down menu and clicks the Submit button, the information will be passed on the end of the URL. If the user selected North Carolina, for instance, the passed information would look similar to the following:

```
http://www.purejavascript.com/cgi-bin/sampleform.cgi?state=NC
```

The POST method, on the other hand, works differently. When POST is used, the browser contacts the URL specified in the action property and sends the data in the body of the HTTP request. For those of you familiar with the HTTP standard, you know that information is passed back to the browser in two main parts: the *head* and the *body*. When a browser sends a POST form, it performs a task similar to the server in that it sends the information in the body of the request and not on the URL.

There are different cases for using the two methods. If you are sending large amounts of form information to the server, the POST method should be used. Normally a server will have problems handling large amounts of data using the GET method. The POST method is also useful for keeping your data from being easily seen because the form information is sent in a data block.

Keep in mind that JavaScript is not a complete substitute for server-side form processing programs. It should be used more as a complement to these programs. By combining the use of JavaScript and server-side programs, a developer can create a very effective and efficient means of processing forms.

Before programmers can use JavaScript with forms, they need to know how to get and parse forms for information. The next section takes a look at methods of extracting information from forms using JavaScript.

The Forms Array

Another JavaScript built-in object used to access components within a page is the Form array. The Form array, which is a property of the document object, is an array containing a list of the forms within a given document. Because it is an array, each form in the document can be referenced by the index number that represents its position in the document.

For instance, if you had a document containing three forms and you wanted to access a property in the second form, you would reference it with the following syntax:

```
document.forms[1].property
```

In this example, the *document* object refers to the document in which the form is located, and the *property* element refers to the property you are trying to access.

Listing 4.7 is an HTML page that contains two forms. In addition to the forms on this page, two JavaScript functions are included in the <head> portion of the page that show different methods of accessing forms and perform some input validation. Each of the forms contains a text area for the user to insert text, as well as a Submit button. When the user attempts to submit the form, an onClick event is fired and the contents of the form are passed to a JavaScript function for processing.

Listing 4.7 Using the *Forms* Array to Access Multiple Forms on a Page

```
<html>
<head>
<title>Forms Array Example</title>
<script language="JavaScript" type="text/javascript">
<!--

// Function verifyZip checks for a valid ZIP Code.  If user enters invalid
// ZIP Code, then an alert box is used to inform the user. Function
// takes the length as an input parameter.
function verifyZip(length){

  // Create variable and store the form value for the ZIP input.
  var zipEntry = document.forms[0].zip.value;

  // Parse the input for an integer number using 10 as the radix.
  var zipNum = parseInt(zipEntry, 10);

  // Check to see that the length is 5.
  if (document.forms[0].zip.value.length == length){
    // Verify that the ZIP is a number.
    if(zipNum != 0 && isNaN(zipNum) == false){
      alert(zipEntry + " is a valid zip code");
    } else {
      // Inform the user if the ZIP is not valid.
      alert("Invalid Zip Code Entered. Please Re-enter");
    }
  } else {
    alert("Invalid Zip Code Entered. Please Re-enter");
  }
}

// Function myName displays the name the user entered.
```

```
function myName(){
  // Get the form value of the name entered.
  var name = document.form2.name.value;
  alert("You Entered:  " + name);
}


// -->
</script>
</head>
<body>
<p>
<center><b>Forms Example</b></center>
<br><br><br>
<table>
<form name="form1" method="post">
  <tr>
    <td align="right">Enter a 5 Digit Zip Code:</td>
    <td align="left">
      <input type= "text" name="zip" size="15">
      <input type="button" name="button1"
    ➥value="Verify" onclick="verifyZip(5)">
    </td>
  </tr>
</form>
<form name="form2" action="" method="post">
  <tr>
    <td align="right">Enter Your Name:</td>
    <td align="left">
      <input type="text" name="name" size="15">
      <input type="button" name="button2" value="Show Name"
             onclick="myName(this.form)">
    </td>
  </tr>
</form>
</table>
</body>
</html>
```

In the first form, validation is performed on the input. The user is asked to enter a five-digit ZIP Code. Once entered, the user can push the verify button, which calls the verifyZip function. This function uses the forms array index number to access the user input. Figure 4.8 shows this example of accessing the forms array.

NOTE

Remember that form indexes are zero indexed and are stored in the array in sequential order. The first form in the document is forms[0], the second form is forms[1], the third form is forms[2], and so on.

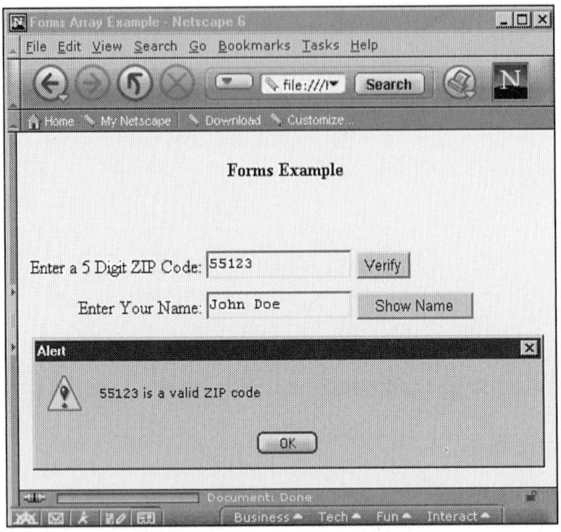

Figure 4.8

The output result for processing the first form.

When a script has the input, it can perform checks to make sure that it is the correct length and that a numeric value was entered. If the correct information has been entered, a message is displayed informing the user the input was valid. If incorrect information was entered, an error message is displayed informing the user of an invalid entry.

The second form takes a name as input and passes it to the showName function, which displays the name in a window when the Show Name button is chosen. Notice that the function accesses the form information differently than the first function. Instead of using the forms array, it references the form by its name value.

In this example, the variable *name* is set using the name attribute of the <form> tag instead of the index number of the Forms array. Either method of accessing a form element is valid. However, if a document contains many forms, it might be easier to use the form name instead of counting the Forms array index numbers. Accessing a form through the name attribute also tends to make the script easier to understand.

This example demonstrates some uses of combining forms and JavaScript. Another useful function of JavaScript and forms is information manipulation. For instance, if the form processing program on the server-side only processes phone numbers without the hyphen, developers can program their scripts to strip all hyphens out of phone numbers before submission.

Accessing and Writing Information

Just as the document object contains a forms array, the form object contains an elements array. The elements array works similar to the forms array in that items are indexed in the order they appear, and you can access a specific element by its name instead of index number. Listing 4.8 demonstrates the two different ways of accessing form elements.

Listing 4.8 Using Different Methods of Accessing Form Elements

```html
<html>
<head>
<title>Example of accessing form elements</title>

<script language="JavaScript" type="text/javascript">
<!--

// Function displays the car information entered.
function showCar(){

  // Access the car information by using the elements array.
  var car = document.pref.elements[0].value;
  alert("Your favorite car is: " + car);
}

// Function displays the color information entered.
function showColor(){

  // Access the color value directly by form name.
  var color = document.pref.color.value;
  alert("Your favorite color is: " + color);
}

// -->
</script>
</head>
<body>

<form name="pref" method="post">
Enter the name of your favorite car:
  <input type="text" name="car" size="25">
  <input type="button" name="carButton" value="Show Car"
         onclick="showCar(this.form)">
<br>
Enter your favorite color:
  <input type="text" name="color" size="15">
  <input type="button" name="colorButton" value="Show Color"
         onclick="showColor(this.form)">
</form>

</body>
</html>
```

The information entered into each text box becomes an element of the form. Using the elements array, a script can access each individual element of the array. As you can

see in the `showCar` function, the car element is referred to by `document.pref.`
`elements[0].value`. This is accessing the first element of the `elements` array in this
specific form. The button would be the second element and would be referenced by
`document.pref.elements[1].value`, and so on for other elements throughout the
form.

The `showColor` function references the `color` object differently: by using the `color`
object name with `document.pref.color.value`. If you were to use the elements array,
this value would be referenced by `document.pref.elements[2].value`. Referencing
by element name is much safer and easier to keep track of, and it can prevent future
problems. For example, suppose that you have a Web page containing two frames, A
and B, respectively. Frame A contains a JavaScript program that references elements
within frame B using the `elements` array. If the Web page in frame B were to change
but still contain form elements, your JavaScript program in frame A would be accessing incorrect form elements. Another reason for using element names is that if new
form elements are inserted in the future, all the element numbering would not have to
be changed.

TIP

Referencing by the `elements` array can be useful if you want to keep your program generic, but if you want better maintainability and ease of use, referencing
by `name` is the preferred choice.

In addition to accessing form elements, you can also write or modify form information.
This can be a very useful technique for automatic form correction. Just about any
object that carries information within a form can be modified.

Take a look at a simple example of writing information to forms. Listing 4.9 contains
a form with one text box with a question and one Submit button. The user is asked to
enter the answer to the question. If the answer is correct, an information box appears
indicating so. If it is wrong, an alert box appears informing the user that he entered the
wrong answer, and the correct answer is automatically written to the text box.

Listing 4.9   Writing Information to JavaScript Forms

```
<html>
<head>
<title>Example of Writing Form Elements</title>

<script language="JavaScript" type="text/javascript">
<!--

// Function checks to see if the text submitted is the
// correct answer.
function checkText(){

    // Perform an equality check to see if the input is correct.
    if( document.FormExample3.textbox.value == "Bugs Bunny"){
```

```
      alert("You are correct!");
   } else {

   // If the original input was incorrect, output the
   // correct information and inform the user.
      document.FormExample3.textbox.value = "Bugs Bunny";
      alert("That is incorrect. The correct answer is now in the text box.");
   }
}

// -->
</script>
</head>
<body>

<form name="FormExample3" method="post">
What Looney Tunes Character is gray and has long ears?
   <input type="text" name="textbox" size="25">
   <input type="button" name="Bugs" value="Submit"
 ➥onclick="checkText(this.form)">
</form>
</body>
</html>
```

Building on the foundation of the code in Listing 4.9, it's possible to create a JavaScript method that creates a customized pull-down menu based on specific user input.

Form Example

Listing 4.10 presents a sample Web page that allows a user to enter his personal information to submit. After all the information is entered and the user clicks the Submit button, all the form data is validated on the client-side before passing the data to the server for further processing.

Listing 4.10   Example Using a Form for Client-Side Validation

```
<html>
<head>
<title>Form Validation Example</title>
<script language="JavaScript" type="text/javascript">
<!--

// Function checks to see that the personal
// information entered is valid.
function validatePersonalInfo(){

   // Declare variables to hold input values.
   var _first = document.info.fname.value;
   var _last = document.info.lname.value;
   var _street = document.info.street.value;
```

Listing 4.10 *Continued*

```
var _city = document.info.city.value;
  var _zip = document.info.zip.value;
  var _phone = document.info.phone.value;
  var _email = document.info.email.value;

  // Verify that the all input fields are filled in.
  if(_first.toString() == ""){alert("Please enter a first name.");}
  if(_last.toString() == ""){alert("Please enter a last name.");}
  if(_street.toString() == ""){alert("Please enter your street name.");}
  if(_city.toString() == ""){alert("Please enter your city.");}
  if(_zip.toString() == ""){alert("Please enter your ZIP.");}
  if(_phone.toString() == ""){alert("Please enter your phone number.");}
  if(_email.toString() == ""){alert("Please enter your email.");}

  else{
    // Check that the ZIP and phone numbers are valid inputs.
    var checkZip = checkNum(5);
    var phoneInput = document.info.phone.value;

    // Initialize variables.
    var validPhone = false;
    var validZip = false;

    if(checkZip == true){
      validZip = true;
    }
    else{
      alert("Invalid ZIP Code: " + validZip);
    }

    // If the phone number is not valid, then inform user.
    if(!checkPhone(phoneInput)){
      alert("Phone number is invalid." + validPhone);
    }
    else{
      validPhone = true;
    }

    if(validZip && validPhone){
      alert("Your form has been verified");
    }
  }
}

// Strips hyphens out of phone number and verifies that
// phone number is valid. Any phone number in the format
// xxxxxxxxxx, xxx-xxx-xxxx, or (xxx)xxx-xxxx will be valid.
```

```
function checkPhone(str){
  var regexp = /^(\d{10}|\d{3}-\d{3}-\d{4}|\(\d{3}\)\d{3}-\d{4})$/;
  return regexp.test(str);
}


// Function checks that the ZIP Code is valid.
function checkNum(length){
  var zipEntry = document.info.zip.value;
  var zipNum = parseInt(zipEntry, 10);

  if (document.info.zip.value.length == length){
    if(zipNum != 0 && isNaN(zipNum) == false){
      // Valid ZIP Code
      return true;
    }
    else {
      // Invalid ZIP Code
      return false;
    }
  }
  else {
    //Too Many digits- Invalid
    return false;
  }
}


// -->
</script>
</head>
<body>
<p>
<center><b>Form Validation Example</b></center>
<p>This page demonstrates how JavaScript can do form validation on a Web page.
Using JavaScript to do validation on the client-side can greatly reduce
processing time by reducing the chance of submitting incorrect forms.
<hr>
<br>
<b>Personal Information:</b>
<form name="info" method="post">
<table>
  <tr>
    <td align="left">first name:</td>
    <td align="left">
      <input type="text" name="fname" size="15">
      last name:
      <input type="text" name="lname" size="20">
    </td>
  </tr>
  <br>
```

Listing 4.10   Continued

```
<tr>
   <td align="left">Street:</td>
   <td align="left">
     <input type="text" name="street" size="30">
   </td>
 </tr>
 <br>
 <tr>
   <td align="left">City:</td>
   <td align="left">
     <input type="text" name="city" size="15">
     State:
     <select name="state">
       <option value="AL">AL</option>
       <option value="AK">AK</option>
       <option value="AZ">AZ</option>
       <option value="AR">AR</option>
       <option value="CA">CA</option>
       <option value="CO">CO</option>
       <option value="CT">CT</option>
       <option value="DE">DE</option>
       <option value="FL">FL</option>
       <option value="GA">GA</option>
       <option value="HI">HI</option>
       <option value="ID">ID</option>
       <option value="IL">IL</option>
       <option value="IN">IN</option>
       <option value="IA">IA</option>
       <option value="KS">KS</option>
       <option value="KY">KY</option>
       <option value="LA">LA</option>
       <option value="ME">ME</option>
       <option value="MD">MD</option>
       <option value="MA">MA</option>
       <option value="MI">MI</option>
       <option value="MN">MN</option>
     </select>

     ZIP:
     <input type="text" name="zip" size="7">
   </td>
 </tr>
 <br>
 <tr>
   <td align="left">Phone (w/area code):</td>
   <td align="left">
     <input type="text" name="phone" size=20>
   </td>
 </tr>
```

```
    <br>
    <tr>
      <td align="left">Email:</td>
      <td align="left">
        <input type="text" name="email" size="20">
      </td>
    </tr>
    <br>
</table>
<center>
  <input type="button" value="Submit" onclick="validatePersonalInfo()">
</center>
</form>
</body>
</html>
```

Figure 4.9 shows how the personal information form looks.

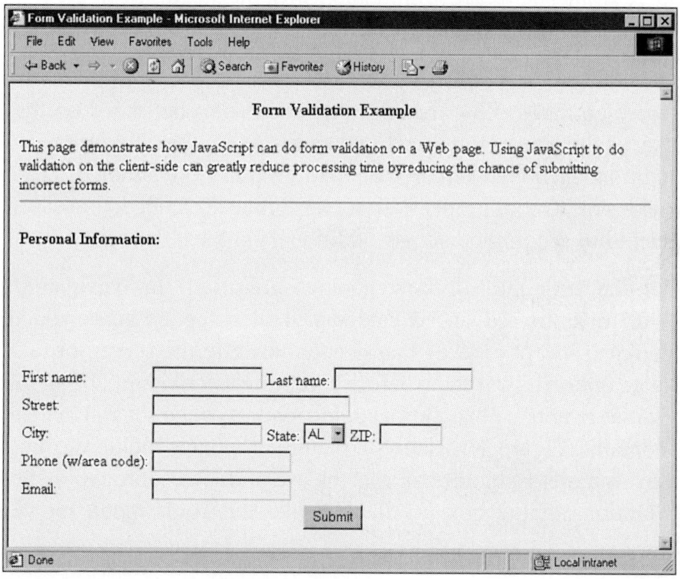

Figure 4.9

Form example using client-side validation.

The form begins by validating that all the input fields have been filled. If any of the fields are left empty, an alert box will appear indicating that the field requires input. Two main inputs require special validation: the ZIP Code and the phone number.

The first function called is `ValidatePersonalInfo`. This main function checks to see that all the user entries are valid. If so, an alert box is returned indicating that the form has been validated. Before the form can be completely validated, the ZIP Code and phone number must be checked. The ZIP Code verification is performed by the sub-function called `checkNum`. This function takes one parameter—the string length. For the ZIP Code, we are restricting the string length to five digits. If this is found to be true, the ZIP Code is validated.

The second sub-function called is `checkPhone`. The `checkPhone` function takes the input for the phone number and checks it against three different standard phone number formats. If any are found to be valid, the function returns `true`. After both checks are performed, the form is determined to contain valid information.

Cookie Handling

A *cookie* is a small bit of organized information that is stored by a browser in a text file on the user's computer. Cookies are typically used to store information pertinent to a specific site that is currently used and can be reused in the future.

The location of cookie text file differs according to the browser being used. In Navigator, all cookies are stored in a file named `cookies.txt`. In Internet Explorer, each cookie is stored as its own individual text file in the Cookies folder, which is located by default in the \Windows or \Winnt folder.

There are limitations to cookies. The size of a cookie is limited to 4KB. Also, Navigator browsers only allow for 300 total cookies to be stored on the user's computer. This keeps the size of the `cookies.txt` file or Cookies folder to a 1200KB maximum. In addition, each Web server is only allowed to store a total of 20 cookies. If the 300 total cookies or 20 cookies per Web server limit is exceeded, the least recently used cookie is deleted to accommodate any additional cookies.

Browsers let the user control how cookies are used. In Navigator, under Edit, Preferences, there is an Advanced category. This category gives you the option to accept all cookies, accept cookies that get sent back to the server, or disable cookies. There is also an option to warn you before accepting a cookie. Enabling this option will force the browser to notify you when a cookie requests to be set and inform you of what the cookie contains. Figure 4.10 shows a picture of what a cookie warning would look like. Similarly, Internet Explorer controls the use of cookies through its Security tab on its Internet Options dialog box (available under the Tools menu for version 5.5 on Windows).

NOTE

When a cookie is first set, it is stored in the browser's memory. It isn't until the browser is exited that the cookie gets written to the file.

The `cookie` object is part of the `Document` object. Cookies can be created, set, and modified by setting the appropriate values of the `cookie` property. A cookie has four name attributes: `expires`, `path`, `domain`, and `secure`.

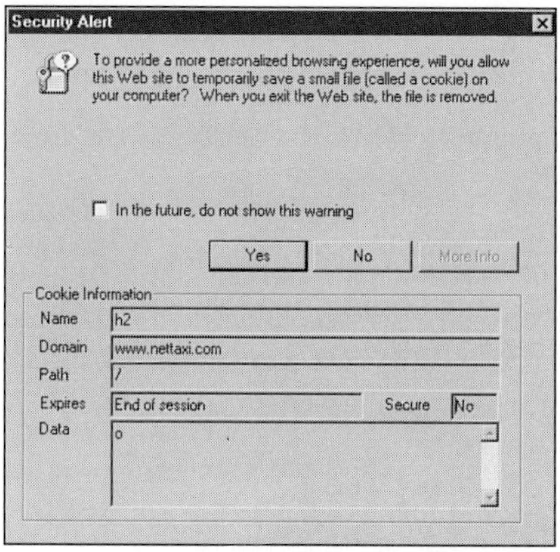

Figure 4.10

Cookie warning example.

By default, a cookie lasts only during the current browsing session. When the browsing session is over, the cookie is destroyed. For a cookie to last beyond the current browsing session, the `expires` attribute must be set. This attribute specifies the life of a cookie. The value of this attribute can be set to any valid date string. If the `expires` attribute is set, the cookie is written to the cookie text file after the current browsing session is over. If no `expires` attribute is set, the cookie will expire when the user's browsing session ends.

The `path` attribute specifies the domain associated with the cookie. The level of association begins at the specified path and goes down into any subfolders. For example, suppose that `http://www.purejavascript.com/examples/cookie.html` was setting a cookie and wanted the cookie to be shared across Web pages on the `pure-javascript.com` domain. To do this, the cookie `path` attribute needs to be set to `"/"`. This allows the cookie to be accessed from any page on the `www.purejavascript.com` Web server. If the path was set to `"/examples"`, the cookie would only be valid to pages in the examples folder and its subfolders.

NOTE

If the `secure` attribute is specified, the cookie will be only be transmitted over a secure channel (HTTPS). If `secure` is not specified, the cookie can be transmitted over any communications channel.

Understanding the cookie attributes is the first step in being able to read and write cookies. Now that you do understand this, look at how to read cookies.

Reading Cookies

As stated before, cookies are part of the document object. The first thing you have to do is to read the cookie property. This can be done with the following statement:

```
var cookieName = document.cookie;
```

This statement creates the variable cookieName and assigns it the cookie property of the document object. When you have accessed this property, you must extract the various attributes of the cookie. The cookie property itself returns a string containing all the cookies pertaining to the current document.

Cookies are interpreted in name/value pairs. The string returned from the cookie property contains the list of cookie name/value pairs. To read an individual attribute, you must parse through its string. You can use built-in JavaScript string methods to accomplish this.

Look at the example in Listing 4.11 to see how to read a cookie. When calling this function in your code, you simply need to pass the name of the cookie you are looking for.

Listing 4.11   Getting a Cookie Value

```
<script language="JavaScript" type="text/javascript">
<!--

// Declare variable to hold all the cookies contained
// in the document.
var cookies = document.cookie;

// Function that gets a cookie's value by searching
// for the name of the cookie.
function readCookie(name) {

  // Declare variable to set the "name=" value.
  var start = cookies.indexOf(name + "=");

  // Get the index if the cookie name is found.
  if (start == -1){
    alert("Cookie not found");
  }
  // Get the first character of the cookie.
  start = cookies.indexOf("=", start) + 1;

  // Read to the end of the cookie.
  var end = cookies.indexOf(";", start);

  if (end == -1){
    end = cookies.length;
```

```
  }

  // Get the cookie value, reversing the escaped format by
  // using the unescape method.
  var value = unescape(cookies.substring(start, end));

  if(value == null){
    alert("No cookie found");
  }
  else{
    alert("Cookie value is: " + value);
  }
}
// -->
</script>
```

Writing Cookies

Cookie values can be created, modified, and set. Remember that cookies are read as name/value pairs. Therefore, when you write a cookie, its attributes must be written as a name/value pair.

To set a cookie value, you first create a cookie and assign it a name. Then you must set each individual attribute for the new cookie. Keep in mind that when you set the expires attribute, you must have a valid date string. It is best to use the JavaScript Date methods to create a date string, which can be assigned. Additional cookie attributes can be set similarly. The following is an example of how this is done:

```
document.cookie = "name=" + form.cookie.value + "; expires=" + month;
```

If you want to modify a specific value in the cookie, just set its attributes again. You can delete a cookie's value by modifying that attribute.

Windows in Action

A window object is used in all your JavaScript programs, whether you specify it or not. The window object is one level higher than the document object in the JavaScript object hierarchy and provides a developer with the ability to manipulate the current window as well as create new window instances.

The ability to create new windows allows developers to add functionality to their sites. Some sites have advertisers create new windows to show their advertisement banners, whereas others, such as ESPN (shown in Figure 4.11), use this as a method to play games in windows while their users continue to browse.

The Parent/Child Relationship

Windows use what is described as a parent/child relationship when they are initiated. This means that if window B is created from within window A, window B is considered a child of window A, which is its parent. Any actions performed on the child by its parent must be referenced through its parent. Look at the following code:

```
<html>
<head>
<script language="JavaScript" type="text/javascript">
<!--
// Function creates a new window called myChild
// with the index.html file in it.
function create(){
  open("index.html", "myChild");
}
// -->
</script>
</head>
<body>
<form name="form1">
  <input type="button" value="Create Child" onclick='create()'>
</form>
</body>
</html>
```

Figure 4.11

Pop-up window for a game.

The function `create` simply creates a new window that would be considered a child of the original window. The name of the child is specified in the second parameter of the `window.open` function, which is `"myChild"`. Any values in the child window are referenced using the name of the parent window. If the child window has a child of its own, this would be considered a grandchild of the parent. For a grandparent to perform actions on its grandchild, it must first reference its immediate parent and then its grandparent. Suppose that the grandchild is named Jane, its parent is named Bob, and the grandparent is named Joe. For Jane to be manipulated by Joe's window, it must reference the value by the following:

```
joe.bob.jane.document.form1.textBox.value
```

The parent has total control of its immediate child window and any subsequent child (grandchild) windows. If the parent window is destroyed, all control for the remaining child windows is lost.

A child window can find out who its parent is by using the `opener` method. The `opener` method will tell the child from which window it was created. You use the `opener` method as shown in the following:

```
var name = window.opener.document.name;
```

This will return the name of the parent document to the `name` variable.

You can use multiple instances of `opener` if you have several levels of windows. If a grandchild wanted to reference its grandparent, it could do so by simply adding another level:

```
window.opener.opener.document.form1.textbox.value
```

For a window to refer to its own properties, you can use the window `self` property. Suppose that you wanted to set a `textbox` value within a form document in a window. You could refer to the value as shown in the following:

```
self.document.formName.textbox.value = "JavaScript is cool";
```

Creating Windows

JavaScript provides a built-in method to create new instances of windows. The `open` method can be used to create any primary or secondary window. The following is an example of how `open` can be used.

```
window.open("web.html", "newWin", "resizeable,menubar,toolbar");
```

This creates a window that is resizable, contains a menu bar, and has a toolbar. The `"web.html"` is the file that will open in the newly created window. `"newWin"` represents the name of the window object. Many different features can be added to a window. This example only shows a few. Other features include, `outerHeight`, `outerWidth`, `innerHeight`, `innerWidth`, `alwaysRaised`, `alwaysLowered`, `location`, `screenY`, and `screenX`. The features are specified in the parameters of the `open` function.

NOTE

Be careful not to include any spaces between window features; this will cause errors to occur in your window creation. Refer to the `windows` object in Chapter 8, "Client-Side," for more details on other windows properties.

After you create a new window, you can manipulate it. JavaScript also provides you with the ability to interact between multiple windows. As long as a `window` property is referenced correctly, you can modify objects in other windows. Remember the parent-child relationship when referencing `window` objects.

Limitations

In older versions of JavaScript, windows could only be referenced from the top down. This meant that a parent window would know the properties of its child windows, but not vice versa. In JavaScript version 1.2 and later, this problem is resolved. As mentioned earlier, using the `opener` property will resolve any child/parent referencing conflicts.

Window Example

The next example shows how you can send information between two windows. It begins with the parent window. Figure 4.12 shows both the parent and child windows open with the parent window on the top.

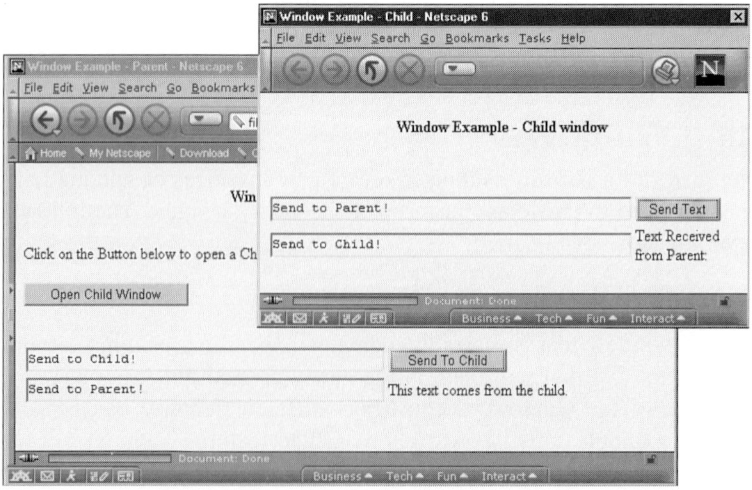

Figure 4.12

Window example showing how information can be sent between windows.

Look at the code for the parent window in Listing 4.12.

Listing 4.12 *Parent Code for Window Example*

```
<html>
<head>
<title>Window Example - Parent</title>
<script language="JavaScript" type="text/javascript">
<!--

// Function creates and opens a new child window.
function openWin(){
  // Open a new window named "ChildWin".
  childWin=open("child.html", "ChildWin","toolbar,scrollbars,menubar,status,
              ➥width=500,height=200");
}

// Function sends a value from the parent window to the
// child window.
function sendToChild(){
  childWin.document.childForm.childText.value =
            ➥document.parentForm.parenttext.value;
}

// -->
</script>
</head>

<body>
<p>
<center>
  <b>Window Example - Parent Window</b>
  <br><br><br>
</center>
<form name="parentForm">
  Click on the Button below to open a Child window:
  <br><br>
  <input type="button" name="submit" value="Open Child Window"
       onclick="openWin()">
  <br><br><br>
  <table>
    <tr>
      <td align="left">
        <input type="text" name="parenttext" size="45">
      </td>
      <td align="left">
        <input type="button" name="submit" value="Send To Child"
              onclick="sendToChild()">
      </td>
    </tr>
    <tr>
```

Listing 4.12 Continued

```
    <td align="left">
       <input type="text" name="received" size="45">
     </td>
     <td align="left">
        This text comes from the child.
     </td>
   </tr>
  </table>
</form></body>
</html>
```

This parent window has a button, which, when clicked, opens a child window. It also has two text fields, one for sending text to the child and one for receiving text from the child. The user will first click the button to create a new window. This is the child window. When the user enters text into the first text box and clicks the Send Text button, the input is sent to the child and appears in its appropriate text box. Take a look now at what the child window looks like in Listing 4.13.

Listing 4.13 Child Window Code for Window Example

```
<html>
<head>
<title>Window Example - Child</title>
<script language="JavaScript" type="text/javascript">
<!--

// Function sends a value from the child window to the parent window.

function sendToParent(){
  window.opener.document.parentForm.received.value =
    ➥document.childForm.sendText.value;
}

// -->
</script>
</head>

<body>
<p>
<center>
  <b>Window Example - Child window</b>
  <br><br><br>
</center>
<form name="childForm">
  <table>
    <tr>
      <td align="left">
```

```
      <input type="text" name="sendText" size="45">
    </td>
    <td align="left">
      <input type="button" name="submit" value="Send Text"
             onclick="sendToParent()">
    </td>
  </tr>
  <br>
  <tr>
    <td align="left">
      <input type="text" name="childText" size="45">
    </td>
    <td align="left">
      Text Received from Parent:
    </td>
  </tr>
 </table>
</form>
</body>
</html>
```

The child window is similar to the parent except that there is no option to open another window. The child window has one text field for sending text to the parent window and one text field for receiving text from the parent. In the JavaScript code, you can see the use of the opener property to reference its parent. Remember, you cannot reference windows directly upward. The parent can call a child by name, but a child cannot call the parent by its name.

Manipulating windows provides you with the ability to greatly expand your site's functionality. Many window properties can be specified or modified to your individual needs. Do be careful on how you implement these windows, however, because often times too many (or any for that matter) pop-up windows can be annoying. Be sure that you really need it.

Dynamic Documents

As Web sites became more advanced, the need for dynamic content grew. In the beginning, the only type of presentation technologies available was plain HTML. It allowed various type of formatting so content could be displayed in a pleasant manner, but soon more was needed—enter scripting languages. The combination of JavaScript and HTML was a big step, and that coupled with support for CSS meant that a developer could create static content with HTML and then have control over it with JavaScript and CSS.

The Web has come a long way in a very short period. The first generation was called Dynamic HTML or DHTML for short. As we just mentioned, DHTML wasn't one specific technology, but a core set of three technologies working together to provide a toolset for developers to create dynamic content. But things have moved on even more since then.

In today's newest browsers we have the *Document Object Model (DOM)* at our disposal. This is an attempt to standardize the method in which you access elements within a given document, such as an HTML or XHTML document. This is definitely the way of the future, but it does not remove the fact that some of the older browsers are still around.

Within this section of the chapter, we are going to take a look at both the old (DHTML) and new (scripting the DOM) ways of doing things. We will also show you how to build cross-browser scripts that will work in all version 4+ browsers. With the rate of adoption of the DOM, this will most likely be the last edition of this book that covers the old way, but for now it is definitely still needed.

The Old Way

Netscape initially tackled three-dimensional positioning with the `<layer>` and `<ilayer>` tags in Navigator 4. Internet Explorer 4, on the other hand, implemented three-dimensional positioning through their *DHTML Object Model* implementation by extending the functionality of the existing HTML tags, such as `<div>`.

With the release of these version 4 browsers, developers had two ways of creating layers within documents, but they were browser-specific. Cascading Style Sheets, which is also needed for creating dynamic documents, has been implemented in both browsers. CSS provides the base positioning. There are some differences in implementation, in both level and interpretation, so this area is still in a state of change, but things are getting much better.

Navigator 4 Layers

The concept of layers was introduced in Navigator 4, but not only in the HTML, but also through the new Layers object in JavaScript 1.2. Similar to many things at the time, these `layers` were only supported in Navigator 4—not Internet Explorer. They did have some usefulness, however, by providing the ability to control the stacking and movement of elements within a single window.

On the HTML side, one of the new tags created was the `<layer>` tag. This tag allowed you use JavaScript for layer manipulation. The following shows an example of using this tag.

```
<layer id="myLayer" width="220" height="100" bgcolor="red" top="150"
      left="100" visibility="show">
  This is a Navigator 4 tag
</layer>
```

The positioning of layers could be either absolute or relative, as with most elements. With *absolute* positioning, you can specify the position within its containing layer. *Relative* positioning is when the object appears in its natural location within the flow of the document.

The `<layer>` tag used absolute positioning, and contained properties that let a developer specify the exact position in the document. Now the second tag they introduced allowed for relative positioning. The `<ilayer>` tag was considered an inflow or inline layer.

The HTML tags were only half of what was added by Netscape for this functionality. In addition to this, they also added the `Layer` object and the `document.layers` array to JavaScript for accessing and manipulating these layers. This object contained its own methods and properties for performing these tasks.

Even though it is not defined in the HTML 4 Recommendation, Navigator 4 required that you have the `name` attribute set in the tags, be it `<layer>`, `<ilayer>`, or `<div>` (which was used to define groups of tags) for this to work. The syntax is rather simple for accessing layers in this manner. For instance, if you are wanting to access a layer called `layer1`, you could accomplish this through the following syntax:

```
document.layers['layer1']
```

Because these types of layers represent the old method of performing document dynamics, we are not going to go into any more detail here. We will, however, include a cross-browser example later in the chapter in the section called "Dynamic Documents" that will help show how dynamic documents in Navigator 4 works. But moving forward, you should pay close attention to the new method, which is what has been implemented in Netscape 6.

NOTE

Want some more information on Navigator's `Layer` object? Check out its entry in Chapter 8.

Internet Explorer 4's DHTML Object Model

Internet Explorer 4 took a broader approach to DHTML by allowing developers the ability not only to access layers, which they defined primarily using `<div>` tags, but also to access almost all tags within a given document. On the layer front, the `<div>` approach was the way to go because it was a tag that was part of the HTML Recommendation. The tag is essentially used to define data blocks within a document—blocks that can later be scripted, styled, and manipulated.

In addition to this tag, there was also the `<span>` tag. Whereas the `<div>` tag provided a way to organize numerous tags together as a single group, `<span>` was used to group a set of characters inline, within the body of another tag.

Similar to Navigator, Internet Explorer needed a method to access these elements and manipulate them. Microsoft did not implement the `Layer` object, but rather the `document.all` collection. This collection provided the means by which you could access elements within your document. However, unlike the `document.layers` method, it did not rely on the non-standard `name` attribute of the `<div>` tag, but rather on the standardized `id` attribute instead. Using the same *layer1* as our example, you would access this layer in Internet Explorer 4 or 5 using the following syntax:

```
document.all['datablock1']
```

Even though both the Netscape and Internet Explorer methods differ, both have been deprecated in favor of the DOM approach.

The New Way

The Document Object Model (DOM) is a very broad topic, and covers all aspects of representing documents within an object model designed for accessibility and flexibility. In this section, we will discuss the basics of the DOM, its structure, and how it can be used in relation to JavaScript. This is meant to be an overview of the DOM.

NOTE

If you really want to learn more about the DOM and all its details, take a look at the W3C DOM Level 1 and Level 2 Recommendation and the new work involved around the future Level 3.

What Is the DOM?

The DOM refers to the Document Object Model, which provides access to all elements and their attributes within a document through a hierarchical structure. The DOM API can be used to create, delete, and modify elements and content. Although the DOM was designed to work with any programming language, it is most commonly associated with XML and HTML. The primary focus here will be within the scope of the JavaScript binding that it defines.

The DOM Level 1 is supported starting in Netscape 6, Internet Explorer 5 and Opera 5, whereas parts of Level 2 are also supported in these browsers. As usual, each browser will have its own quirks on how parts of the DOM work. Earlier versions of these browsers also support various aspects of the DOM, but not completely.

Manipulating the DOM

Before getting into discussions on how to use the DOM, we need to set up a little vocabulary. When talking about the DOM, three terms are often used. They are node, element, and attribute. Each document contains a bunch of *nodes*, which represents either a piece of text or a tag and its attributes. A tag (that is, `<img>`) is also referred to as an *element* in terms of the DOM. Each element might or might not have an *attribute*. For example in the following HTML code, we have the `<img>` element containing attributes of `src` and `name`:

```
<html>
<body>
<img src="dog.gif" name="myDog" alt="Dog">
</body>
</html>
```

The DOM allows a program to access all the elements in a document through a "tree" like object structure. The structure begins with a root object; typically in an HTML file, this would be the `<html>` tag. Within the root object, additional objects are contained in a parent-child type relationship. A child would be considered as any node nested within another node. In the previous example, the <html> node would be a parent to the <body> node. The <img> node would be considered a child to the body node, and so on.

Nodes can be accessed directly by name (if they have a name attribute) by using built-in DOM methods or through parent-child relationship properties. To access a node by name, use the getElementById() method of the Document object. If using the parent-child assesors, the Document.parentNode[], Document.childNodes[], and Document.getSibling[] arrays will be the most useful.

Elements and attributes can be added, modified, or deleted through the DOM. To create a new element, the createElement() method is used. Looking at the following example, we see how to create a new anchor element and add attributes to it:

```
var myNewLink = document.createElement('a');
myNewLink.setAttribute('href', 'home.html');
myNewLink.setAttribute('name', 'Homepage');
```

There are many built-in methods and properties for manipulating the DOM. To see a list of all the properties, refer to the W3C DOM Recommendation available at http://www.w3.org/DOM or the DOM browser support information for Netscape, Internet Explorer, or Opera browsers.

DOM Cascading Style Sheets

The DOM can also be used with CSS, which is often used to create Web pages requiring positioning, formatting, or dynamic content. It allows you to define constructs on how your content is presented, and the DOM can be used to expose these constructs to an object model. Once exposed, it allows a JavaScript program to create, modify, or remove CSS properties.

All CSS items should be available within the document interface. In addition, the CSSStyleSheet interface can also be used to access the rules for a particular style sheet. To determine whether the DOM has support for CSS, the hasFeature() method can be called passing CSS for the first argument (feature) and the version (Level) number.

DOM Example

Now that we have discussed what the DOM is, some of its methods, and how to manipulate it, let's take a look at an example. Listing 4.14 demonstrates three different parts; the first of which is how to add text dynamically within a document. The second shows how to modify an HTML ordered list to an unordered list, and the third part shows how a link can be added to a document dynamically.

Listing 4.14 Example of Different DOM Uses

```
<html>
<head>
  <script "type="text/javascript" language="JavaScript">
  <!--
```

Listing 4.14   Continued

```
// adds a piece of text to a document
function addtext(text){
  if (document.createTextNode){
    var mytext=document.createTextNode(text);
    document.getElementById("example").appendChild(mytext);
  }
}


// changes an ordered list to an unordered list
function changeList(){
  var oldListItems = myList.innerHTML;
  var newNode = document.createElement("UL");
  myList.replaceNode(newNode);
  newNode.innerHTML = oldListItems;
}


// adds link to the document
function addLink(){
  var myLink = document.createElement('a');
  myLink.setAttribute('href', 'http://www.amazon.com');
  myLink.setAttribute('name','Amazon');
  text = document.createTextNode(' Amazon.com ');
  myLink.appendChild(text);
  document.getElementById('firstlink').appendChild(myLink);
}
// -->
</script>
</head>
<body>
<h3>This is an example of how to use the DOM to perform various tasks</h3>
<!-- First DOM Example -->
<p>
This example shows how to dynamically add new text into a document.
<div id="example" onClick="addtext('*This is new text* ')">
  <b>Click here</b> to add the new text.
</div>
<p>
<hr>
This example shows how to modify the ordered list to an unordered list.
<br>
( works in IE 5 )<br>

<!-- Second DOM Example -->
<form name="form1">
  <ol id=myList>
    <li>Item 1</li>
    <li>Item 2</li>
    <li>Item 3</li>
```

```
    </ol>
    <input type="button" value="Change List Type" onclick="changeList()">
</form>
<p>

<!-- Third DOM Example -->
This example shows how to dynamically add a new link
<div id="firstlink" onClick="addLink()">
    <b>Click here</b> to add the new text.
</div>
<hr>

</body>
</html>
```

Cross Browser DHTML

So far, we have discussed the two ways of creating and handling dynamics in HTML documents: the old DHTML way, and the new DOM way. Earlier in the chapter, we talked about the old way and then showed the basic syntax of how it worked. Later, we discussed the newer DOM method and included an example. Now, we are going to show you a single piece of code that will show and hide a data block, or layer if you will, that works not only in the older version 4 browsers using the DHTML methods, but also in the newer version 5 and 6 browsers using the DOM approach.

As you will see in our example, we will use <div> tags to create our blocks, CSS to perform some basic styling, and finally JavaScript to determine the type of browser the user has and how to handle the scripting of the data blocks. In this example we will create a data block, or layer, and two form buttons. When one button is clicked the block will disappear. When the other one is clicked, it will reappear.

There are several aspects of this listing to review, starting with the simple aspects first. The HTML used is nothing more than a simple form with two buttons that call JavaScript functions on onclick events. Directly below this form is an even more simple <div> block that only contains the text "My block". Also notice that we use the onload event handler within the <body> tag to call a JavaScript function. This code looks similar to

```
<body onload="checkBrowser()">
    <form>
        <input type="button" value="Hide"
               onclick="changeState('datablock','hidden')">
        <input type="button" value="Show"
               onclick="changeState('datablock','visible')">
    </form>
    <div name="datablock" id="datablock">
        <p>My block</p>
    </div>
</body>
```

As for the function, its purpose is to set the proper variables that represent our scripting syntax. It looks like the following, where `ieVer` represents the major version number of any IE browser accessing the page. As for the `"Gecko"` reference, that is part of the user agent string within browsers built from Mozilla.org's Gecko rendering engine, such as Netscape 6.

```
function checkBrowser(){
  // IE 4
  if((ieVer < 5) && (ieVer > 0)){
    block = ".all";
    style = ".style";
    isDHTML = "true";

  // Navigator 4
  }else if(navigator.userAgent.indexOf("Nav") != -1){
    block = ".layers";
    style = "";
    isDHTML = "true";

  // IE 5+ and Netscape 6+
  }else if((navigator.userAgent.indexOf("Gecko") != -1) ||
          (ieVer >= 5)){
    isDOM = "true";
  }
}
```

Within Navigator, as we had mentioned, this is accomplished by including the property you want to access immediately after the `document.layers['`*layerName*`']` declaration. For Internet Explorer, however, this is accessed through the additional `style` collection, so your syntax will be something similar to `document.all['`*layerName*`'].style.`*property*.

These two methods might seem to pose a problem for writing your code because it appears we will have to write two different sets of code for each browser. Within the JavaScript language, however, there is a top-level `eval()` function that takes a string passed to it, and evaluates it as JavaScript code. This allows us, for instance, to dynamically build a piece of JavaScript code, such as our layer reference, and pass it to the `eval()` function to be executed.

This only takes care of the older DHTML method, so we also need to take what we learned earlier and use it to access the DOM for the newer browsers. We accomplish this by using the `getElementById()` method to return a pointer to the layer, and then using the *element*`.style.visibility` property to hide or show the layer. You will also notice in the function that we set an `isDHTML` and an `isDOM` variable, which we will use later.

The last function takes care of all this and is the one called by our form buttons—`changeState()`. This function takes two parameters—the first one is the name of the layer it is supposed to effect, and the second is the visibility value that the layer should be changed to. Because we have to access and change the layer properties using different methods, our function will look similar to

```
function changeState(dblock, state){
  if(isDHTML == "true"){
    eval("document" + block + "['" + dblock + "']" + style +
        ".visibility = '" + state + "'");
  }else if(isDOM == "true"){
    var blockElement = document.getElementById(dblock);
    blockElement.style.visibility = state;
  }
}
```

At this point, we have gone over most of the code with the exception of some variable declarations and a single style sheet property setting. Listing 4.15 contains the complete example.

Listing 4.15   Manipulating Layers in All Supporting Browsers

```
<html>
<head>
  <style type="text/css">
  <!--
    #datablock{
    background-color: lightblue;
    }
  -->
  </style>
  <script type="text/javascript" language="JavaScript1.2">
  <!--
    // global variables for browser
    var block = new String();
    var style = new String();
    var isDHTML = new Boolean(false);
    var isDOM = new Boolean(false);

    // determine IE version
    var ieVer = parseInt(navigator.userAgent.charAt(parseInt(
                ➡navigator.userAgent.indexOf("MSIE")) + 5));

    // set appropriate variables depending on scripting method
    function checkBrowser(){
      if((ieVer < 5) && (ieVer > 0)){
        block = ".all";
        style = ".style";
        isDHTML = "true";
      }else if(navigator.userAgent.indexOf("Nav") != -1){
        block = ".layers";
        style = "";
```

```
          isDHTML = "true";
        }else if((navigator.userAgent.indexOf("Gecko") != -1) ||
               (ieVer >= 5)){
          isDOM = "true";
        }
      }

      // Take the state passed in, and change it.
      function changeState(dblock, state){
        if(isDHTML == "true"){
          eval("document" + block + "['" + dblock + "']" + style +
               ".visibility = '" + state + "'");
        }else if(isDOM == "true"){
          var blockElement = document.getElementById(dblock);
          blockElement.style.visibility = state;
        }
      }
    //-->
    </script>
  </head>
  <body onload="checkBrowser()">
    <form>
      <input type="button" value="Hide"
             onclick="changeState('datablock','hidden')">
      <input type="button" value="Show"
             onclick="changeState('datablock','visible')">
    </form>
    <div name="datablock" id="datablock">
      <p>My block</p>
    </div>
  </body>
</html>
```

XML-Based User Interface Language (XUL)

In this section, we will discuss the basics of a new language called the XML-based *User Interface Language (XUL)*. XUL works across many different platforms within the Gecko rendering engine and with various programming languages. We will attempt to cover XUL from a high level and provide some insight into how JavaScript can be used in conjunction with XUL.

What Is XUL?

XUL is an XML-based programming language used for defining objects and layouts in a user interface. XUL was created to provide a XML shorthand for describing the contents of windows and dialogs and is heavily used within the Mozilla and Netscape 6 browsers.

File Structure and Syntax

XUL files typically are denoted with a .xul file extension. The language is tag based and similar to XML; and in fact, XUL looks like a cross between XML and HTML, with some additional specialized tags. Like XML, XUL is also case sensitive.

The beginning of an XUL file could look similar to the following code:

```
<?xml version="1.0"?>
<?xml-stylesheet href="chrome://global/skin/" type="text/css"?>
<!DOCTYPE window>
<window xmlns="http://www.mozilla.org/keymaster/gatekeeper/there.is.only.xul">
```

The first line denotes that this is an XML file and specifies the version, while the second line defines which style sheets will be used for this particular file. The third line designates the type of document it is, while the fourth line allocates a namespace to the XUL file listed at the end of the URL.

NOTE

Want more information on namespaces in XML? Check out
http://www.w3.org/TR/1999/REC-xml-names-19990114.

XUL and JavaScript

XUL by itself does not perform any specific function. For a browser to use XUL, a programming language is needed to tie the different interface components together. For the purpose of this book, JavaScript will be used as the binding language.

JavaScript can be inserted within an XUL document. To denote portions of the document that pertain to JavaScript, the <html:script></html:script> tag is used. Any JavaScript code is inserted between the opening and the closing tags. For more complex functionality requiring a greater deal of scripting, JavaScript code can be separated into its own file (denoted with a .js extension). This file is then included in the XUL file by specifying the src attribute of the <html:script> tag. The following shows an example of this:

```
<html:script language="JavaScript" src="myscript.js"/>
```

XUL works primarily with widgets. These are things such as menus, toolbars, buttons, scrollbars, and so on. These widgets can use JavaScript to interact with the user. For example, suppose that you create a new button widget and want to perform a specific function when the button is pressed. Using the JavaScript onclick event handler, you can determine when the new button has been pressed. This works for other events as well.

XUL Example

Let's look at an example of an XUL file, which creates a new menu. Listing 4.16 shows a very simple XUL program that uses the menubar widget.

Listing 4.16   XUL Example

```
<?xml version="1.0"?>
<?xml-stylesheet href="chrome://global/skin/" type="text/css"?>
<!DOCTYPE window>
<html:script src="myScript.js"/>
<window id="new-window" title="new menus"
 ➡xmlns="http://www.mozilla.org/keymaster/gatekeeper/there.is.only.xul">
<menubar>
    <menu value="aNewMenu">
      <menupop>
         <menuitem value="First New Item" onclick="shoeFirst();"/>
         <menuitem value="Second New Item" onclick="showSecond();"/>
         <menuseparator/>
         <menuitem value="Last New Item" onclick="showLast();"/>
      </menupop>
    </menu>
</menubar>
</window>
```

The example creates a new menu, *aNewMenu*, and adds three options to it. A separator is used to distinguish between the first two items and the last item. Each item performs a specific JavaScript function, which is defined in a separate file named "myScript.js".

Moving On

In this chapter, we discussed a number of different items related to Client-side scripting with JavaScript. In this edition, we've expanded to new technologies including the Document Object Model and XUL. Scripting technology is becoming more advanced every day. With the advent of DOM and XML, developers are able to create a wide variety of dynamic Web content.

CHAPTER 5

JavaScript on the Server-Side

So far, you have taken an in-depth look into the JavaScript language. You have examined some of the functionality JavaScript has and some of its applications. The remaining chapters will discuss how to approach JavaScript as a programming language, and how to maximize your coding efforts by understanding the environments in which it is interpreted.

In addition to applying JavaScript on the client-side, there is also server-side usage. This feature, which is implemented in Netscape and iPlanet's Enterprise line of servers and within Microsoft's ASP environment in their Internet Information Server (IIS) servers, allows developers to build robust Web-based applications. The use of these Web-based programs can be limitless, but is most commonly used to maintain user sessions and interact with databases to build pages dynamically.

NOTE

Netscape and Sun have joined forces to jointly create various server applications under the name iPlanet (http://www.iplanet.com). This alliance occurred after the release of Netscape Enterprise Server 3.6, which is why the 4.0 server is referred to as iPlanet Enterprise Server. From this point on, we will simply refer to this server-side JavaScript environment as the Enterprise Server environment to avoid confusion.

In this chapter, you will take a closer look at server-side JavaScript. You'll see how it is different from client-side and learn how to deploy your applications. You will analyze the various uses of the technology and learn how to manage your programs. Overall, this chapter will be a primer for any server-side JavaScript you might be deploying on your site.

How Does Server-Side Differ from Client-Side?

Server-side JavaScript is not only different from client-side because of the environment in which it is interpreted, but it also has divergent concepts that are applied. These distinctions can be placed into two major categories, each of which will be further broken down in this chapter. The initial categories are

- Differences in the server-side environments
- Actual programming differences from client-side

As a developer, you should be aware of these items before you begin writing server-side applications. Server-side is conceptually different from client-side, even though much of the language semantics and syntax are shared.

Server-Side Environments

One of the first things you should understand about using JavaScript on the server-side is the fact that the implementations within the Enterprise and IIS servers are different. This difference is much greater than that on the client-side, where differences appear in object models and means of implementation.

On the Enterprise front, we find that the Netscape and iPlanet alliance has created objects, properties, and methods that conform to standard server-side functionality no matter what the platform. You will find language elements that allow you to access the file system, send mail, and retrieve data from databases. None of these items are specific to any platform and are generic enough to be used across all the platforms supported by the server.

Microsoft, on the other hand, has taken a very Windows-centric approach to implementing a server-side version of its JScript language. It has many objects and related elements pertaining to the Windows environment. And lately, it has extended support for the JScript language to be included as a major language within its .NET framework. We will touch on these areas in this chapter.

Programming Differences

The next items to analyze in server-side JavaScript are the programming differences that occur. Besides the functionality added on the server-side, JavaScript also has some key programming differences. These include, but are not limited to, the following:

- Within the Enterprise Server environment, scripts to be executed on the server-side are contained between beginning <server> and ending </server> tags.
- Within the Microsoft ASP environments, the JScript language must first be specified. By default, the VBScript language is the dialect of choice.
- Additional objects, methods, properties, and events are available on the server-side.

- None of the client-side–specific language elements are available on the server-side, however the elements core to the language are.

Unlike the client-side scripts, which are contained between beginning `<script>` and ending `</script>` tags, all scripts to be executed on the server-side within the Enterprise Server are contained between beginning `<server>` and ending `</server>` tags. This tells the Enterprise server to execute all the code between these tags. As a programmer, this allows you to have client-side code on the same page without it being interpreted by the server.

On the Microsoft side of the server-side implementation, several different languages are available to the developer for writing their applications. Because of this, it is necessary to specify JScript as the language used on your page. This is accomplished in two ways.

- Including the following line as the first line on your ASP page. It sets JScript as the default language for that page.

```
<%@LANGUAGE="JScript"%>
```

- Using beginning and ending `<script>` tags with the `runat` ASP-specific attribute set to `server` and the `language` attribute set to `JScript`.

```
<script language="JScript" runat="server">
  // your code here
</script>
```

JavaScript on the server-side has objects for sending mail, opening connections to a database, managing a pool of connections, accessing the file system, and handling returned data. This syntax expansion on the server-side makes JavaScript a rich language for developing the robust applications on the server that you need.

A final difference is the fact that pure client-side language elements are not available on the server-side. This is nothing more than a reflection of the environment in which the scripts are interpreted, but it can be strange for the experienced JavaScript programmer who has not experienced the language on the server-side. For instance, there is no `navigator` or Form object. These are all specific to the client that is interpreting the script.

NOTE

Because there are differences in the server-side and client-side implementations, refer to Part III, "JavaScript Reference," to determine if the object, method, property, or event you want to use is supported.

Netscape's Server-Side JavaScript

Netscape was the first to implement JavaScript on the server-side, so it is no surprise that its implementation of the language builds upon the foundations developed within the browser. In this section, we will discuss what versions of their servers support JavaScript and how you run and manage applications developed in this language.

Server Support

Before you start developing any server-side JavaScript application within the Enterprise Server environment, you should first make sure of the level of support you have access to. As you are beginning to see, things have changed a lot with JavaScript over the years, and you want to make sure that you have the resources necessary to perform the tasks you need to accomplish. Table 5.1 has a list of the various versions of JavaScript on the server-side within the Enterprise Server environment.

Table 5.1   Server-side JavaScript Support

JavaScript Version	Enterprise Server Version
1.1	Netscape Enterprise Server 2.0
1.2	Netscape Enterprise Server 3.0
1.4	iPlanet Web Server, Enterprise Edition 4.0
1.5	iPlanet Web Server, Enterprise Edition 5.0

Compiling Your Scripts

Unlike client-side JavaScript, the server-side implementation within the Enterprise Servers require you to compile your scripts into .web files. These files, which are stored in byte code, contain all the files necessary for your Web-based application. The .web files would include any .html files that contain your server-side code, as well as any external source JavaScript .js files that you might be using.

Netscape has provided a command-line tool, the JavaScript Application Compiler (jsac), which is located in the bin directory of your installation, to compile your applications. The minimum requirement for compiling the application is the .html file that contains your code. The tool itself takes a variety of parameters, defined in Table 5.2, to build your .web file.

NOTE

In Table 5.2, all the options are listed as *-option*. The tool also accepts the syntax of */option*. In addition, all paths should use a backslash (\) for directory mappings because the forward slash maps to the use of an option.

Table 5.2   Command-Line Parameters Available to `jsac`

Option	Description
`-a version`	This option allows you to specify the version of the interpreter against which to compile the application. At the time of this writing, this option has only one value, 1.2, and is used to tell the compiler how to handle comparison operators, which were different in JavaScript 1.2.
`-c`	Verifies the syntax in your script, but does not create a .web file. Do not use this option with the -o option.

Option	Description
-d	Displays the JavaScript contents of your files.
-f *filelist*	This specifies a text file that contains the names of all the files you want to include in your build. The primary reason for this option is for those operating systems that have a limit to the number of characters you can specify on a single command line. Each filename in the file should be separated by a space. If your filename has a space in it, include the name within quotes.
-h	Displays help for the tool. Do not use with any other options.
-i *inputfile*	Specifies the name of a single input .html file. See -f when including multiple files.
-l *characterset*	Allows you to specify the character set used when compiling your application. This would be something similar to iso-8859-1.
-o *outputfile*	Specifies the name of the output .web file you are creating. Do not use this with the -c option.
-p *path*	Designates the root for any relative path filenames you specify.
-r *errorfile*	This option allows you to specify a file to which to have all errors written.
-v	Displays verbose information about the execution of the compile.

Using these options, a typical build of an application might look something similar to the following.

```
jsac -o myApp.web -v index.html results.html jsbeans.js
```

It specifies to display the build process verbose, defines the output file as myApp.web, and gives the filenames of the files to include.

Here is another example that specifies a full path to the input file as well as sets an error file to log any errors during the compilation process.

```
jsac -o myApp.web -v -i /js/myapps/index.html -r /js/logs/myapperror.log
```

As many programmers know, it is very important to know your command-line options. Knowing how to troubleshoot by compiling a project can often be just as challenging as creating one.

The Server Side JavaScript Application Manager

The Server Side JavaScript Application Manager, shown in Figure 5.1, is the program used to manage server-side applications within the Enterprise Server environment. From within this common interface, you can start, stop, restart, run, debug, modify, and remove applications created for a Web site. It is a dashboard to all the server-side JavaScript applications installed.

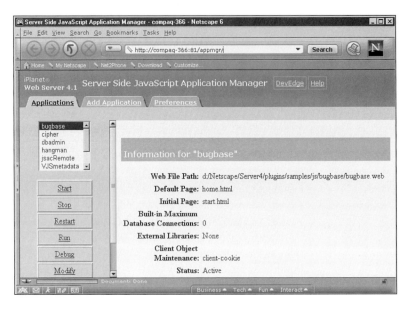

Figure 5.1
Enterprise Server's Server Side JavaScript Application Manager.

This manager is much more than a start and stop location for applications. In fact, it is most useful for verifying current status and information, debugging, and setting configuration options. After an application has been compiled and added to the Server Side JavaScript Application Manager, this interface is used to maintain all aspects of the program—not including the actual coding, of course. However, before you can use the JavaScript Application Manager, you must do a few things.

Configuration

Before the Server Side JavaScript Application Manager is available for use, it must be enabled within an instance of Enterprise Server. This can be done easily from the Server Manger.

Once logged in to the Administration Server, simply select the option that represents the instance of the Web server on which you want to enable server-side JavaScript. When you have accessed the Server Manager for this instance, click the Programs button in the menu bar. Next, click the link to Server Side JavaScript in the navigation bar to the left of the page. This takes you to the main screen, shown in Figure 5.2.

When you have access to this page, there are three options:

- Activate the server-side JavaScript environment
- Require a password for access to the JavaScript Application Manager
- Select a JavaScript Thread Pool option

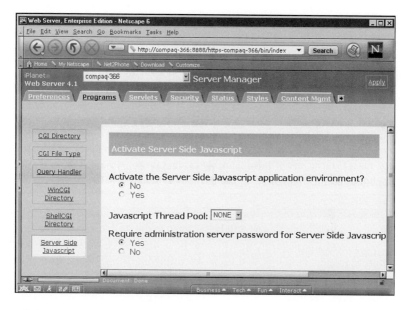

Figure 5.2

Enabling server-side JavaScript through the Server Manager.

The first thing you need to select in this screen is to activate the server-side JavaScript environment. Next, consider using the Administration password to access the JavaScript Application Manager. This is highly recommended because it is a major security risk to unprotect applications. Without the password, a person could stop, or even worse, modify the settings for applications. And finally, if you plan on using server-side JavaScript to connect to databases, you can specify a thread pool. For more information on thread pooling, click the Help button on this screen.

When server-side JavaScript is enabled and you have made a decision on whether to password protect the application manager, click the OK button. This will take you to the Save And Apply Changes page, where you should click Save And Apply to activate these options. An alert box will be displayed, confirming a successful or unsuccessful change.

PROBLEMS?

If problems are encountered here, check the following:

- Are any NSAPI (Netscape Server Application Programming Interface) plug-ins running that might conflict with server-side JavaScript?
- Is any kind of third-party software being used to dynamically build the Web pages for this site that might have conflicting or overlapping settings?
- Has someone hand modified the obj.conf file recently?

For the first two, think specifically about those applications or NSAPI plug-ins that parse pages. Consider turning off Parsed HTML if it is enabled. This can be done within the Web server instance's administration by clicking the Content Management menu item and then clicking the Parse HTML link in the navigation.

Finally, if there are still troubles or if the third bullet point came into play, consider loading a previous version of the `obj.conf` file. This can be done by clicking the Server Preferences menu item, and then selecting the Restore Configuration link in the navigation. Check under the `obj.conf` column and roll it back one version at a time until it works. Note that you are undoing any prior changes of the configuration file. Doing so might break another process while trying to fix the JavaScript ApplicationManager.

When a successful saving of the configuration file (`obj.conf`) and restarting of the Web server has been accomplished, you will be returned to the Active Server Side JavaScript page. At the top of the page, there will now be a link to the Server Side JavaScript Application Manager. This link will be in the following form, where `machinename` is replaced with the name of your machine and domain if applicable.

`http://machinename/appmgr`

Now that everything is configured to run the application manager, click the link. This will launch another page and load the Server Side JavaScript Application Manager. When on this page, click the Preferences tab. This will display a page to set up some defaults when adding new applications and set a couple of preferences.

Table 5.3 defines the options available when setting the default values for new applications.

Table 5.3   Default Application Settings That Can Be Set for the JavaScript Application Manager

Setting	Description
Web File Path	This is the default path to your `.web` file. If you store all your applications in a subdirectory of `/ssjsapps/myprojects`, you should choose this option.
Default Page	This option specifies the default page of your application. For practical purposes, you might want to set this to `index.html`.
Initial Page	This specifies the initial page of your application. For example, if your application has global settings that are only loaded when the application is first started and you have stored this in a file called `global.html`, you should set this option to this file.
Built-In Maximum Database Connections	Those of you who are using databases that charge on a per connection basis will like this feature. It is the default that restricts your applications to a set number of maximum connections.

Setting	Description
External Libraries	This contains the absolute path to any external libraries that your application might be using.
Client Object Maintenance	This default option is used to determine if you are going to maintain user sessions in your application. The possible choices are Client Cookie, Client-URL, Server-IP, Server-Cookie, and Server-URL.

After specifying the options for the Default Values When Adding Applications section, specify your preferences. Within the Preferences section, there are two items to set:

- *Confirm On*—This option determines if a confirmation dialog box is to pop up before you perform a task. The list of tasks this can be enabled for are Remove, Start, Stop, and/or Restart an application.
- *Debug Output*—This option allows you to choose if you want to do your debugging in the Same Window or Other Window of the application.

After these settings are completed, click the OK button. This will finish the configuration of the Server Side JavaScript Application Manager. Additional help or documentation can be accessed by clicking the links within the user interface.

Script Management

Managing scripts might be one of the most overlooked aspects of deploying a Web-based application. The mentality seems to be, "It was written to never break." This, as we all know, simply never holds up in the real world. Even applications that worked perfectly for years will eventually hit a bump. It might be after an upgrade to a new server, or maybe a new browser has come out that implements some client-side JavaScript differently than expected. Either way, it will happen, so expect it.

The Server Side JavaScript Application Manager provides a common location to manage applications as well as perform maintenance on them. You can access the online documentation at DevEdge and launch the help window with documentation before clicking any of the available tabs.

When the Applications tab is selected, you will see the list of applications currently installed. These are located in a scrolling text area at the top of the section. After an application is selected, any of the options defined in Table 5.4 can be used.

Table 5.4   Application Options in the Controls Section

Control Option	Description
Start	Starts the application and makes it available for your users to use.
Stop	Stops the selected application.
Restart	Stops and restarts the selected application.
Run	Launches a separate window and loads the URL to the selected application. This allows you to quickly test your application to ensure that it is working properly.

Table 5.4   Continued

Control Option	Description
Debug	Launches either one or two windows, depending on how you set your preferences, to debug your application.
Modify	Allows you to modify any of the settings you have for that application.
Remove	Removes the application from your list of managed applications.

This section discusses the ability to manage applications. When an application is selected, its information is displayed as well as its current status. Now take a look at using the Debug feature, which is a valuable tool for any server-side JavaScript developer.

To launch the Debugging window, select the application to debug, and then click the Debug button. Depending on how the preferences are set, you will see one or two main windows. If there is only one window, it will be split into two frames.

One of these elements is the Debugging window, seen as a single window in Figure 5.3. As a program runs, the contents of this window will change as JavaScript code is processed within the application. This tool provides a look at the information being passed back and forth. It is possible to see variables being set, as well as objects created and their various states.

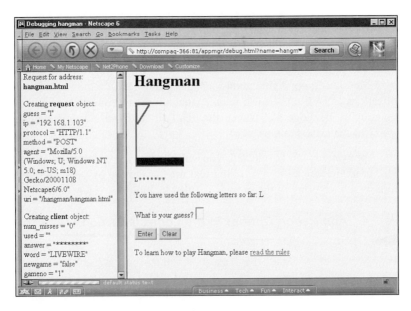

Figure 5.3

The Debugging window is used to display various bits of information about the application being debugged.

As a programmer, you often will want to know the value of variables you create and return values of methods. Server-side JavaScript makes this possible by using the debug() method in scripts to write information to the Trace Information window during runtime. This method is similar to the write() server-side method, where a string or variable is passed, and the interpreter writes the data passed to the window. A typical use of this method might look similar to the following:

```
debug("myFunction entered and was passed: " + myVar);
```

NOTE

For more information on using the debug() method, see its entry in Chapter 9, "Server-Side."

In addition to knowing how to debug applications, it is important to understand the error messages you might run across. There are two main types of errors. One type of error, which is common for syntax mistakes, is a standard server-side JavaScript error. This error will return the object in which the error occurred, the error message, the filename of the application, and the line number.

The second types of errors are those generated by databases. These errors can have several different types of information returned, but usually contain the following:

- *Database/Function*—This error alerts the programmer that a database error occurred, and it lists the function in which it occurred.
- *LiveWire Services Error*—This error, generated by the LiveWire database connection service, states that an error occurred and lists a message as to why.
- *Vendor Error*—This error is also returned by the LiveWire service, but it reports an error specific to the database to which you are connecting. You will need to know your database error codes to decipher this error.
- *Standard Server-Side JavaScript Error*—This error is the same as the first type, except that it is specific to your use of a database connection.

In addition to the Debugging window, there is a main window, or frame. When debugging an application, this window contains the application itself. The combination of this window and the Debugging window allows a developer to step through, as a user would, and see what is going on in the background. With the Debug feature of the Server-Side JavaScript Application Manager, a developer can correct and work through almost any problem he might encounter.

Microsoft's ASP Environment

Like Netscape, Microsoft soon saw the value in implementing JScript on the server-side and within its .NET framework. The ability to give developers a single language for both client-side and server-side was too compelling. So, with the release of IIS 3.0, ASP 1.0 was made available, and within that release, JScript was at the disposal of developers. Since that time we have seen the release of IIS 4.0 and 5.0, along with ASP 2.0, 3.0, and ASP+ (now referred to as ASP.NET).

Server Support

Before you start developing any server-side JScript application within the ASP environment, you should first make sure of the level of support you have access to. Table 5.5 has a list of the various versions of JScript on the server-side within IIS.

Table 5.5   Server-side JScript Support

JScript Version	IIS Support	ASP Version
2.0	3.0	1.0
3.0	4.0	2.0
5.0	5.0	3.0
6.0	6.0	ASP.NET (previously known as ASP+)

Using the JScript Language

Before we go any further, there is one interesting thing to note about Microsoft's implementation of JScript. Unlike, at least currently, other browsers and environments that support an ECMAScript-based scripting language, the JScript engine within Microsoft's applications can be upgraded. This means that you might only be currently running IIS 4.0, but it is possible to download and install the JScript 5.6 engine.

Actually using the JScript language is fairly easy. As we touched on in Chapter 1, "What Is JavaScript to a Programmer?" there are a few extra objects, listed in Table 5.6, that you need to be aware of. Other than these, you can use the normal objects, properties, and methods you are accustomed to using.

Table 5.6   Server-side JScript Objects

Object	Description
Application	Contains elements that allow you to share information across all users of a given application.
ASPError	Contains elements that allow you to obtain information on errors that might have occurred within your ASP application.
ObjectContext	Contains elements that allow you to either commit or abort a transaction that has been initiated by your script.
Request	Contains elements specific to the browser making the request to IIS.
Response	Contains elements specific to the server returning a request to the user's browser.
Server	Contains elements specific to the environment in which the script is running. This includes access to the various environment variables.
Session	Contains elements specific to a user's session.

> **NOTE**
>
> See Chapter 9 for more information on these objects and their properties, methods, events, and collections.

Checking Your Environment

Before you start trying to build ASP applications using JScript, there are a few items that you should be aware of. These items might differ slightly across the various versions of IIS, but conceptually they are consistent.

- Make sure that your installation of IIS is configured to load and execute .asp files with the asp.dll.
- Make sure that your Home Directory permissions allow for Script or Execute permissions.
- Make sure that you have either explicitly set JScript as the language on your pages, or that you have set it as the default language within the properties of your instance of IIS.

Although these items seem minor, failure to have these set can prevent your scripts from running. By default, everything, with the exception of the default language being JScript, should be set up correctly. To test, you can use the code in Listing 5.1. If you are able to serve the page through IIS to a browser and see `"It Worked!"`, you will be able to proceed with the ASP examples later in this chapter.

Listing 5.1   Sample Code to Test if ASP Is Properly Functioning Within Your Instance of IIS

```
<html>
<head>
  <title>JScript within ASP Test</title>
</head>
<body>
  <script language="JScript" runat="server">

  // Write "It Worked!" to the users page.
  Response.Write("It Worked!");

  </script>
</body>
</html>
```

Uses of Server-Side JavaScript

Now that you have seen some of the differences of server-side and client-side JavaScript and how to create your applications within the appropriate environments, take a look at some of Server-Side JavaScript's uses. This section does not try to outline all the uses you might encounter, but rather discusses some of the more common aspects of using server-side JavaScript. We have included examples for both environments specific to the server-side implementation, so this should give you a good taste of what you can do with this powerful language.

Within Enterprise Server

Because both the Enterprise and IIS environments differ as do their implementation of the JavaScript language, we will first take a look at examples specific to Enterprise Server. In this section, we will explore the following:

- Database connectivity
- E-mail
- Working with Files

Database Connectivity

One of the major features of server-side JavaScript is its capability to connect to databases. As you know, Netscape has paved the way for the use of standardized technology, and you can expect nothing less when connecting to databases. It provides native-support, industry-leading databases such as DB2, Informix, Oracle, and Sybase databases, as well as access through ODBC for other databases, such as Microsoft's SQL Server.

The functionality server-side JavaScript provides for connecting to databases is done through its LiveWire service, which no longer has to be installed as a separate component. This service provides JavaScript objects that can be used to connect to various databases. Once connected, you are able to run the SQL statements necessary to perform the operations you want.

NOTE

When Netscape released version 2 of Enterprise Server, LiveWire was a blanket term for "server-side JavaScript." By the time version 3 of Enterprise Server was released, the acceptance of JavaScript as an industry standard had increased. To maintain some consistency across terminology, the term LiveWire has now, starting with version 3 of Enterprise Server, been associated with the service that allows developers to write code to interact with databases.

Connections to a database are maintained in a *pool*. Before you open a connection to a database and have the ability to run queries against it, you must create an instance of the DbPool object. When the instance is created, you can obtain connections from the pool as needed. The pool object itself takes all the parameters necessary to make the connection. It is possible to create a pool without specifying any parameters. However, you must pass the parameters when the first connection is attempted.

The following code is the syntax for creating a DbPool object. Each parameter is defined in the bulleted list following the example.

```
var myPool = new DbPool (DBType, DBInstance, UID, PWD, DBName, MaxConn,
➥CommitFlag);
```

- DBType—The type of database it is. Possible values are ORACLE, SYBASE, INFORMIX, DB2, or ODBC.
- DBInstance—This is the instance name of the database. For ODBC it is the DSN entry name.
- UID—The username or ID you want the connections to connect as.
- PWD—The password for the user you are connecting as.
- DBName—The name of the database into which you want to log. For Oracle, DB2, and ODBC connections, this should be a blank, " ", string. In Oracle, the name of the database for these connections is set up in the tnsnames.ora file and is defined by the DSN for ODBC connections. DB2 does not have a database name and is referenced only by the DBInstance.
- MaxConn—The maximum number of connections to the pool. This is effectively the number of connections the pool will open to the database.
- CommitFlag—This flag determines if a pending transaction is committed when the connection is released. If it is set to false, the transaction is rolled back. If it is set to true, it is committed.

Because it is possible to create an instance of this object by passing a limited set of these parameters, as well as passing none, you should reference the DbPool entry in Chapter 9 before using this object.

After you have created a pool, you can use the connections within that pool as needed. To pull a connection, use the connection() method on your pool. This will return an available connection to use for processing. The syntax and a description of the parameters are as follows:

```
var myConn = myPool.connection(name, timeout);
```

- name—This is a name you can give your connection. Because you actually store the connection in a variable, this name's primary function becomes one for debugging purposes.
- timeout—A numeric value for the number of seconds you give the instance to connect.

After the connection has been made, you are able to perform the necessary processing you require for your application. For more information on the methods available, check entries for the Connection, Cursor, and database objects in Chapter 9.

USER SESSIONS AND DATABASE ACCESS

An extensive discussion of how to manage user sessions and database connections as various users access your application is beyond the scope of this book. However, there are some items you should be aware of when performing these tasks.

You should know how database queries are handled. You should understand how the information is returned from your specific database and how to process the information.

You should also know how to appropriately manage user connections to your application. It is possible your application will have to manage many connections from many users at the same time. If your sessions and connections get crossed, you might send the wrong information to the wrong user.

Maintaining and managing your user sessions and database connections can be a very important factor and you should take great care when working with them.

E-Mail

Another feature that can be exploited and implemented within server-side JavaScript applications is the ability to send mail. The properties and methods needed to perform these tasks are contained in the `SendMail` object.

NOTE

Refer to the Chapter 9, "Server-Side," for more information on the `SendMail` object.

Using the `SendMail` object is very straightforward. Simply set the same properties contained in the everyday e-mail you send and invoke the `send()` method. If an error is encountered, it can be analyzed by using the error methods supplied. Listing 5.2 shows an example use of this object to create a page for users to send e-mail. Figure 5.4 shows what is displayed to the user when she encounters this page, and Figure 5.5 shows the results of submitting a successful e-mail.

Listing 5.2   Example of Using the `SendMail` Object

```
<html>
<head>
  <title> Using the SendMail object</title>
</head>
<body>
<server>

  // See if they have submitted or just need the form.
  if(request.method == "POST"){

      // Create an instance of the SendMail object.
      var myMail = new SendMail();

      // Assign the properties their values.
      myMail.To = request.toAddress;
      myMail.From = request.fromAddress;
      myMail.Subject = request.subject;
      myMail.Body = request.body;
      myMail.Smtpserver = "mail.purejavascript.com";
      myMail.Errorsto = "errors@purejavascript.com"

      // Try to send the mail.
      if(!myMail.send()){
```

```
        // If there was an error, give the user the e-mail address of who they
        // should contact about the error, as well as the error code and
        // message.
        write("Error sending your message. Please send e-mail to ");
        write(myMail.Errorsto + " with the following error message");
        write("Error " + myMail.errorCode() + ": " + myMail.errorMessage());
    }else{

        // If there was not an error, tell the user they were successful.
        write("Your message was sent successfully!");
    }
}else{

    // If this page was called and a form was not submitted, write the
    // email form to the page for the user to use.
    write('<form name="myForm" method="post">');
    write('<table border="1"><tr><td>');
    write('<table border="0">');
    write('<tr align="left" valign="top">');
    write('<td><b>To:</b></td>');
    write('<td><input type="text" name="toAddress" size="30"></td>');
    write('</tr>');
    write('<tr align="left" valign="top">');
    write('<td><b>From:</b></td>');
    write('<td><input type="text" name="fromAddress" size="30"></td>');
    write('</tr>');
    write('<tr align="left" valign="top">');
    write('<td><b>Subject:</b></td>');
    write('<td><input type="text" name="subject" size="30"></td>');
    write('</tr>');
    write('<tr align="left" valign="top">');
    write('<td><b>Body:</b></td>');
    write('<td><textarea name="body"');
    write(' cols="60" rows="10" wrap="soft"></textarea>');
    write('</td>');
    write('</tr>');
    write('<tr align="left" valign="top">');
    write('<TD colspan=2 align="right"><input type="submit"');
    write(' value="Send Mail">');
    write('</td>');
    write('</tr>');
    write('</table>');
    write('</td></tr></table>');
    write('</form>');
    }
</server>
</body>
</html>
```

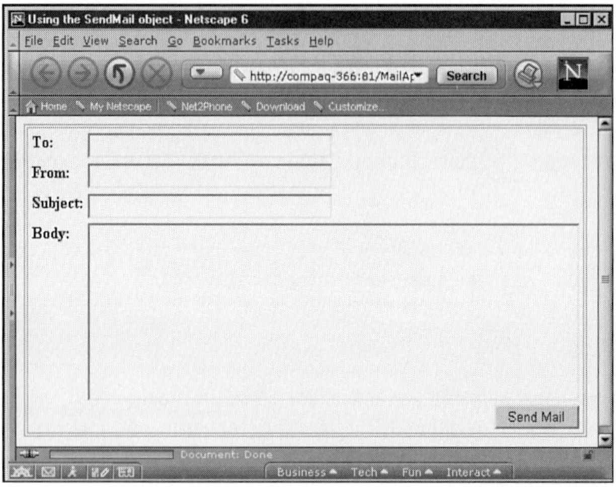

Figure 5.4

Building an e-mail page for your applications.

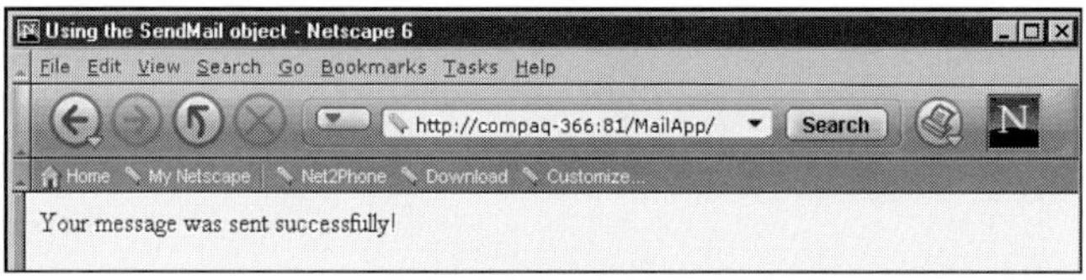

Figure 5.5

The results of submitting an e-mail successfully.

As the example demonstrates, the SendMail object makes it easy to create a page through which users can send mail. In a true, fully developed, Web-based application, a programmer should add code to check for errors in the submission. This would be an appropriate time to use client-side JavaScript to ensure that basic requirements, such as syntactically correct e-mail addresses, are entered.

Working with Files

The File object allows you to perform various system tasks, such as reading and writing to a file on your disk. The File object itself has many methods and a prototype property that allows a programmer to create new properties and methods of the object.

NOTE

Refer to Chapter 9 for more information on the File object.

Similar to the SendMail object, the use of the File object is straightforward. The methods provided allow you to perform the various tasks needed on the files in your file system.

Part of the functionality of working with these files allows a programmer to specify how he wants to open the file. A file can be opened to read, write, append, or open in binary mode. These options are specified in the open() method in the following form.

```
myFile.open("option");
```

NOTE

Refer to Chapter 9 for more information on the options that can be passed to this method.

In your applications, you might want to display the contents of a file. This program could be an administration application that reads a file and displays its contents on a page. Listing 5.3 contains an application that displays the contents of a selected log file on the file system.

Listing 5.3 Using the `File` Object to Display the Contents of a File

```
<html>
<head>
  <title> Using the File object</title>
</head>
<body>
<server>

  // See if they have submitted or just need the form.
  if(request.method == "POST"){

    // Create an instance of the File object and pass it the file
    // the user specified they wanted to view.
    var myLog = new File(request.file);

    // Try to open the file.
    if(!myLog.open("r")){

      // If there was an error, tell the user.
      write("There was an error opening the file: " + request.file);
    }else{

      // If there was not an error, then open the file and display it.
      write('<h3>The contents of ' + request.file + ' are as follows:</h3>');
      while(!myLog.eof()){
        write(myLog.readln());
      }
    }
  }else{

    // If this page was called then write the select box to the page for
    // the user to use select which log they want to see.
```

```
    write('<form name="myForm" method="post">');
    write('<select name="file">');
    write('<option value="/logs/admin.log">Admin Log</option>');
    write('<option value="/logs/user.log">User Log</option>');
    write('<option value="/logs/error.log">Error Log</option>');
    write('</select>');
    write('<input type="submit" value="View Log">');
    write('</form>');
  }
</server>
</body>
</html>
```

In this example, a user has the ability to select a file for viewing. After submitting the request, the example tries to open the file for reading. If it is unsuccessful, an error with the filename is returned to the user. If the file opens, the contents are displayed in the document.

Within IIS

On the IIS side of the fence, it is important to show how the language syntax differs from Enterprise Server's implementation, but remains true to the JavaScript language. Within this section we will explore examples in the follow areas:

- Form submissions
- Session handling

Form Submissions

One of the nice things about JavaScript on the server-side within both the Enterprise and IIS environments is the ease with which you can process form data. Within IIS this is accomplished through the use of the Request object and its associated properties, methods, and collections, which are detailed in Chapter 9.

To use this object, we must create a form that will pass some information. For simplicity's sake, we will prompt the user for his first and last name. Listing 5.4 contains the HTML for this page.

Listing 5.4   HTML for Our Form

```
<html>
<head>
  <title>ASP Form Example</title>
</head>
<body>
<form action="process.asp" method="post">
  First Name:<input name="first" width="10"><br>
  Last Name:<input name="last" width="10"><br>
  <input type="submit" value="Submit">
</form>
</body>
</html>
```

Now that the form has been created, we must create the `process.asp` file to handle its submission. Within this file, we will use the `Write()` method of the `Response` object to output the values of the passed information. As we mentioned before, JScript has several objects specific to their IIS implementation for processing data. The `Response` object, which is detailed in Chapter 9.

We will use the `Request.Form` collection, which takes the name of the form element you are trying to access. In our example, this will be for `first` and `last`. Listing 5.5 shows the code we can use to complete this task.

Listing 5.5   ASP Code Using JScript to Process Our Form

```
<html>
<head>
  <title>ASP Form Example: Results</title>
</head>
<body>
<script language="JScript" runat="server">

  // write the first and last name entered in the form
  Response.Write("You entered (last, first format): ");
  Response.Write(Request.Form("last") + ", " + Request.Form("first"));

</script>
</body>
</html>
```

Server Variables

Another use of ASP is to access and use various server variables. For instance, on many occasions a Web developer might need to determine the browser making the request. He might want to direct the user agent to a specific site, or possibly post a warning message.

In Listing 5.6 we use the `Request.ServerVariables` collection to access the `HTTP_USER_AGENT` variable. After loading into a variable, we use the `indexOf()` method to see if it is Internet Explorer. We then print out a message stating if it is Internet Explorer or not followed by the entire user-agent string.

Listing 5.6   Using the `Request.ServerVariables` Collection

```
<html>
<head>
  <title>ASP Form Example: Results</title>
</head>
<body>
<script language="JScript" runat="server">

  // store user agent string in variable
  var ua = new String(Request.ServerVariables("HTTP_USER_AGENT"));
```

```
  // Check to see if its Internet Explorer.
  if(ua.indexOf("MSIE") != -1){
    Response.Write("Welcome!<br />");
    Response.Write("User-agent: ");
    Response.Write(Request.ServerVariables("HTTP_USER_AGENT"));

  // Browser is not IE, so do something different.
  }else{
    Response.Write("You are not using an Internet Explorer browser<br />");
    Response.Write("User-agent: " +
Request.ServerVariables("HTTP_USER_AGENT"));
  }

</script>
</body>
</html>
```

Moving On

Up until this point, we have covered the use of JavaScript on both the client and server-side. For many of you, this represents the borders of what can be accomplished with JavaScript. However, Chapter 6, "Windows Scripting," will map out yet another environment where JavaScript (or JScript rather) has taken hold—the Windows Script Host environment.

CHAPTER 6

Windows Scripting

As many developers know, a big deficiency with Windows was its lack of scripting support for automating tasks. Most other operating systems had some type of built-in scripting engine. Of course there was the batch file support in MS-DOS, but it was very limited in its capability and not very useful in the Windows environment.

Microsoft realized this limitation and introduced the Windows Script specification within Internet Explorer 3.0. This provided an interface for developers to build scripting engines for different browsers. From the Windows Script Interfaces grew what is known today as the Windows Script Host.

Windows Script Host

Windows Script Host (WSH) provides the ability to automate tasks for the Windows environment. Before WSH, batch files were available in MS-DOS. However, they weren't very powerful and provided little use in the Windows environment. A scripting language was needed for Windows, and WSH was the answer. Suppose that you wanted to get the computer name, add a desktop shortcut, and map a network drive without doing each task individually. With Windows Script Host, all these tasks can be performed through a single script.

WSH can be used with a few different programming languages. VBScript and JScript are supported in the default engine on Windows 98 and NT/2000. This book focuses on the JScript language and will use it in the examples.

The latest version of WSH is 5.6. Although it is still a beta version, the scripting engine can be downloaded from Microsoft's Web site. The added benefits of this version are improved argument handling, remote script capability, treating processes as objects, access to the current working directory, and an improved security model.

The way Windows Script Host works is you create a script using various methods and properties from the WSH objects and save it to a file with the `.wsf` extension. This specifies that the file is a Windows Script Host file. Let's take a look at an example of a simple WSH file. Listing 6.1 shows a WSH file that will display the username of the local machine in which the script is run.

Listing 6.1   Example of a WSH File

```
<job>
<script language="JScript">

var WshNetwork = WScript.CreateObject("Wscript.Network");
WScript.Echo("The User name is: " + WshNetwork.UserName);

</script>
</job>
```

The syntax of a WSH script is fairly simple. You enclose your functionality between the opening and closing `<job><script>` tags. This is similar to a normal JScript or JavaScript program. This script can be run a few different ways. These ways are discussed later in the chapter.

Architecture

The architecture of the Windows Script Host is fairly basic. There are only a few components, which operate together, to make WSH scripts come alive. They are the script itself, the Windows Shell, the Windows Registry, and the WSH engine. Figure 6.1 shows a diagram indicating how the components interact with each other to process the script.

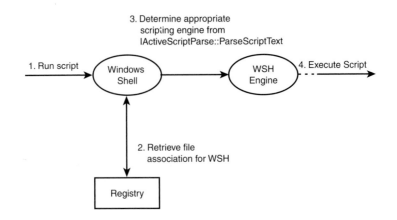

Figure 6.1

WSH architecture.

As you can see, the Windows Shell is the first component to encounter the script file. The shell must then determine what this file is and does so by looking up the file association in the Registry. When it has this information, it can then pass the file to the Windows Script Host Engine, which will use the `IActiveScriptParse::ParseScriptText` method to determine whether this particular script will go to a JavaScript engine, Visual Basic Script engine, Perl engine, and so on.

Object Model

The WSH is based on an object model hierarchy, which consists of 14 objects. Every object stems from the `WScript` object (root object). The WSH Object model is shown in Figure 6.2.

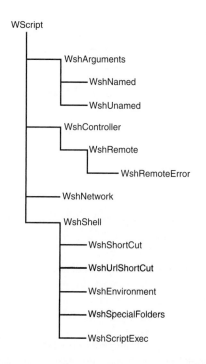

Figure 6.2

WSH object model hierarchy.

Not every object can be instantiated directly. The WScript object is available in every WSH script and does not need to be instantiated. Other objects that can be instantiated are the `WshController`, `WshNetwork`, and `WshShell`. To create these objects, use the `CreateObject` method. All other child objects are indirectly created through the top-level objects. The WSH object model exposes various COM objects, which can be manipulated.

Benefits and Limitations

WSH has both its benefits and limitations. Using JScript or VBScript, WSH provides you direct access to a computer and it's Windows resources. You can directly manipulate the Windows Registry, set default printers, run remote scripts and more. The WSH is a low memory scripting host that works well with scripts that require little user interaction. So for things such as entering logon scripts and batch processes, and performing administrative tasks, WSH is a great tool to use.

However, with it's power comes disadvantages. Providing a script direct access to your local computers' resources can be very dangerous. Should a developer decide to write a malicious script, a lot of damage can be caused. For this reason, some choose for their Windows environment to disable WSH.

WSH is limited in some aspects. The graphical components are limited. There are no custom dialogs or anything of that sort. For better UI's, your program will need to rely on the tools available with whichever language you choose to write your script in.

Windows Script Components

Many different components are tied together to create the whole Windows Script Host object model. In this section we will discuss some of these objects and their capabilities in more detail.

Objects

In the Object Model, you saw that many different objects comprise the Windows Script Host. Each object has its own methods and properties associated with it. The main objects from which all other minor objects stem are `WScript`, `WshController`, `WshNetwork`, and `WshShell`.

The three most commonly used ones that we'll discuss are `WScript`, `WshShell`, and `WshNetwork`. They provide the majority of the top-level functionality for Windows Script Host. Let us take a look at what each of them can do.

WScript

The `WScript` object is the root-level object from which all other objects are created. It does not need to be instantiated and is available from any script file. It can be used for a number of different tasks. You can use it as an informational object to get script filenames, command-line arguments, and host information. It can also be used to create objects, connect to and disconnect from objects, sink events, stop script execution, and output information. Listing 6.1 displays the simplest form of using the `WScript` object by using its `Echo` method to output the username.

As mentioned earlier, WScript can create any type of child object by using the `CreateObject` method. Suppose that you wanted to create a new `WshShell` object. You could do so by using the following line.

```
WshShellObj = WScript.CreateObject("WScript.Shell");
```

By now you are probably saying to yourself, "This is great, but what can I do with a new WshShell object?" Keep reading and you will find out. (See Chapter 15, "Windows Script Host," for details on all the methods and properties associated with the WScript object.)

WshShell

WshShell is a very useful object. It is used for manipulating the Windows Registry, creating shortcuts, starting new shell processes, and reading system information. It provides the ENVIRONMENT collection for your program, which allows you to access or manipulate environment variables. (See Chapter 15 for details on all the methods and properties associated with the WshShell object.)

Let's look at a simple example in Listing 6.2, which creates a shortcut on the desktop to the Amazon.com Web site. Using the CreateObject method of the root WScript object, we can create a WshShell object named WshShellObj. Next we need to specify that the shortcut is to be created on the desktop. To accomplish this, the SpecialFolders method is used with "*Desktop*" as the parameter. Then we call the CreateShortcut method and pass it the path for our shortcut. Finally the target path for the shortcut is specified and the shortcut is saved.

Listing 6.2   Example of Creating a Shortcut with the WshShell **Object**

```
<job>
<script language="JScript">

// Create a WshShell object.
WshShellObj = WScript.CreateObject("WScript.Shell");

// Specify the Desktop as a folder.
myDesktop = WshShellObj.SpecialFolders("Desktop");

// Create a shortcut to the Amazon.com website.
var urlShortcut = WshShellObj.CreateShortcut(myDesktop + "\\Amazon.url");
urlShortcut.TargetPath = "http://www.amazon.com";
urlShortcut.Save();

</script>
</job>
```

WshNetwork

The WshNetwork object is used to perform many different network-related tasks. With this object, you can add printer connections, obtain the computer name, map network drives, set default printers, get user domains, and more. These types of tasks can be very useful to a Windows network administrator. (See Chapter 15 for details on all the methods and properties associated with the WshNetwork object.)

Let's look at an example. Suppose that a new network printer has been added and the network administrator wants to make it as easy as possible for users to add this printer to their machine. The administrator could create a WSH script that all users can run to add the printer to their machines. In Listing 6.3, we see the code to add a new printer.

Listing 6.3   Adding Printer with *WshNetwork* **Object**

```
<job>
<script language="JScript">

// Create Arguments object.
WshArgObj = WScript.Arguments;

// Read in the username and password.
var userName = WshArgObj.Item(0);
var passwd = WshArgObj.Item(1);

// Create a new Network object and add printer.
var WshNetwork = new CreateObject("Wscript.Network");
var printer = "\\printers\NewPrinter";
var localName = "myNewPrinter";
WshNetwork.AddPrinterConnection(localName, printer, userName, passwd);

</script>
</job>
```

Because user input is required for this particular script, it is recommended that the command line method, cscript.exe, is used to execute the script. (For more information on differences between cscript.exe and wscript.exe, refer to the "Methods of Executing Script" section). The user would specify his username and password as the arguments. So assuming that the file is named "addPrinter.wsf", it would be executed in an MS-DOS Windows as follows:

```
cscript addPrinter.wsf Betty pass123
```

Methods of Executing Scripts

To run a WSH script, you need to have the Windows Scripting Engine installed on your operating system. This is included in Windows 98 and NT/2000. For Windows 95 users, the WSH engine can be added by downloading the engine from the Microsoft site and installing it. See http://msdn.microsoft.com/scripting for more information.

Once installed, WSH scripts can be run in two different modes. They are Windows-based and DOS-(command) based. The mode in which you run your scripts depends on what tasks you intend to accomplish. If you intend to have some user interaction and want to use graphical components, the Windows-based execution is preferred (wscript.exe). If your script needs to perform tasks, which can only be done in MS-DOS or require little user interaction, the command-based execution should be used (cscript.exe). Both methods of execution can be run from a command line and have certain options that can be specified. They are listed in Table 6.1.

Table 6.1 `wscript.exe` *and* `cscript.exe` *Options*

Type	Description
`//B`	Specifies the batch mode. Suppresses user prompts and script error messages.
`//D`	Enables the debugger.
`//E:engine`	Runs the script with the specific script engine.
`//H:cscript`	Uses `cscript.exe` as the default execution method.
`//H:wscript`	Uses `wscript.exe` as the default execution method.
`//I`	Specifies the interactive mode. Displays user prompts and script errors.
`//Job:<jobID>`	Executes a specified jobID from the `.wsf` file.
`//logo`	Displays an execution banner.
`//nologo`	Prevents display of the execution banner.
`//S`	Saves current command-line options.
`//T:nn`	Sets the maximum number of seconds that a script can run.
`//U`	Not available with `wscript.exe`.
`//X`	Launches a program in the debugger.
`//?`	Help. Displays information for command parameters.

To execute a script generically from the command line, adhere to the following syntax:

```
wscript <filename> [//options] [arguments]
cscript <filename> [//options] [arguments]
```

Arguments should be separated with a space. WSH also supports drag-and-drop functionality for arguments. You can drag and drop a file onto a WSH file, and—provided that your script is written to parse the argument—it will treat your dragged filename as an argument.

Windows-Based Scripts

Windows-based WSH scripts allow you to take advantage of the limited graphical capabilities in WSH. This is particularly useful if your script requires visual user interaction. Keep in mind though that WSH doesn't have very complex dialog boxes. The graphical components are mostly limited to the tools available in VBScript or JScript and pop-up dialogs.

There are three methods to execute a Windows-based script. The easiest is to locate the script file in Windows Explorer and then double-click it to start. The second method is to use the "Run" option from the Windows Start Menu. Choose the WSH file in the "Run" option and then click the OK button to run. This is shown in Figure 6.3. The third method is to run your script from the command line using `wscript.exe`.

Any of these methods will work, and it is just a matter of personal preference. Let's take a look at the example in Listing 6.4.

Figure 6.3

Running script from the Run option.

Listing 6.4 **Simple** `Hello World` **Script**

```
<job>
<script language="JScript">

// Output the Hello World text.
WScript.Echo("Hello World!");

</script>
</job>
```

If we were to run the script as a Windows-based script, the output would display a pop-up window as shown in Figure 6.4.

Figure 6.4

The WSH pop-up display box.

Command-Based Scripts

WSH scripts can also be run from the command prompt. This is performed in the DOS environment using the cscript executable. For example, if you wanted to run a script called "`hello.wsf`", you would type the following at a command prompt:

cscript hello.wsf

This example assumes that you are running the script from the same directory it is located. Otherwise, the path to the file will need to be specified. Any arguments or options passed to the script would be added after the script name. So, if you wanted to use the Interactive mode options and pass a string as the first argument, your script call would look similar to this:

`cscript hello.wsf //I /arg1`

Command-based scripts can also display output, similar to Windows-based scripts. However, unlike the Windows-based pop-up window, the command script output is suppressed to the same DOS Window in which the script is run. This is one of the disadvantages to the command-based scripts. No graphical components are provided. In Figure 6.5, an example of the well-known Hello World program is executed displaying the "Hello World" text to the screen.

Figure 6.5

Command-based output display.

Remote Scripting

With the latest version of WSH (version 5.6), it is possible to execute scripts remotely. This allows you to remotely administer various automation tasks to computers across the network. These tasks can even be executed simultaneously. You can remotely start, stop, and get the status of WSH scripts. If an error occurs through the WshRemoteError object, you can get the character, line number, error description, and even source code for the error.

When a remote script is executed, the local machine actually copies the script to the remote machine before execution. Before a remote script can be executed though, the remote machine must be set up with the proper security settings. To set up remote scripting on your machine, you need to follow three simple steps. First install WSH, version 5.6 (if not already installed). The second step is to add yourself to the remote machine's local administrators group. The third step is to enable remote WSH through the Poledit.exe executable. After this is taken care of, your machine is ready for remote scripting!

There is a caveat to remote scripting. Remote scripting can only be run in the Windows 2000/NT environment. The Windows 9x scripting engine does not support this functionality. This is because you cannot authenticate users who are not on the NT domain.

How to Use Remote Scripting

So how do you use remote scripting? The WSH has provided the WshRemote object and various properties and methods to control the execution of your remote scripts. The WshRemote object is created through the WshController object. First create an instance of the `WshController` with the `CreateObject` method. After you have the controller object, you can use the `CreateScript` method to specify which script you want to execute remotely. This method actually returns a `WshRemote` object that can be used with its `execute()` method to run the script remotely.

As with most computer programs, not all the scripts will run without errors. This is not a problem though. The WSH object model includes the `WshRemoteError` object, which can be used to obtain various error information. It is not an object that is directly instantiated, but an object that is available as a child object of the `WshRemote` object.

Remote Scripting Example

Lets take a look at an example of remote scripting. In Listing 6.5, a maintenance script is to be run remotely on a machine named `"blue2"`. A Controller object, `WshCtrlObj`, is first created. Then an instance of the `WshRemote` object is created using the `CreateScript` method. The path of the script to be run and the machine name are passed as parameters. We set some events to be caught and execute the script. A print statement is added just to check the status. Our current script sleeps while waiting for the remote script to finish execution. Should any errors occur, the function `remote_error` can be used to display all the error information.

Listing 6.5   Remote Scripting Example

```
<job>
<script language="JScript">

// Create a WshController object.
WshCtrlObj = WScript.CreateObject("WScript.Controller");

// Create a WshRemote object.
remoteScript = WshCtrlObj.CreateScript("c:\remote_tasks\maintenance.wsf",
➥ "blue2");

// Catch events.
WScript.ConnectObject(RemoteScript, "RemoteScript_");

// Start the script.
remoteScript.Execute();

// Print the current status.
WScript.Echo("The current status of the remote script is: " +
➥ remoteScript.Status);

while (remoteScript.Status !=2) {
    WScript.Sleep(100);
}

// Catch errors.
function remote_Error(){
```

```
var myError = remoteScript.Error;
var errorString  = "An Error occurred in the remote execution\n";
errorString += The remote error: " + myError.Description + "\n";
errorString += "occurred at line number: " + myError.Line + "\n";
errorString += " ,character: " + myError.Character + "\n";
errorString += "The Source for the Error is: " + myError.Source +"\n";
WScript.Echo(errorString);
}

</script>
</job>
```

Moving On

In this chapter, we have discussed many aspects of the Windows Script Host. We have taken a look at the object model and a few specific objects in detail. We discussed the two methods of running WSH scripts and even how to run scripts remotely. Although the WSH 5.6 is still in beta version, a lot of things can be done with it. Look for even more to be added as WSH continues to evolve.

PART III

JAVASCRIPT REFERENCE

CHAPTER 7

Core Language

This chapter is a detailed reference of all the items and elements that make up the core JavaScript and JScript languages as well as information in the ECMA-262, 3rd Edition standard (ECMAScript). Because the details of JavaScript, JScript, and ECMAScript varies slightly, so does each one's definition of core. Because of these variations, this chapter covers items that are considered core in one standard, but might not exist in the other standards. Every nuance of the languages is covered, giving you a one-stop place to get answers to all your questions. Each entry includes version, environment support, syntax, a description, and an example, as well as many other details.

The chapter is in alphabetical order, by objects, to provide you with quick, easy access to the major parts of the language. The methods, properties, functions, and event handlers of every object appear alphabetically after the respective parent object, using the simple dot notation that makes the language so easy to learn. For example, the sin() function is found after the Math object as Math.sin().

@_alpha
> JScript3.0+
> IE 4+

Syntax
`@_alpha`

Description
The @_alpha variable is used in JScript conditional compilation to determine if a DEC Alpha processor is being used. When the variable is not true, it behaves as NaN although it is technically undefined.

Example

Listing 7.1 alerts the user when a DEC Alpha processor is used.

Listing 7.1   Detect a DEC Alpha Processor

```
<script type="text/jscript" language="JScript">
<!--
@if (@_alpha)
  alert("You are using a DEC Alpha processor.");
@else
  alert("You are NOT using a DEC Alpha processor.");
@end

// -->
</script>
```

@_jscript

> JScript3.0+
> IE 4+

Syntax

```
@_jscript
```

Description

The @_jscript variable is used in JScript conditional compilation to determine if JScript is being used. This variable is always true.

Example

Listing 7.2 displays an alert box based on the value of the @_jscript variable.

Listing 7.2   Detect a JScript

```
<script type="text/jscript" language="JScript">
<!--
@if (@_jscript)
  alert("The @ jscript variable is true.");
@else
  alert("The @_jscript variable is NOT true.");
@end

// -->
</script>
```

@_jscript_build

> JScript3.0+
> IE 4+

Syntax

```
@_jscript_build
```

Description

The @_jscript_build variable is used in JScript conditional compilation to hold the build number of the JScript scripting engine.

CAUTION

Before accessing the @_jscript_build variable, use the @cc_on statement to define the variable. More information about the @cc_on statement can be found later in this chapter.

Example

Listing 7.3 uses the @_jscript_build variable to display the build number of the JScript engine that is being used.

Listing 7.3   Retrieve JScript Build Number

```
<script type="text/jscript" language="JScript">
<!--

//Set conditional compilation so @_jscript_build variable will be defined.
@cc_on

//Display the JScript build number using the @_jscript_build variable.
document.write("The JScript engine build number is ",@_jscript_build);

// -->
</script>
```

@_jscript_version
JScript3.0+
IE 4+

Syntax

```
@_jscript_version
```

Description

The @_jscript_version variable is used in the JScript conditional compilation to hold the JScript version number in *major.minor* format.

CAUTION

Before accessing the @_jscript_version variable, use the @cc_on statement to define the variable.

Example

Listing 7.4 uses the @_jscript_version variable to display the JScript version that is being used.

Listing 7.4   Determine JScript Version

```
<script type="text/jscript" language="JScript">
<!--

//Set conditional compilation so @_jscript_version variable will be defined.
@cc_on

//Display the JScript verision number using the @_jscript_version variable
document.write("The JScript version is ",@_jscript_version).


// -->
</script>
```

@_mac

> JScript3.0+
>
> IE 4+

Syntax

@_mac

Description

The @_mac variable is used in JScript conditional compilation to determine if an Apple Macintosh system is being us ed. When the variable is not true, it behaves as NaN although it is technically undefined.

Example

Listing 7.5 alerts the user when an Apple Macintosh system is used.

Listing 7.5   Detect an Apple Macintosh System

```
<script type="text/jscript" language="JScript">
<!--

@if (@_mac)
  alert("You are using an Apple Macintosh system.");
@else
  alert("You are NOT using an Apple Macintosh system.");
@end

// -->
</script>
```

@_mc680x0

IE 4+

JScript3.0+

Syntax

@_mc680x0

Description

The @_mc680x0 variable is used in JScript conditional compilation to determine if a Motorola 680x0 processor is being used. When the variable is not true, it behaves as NaN although it is technically undefined.

Example

Listing 7.6 alerts the user when a Motorola 680x0 processor is used.

Listing 7.6   Detect a Motorola 680x0 Processor

```
<script type="text/jscript" language="JScript">
<!--

@if (@_mc680x0)
  alert("You are using a Motorola 680x0 processor.");
@else
  alert("You are NOT using a Motorola 680x0 processor.");
@end

// -->
</script>
```

@_PowerPC

IE 4+

JScript3.0+

Syntax

@_PowerPC

Description

The @_PowerPC variable is used in JScript conditional compilation to determine if a Motorola PowerPC processor is being used. When the variable is not true, it behaves as NaN although it is technically undefined.

Example

Listing 7.7 alerts the user when a Motorola PowerPC processor is used.

Listing 7.7   Detect a Motorola PowerPC Processor

```
<script type="text/jscript" language="JScript">
<!--

@if (@_PowerPC)
  alert("You are using a Motorola PowerPC processor.");
@else
  alert("You are NOT using a Motorola PowerPC processor.");
@end

// -->
</script>
```

@_win16

> IE 4+
> JScript3.0+

Syntax

```
@_win16
```

Description

The @_win16 variable is used in JScript conditional compilation to determine if a win16 system is being used. When the variable is not true, it behaves as NaN although it is technically undefined.

Example

Listing 7.8 alerts the user when a win16 system is used.

Listing 7.8   Detect a win16 System

```
<script type="text/jscript" language="JScript">
<!--

@if (@_win16)
  alert("You are using a 16 bit Windows system.");
@else
  alert("You are NOT using a 16 bit Windows system.");
@end

// -->
</script>
```

@_win32

> JScript3.0+
> IE 4+

Syntax

```
@_win32
```

Description

The @_win32 variable is used in JScript conditional compilation to determine if a win32 system is being used. When the variable is not true, it behaves as NaN although it is technically undefined.

Example

Listing 7.9 alerts the user when a win32 system is used.

Listing 7.9   Detect a win32 System

```
<script type="text/jscript" language="JScript">
<!--

@if (@_win32)
  alert("You are using a 32 bit Windows system.");
@else
  alert("You are NOT using a 32 bit Windows system.");
@end
// -->
</script>
```

@_x86

JScript3.0+

IE 4+

Syntax

```
@_x86
```

Description

The @_x86 variable is used in JScript conditional compilation to determine if a Intel processor is being used. When the variable is not true, it behaves as NaN although it is technically undefined.

Example

Listing 7.10 alerts the user when an Intel processor is used.

Listing 7.10   Detect an Intel Processor

```
<script type="text/jscript" language="JScript">
<!--

@if (@_x86)
  alert("You are using an Intel processor.");
```

Listing 7.10   Continued

```
@else
  alert("You are NOT using an Intel processor.");
@end

// -->
</script>
```

@cc_on

> JScript3.0+
>
> IE 4+

Syntax

```
@cc_on
```

Description

The @cc_on statement is used to activate JScript conditional compilation in the script-ing engine.

Example

Listing 7.11 shows where the @cc_on statement would be used within JScript code to get the JScript version.

Listing 7.11   Activate Conditional Compilation

```
<script type="text/jscript" language="JScript">
<!--

//Set conditional compilation so @_jscript_version variable will be defined.
@cc_on

//Display the JScript version number using the @_jscript_version variable
document.write("The JScript version is ",@_jscript_version).

// -->
</script>
```

@if

> JScript3.0+
>
> IE 4+

Syntax

```
@if (condition1)
  statement1
@elif (condition2)
  statement2
```

```
@else
  statement3
@end
```

Description

The `@if` statement operates much the same as a typical `if` conditional statement, but it evaluates compiled variables and has a slightly different syntax. If the expression in *condition1* evaluates to `true`, *statement1* is executed. Otherwise, the *condition2* is evaluated to determine whether *statement2* should be evaluated. The `@elif` statement operates the same as the JavaScript `else...if` statement, even though it looks different. You can use as many `@elif` statements as needed or none at all. Only one `@else` statement should be used to catch conditions that don't meet any of the previous conditionals. Similar to the `@elif` statement, the `@else` statement is optional. The `@end` statement is required at the end of all `@if` conditionals.

Example

Listing 7.12 displays a message based on the type of processor being used.

Listing 7.12   Using `@if` to Display Processor Type

```
<script type="text/jscript" language="JScript">
<!--

//Alert the user as to which type of processor they are using.
@if(@_jscript)
  alert("You are using a DEC Alpha processor.");
@elif(@_mc680x0)
  alert("You are using a Motorola 680x0 processor.");
@elif(@_PowerPC)
  alert("You are using a Motorola PowerPC processor.");
@elif(@_x86)
  alert("You are using an Intel processor.");
@else
  alert("I don't know what type of processor you have!");
@end

// -->
</script>
```

@set

> JScript3.0+
> IE 4+

Syntax

```
@set @varName = value
```

Description

The @set property allows the creation of JScript variables. The name of the variable must start with an ampersand character. If the variable is used before being defined, its value will be NaN.

Example

Listing 7.13 uses the @set property to create a custom compiled variable called @number and assigns the number 25 to the variable. The variable is then used to display a sentence in the browser.

Listing 7.13   Create Custom Compiled Variable Using the @set Property

```
<script type="text/jscript" language="JScript">
<!--

//Create a custom compiled variable called @number and set it to 25
@set @number = 25.

//Display a sentence in the browser based on the value stored in the
//custom compiled variable @number.
@if(@number == 25)
  document.write("Number is equal to ",@number);
@else
  document.write("Number is not equal to 25.");
@end

// -->
</script>
```

Operators

- (Subtraction)

JavaScript 1.0+, ECMAScript 1E+, JScript 1.0+
Nav2+, NES2+, IE 3+, Opera3+

Syntax

num1 - num2

Description

The number to the right of the operator is subtracted from the number to the left of the operator. If either operand is a string, an attempt is made to convert the string to a number before performing the operation.

Example

The code in Listing 7.14 creates a string out of the number "45". The string is converted to a number before being subtracted from the number 25. The result of the subtraction operation (20) is displayed.

Listing 7.14   Using the Subtraction Operator

```
<script type="text/javascript" language="JavaScript">
<!--

//Declare the number 45 as a string
aString = new String("45");

//Subtract 25 from 45
answer = aString - 25;
document.write("answer = (45-25)<br>");

//Answer is equal to 20
document.write("answer = ",answer);

// -->
</script>
```

- (Unary Negation)

JavaScript 1.0+, ECMAScript 1E+, JScript 1.0+
Nav2+, NES2+, IE 3+, Opera3+

Syntax

-num

Description

The unary negation operator changes the sign of *num*. When negating a variable, the contents of the variable do not change; only the value returned is negated. If the operand is a string, it is converted to a number before performing the unary negation operation.

Example

The code in Listing 7.15 creates a string "36". The string is converted to a number before being negated. The result of the negation is -36.

Listing 7.15   Using the Negation Operator

```
<script type="text/javascript" language="JavaScript">
<!--

//Declare the number 36 as a string
aString = new String("36");

//negate the number
answer = -aString;
document.write("answer = -aString<br>");
```

Listing 7.15   Continued

```
//Answer is equal to -36
document.write("answer = ",answer);


// -->
</script>
```

-- (Decrement)

JavaScript 1.0+, ECMAScript 1E+, JScript 1.0+
Nav2+, NES2+, IE 3+, Opera3+

Syntax

```
--variable
variable--
```

Description

The pre-decrement operator, defined in the first syntactical definition, decrements *variable* by 1. The new decremented value is returned by the operation.

The second syntactical definition contains the post-decrement operator. This operator is similar to the pre-decrement operator in that it decrements *variable* by 1. However, the original value is returned by the operation before being decremented.

In both cases, if the operand is a string, it is converted to a number before performing the operation.

Example

Listing 7.16 demonstrates how the pre-decrement and post-decrement operators work. Notice that the variable num holds a string that is converted before performing the decrement operations. The result from executing this code is shown in Figure 7.1.

Listing 7.16   Using the Decrement Operator

```
<script type="text/javascript" language="JavaScript">
<!--

// Store value in variable before pre-decrement
document.write("<h3>Before Pre-decrement</h3>");
num = new String("807");    //num holds the string 807
document.write("num=",num,"<br>");    //807 is displayed.

// Pre-decrement the value stored in num
returnValue = --num;
document.write("<h3>After Pre-decrement</h3>");
document.write("num=",num,"<br>");    //806 is displayed.

//806 is displayed by returnValue
document.write("Value returned from operation is ",returnValue,"<br>");
```

```
// Post-decrement the value stored in num
returnValue = num--;
document.write("<h3>After Post-decrement</h3>");
document.write("num=",num,"<br>");    //805 is displayed.

//806 is displayed by returnValue
document.write("Value returned from operation is ",returnValue,"<br>");

// -->
</script>
```

Figure 7.1
The difference between pre-decrement and post-decrement.

! (Logical NOT)
JavaScript 1.0+, ECMAScript 1E+, JScript 1.0+
Nav2+, NES2+, IE 3+, Opera3+

Syntax
!operand

Description
The ! operator inverts the boolean value returned from the *operand*. So, if *operand* evaluates to true, the result of the operation is false. If the *operand* evaluates to false, the result is true. When the *operand* evaluates to a non-Boolean value, it is converted to true or false before performing the inversion.

Example
In Listing 7.17 the character "1" is converted to the Boolean true before inverting the value with the NOT operand. The variable theReverseTruth is assigned false.

Listing 7.17   Using the Logical NOT *Operator*

```
<script type="text/javascript" language="JavaScript">
<!--

//Create a variable that contains 1
theTruth = new String("1");

//Invert the value stored in the previous variable
theReverseTruth = !theTruth;

//Output the values stored in the two variables
document.write("theTruth = ",theTruth,"<br>");
document.write("theReverseTruth = ",theReverseTruth);

// -->
</script>
```

!= (Not Equal)

JavaScript 1.0+, ECMAScript 1E+, JScript 1.0+
Nav2+, NES2+, IE 3+, Opera3+

Syntax

expression1 != *expression2*

Description

The not equal operator compares the first expression to the second expression. If the expressions are not equal, true is returned from the operation. If they are equal, false is returned.

JavaScript and Microsoft JScript interpreters attempt to convert the expressions to the same data type before evaluating the not equal operation using the following rules:

- true is converted to the number 1, and false is converted to zero before being compared.
- If either of the operands is NaN, the equality operator returns false.
- Null and undefined are equal.
- Null and undefined are not equal to 0 (zero), "" (empty string), or false.
- If a string and a number are compared, attempt to convert the string to a number and then check for equality.
- If an object and a string are compared, attempt to convert the object to a string and then check for equality.
- If an object and a number are compared, attempt to convert the object to a number and then check for equality.
- If both operands of an equality operation are objects, the address of the two objects are checked for equality.

CAUTION

In JavaScript 1.2, the decision was made to NOT do type conversion on the operands of the not equal operator. JavaScript reverted back to using type conversion with this operator in 1.3 and later.

Example

In the following example, the string `"523"` is converted to a number (except in JavaScript 1.2, in which type conversion is not performed), so that two numbers are compared. Because the left operand is equal to the right operand, the phrase `"The string 523 is EQUAL to the number 523"` is written to the browser window.

Listing 7.18   Using the Not Equal Operator

```
<script type="text/javascript" language="JavaScript">
<!--

//Before comparing this string to the number the
//string will be converted to a number.
if("523" != 523)
{
  //If the two numbers are not equal then display this sentence.
  document.write("The string 523 is NOT equal to the number 523");
}
else
{
  //If the two numbers are equal then display this sentence.
  document.write("The string 523 is EQUAL to the number 523");
}

// -->
</script>
```

!== (Non-Identity)

JavaScript 1.3+, ECMAScript 3E+, JScript 1.0+
Nav4.06+, IE 3+, Opera5+

Syntax

expression1 !== *expression2*

Description

The non-identity operator compares the first expression to the second expression. If the value on the left is not equal to the value on the right side of the operator, `true` is returned from the operation. If the values are equal, `false` is returned.

NOTE

No type conversion is performed on the expressions before the comparison is made.

Example

In Listing 7.19, the string `"8765"` is NOT converted to a number, so the two expressions are not the same type. Because the two operands are not the same type, they are not equal, so the phrase `"The string 8765 is NOT equal to the number 8765"` is written to the browser window.

Listing 7.19   Using the Not-Identity Operator

```
<script type="text/javascript" language="JavaScript">
<!--

//Compare the string to the number but do not
//convert the string to a number.
if("8765" !== 8765)
{
  //If the string and number are not equal then display this sentence.
  document.write("The string 8765 is NOT equal to the number 8765");
}
else
{
  //If the string and number are equal then display this sentence.
  document.write("The string 8765 is EQUAL to the number 8765");
}

// -->
</script>
```

% (Modulus)

JavaScript 1.0+, ECMAScript 1E+, JScript 1.0+
Nav2+, NES2+, IE 3+, Opera3+

Syntax

num1 % *num2*

Description

The modulus operator begins the same as the division operator, by dividing the left value by the right; but instead of returning the normal result of division, only the remainder is returned by the operation. If either operand is a string, an attempt is made to convert the string to a number before performing the operation.

Example

In Listing 7.20, the variable answer is assigned the value 1 because 7 is divided by the number 2 three times plus a remainder of 1. This remainder is stored in the variable answer.

Listing 7.20   Using the Modulus Operator

```
<script type="text/javascript" language="JavaScript">
<!--

//1 is stored in the variable answer.
answer = 7 % 2;

//Display the value in the variable answer
document.write("answer = ",answer);

// -->
</script>
```

%= (Modulus Assignment)

JavaScript 1.0+, ECMAScript 1E+, JScript 1.0+
Nav2+, NES2+, IE 3+, Opera3+

Syntax

variable %= value

Description

The modulus assignment operator divides the value stored in the left variable by the right value. The remainder is returned by the operation and stored in the variable to the left of the operator. If value is a string, an attempt is made to convert the string to a number before performing the modulus and assignment.

Example

In Listing 7.21, the variable answer is initially assigned the value 17. The number 17 is divided by the number 3. The remainder portion (modulos) of the result of the division is stored in the variable answer, overwriting the number 3.

Listing 7.21   Using the Modulus Assignment Operator

```
<script type="text/javascript" language="JavaScript">
<!--

//Initialize the variable answer with 3.
answer = 17;

//The number 2 is stored in the variable answer.
answer %= 3;
```

Listing 7.21   Continued

```
//Display the value stored in the variable answer.
document.write("answer = ",answer);


// -->
</script>
```

& (Bitwise AND)

JavaScript 1.0+, ECMAScript 1E+, JScript 1.0+
Nav2+, NES2+, IE 3+, Opera3+

Syntax

num1 & *num2*

Description

The bitwise AND operator looks at the integer numbers on both sides of the operator as 32-bit binary numbers. The bitwise AND (&) operator individually evaluates each of the 32 bits representing the number on the left of the operator to the corresponding bit of the number on the right of the operator using the truth table shown in Table 7.1. The 32-bit binary result of the logical AND operation is converted to an integer value and returned from the bitwise AND operation.

Table 7.1   Bitwise AND Truth Table

First Value	Second Value	Result
true	true	true
true	false	false
false	true	false
false	false	false

Example

The code in Listing 7.22 uses the bitwise AND operator on the numbers 11 and 6. The result of the bitwise AND operation is 2.

Listing 7.22   Using the Bitwise AND Operator

```
<script type="text/javascript" language="JavaScript">
<!--

// integer = 32-bit binary representation
// 11 = 00000000000000000000000000001011
//  6 = 00000000000000000000000000000110
//  2 = 00000000000000000000000000000010

// answer is equal to 2
answer = 11 & 6;
```

```
//Display the value stored in the variable answer.
document.write("11 & 6 = ",answer);

// -->
</script>
```

&& (Logical AND)

JavaScript 1.0+, ECMAScript 1E+, JScript 1.0+
Nav2+, NES2+, IE 3+, Opera3+

Syntax

expression1 && *expression2*

Description

The logical AND operator returns true if the expression on the left and the expression on the right of the operator evaluate to true. If either the left, right, or both evaluates to false, the result of the operation is false.

Be sure to note that the implementation of the logical AND operator in JavaScript is more complex than what was just mentioned. The AND operation begins by evaluating the left expression. If the left expression evaluates to false, the basic logic of the AND operator is complete, so the right expression is never evaluated. But if the left expression evaluates to true, the right expression must be evaluated to determine the final result of the AND operation. In either case, the final result returned by the AND operation is actually determined by the result of the last expression to be evaluated.

Example

Listing 7.23 demonstrates the complications associated with the logical AND operator. The first expression evaluates to false, causing the logical AND operation to evaluate to false and the message "The && evaluated FALSE!" is displayed. Because the first expression evaluates to false, the second expression, which assigns the number 5 to the variable x, is not evaluated and x remains equal to 3.

Listing 7.23   The Complicated Logical AND Operator

```
<script type="text/javascript" language="JavaScript">
<!--

//Initialize the variable x with the number 3.
x = 3;

//The assignment of 5 to the variable x never occurs
//since the expression (2==x) evaluates to false in the if statement.
if((2==x) && (x=5))
{
  document.write("The && evaluated TRUE!<br>");
```

Listing 7.23   Continued

```
}
else
{
  document.write("The && evaluated FALSE!<br>");
}

// x is still equal to 3
document.write("x=",x,"<br>");

// -->
</script>
```

&= (Bitwise AND Assignment)

JavaScript 1.0+, ECMAScript 1E+, JScript 1.0+
Nav2+, NES2+, IE 3+, Opera3+

Syntax

variable &= value

Description

The bitwise AND plus assignment operator looks at the integer numbers on both sides of the operator as 32-bit binary numbers. The bitwise AND (&) operator individually evaluates each of the 32 bits representing the number on the left of the operator to the corresponding bit of the number on the right of the operator using the truth table shown in Table 7.2. The 32-bit binary result of the bitwise AND operation is converted to an integer value and stored in the variable to the left of the operator.

Table 7.2   Bitwise AND Truth Table

First Value	Second Value	Result
true	true	true
true	false	false
false	true	false
false	false	false

Example

In Listing 7.24, the bitwise AND plus assignment operator is used on the numbers 12 and 6 to generate a result of 4.

Listing 7.24   Using the Bitwise AND Plus Assignment Operator

```
<script type="text/javascript" language="JavaScript">
<!--

// integer = 32-bit binary representation
// 12 = 00000000000000000000000000001100
```

```
//  6 = 00000000000000000000000000000110
//  4 = 00000000000000000000000000000100

//Initialize the variable x with the number 6.
x = 6;

//x is now equal to 4.
x &= 12;

//Display the value stored in the variable x.
document.write("x = ",x);

// -->
</script>
```

* (Multiplication)

JavaScript 1.0+, ECMAScript 1E+, JScript 1.0+
Nav2+, NES2+, IE 3+, Opera3+

Syntax

*num1 * num2*

Description

The multiplication operator (*) multiplies the left operand by the right operand. If either of the operands is a string, an attempt is made to convert the string to a number.

Example

In Listing 7.25, the string "5" is converted to a number before being multiplied by the number 6. The result of 30 is displayed in the browser window.

Listing 7.25   Using the Multiplication Operator

```
<script type="text/javascript" language="JavaScript">
<!--

//Initialize the variable aString.
aString = new String("5");

//Perform mulitplication operation.
x = aString * 6;
document.write("x = ",x);

// -->
</script>
```

*= (Multiplication Assignment)

JavaScript 1.0+, ECMAScript 1E+, JScript 1.0+
Nav2+, NES2+, IE 3+, Opera3+

Syntax

```
variable *= value
```

Description

The number stored in the variable to the left of the operator is multiplied by the number to the right of the operator. The result of the multiplication is written into the variable to the left of the operand. If either of the operands is a string, it is converted to a number.

Example

In Listing 7.26, the string `"5"` is converted to a number before being multiplied by the number 7. The result of the multiplication, which is 35, is stored in the variable x.

Listing 7.26   Using the Multiplication Plus Assignment Operator

```
<script type="text/javascript" language="JavaScript">
<!--

//Initialize the variable x with the number 7
//and the variable aString with "5".
x = 7;
aString = new String("5");

//Perform mulitplication and assignment operation.

//Display the value stored in the variable x.
document.write("x = ",x);

// -->
</script>
```

, (Comma)

JavaScript 1.0+, ECMAScript 1E+, JScript 1.0+
Nav2+, IE 3+, Opera3+

Syntax

```
expression1, expression2,...,expressionN3
```

Description

The comma allows multiple expressions to be evaluated as one expression. The only value returned from this operation is the return value of the right-most expression.

Example

In Listing 7.27, the comma is used to execute multiple assignment statements on one line. The number 3 is stored in y, and then 9 is stored in z. Because z=9 is the last statement in the group of comma-separated statements, its value is returned and stored in the variable x. The final values stored in each variable is displayed (x=9, y=3, z=9).

Listing 7.27   Using the Comma to Separate Multiple Statements

```
<script type="text/javascript" language="JavaScript">
<!--

//Assign values to all three variables.
x = (y = 3, z = 9);

//Display the values stored in all three variables.
document.write("x = ",x,"<br>y = ",y,"<br>z = ",z);

// -->
</script>
```

/ (Division)

JavaScript 1.0+, ECMAScript 1E+, JScript 1.0+
Nav2+, NES2+, IE 3+, Opera3+

Syntax

num1 / num2

Description

The left number is divided by the right number. If either of the operands is a string, it is converted to a number.

Example

In Listing 7.28, the string `"168"` is converted to a number before being divided by the number 14. The result (12) of the division is stored in the variable x and displayed in the browser window.

Listing 7.28   Using the Division Operator

```
<script type="text/javascript" language="JavaScript">
<!--

//Initialize the variable aString with "168".
aString = new String("168");

//Create the variable x and set it equal to the number 12.
x = aString / 14;

//Display the value stored in the variable x.
document.write("x = ",x);

// -->
</script>
```

/* / (Multi-line Comment)

JavaScript 1.0+, ECMAScript 1E+, JScript 1.0+
Nav2+, IE 3+, Opera3+

Syntax

```
/* comments */
```

Description

Every character that appears within the two comment tags is ignored by the JavaScript interpreter. Placing the tags on different lines allows comments to span multiple lines. Be careful not to nest comment tags within comment tags because this will lead to errors.

Example

Listing 7.29 demonstrates the use of multiple-line comments in JavaScript code.

Listing 7.29   Using the Multi-Line Comments

```
<script type="text/javascript" language="JavaScript">
<!--

document.write("<h2>Multi-line Comments</h2>");

/* Even though this sentences spans multiple lines it is treated
as a comment because it begins and ends with comment tags.
document.write("Not displayed!");
Notice that even the JavaScript statement above is treated as a comment*/

// -->
</script>
```

// (Comment)

JavaScript 1.0+, ECMAScript 1E+, JScript 1.0+
Nav2+, IE 3+, Opera3+

Syntax

```
// comment
```

Description

Every character that appears after this tag and on the same line as the tag is ignored by the JavaScript interpreter.

Example

Listing 7.30 demonstrates the use of the single line comment in JavaScript code.

Listing 7.30   *Using Single Line Comments*

```
<script type="text/javascript" language="JavaScript">
<!--

document.write("<h2>Single Line Comments</h2>");

//Everything on the following line is considered a comment.
//document.write("Not Displayed!");

// -->
</script>
```

/= (Division Assignment)

JavaScript 1.0+, ECMAScript 1E+, JScript 1.0+
Nav2+, NES2+, IE 3+, Opera3+

Syntax

variable /= value

Description

The number stored in the variable on the left of the operator is divided by the number on the right. The result of the division overwrites the value in the variable on the left of the operator. If either of the operands is a string, it is converted to a number.

Example

In Listing 7.31, the string "8" is converted to a number before being used to divide by the number 32. The result of the division, which is 4, is stored in the variable x.

Listing 7.31   *Using the Division and Assignment Operator*

```
<script type="text/javascript" language="JavaScript">
<!--

//Initialize the variables x and aString.
x = 32;
aString = new String("8");

//The variable x is now equal to the number 4.
x /= aString;

//Display the value stored in the variable x.
document.write("x = ",x);

// -->
</script>
```

?: (Conditional)

JavaScript 1.0+, ECMAScript 1E+, JScript 1.0+
Nav2+, NES2+, IE 3+, Opera3+

Syntax

expression ? *v value1* : *value2*

Description

An expression that evaluates to a Boolean is always placed to the left of the question mark (?). If the expression evaluates to `true`, *value1* is returned from the operation. If the expression evaluates to `false`, *value2* is returned.

The same functionality of the conditional operator can be achieved with an `if...else` statement.

Example

In Listing 7.32, the conditional operator is shown along with a similar standard `if` statement. Both the conditional operator and the `if` statement have the same result, except that the conditional operator takes up less space. The string "The hamburgers are done!" are displayed for both operators.

Listing 7.32 The Conditional Operator and `if` Statement Are Compared

```
<script type="text/javascript" language="JavaScript">
<!--

// Set the cooking status flag to "YES".
doneCooking = "YES"

//Create 2 empty variables.
var message1;
var message2;

//Standard if statement
if (doneCooking == "YES")
  message1 = "The hamburgers are done!";
else
  message1 = "The hamburgers are still cooking.";

//Same statement using conditional operator
message2 = (doneCooking == "YES") ?
  "The hamburgers are done!" :
  "The  hamburgers are still cooking.";

// Print the message to the screen.  Notice both messages are the same!
document.write("The if statement returns: ",message1,"<br>");
document.write("The conditional operator returns: ",message2);
```

```
// -->
</script>
```

^ (Bitwise Exclusive OR)

JavaScript 1.0+, ECMAScript 1E+, JScript 1.0+
Nav2+, NES2+, IE 3+, Opera3+

Syntax

num1 ^ num2

Description

The bitwise exclusive OR (XOR) operator looks at the integer numbers on both sides of the operator as 32-bit binary numbers. The bitwise exclusive OR uses a special version of the logical OR operator, called exclusive OR, to evaluate each individual bit of a binary number.

Each of the 32 bits representing the number on the left of the operator is compared to the corresponding bit of the number on the right of the operator using the exclusive OR truth table shown in Table 7.3. The 32-bit binary result of the operation is converted to an integer value and returned.

Table 7.3   Bitwise Exclusive OR Truth Table

First Value	Second Value	Result
true	true	false
true	false	true
false	true	true
false	false	false

Example

The code in Listing 7.33 uses the bitwise exclusive OR operator on the numbers 6 and 3. The result of executing the code is the number 5, which is written to the browser window.

Listing 7.33   Using the Bitwise Exclusive OR Operator

```
<script type="text/javascript" language="JavaScript">
<!--

// integer = 32-bit binary representation
// 6 = 00000000000000000000000000000110
// 3 = 00000000000000000000000000000011
// 5 = 00000000000000000000000000000101

//Display the number 5 in the browser.
document.write("6 ^ 3 = ", (6 ^ 3) );
```

Listing 7.33   Continued

```
// -->
</script>
```

^= (Bitwise Exclusive OR Assignment)

JavaScript 1.0+, ECMAScript 1E+, JScript 1.0+
Nav2+, NES2+, IE 3+, Opera3+

Syntax

variable ^= value

Description

The bitwise exclusive OR assignment operator (^=) looks at the integer numbers on both sides of the operator as 32-bit binary numbers. The bitwise exclusive OR assignment operator uses a special version of the logical OR operator, called exclusive OR, to evaluate each individual bit of a binary number.

Each of the 32 bits representing the number on the left of the operator is compared to the corresponding bit of the number on the right of the operator using the exclusive OR truth table shown in Table 7.4. The 32-bit binary result of the operation is converted to an integer value and stored in the variable to the left of the operator.

Table 7.4   Exclusive OR Truth Table

First Value	Second Value	Result
true	true	false
true	false	true
false	true	true
false	false	false

Example

Listing 7.34 uses the bitwise exclusive OR assignment operator on the numbers 10 and 6 to generate the result 12.

Listing 7.34   Using the Bitwise Exclusive OR Assignment Operator

```
<script type="text/javascript" language="JavaScript">
<!--

// integer = 32-bit binary representation
// 10 = 00000000000000000000000000001010
//  6 = 00000000000000000000000000000110
// 12 = 00000000000000000000000000001100

//Initialize the variable x with the number 10.
x = 10;
```

```
//The variable x is now equal to 12.
x ^= 6;

//Display the value stored in the variable x.
document.write("x = ",x);

// -->
</script>
```

I (Bitwise OR)

JavaScript 1.0+, ECMAScript 1E+, JScript 1.0+
Nav2+, NES2+, IE 3+, Opera3+

Syntax

num1 | num2

Description

The bitwise OR operator looks at the integer numbers on both sides of the operator as 32-bit binary numbers. The truth table of the logical OR (||) operator, shown in Table 7.5, is used to individually evaluate each of the 32 bits representing the number on the left of the operator to the corresponding bit of the number on the right of the operator. The 32-bit binary result of the bitwise OR operation is converted to an integer value and returned from the operation.

Table 7.5   Logical OR Truth Table

First Value	Second Value	Result
true	true	true
true	false	true
false	true	true
false	false	false

Example

The code in Listing 7.35 uses the bitwise OR operator on the numbers 9 and 5. Executing the code displays the number 13 in the browser window.

Listing 7.35   Using the Bitwise OR Operator

```
<script type="text/javascript" language="JavaScript">
<!--

// integer = 32-bit binary representation
//   9 = 00000000000000000000000000001001
//   5 = 00000000000000000000000000000101
//  13 = 00000000000000000000000000001101
```

Listing 7.35 Continued

```
Display the number 13 in the browser window.
document.write("9 | 5 = ", (9 | 5) );


// -->
</script>
```

|| (Logical OR)

JavaScript 1.0+, ECMAScript 1E+, JScript 1.0+
Nav2+, NES2+, IE 3+, Opera3+

Syntax

expression1 || expression2

Description

The logical OR operator returns true if the left operand, right operand, or both operands evaluates to true. If both the operands evaluate to false, the result of the operation is false.

The implementation of the logical OR operator in JavaScript and JScript is more complex than what was just mentioned. The OR operation begins by evaluating the left operand. If the left operand evaluates to true, the basic logic of the OR operator is complete, so the right operand is never evaluated. But if the left operand evaluates to false, the right operand must be evaluated to determine the final result of the OR operation. In either case, the final result returned by the OR operation is actually the result of the last operand to be evaluated.

Example

Listing 7.36 demonstrates the complications associated with the logical OR operator. The first expression evaluates to true, causing the logical OR operation to evaluate to true. Because the first expression evaluates to true, the second expression, which assigns the number 7 to the variable x, is not evaluated so x remains equal to 8.

Listing 7.36 The Complicated Logical OR Operator

```
<script type="text/javascript" language="JavaScript">
<!--

//Initialize the variable x with the number 8.
x = 8;

//The assignment of 7 to the variable x never occurs
//since the first expression (8==x) evaluates to true.
if((8==x) || (x=7))
{
   document.write("The || evaluated TRUE!<br>");
}
```

```
else
{
  document.write("The || evaluated FALSE!<br>");
}

// x is equal to 8.
document.write("x=",x,"<br>");

// -->
</script>
```

|= (Bitwise OR Assignment)

JavaScript 1.0+, ECMAScript 1E+, JScript 1.0+
Nav2+, NES2+, IE 3+, Opera3+

Syntax

variable |= *value*

Description

The bitwise OR assignment operator looks at the integer numbers on both sides of the operator as 32-bit binary numbers. The logical OR (||) operator individually evaluates each of the 32 bits representing the number on the left of the operator to the corresponding bit of the number on the right of the operator. The 32-bit binary result of the logical OR operation is converted to an integer value and stored in the variable on the left of the operator.

Example

Listing 7.37 uses the bitwise OR assignment operator on the numbers 2 and 5 to generate the number 7.

Listing 7.37   Using the Bitwise OR and Assignment Operator

```
<script type="text/javascript" language="JavaScript">
<!--

// integer = 32-bit binary representation
// 2 = 00000000000000000000000000000011
// 5 = 00000000000000000000000000000101
// 7 = 00000000000000000000000000000111

//Initialize the variable x with the number 2.
x = 2;

//Perform the bitwise OR assignment operation.
x |= 5;
```

Listing 7.37   Continued

```
//Display the value stored in the variable x.
document.write("x = ",x);


// -->
</script>
```

~ (Bitwise NOT)

JavaScript 1.0+, ECMAScript 1E+, JScript 1.0+
Nav2+, NES2+, IE 3+, Opera3+

Syntax

~operand

Description

The bitwise NOT operator begins by looking at the number to the right of the operator as a 32-bit binary number. Each bit of the given number is reversed so that all ones become zeros and all zeros become ones. The 32-bit binary result is converted to an integer value and returned from the bitwise NOT operation.

The result of inverting a number can be very confusing because of the way signed numbers are represented. Just remember that applying the bitwise NOT operator to a positive number will return the original number with the sign changed, minus one.

Example

The code in Listing 7.38 demonstrates the use of the bitwise NOT operator. Notice that the result of the operation is –3 , which is the original number (2) with the sign reversed (–2) minus 1.

Listing 7.38   The Complicated Bitwise NOT Operator

```
<script type="text/javascript" language="JavaScript">
<!--

// integer = 32-bit binary representation
//   2 = 00000000000000000000000000000010
//  -3 = 11111111111111111111111111111101


//Display the result of the Bitwise NOT Operator.
document.write("~2 = ",(~2));    //Displays -3

// -->
</script>
```

+ (Addition)

JavaScript 1.0+, ECMAScript 1E+, JScript 1.0+
Nav2+, NES2+, IE 3+, Opera3+

Syntax

operand1 + operand2

Description

The addition operator provides two types of functionality depending on the data type of the operands. The first type of functionality is simple addition, in which the value on the left of the addition operator is added to the value on the right. For this type of addition, both operands must be numbers.

The second type of functionality provided by the addition operator is string concatenation. If either of the operands is a string, string concatenation is performed by first converting any non-string operand to a string. String concatenation is then performed by appending the string to the right of the operator to the end of the string located to the left of the operator.

Example

Listing 7.39 demonstrates the addition of numbers as well as string concatenation. Compare the Listing 7.39 to the result of executing the code as seen in Figure 7.2 to understand how addition is handled with various variable types.

Listing 7.39   *Addition of Numbers and String Concatenation*

```
<script type="text/javascript" language="JavaScript">
<!--

//Initialize the variable aString.
aString = new String("67");

//answerNum contains the number 90.
answerNum = 67 + 23;

//answerStr contains the string "6723".
answerStr = aString + 23;

//Print the result to the screen.
document.write("answerNum =",answerNum,"<br>");   //Displays 90
document.write("answerStr =",answerStr);          //Displays 6723

// -->
</script>
```

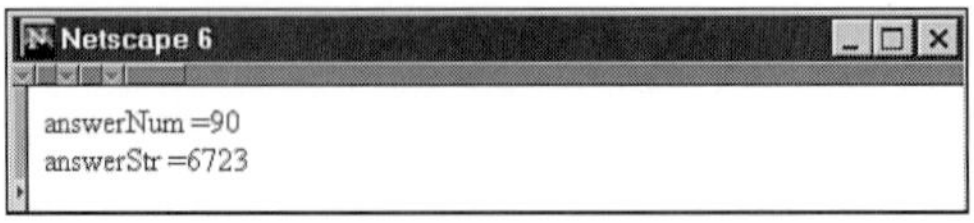

Netscape 6

answerNum =90
answerStr =6723

Figure 7.2

Using the addition operator to add numbers and concatenate strings.

++ (Increment)

JavaScript 1.0+, ECMAScript 1E+, JScript 1.0+
Nav2+, NES2+, IE 3+, Opera3+

Syntax

```
++variable        (Pre-Increment)
variable++        (Post-Increment)
```

Description

The pre-increment operator increments *variable* by 1. The new incremented value is returned by the operation.

The post-increment operator is similar to the pre-increment operator in that it increments *variable* by 1. However, the original value is returned by the operation before being incremented.

In both cases, if the operand is a string, it is converted to a number before performing the operation.

Example

Listing 7.40 demonstrates how the pre-increment and post-increment operators work. Notice that the variable num holds a string that is converted before performing the increment operation. The result of executing this code is shown in Figure 7.3.

Listing 7.40   Using the Increment Operator

```
<script type="text/javascript" language="JavaScript">
<!--

/* Store value in variable before pre-increment */
document.write("<h3>Before Pre-increment</h3>");
num = new String("807");   //num holds the string 807
document.write("num=",num,"<br>");   //807 is displayed.

/* Pre-increment the value stored in num */
returnValue = ++num;
document.write("<h3>After Pre-increment</h3>");
document.write("num=",num,"<br>");   //808 is displayed.
```

```
//808 is displayed by returnValue.
document.write("Value returned from operation is ",returnValue,"<br>");

/* Post-increment the value stored in num */
returnValue = num++;
document.write("<h3>After Post-increment</h3>");
document.write("num=",num,"<br>");      //809 is displayed.

//808 is displayed by returnValue.
document.write("Value returned from operation is ",returnValue,"<br>");

// -->
</script>
```

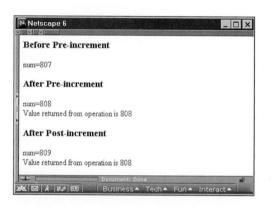

Figure 7.3

The difference between pre-increment and post-increment.

+= (Addition Assignment)

JavaScript 1.0+, ECMAScript 1E+, JScript 1.0+
Nav2+, NES2+, IE 3+, Opera3+

Syntax

variable += value

Description

The addition assignment operator provides two types of functionality depending on the data type of the operands. The first type of functionality is simple addition in which the value stored in the variable on the right of the addition assignment operator is added to the value on the left. The result of the addition overwrites the value stored in the variable on the left of the operator. If either of the operands is not a number or string, it will be converted to a number.

The second type of functionality provided by the addition assignment operator is string concatenation. If either of the operands is a string, string concatenation is performed by first converting any non-string operand to a string. String concatenation is then performed by appending the string to the right of the operator to the end of the string located to the left of the operator. The new string is stored in the variable on the left of the operator.

Example

In Listing 7.41, the addition assignment operator is used to add two numbers together as well as concatenate two strings.

Listing 7.41   Using the Addition and Assignment Operator

```
<script type="text/javascript" language="JavaScript">
<!--

//Initialize the variables num and str.
num = 42;
str = new String("42");

//Use the addition/assignment operator.
num += 8;    //num contains the number 50.
str += 8;    //str contains the string "428".

//Display the results of the addition/assignment operator.
document.write("num = ",num,"<br>str = ",str);

// -->
</script>
```

< (Less Than)

JavaScript 1.0+, ECMAScript 1E+, JScript 1.0+
Nav2+, NES2+, IE 3+, Opera3+

Syntax

num1 < num2

Description

The less than operator compares the value on the left of the operator to the value on the right. If the value on the left is less than the value on the right, `true` is returned from the operation. If the value on the left of the operator is greater than or equal to the value on the right, `false` is returned. If either of the operands is not a number or string, it will be converted to a number before performing the comparison.

Example

In Listing 7.42, the string "45" is converted to a number before performing the comparison. Because the number 45 is less than the number 68, the phrase "45 is less than 68" is returned.

Listing 7.42   Using the Less Than Operator

```
<script type="text/javascript" language="JavaScript">
<!--

//Initialize the variable str with "45".
str = new String("45");

//Compare the variable to the number 68.
if(str < 68)
  document.write("45 is less than 68");
else
  document.write("Returned FALSE!");

// -->
</script>
```

<< (Shift Left)

JavaScript 1.0+, ECMAScript 1E+, JScript 1.0+
Nav2+, NES2+, IE 3+, Opera3+

Syntax

num1 << num2

Description

The shift left operator looks at the integer on the left of the operator as a 32-bit binary number. The number of positions specified by *num2* shifts all the bits of num1 to the left. As the bits are shifted to the left, zeros are filled in on the right. Because the number can only be 32-bits long, the extra bits on the left are lost. The 32-bit binary result of the shifting operation is converted to an integer value and returned from the shift left operation.

NOTE

The result generated from the shift left operator can be quickly calculated by multiplying the number by 2 raised to the *x* power, where *x* is the number of positions shifted.

Example

Listing 7.43 shifts the bits that make up the number 2 to the left two positions, which results in the number 8.

Listing 7.43   Using the Shift Left Operator

```
<script type="text/javascript" language="JavaScript">
<!--

// integer = 32-bit binary representation
// 2 = 00000000000000000000000000000010
// 8 = 00000000000000000000000000001000

//Assign the number 8 to the variable x.
x = 2 << 2;

//Display the value stored in the variable x.
document.write("2 << 2 = ",x);

// -->
</script>
```

<<= (Shift Left Assignment)

JavaScript 1.0+, ECMAScript 1E+, JScript 1.0+
Nav2+, NES2+, IE 3+, Opera3+

Syntax

variable <<= num

Description

The shift left assignment operator looks at the integer stored in the variable to the left of the operator as a 32-bit binary number. All the bits in this number are shifted to the left by the number of positions specified by the integer to the right of the operator. As the bits are shifted to the left, zeros are filled in on the right. Because the number can only be 32-bits long, the extra bits on the left are lost. The 32-bit binary result of shifting operation is converted to an integer value and stored in the variable to the left of the operator.

Example

In Listing 7.44, the 32-bit binary version of the number 3, which is stored in the variable x, is shifted two positions to the left. The result of this operation, the number 12, is stored in the variable x.

Listing 7.44   Using the Shift Left Assignment Operator

```
<script type="text/javascript" language="JavaScript">
<!--
```

```
// integer = 32-bit binary representation
//  3 = 00000000000000000000000000000011
// 12 = 00000000000000000000000000001100


//Initialize the variable x with the number 3.
x = 3;


//The variable x is now equal to the number 12.
x <<= 2;


//Display the value stored in the variable x.
document.write("x = ",x);


// -->
</script>
```

<= (Less Than or Equal)

JavaScript 1.0+, ECMAScript 1E+, JScript 1.0+
Nav2+, NES2+, IE 3+, Opera3+

Syntax

num1 <= num2

Description

The less than or equal operator compares the number on the left of the operator to the number on the right. If the number on the left is less than or equal to the number on the right, `true` is returned from the operation. If the number on the left of the operator is greater than the number on the right, `false` is returned.

Example

In Listing 7.45, the string `"34"` would be converted to a number before performing the comparison. Because the number 34 is less than the number 77, the phrase `"34 is less than or equal to 77"` would be returned.

Listing 7.45   Using the Less Than or Equal Operator

```
<script type="text/javascript" language="JavaScript">
<!--

//Initialize the variable str to "34".
str = new String("34");

//Compare the value stored in the variable to the number 77.
if(str <= 77)
  document.write("34 is less than or equal to 77");
```

Listing 7.45   Continued

```
else
  document.write("Returned FALSE!");

// -->
</script>
```

= (Assignment)

JavaScript 1.0+, ECMAScript 1E+, JScript 1.0+
Nav2+, NES2+, IE 3+, Opera3+

Syntax

variable = value

Description

The value to the right of the operator is stored in the variable to the left of the operator.

Example

In Listing 7.46, the assignment operator is used to assign various types of values to variables. The type of operator is then used to determine the type value stored in the variables. The types are then displayed in the browser (*x* is a number, *y* is a string, and *z* is a boolean).

Listing 7.46   Using the Assignment Operator

```
<script type="text/javascript" language="JavaScript">
<!--

//Number
x = 456;                    //x contains a number.
document.write("x is a ",typeof x,"<br>");

//String
y = new String("Hello")    //y contains a String.
document.write("y is a ",typeof y,"<br>");

//Boolean
z = true;                   //z contains a Boolean.
document.write("z is a ",typeof z);

// -->
</script>
```

-= (Subtraction Assignment)

JavaScript 1.0+, ECMAScript 1E+, JScript 1.0+
Nav2+, NES2+, IE 3+, Opera3+

Syntax

```
variable -= value
```

Description

The number to the right of the operator is subtracted from the number stored in the variable to the left of the operator. The result of the operation overwrites the value stored in the variable to the left of the operator. If either operand is a string, an attempt is made to convert the string to a number before performing the subtraction.

Example

In Listing 7.47, the string "878" is converted to a number before the subtraction operation begins. The number 55 is subtracted from 878 and the result, 823, is stored in the variable answer.

Listing 7.47   Using the Subtraction Assignment Operator

```javascript
<script type="text/javascript" language="JavaScript">
<!--

//Initialize the variable aString with "878".
aString = new String("878");

//Assign the number 823 to the variable answer.
answer -= 55;

//Display the values stored in the variable answer.
document.write("answer = ",answer);

// -->
</script>
```

== (Equal)

JavaScript 1.0+, ECMAScript 1E+, JScript 1.0+
Nav2+, NES2+, IE 3+, Opera3+

Syntax

```
expression1 == expression2
```

Description

The equal operator compares the value on the left of the operator to the value on the right of the operator. If the values are equal, true is returned from the operation. If the values are not equal, false is returned from the operation.

JavaScript attempts to convert the operands to the same data type before comparing the values for all versions of JavaScript except 1.2. JavaScript adheres to the following rules when performing type conversion:

- True is converted to the number 1, and false is converted to 0 before being compared.
- If either of the operands is NaN, the equality operator returns false.
- Null and undefined are equal.
- Null and undefined are not equal to 0 (zero), "" (empty string), or false.
- If a string and a number are compared, attempts to convert the string to a number and then checks for equality.
- If an object and a string are compared, attempts to convert the object to a string and then checks for equality.
- If an object and a number are compared, attempts to convert the object to a number and then checks for equality.
- If both operands of an equality operation are objects, the address of the two objects are checked for equality.

CAUTION

In JavaScript 1.2, the decision was made to NOT do type conversion on the operands of the equal operator. JavaScript reverted back to using type conversion with this operator in 1.3 and later.

Example

In Listing 7.48, the string "749" is converted to a number (except in JavaScript 1.2, in which type conversion is not performed) so that two numbers are compared. Because the left operand is equal to the right operand, the phrase "The string 749 is EQUAL to the number 749" is written to the browser window.

Listing 7.48 Using the Equal Operator

```
<script type="text/javascript" language="JavaScript">
<!--

//The string is converted to a number before performing the comparison.
if("749" == 749)
{
  document.write("The string 749 is EQUAL to the number 749");
}
else
{
  document.write("The string 749 is NOT equal to the number 749");
}

// -->
</script>
```

=== (Identity)

JavaScript 1.3+, ECMAScript 3E+, JScript 1.0+
Nav4.06+, IE 3+, Opera5+

Syntax

```
expression1 === expression2
```

Description

The identity operator compares the first operand to the second operand. If the value on the left is equal to the value on the right side of the operator, `true` is returned from operation. If the values are not equal, `false` is returned.

NOTE

No type conversion is performed on the operands before the comparison is made.

Example

In Listing 7.49, the string `"326"` is NOT converted to a number, so the two operands are not the same type. Because the two operands are not the same type, they are not equal, so the phrase `"The string 326 is NOT equal to the number 326"` is written to the browser window.

Listing 7.49   Using the Identity Operator

```
<script type="text/javascript" language="JavaScript">
<!--

//A string is compared to a number.
if("326" === 326)
{
  document.write("The string 326 is NOT equal to the number 326");
}
else
{
  document.write("The string 326 is EQUAL to the number 326");
}
// -->
</script>
```

> (Greater Than)

JavaScript 1.0+, ECMAScript 1E+, JScript 1.0+
Nav2+, NES2+, IE 3+, Opera3+

Syntax

```
num1 > num2
```

Description

The greater than operator compares the value on the left of the operator to the value on the right. If the value on the left is greater than the value on the right, `true` is returned from the operation. If the value on the left of the operator is less than or equal to the value on the right, `false` is returned. If either of the operands is not a number, it is converted to a number before performing the comparison.

Example

In Listing 7.50, the string `"112"` would be converted to a number before performing the comparison. Because the number 112 is greater than the number 68, the phrase `"112 is greater than 68"` is returned.

Listing 7.50   Using the Greater Than Operator

```
<script type="text/javascript" language="JavaScript">
<!--

//Initialize the variable str with the string "112".
str = new String("112");

//Compare the value in the variable to a number.
if(str > 68)
  document.write("112 is greater than 68");
else
  document.write("Returned FALSE!");

// -->
</script> >
```

>= (Greater Than or Equal)
JavaScript 1.0+, ECMAScript 1E+, JScript 1.0+
Nav2+, NES2+ IE 3+, Opera3+

Syntax

variable >= value

Description

The greater than or equal operator compares the number on the left of the operator to the number on the right. If the number on the left is greater than or equal to the number on the right, `true` is returned from the operation. If the number on the left of the operator is less than the number on the right, `false` is returned.

Example

In Listing 7.51, the string `"95"` would be converted to a number before performing the comparison. Because the number 95 is greater than the number 44, the phrase `"95 is greater than or equal to 44"` is returned.

Listing 7.51   Using the Greater Than Or Equal Operator

```
<script type="text/javascript" language="JavaScript">
<!--
```

```
//Initialize the variable str.
str = new String("95");

//Compare the value stored in the variable to the number 44.
if(str >= 44)
  document.write("95 is greater than or equal to 44");
else
  document.write("Returned FALSE!");

// -->
</script>
```

>> (Shift Right with Sign)
JavaScript 1.0+, ECMAScript 1E+, JScript 1.0+
Nav2+, NES2+, IE 3+, Opera3+

Syntax

num1 >> num2

Description

The shift right with sign operator looks at the integer to the left of the operator, *num1*, as a 32-bit binary number. All the bits in this number are shifted to the right by the number of positions specified by *num2*. As the bits are shifted to the right, either ones or zeros are filled in on the left. If the original number is positive, zeros are added to the left side of the binary number. On the other hand, if the original number is negative, ones are used. Because the result can only be 32-bits long, the extra bits on the right are lost. The 32-bit binary result of shifting operation is converted to an integer value and returned from the shift right with sign operation.

NOTE

The result generated from the shift right with sign operator can be quickly calculated by dividing the number by 2 raised to the *x* power, where *x* is the number of positions shifted. Discard the remainder.

Example

Listing 7.52 shifts the bits that make up the number 14 to the right two positions, which results in the number 3. The code also shifts the bits that make up the number -14 to the right one position, which results in the number -2.

Listing 7.52   Using the Shift Right with Sign Operator

```
<script type="text/javascript" language="JavaScript">
<!--
```

Listing 7.52   Continued

```
// integer = 32-bit binary representation
// 14 = 00000000000000000000000000001110
//  3 = 00000000000000000000000000000011

//The number 3 is assigned to the variable x.
x = 14 >> 2;

//Display the value stored in the variable.
document.write("14 >> 2 = ",x);

//- - - - - - - - - - - - - - - - - - - - - - - - - - - - - - - - - - - - - - - - -
document.write("<br>");

// integer = 32-bit binary representation
// -4 = 11111111111111111111111111111100
// -2 = 11111111111111111111111111111110

//The number -2 is stored in the variable y.
y = -4 >> 1;    //y is equal to -2.

//Display the value stored in the variable y.
document.write("-4 >> 1 = ",y);

// -->
</script>
```

>>= (Shift Right with Sign Assignment)

JavaScript 1.0+, ECMAScript 1E+, JScript 1.0+
Nav2+, NES2+, IE 3+, Opera3+

Syntax

variable >>= v value

Description

The shift right with sign assignment operator (>>=) looks at the integer to the left of the operator as a 32-bit binary number. All the bits in this number are shifted to the right by the number of positions specified by the integer to the right of the operator. As the bits are shifted to the right, either ones or zeros are filled in on the left. If the original number is positive, zeros are added to the left side of the binary number. On the other hand, if the original number is negative, ones are used. Because the result can only be 32-bits long, the extra bits on the right are lost. The 32-bit binary result of shifting operation is converted to an integer value and stored in the variable to the left of the operator.

Example

In Listing 7.53, the 32-bit binary version of the number 15, which is stored in the variable x, is shifted one position to the right. The result of this operation, the number 7, is stored in the variable x.

Listing 7.53   *Using the Shift Right with Sign Assignment Operator*

```
<script  type="text/javascript" language="JavaScript">
<!--

// integer = 32-bit binary representation
// 15 = 00000000000000000000000000001111
//  7 = 00000000000000000000000000000111

//Initialize the variable x with the number 15.
x = 15;

//The variable x is now equal to 7.
x >>= 1;

//Display the values stored in the variable x.
document.write("x = ",x);

// -->
</script>
```

>>> (Shift Right Zero Fill)

JavaScript 1.0+, ECMAScript 1E+, JScript 1.0+
Nav2+, NES2+, IE 3+, Opera3+

Syntax

num1 >>> num2

Description

The shift right zero fill operator looks at the integer to the left of the operator as a 32-bit binary number. All the bits in this number are shifted to the right by the number of positions specified by the integer to the right of the operator. As the bits are shifted to the right, zeros are filled in on the left, regardless of the sign of the original integer. Because the result can only be 32-bits long, the extra bits on the right are lost. The 32-bit binary result of this shifting operation is converted to an integer value and returned from the shift right zero fill operation.

Example

Listing 7.54 shifts the bits that make up the number 13 to the right one position, which results in the number 6. The number 1073741822 results from shifting the bits that make up the number –8 two positions to the right.

Listing 7.54   Using the Shift Right Zero Fill Operator

```javascript
<script type="text/javascript" language="JavaScript">
<!--

// integer = 32-bit binary representation
// 13 = 00000000000000000000000000001101
//  6 = 00000000000000000000000000000110

//Assign the number 6 to the variable x.
x = 13 >>> 1;

//Display the value stored in the variable x.
document.write("13 >>> 1 = ",x);

//------------------------------------
document.write("<br>");

// integer = 32-bit binary representation
//         -8 = 11111111111111111111111111111000
// 1073741822 = 00111111111111111111111111111110

//Assign the number 1073741822 to the variable y.
y = -8 >>> 2;

//Display the value stored in the variable y.
document.write("-8 >>> 2 = ",y);

// -->
</script>
```

>>>= (Shift Right Zero Fill Assignment)

JavaScript 1.0+, ECMAScript 1E+, JScript 1.0+
Nav2+, NES2+, IE 3+

Syntax

variable >>>= value

Description

The shift right zero fill assignment operator (>>>=) looks at the integer to the left of the operator as a 32-bit binary number. All the bits in this number are shifted to the right by the number of positions specified by the integer to the right of the operator. As the bits are shifted to the right, zeros are filled in on the left, regardless of the sign of the original integer. Because the result can only be 32-bits long, the extra bits on the right are lost. The 32-bit binary result of this shifting operation is converted to an integer value and stored in the variable to the left of the operator.

Example

In Listing 7.55, the 32-bit binary version of the number –6, which is stored in the variable x, is shifted one position to the right. The result of this operation, the number 1073741822, is stored in the variable x.

Listing 7.55   Using the Shift Right Zero Fill Assignment Operator

```
<script type="text/javascript" language="JavaScript">
<!--

// integer = 32-bit binary representation
//         -6 = 11111111111111111111111111111010
// 1073741822 = 00111111111111111111111111111110
//Initialize the variable x with the number -6.
x = -6;

//The variable x now contains the number 1073741822.
x >>>= 2;

//Display the value stored in the variable x.
document.write("x = ",x);

// -->
</script>
```

abstract

JavaScript 1.2+, ECMAScript 2E+, JScript 5+
Nav4+, NES 3+, IE5+, Opera5+

Syntax

```
Reserved Keyword
```

Description

The abstract keyword has not been implemented in JavaScript to date, but has been reserved for future use.

Example

This keyword has not been implemented, therefore no example is provided.

ActiveXObject

JScript3.0+
IE4+

Syntax

```
var variable = new ActiveXObject(serverName.typeName,location)
```

Description

The `ActiveXObject` creates a reference to an object that is connected to another application or programming tool through automation interfaces. The arguments used by this object are listed in Table 7.6.

Table 7.6   *Arguments Associated with* `ActiveXObject`

Argument	Description
serverName	The name of the application that provides the object.
typeName	The type or class of the object to create.
location	The name of the network server where the object is to be created. This argument is optional.

Example

Listing 7.56 uses the `ActiveXObject` to create a multiplication table in a Microsoft Excel document. Excel will be started automatically.

Listing 7.56   *Create a Multiplication Table in an Excel Document*

```
<script type="text/jscript" language="JScript">
<!--

var ExcelSheet = new ActiveXObject("Excel.Sheet");

// Make Excel visible through the Application object.
ExcelSheet.Application.Visible = true;

//Create multiplication table in Excel.
for(i=1;i<11;i++)
{
  // numbers to be multiplied in first two rows.
  ExcelSheet.ActiveSheet.Cells(i,1).Value = i;
  ExcelSheet.ActiveSheet.Cells(i,2).Value = 9;

  // Create Excel string to handle multiplication.
  var aString = new String("=A");
  aString += i;
  aString += "*B";
  aString += i;
  ExcelSheet.ActiveSheet.Cells(i,3).Value = aString;
}

// -->
</script>
```

Arguments

JavaScript 1.1+, ECMAScript 1E+, JScript 1.0+
Nav3+, IE3+, Opera5+

Syntax

```
arguments
arguments [index]
```

Description

The `Arguments` object is an array that contains all the arguments passed into the currently executing function as well as a few other useful properties. This object is automatically created and initialized when a function is invoked and goes out of scope as soon as the code function finishes executing. To access arguments passed into a function, simply use array brackets to specify an *index*. Table 7.7 lists the properties associated with the `Argument` object.

NOTE

To use the `Arguments` object, you do not specify the function using dot notation as you might expect. This is because this object is different from the `Function`. `arguments[]` array associated with a `Function` object. Using this `Arguments` object gives you the ability to access the arguments of functions that have no name.

Table 7.7   Properties Associated with the `Arguments` **Object**

Property	Description
`callee`	Contains the function that is currently executing
`caller`	Contains the `Arguments` object of the calling function
`length`	The length of the arguments array

Example

In Listing 7.57, a function is created to display an individual's favorite food in an alert box. The function is called when the buttons are pressed. The arguments passed to this function are accessed within the function with the `Arguments` object array brackets.

Listing 7.57   Using the `Arguments` **Object to Display People's Favorite Foods**

```
<html>
<body>
Select a person's name to discover their favorite food!

<form>
<input type="button"
       value="Meredith"
       OnClick=displayFood(this,"pizza")>
```

Listing 7.57   Continued

```
<input type="button"
       value="Allison"
       OnClick=displayFood(this,"beans")>
<input type="button"
       value="BayLeigh"
       OnClick=displayFood(this,"carrots")>
<input type="button"
       value="Michael"
       OnClick=displayFood(this,"corn")>
<input type="button"
       value="Rob"
       OnClick=displayFood(this,"hotdogs")>
</form>

<script type="text/javascript" language="JavaScript">
<!--

//Create a function that displays a person's favorite food.
function displayFood()
{
  //Create a string that contains the name of the person.
  var aString = arguments[0].value;
  aString += "'s favorite food is ";

  //Add the favorite food to the end of the string.
  aString += arguments[1];

  //Display the string in an alert box.
  alert(aString);
}

// -->
</script>

</body>
</html>
```

Arguments.callee

JavaScript 1.2+, ECMAScript 1E+, JScript 5.5+
Nav4+, IE5.5+, Opera5+

Syntax

```
arguments.callee
```

Description

The `callee` property of the `Arguments` object contains the function that is currently executing. This is useful if the function has no name.

Example

In Listing 7.58, a function is created to display an individual's favorite food in an alert box. The function is called when the buttons are clicked. The code that makes up the executing function is displayed using the `callee` property.

Listing 7.58 *Using the* `callee` *Property of the* Arguments *Object*

```
<html>
Learn what functions are used when you press the buttons
below that represent a person's favorite food!

<form>
<input type="button"
       value="Meredith"
       OnClick=displayFood(this,"pizza")>
<input type="button"
       value="Allison"
       OnClick=displayFood(this,"beans")>
<input type="button"
       value="BayLeigh"
       OnClick=displayFood(this,"carrots")>
<input type="button"
       value="Michael"
       OnClick=displayFood(this,"corn")>
<input type="button"
       value="Rob"
       OnClick=displayFood(this,"hotdogs")>
</form>

<script type="text/javascript" language="JavaScript">
<!--

//Create a function that displays a person's favorite food.
function displayFood()
{
  //Create a string that contains the name of the person.
  var aString = arguments[0].value;
  aString += "'s favorite food is ";

  //Add the favorite food to the end of the string.
  aString += arguments[1];

  //Display the string in an alert box.
  alert(aString);

  //Display the function using the callee property.
  alert(arguments.callee.toString());
}
```

Listing 7.58   Continued

```
// -->
</script>
</html>
```

Arguments.caller

JavaScript 1.2+
Nav4+

Syntax

```
arguments.caller
```

Description

The caller property of the Arguments object contains the Arguments object of the calling function. If the given function was not executed from within another function, null is stored in this property.

Example

Listing 7.59 creates two functions. One displays an individual's favorite food in an alert box, whereas the other displays the number of arguments associated with the calling function. Anytime a button is clicked, an alert box displays the favorite food. This function then calls the second function to display an alert box saying two arguments were passed into the first function.

Listing 7.59   Using the caller Property of the Arguments Object

```
<html>
Select a person's name to discover their favorite food!

<form>
<input type="button"
       value="Meredith"
       OnClick=displayFood(this,"pizza")>
<input type="button"
       value="Allison"
       OnClick=displayFood(this,"beans")>
<input type="button"
       value="BayLeigh"
       OnClick=displayFood(this,"carrots")>
<input type="button"
       value="Michael"
       OnClick=displayFood(this,"corn")>
<input type="button"
       value="Rob"
       OnClick=displayFood(this,"hotdogs")>
</form>
```

```
<script type="text/javascript" language="JavaScript">
<!--

//Display the number of arguments in the function that calls this function.
function displayArgLength()
{
  var argLengthStr = "The calling function contained ";
  argLengthStr += arguments.caller.length;
  argLengthStr += " arguments.";
  alert(argLengthStr);
}

//Create a function that displays a person's favorite food.
 function displayFood()
{
  //Create a string that contains the name of the person.
  var aString = arguments[0].value;
  aString += "'s favorite food is ";

  //Add the favorite food to the end of the string.
  aString += arguments[1];

  //Display the string in an alert box.
  alert(aString);

  displayArgLength();
}

// -->
</script>
 </html>
```

Arguments.length

JavaScript 1.1+, ECMAScript 1E+, JScript 5.5+
Nav3+, IE5.5+, Opera5+

Syntax

```
arguments.length
```

Description

The length property of the Arguments object contains the number of arguments that were passed into the function to which the Arguments object is associated. If fewer arguments are passed in than are specified in the definition of the function, the length property will only contain the number of arguments passed into the function. This number matches the number of elements in the arguments array associated with the Arguments object.

Example

In Listing 7.60, the `length` property of the `Arguments` object is used to process any number of arguments passed into the `displayFood()` function.

Listing 7.60   Using the `length` Property to Access Elements of the
`Arguments` **Object**

```
<html>
Select a person's name to discover their favorite foods!

<form>
<input type="button"
       value="Meredith"
       OnClick=displayFood(this,"pizza","salad","cake")>
<input type="button"
       value="Allison"
       OnClick=displayFood(this,"beans","potatoes")>
<input type="button"
       value="BayLeigh"
       OnClick=displayFood(this,"carrots")>
<input type="button"
       value="Michael"
       OnClick=displayFood(this,"corn","beans")>
<input type="button"
       value="Rob"
       OnClick=displayFood(this,"hotdogs")>
</form>

<script type="text/javascript" language="JavaScript">
<!--

//Create a function that displays a person's favorite foods.
function displayFood()
{
  //Create a string that contains the name of the person.
  var aString = arguments[0].value;
  aString += "'s favorite foods are: ";

  //Add all the favorite foods to the end of the string.
  for(var i=1; i<arguments.length; i++)
  {
    aString += arguments[i];
    aString += ", ";
  }

  //Display the string in an alert box.
  alert(aString);
}
```

```
// -->
</script>
```

Array

JavaScript 1.1+, ECMAScript 1E+, JScript 3.0+
Nav3+, NES3+, IE 4+, Opera3+

Syntax

```
var variable = new Array()
var variable = new Array(int)
var variable = new Array(arg1, ..., argN)
```

Description

Although arrays can be created with the basic JavaScript object, the `Array` object provides a much easier way to create and manage arrays.

Table 7.8 lists the argument and return values associated with this object's constructors. These constructors create a new array and, in two cases, initialize the `Array` object based on the arguments passed in the parameter list. The constructor that has no arguments sets the `length` property to `0`.

Table 7.8 *Arguments and Return Values Associated with the* `Array` *Object*

Type	Item	Description
Arguments	int	When the array constructor contains one argument, an array is created, and its `length` property is set to the value `int`.
	arg1,...argN	When the parameter list of the array constructor contains more than one argument, an array is created and the array is populated with the arguments. The array `length` property is set to the number of arguments in the parameter list.
Returns		The newly created array is returned from the constructor.

Table 7.9 lists the properties and methods used by the `Array` object.

Table 7.9 *Properties and Methods Used by the* `Array` *Object*

Type	Item	Description
Property	constructor	Specifies the function that creates the `Array` object's prototype.
	index	Contains the original string against which a regular expression was matched (read-only).

Table 7.9   Continued

Type	Item	Description
	input	Contains the position of a regular expression match in a string (read-only).
	lastIndex	Contains the position after the last regular expression match in a string (read-only).
	length	Contains the number of elements in the array.
Methods	concat()	Concatenates an array onto the end of an array.
	join()	Concatenates all elements of an array into one string.
	pop()	Deletes the last element from an array.
	push()	Adds elements to the end of an array.
	reverse()	Reverses the order of the elements in the array.
	shift()	Deletes elements from the front of an array.
	slice()	Returns a subsection of the array.
	sort()	Sorts elements in array.
	splice()	Inserts and removes elements from an array.
	toSource()	Converts elements to a string with square brackets.
	toString()	Converts elements to a string.
	unshift()	Addselements to the front of an array.
	unwatch()	Removes a watchpoint.
	watch()	Sets a watchpoint.

Example

Listing 7.61 creates an array of numbers using the Array constructor. Once created, the elements are displayed on the screen using bracket notation ([ ]).

Listing 7.61   Creating an Array and Accessing Its Elements

```
<html>

<h2>Creating and Accessing Arrays</h2>

<script type="text/javascript" language="JavaScript">
<!--

//Create a new array that contains 3 numbers.
numArray = new Array(45,67,34);
document.write("Created an array of numbers that contains 45, 67, and 34<br>");

//Display the contents of the array.
document.write("[0]=",numArray[0],"<br>"); // will display 45
document.write("[1]=",numArray[1],"<br>"); // will display 67
document.write("[2]=",numArray[2]);        // will display 34
```

```
// -->
</script>

</html>
```

Array.concat( )
JavaScript 1.2+, ECMAScript 3E+, JScript 3.0+
Nav4+, NES3+, IE 4+, Opera5+

Syntax
array.concat (*arg1,...argN*)

Description

The concat() method adds the elements listed in the parameter list to the end of the existing array and returns the result. The original is not changed by this method. Should any of the arguments be Array, the elements of that array are concatenated to the array that called the method.

Table 7.10 lists the argument and return values associated with this method.

Table 7.10 **Arguments and Return Values Associated with** concat()

Type	Item	Description
Arguments	arg1,...argN	The parameter list of the concat() method contains one or more elements to be concatenated to the end of the array.
Returns		The original array with the new concatenated elements is returned from the method.

Example

Listing 7.62 uses the concat() method to display the total inventory of two grocery store shelves. Notice how the multidimensional arrays wereconcatenated together in Figure 7.4.

Listing 7.62 **Using** concat() **to Display Inventory**

```
<script type="text/javascript" language="JavaScript">
<!--
//Display the elements in the array.
function displayElements(theArray)
{
  //Access each element in the array.
  for(i=0; i<theArray.length; i++)
  {
    //Display the element.
    document.write("  - ",theArray[i][1]," ");
```

Listing 7.62 Continued

```
        document.write(theArray[i][0],"<br>");
    }
}


//Create a grocery shelf using an array to represent
//the items on each shelf.
shelf1 = new Array(["apples",10],["oranges",25]);
document.write("Shelf 1 contains:<br>");

//Display the items on shelf 1.
displayElements(shelf1);

//Create a second grocery shelf using an array to represent
//the items on each shelf.
shelf2 = new Array(["grapes",50],["bananas",3],["lemons",8]);
document.write("Shelf 2 contains:<br>");

//Display the items on shelf 2.
displayElements(shelf2);

//Create a master inventory list by concatenating
//the two shelf arrays into one array.
inventory = shelf1.concat(shelf2);

//Display all the items on all the shelves.
document.write("<br>The total inventory contains:<br>");
displayElements(inventory);
// -->
</script>
```

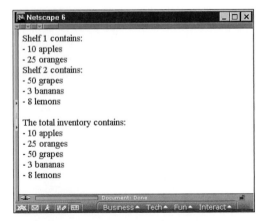

Figure 7.4

Concatenate the items on two grocery store shelves.

Array.constructor

JavaScript 1.1+, ECMAScript 1E+, JScript 3.0+
Nav3+, NES3+, IE 4+, Opera3+

Syntax

`array.constructor`

Description

The `constructor` property of the `Array` object is used to create the object's prototype.

Example

Listing 7.63 demonstrates the `constructor` property as it relates to the `Array` object.

Listing 7.63   The Array's `constructor` *Property*

```javascript
<script type="text/javascript" language="JavaScript">
<!--
// Create a new array object using the constructor property.
myArray = new Array("Mike","Eric","Ory","Jason","Jonathon","Kevin");
if(myArray.constructor == Array){
  document.write("Object was created");
}
// -->
</script>
```

Array.index

JavaScript 1.2+, JScript 3.0+
Nav4+, NES3+, IE 4+, Opera4+

Syntax

`array.index`

Description

The `index` property is a read-only property that contains the position of a regular expression match within a string. This property only appears in the `Array` object that is returned from the following regular expression related methods:

- `RegExp.exec()`
- `String.match()`
- `String.replace()`

Example

Listing 7.64 creates a regular expression string that contains the search string `"red"`. The `exec()` method is used to find the regular expression within a string. The `index` property is then used to display `"The word 'red' was found at position 4"`, which contains the position character position (4) within the string where the word `"red"` was found.

Listing 7.64 *Using the* index *Property to Display the Position of a Match*

```
<script type="text/javascript" language="JavaScript">
<!--
myReg=/red/;
myArray = myReg.exec("The red ball.");
document.write("The word 'red' was found at position ",myArray.index);
// -->
</script>
```

Array.input

JavaScript 1.2+, JScript 3.0+
Nav4+, NES3+, IE 4+, Opera4+

Syntax

array.input

Description

The input property is a read-only property that contains the string against which the regular expression was matched. This property only appears in the Array object that is returned from the following regular expression related methods:

- RegExp.exec()
- String.match()
- String.replace()

Example

Listing 7.65 creates a regular expression string that contains the search string "red". The exec() method is used to find the regular expression within a string. The input property is then used to display the string that was searched.

Listing 7.65 *Using the* index *Property to Display the Regular Expression*

```
<script type="text/javascript" language="JavaScript">
<!--
myReg=/red/;
myArray = myReg.exec("The red ball.");
document.write("The word red was found in the string '", myArray.input, "'");
// -->
</script>
```

Array.join()

JavaScript 1.1+, ECMAScript 1E+, JScript 3.0+
Nav3+, NES3+, IE 4+, Opera3+

Syntax

array.join()
array.join(*string*)

Description

The join() method converts all the elements of the array to strings and then concatenates all the strings into one string. If an argument is provided in the parameter list, it is used to separate the elements in the string returned by the method. Table 7.11 lists the argument and return values associated with this method.

Table 7.11   Arguments and Return Values Associated with join()

Type	Item	Description
Arguments	string	A string that is used to separate the elements of the array in the string returned from the method.
Returns		All the elements of the array are concatenated into one string and returned from the method.

Example

Listing 7.66 creates an array of fruits. The contents of this array are displayed on the screen using the join() method. A dash is specified as the delimiter used to separate the array elements when they are written to the screen as a string.

Listing 7.66   Using the join() **Method to Display the Elements of an Array**

```
<script type="text/javascript" language="JavaScript">
<!--

//Create an array that contains 3 fruits.
fruit = new Array("Apple","Orange","Grape");

//List the contents of the fruit array as a string
//with a dash separating each item.
aString = fruit.join("-");   //aString = "Apple-Orange-Grape"

//Display the string generated from using the join() method.
document.write("The fruit array contains: ",aString);

// -->
</script>
```

Array.lastIndex

JavaScript 1.2+, JScript 3.0+
Nav4+, NES3+, IE 4+

Syntax

array.lastIndex

Description

The lastIndex property is a read-only property that contains the position following the last character in a regular expression match. This property only appears in the Array object that is returned from the following regular expression related methods:

- RegExp.exec()
- String.match()
- String.replace()

Example

Listing 7.67 creates a regular expression string that contains the search string "red". The exec() method is used to find the regular expression within a string. The lastIndex property is then used to display the number 7, which is the position following the word "red" that was found in the string.

Listing 7.67   Using the lastIndex *Property to Display the Position Following the Match*

```
<script type="text/javascript" language="JavaScript">
<!--
myReg=/red/;
myArray = myReg.exec("The red ball.");
document.write("The lastIndex property is set to ",myArray.lastIndex);
// -->
</script>
```

Array.length
JavaScript 1.1+, ECMAScript 1E+, JScript 3.0+
Nav3+, NES3+, IE 4+, Opera3+

Syntax

array.length

Description

The length property holds the number of elements in the array. This property is a read/write variable. If the length property is overwritten with a number that is larger than the original number, new elements are added to the end of the array and assigned undefined values. If the length property is overwritten with a number that is smaller than the original number, elements at the end of the array are lost.

Example

Listing 7.68 creates an array of coins. The number of coins in the array is then reduced from 4 to 3 by modifying the length property so the array contains only three elements. Because the quarter was the last element in the array, it was removed when the length property was changed.

Listing 7.68 *Using the* `length` *Property to Reduce the Number of Elements in an Array*

```
<script type="text/javascript" language="JavaScript">
<!--

//Create an array of coins.
coins = new Array("Penny","Nickel","Dime","Quarter");

x = coins.length;   //x contains 4.
coins.length = 3    //"Quarter" was removed from array.

//Display the contents of the array.
document.write("The coins array contains: ", coins.join(','));

// -->
</script>
```

Array.pop()

JavaScript 1.2+, ECMAScript 3E+, JScript 5.5+
Nav4+, NES3+, IE5.5+, Opera5+

Syntax

array.pop()

Description

The pop() method "pops" elements off the end of the array by deleting the last element of the array and setting the array's length property to one less than its current value. The element popped off the end of the array is returned from the method. Table 7.12 shows the return value associated with this method.

Table 7.12 *Arguments and Return Values Associated with* `pop()`

Type	Item	Description
Returns		The last element in the array is returned from the method.

Example

In Listing 7.69, an array of pages is created to represent a stack of papers. The pop() method removes and returns the top-most paper. After the pop() method is executed, the variable currentPaper contains "Page3", and the array's length property is 2.

Listing 7.69 *Using the* `pop()` *Method to Remove Elements from the End of an Array*

```
<script type="text/javascript" language="JavaScript">
<!--
```

Listing 7.69   Continued

```
//Create an array of papers and remove the top page.
pileOfPapers = new Array("Page1","Page2","Page3");
currentPaper = pileOfPapers.pop();  //Removed Page3
document.write(currentPaper," was removed from the pile.");


// -->
</script>
```

Array.prototype

JavaScript 1.1+, ECMAScript 1E+, JScript 3.0+
Nav3+, NES3+, IE 4+, Opera5+

Syntax

```
Array.prototype.property
```

```
Array.prototype.method
```

Description

The `prototype` property allows you to add new properties and methods (designated as property/method in the Syntax section) to the `Array` object that can be used throughout your code.

Example

In Listing 7.70, the `prototype` property is used to provide a `pop()` method for working with arrays. Even though a `pop()` method is already available, a new `pop()` method will be created. This method overrides the functionality of the `Array.pop()` method. The new `pop()` method is used at the end of the code to remove an the "Peach" element from the array of juice flavors. The contents of the *flavorArray* are displayed before and after the new `pop()` method is executed to show that the "Peach" flavor was removed.

Listing 7.70   Assigning a New Method to the Array Object with the Prototype Property

```
<script type="text/javascript" language="JavaScript">
<!--

//This function removes the last element in the array.  This last
//element is returned from the function.
function pop()
{
  if(this.length != 0)
  {
    var lastElement = this[this.length-1];  //Get last element.
    this.length = this.length-1;            //Remove last element from array.
    return(lastElement);                    //Return the last element.
```

```
  }
}

//Make the pop() function available to all Array objects.
//This will override the pop() method provided by the Array object in Netscape.
Array.prototype.pop = pop;

//Create an Array of juice flavors.
var flavorArray = new Array("Strawberry","Blueberry","Peach");

//Display the contents of the flavor array.
document.write("The flavor array initially contains: ");
document.write(flavorArray.join(', '),"<br>");

//Remove Peach from the array.
var removedElement = flavorArray.pop();
document.write(removedElement," was removed from the flavor array.<br>");

//Display the contents of the flavor array after the pop() method.
document.write("The flavor array now contains: ");
document.write(flavorArray.join(', '),"<br>");

// -->
</script>
```

Array.push()

JavaScript 1.2+, ECMAScript 3E+, JScript 5.5+
Nav4+, NES3+, IE5.5+, Opera5+

Syntax

array.push (*arg1,...argN*)

Description

The push() method "pushes" the elements specified in the parameter list on to the end of the array in the order they were listed. Table 7.13 shows the arguments and return values associated with this method.

Table 7.13 *Arguments and Return Values Associated with* push()

Type	Item	Description
Arguments	arg1,...argN	One or more elements to be added to the end of the array
Returns		The last element added to the end of the array, which is also the last argument in the parameter list

Example

In Listing 7.71, an array of pages is created to represent a stack of papers. The push() method puts two more pages on the end of the array. After the push() method is executed, the variable currentPaper contains "Page4", and the array's length property is 4.

Listing 7.71 **Using the** push() *Method to Add Elements to the End of an Array*

```
<script type="text/javascript" language="JavaScript">
<!--

//Create an array of papers.
pileOfPapers = new Array("Page1","Page2");

//Add 2 more pages to the end of the array.
currentPaper = pileOfPapers.push("Page3","Page4");

//Display the papers in the pile.
document.write(pileOfPapers.join(','()," are in the pile.");

// -->
</script>
```

Array.reverse()

JavaScript 1.1+, ECMAScript 1E+, JScript 3.0+
Nav3+, NES3+, IE 4+, Opera5+

Syntax

```
array.reverse()
```

Description

The reverse() method reverses the order of the elements in the array according to the array index numbers.

Example

Listing 7.72 creates an array representing a line of people. The reverse() method is called to reverse the order of the names so that Polly is the first element, Leslie is the second element, and Cheryl is the last element.

Listing 7.72 *Reversing Element Positions in an Array with the* reverse() *Method*

```
<script type="text/javascript" language="JavaScript">
<!--
```

```
//Create an array of names representing people in a grocery store line.
lineOfPeople = new Array("Cheryl","Leslie","Polly");
lineOfPeople.reverse();    //Reverse the items in the array.

//Display the names in the array. Notice the reversed ordering.
document.write("lineOfPeople[0]=",lineOfPeople[0],"<br>");
document.write("lineOfPeople[1]=",lineOfPeople[1],"<br>");
document.write("lineOfPeople[2]=",lineOfPeople[2],"<br>");

// -->
</script>
```

Array.shift()

JavaScript 1.2+, ECMAScript 3E+, JScript 5.5+
Nav4+, NES3+, IE5.5+, Opera5+

Syntax

```
array.shift()
```

Description

The shift() method deletes and returns the first element of the array. Once deleted, all the remaining elements are shifted down one spot, so the first position is filled by the element that was previously in the second position. Table 7.14 shows the return value associated with this method.

Table 7.14 Return Value Associated with shift()

Type	Item	Description
Returns		The first element of the array, before the elements are shifted, is returned from the method.

Example

Listing 7.73 creates an array representing people waiting for a table at a restaurant. The shift() method pulls the first name off the list and shifts all the other names down one position. After the shift() method is executed, the variable personToSeat now contains Kent. Jon is shifted to lineOfPeople[0] and Jeremy to lineOfPeople[1].

Listing 7.73 Removing the First Element from an Array with the shift() Method

```
<script type="text/javascript" language="JavaScript">
<!--

//Create an array representing a line of people at a restaurant.
lineOfPeople = new Array("Kent","Jon","Jeremy");
personToSeat = lineOfPeople.shift();   //Kent pulled from array
```

Listing 7.73 **Continued**

```
//Display name of person removed from array.
document.write("Please seat ",personToSeat,"<br>");

//Display people left in the array.
document.write("People waiting for a seat: ",lineOfPeople.join(', '));
// -->
</script>
```

Array.slice()

JavaScript 1.2+, ECMAScript 3E+, JScript 3.0+
Nav4+, NES3+, IE 4+, Opera5+

Syntax

```
array.slice (start)
array.slice(start, stop)
```

Description

The slice() method returns a new array that contains the elements of the original array starting at position start and ending at the element position *before* stop. If no stop position is specified, the new array will contain the elements of the original array, starting at the position stated in start through the end of the array. Table 7.15 lists the arguments and return values associated with this method.

Table 7.15 **Arguments and Return Values Associated with** slice()

Type	Item	Description
Arguments	start	The position in the array where the slice is to begin. Negative numbers can be used to count from the last element to the first. For example, –1 is the last element in the array, and –2 is the second to the last element in the array.
	stop	The position in the array where the slice is to stop. Similar to the start parameter, the stop parameter can be negative.
Returns		A new array is returned from this method that contains the elements of the original array from index positions specified by start and stop.

Example

In Listing 7.74, an array of numbers is created. A new array of numbers is derived from the original array of numbers using the slice() method. After the slice() method is executed, the array newNumArray contains the elements 23 and 759.

Listing 7.74   Selecting a Subsection from an Array with the `slice()`
Method

```
<script type="text/javascript" language="JavaScript">
<!--

//Create an array of 4 numbers and display the contents.
numArray = new Array(345,23,759,5);
document.write("numArray contains the numbers: ",numArray.join(', '),"<br>");

//Create a new array from part of the original array.
newNumArray = numArray.slice(1,3);     // new array contains [23,759].

//Display the contents of the new array.
document.write("newNumArray contains the numbers: ",newNumArray.join(',
'),"<br>");

// -->
</script>
```

Array.sort()

JavaScript 1.1+, ECMAScript 1E+, JScript 3.0+
Nav3+, NES3+, IE 4+, Opera5+

Syntax

```
array.sort()
array.sort (function)
```

Description

The `sort()` method rearranges the elements of the array based on a sorting order. Table 7.16 lists the argument associated with this method. If the method has no parameters, JavaScript attempts to convert all the elements of the array to strings and then sort them alphabetically. If the array should be sorted some other way, a `function` must be provided to handle the new sorting algorithm.

Table 7.16   Argument Associated with `sort()`

Type	Item	Description
Argument	`function`	A function designated to handle the sorting of the array.

As mentioned before, if the array should be sorted some other way than jscriptbetically, a `function` must be provided to handle the new sorting algorithm. The function specified must operate based on the following rules:

- The function must accept two arguments that are to be compared.
- The function must return a number indicating the order of the two arguments in relation to each other.

- If the first argument should appear before the second argument, a number less than zero should be returned from the function.
- If the first argument should appear after the second argument, a number greater than zero should be returned from the function.
- If both arguments are equivalent, zero should be returned from the function.

When the function specified by the sort() method returns zero, signifying that the arguments are equal, the arguments remain in the same order relative to each other after the function has been called.

Example

To help solidify how this method operates, Listing 7.75 demonstrates how to use the method to sort an array based on the number of characters in each argument. Notice how the sort() method changes the order of the elements of the array in Figure 7.5.

Listing 7.75   Sorting an Array Based on Argument Lengths

```
<script type="text/javascript" language="JavaScript">

<!--
//Display the contents of an array.
function contentsOfArray(theArray)
{
  document.write("the array contains:<br>");
  //Access each element in the array.
  for(i=0; i<theArray.length; i++)
  {
    document.write("Position ",i," = ",theArray[i],"<br>");
  }
}


//Sort arguments based on their length.
function sortOnArgLen(arg1,arg2)
{
  if(arg1.length < arg2.length)
    return -1;
  if(arg1.length > arg2.length)
    return 1;
  if(arg1.length == arg2.length)
    return 0;
}


//Create and display an array of shapes.
shapes = new Array("triangle","rectangle","square");
document.write("Before the sort method ");
contentsOfArray(shapes);
```

```
//Sort the array.
shapes.sort(sortOnArgLen);
document.write("<br>After the sort method ");
contentsOfArray(shapes);
// -->
</script>
```

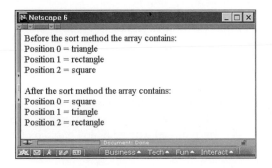

Figure 7.5

Sort the array elements based on the character length of each element.

Array.splice()

JavaScript 1.2+, ECMAScript 3E+, JScript 5.5+
Nav4+, IE5.5+, Opera5+

Syntax

array.splice(start,delete,arg3,...,argN)

Description

The splice() method provides a way for elements to be either added or deleted from the array. When the delete parameter contains a number other than zero, the elements beginning at start and ending at start+delete are deleted from the array. If delete is zero, no elements are deleted. All elements from start to the end of the array are deleted when delete is not specified. If arguments follow the delete parameter, they are added to the array as elements beginning at the position specified by start. Existing elements are shifted up to allow room for the new elements.

NOTE

There was a bug in Navigator 4 when just one element was deleted from an array. Rather than returning an array that contained the deleted element, the actual element was returned from the method. In addition, when no elements were deleted from the array, null was returned instead of an empty array.

Table 7.17 lists the arguments and return values associated with the splice() method.

Table 7.17   **Arguments and Return Values Associated with** `splice()`

Type	Item	Description
Arguments	`start`	The position in the array where the slice is to begin.
	`delete`	The number of elements to be deleted from the array, beginning at the position specified by `start`.
	`arg3,...,argN`	New array elements to be inserted into the array, starting at the position specified by `start`.
Returns		If any elements are deleted from the array, they are returned from the method as an array.

Example

To help understand how the `splice()` method works, Listing 7.76 uses the `delete` and `insert` capabilities of the method to simulate a food order at a restaurant. In Figure 7.6, notice how the hamburger was replaced with a hot dog based on the customer's change in appetite.

Listing 7.76   **Using** `splice()` **to Simulate a Food Order**

```
<script type="text/javascript" language="JavaScript">
<!--
//Display the current order.
function printOrder(theArray)
{
  document.write("The current order is:<br>");
  //Access each element in the array.
  for(i=0; i<theArray.length; i++)
  {
    document.write("- ",theArray[i],"<br>");
  }
}


//Create and display a food order.
foodOrder = new Array("hamburger","fries","drink");
document.write("<h3>The initial order taken</h3>");
printOrder(foodOrder);

//Replace the hamburger with a hotdog.
foodOrder.splice(0,1,"hotdog");
document.write("<h3>The customer wants a hotdog ");
document.write("instead of the hamburger.</h3>");

//Print the new order.
printOrder(foodOrder);
// -->
</script>
```

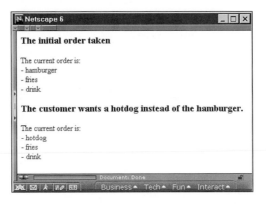

Figure 7.6

The food order changed using the `splice()` method.

Array.toSource()
JavaScript1.3+, JScript3.0
Nav4.06+, IE4

Syntax
`array.toSource()`

Description
The `toSource()` method returns one string representing the source of the `Array` object. The string that is returned contains all the elements in the array separated with commas. The entire string is enclosed with brackets (`[]`) to show it is an array. If another array is contained within an array, its contents are also part of the string with its own set of brackets.

Example
Listing 7.77 creates an `Array` object of colors and an `Array` object of numbers. The array of numbers is included in the array of colors. The `toSource()` method is then applied to the `Array` object to return the source string.

```
["Blue", "Green", "Red", [3, 6, 7]]
```

Listing 7.77   *Accessing the source of an* Array *object with the* toSource() *Method*

```
<script type="text/javascript" language="JavaScript">
<!--

//Create an array of numbers.
numbers = new Array(3,6,7);
```

Listing 7.77   Continued

```
//Create an array of colors and a subarray of numbers.
colors = new Array("Blue","Green","Red",numbers);

//Force JavaScript to display the array contents in a string.
aString = colors.toSource();  //Create a string from the array contents.
document.write(aString); //Display the string.

// -->
</script>
```

Array.toString()

JavaScript 1.1+, ECMAScript 1E+, JScript 3.0+
Nav3+, IE 4+, Opera5+

Syntax

`array.toString()`

Description

The `toString()` method returns one string that contains all the elements in the array separated with commas. You might be wondering why anyone would need this method when the `join()` method can do this and more. The reason is that the `toString()` method is what JavaScript uses to automatically convert an array to a string when the array is used in string context.

CAUTION

JavaScript 1.2 did not use commas to separate the elements. Instead, each element was enclosed in square brackets.

Table 7.18 shows the return value associated with the `toString()` method.

Table 7.18   Return Value Associated with `toString()`

Type	Item	Description
Returns		A string that contains all the elements of the array

Example

Listing 7.78 creates an array of colors and then uses the `toString()` method to put the contents of the array into a string which is then displayed in the browser.

Listing 7.78   Forcing JavaScript to Use an Array's `toString()` Method

```
<script type="text/javascript" language="JavaScript">
<!--
```

```
//Create an array of colors.
colors = new Array("Blue","Green","Red");

//Force JavaScript to display the array contents in a string.
document.write(colors.toString()); //returns "Blue,Green,Red"
// -->
</script>
```

Array.unshift()

JavaScript 1.2+, ECMAScript 3E+, JScript 5.5+
Nav4+, NES3+, Opera5+

Syntax

`array.unshift(arg1,...argN)`

Description

The unshift() method adds the arguments listed in the parameter list to the front of the array as new elements. Existing elements are shifted up to allow room for the new elements. Table 7.19 lists the arguments and return values associated with this method.

Table 7.19 Arguments and Return Values Associated with unshift()

Type	Item	Description
Arguments	arg1,...argN	Elements to be added to the array
Returns		The length of the array after adding the new elements.

Example

Listing 7.79 creates an array of school grades. Two new grades, 100 and 93, are added to the front of the array using the unshift() method. After the unshift() method has executed, the grades array contains [100,93,95,87], and newLength contains the new length of the array, 4.

Listing 7.79 *Adding Elements to the Front of an Array Using the* unshift() ***Method***

```
<script type="text/javascript" language="JavaScript">
<!--

//Create an array of test grades.
grades = new Array(95,87);

//Add two more grades to the array.
newLength = grades.unshift(100,93);

//Display the grades stored in the array.
for(i=0; i<newLength; i++)
```

Listing 7.79   Continued

```
{
  document.write("grades[",i,"]=",grades[i],"<br>");
}

// -->
</script>
```

Array.unwatch()

JavaScript 1.2+
Nav4+, NES3+

Syntax

Array.unwatch *(property)*

Description

The unwatch() method of the Array object, is used to turn off the watch on a particular property specified by *property*.

Example

Listing 7.80 shows how the unwatch() method is used to stop watching the user defined property *p*.

Listing 7.80   Example of the unwatch() **method of the** Array **object**

```
<script type="text/javascript" language="JavaScript">
<!--
function alertme(id,oldValue,newValue)
{
  document.writeln("myArray." + id + " changed from " + oldValue + " to ");
  document.writeln(newValue + "<br>");
  return newValue;
}

var myArray = new Array();
Array.prototype.p = 1;
myArray.watch("p",alertme);

myArray.p = 2;
myArray.unwatch("p");
myArray.p = 3;
myArray.watch("p",alertme);
myArray.p = 4;
// -->
</script>
```

Array.valueOf()

JavaScript1.1+, ECMAScript 1E+, JScript3.0+
Nav3+, NES2+, IE4+, Opera3+

Syntax

```
array.valueOf ()
```

Description

The valueOf() method returns the primitive value of the object. In terms of an instance of an Array object, this method returns the array elements separated by commas. If an array contains another array, the contents are flattened when this method is used.

Example

Listing 7.81 creates an Array object of colors and an Array object of numbers. The array of numbers is included in the array of colors. Because the valueOf() method returns the actual elements in the array, "Blue,Green,Red,3,6,7" is written to the browser.

Listing 7.81   Using the valueOf() **Method to Return the Value of the** Array **Object**

```
<script type="text/javascript" language="JavaScript">
<!--

//Create an array of numbers.
numbers = new Array(3,6,7);

//Create an array of colors and a subarray of numbers.
colors = new Array("Blue","Green","Red",numbers);

//Display the primitive value of the array.
document.write(colors.valueOf()); //Display the array elements.

// -->
</script>
```

Array.watch()

JavaScript 1.2+
Nav4+, NES3+

Syntax

```
Array.watch(property,function)
```

Description

The watch()method of the Array object is used to turn on the watch of a particular property specified by *property*. Any time the specified property is changed after the watch() method has been called, the specified function is called.

Example

Listing 7.82 shows how the watch() method is used to start watching the user-defined property p.

Listing 7.82   Example of the* watch() *Method of the* Array *Object

```
<script type="text/javascript" language="JavaScript">
<!--
function alertme(id,oldValue,newValue)
{
  document.writeln("myArray." + id + " changed from " + oldValue + " to ");
  document.writeln(newValue + "<br>");
  return newValue;
}

var myArray = new Array();
Array.prototype.p = 1;
myArray.watch("p",alertme);

myArray.p = 2;
// -->
</script>
```

Automation

> JScript3.0+
> IE4+

Syntax

Core JScript Object

Description

Automation objects are objects that are connected to other applications or programming tools through automation interfaces. These objects give JScript developers access to properties and methods applications from within the JScript code. See ActiveXObject() and GetObject() for details on using automation objects.

Example

See ActiveXObject() and GetObject() for examples of using automation objects.

boolean

> JavaScript1.2, ECMAScript 2E+, JScript 5+
> Nav4+, NES3+, IE5+, Opera5+

Syntax

```
Reserved Keyword
```

Description

The `boolean` keyword has not been implemented in server-side JavaScript to date, but has been reserved for future use. Note that this keyword is not the same as the `Boolean` object.

Example

This keyword has not been implemented; therefore, no example is provided.

Boolean

JavaScript 1.1+, ECMAScript 1E+, JScript 3.0+
Nav3+, NES3+, IE 4+, Opera5+

Syntax

```
var variable = new Boolean(value)
var variable = Boolean(value)
```

Description

The `Boolean` object is a wrapper object that holds a primitive boolean value, as well as provides a method for converting the value to a string. A primitive `boolean` can have only one of two states: `true` or `false`. Internally, JavaScript uses the number 1 to represent `true` and 0 to represent `false`, but provides the `toString()` method to return the strings `"true"` and `"false"`.

A `Boolean` object is created with the `Boolean()` constructor and the `new` operator or by the `Boolean()` function. The argument, return value, and method associated with this object are listed in Table 7.20.

Table 7.20   The Argument, Return Value, Properties, and Methods Associated with the `Boolean` Object

Type	Item	Description
Argument	value	The value to be converted to a Boolean value and stored in the object. The values `null`, `NaN`, `""` (empty string), and `0` (zero) are converted to `false`. All other values (including the string `"false"`) are converted to `true`.
Returns		If the `new` operator is used, the new `Boolean` object is returned. If the `Boolean()` function is used, the primitive Boolean value is returned.
Properties	constructor	Specifies the function that creates the `Boolean` object's prototype.
	prototype	Represents the prototype of this class.

Table 7.20   *Continued*

Type	Item	Description
Methods	toSource	Returns a string representation of the `Boolean` object.
	toString()	This method returns a string representation of the primitive Boolean value stored in the object. If the object contains `true`, the string `"true"` is returned. Similarly, if the object contains `false`, the string `"false"` is returned.
	unwatch()	Removes a watch point.
	valueOf()	Returns a Boolean value contained in the object.
	watch	Sets a watch point.

Example

In Listing 7.83, a `Boolean` object and a primitive Boolean value are created. There are a couple of key points to notice when examining the results generated by the code, shown in Figure 7.7. First, the `Boolean()` constructor converts the string `"false"` to the Boolean value `true`. Second, `boolObj` is a `Boolean` object, whereas `boolVal` is just a variable holding a primitive Boolean value.

Listing 7.83   *A* `Boolean` *Object Versus a Primitive Boolean Value*

```
<script type="text/javascript" language="JavaScript">
<!--

//Create a Boolean object.
boolObj = new Boolean("false");
document.write("boolObj = ",boolObj);         //Display true.
document.write(" [",typeof boolObj,"]<br>");  //Display object.

//Create a primitive boolean value.
boolVal = Boolean(false);
document.write("boolVal = ",boolVal);         //Display false.
document.write(" [",typeof boolVal,"]");      //Display boolean.

// -->
</script>
```

Figure 7.7

Boolean object versus primitive boolean value.

Boolean.constructor

JavaScript 1.1+, ECMAScript 1E+, JScript 3.0+
Nav3+, NES3+, IE 4+, Opera3+

Syntax

```
Boolean.constructor
```

Description

The constructor property of the Boolean object is used to create the object's proto-type.

Example

Listing 7.84 demonstrates the constructor property as it relates to the Boolean object.

Listing 7.84 **The Boolean's** contructor **Property**

```
<script type="text/javascript" language="JavaScript">
<!--
// Create a new boolean object using the constructor property.
myBoolean = new Boolean(true);
if(myBoolean.constructor == Boolean){
  document.write("Object was created");
}
// -->
</script>
```

Boolean.prototype

JavaScript 1.1+, ECMAScript 1E+, JScript 3.0+
Nav3+, IE 4+, Opera5+

Syntax

```
Boolean.prototype.property
```

```
Boolean.prototype.method
```

Description

The prototype property allows you to add new properties and methods to the Boolean object that can be used throughout your code.

Example

In Listing 7.85, the prototype property is used to create a new method, called letter(), which can be used by all Boolean objects. The letter() method uses the letterBoolean() function to return true or false based on the status of the object.

Listing 7.85   Assigning a New Method to the Boolean **Object with the** prototype **Property**

```
<script type="text/javascript" language="JavaScript">
<!--

//This function returns the string "T" or "F" based on the value stored in the
//Boolean object that uses this function.
function letterBoolean()
{
  if(this == true)
    return("T");
  else
    return("F");
}

//Make the letterBoolean function available to all Boolean objects.
Boolean.prototype.letter = letterBoolean;

//Create a Boolean object with an initial setting of true.
var myBooleanObj = new Boolean(true);   //myBooleanObj equal to true

//Display the state of the Boolean object using the letter method.
document.write("myBooleanObj is set to ",myBooleanObj.letter());   //Return "T"

// -->
</script>
```

Boolean.toSource()

JavaScript1.3+, JScript3.0
Nav4.06+, IE4

Syntax

```
boolean.toSource()
```

Description

The toSource() method returns one string representing the source of the Boolean object. The string that is returned is enclosed in parentheses.

Example

Listing 7.86 creates a Boolean object to represent true. The toSource() method is then applied to the Boolean object to return the source string "(new Boolean(true))".

Listing 7.86   Accessing the Source of a Boolean **Object with the** toSource() **Method**

```
<script type="text/javascript" language="JavaScript">
<!--
```

```
//Create a Boolean object representing true.
bool = new Boolean(1);

//Display the source of the Boolean object.
document.write(bool.toSource());

// -->
</script>
```

Boolean.toString()

JavaScript 1.1+, ECMAScript 1E+, JScript 3.0+
Nav3+, IE 4+, Opera5+

Syntax

boolean.toString()

Description

The toString()method returns the string representation ("true" or "false") of the primitive Boolean value stored in the Boolean object. The return value associated with this object is listed in Table 7.21.

Table 7.21 Return Value Associated with toString()

Type	Description
Returns	If true, the string "true" is returned. If false, the string "false" is returned.

Example

In Listing 7.87, the toString() method is used to force a comparison of strings rather than Boolean values. Without the toString() method, the if comparison would find the Boolean value not equal to the string value.

Listing 7.87 Force the Desired Comparison Using Boolean's toString()
Method

```
<script type="text/javascript" language="JavaScript">
<!--

//Create a Boolean object that contains the boolean value "false".
boolObj = new Boolean(false);

//Force JavaScript to convert the boolObj object to the string "false"
//before comparing to the string "false".
if(boolObj.toString() == "false")     //Evalutes to true,
  alert("EQUAL");                      //so display "EQUAL" on screen.
```

Listing 7.87   Continued

```
else
  alert("NOT Equal");

// -->
</script>
```

Boolean.unwatch()

JavaScript 1.2+
Nav4+, NES3+

Syntax

Boolean.unwatch (*property*)

Description

The unwatch() method of the Boolean object is used to turn off the watch on a particular property specified by *property*.

Example

Listing 7.88 shows how the unwatch() method is used to stop watching the user-
defined property p.

Listing 7.88   Example of the unwatch() *method of the* Boolean *Object*

```
<script type="text/javascript" language="JavaScript">
<!--
function alertme(id,oldValue,newValue)
{
  document.writeln("myBoolean." + id + " changed from " + oldValue + " to ");
  document.writeln(newValue + "<br>");
  return newValue;
}

var myBoolean = new Boolean();
Boolean.prototype.p = 1;
myBoolean.watch("p",alertme);

myBoolean.p = 2;
myBoolean.unwatch("p");
myBoolean.p = 3;
myBoolean.watch("p",alertme);
myBoolean.p = 4;
// -->
</script>
```

Boolean.valueOf()

JavaScript1.1+, ECMAScript 1E+, JScript3.0+, Nav3+, NES2+, IE4+, Opera3+

Syntax

```
boolean.valueOf()
```

Description

The valueOf() method returns the primitive value of the object. In terms of an instance of a Boolean object, this method returns a Boolean value contained in the object.

Example

Listing 7.89 creates a Boolean object representing true. Because the valueOf() method returns the Boolean value in the object, "true" is written to the browser.

Listing 7.89   Using the valueOf() ***Method to Return the Value of the*** Boolean ***Object***

```
<script type="text/javascript" language="JavaScript">
<!--

//Create a Boolean object representing true.
bool = new Boolean(1);

//Display the source of the Boolean object.
document.write(bool.valueOf());

// -->
</script>
```

Boolean.watch()

JavaScript 1.2+
Nav4+, NES3+

Syntax

```
Boolean.watch (property,function)
```

Description

The watch()method of the Boolean object is used to turn on the watch of a particular property specified by *property*. Any time the specified property is changed after the watch() method has been called, the specified function is called.

Example

Listing 7.90 shows how the watch() method is used to start watching the user-defined property p.

Listing 7.90 *Example of the* watch() *Method of the* Boolean *Object*

```
<script type="text/javascript" language="JavaScript">
<!--
function alertme(id,oldValue,newValue)
{
  document.writeln("myBoolean." + id + " changed from " + oldValue + " to ");
  document.writeln(newValue + "<br>");
  return newValue;
}

var myBoolean = new Boolean();
Boolean.prototype.p = 1;
myBoolean.watch("p",alertme);

myBoolean.p = 2;
// -->
</script>
```

break

JavaScript 1.1+, ECMAScript 1E+, JScript 1.0+
Nav3+, IE 3+, Opera3+

Syntax

```
break label;
```

Description

The keyword break provides a way to exit out of loop structures and switch conditionals prematurely. Most of the time, the word break appears on a line by itself, but there are times when a label will follow the keyword (see Table 7.22). When a label is used, code execution completely breaks out of the area designated by label and proceeds to the code that follows the area. To label a statement, simply place the label name followed by a colon (:) in front of the code that needs to be broken out of during code execution.

Table 7.22 *Argument Associated with the* break *Keyword*

Type	Item	Description
Argument	label	A label that designates code from which to break.

Example

Listing 7.91 demonstrates the effect of using labels and break statements when working with nested loops. Figure 7.8 shows the result of executing this code.

Listing 7.91 *Using* break*s and Labels*

```
<script type="text/javascript" language="JavaScript">
<!--
```

```
//Loop through the outer loop (forLoop1) 4 times.
forLoop1:
for (var counter1 = 1; counter1 <= 5; counter1++)
{
  //Go through this inner loop 4 times for each time through the outer loop.
  for (var counter2 = 1; counter2 <= 5; counter2++)
  {
    //Display the values in each for loop's counter.
    document.write("Counter1=",counter1);
    document.write(" Counter2=",counter2,"<br>");

    //Break out of inner loop the 3rd time through the inner loop.
    if (counter2 == 3)
      break;

    //Break out of the outer loop the 3rd time through the outer loop.
    if (counter1 == 3)
      break forLoop1;
  }
}

document.write("All done!");

//-->
</script>
```

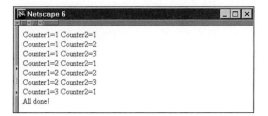

Figure 7.8

Using labels and the break *statement in nested loops.*

Notice how the break statement with no label, in Figure 7.8, breaks out of just the inner loop. When the break statement is used with a label, JavaScript knows at what level to break.

byte

JavaScript1.2+, ECMAScript 2E+, JScript 5+
Nav4+, NES3+, IE5+, Opera5+

Syntax

```
Reserved Keyword
```

Description

The byte keyword has not been implemented in server-side JavaScript to date, but has been reserved for future use.

Example

This keyword has not been implemented; therefore, no example is provided.

case

JavaScript1.2+, ECMAScript 2E+, JScript3.0+
Nav4+, NES3+, IE4+, Opera5+

Syntax

```
Reserved Keyword
```

Description

The case keyword has not been implemented in server-side JavaScript to date, but has been reserved for future use.

Example

This keyword has not been implemented; therefore, no example is provided.

char

JavaScript1.2+, ECMAScript 2E+, JScript 5+
Nav4+, NES2+, IE5+, Opera5+

Syntax

```
Reserved Keyword
```

Description

The char keyword has not been implemented in server-side JavaScript to date, but has been reserved for future use.

Example

This keyword has not been implemented; therefore, no example is provided.

class

JavaScript1.2+, ECMAScript 1E+, JScript3.0+
Nav4+, NES3+, IE4+, Opera5+

Syntax

```
Reserved Keyword
```

Description

The word class is reserved for future use, so there is no definition at this time.

Example

No example can be provided because `class` is reserved for future use.

const

JavaScript1.2, ECMAScript 1E+, JScript 5+
Nav4+, NES3+, IE5+, Opera5+

Syntax

`Reserved Keyword`

Description

The word `const` is reserved for future use, so there is no definition at this time.

Example

No example can be provided because `const` is reserved for future use.

continue

JavaScript 1.1+, ECMAScript 1E+, JScript 3.0+
Nav3+, IE 4+, Opera3+

Syntax

`continue label;`

Description

The `continue` statement forces the execution of the code within a loop to continue at the beginning of the loop. Normally, the `continue` keyword appears on a line by itself, but there are times when a label will follow the keyword (see Table 7.23). When a label is used, code execution immediately jumps to the beginning of the loop designated by the label and begins executing code.

Table 7.23   Argument Associated with the `continue` **Keyword**

Type	Item	Description
Argument	`label`	A label that designates code to execute.

The beginning of a loop varies depending on the type of loop structure. Table 7.24 shows where each looping structure jumps to when a `continue` structure is encountered.

Table 7.24   Where the `continue` **Statement Jumps**

Looping Structure	`Continue` Jumps to
`for`	Expression in parentheses following `for` keyword
`while`	Expression in parentheses following `while` keyword
`do...while`	Expression in parentheses following `while` keyword
`for...in`	Next property name in object

CAUTION

There is a bug in Navigator 4 that causes the expression in parentheses following the `while` keyword in a `do...while` loop to not get executed when jumped to using a `continue` statement. Instead, execution of code starts at the top of loop, after the `continue` statement. This problem can be avoided by using a `while` loop.

To label a statement, simply place the label name followed by a colon (`:`) in front of the code where code execution needs to continue.

Example

Listing 7.92 demonstrates the use of labels and `continue`. This example is a bit complicated, so take time to compare Listing 7.79 to the output in Figure 7.9. Notice how the phrase `"Bottom of innerLoop"` was not printed after the `"Continue at top of innerLoop."` because code execution jumped back to beginning of the inner-most loop. When a label was attached to the `continue` keyword, code execution jumped back to the beginning of the loop labeled `outerLoop`.

Listing 7.92 Using the `continue` Statement

```
<script type="text/javascript" language="JavaScript">
<!--

//Loop through the outerLoop twice.
outerLoop:
  for (var counter1 = 1; counter1 <= 2; counter1++)
  {
    document.write("Top of outerLoop.<br>");

    //Loop through the innerLoop twice.
    innerLoop:
      for (var counter2 = 1; counter2 <= 2; counter2++)
      {
        //Display the values in each for loop's counter.
        document.write("Top of innerLoop.<br>");
        document.write("Counter1=",counter1,"<br>");
        document.write("Counter2=",counter2,"<br>");

        //If this is the second time through the innerLoop,
        //don't go any further and jump back to the top of the innerLoop.
        if (counter2 == 2)
        {
          document.write("Continue at top of innerLoop.<br>");
          continue;
        }

        //If this is the second time through the outerLoop,
        //don't go any further and jump back to the top of the outerLoop.
```

```
      if (counter1 == 2)
      {
        document.write("Continue at top of outerLoop.<br>");
        continue outerLoop;
      }
      document.write("Bottom of innerLoop.<br>");
    }
    document.write("Bottom of outerLoop.<br>");
  }

document.write("All done!");

//-->
</script>
```

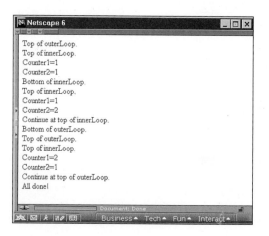

Figure 7.9

The result of using the `continue` *statement.*

Date

JavaScript 1.0+, ECMAScript 1E+, JScript 1.0+
Nav2+, NES2+, IE 3+, Opera3+

Syntax

```
var variable = new Date();
var variable = new Date(milliseconds1);
var variable = new Date(string)
var variable = new Date(year, month, day, hours, minutes, seconds,
milliseconds2)
```

Description

The Date object represents all aspects of a date and time from year to milliseconds. If arguments are provided when creating the Date object, the new object will contain the date specified; otherwise the object will be set to the current date. The arguments and methods are listed in Table 7.25.

CAUTION

If the Date() constructor can also be called as a function by excluding the new operator. With this is done a string representation of the date is returned rather than a Date object

Table 7.25 **Arguments and Methods Associated with the** Date *Object*

Type	Item	Description
Argument	constructor	Specifies the function that creates the Boolean object's prototype.
	milliseconds1	The desired date is calculated from the number of milliseconds between midnight January 1, 1970 GMT and the desired date.
	string	The desired date is calculated from the string representation. The format of the string should match the parse() method of the Date object.
	year	A four-digit representation of the year.
	month	The month represented as an integer, where 0 represents January and 11 represents December.
	day	The day of the month represented as an integer from 1 to 31. Optional argument.
	hours	The hour represented as an integer where 0 represents 12 a.m. (midnight) and 23 represents 11 p.m. Optional argument.
	minutes	The minutes in the hour represented as an integer from 0 to 59. Optional argument.
	seconds	The seconds in the minute represented as an integer from 0 to 59. Optional argument.
	milliseconds2	The milliseconds in the second represented as an integer from 0 to 999. Optional argument.
Methods	getDate()	Returns the day of the month.
	getDay()	Returns the day of the week.
	getFullYear()	Returns the year in local time with four digits.
	getHours()	Returns the hour.
	getMilliseconds()	Returns the milliseconds.

getMinutes()	Returns the minutes.
getMonth()	Returns the month.
getSeconds()	Returns the seconds.
getTime()	Returns the date and time in milliseconds.
getTimezoneOffset()	Returns the time zone offset from GMT in minutes.
getUTCDate()	Returns the day of the month converted to universal time.
getUTCDay()	Returns the day of the week converted to universal time.
getUTCFullYear()	Returns a four-digit representation of the year converted to universal time.
getUTCHours()	Returns the hour converted to universal time.
getUTCMilliseconds()	Returns the milliseconds converted to universal time.
getUTCMinutes()	Returns the minutes converted to universal time.
getUTCMonth()	Returns the month converted to universal time.
getUTCSeconds()	Returns the seconds converted to universal time.
getVarDate()	Returns the date in VT_DATE format.
getYear()	Returns the year as either four digits or two digits.
parse()	Converts a string, representing a date and time, into milliseconds.
setDate()	Sets the day of the month.
setFullYear()	Sets the year as a four-digit number.
setHours()	Sets the hour.
setMilliseconds()	Sets the milliseconds.
setMinutes()	Sets the minutes.
setMonth()	Sets the month.
setSeconds()	Sets the seconds.
setTime()	Sets the date and time from a millisecond representation of a date and time.
setUTCdate()	Sets the day of the month in universal time.
setUTCFullYear()	Sets the year as a four-digit number in universal time.
setUTCHours()	Sets the hour in universal time.
setUTCMilliseconds()	Sets the milliseconds in universal time.
setUTCMinutes()	Sets the minutes in universal time.
setUTCMonth()	Sets the month in universal time.

Table 7.25   Continued

Type	Item	Description
	setUTCSeconds()	Sets the seconds in universal time.
	setYear()	Sets the year as either a four-digit number or a two-digit number.
	toGMTString()	Returns the data and time as a string in universal time (GMT).
	toLocalString()	Returns the date and time as a string in local time format.
	toSource()	Returns the source of the Date object.
	toString()	Returns the date and time as a string in local time.
	toUTCString()	Returns the data and time as a string in universal time (GMT).
	unwatch	Removes a watchpoint.
	UTC()	Converts a universal date and time (GMT) to milliseconds.
	watch	Sets a watchpoint.

Example

Listing 7.93 demonstrates how to create Date objects using various arguments in the Date() constructor.

Listing 7.93   *Creating* Date *Objects*

```
<script type="text/javascript" language="JavaScript">
<!--

//Create a new Date object using all arguments.
theDate1 = new Date(2002,9,29,20,5,8,10);

//Create a new Date object using just milliseconds.
theDate2 = new Date(theDate1.getTime());

//Create a new Date object using a string.
theDate3 = new Date(theDate1.toString());

//Display all the date objects.
document.write("theDate1-> ",theDate1.toString());
document.write("<br>theDate2-> ",theDate2.toString());
document.write("<br>theDate3-> ",theDate3.toString());

// -->
</script>
```

Date.constructor

JavaScript 1.1+, ECMAScript 1E+, JScript 3.0+
Nav3+, NES3+, IE 4+, Opera3+

Syntax

`Date.constructor`

Description

The `constructor` property of the `Date` object is used to create the object's prototype.

Example

Listing 7.94 demonstrates the `constructor` property as it relates to the `Date` object.

Listing 7.94   **The** `Date`**'s** `contructor` **Property**

```
<script type="text/javascript" language="JavaScript">
<!--
// Create a new date object using the constructor property.
myDate = new Date();
if(myDate.constructor == Date){
  document.write("Object was created");
}
// -->
</script>
```

Date.getDate()

JavaScript 1.0+, ECMAScript 1E+, JScript 1.0+
Nav2+, NES2+, IE 3+, Opera3+

Syntax

`date.getDate ()`

Description

The `getDate()`method returns the day of the month expressed as an integer from 1 to 31.

Example

The code in Listing 7.95 displays the current day of the month expressed as an integer from 1 to 31 using the `getDate()` method.

Listing 7.95   **Using the** `getDate()` **Method to Return the Day of the Month**

```
<script type="text/javascript" language="JavaScript">
<!--
```

Listing 7.95   Continued

```
//Create a Date object that contains the current date and time.
theDate = new Date();

//Display the date.
document.write("The date is ",theDate.getDate());

// -->
</script>
```

Date.getDay()

JavaScript 1.0+, ECMAScript 1E+, JScript 1.0+
Nav2+, NES2+, IE 3+, Opera3+

Syntax

*date.*getDay()

Description

The getDay()method returns the day of the week expressed as an integer from 0 (Sunday) to 6 (Saturday).

Example

The code in Listing 7.96 uses the getDay() method to return the day of the week expressed as an integer. This number is then converted to a string representation of the day of the week.

Listing 7.96   Using the getDay() *Method to Return the Day of the Week*

```
<script type="text/javascript" language="JavaScript">
<!--

//This function converts the day from a number to
//a string and returns the string.
function getDayString(num)
{
  var day;     //Create a local variable to hold the string.
  switch(num)
  {
    case 0:
      day="Sunday";
      break;
    case 1:
      day="Monday";
      break;
    case 2:
      day="Tuesday";
      break;
```

```
    case 3:
      day="Wednesday";
      break;
    case 4:
      day="Thursday";
      break;
    case 5:
      day="Friday";
      break;
    case 6:
      day="Saturday";
      break;
    default:
      day="Invalid day";
  }
  return day;
}

//Create a Date object that contains the current date and time.
theDate = new Date();

//Display the day.
document.write("Today is ",getDayString(theDate.getDay()));
// -->
</script>
```

Date.getFullYear()

JavaScript 1.2+, ECMAScript 1E+, JScript 3.0+
Nav4+, IE 4+, Opera5+

Syntax

date.getFullYear()

Description

The getFullYear()method returns the year in local time as a full four-digit number.

Example

The code in Listing 7.97 displays the year using the getFullYear() method.

Listing 7.97   Using the getFullYear() *Method to Return the Year*

```
<script type="text/javascript" language="JavaScript">
<!--

//Create a Date object that contains the current date and time.
theDate = new Date();
```

Listing 7.97   Continued

```
//Display the full year.
document.write("The year is ",theDate.getFullYear());


// -->
</script>
```

Date.getHours()

JavaScript 1.0+, ECMAScript 1E+, JScript 1.0+
Nav2+, NES2+, IE 3+, Opera3+

Syntax

date.getHours()

Description

The getHours() method returns the hour portion of the date expressed as an integer from 0 (12:00 a.m. midnight) to 23 (11:00 p.m.).

Example

The code in Listing 7.98 displays the current hour as an integer from 0 to 23 using the getHours() method.

Listing 7.98   *Using the* getHours() *Method to Return the Current Hour*

```
<script type="text/javascript" language="JavaScript">
<!--

//Create a Date object that contains the current date and time.
theDate = new Date();

//Display the hour.
document.write("The hour is ",theDate.getHours());


// -->
</script>
```

Date.getMilliseconds()

JavaScript 1.2+, ECMAScript 1E+, JScript 3.0+
Nav4+, IE 4+, Opera5+

Syntax

date.getMilliseconds()

Description

The getMilliseconds() method returns the millisecond portion of the date expressed as an integer from 0 to 999.

Example

The code in Listing 7.99 displays the milliseconds in the Date object using the getMilliseconds() method.

Listing 7.99   Using the getMilliseconds() Method to Return the Current Millisecond

```
<script type="text/javascript" language="JavaScript">
<!--

//Create a Date object that contains the current date and time.
theDate = new Date();

//Display the milliseconds.
document.write("The millisecond is ",theDate.getMilliseconds());

// -->
</script>
```

Date.getMinutes()

JavaScript 1.0+, ECMAScript 1E+, JScript 1.0+
Nav2+, NES2+, IE 3+, Opera3+

Syntax

date.getMinutes()

Description

The getMinutes() method returns the minutes portion of the Date object expressed as an integer from 0 to 59.

Example

The code in Listing 7.100 displays the current minute using the getMinutes() method.

Listing 7.100   Using the getMinutes() Method to Return the Current Minute

```
<script type="text/javascript" language="JavaScript">
<!--

//Create a Date object that contains the current date and time.
theDate = new Date();

//Display the minutes.
document.write("The minute is ",theDate.getMinutes());

// -->
</script>
```

Date.getMonth()

JavaScript 1.0+, ECMAScript 1E+, JScript 1.0+
Nav2+, NES2+, IE 3+, Opera3+

Syntax

date.getMonth()

Description

The getMonth() method returns the month portion of the Date object expressed as an integer from 0 (January) to 11 (December).

Example

The code in Listing 7.101 displays the current month using the getMonth() method.

Listing 7.101 *Using the* getMonth() *Method to Return the Current Month*

```
<script type="text/javascript" language="JavaScript">
<!--

//This function converts the month from a number to
//a string and returns the string.
function getMonthString(num)
{
  var month;      //Create a local variable to hold the string.
  switch(num)
  {
    case 0:
      month="January";
      break;
    case 1:
      month="February";
      break;
    case 2:
      month="March";
      break;
    case 3:
      month="April";
      break;
    case 4:
      month="May";
      break;
    case 5:
      month="June";
      break;
    case 6:
      month="July";
```

```
      break;
    case 7:
      month="August";
      break;
    case 8:
      month="September";
      break;
    case 9:
      month="October";
      break;
    case 10:
      month="November";
      break;
    case 11:
      month="December";
      break;
    default:
      month="Invalid month";
  }
  return month;
}

//Create a Date object that contains the current date and time.
theDate = new Date();

//Display the month.
document.write("The month is ",getMonthString(theDate.getMonth()));

// -->
</script>
```

Date.getSeconds()

JavaScript 1.0+, ECMAScript 1E+, JScript 1.0+
Nav2+, NES2+, IE 3+, Opera3+

Syntax

date.getSeconds()

Description

The getSeconds() method returns the seconds portion of the Date object expressed as an integer from 0 to 59.

Example

The code in Listing 7.102 displays the current seconds using the getSeconds() method.

Listing 7.102 Using the `getSeconds()` **Method to Return the Current Second**

```
<script type="text/javascript" language="JavaScript">
<!--

//Create a Date object that contains the current date and time.
theDate = new Date();

//Display the seconds.
document.write("The second is ",theDate.getSeconds());

// -->
</script>
```

Date.getTime()

JavaScript 1.0+, ECMAScript 1E+, JScript 1.0+
Nav2+, NES2+, IE 3+, Opera3+

Syntax

date.getTime()

Description

The getTime() method returns the equivalence of the Date object in milliseconds. The milliseconds are expressed as an integer representing the number of milliseconds between midnight January 1, 1970 (GMT) to the date and time specified in the Date object.

> **TIP**
>
> It is much easier to compare two different dates as milliseconds by using the getTime() method, rather than having to examine the individual parts of the date.

Example

The code in Listing 7.103 displays, 946684800000, the number of milliseconds that passed between midnight January 1, 1970 and midnight January 1, 2000 using the getTime() method.

Listing 7.103 Using the `getTime()` **Method to Return the Milliseconds Between 1970 and 2000**

```
<script type="text/javascript" language="JavaScript">
<!--

//Create a Date object that contains midnight January 1, 1970.
Date1970 = new Date(1970,1,1,0,0,0,0);
```

```
//Create a Date object that contains midnight January 1, 2000.
date2000 = new Date(2000,1,1,0,0,0,0);
//Display the elapsed milliseconds.
document.write(date2000.getTime()-date1970.getTime());
document.write(" milliseconds passed between 1-1-1970 and 1-1-2000");

// -->
</script>
```

Date.getTimezoneOffset()

JavaScript 1.0+, ECMAScript 1E+, JScript 1.0+
Nav2+, NES2+, IE 3+, Opera3+

Syntax

```
date.getTimezoneOffset()
```

Description

The getTimezoneOffset() method returns the difference between the time zones of local time and Greenwich Mean Time (GMT). This difference is returned as an integer representing the number of minutes between the time zone of the local time and GMT. Although this is a method of a Date object, the actual date and time associated with the date is irrelevant because the time zone difference is based on the environment settings in which the JavaScript code is run.

Example

The code in Listing 7.104 displays the time zone offset by using the getTimezoneOffset() method. Notice that when the date and time are changed, the time zone offset remains the same because the contents of the Date object are not used in the calculation.

Listing 7.104   Using the getTimezoneOffset() *Method to Return the Time Zone Offset*

```
<script type="text/javascript" language="JavaScript">
<!--

//Create 2 very different date objects.
aDate1 = new Date(1990,1,1,0,0,0,0);
aDate2 = new Date(1994,2,13,8,24,45,300);

//Display the timezone offsets.
document.write("The timezone offset of aDate1 is ");
document.write(aDate1.getTimezoneOffset()," minutes.<br>");
document.write("The timezone offset of aDate2 is "
document.write(aDate2.getTimezoneOffset()," minutes.");

// -->
</script>
```

Date.getUTCDate()

JavaScript 1.2+, ECMAScript 1E+, JScript 3.0+
Nav4+, IE 4+, Opera5+

Syntax

date.getUTCDate()

Description

The getUTCDate() method returns the day of the month converted to universal time and expressed as an integer from 1 to 31.

Example

The code in Listing 7.105 displays the day of the month in universal time using the getUTCDate() method.

Listing 7.105   Using the getUTCDate() **Method to Return the Day of the Month**

```
<script type="text/javascript" language="JavaScript">
<!--

//Create a Date object that contains the current date and time.
theDate = new Date();

//Display the UTC date.
document.write("The UTC date is ",theDate.getUTCDate());

// -->
</script>
```

Date.getUTCDay()

JavaScript 1.2+, ECMAScript 1E+, JScript 3.0+
Nav4+, IE 4+, Opera3+

Syntax

date.getUTCDay()

Description

The getUTCDay() method returns the day of the week converted to universal time and expressed as an integer from 0 (Sunday) to 6 (Saturday).

Example

The code in Listing 7.106 uses the getUTCDay() method to return the day of the week expressed as an integer in universal time. The number is then converted to a string equivalent to the day of the week.

Listing 7.106 Using the `getUTCDay()` ***Method to Return the Day of the Week***

```
<script type="text/javascript" language="JavaScript">
<!--

//This function converts the day from a number to
//a string and returns the string.
function getDayString(num)
{
  var day;    //Create a local variable to hold the string.
  switch(num)
  {
    case 0:
      day="Sunday";
      break;
    case 1:
      day="Monday";
      break;
    case 2:
      day="Tuesday";
      break;
    case 3:
      day="Wednesday";
      break;
    case 4:
      day="Thursday";
      break;
    case 5:
      day="Friday";
      break;
    case 6:
      day="Saturday";
      break;
    default:
      day="Invalid day";
  }
  return day;
}

//Create a Date object that contains the current date and time.
theDate = new Date();

//Display the UTC day.
document.write("The UTC day is ",getDayString(theDate.getUTCDay()));

// -->
</script>
```

Date.getUTCFullYear()

JavaScript 1.2+, ECMAScript 1E+, JScript 3.0+
Nav4+, IE 4+, Opera5+

Syntax

date.getUTCFullYear()

Description

The getUTCFullYear() method returns the year as a full four-digit number converted to universal time.

Example

The code in Listing 7.107 displays the year in universal time using the getUTCFullYear() method.

Listing 7.107   Using the getUTCFullYear() ***Method to Return the Year***

```
<script type="text/javascript" language="JavaScript">
<!--

//Create a Date object that contains the current date and time.
theDate = new Date();

//Display the full UTC year.
document.write("The UTC year is ",theDate.getUTCFullYear());

// -->
</script>
```

Date.getUTCHours()

JavaScript 1.2+, ECMAScript 1E+, JScript 3.0+
Nav4+, IE 4+, Opera5+

Syntax

date.getUTCHours()

Description

The getUTCHours() method returns the hour portion of the date, converted to universal time and expressed as an integer from 0 (12:00 a.m. midnight) to 23 (11:00 p.m.).

Example

The code in Listing 7.108 displays the current hour in universal time using the getUTCHours() method.

Listing 7.108 Using the getUTCHours() *Method to Return the Current Hour*

```
<script type="text/javascript" language="JavaScript">
<!--

//Create a Date object that contains the current date and time.
theDate = new Date();

//Display the hour.
document.write("The UTC hour is ",theDate.getUTCHours());

// -->
</script>
```

Date.getUTCMilliseconds()

JavaScript 1.2+, ECMAScript 1E+, JScript 3.0+
Nav4+, IE 4+, Opera5+

Syntax

date.getUTCMilliseconds()

Description

The getUTCMilliseconds() method returns the milliseconds portion of the date, converted to universal time and expressed as an integer from 0 to 999.

Example

The code in Listing 7.109 displays the current milliseconds in universal time using the getUTCMilliseconds() method.

Listing 7.109 Using the getUTCMilliseconds() *Method to Return the Current Milliseconds*

```
<script type="text/javascript" language="JavaScript">
<!--

//Create a Date object that contains the current date and time.
theDate = new Date();

//Display the UTC milliseconds.
document.write("The UTC millisecond is ",theDate.getUTCMilliseconds());

// -->
</script>
```

Date.getUTCMinutes()

JavaScript 1.2+, ECMAScript 1E+, JScript 3.0+
Nav4+, IE 4+, Opera5+

Syntax

```
date.getUTCMinutes()
```

Description

The getUTCMinutes() method returns the minutes portion of the Date object, converted to universal time and expressed as an integer from 0 to 59.

Example

The code in Listing 7.110 displays the current minutes in universal time using the getUTCMinutes() method.

Listing 7.110   Using the getUTCMinutes() Method to Return the Current Minutes

```
<script type="text/javascript" language="JavaScript">
<!--

//Create a Date object that contains the current date and time.
theDate = new Date();

//Display the UTC minutes.
document.write("The UTC minute is ",theDate.getUTCMinutes());

// -->
</script>
```

Date.getUTCMonth()

JavaScript 1.2+, ECMAScript 1E+, JScript 3.0+
Nav4+, IE 4+, Opera5+

Syntax

```
date.getUTCMonth()
```

Description

The getUTCMonth() method returns the month portion of the Date object, converted to universal time and expressed as an integer from 0 (January) to 11 (December).

Example

The code in Listing 7.111 uses the getUTCMonth() method to return the current month, expressed as an integer, in universal time. The integer is converted to a string representation of the month.

Listing 7.111   Using the getUTCMonth() Method to Return the Current Month

```
<script type="text/javascript" language="JavaScript">
<!--
```

```
//This function converts the month from a number to
//a string and returns the string.
function getMonthString(num)
{
  var month;      //Create a local variable to hold the string.
  switch(num)
  {
    case 0:
      month="January";
      break;
    case 1:
      month="February";
      break;
    case 2:
      month="March";
      break;
    case 3:
      month="April";
      break;
    case 4:
      month="May";
      break;
    case 5:
      month="June";
      break;
    case 6:
      month="July";
      break;
    case 7:
      month="August";
      break;
    case 8:
      month="September";
      break;
    case 9:
      month="October";
      break;
    case 10:
      month="November";
      break;
    case 11:
      month="December";
      break;
    default:
      month="Invalid month";
  }
  return month;
}
```

Listing 7.111 Continued

```
//Create a Date object that contains the current date and time.
theDate = new Date();

//Display the UTC month.
document.write("The UTC month is ",getMonthString(theDate.getUTCMonth()));

// -->
</script>
```

Date.getUTCSeconds()

JavaScript 1.2+, ECMAScript 1E+, JScript 3.0+
Nav4+, IE 4+, Opera5+

Syntax

date.getUTCSeconds()

Description

The getUTCSeconds() method returns the seconds portion of the Date object, converted to universal time and expressed as an integer from 0 to 59.

Example

The code in Listing 7.112 displays the current second in universal time using the getUTCSeconds() method.

Listing 7.112   Using the getUTCSeconds() Method to Return the Current Second

```
<script type="text/javascript" language="JavaScript">
<!--

//Create a Date object that contains the current date and time.
theDate = new Date();

//Display the UTC seconds.
document.write("The UTC seconds is ",theDate.getUTCSeconds());

// -->
</script>
```

Date.getVarDate()

JScript 3.0+
IE 4+

Syntax

date.getVarDate()

Description

The getVarDate() method returns the date value in VT_DATE format, which can be used with Visual Basic and VBScript when interacting with COM objects, ActiveX objects, and so on. The format is dependent on regional settings.

Example

The code in Listing 7.113 displays the date using the getVarDate() method.

Listing 7.113 *Using the* getVarDate() *Method*

```
<script type="text/jscript" language="JScript">
<!--
//Create a Date object that contains the current date and time.
theDate = new Date();

//Display the date.
document.write("The date is ",theDate.getVarDate());
// -->
</script>
```

Date.getYear()

JavaScript 1.0+, ECMAScript 1E+, JScript 1.0+
Nav2+, NES2+, IE 3+, Opera3+

Syntax

date.getYear()

Description

The getYear()method returns the year portion of the Date object. Unfortunately, the year is represented as either a two-digit number or a four-digit number, depending on the browser version. For example, the year 1983 might be returned from the methods as 1983 or just 83.

NOTE

The getYear() method is obsolete. The getFullYear() method should be used instead of getYear().

Example

The code in Listing 7.114 displays the year using the getYear() method associated with your specific browser.

Listing 7.114 *Using the* getYear() *Method to Return the Current Year*

```
<script type="text/javascript" language="JavaScript">
<!--
```

Listing 7.114   Continued

```
//Create a Date object that contains the current date and time.
theDate = new Date();

//Display the year.
document.write("The year is ",theDate.getYear());

// -->
</script>
```

Date.parse()

JavaScript 1.0+, ECMAScript 1E+, JScript 1.0+
Nav2+, NES2+, IE 3+, Opera5+

Syntax

```
Date.parse (date)
```

Description

The parse() method returns the time, represented in milliseconds between the date argument string and midnight, January 1, 1970, GMT. Notice that this method is associated with the "Date" object rather than a date that was declared. The string date should use the format written by the Date toGMTString() method, which resembles the following:

```
Mon, 24 Oct 1982 12:03:27 -0200
```

The method will also accept strings that lack all or any portion of the time and time zone.

Example

The code in Listing 7.115 displays the milliseconds from 1970 to the string representation of the date and time.

Listing 7.115   Using the parse() *Method*

```
<script type="text/javascript" language="JavaScript">
<!--
//Convert the string representation of the date "Sun, 24 Oct 1982 12:03:27"
//to milliseconds and display the milliseconds.
document.write("The milliseconds of the string ";
document.write("'Sun, 24 Oct 1982 12:03:27': ");
document.write(Date.parse("Sun, 24 Oct 1982 12:03:27"));

// -->
</script>
```

Date.prototype
JavaScript 1.1+, ECMAScript 1E+, JScript 3.0+
Nav3+, NES3+, IE 4+, Opera5+

Syntax

Date.prototype.*property*

Date.prototype.*method*

Description

The prototype property allows you to add new properties and methods to the Date
object that can be used throughout your code.

Example

In Listing 7.116, the prototype property is used to create a new method, called
getDayString, which can be used by all Date objects. The getDayString() method
uses the getDayString() function to return a string representation of the day of the
week (for example, Sunday, Monday, Tuesday,...). This new functionality is used to
display the name of the current day.

**Listing 7.116   *Creating a New Method to Get the String Representation
of the Day***

```
<script type="text/javascript" language="JavaScript">
<!--

//This function returns a string representation of the day.
function getDayString()
{
  var day
  switch(this.getDay())
  {
    case 0:
      day="Sunday";
      break;
    case 1:
      day="Monday";
      break;
    case 2:
      day="Tuesday";
      break;
    case 3:
      day="Wednesday";
      break;
    case 4:
      day="Thursday";
      break;
```

Listing 7.116   Continued

```
    case 5:
      day="Friday";
      break;
    case 6:
      day="Saturday";
      break;
    default:
      day="Invalid day";
  }
  return(day);
}

//Make the getDayString function available to all Date objects.
Date.prototype.getDayString = getDayString;

//Create a Date object with current date and time.
var currentDate = new Date();

//Display the day as a string.
document.write("<h2>Today is ",currentDate.getDayString(),"</h2>");


// -->
</script>
```

Date.setDate()

JavaScript 1.0+, ECMAScript 1E+, JScript 1.0+
Nav2+, NES2+, IE 3+, Opera3+

Syntax

*date.*setDate(*day*)

Description

The setDate() method sets the day of the month in the Date object to the argument day, an integer from 1 to 31. The method returns an integer representing the number of milliseconds between midnight January 1, 1970 (GMT) to the date and time specified in the Date object after the day of the month has been adjusted.

CAUTION

Prior to JavaScript 1.2, this method returned nothing.

Example

The code in Listing 7.117 displays the current date in milliseconds before setting the day to 4. Notice that the milliseconds specified after the setDate() method are the same as the result returned from the method.

Listing 7.117 **Setting the Day of the Month with the** setDate() **Method**

```
<script type="text/javascript" language="JavaScript">
<!--

//Create a Date object.
theDate = new Date();

//Set the day of the month and display the milliseconds.
document.write("Initial milliseconds=",theDate.getTime());
document.write("<br>setDate returned ");
document.write(theDate.setDate(4)," milliseconds.")
document.write("<br>Final milliseconds=",theDate.getTime());

// -->
</script>
```

Date.setFullYear()

JavaScript 1.2+, ECMAScript 1E+, JScript 3.0+
Nav4+, IE 4+, Opera5+

Syntax

date.setFullYear(*year*)

Description

The setFullYear() method sets the year in the Date object to the argument year, a four-digit integer. The method returns an integer representing the number of milliseconds between midnight January 1, 1970 (GMT) to the date and time specified in the Date object after the year has been adjusted.

Example

The code in Listing 7.118 displays the current date in milliseconds before setting the year to 2003. Notice that the milliseconds specified after the setFullYear() method are the same as the result returned from the method.

Listing 7.118 **Setting the Day of the Week with the** setFullYear() **Method**

```
<script type="text/javascript" language="JavaScript">
<!--

//Create a Date object.
theDate = new Date();

//Set the year and display the milliseconds.
document.write("Initial milliseconds=",theDate.getTime());
document.write("<br>setFullYear returned ");
```

Listing 7.118 **Continued**

```
document.write(theDate.setFullYear(2003)," milliseconds.")
document.write("<br>Final milliseconds=",theDate.getTime());


// -->
</script>
```

Date.setHours()

JavaScript 1.0+, ECMAScript 1E+, JScript 1.0+
Nav2+, NES2+, IE 3+, Opera3+

Syntax

`date.setHours (hours)`

Description

The setHours() method sets the hour in the Date object to the argument hours, an integer from 0 (12:00 a.m. midnight) to 23 (11:00 p.m.). The method returns an integer representing the number of milliseconds between midnight January 1, 1970 (GMT) to the date and time specified in the Date object after the hour has been adjusted.

Example

The code in Listing 7.119 displays the current date in milliseconds before setting the hour to 7 (8:00 a.m.). Notice that the milliseconds specified after the setHours() method are the same as the result returned from the method.

Listing 7.119 **Setting the Hour with the** setHours() **Method**

```
<script type="text/javascript" language="JavaScript">
<!--

//Create a Date object.
theDate = new Date();

//Set the hour and display the milliseconds.
document.write("Initial milliseconds=",theDate.getTime());
document.write("<br>setHours returned ");
document.write(theDate.setHours(7)," milliseconds.")
document.write("<br>Final milliseconds=",theDate.getTime());

// -->
</script>
```

Date.setMilliseconds()

JavaScript 1.2+, ECMAScript 1E+, JScript 3.0+
Nav4+, IE 4+, Opera5+

Syntax

*date.*setMilliseconds(*milliseconds*)

Description

The setMilliseconds() method sets the milliseconds in the Date object to the argument milliseconds, an integer from 0 to 999. The method returns an integer representing the number of milliseconds between midnight January 1, 1970 (GMT) to the date and time specified in the Date object after the milliseconds have been adjusted.

Example

Listing 7.120 displays the current date in milliseconds before setting the milliseconds to 792. Notice that the milliseconds specified after the setMilliseconds() method are the same as the result returned from the method.

Listing 7.120 *Setting the Milliseconds with the* setMilliseconds()
Method

```
<script type="text/javascript" language="JavaScript">
<!--

//Create a Date object.
theDate = new Date();

//Set the milliseconds.
document.write("Initial milliseconds=",theDate.getTime());
document.write("<br>setMilliseconds returned ");
document.write(theDate.setMilliseconds(792)," milliseconds.")
document.write("<br>Final milliseconds=",theDate.getTime());

// -->
</script>
```

Date.setMinutes()

JavaScript 1.0+, ECMAScript 1E+, JScript 1.0+
Nav2+, NES2+, IE 3+, Opera3+

Syntax

*date.*setMinutes (*minutes*)

Description

The setMinutes() method sets the minutes in the Date object to the argument minutes, an integer from 0 to 59. The method returns an integer representing the number of milliseconds between midnight January 1, 1970 (GMT) to the date and time specified in the Date object after the minutes have been adjusted.

Example

The code in Listing 7.121 displays the current date in milliseconds before setting the minutes to 43. Notice that the milliseconds specified after the setMinutes() method are the same as the result returned from the method.

Listing 7.121 Setting the Minutes with the* setMinutes() *Method

```
<script type="text/javascript" language="JavaScript">
<!--

//Create a Date object.
theDate = new Date();

//Set the minutes and display the milliseconds.
document.write("Initial milliseconds=",theDate.getTime());
document.write("<br>setMinutes returned ");
document.write(theDate.setMinutes(43)," milliseconds.")
document.write("<br>Final milliseconds=",theDate.getTime());

// -->
</script>
```

Date.setMonth()

JavaScript 1.0+, ECMAScript 1E+, JScript 1.0+
Nav2+, NES2+, IE 3+, Opera3+

Syntax

date.setMonth (*month*)

Description

The setMonth() method sets the month in the Date object to the argument month, an integer from 0 (January) to 11 (December). The method returns an integer representing the number of milliseconds between midnight January 1, 1970 (GMT) to the date and time specified in the Date object after the month has been adjusted.

CAUTION

Prior to JavaScript 1.2, this method returned nothing.

Example

The code in Listing 7.122 displays the current date in milliseconds before setting the month to 2 (March). Notice that the milliseconds specified after the setMonth() method are the same as the result returned from the method.

Listing 7.122   Setting the Month with the setMonth() *Method*

```
<script type="text/javascript" language="JavaScript">
<!--

//Create a Date object.
theDate = new Date();

//Set the month and display the milliseconds.
document.write("Initial milliseconds=",theDate.getTime());
document.write("<br>setMonth returned ");
document.write(theDate.setMonth(2)," milliseconds.")
document.write("<br>Final milliseconds=",theDate.getTime());

// -->
</script>
```

Date.setSeconds()

JavaScript 1.0+, ECMAScript 1E+, JScript 1.0+
Nav2+, NES2+, IE 3+, Opera3+

Syntax

*date.*setSeconds(*seconds*)

Description

The setSeconds() method sets the seconds in the Date object to the argument seconds, an integer from 0 to 59. The method returns an integer representing the number of milliseconds between midnight January 1, 1970 (GMT) to the date and time specified in the Date object after the seconds have been adjusted.

CAUTION

Prior to JavaScript 1.2, this method returned nothing.

Example

The code in Listing 7.123 displays the current date in milliseconds before setting the seconds to 16. Notice that the milliseconds specified after the setSeconds() method are the same as the result returned from the method.

Listing 7.123   Setting the Seconds with the setSeconds() *Method*

```
<script type="text/javascript" language="JavaScript">
<!--

//Create a Date object.
theDate = new Date();
```

Listing 7.123 Continued

```
//Set the seconds and display the milliseconds.
document.write("Initial milliseconds=",theDate.getTime());
document.write("<br>setSeconds returned ");
document.write(theDate.setSeconds(16)," milliseconds.")
document.write("<br>Final milliseconds=",theDate.getTime());

// -->
</script>
```

Date.setTime()

JavaScript 1.0+, ECMAScript 1E+, JScript 1.0+
Nav2+, NES2+, IE 3+, Opera3+

Syntax

```
date.setTime (milliseconds)
```

Description

The setTime() method sets the time in the Date object to the argument milliseconds, an integer representing the number of milliseconds between midnight January 1, 1970 (GMT) to the desired date and time.

Example

The code in Listing 7.124 uses the setTime() method to set the date to November, 17, 2005 using milliseconds.

Listing 7.124 Setting the Date with the setTime() Method

```
<script type="text/javascript" language="JavaScript">
<!--

//Create a Date object.
theDate = new Date();

//Set the date to Nov. 17, 2005.
theDate.setTime(1132203600000);

//Display the date.
document.write(theDate.toString());

// -->
</script>
```

Date.setUTCDate()

JavaScript 1.2+, ECMAScript 1E+, JScript 3.0+
Nav4+, IE 4+, Opera5+

Syntax

date.setUTCDate(*day*)

Description

The setUTCDate() method sets the day of the month in the Date object to the argument day, an integer from 1 to 31 (universal time). The method returns an integer representing the number of milliseconds between midnight January 1, 1970 (GMT) to the date and time specified in the Date object after the day of the month has been adjusted.

Example

The code in Listing 7.125 displays the current date in milliseconds (universal time) before setting the day to 6. Notice that the milliseconds specified after the setUTCDate() method are the same as the result returned from the method.

Listing 7.125   Setting the Date with the setUTCDate() *Method*

```
<script type="text/javascript" language="JavaScript">
<!--

//Create a Date object.
theDate = new Date();

//Set the day of the month and display the milliseconds.
document.write("Initial milliseconds=",theDate.getTime());
document.write("<br>setUTCDate returned ");
document.write(theDate.setUTCDate(6)," milliseconds.")
document.write("<br>Final milliseconds=",theDate.getTime());

// -->
</script>
```

Date.setUTCFullYear()

JavaScript 1.2+, ECMAScript 1E+, JScript 3.0+
Nav4+, IE 4+, Opera5+

Syntax

date.setUTCFullYear(*year*)

Description

The setUTCFullYear() method sets the year in the Date object to the argument year, a four-digit integer (universal time). The method returns an integer representing the number of milliseconds between midnight January 1, 1970 (GMT) to the date and time specified in the Date object after the year has been adjusted.

Example

The code in Listing 7.126 displays the current date in milliseconds (universal time) before setting the year to 2004. Notice that the milliseconds specified after the setUTCFullYear() method are the same as the result returned from the method.

Listing 7.126   Setting the Year with the setUTCFullYear() Method

```
<script type="text/javascript" language="JavaScript">
<!--

//Create a Date object.
theDate = new Date();

//Set the year and display the milliseconds.
document.write("Initial milliseconds=",theDate.getTime());
document.write("<br>setUTCFullYear returned ");
document.write(theDate.setUTCFullYear(2004)," milliseconds.")
document.write("<br>Final milliseconds=",theDate.getTime());

// -->
</script>
```

Date.setUTCHours()

> JavaScript 1.2+, ECMAScript 1E+, JScript 3.0+
> Nav4+, IE 4+, Opera5+

Syntax

date.setUTCHours(*hours*)

Description

The setUTCHours() method sets the hour in the Date object to the argument hours, an integer from 0 (12:00 a.m. midnight) to 23 (11:00 p.m.) universal time. The method returns an integer representing the number of milliseconds between midnight January 1, 1970 (GMT) to the date and time specified in the Date object after the hour has been adjusted.

Example

The code in Listing 7.127 displays the current date in milliseconds (universal time) before setting the hour to 5 (5:00 a.m.). Notice that the milliseconds specified after the setUTCHours() method are the same as the result returned from the method.

Listing 7.127   Setting the Hour with the setUTCHours() Method

```
<script type="text/javascript" language="JavaScript">
<!--

//Create a Date object.
theDate = new Date();
```

```
//Set the hour and display the milliseconds.
document.write("Initial milliseconds=",theDate.getTime());
document.write("<br>setUTCHours returned ");
document.write(theDate.setUTCHours(5)," milliseconds.")
document.write("<br>Final milliseconds=",theDate.getTime());

// -->
</script>
```

Date.setUTCMilliseconds()

JavaScript 1.2+, ECMAScript 1E+, JScript 3.0+
Nav4+, IE 4+, Opera5+

Syntax

date.setUTCMilliseconds(*milliseconds*)

Description

The setUTCMilliseconds() method sets the milliseconds in the Date object to the argument milliseconds, an integer from 0 to 999 (universal time). The method returns an integer representing the number of milliseconds between midnight January 1, 1970 (GMT) to the date and time specified in the Date object after the milliseconds have been adjusted.

Example

The code in Listing 7.128 displays the current date in milliseconds (universal time) before setting the milliseconds to 258. Notice that the milliseconds specified after the setUTCMilliseconds() method are the same as the result returned from the method.

Listing 7.128   Setting the Milliseconds with the setUTCMilliseconds() *Method*

```
<script type="text/javascript" language="JavaScript">
<!--

//Create a Date object.
theDate = new Date();

//Set the milliseconds.
document.write("Initial milliseconds=",theDate.getTime());
document.write("<br>setUTCMilliseconds returned ");
document.write(theDate.setUTCMilliseconds(258)," milliseconds.")
document.write("<br>Final milliseconds=",theDate.getTime());

// -->
</script>
```

Date.setUTCMinutes()

JavaScript 1.2+, ECMAScript 1E+, JScript 3.0+
Nav4+, IE 4+, Opera5+

Syntax

date.setUTCMinutes(*minutes*)

Description

The setUTCMinutes() method sets the minutes in the Date object to the argument minutes, an integer from 0 to 59 (universal time). The method returns an integer representing the number of milliseconds between midnight January 1, 1970 (GMT) to the date and time specified in the Date object after the minutes have been adjusted.

Example

The code in Listing 7.129 displays the current date in milliseconds (universal time) before setting the minutes to 19. Notice that the milliseconds specified after the setUTCMinutes() method are the same as the result returned from the method.

Listing 7.129   *Setting the Minutes with the* setUTCMinutes() *Method*

```
<script type="text/javascript" language="JavaScript">
<!--

//Create a Date object.
theDate = new Date();

//Set the minutes and display the milliseconds.
document.write("Initial milliseconds=",theDate.getTime());
document.write("<br>setUTCMinutes returned ");
document.write(theDate.setUTCMinutes(19)," milliseconds.")
document.write("<br>Final milliseconds=",theDate.getTime());

// -->
</script>
```

Date.setUTCMonth()

JavaScript 1.2+, ECMAScript 1E+, JScript 3.0+
Nav4+, IE 4+, Opera5+

Syntax

date.setUTCMonth(*month*)

Description

The setUTCMonth() method sets the month in the Date object to the argument month, an integer from 0 (January) to 11 (December) universal time. The method returns an integer representing the number of milliseconds between midnight January 1, 1970 (GMT) to the date and time specified in the Date object after the month has been adjusted.

Example

The code in Listing 7.130 displays the current date in milliseconds (universal time) before setting the month to 4 (May). Notice that the milliseconds specified after the setUTCMonth() method are the same as the result returned from the method.

Listing 7.130   Setting the Month with the setUTCMonth() ***Method***

```
<script type="text/javascript" language="JavaScript">
<!--

//Create a Date object.
theDate = new Date();

//Set the month and display the milliseconds.
document.write("Initial milliseconds=",theDate.getTime());
document.write("<br>setUTCMonth returned ");
document.write(theDate.setUTCMonth(4)," milliseconds.")
document.write("<br>Final milliseconds=",theDate.getTime());

// -->
</script>
```

Date.setUTCSeconds()

JavaScript 1.2+, ECMAScript 1E+, JScript 3.0+
Nav4+, IE 4+, Opera5+

Syntax

date.setUTCSeconds(*seconds*)

Description

The setUTCSeconds() method sets the seconds in the Date object to the argument seconds, an integer from 0 to 59 (universal time). The method returns an integer representing the number of milliseconds between midnight January 1, 1970 (GMT) to the date and time specified in the Date object after the seconds have been adjusted.

Example

The code in Listing 7.131 displays the current date in milliseconds (universal time) before setting the seconds to 46. Notice that the milliseconds specified after the setUTCSeconds() method are the same as the result returned from the method.

Listing 7.131   Setting the Seconds with the setUTCSeconds() *Method*

```
<script type="text/javascript" language="JavaScript">
<!--

//Create a Date object.
theDate = new Date();

//Set the seconds and display the milliseconds.
document.write("Initial milliseconds=",theDate.getTime());
document.write("<br>setUTCSeconds returned ");
document.write(theDate.setUTCSeconds(46)," milliseconds.")
document.write("<br>Final milliseconds=",theDate.getTime());

// -->
</script>
```

Date.setYear()

JavaScript 1.0+, ECMAScript 1E+, JScript 1.0+
Nav2+, NES2+, IE 3+, Opera3+

Syntax

date.setYear(*year*)

Description

The setYear() method sets the year in the Date object to the argument year. The argument can be either a four-digit or two-digit integer. To create a two-digit representation, subtract 1900 from the desired date. So if "92" was passed in as an argument then the year 1992 would be set. The method returns an integer representing the number of milliseconds between midnight January 1, 1970 (GMT) to the date and time specified in the Date object after the year has been adjusted.

NOTE

The getYear() method is obsolete. The setFullYear() method should be used instead of setYear().

CAUTION

Prior to JavaScript 1.2, this method returned nothing.

Example

The code in Listing 7.132 displays the current date in milliseconds before setting the year to 1983. Notice that the milliseconds specified after the setYear() method are the same as the result returned from the method.

Listing 7.132   Setting the Year with the setYear() **Method**

```
<script type="text/javascript" language="JavaScript">
<!--

//Create a Date object.
theDate = new Date();

//Set the year and display the milliseconds.
document.write("Initial milliseconds=",theDate.getTime());
document.write("<br>setYear returned ");
document.write(theDate.setYear(83)," milliseconds.")
document.write("<br>Final milliseconds=",theDate.getTime());

// -->
</script>
```

Date.toGMTString()

JavaScript 1.0+, ECMAScript 1E+, JScript 1.0+
Nav2+, NES2+, IE 3+, Opera3+

Syntax

date.toGMTString()

Description

The toGMTString() method returns a string representing the universal time of the Date object. The date is converted to the GMT time zone before being converted to a string. The format of the string will look similar to the following:

```
Mon, 24 Oct 1982 12:03:27 GMT
```

Example

The code in listing 7.133 creates a Date object that contains the current date and time. The toGMTString() method returns the date as a string in GMT.

Listing 7.133   Converting Date and Time to GMT with the toGMTString() **Method**

```
<script type="text/javascript" language="JavaScript">
<!--

//Create a Date object.
theDate = new Date();

//Display date and time string in GMT.
document.write(theDate.toGMTString());

// -->
</script>
```

Date.toLocaleString()

JavaScript 1.0+, ECMAScript 1E+, JScript 1.0+
Nav2+, IE 3+, Opera5+

Syntax

date.toLocaleString()

Description

The toLocaleString() method returns a string representation of the Date object in the local time zone. The format of the string can vary greatly, depending on the user's date and time format settings.

Example

The code in Listing 7.134 creates a Date object that contains the current date and time. The toLocaleString() method returns the date and time as a string using the local time zone.

Listing 7.134   Converting Date and Time to the Local Time Zone with the toLocaleString() **Method**

```
<script type="text/javascript" language="JavaScript">
<!--

//Create a Date object.
theDate = new Date();

//Display date and time string.
document.write(theDate.toLocaleString());

// -->
</script>
```

Date.toSource()

JavaScript1.3, JScript3.0
Nav4.06+, IE4

Syntax

date.toSource()

Description

The toSource() method converts the Date object to a string that represents the source of the Date instance that was created.

> **NOTE**
>
> The `toSource()` method is usually called internally by JavaScript and not explicitly in code.

Example

Listing 7.135 creates a date object March 16, 2002. The `toSource()` method is then applied to the date object to return the source string `"(new Date(1018986503234))"` with the date expressed in milliseconds.

Listing 7.135   Accessing the Source of a Date **Object with the** toSource() **Method**

```
<script type="text/javascript1.3" language="JavaScript1.3">
<!--

//Create a Date object for April 16, 2002.
theDate = new Date(2002,3,16,15,48,23,234);


//Display "Tue Apr 16 15:48:23 GMT-0400 (Eastern Daylight Time) 2002".
document.write(theDate.toString());

//Display source of date object.
document.write(theDate.toSource());  //Display "(new Date(1018986503234))".

// -->
</script>
```

Date.toString()

JavaScript 1.0+, ECMAScript 1E+, JScript 1.0+
Nav2+, NES2+, IE 3+, Opera5+

Syntax

date.toString()

Description

The `toString()` method returns a string representation of the Date object in the local time zone.

> **NOTE**
>
> How does the `toString()` method differ from `toGMTString()` and `toLocaleString()`? Unlike the `toGMTString()` method, the `toString()` method

displays the date in the local time zone. The `toString()` does not always display the date in the local format of the `toLocaleString()` method.

Example

The code in Listing 7.136 creates a `Date` object from the current date and time. The `toString()` method is then used to display the date as a string in the local time zone.

Listing 7.136   Accessing Date as a String with the `toString()` Method

```
<script type="text/javascript" language="JavaScript">
<!--

//Create a Date object.
theDate = new Date();

//Display date and time string.
document.write(theDate.toString());

// -->
</script>
```

Date.toUTCString()

JavaScript 1.2+, ECMAScript 1E+, JScript 3.0+
Nav4+, IE 4+, Opera3+

Syntax

`date.toUTCString()`

Description

The `toUTCString()` method returns a string representing the universal time of the `Date` object. The date is converted to the GMT time zone before being converted to a string. This method is exactly the same as the `toGMTString()`.

Example

The code in Listing 7.137 creates a `Date` object and initializes it to the current date and time. The `toUTCString()` method is then used to display the current date and time as a string in universal time.

Listing 7.137   Accessing Date in Universal Time with the `toUTCString()` Method

```
<script type="text/javascript" language="JavaScript">
<!--

//Create a Date object.
theDate = new Date();
```

```
//Display date and time string in universal time.
document.write(theDate.toUTCString());

// -->
</script>
```

Date.unwatch()

JavaScript 1.2+

Nav4+, NES3+

Syntax

*Date.*unwatch(*property*)

Description

The unwatch() method of the Date object is used to turn off the watch on a particular property specified by *property*.

Example

Listing 7.138 shows how the unwatch() method is used to stop watching the user-defined property p.

Listing 7.138 **Example of** unwatch() **Method of the** Date **Object**

```
<script type="text/javascript" language="JavaScript">
<!--
function alertme(id,oldValue,newValue)
{
  document.writeln("myDate." + id + " changed from " + oldValue + " to ");
  document.writeln(newValue + "<br>");
  return newValue;
}

var myDate = new Date();
Date.prototype.p = 1;
myDate.watch("p",alertme);

myDate.p = 2;
myDate.unwatch("p");
myDate.p = 3;
myDate.watch("p",alertme);
myDate.p = 4;
// -->
</script>
```

Date.UTC()

JavaScript 1.0+, ECMAScript 1E+, JScript 1.0+
Nav2+, NES2+, IE 3+, Opera3+

Syntax

Date.UTC(*year*, *month*, *day*, *hours*, *minutes*, *seconds*, *milliseconds*)

Description

Because the Date constructor creates new dates in local time, the UTC() method is provided to create dates in universal time (GMT). The method accepts arguments to allow
you to set all aspects of a date and time, from the year to milliseconds. An integer, representing the number of milliseconds between midnight January 1, 1970 (GMT) to the
date and time specified, is returned from the method. The integer can then be used to
create a new Date object. The arguments and return value are in Table 7.26.

CAUTION

The milliseconds returned from the method are incorrect in Navigator 2.

Table 7.26   Arguments and Return Value Associated with UTC()

Type	Item	Description
Argument	year	A four-digit representation of the year.
	month	The month represented as an integer where 0 repre-sents January and 11 represents December.
	day	The day of the month represented as an integer from 1 to 31. Optional argument.
	hours	The hour represented as an integer where 0 repre-sents 12 a.m. (midnight) and 23 represents 11 p.m. Optional argument.
	minutes	The minutes in the hour represented as an integer from 0 to 59. Optional argument.
	seconds	The seconds in the minute represented as an inte-ger from 0 to 59. Optional argument.
	milliseconds	The milliseconds in the second represented as an integer from 0 to 999. Optional argument.
Returns		An integer, representing the number of milliseconds between midnight January 1, 1970 (GMT) to the date and time specified, is returned from the method.

Example

The code in Listing 7.139 creates a new Date object initialized to September 29, 2002
(universal time). The newly created date and time are then displayed in the browser.

Listing 7.139   Creating a Date in Universal Time with the UTC() *Method*

```
<script type="text/javascript" language="JavaScript">
<!--

//Create a Date object in universal time.
theDate = new Date(Date.UTC(2002,9,29,20,5,8,10));

//Display date and time string.
document.write(theDate.toUTCString());

// -->
</script>
```

Date.valueOf()

JavaScript1.1+, ECMAScript 1E+, JScript3.0+
Nav3+, NES2+, IE4+, Opera3+

Syntax

date.valueOf()

Description

The valueOf() method returns the primitive value of the object. In terms of an instance of a Date object, this method returns the equivalence of the Date object in milliseconds. The milliseconds are expressed as an integer representing the number of milliseconds between midnight January 1, 1970 (GMT) to the date and time specified in the Date object.

Example

Listing 7.140 creates a Date object representing the current date and time. The result of the valueOf() method on this date object is displayed in the browser.

Listing 7.140   Using the valueOf() *Method to Return the Value of the* Date *Object*

```
<script type="text/javascript" language="JavaScript">
<!--

//Create a Date object.
theDate = new Date();

//Display the source of the Dateobject.
document.write(theDate.valueOf());

// -->
</script>
```

Date.watch

JavaScript 1.2+
Nav4+, NES3+

Syntax

```
Date.watch (property,function)
```

Description

The watch() method of the Date object is used to turn on the watch on a particular property specified by *property*. Any time the specified property is changed after the watch() method has been called, the specified function is called.

Example

Listing 7.141 shows how the watch() method is used to start watching the user-defined property p.

Listing 7.141   Example of the watch() Method of the Date Object

```
<script type="text/javascript" language="JavaScript">
<!--
function alertme(id,oldValue,newValue)
{
  document.writeln("myDate." + id + " changed from " + oldValue + " to ");
  document.writeln(newValue + "<br>");
  return newValue;
}

var myDate = new Date();
Date.prototype.p = 1;
myDate.watch("p",alertme);

myDate.p = 2;
// -->
</script>
```

debugger

JavaScript 1.2+, JScript 3.0+
Nav4+, NES3+, IE4+, Opera5+

Syntax

```
Reserved Keyword
```

Description

The keyword debugger is reserved for future use.

Example

This keyword has not been implemented; therefore no example is provided.

decodeURI()

    JavaScript 1.5+, ECMAScript 3E+, JScript 5.5+
    Nav6+, NES6+, IE5.5+

Syntax

```
decodeURI (URIString)
```

Description

The decodeURI() function is used to replace each escape sequence in the *URIString* (uniform resource identifiers) with the character that it represents based on the UTF-8 standard. The function returns the decoded string.

NOTE

Escape sequences that do not get encoded by the encodeURI() function (,, /, ?, :, @, &, =, +, $) cannot be decoded using the decodeURI() function. To decode these reserved characters, use the decodeURIComponent() function.

Example

In Listing 7.142 the string "The apple is red." is encoded using the encodeURI() function. The result is the same string, but with the spaces replaced with "%20", the encoded equivalent. This encoded URI string is then decoded back to its original form using the decodeURI() function.

Listing 7.142   Using the* decodeURI() *Function

```
<script type="text/javascript" language='JavaScript'>
<!--

myString="The apple is red";
document.write("The original sentence: " + myString + "<br><br>");

myString = encodeURI(myString);
document.write("The encoded sentence: " + myString + "<br><br>");

myString = decodeURI(myString);
document.write("The decoded sentence: " + myString + "<br><br>");

// -->
</script>
```

decodeURIComponent()

JavaScript 1.5+, ECMAScript 3E+, JScript 5.5+
Nav6+, NES6+, IE5.5+

Syntax

decodeURIComponent(*URIComponentString*)

Description

The decodeURIComponent() function is used to replace each escape sequence in the *URIComponentString* (uniform resource identifiers) with the character that it represents based on the UTF-8 standard. The function returns the decoded string.

NOTE

The decodeURIComponent() function differs from the decodeURI() function in that it decodes some reserved characters (,, /, ?, :, @, &, =, +, $) that are not decoded by the decodeURI() function. For this reason, the decodeURIComponent method is designed to only decode URI strings that were originally encoded using the encodeURIComponent() function.

Example

In Listing 7.143 the phrase "fork, spoon, & knife" is encoded using the encodeURIComponent() function. The result is the same string but with the spaces, commas, and '&' characters encoded. This encoded URI component string is then decoded using the decodeURI() function. But notice that this function only decodes the spaces. In order to decode the commas and '&' character, the decodeURIComponent() function must be used.

Listing 7.143   *Using the* decodeURIComponent() *Function*

```
<script type="text/javascript" language='JavaScript'>
<!--

myString="fork, spoon, & knife";
document.write("The original phrase: " + myString + "<br><br>");

myString = encodeURIComponent(myString);
document.write("The encoded phrase: " + myString + "<br><br>");

myString = decodeURI(myString);
document.write("The decoded phrase: " + myString + "<br><br>");

myString = decodeURIComponent(myString);
document.write("The decoded component phrase: " + myString + "<br><br>");
```

```
// -->
</script>
```

default
JavaScript1.2+, JScript3.0+
Nav4+, NES3+, IE4+, Opera5+

Syntax
```
Reserved Keyword
```

Description
The `default` keyword has not been implemented in JavaScript to date, but has been reserved for future use.

Example
This keyword has not been implemented; therefore no example is provided.

delete
JavaScript 1.0+, ECMAScript 1E+, JScript 3.0+
Nav2+, NES3+, IE 4+, Opera3+

Syntax
```
delete property
```

Description
The `delete` operator deletes properties from objects and array elements from arrays by making them undefined. Actual memory deallocation is done by JavaScript garbage collection. Some objects, such as variables created by the `var` statement, are not affected by the `delete` operator.

CAUTION
Prior to JavaScript 1.2, the `delete` operator set the object property to `null` rather than `undefined`.

Example
The code in Listing 7.144 demonstrates how to use the `delete` operator to delete a `Date` object. Notice that the last `document.write()` statement does not write anything to the browser because `theDate` is undefined after using the `delete` operator.

Listing 7.144   *Using the* `delete` *Operator*
```
<script type="text/javascript" language="JavaScript">
<!--
```

Listing 7.144   Continued

```
//Create a Date object in universal time.
theDate = new Date();

//Display the date object.
document.write("theDate=",theDate,"<br>Deleting theDate!<br>");

//Delete theDate.
delete theDate;

//Attempt to display theDate.
document.write("theDate=",theDate);    //theDate is undefined.

// -->
</script>
```

do

ECMAScript 3.0+, ECMAScript 2E+, JScript 5.5+
Nav4+, NES3+, IE 5.5+, Opera5+

Syntax

```
Reserved Keyword
```

Description

The do keyword is utilized in the do...while loop structure, thus it cannot be used as a variable name.

Example

This keyword is reserved. See the do...while entry for more information on its use.

do...while

JavaScript 1.0+ , ECMAScript 1E+, JScript 3.0+
Nav2+, NES3+, IE 4+, Opera 3+

Syntax

```
do{
  statement;
}while(expression);
```

Description

The do...while loop always executes the loop once before evaluating the expression for the first time. Once the loop has executed for the first time, the expression, in parenthesis, is evaluated. If true, the loop is executed again. When the expression evaluates to `false`, the next line of code following the `while` structure is executed. A statement must be included in the loop that modifies a variable in the expression to prevent an infinite loop. Also, notice that a semicolon (`;`) must be placed after the right parenthesis.

Example

Listing 7.145 uses the `do...while` loop to control access through a gate. Only three individuals are allowed through the gate.

Listing 7.145   The `do...while` Loop

```
<script type="text/javascript" language="JavaScript">
<!--

names = new Array("Mendy","Michael","Jeff","Bill","Mike");
x = 0; //array counter

document.write("Allow these 3 individuals through gate:<br>");

//Print names of the first 3 individuals who can pass through gate.
do
{
  document.write((x+1),". ",names[x],"<br>");
  x++;   //increment counter
}
while(x<3);

// -->
</script>
```

double

JavaScript1.2+, ECMAScript 2E+, JScript 5.0+
Nav4+, NES3+, IE5+, Opera5+

Syntax

Reserved Keyword

Description

The `double` keyword has not been implemented in server-side JavaScript to date, but has been reserved for future use.

Example

This keyword has not been implemented; therefore no example is provided.

else

JavaScript 1.0+, JScript 1.0+, ECMAScript 1E+
Nav2+, IE3+

Syntax

Reserved Keyword

Description

The `else` statement is used to perform alternative logic should the corresponding `if` statement not evaluate to `true`.

Example

Listing 7.146 shows an example of the basic logic to the `else` statement. If the `if` condition does not equate to `true`, the `else` statement is executed.

Listing 7.146   Example of the `else` Keyword

```
if (something == true)
{
  // Do something.
}
else{
  // Do something else.
}
```

encodeURI()

JavaScript 1.5+, ECMAScript 3E+, JScript 5.5+
Nav6+, NES6+, IE5.5+

Syntax

encodeURI (*URIString*)

Description

The `encodeURI()` function is used to encode a *URI (uniform resource identifier)* by replacing specific characters with escape sequences representing UTF-8 encoding.

NOTE

Certain characters will not be encoded with the `encodeURI()` function. They are shown in Table 7.27.

Table 7.27   Unencoded Characters

Type	Character
Reserved characters	,, /, ?, :, @, &, =, +, $
unescaped characters	alphabetic, decimal, -, ., !, ~, *, ', (,)
score	#

Example

In Listing 7.147, the string "The apple is red." is encoded using the encodeURI() function. The result is the same string, but with the spaces replaced with "%20", which is the encoded equivalent.

Listing 7.147 *Using the* encodeURI() *Function*

```
<html>
<script type="text/javascript" language='JavaScript'>
<!--

myString="The apple is red";
document.write("The original sentence: " + myString + "<br><br>");

myString = encodeURI(myString);
document.write("The encoded sentence: " + myString + "<br><br>");

// -->
</script>
</html>
```

encodeURIComponent()

JavaScript 1.5+, ECMAScript 3E+, JScript 5.5+
Nav6+, NES6+, IE5.5+

Syntax

encodeURIComponent (*URIComponentString*)

Description

The encodeURIComponent() function is used to replace certain characters in the *URIComponentString* (uniform resource identifier) with escape sequences representing its UTF-8 character encoding. This function assumes a URI component, and therefore will encode reserved characters.

NOTE

Certain characters will not be encoded with the encodeURIComponent() function. They are shown in Table 7.28.

Table 7.28 *Unencoded Characters*

Type	Character
unescaped characters	alphabetic, decimal, -, ., !, ~, *, ', (,)
score	#

Example

In Listing 7.148, the phrase `"fork, spoon, & knife"` is encoded using the `encodeURIComponent()` function. The result is the same string, but with the spaces, commas, and & characters encoded.

Listing 7.148   Using the `encodeURIComponent()` *Function*

```
<html>
<script type="text/javascript" language='JavaScript'>
<!--

// Create a string object.
myString="fork, spoon, & knife";
document.write("The original phrase: " + myString + "<br><br>");

// URI Encode the string and display.
myString = encodeURIComponent(myString);
document.write("The encoded phrase: " + myString + "<br><br>");

// -->
</script>
</html>
```

enum

> JavaScript 1.3+, ECMAScript 1E+, JScript 3.0+
> Nav4.06+, IE4+

Syntax

```
Reserved Keyword
```

Description

The enum keyword is initially introduced in JavaScript 1.3 and is reserved for future use.

Example

This entry has not yet been implemented in the JavaScript language, and no example is provided.

Enumerator

> JScript3.0+
> IE4+

Syntax

```
var variable = new Enumerator(collection)
```

Description

The Enumerator object provides access to items in a collection by allowing iteration through a collection. Accessing items in a collection requires moving the Enumerator object to the first element or the next element using special methods. Unlike arrays, enumerators cannot access a specific position. To create an Enumerator object, use the Enumerator() constructor. This constructor requires that a collection be passed in as an argument. The methods associated with the Enumerator object are listed in Table 7.29.

Table 7.29 *Methods Associated with the* Enumerator *Object*

Method	Description
atEnd()	Determines whether Enumerator is at the end of the collection
item()	Returns the current item in the collection
moveFirst()	Resets the Enumerator to the first item in the collection
moveNext()	Moves Enumerator to the next item in the collection

Example

Listing 7.149 creates an Enumerator object for accessing items in the Drives collection.

Listing 7.149 *Creating an* Enumerator *Object*

```
var fileSysObj = new ActiveXObject("Scripting.FileSystemObject");
var en = new Enumerator(fileSysObj.Drives);
```

Enumerator.atEnd()

JScript 3.0+
IE4+

Syntax

enumeratorobj.atEnd()

Description

The atEnd() method of the Enumerator object returns true if the enumerator is pointing to the last element in the collection; otherwise, it returns false. true is also returned if the collection is empty or undefined.

Example

The atEnd() method is used in Listing 7.150 to determine when to stop looping through the for loop.

Listing 7.150   Stop Looping with the atEnd() Method

```
<html>

<h1>Drive Letters and drive types:</h1>

<script language="JScript">
<!--

// Create enumerator object.
var fileSysObj = new ActiveXObject("Scripting.FileSystemObject");
var en = new Enumerator(fileSysObj.Drives);

// Display drive letter and type for each drive.
// Loop on each Enumerator object. While not at the end of
// Enumeration, continue looping on the next item.
for (;!en.atEnd();en.moveNext())
{
  document.write("Drive ",en.item().DriveLetter);
  document.write(" is of type ",en.item().DriveType,"<br>");
}

// -->
</script>
</html>
```

Enumerator.item()

> JScript 3.0+
> IE4+

Syntax

enumeratorobj.item()

Description

The item() method of the Enumerator object returns the element to which the enumerator is pointing in the collection. If the collection is empty or undefined, undefined is returned.

Example

The item() method is used in Listing 7.151 to access the drive letter and drive type of the current drive.

Listing 7.151   Accessing Drives with the item() Method

```
<html>

<h1>Drive Letters and drive types:</h1>
```

```
<script language="JScript">
<!--

// Create enumerator object.
var fileSysObj = new ActiveXObject("Scripting.FileSystemObject");
var en = new Enumerator(fileSysObj.Drives);

// Display drive letter and type for each drive.
for (;!en.atEnd();en.moveNext())
{
  document.write("Drive ",en.item().DriveLetter);
  document.write(" is of type ",en.item().DriveType,"<br>");
}

// -->
</script>
</html>
```

Enumerator.moveFirst()

JScript 3.0+
IE4+

Syntax

enumeratorobj.moveFirst()

Description

The moveFirst() method of the Enumerator object moves the enumerator to the beginning of the collection. If the collection is empty or undefined, undefined is returned.

Example

In Listing 7.152, the enumerator is used to access the drive letters and types. The moveFirst() method moves the enumerator back to the beginning of the collection so that the drive status can be determined for each drive.

Listing 7.152   Moving the Enumerator to the Beginning of the Collection Using the moveFirst() Method

```
<html>

<h1>Drive Letters and drive types:</h1>

<script language="JScript">
<!--

// Create enumerator object.
var fileSysObj = new ActiveXObject("Scripting.FileSystemObject");
var en = new Enumerator(fileSysObj.Drives);
```

Listing 7.152   Continued

```
// Display drive letter and type for each drive.
for (;!en.atEnd();en.moveNext())
{
  document.write("Drive ",en.item().DriveLetter);
  document.write(" is of type ",en.item().DriveType,"<br>");
}

document.write("<h1>Drive Status:</h1>");

// Move enumerator to the beginning of the collection.
en.moveFirst();

// Determine if drive is ready.
for (;!en.atEnd();en.moveNext())
{
  if(en.item().IsReady)
  {
    document.write("Drive ",en.item().DriveLetter);
    document.write(" is ready!<br>");
  }
  else
  {
    document.write("Drive ",en.item().DriveLetter);
    document.write(" is not ready!<br>");
  }
}

// -->
</script>
</html>
```

Enumerator.moveNext()

> JScript 3.0+
>
> IE4+

Syntax

`enumeratorobj.moveNext()`

Description

The `moveNext()` method of the `Enumerator` object moves the enumerator to the next item in the collection. If the collection is empty, `undefined` is returned.

Example

The `moveNext()` method is used in Listing 7.153 to move the enumerator to the next drive in the collection.

Listing 7.153 *Move to the Next Drive Using* moveNext()

```
<html>

<h1>Drive Letters and drive types:</h1>

<script language="JScript">
<!--

// Create enumerator object.
var fileSysObj = new ActiveXObject("Scripting.FileSystemObject");
var en = new Enumerator(fileSysObj.Drives);

// Display drive letter and type for each drive.
for (;!en.atEnd();en.moveNext())
{
  document.write("Drive ",en.item().DriveLetter);
  document.write(" is of type ",en.item().DriveType,"<br>");
}

// -->
</script>
</html>
```

Error

JScript 5.0+
IE5+

Syntax

```
var variable = new Error();
var variable = new Error(num);
var variable = new Error(num, description);
```

Description

The Error object contains information about errors. The Error() constructors can be used to create custom error messages. The arguments and properties associated with the Error object are listed in Table 7.30.

Table 7.30 *Arguments and Properties Associated with the* Error *Object*

Type	Item	Description
Argument	number	A number assigned to an error—Zero, if no number is provided in the constructor.
	description	A string that describes the error—empty string, if no string is provided in the constructor.
Property	description	Sets or returns the description string associated with a specific error.

Table 7.30 Continued

Type	Item	Description
	message	A string that contains the error message.
	name	Returns a string containing the name of the error.
	number	Sets or returns the number associated with a specific error.

NOTE

An error number is a 32-bit value where the upper 16-bit word is the facility code and the lower word is the actual error code. The facility code refers to the component that caused the error.

Example

Listing 7.154 creates an Error object.

Listing 7.154   Creating an Error Object

```
var myError = Error(35,"My Error");
```

Error.description

JScript 5.0+
IE5+

Syntax

```
errorobj.description
errorobj.description = string
```

Description

The description property associated with the Error object contains the description of the error. This method is read/write so that you can assign descriptions using this property.

Example

Listing 7.155 creates an Error object and then displays the description.

Listing 7.155   Display description property of an Error

```
<html>

<script language="JScript">
<!--

// Create an Error object.
var myError = new Error(45,"A really big error!");
```

```
// Display description associated with the custom error.
document.write("The custom error description is '");
document.write(myError.description,"'");

// -->
</script>
</html>
```

Error.message

JScript 5.5+
IE5.5+

Syntax

errorobj.message
errorobj.message = *string*

Description

The message property associated with the Error object returns a string containing an error message displayed to users. This is the same as the *description* property.

Example

Listing 7.156 creates an Error object and then displays the message.

Listing 7.156   Display the Message of an Error with the message Property

```
<html>

<script language="JScript">
<!--

// Create an Error object.
var myError = new Error(45,"The error message!");

// Display message associated with the custom error.
document.write("The custom error message is '");
document.write(myError.message,"'");

// -->
</script>
</html>
```

Error.name

JScript 5.5+
IE5.5+

Syntax

errorobj.name

Description

The name property associated with the Error object returns a name or exception type of an error. If the error is a runtime error, the name property is set to one of the exception types shown in Table 7.31.

Table 7.31   Runtime Exception Errors

Exception Type	Description
ConversionError	Occurs with invalid object conversions.
RangeError	Occurs when a function is supplied arguments outside its allowable range.
ReferenceError	Occurs when an invalid reference has been made.
RegExpError	Occurs with a regular expression compilation error.
SyntaxError	Occurs with invalid syntax.
TypeError	Occurs when actual type of an operand does not match expected type.
URIError	Occurs when an illegal URI is detected.

Example

Listing 7.157 creates an Error object and then displays the name property.

Listing 7.157   Displays the Name of an Error with the name Property

```
<html>

<script language="JScript">
<!--

// Create an Error object.
var myError = new Error(45,"The error message!");

// Display name associated with the custom error.
document.write("The error name is '");
document.write(myError.name,"'");

// -->
</script>
</html>
```

Error.number

JScript 5.0+
IE5+

Syntax

errorobj.number
errorobj.number = *number;*

Description

The number property associated with the Error object contains the error number of the error. This method is read/write, so you can assign an error number using this property.

Example

Listing 7.158 creates an Error object and then displays the error number.

Listing 7.158   Displays Error Number Associated with Custom Error Using the number Property

```
<html>

<script language="JScript">
<!--

// Create an Error object.
var myError = new Error(45,"A really big error!");

// Display error number associated with the custom error.
document.write("The custom error number is ");
document.write(myError.number);

// -->
</script>
</html>
```

escape()

JavaScript 1.0+, ECMAScript 1E+, JScript 3.0+
Nav2+, NES2+, IE4+, Opera3+

Syntax

```
escape (string)
escape(expression)
```

Description

The escape() function takes any string object or expression and returns a string object in which all non-alphanumeric characters are converted to their numeric equivalent in the form %XX. The XX is a hexadecimal number representing the non-alphanumeric character.

Example

Listing 7.159 shows how to use the escape() function. It takes a string of text and returns the escaped value.

Listing 7.159   Example of How to Use escape()

```
<script type="text/javascript" language="JavaScript">
var newString = escape("Tom & Jerry Show");
</script>
```

This returns: "Tom%20%26%20Jerry%20show". Notice that the spaces were replaced with "%20" and the & sign was replaced with %26.

Listing 7.160 shows how to return the escape() function's interpretation of user input.

Listing 7.160   Example of Returning a Value from the escape() **Function**

```
<html>
<body>
<script type="text/javascript" language="JavaScript">
<!--
// Writes the value of input after escape has been performed.
function showEscapeVal(){
    alert("The escape value is: " + escape(document.form1.input1.value));
}
// -->
</script>

<form name="form1">
Enter input:
<input type="text" name="input1" size="30">
<input type="button" value="Show Escape Value" onClick='showEscapeVal()'>
</form>

</body>
</html>
```

eval()

JavaScript 1.0+, JScript 1.0+
Nav2+, NES2+, IE3+, Opera3+

Syntax

```
eval (command)
eval(string)
```

Description

The eval() function accepts a string of JavaScript statements and evaluates it as JavaScript source code. eval() returns the value of the executed JavaScript statement.

> ## NOTE
>
> `eval()` has evolved with JavaScript. In the early releases of JavaScript, version 1.0, `eval()` was only a built-in function. When version 1.1 was released, though, it was made a method as well. But when JavaScript version 1.2 was initially released, it was changed back to being just a built-in function. However, `eval()` was once again changed to a built-in function and method with the release of Navigator 4.02 and later.

Example

Listing 7.161 shows how to use `eval()` to execute a JavaScript command input by a user. Simply enter a valid JavaScript command into the text box and click the Execute button. When the button is clicked, the `run()` function is called, which performs an eval on the user input.

Listing 7.161   Simple Use of the `eval()` Function

```
<html>
<body>
<script type="text/javascript" language="JavaScript">
<!--
// Executes the JavaScript command entered in the text box.
function run(){
     eval (document.form1.input1.value);
}
// -->
</script>

<form name="form1">
Enter a Javascript command in the text field and click
the "execute" button to execute the command.
<br><br>
Command:<input type="text" name="input1" size="30">
<br>
<input type="button" value="execute" onClick='run()'>
</form>

</body>
</html>
```

export

JavaScript 1.2+, ECMAScript 1E+
Nav4+

Syntax

```
export
```

Description

`export` is a keyword used by scripts implementing security features that makes objects, properties, and methods accessible to other unsigned scripts.

Example

Listing 7.162 shows how to use the `export` keyword. In the JavaScript code, the `export` keyword is used to make the variables, name, city, and `showName()` function available to other unsigned scripts. Other scripts would access the information using the `import` keyword.

Listing 7.162   *Example of Using* export

```
<html>
<body>
<script type="text/javascript" language="JavaScript">
<!--
// Declare variables.
var name = "John Smith";
var city = "Atlanta";

function showName(){
    alert("Your name is: " + name);
}

// Makes two variables and showName function available to other scripts.
export name, city, showName

// -->
</script>

</body>
</html>
```

extends

JavaScript 1.3+, ECMAScript 1E+
Nav4.06+

Syntax

`Reserved Keyword`

Description

The `extends` keyword was initially introduced in JavaScript 1.3, and it is reserved for future use.

Example

This entry has not yet been implemented in the JavaScript language.

false

JavaScript 1.2+
Nav4+, NES3+

Syntax

Reserved Keyword

Description

The false keyword has not been implemented in JavaScript to date. It has been reserved for future use.

Example

This keyword has not been implemented; therefore, no example is provided.

final

JavaScript 1.2+
Nav4+, NES3+

Syntax

Reserved Keyword

Description

The final keyword has not been implemented in JavaScript to date. It has been reserved for future use.

Example

This keyword has not been implemented; therefore, no example is provided.

float

JavaScript 1.2+
Nav4+, NES3+

Syntax

Reserved Keyword

Description

The float keyword has not been implemented in JavaScript to date. It has been reserved for future use.

Example

This keyword has not been implemented; therefore, no example is provided.

for

JavaScript 1.0+, ECMAScript 1E+, JScript 1.0+
Nav2+, NES2+, IE3+

Syntax

```
for( [initial statement;]  [condition;] [num;]){

  code;

}
```

Description

The for keyword is used to create a loop that consists of three optional expressions, enclosed in parentheses and separated by semicolons, followed by a block of statements executed in the loop.

The *initial statement* is a JavaScript statement or variable declaration. The *condition* is an optional statement that is evaluated through each iteration of the loop. If a *condition* is satisfied, all statements contained in the loop are executed. The *num* designates whether the loop increments or decrements every loop iteration. And finally, the *code* contains JavaScript statements that are executed each time the condition is satisfied.

Example

Listing 7.163 shows an example of a loop that performs a document.write nine times. An initial variable i is declared and set equal to zero. The variable is then evaluated against the condition that it is less than nine. If this evaluates to true, the variable is incremented and the document.write expression is performed.

Listing 7.163   Example of the for Loop

```
<html>
<body>
<script type="text/javascript" language="JavaScript">
<!--

// Loop nine times and display text indicating each iteration.
    for (i=0; i<9; i++){
        document.write("Loop iteration " + i + "<br>");
    }

// -->
</script>

</body>
</html>
```

for...in
JavaScript 1.0+, ECMAScript 1E+, JScript 1.0+
Nav2+, NES2+, IE3+, Opera3+

Syntax

```
for(variable in object){

code;

}
```

Description

The for...in object iterates a specified variable over all the properties of an object. The statements, contained in the body, are executed once for each property. The *variable* is a variable iterated over each property in the *object*. The *code* contains JavaScript statements to be executed.

Example

Listing 7.164 shows how to use the for...in object. The showProperties function takes an object type and object name as arguments. A for...in loop is then executed on the object displaying each of the object's properties and their values.

Listing 7.164   Using the for...in Object

```
<html>
<body>
<script type="text/javascript" language = "JavaScript">
<!--
// Function displays the properties for the specified object.
function showProperties(obj, objName) {
    var result;
    for (var i in obj) {
        result += i + " = " + obj[i] + "<br>";
    }
    document.write("The properties for the " + objName + " object:" +
                   "<br><br>");
    document.write(result);
}
// -->
</script>
<form name="form1">
<input type="button" value="Get Button Properties" name="button1"
onClick='showProperties(this, this.name)'>
</form>
</body>
</html>
```

function

JavaScript 1.0+, ECMAScript 1E+, JScript 1.0+
Nav2+, NES2+, IE3+, Opera3+

Syntax

```
function name(parm1, parm2, ..., parmN)
```

```
function name()
```

Description

The function keyword is used for specifying JavaScript functions. JavaScript functions typically contain a series of JavaScript statements that are grouped together to perform a specific task. The *name* is the name of the function and *parm1–parmN* are any optional parameters.

Example

Listing 7.165 shows how the function keyword is used. The function keyword defines the sendMessage function.

Listing 7.165   Example of the function Keyword

```
<html>
<script type="text/javascript" language="JavaScript">
<!--
function sendMessage(){
    alert("The function key word is used to declare the sendMessage
function");
}
// -->
</script>
</html>
```

Function()

JavaScript 1.0+, ECMAScript 1E+, JScript 2.0+
Nav2+, NES2+, IE3+, Opera3+

Syntax

```
var variable = new Function()
var variable = new Function(int)
var variable = new Function(arg1, ..., argN)
```

Description

Function() is a constructor that creates a Function object. Table 7.32 lists the different methods and properties of the Function object.

Table 7.32 **Properties and Methods of the** Function **Object**

Type	Item	Description
Property	arguments	Array reflecting function arguments
	arity	Number of arguments expected by function
	callee	Specifies the body of the current executing function
	caller	Reference to function caller
	constructor	Specifies the function which creates the Function object's prototype
	length	Returns the number of arguments expected by a function
	prototype	Prototype for a class of objects
Method	apply()	Applies method to multiple objects
	call()	Allows calling of methods belonging to other functions
	toSource()	Created a copy of the function object
	toString()	Converts function back to string that defines it
	valueOf()	Returns a string representation of the function source code

Example

Listing 7.166 shows how a new Function object can be created with a single line. In this example, the function, when called, will change the background color of the page to blue.

Listing 7.166 **Setting the Background Color with a New** Function **Object**

```
<script type="text/javascript" language="JavaScript">
<!--

// Create a function to change background color.
var setBGColor = new Function(document.bgColor='blue');

// -->
</script>
```

Function.apply()

JavaScript 1.3+, ECMAScript 1E+
Nav4.06+, IE3+, Opera3+

Syntax

function.apply()

Description

The apply() method of the Function object is used to apply a method of one object to another object. Using the apply() method keeps developers from having to rewrite methods for different objects.

Example

Listing 7.167 shows how the apply() method can be used between two objects. The bigHome function adds a new property, numRooms, to the home object.

Listing 7.167   Using the apply() Method

```
<html>
<body>
<script type="text/javascript" language="JavaScript">
<!--

// Function defines a home with two properties.
function home(number, street){
    var num = number;
    var str = street;
    document.write("house number is: " + num + "<br>");
    document.write("Street name is: " + str + "<br>");
}

// Function adds an additional property to the basic home.
// Applies the home function.
function bigHome(number, street, rooms){
    var numRooms = rooms;
    home.apply(home,arguments);
    document.write("The number of rooms is: " + numRooms + "<br>");
}

myHome = new bigHome(101, Main, 5);
// -->
</script>
</body>
</html>
```

Function.arguments

JavaScript 1.1+, JScript 2.0+, ECMAScript 1E+
Nav3+, NES2+, IE3+, Opera3+

Syntax

function.arguments

Description

The arguments property of the Function object is an array that holds the arguments that are passed to a function. The number of arguments passed to a defined function can be more than the number of parameters if the arguments array is used. The arguments array can only be accessed while inside the function. Any attempt to access the arguments array outside the function will result in an error.

Example

Listing 7.168 shows how the arguments array is used. A document.write is performed, which calls the foo function. The foo function is passed two arguments and calls the foobar function with the parameter 123. The foobar function outputs the number of arguments it has and outputs the second argument to the function that called it, in this case the foo function.

Listing 7.168   Using the arguments **Property**

```
<html>
<body>
<script type="text/javascript" language="JavaScript">
<!--
// Function foo, calls function foobar with the parameter 123.
function foo(a,b) {
    foobar(123);
    document.write("Done with function foo" + "<br>");
}

// Function foobar writes output to the document
// using the arguments property of function.
function foobar(x) {
    document.write(foobar.arguments.length + "<br>");
    document.write(foobar.arguments.caller.b + "<br>");
}

document.write(foo(21,44) + "\n");
// -->
</script>
</body>
</html>
```

Function.arity

JavaScript 1.2
Nav4+, NES3+

Syntax

```
function.arity
```

Description

The `arity` property of the `Function` object represents the number of declared arguments a function expects to receive. This is valid when the language attribute of the script tag is set to `JavaScript1.2`. *This property is deprecated in JavaScript 1.4.* In JavaScript 1.5, this property is replaced with the `length` property.

Example

Listing 7.169 shows how `arity` can be used. The first line written to the user's page contains the number of arguments passed to the function. The second line is the result of running the script.

Listing 7.169   Example of Using `arity`

```
<html>
<body>
<script type="text/javascript" language="JavaScript">
<!--
// Function subtracts the second number from the first.
function subtract(first, second){
  var result = first - second;
  return result;
}

// Write the results to the screen.
document.write("arity = " + subtract.arity + "<br>")
document.write("The result of the subtract function is: " + subtract(4,3));

// -->
</script>
</body>
</html>
```

Function.call()

JavaScript 1.3+
Nav4.06+, IE3+, Opera3+

Syntax

```
function.call(this)
```

```
function.call(this, arg1, arg2, ..., argN)
```

Description

The `call()` method of the `Function` object allows you to call another object's method. Optional arguments can be passed to the method as shown in the second syntactical definition.

Example

Listing 7.170 shows an example of the call() method. The script creates a person and author object. The author object uses the call() method to perform some of its creation.

Listing 7.170   Using the call() *Method of the* Function *Object*

```
<script type="text/javascript" language="JavaScript">
<!--

// Create a person object to handle the creation
// of people.
function person (author, name){
  this.name = name;
  this.author = true;
}

// Create an author object.
function authors(name, books){
  this.books = books;
  person.call(this, name);
}

authors.prototype = new person();

// Create a new author.
var myAuthor = new authors("Allen", 5);

// -->
</script>
```

Function.callee

JavaScript 1.2+
Nav4+, IE5+

Syntax

function.callee

Description:

The callee property of the Function object was actually a property of Function.arguments in JavaScript versions through 1.3. In JavaScript 1.4 and later, it is a local property. It is used to specify the function body of the currently executing function. It is only available within the body of a function.

Example

Listing 7.171 shows how the `callee` property is used to get the value of the `Function.callee` property.

Listing 7.171 *Accessing the* `callee` *Property*

```
<html>
<script type="text/javascript" language="JavaScript">
<!--
function display() {
  alert( display.callee );
}
// -->
</script>

<body>
<form name="form1">
<input type="button" value="Get callee property" onClick='display()'>
</form>

</body>
</html>
```

Function.caller

> JavaScript 1.1+, JScript 2.0+
> Nav3+, NES2+, IE3+, Opera3+

Syntax

`function.caller`

Description:

The `caller` property of the `Function` object is used to reference the function that called the currently executing function. *This property is deprecated in JavaScript 1.3.* In JavaScript versions 1.4 and 1.5, this property is no longer used.

Example

Listing 7.172 shows how the `caller` property is used to get the name of the function calling `John()`.

Listing 7.172 *Accessing the* `caller` *Property*

```
<html>
<script type="text/javascript" language="JavaScript">
<!--

// Define a simple function Alice(), which calls the John() function.
function Alice(){
```

```
        var Boss = true;
        John();
}

// Function outputs its caller.
function John(){
    myBoss = John.caller.name;
    document.write("The boss is: " + myBoss + "<br>");
}
// -->
</script>

</html>
```

Function.constructor

JavaScript 1.1+, JScript 2.0+
Nav3+, NES2+, IE4+

Syntax

function.constructor

Description

The constructor property of the Function object is used to create the object's proto-type.

Example

Listing 7.173 shows how the constructor property is used. A function object named drive is defined. Then using the constructor property, we determine whether drive is a Function object.

Listing 7.173   *Accessing the* constructor *Property*

```
<html>
<script type="text/javascript" language="JavaScript">
<!--

function drive() {
  return "something";
}

if(drive.constructor == Function)
{
    document.write("Constructor matches");
}

// -->
</script>
</html>
```

Function.length

JavaScript 1.1+, ECMAScript 1E+
Nav3+

Syntax

```
function.length
```

Description:

The length property of the Function object is used to specify the number of arguments in which the function expects. This is not to be confused with the arguments.length property that provides the number of arguments actually passed into a function.

Example

Listing 7.174 shows how the length property is used.

Listing 7.174   Accessing the length Property

```
<html>
<script type="text/javascript" language="JavaScript">
<!--
// Function to display the args.
function show(parm1, parm2) {
  alert( "Length is: " + length );
}
// -->
</script>

<body>
Click the button to get the number of arguments the show function expects
<br><br>
<form name="form1">
<input type="button" value="Get length property" onClick='show(1,2)'>
</form>
</body>
</html>
```

Function.prototype

JavaScript 1.1+, ECMAScript 1E+, JScript 2.0+
Nav3+, NES2+, IE3+, Opera3+

Syntax

```
function.prototype.property
```

```
function.prototype.method
```

Description

The `prototype` property of the `Function` object refers to the object that serves as the prototype from which classes are created. `prototype` allows you to add new properties or methods to an existing class by adding them to the prototype associated with the constructor of that class.

Example

Listing 7.175 shows how the `prototype` property is used. The function `setTask`, which simply sets the `task` variable, is defined. Then a new prototype called `duty` is created for the `String` object. The `duty` prototype is set to call the `setTask` function. Now all `String` objects in the example have the `setTask` method.

Listing 7.175 *Example for the* `prototype` *Property*

```
<html>
<body>
<script type="text/javascript" language="JavaScript">
<!--

var mytask = new String();

// sample function that sets the task string
function setTask(str){
    var task="Girls go shopping";

    if(str != null){
     task = str;
    }
    return task;
}

String.prototype.duty = setTask;

document.write("The first task is: " + mytask.duty("Nothing") + "<br>");
document.write("The next task is: " + mytask.duty());
// -->
</script>
</body>
</html>
```

Function.toSource()

JavaScript 1.3+
Nav4.06+, IE3+, Opera3+

Syntax

`function.toSource()`

Description

The toSource() method of the Function object allows you to create a copy of an object.

Example

Listing 7.176 uses the toSource() method on a newly created string. Running this script in a browser returns the following:

```
(new String("This is the source"))
```

Listing 7.176   Using the toSource() ***Method***

```
<html>
<body>
<script type="text/javascript" language="JavaScript">
<!--

// Create a new String instance.
var aString = new String("This is the source");

// Call the toSource() method.
bString = aString.toSource();

// Write the returned value of calling the toSource()
// method to the page.
document.write(bString);

// -->
</script>

</body>
</html>
```

Function.toString()

JavaScript 1.1+, ECMAScript 1E+, JScript 2.0+
Nav3+, NES2+, IE4+, Opera3+

Syntax

```
function.toString()
```

Description

The toString() method of the Function object is used to convert a function to a text string. The method converts the function back to the JavaScript source that defines the function. The converted string includes all aspects of the defined function.

Example:

Listing 7.177 shows how the toString() method is used to convert a function to a text string.

Listing 7.177   *Use of the* toString() *Method*

```
<html>
<body>
<script type="text/javascript" language="JavaScript">
<!--

// Function just writes some text output.
function writeText(){
    document.write("Some dummy text");
}

// Call the toString() method.
var func = writeText.toString();

// Write the results to the page.
document.write("The string representation of the writeText");
document.write(" function looks like: " + "<br><br><b>");
document.write(func + "</b>");
// -->
</script>

</body>
</html>
```

Function.valueOf()

JavaScript 1.1+, JScript 2.0+
Nav3+, IE4+, Opera5+

Syntax

```
function.valueOf()
```

Description

The valueOf() method of the Function object is used to obtain a string representation of the function source code. Typically this is a method used internally by the JavaScript interpreter and not explicitly in code. However it can be called directly if needed.

Example

Listing 7.178 shows how the valueOf() method is used. A function called myTest simply calls the valueOf() method to get the string representation of the myTest function.

Listing 7.178   Using the `valueOf()` *Method*

```
<html>
<body>
<script type="text/javascript" language="JavaScript">
<!--

document.write("Below is the value returned from calling valueOf() on" +
" the myTest function." + "<br><br>");

// Execute function myTest.
document.write( "<b>" + myTest() );

function myTest()
{
    var temp;
    return (myTest.valueOf() );
}

// -->
</script>
</body>
</html>
```

GetObject

> JScript 3.0+
> IE4+

Syntax

GetObject (*path*)

GetObject(*path*, *app.type*)

Description

The `GetObject` function returns a reference to an `Automation` object from a file. The function can take up to two parameters. The *path* parameter represents the full path and name to the file containing the object you want to retrieve.

NOTE

Some of the applications you can retrieve objects from allow you to activate only part of the file. This can be achieved by placing an exclamation point, !, at the end of the *path* followed by the string that specifies the part you want to activate.

The *app.type* attribute is the program ID or formal definition of the object. The *app* portion represents the name of the application providing the object, and the *type* designates the type of object to create. If this parameter is not passed, the `Automation` object will try to determine which application to start.

NOTE

Use the ActiveXObject function if you want to create an instance without starting the object with a file loaded.

Example

Listing 7.179 shows the syntax that can be used to return an Automation object from a file. The second entry shows how you can activate only part of the object.

Listing 7.179   Using the GetObject Function

```
// Returning an object for this Excel file
var myObj = GetObject("C:\\TEMP\\TESTOBJ.XLS");

// Activating the first sheet in the file
var myObjRef = GetObject("C:\\TEMP\\TESTOBJ.XLS!sheet1");
```

Global

JavaScript 1.0+, JScript 3.0+, ECMAScript 1E+
Nav2+, NES2+, IE3+, Opera3+

Syntax

Core JavaScript Object

Description

The Global object is a core object in the JavaScript language. Properties and functions that are not associated with any other object belong to this object. Table 7.33 shows the properties and methods of this object

Table 7.33   Properties and Functions of the Global Object

Type	Item	Description
Property	Infinity	Keyword that represents positive infinity
	NaN	Represents an object not equal to any number
	Number	Converts an object into a Number
	String	Converts an object into a String
	undefined	Represents an undefined value
Method	decodeURI()	Decodes a uniform resource identifier
	decodeURIComponent()	Decodes a uniform resource identifier encoded by the encodeURIComponent() method.
	encodeURI()	Encodes a complete uniform resource identifier

Table 7.33   *Continued*

Type	Item	Description
	encodeURIComponent()	Encodes a uniform resource identifier component
	escape()	Returns a string object in which all non-alphanumeric characters are converted to their numeric equivalent
	eval()	Accepts a string of JavaScript statements and evaluates it as JavaScript source code
	isFinite()	Method used to determine whether a variable has finite bounds
	isNaN()	Method used to determine whether a variable is a valid number or not
	parseFloat()	Method used to convert a string to a number of type float
	parseInt()	Method used to convert a string to an integer
	unescape()	Method that takes a hexadecimal value and returns the ISO-Latin-1 ASCII equivalent

Example

See the separate entries for each of these properties and functions for examples. Note that the properties and functions are not referred to with a preceding Global reference, when being used.

Global.decodeURI()

JavaScript 1.5+, ECMAScript 3E+, JScript 5.5+
Nav6+, NES6+, IE5.5+

Syntax

decodeURI (*URIString*)

Description

The decodeURI() function is used to replace each escape sequence in the *URIString* (uniform resource identifier) with the character that it represents based on the UTF-8 standard. (See http://www.utf-8.org/ for more information on UTF-8.) The function returns the decoded string.

NOTE

Escape sequences that do not get encoded by the encodeURI() function (,, /, ?, :, @, &, =, +, $) cannot be decoded using the decodeURI() function. To decode these reserved characters, use the decodeURIComponent() function.

Example

In Listing 7.180, the string "The apple is red." is encoded using the encodeURI() function. The result is the same string but with the spaces replaced with "%20", the encoded equivalent. This encoded URI string is then decoded back to its original form using the decodeURI() function.

Listing 7.180   Using the decodeURI() Function

```
<html>
<script type="text/javascript" language='JavaScript'>
<!--

// Create a string.
myString="The apple is red";
document.write("The original sentence: " + myString + "<br><br>");

// Encode the string.
myString = encodeURI(myString);
document.write("The encoded sentence: " + myString + "<br><br>");

// Decode the string.
myString = decodeURI(myString);
document.write("The decoded sentence: " + myString + "<br><br>");

// -->
</script>
</html>
```

Global.decodeURIComponent()

JavaScript 1.5+, ECMAScript 3E+, JScript 5.5+
Nav6+, NES6+, IE5.5+

Syntax

decodeURIComponent (*URIComponentString*)

Description

The decodeURIComponent() function is used to replace each escape sequence in the *URIComponentString* (uniform resource identifier) with the character that it represents based on the UTF-8 standard. The function returns the decoded string.

NOTE

The decodeURIComponent() function differs from the decodeURI() function in that it decodes some reserved characters (,, /, ?, :, @, &, =, +, $) that are not decoded by the decodeURI() function. For this reason, the decodeURIComponent method is designed to only decode URI strings that were originally encoded using the encodeURIComponent() function.

Example

In Listing 7.181, the phrase `"fork, spoon, & knife"` is encoded using the `encodeURIComponent()` function. The result is the same string, but with the spaces, commas, and & characters encoded. This encoded URI component string is then decoded using the `decodeURI()` function. But notice that this function only decodes the spaces. In order to decode the commas and the & character, the `decodeURIComponent()` function must be used.

Listing 7.181   *Using the* `decodeURIComponent()` *Function*

```
<html>
<script type="text/javascript" language='JavaScript'>
<!--

// Create a string object.
myString="fork, spoon, & knife";
document.write("The original phrase: " + myString + "<br><br>");

// Encode the string using the enocdeURIComponent function.
myString = encodeURIComponent(myString);
document.write("The encoded phrase: " + myString + "<br><br>");

// Decode the string with the decodeURI function.
myString = decodeURI(myString);
document.write("The decoded phrase: " + myString + "<br><br>");

// Decode the string using the decodeURIComponent function.
myString = decodeURIComponent(myString);
document.write("The decoded component phrase: " + myString + "<br><br>");

// -->
</script>
</html>
```

Global.encodeURI()

JavaScript 1.5+, ECMAScript 3E+, JScript 5.5+
Nav6+, NES6+, IE5.5+

Syntax

`encodeURI (URIString)`

Description

The `encodeURI()` function is used to encode a URI by replacing specific characters with escape sequences representing UTF-8 encoding.

> **NOTE**
>
> Certain characters will not be encoded with the `encodeURI()` function. They are shown in Table 7.34.

Table 7.34   Unencoded characters

Type	Character
Reserved characters	, , /, ?, :, @, &, =, +, $
unescaped characters	alphabetic, decimal, -,_., !, ~, *, ', (,)
score	#

Example

In Listing 7.182, the string `"The apple is red."` is encoded using the `encodeURI()` function. The result is the same string, but with the spaces replaced with `"%20"`, the encoded equivalent.

Listing 7.182   Using the `encodeURI()` **Function**

```
<html>
<script type="text/javascript" language='JavaScript'>
<!--

// Create a string object.
myString="The apple is red";
document.write("The original sentence: " + myString + "<br><br>");

// Encode the string object and then output the result.
myString = encodeURI(myString);
document.write("The encoded sentence: " + myString + "<br><br>");

// -->
</script>
</html>
```

Global.encodeURIComponent()

JavaScript 1.5+, ECMAScript 3E+, JScript 5.5+
Nav6+, NES6+, IE5.5+

Syntax

`encodeURIComponent (URIComponentString)`

Description

The `encodeURIComponent()`function is used to replace certain characters in the `URIComponentString` (uniform resource identifier) with escape sequences representing their UTF-8 character encoding. This function assumes a URI component and therefore will encode reserved characters.

> **NOTE**
>
> Certain characters will not be encoded with the encodeURIComponent() function. They are shown in Table 7.35.

Table 7.35   Unencoded Characters

Type	Character
unescaped characters	alphabetic, decimal, -,_., !, ~, *, ', (,)
score	#

Example

In Listing 7.183, the phrase "fork, spoon, & knife" is encoded using the encodeURIComponent() function. The result is the same string, but with the spaces, commas, and & characters encoded.

Listing 7.183   Using the encodeURIComponent() Function

```
<html>
<script type="text/javascript" language='JavaScript'>
<!--

// Create a new string object.
myString="fork, spoon, & knife";
document.write("The original phrase: " + myString + "<br><br>");

// Encode the string and output the result.
myString = encodeURIComponent(myString);
document.write("The encoded phrase: " + myString + "<br><br>");

// -->
</script>
</html>
```

Global.escape()

JavaScript 1.0+, ECMAScript 1E+, JScript 1.0+
Nav2+, NES2+, IE3+, Opera3+

Syntax

```
escape (string)
escape(expression)
```

Description

The escape() method takes any string object or expression and returns a string object in which all non-alphanumeric characters are converted to their numeric equivalent in the form %*XX*. The *XX* is a hexadecimal number representing the non-alphanumeric character.

Example

Listing 7.184 shows how to use the `escape()` method and what it returns. It takes a string of text and returns the escaped value.

Listing 7.184   Example of How to Use `escape()`

```
<script type="text/javascript" language="JavaScript">
var newString = escape("Tom & Jerry Show");
</script>
```

This returns: `"Tom%20%26%20Jerry%20show"`. Notice that the spaces were replaced with `"%20"` and the & sign was replaced with `%26`.

Listing 7.185 shows how to return the `escape()` method's interpretation of user input.

Listing 7.185   Example of Taking User Input and Passing Data to the `Escape` **Method**

```
<html>
<body>
<script type="text/javascript" language="JavaScript">
<!--
// Writes the value of input after escape has been performed.
function showEscapeVal(){
    document.write(escape(document.form1.input1.value);
}
// -->
</script>

<form name="form1">
<input type="text" name="input1" size=30>
</form>

</body>
</html>
```

Global.eval()

JavaScript 1.0+, JScript 1.0+, ECMAScript 1E+
Nav2+, NES2+, IE3+, Opera3+

Syntax

```
eval (command)
eval(string)
```

Description

The eval() function accepts a string of JavaScript statements and evaluates it as JavaScript source code. eval() returns the value of the executed JavaScript statement.

> **NOTE**
>
> eval() has evolved with JavaScript. In the early releases of JavaScript, version 1.0, eval() was only a built-in function. When version 1.1 was released though, it was made a method as well. But when JavaScript version 1.2 was initially released, it was changed back to being just a built-in function. However, eval() was once again changed to a built-on function and method, with the release of Navigator 4.02 and later. With JavaScript 1.4 and later, the eval() method is a top level function not associated with any object.

Example

Listing 7.186 shows how to use eval() to execute a JavaScript command input by a user. Simply enter a valid JavaScript command into the text box and click the Execute button. When the button is clicked, the run() function is called, which performs an eval on the user input.

Listing 7.186   Simple Use of the eval() Function

```
<html>
<body>
<script type="text/javascript" language="JavaScript">
<!--
// Executes the JavaScript command entered in the text box.
function run(){
    eval (document.form1.input1.value);
}
// -->
</script>

<form name="form1">
Enter a JavaScript command in the text field and click
the "execute" button to execute the command.
<br><br>
Command:<input type="text" name="input1" size="30">
<br>
<input type="button" value="execute" onClick='run()'>
</form>

</body>
</html>
```

Global.Infinity
JavaScript 1.3+, JScript 3.0+, ECMAScript 1E+
Nav4.06+, IE4+, Opera3+

Syntax

```
Infinity
```

Description

`Infinity` is a JavaScript keyword that represents positive infinity.

Example

Listing 7.187 shows how the `Infinity` keyword is used. An input text box is provided to enter a value to be compared to `Infinity`. If any number is entered, it will result in being less than `Infinity`. However, if the word `Infinity` is entered, it will result in being equal to `Infinity`.

Listing 7.187   Example of Using the `Infinity` Property

```
<html>
<body>
<script type="text/javascript" language="JavaScript">
<!--

// function checks to see if the input is greater, less than, or equal
// to the value input by the user.
function checkNum(){

 input=document.form1.num.value;

   if(input < Infinity){
       alert("Your number is less than Infinity");
   }
   else if(input > Infinity){
      alert("Your number is greater than Infinity");
   }
   else if(input == Infinity){
     alert("Your number if equal to Infinity");
   }

}
// -->
</script>

<form name="form1">
Enter a number to compare against Infinity.
<br><br>
<input type="text" size="35" name="num">
```

Listing 7.187   Continued

```
<br><br>
<input type="button" value="Check Number" onClick='checkNum()'>
</form>
// -->
</script>

</body>
</html>
```

Global.isFinite()

JavaScript 1.3+, ECMAScript 1E+, JScript 3.0+
Nav4.06+, IE4+, Opera3+

Syntax

```
isFinite()
```

Description

The isFinite() method is used to determine whether a variable has finite bounds.

Example

In Listing 7.188, you see how the isFinite() method is used to verify whether the user input value has finite bounds.

Listing 7.188   Example of isFinite() **Method**

```
<html>
<body>

<script type="text/javascript" language="JavaScript">
<!--

// Function to check whether the text entered
// is a number.
function checkNum(){
    var n = document.form1.text1.value;
    if(isFinite(n) == true){
        alert("Your entry had finite bounds");
    }
}
// -->
</script>

<form name="form1">
Enter a number or character into the text box and then click the check value
button to verify if the input is a number.
<br><br>
```

```
<input type="text" name="text1" size="3">
<br><br>
<input type="button" value="Check value" onClick='checkNum()'>
<br>
</form>

</body>
</html>
```

Global.isNaN()

JavaScript 1.1+, JScript 1.0+, ECMAScript 1E+
Nav3+, NES2+, IE3+, Opera3+

Syntax

isNaN (*variable*)

Description

The isNaN()function is used to determine whether *variable* is a valid number.

Example

In Listing 7.189, you see how the isNaN() function can be used to check user input.

Listing 7.189   Example of isNaN() Function

```
<html>
<body>
<script type="text/javascript" language="JavaScript">
<!--

// Function to check whether the user input
// is a valid number.
function checkNum(){
    var n = document.form1.text1.value;
    if(isNaN(n) == true){
       alert("Your entry is not a number");
     }
}
// -->
</script>

<form name="form1">
Enter a number or character into the text box and then click the check value
button to verify if the input is a number.
<br><br>
<input type="text" name="text1" size=3>
<br><br>
<input type="button" value="Check value" onClick='checkNum()'>
```

Listing 7.189   Continued

```
<br>
</form>

</body>
</html>
```

Global.NaN

JavaScript 1.3+, JScript 3.0+, ECMAScript 1E+
Nav4.06+, IE4+

Syntax

NaN

Description

The NaN object represents an object that is not equal to any number, including itself.
NaN stands for *Not a Number*.

Example

Listing 7.190 shows how the NaN object is used in a comparison.

Listing 7.190   Example Using the NaN Object

```
<html>
<body>
<script type="text/javascript" language="JavaScript">
<!--
// Checks to see if the string "a" is a number.
if ("a" != NaN){
    document.write("This is not a number");
}
// -->
</script>

</body>
</html>
```

Global.Number()

JavaScript 1.2+
Nav4+, NES3+, IE4+

Syntax

Number(obj)

Description

The Number() method takes whatever object is passed in as a parameter, *obj*, and converts it to a Number. If the object being converted does not contain a well-formed numeric literal, NaN is returned. When converting a Date object, the time is measured in milliseconds from Jan 1970 GMT.

Example

Listing 7.191 shows how the Number() method is used to convert a Date object into a number.

Listing 7.191   Example Using the Number() *Method*

```
<html>
<script type="text/javascript" language="JavaScript">
<!--

// Create a date object.
var mydate = new Date ("January 1, 2001");

// Convert the date to a Number object.
document.write("Converting the Date object to a number gives you: " +
Number(mydate) );
// -->
</script>

</html>
```

Global.parseFloat()

JavaScript 1.0+, ECMAScript 1E+, JScript 1.0+
Nav2+, NES2+, IE3+, Opera3+

Syntax

parseFloat (*string*)

Description

The parseFloat() method is used to convert a string to a number.

Example

Listing 7.192 shows how the parseFloat() method is used. In the example, parseFloat is called with two different strings. The first string, which contains numerical characters, is converted to a number without any problems. The second string, which contains alphabetic characters, is unable to be converted into a number.

Listing 7.192 **Example of the** parseFloat() *Method*

```
<html>
<body>
<script type="text/javascript" language="JavaScript">
<!--
// Convert the "1245.31" string to a number.
document.write("The string 1245.31 converted is" +
➥parseFloat("1245.31") + "<br>");

// Try to convert the string "test" to a number.
// If not possible, then print error.
if( isNaN(parseFloat("test")) ){
   document.write("Cannot convert test string to a number.");
}
// -->
</script>

</body>
</html>
```

Global.parseInt()

JavaScript 1.0+, ECMAScript 1E+, JScript 1.0+
Nav2+, NES2+, IE3+, Opera3+

Syntax

```
parseInt(string, radix)

parseInt(string)
```

Description

The parseInt() method is used to convert a string to an integer. It can take *string* input with an optional *radix* input. The *radix* input represents the base of the number in the string.

Example

Listing 7.193 shows how parseInt() is used to parse a string. A few different examples are shown for different string types.

Listing 7.193 **Example of the** parseInt() *Method*

```
<html>
<body>
<script type="text/javascript" language="JavaScript">
<!--
// Convert the "859" string to an integer.
```

```
document.write("The string 859 converted to an integer is: ");
document.write(parseInt("859") + "<br>");

// Converts a binary string into a integer.
document.write("The binary string 101101 converted to an integer is: ");
document.write(parseInt("101101", 2) + "<br>");

// Converts a hexidecimal string into an integer.
document.write("The hexidecimal string FA832B converted to an integer is: ");
document.write(parseInt("FA832B", 16) + "<br>");

// -->
</script>

</body>
</html>
```

Global.String()

JavaScript 1.2+
Nav4+, NES3+, IE4+

Syntax

String(obj)

Description

The String() method takes whatever object is passed in as a parameter and converts it to a String. It is the same as using the toString() method.

Example

Listing 7.194 shows how the String() method is used to convert a Date into a String.

Listing 7.194   Example Using the String() Method

```
<html>
<script type="text/javascript" language="JavaScript">
<!--

// Create a new Date object.
var myVar = new Date(473982503723);

// Covert the Date object to a String object.
document.write("Converting the Date object to a String gives you: " +
String(myVar) );

// -->
</script>
</html>
```

Global.unescape()

JavaScript 1.0+, JScript 1.0+, ECMAScript 1E+
Nav2+, NES2+, IE3+, Opera3+

Syntax

```
unescape (string)
```

Description

The unescape() method takes a hexadecimal value and returns the ISO-Latin-1 ASCII equivalent. This method performs the opposite operation of the escape() method and is commonly used to escape user-entered data before form submission.

Example

Listing 7.195 declares a local variable, escapedVal, and passes it to the unescaped() method. The result, "@", is then written to the page.

Listing 7.195   Using the unescape() Method to Convert a Hexadecimal Value to Its ASCII Equivalent

```
<script type="text/javascript" language="JavaScript">
<!--

// Create a variable.
var escapedVal = "%40";

// Evaluate the variable and place the value in a variable.
var unescapedVal = unescape(escapedVal);

document.write('The <i>escapedVal</i> value (' + escapedVal + ") ");
document.write("evaluates to " + unescapedVal);

// -->
</script>
```

Global.undefined

JavaScript 1.3+, JScript 5.5+
Nav4.06+, IE5.5+

Syntax

```
undefined
```

Description

The undefined property represents an undefined value.

Example

Listing 7.196 shows how the `undefined` property can be used to check whether a variable has been assigned.

Listing 7.196   *Example Using the* undefined *Property*

```
<html>
<script type="text/javascript" language="JavaScript">
<!--

var myVar;

// Check for variable initialization.
if (myVar == undefined){
   document.write("The variable, myVar has not been initialized!");
}


// -->
</script>

</html>
```

goto

JavaScript 1.3+
Nav4+

Syntax

```
Reserved Keyword
```

Description

The `goto` keyword has not been implemented in client-side JavaScript to date. It has been reserved for future use.

Example

This keyword has not been implemented; therefore, no example is provided.

if

JavaScript 1.0+, ECMAScript 1E+, JScript 1.0+
Nav2+, NES2+, IE3+, Opera3+

Syntax

```
if(statement){
  code;
}
```

Description

The if statement is used to perform logic statements on specific cases. If *statement* evaluates to true, *code* is executed.

Example

In Listing 7.197, you see how the if statement is being used to determine whether the Tilly boolean value is true.

Listing 7.197   Example of the if Statement

```
<html>
<body>
<script type="text/javascript" language="JavaScript">
<!--

var Tilly = 1;

// Check to see if the variable is true.
if(Tilly == true){
    document.write("Statement is true");
}

// -->
</script>

</body>
</html>
```

if...else

JavaScript 1.0+, ECMAScript 1E+, JScript 1.0+
Nav2+, NES2+, IE3+, Opera3+

Syntax

```
if(statement){
  code;
}else(statement){
  code;
}
```

Description

The if...else statement is used to perform logic statements on specific cases. If *statement* is satisfied, its statements are executed. Otherwise, the else *statement* is evaluated. When *statement* evaluates to true, *code* is executed.

Example

In Listing 7.198, you see how the if...else statement is being used to determine whether the isDog boolean value is true.

Listing 7.198   Example of the `if...else` *Statement*

```
<html>
<body>
<script type="text/javascript" language="JavaScript">
<!--

var isDog = 1;

// Check to see if Dog variable is true or false.
// Output message depending on the case.
if(isDog == true){
    document.write("Statement is true");
}
else{
    document.write("Statement is false");
}
// -->
</script>

</body>
</html>
```

implements

> JavaScript 1.2+
> Nav4+, NES3+

Syntax

`Reserved Keyword`

Description

The `implements` keyword has not been implemented in server-side JavaScript to date. It has been reserved for future use.

Example

This keyword has not been implemented; therefore, no example is provided.

import

> JavaScript 1.0+, ECMAScript 1E+, JScript 1.0+
> Nav2+, IE3+, Opera3+

Syntax

`import`

Description

The `import` keyword allows a script to import properties, functions, and objects from a signed script that has exported the information.

Example

Listing 7.199 shows how the `import` keyword is used to import multiple properties from another script.

Listing 7.199   Example of the `import` Keyword

```
<html>
<body>
<script type="text/javascript" language="JavaScript">
<!--

// Imports the variables name, city and state from another script.
// This makes those properties accessible to myObj.
import myObj.name;
import myObj.city;
import myObj.state;

// -->
</script>

</body>
</html>
```

in

> JavaScript 1.4
> Nav6+, IE5.5+

Syntax

```
Prop in objectName
```

Description

The `in` keyword will return `true` or `false` depending on whether a specified property, *prop,* is in a specified object, *objectName.* The property can be a string or numeric expression representing a property name or array index.

Example

Listing 7.200 shows how the `in` keyword is used to check to see whether the `length` property is in the `String` object.

Listing 7.200   Example of the `in` Keyword

```
<html>
<body>
<script type="text/javascript" language="JavaScript">
<!--
// Create a new String object.
var myStr = new String("Something");
```

```
// Check for "length".
if ("length" in myStr){
    document.write("length in myStr evaluates to true");
}

// -->
</script>
</body>
</html>
```

Infinity

JavaScript 1.3+, JScript 1.0+
Nav4.06+, IE3+, Opera3+

Syntax

```
Infinity
```

Description

`Infinity` is a JavaScript keyword that represents positive infinity.

Example

Listing 7.201 shows how the `Infinity` keyword is used. An input text box is provided to enter a value to be compared to `Infinity`. If any number is entered, it will result in being less than `Infinity`. However, if the word `"Infinity"` is entered, it will result in being equal to `Infinity`.

Listing 7.201   Example of the infinity Keyword

```
<html>
<body>
<script type="text/javascript" language="JavaScript">
<!--

// Function checks to see if the input is greater, less than, or equal
// to the value input by the user.
function checkNum(){

 input=document.form1.num.value;

    if(input < Infinity){
        alert("Your number is less than Infinity");
    }
    else if(input > Infinity){
        alert("Your number is greater than Infinity");
    }
    else if(input == Infinity){
        alert("Your number is equal to Infinity");
    }
```

Listing 7.201   Continued

```
}
// -->
</script>

<form name="form1">
Enter a number to compare against Infinity.
<br><br>
<input type="text" size="35" name="num">
<br><br>
<input type="button" value="Check Number" onClick='checkNum()'>
</form>

</body>
</html>
```

instanceof

JavaScript 1.2+
Nav4+, NES3+

Syntax

```
Reserved Keyword
```

Description

The instanceof keyword is used to determine whether a specified object is of a specified object type. It will return true or false depending on this condition.

Example

Listing 7.202 shows how the instanceof keyword is used to check to see whether the length property is in the String object.

Listing 7.202   Example of the instanceof Keyword

```
<html>
<body>
<script type="text/javascript" language="JavaScript">
<!--

// Create a new String object.
var myStr = new String("Tilly the Dog");

// Check to see if the myStr object is an instance of the
// String object.
if (myStr instanceof String){
    document.write("myStr is an instance of the String object");
}
```

```
// -->
</script>
</body>
</html>
```

int

JavaScript 1.2+
Nav4+, NES3+

Syntax

Reserved Keyword

Description

The int keyword has not been implemented in JavaScript to date. It has been reserved for future use.

Example

This keyword has not been implemented; therefore, no example is provided.

interface

JavaScript 1.2+
Nav4+, NES3+

Syntax

Reserved Keyword

Description

The interface keyword has not been implemented in server-side JavaScript to date. It has been reserved for future use.

Example

This keyword has not been implemented; therefore, no example is provided.

isFinite()

JavaScript 1.3+, ECMAScript 1E+, JScript 3.0+
Nav4.06+, IE4+, Opera3+

Syntax

isFinite()

Description

The isFinite() method is used to determine whether a variable has finite bounds.

Example

In Listing 7.203, isFinite() method is used to verify whether the user input value has finite bounds.

Listing 7.203 *Example of the* isFinite() *Method*

```
<html>
<body>
<script type="text/javascript" language="JavaScript">
<!--

// Function to check whether the input has finite bounds.
function checkNum(){
    var n = document.form1.text1.value;
    if(isFinite(n) == true){
       alert("Your entry has finite bounds");
     }
}
// -->
</script>

<form name="form1">
Enter a number or character into the text box and the click the check value
button to verify if the input has finite bounds.
<br><br>
<input type="text" name="text1" size="3">
<br><br>
<input type="button" value="Check value" onClick='checkNum()'>
<br>
</form>

</body>
</html>
```

isNaN()

> JavaScript 1.1+, JScript 1.0+
> Nav3+, NES2+, IE3+, Opera3+

Syntax

isNaN (*variable*)

Description

The isNaN() function is used to determine whether *variable* is a valid number.

Example

Listing 7.204, shows how the isNaN() function can be used to check user input.

Listing 7.204 *Example of the* `isNaN()` *Function*

```
<html>
<body>
<script type="text/javascript" language="JavaScript">
<!--

// Function to check to see if the user input is a valid number.
function checkNum(){
    var n = document.form1.text1.value;
    if(isNaN(n) == true){
       alert("Your entry is not a number");
      }
}
// -->
</script>

<form name="form1">
Enter a number or character into the text box and then click the check value
button to verify if the input is a number.
<br><br>
<input type="text" name="text1" size=3>
<br><br>
<input type="button" value="Check value" onClick='checkNum()'>
<br>
</form>

</body>
</html>
```

java

JavaScript 1.1+
Nav3+, NES2+, Opera 3+

Syntax

`java`

Description

The `java` object allows you to access any class within the package `java.*`. It is shorter and works the same way as using the `packages.java` property.

Example

Listing 7.205 shows how the `java` property can be used to call the `lang` package and print out a string to the `java` console.

Listing 7.205   Example Using the java *Object*

```
<html>
<script type="text/javascript" language="JavaScript">
<!--

// Use the Java package to write text to the Java Console.
java.lang.System.out.println("Z Me Fly!");


// -->
</script>

</html>
```

javaArray

> JavaScript 1.1+
> Nav4+, NES2+

Syntax

```
var variable = arrayObject
```

```
var variable = package.newInstance(obj)
```

Description

The javaArray object represents a wrapped Java array that can be accessed from within a JavaScript program. In most situations, to create a javaArray type, simply store a java array datatype into a variable in JavaScript and it will automatically create the javaArray object. It can also be created by using the newInstance function and passing in the object to be created as the parameter. Table 7.36 shows the method and property of the javaArray object.

Table 7.36   Property and Method of the javaArray *Object*

Type	Item	Description
Property	length	Specifies the number of elements in the javaArray
Method	toString()	Returns a string representing the specified number object

Example

Listing 7.206 shows how a new javaArray object is created for the String object.

Listing 7.206   Example of a javaArray *Object*

```
<html>

<script type="text/javascript" language="JavaScript">
<!--
```

```
// Create a new java String object.
var myStr = new java.lang.String("Example of javaArray");

// Create the new javaArray by assigning the array returned
// from getBytes to the variable myStrBytes.
var myStrBytes = myStr.getBytes();

document.write("The first byte contains: " + myStrBytes[0] + "<br>");
document.write("The second byte contains: " + myStrBytes[1] + "<br>");
document.write("The third byte contains: " + myStrBytes[2] + "<br>");

// -->
</script>

</html>
```

javaArray.length
JavaScript 1.1+
Nav3+, NES2+, Opera3+

Syntax

javaArrayName.length

Description

The length property of the javaArray object allows you to get the length of the javaArray.

Example

Listing 7.207 shows how the length property can be used to get the length of the *myStrBytes* javaArray object. Using a for loop, we loop through the whole length of the array and print out all its contents.

Listing 7.207   *Example Using the* javaArray length *Property*

```
<html>
<script type="text/javascript" language="JavaScript">
<!--

// Create a new java String object.
var myStr = new java.lang.String("Example of javaArray");
var myStrBytes = myStr.getBytes();

document.write("The length of the array is: " + myStrBytes.length +"<br>");

for (i=0; i < myStrBytes.length; i++)
{
```

Listing 7.207   *Continued*

```
   document.write("The value in myStrBytes index " + i + " is "
➡+ myStrBytes[i] + "<br>");
}

// -->
</script>

</html>
```

javaArray.toString
JavaScript 1.1+
Nav3+, NES2+, Opera3+

Syntax
javaArrayName.toString()

Description
The toString() method of the javaArray object returns the string representation of the javaArray. In JavaScript 1.4, this method is overridden by *java.lang.object.toString*.

Example
Listing 7.208 shows how the toString() method is used to output the string representation of the *myStrBytes*.

Listing 7.208   *Example Using the* toString *Method*

```
<html>
<script type="text/javascript" language="JavaScript">
<!--

// Create a new java String object.
var myStr = new java.lang.String("Example of javaArray");
var myStrBytes = myStr.getBytes();

document.write("The toString representation of the array is: "
➡+ myStrBytes.toString() +"<br>");

// -->
</script>

</html>
```

javaClass
JavaScript 1.1+
Nav3+, NES2+, Opera3+

Syntax

```
javaClass = classname
```

Description

The `javaClass` object provides you a reference to a single class in the Java package. A `javaClass` object is created by assigning a specific class object to a JavaScript defined variable. Once created, the JavaScript defined variable can access static fields and static methods of the instantiated class.

Example

Listing 7.209 shows how the `javaClass` property is used to reference the Color class within the `java.awt` package. After creating the `javaClass` object, `col`, a new color is created using the specified RGB values.

Listing 7.209   Example Using the `javaClass` Object

```
<html>
<body>
<script type="text/javascript" language="JavaScript">
<!--

col = package.java.awt.Color

 // Create color object with RGB values (Maroon).
 myColor = col(80,00,00);

// -->
</script>

</body>
</html>
```

javaObject

JavaScript 1.1+
Nav3+, NES2+, Opera3+

Syntax

```
javaObject = new Packages.JavaClass(parms)
```

Description

The `javaObject` object is a wrapped Java object that can be accessed within JavaScript code. It can be created in a script by assigning the return value of any Java method that returns an object type or by creating a new Java object.

Example

Listing 7.210 shows how the `javaObject` is used to get the `byteValue` of a Java Integer object.

Listing 7.210   Example Using the `javaobject` *Object*

```
<html>

<script type="text/javascript" language="JavaScript">
<!--

// Create a new java Integer object.
myInteger = new java.lang.Integer(492);
myByteVal = myInteger.byteValue();

// Display a specific byteValue.
document.write("This is the byteValue of 492: " + myByteVal);

// -->
</script>

</html>
```

javaPackage
>
> JavaScript 1.1+
> Nav3+, NES2+, Opera3+

Syntax

Packages.*javaPackage*

Description

The `javaPackage` object provides you with a reference to a specified Java Package.

Example

Listing 7.211 shows how the `javaPackage` is used to access the Java Font package and create a font object that has the `UNDERLINE_ON` property.

Listing 7.211   Example Using the `javaPackage` *Object*

```
<html>
<script type="text/javascript" language="JavaScript">
<!--

// Specify the font java package.
var myAWT = Packages.java.awt.font;

// Create a new Font object.
myfont = myAWT.TextAttribute.UNDERLINE_ON;

document.write("My Font is: " + myfont);
```

```
// -->
</script>

</html>
```

JSException

JavaScript 1.1+
Nav4+, NES2+

Syntax

a) public JSException()

b) public JSException(String s)

c) public JSException (String s, String filename, int lineNum,
➡String source, int token)

Description

The JSException object is an exception that is thrown when a piece of JavaScript code returns an error. It is part of the netscape.javascript package. The *s* parameter represents the message string. The *filename* parameter represents the URL of the file containing the error. The *lineNum* parameter represents the line number in the file in which the error occurred. The *source* parameter represents the string containing the code to be executed. The *token* parameter represents the index into the source string where the error occurred. The constructors listed previously are deprecated in JavaScript 1.4. Table 7.37 shows the JSException method.

Table 7.37 Method of the JSException *Object*

Method	Description
getWrappedException()	Returns the exception thrown

Example

Listing 7.212 shows how a JSException is used within a try...catch block. When running the eval() method, if the dog object is not defined, an exception will be thrown. When the catch block catches the exception, it will check to see whether the exception is a JSException. If it is, doRoutineA is called. Otherwise doRoutineB is called.

Listing 7.212 Example of a JSException *Object*

```
try {
    // Execute the specified statement.
    global.eval("dog.weight = 120;");
} catch (Exception e) {
    // If a JSException is caught, execute doRoutineA.
```

Listing 7.212   Continued

```
if (e instanceof JSException) {
   doRoutineA();
} else {
   doRoutineB();
}
}
```

JSException.getWrappedException()

JavaScript 1.4+
Nav6+, IE5.5+

Syntax

```
JSException.getWrappedException()
```

Description

The getWrappedException() method is used to unwrap a JSException. Typically, when JavaScript throws an exception, it is wrapped as an instance of JSException.

Example

Listing 7.213 shows how the getWrappedException() method is used to return the exception thrown as an unwrapped exception.

Listing 7.213   Example Using the getWrappedException() Method

```
import netscape.javascript.*;

public class test {
    public static Object execute(JSObject obj, String jsCode) {
        try {
            obj.eval(jsCode);
        }
        catch (JSException e) {
         // If a JSException is caught, then wrap and return.
            return e.getWrappedException();
        }
        return null;
    }
}
```

JSObject

JavaScript 1.1+
Nav4+, NES2+

Syntax

```
JSObject
```

Description

The JSObject object is a wrapped instance of the netscape.javascript.JSObject class. This wrapped instance allows a Java program to manipulate a JavaScript object. Table 7.38 lists the property and methods associated with the JSObject.

Table 7.38   Property and Methods of the JSObject Object

Type	Item	Description
Property	length	Specifies the number of elements in the javaArray.
Method	call()	Calls a JavaScript method.
	equals()	Checks whether two JSObjects refer to the same instance.
	eval()	Evaluates a JavaScript expression.
	getMember()	Retrieves a JavaScript property value.
	getSlot()	Retrieves a JavaScript array element value.
	getWindow()	Gets a JSObject for the window containing the applet.
	removeMember()	Removes a property of a JavaScript object.
	setMember()	Sets a JavaScript object property value.
	setSlot()	Sets a JavaScript object array element value.
	toString()	Converts a JSObject to a string.

Example

Listing 7.214 shows how a new JSObject object is used to access the properties of the JavaScript *Car* object. In Listing 7.215, the JavaScript code to create a *Car* object is displayed.

Listing 7.214   Example of the JSObject Object

```java
import netscape.javascript.*;

public class car
{
    public String carModel;
    public String carColor;
    public String carYear;

    // Define the class constructor.
    public car(JSObject jsCar)
    {
        this.carModel = (String)jsCar.getMember("model");
        this.carColor = (String)jsCar.getMember("color");
        this.carYear =  (String)jsCar.getMember("year");
    }
}
```

Listing 7.215 **Creating the** `Car` *Object*

```
<html>
<!--
<script type="text/javascript" language="JavaScript">

function Car(model,color,year) {
   this.model = model
   this.color = color
   this.year = year
}

// Create a new Car object.
myCar = new Car("M3","black","2001");

</script>
// -->

</html>
```

JSObject.call()

JavaScript 1.1+
Nav3+, NES2+

Syntax

JSObject.call(methodName, argArray)

Description

The `call()` method allows you to invoke a JavaScript method from within a Java program. Pass it the *methodName* and an array representing an array of Java objects used to pass arguments to the JavaScript method.

Example

Listing 7.216 shows how the `call()` method is used to inform the user of the browser name and version. When the applet is loaded in the browser, the `init()` method contains a call to the JavaScript's test function, which provides the alert. Listing 7.217 shows the HTML code for loading the applet.

Listing 7.216 **Java Applet Showing the** `call` **Method**

```
import java.applet.*;
import netscape.javascript.*;
import java.awt.Graphics;

public class myApplet extends Applet {
   String myString;
```

```
// Initialize the applet.
   public void init() {
      myString = new String("Pure JavaScript!");
      JSObject win = JSObject.getWindow(this);
      String args[] = {""};
      win.call("test", args);
   }

   public void paint(Graphics g) {
      g.drawString(myString, 25, 20);
   }

// Set the myString variable.
   public void setString(String aString) {
       myString = aString;
       repaint();
   }

}
```

Listing 7.217   Example of a JavaScript Program for the `call` ***Method***

```
<html>
<script type="text/javascript" language="JavaScript">
<!--
// Function to check the version of the browser being used.
function test() {
  alert("You are using " + navigator.appName + " " + navigator.appVersion)
}
// -->
</script>

<body>
<applet code="myApplet.class" name="myApplet" width=150 height=25 mayscript>
</applet>

<form name="form1">
<input type="button" value="Set String"
➥onClick="document.myApplet.setString(document.form1.str.value)"><br>
<input type="text" size="20" name="str">
</form>
</body>
</html>
```

JSObject.equals()

JavaScript 1.1+
Nav3+, NES2+

Syntax

```
JSObject.equals()
```

Description

The `equals()` method is used to check whether two `JSObjects` refer to the same instance.

Example

Listing 7.218 shows how the `equals()` method is used to see whether the *win* object and the *joe* object are equal.

Listing 7.218   Example Using the `equals` Method

```
// Function to check whether two objects are equal.
public void check() {
    win = JSObject.getWindow(this);
    joe = JSObject.getMember("address");

    if(joe.equals(win) ){
      System.out.println("Objects are equal");
    }
    else {
      System.out.println("Objects are NOT equal");
    }
}
```

JSObject.eval()
JavaScript 1.1+
Nav3+, NES2+

Syntax

```
JSObject.eval()
```

Description

The `eval()` method is used to execute a JavaScript expression.

Example

Listing 7.219 shows how the `eval()` method is used in the Java program to call an `alert()` JavaScript function indicating that the Applet is painting. Listing 7.220 shows the HTML for loading the Applet.

Listing 7.219   Example of using the `eval()` Method Within Java

```
import java.applet.*;
import netscape.javascript.*;
import java.awt.Graphics;
```

```java
public class myApplet extends Applet {
   String myString;

   // Initialize the applet.
   public void init() {
      myString = new String("Pure JavaScript!");
   }

   public void paint(Graphics g) {
      g.drawString(myString, 25, 20);
      JSObject win = JSObject.getWindow(this);
      win.eval("alert('Painting')");
   }

   // Set the myString variable.
   public void setString(String aString) {
      myString = aString;
      repaint();
   }

}
```

Listing 7.220   Example of JavaScript Loading Applet

```html
<html>
<body>

<!-- Load the applet in the browser -->
<applet code="myApplet.class" name="myApplet" width=150 height=25 mayscript>
</applet>

<form name="form1">
<input type="button" value="Set String"
onClick="document.myApplet.setString(document.form1.str.value)"><br>
<input type="text" size="20" name="str">
</form>

</body>
</html>
```

JSObject.getMember()
        JavaScript 1.1+
        Nav3+, NES2+

Syntax

JSObject.getMember()

Description

The getMember() method is used to retrieve the value of a property of a JavaScript object.

Example

Listing 7.221 shows how the getMember() method is used to get the properties of the new car object created from the JavaScript script.

Listing 7.222 shows the JavaScript code for creating a new Car object.

Listing 7.221   Example Using the getMember() Method to Get the Properties of the Car Object

```
import netscape.javascript.*;

public class car
{
    public String carModel;
    public String carColor;
    public String carYear;

    // Define the class constructor.
    public car(JSObject jsCar)
    {
        this.carModel = (String)jsCar.getMember("model");
        this.carColor = (String)jsCar.getMember("color");
        this.carYear =  (String)jsCar.getMember("year");
    }
}
```

Listing 7.222   Example of Creating a New Car Object

```
<html>
<!--
<script type="text/javascript" language="JavaScript">

function Car(model,color,year) {
   this.model = model
   this.color = color
   this.year = year
}

// Create a new Car object.
myCar = new Car("M3","black","2001");

</script>
// -->

</html>
```

JSObject.getSlot()

JavaScript 1.1+
Nav3+, NES2+

Syntax

```
JSObject.getSlot()
```

Description

The getSlot() method is used to get the value of an array element of a JavaScript object.

Example

Listing 7.223 shows how the getSlot() method is used to get the value of the second array element of a Car object.

Listing 7.223   Example Using the getSlot() **Method**

```
import netscape.javascript.*;

public class car
{
    public car(JSObject jsCar)
    {
        // Get the second array element.
        jsCar.getSlot(2);
    }
}
```

JSObject.getWindow()

JavaScript 1.1+
Nav3+, NES2+

Syntax

```
JSObject.getWindow()
```

Description

The getWindow() method is a static method that returns a handle to the current Navigator window.

Example

Listing 7.224 shows how the getWindow() method is used to assign a window handle to the *win* JSObject.

Listing 7.224   *Example Using the* `getWindow()` *Method*

```
public class myApplet extends Applet {
    public void init() {
        JSObject win = JSObject.getWindow(this);
    }
}
```

JSObject.removeMember()

JavaScript 1.1+
Nav3+, NES2+

Syntax

```
JSObject.removeMember()
```

Description

The `removeMember()` method is used to remove a property of a JavaScript object.

Example

Listing 7.225 shows how the `removeMember()` method is used to remove the *year* property of the `car` object.

Listing 7.226 shows the JavaScript code for creating a new `car` object.

Listing 7.225   *Example Using the* `removeMember()` *Method to Remove the* year *Property*

```
import netscape.javascript.*;

public class car
{

    // Define the class constructor.
    public car(JSObject jsCar)
    {
        jsCar.removeMember("year");
    }
}
```

Listing 7.226   *Example Defining the* Car *Object*

```
<html>
<!--
<script type="text/javascript" language="JavaScript">

function Car(model,color,year) {
    this.model = model
    this.color = color
    this.year = year
}
```

```
// Create a new Car object.
myCar = new Car("M3","black","2001");

</script>
// -->

</html>
```

JSObject.setMember()

JavaScript 1.1+
Nav3+, NES2+

Syntax

```
JSObject.setMember()
```

Description

The setMember() method is used to set the value of a property of a JavaScript object.

Example

Listing 7.227 shows how the setMember() method is used to set the value of the model property in the JavaScript car object (defined in Listing 7.xxx).

Listing 7.227 Example Using the setMember() Method to Set the model Property

```
import netscape.javascript.*;

public class car
{
    public car(JSObject jsCar)
    {
        // Set value of Model property
        jsCar.setMember("model","330ci");
    }
}
```

JSObject.setSlot()

JavaScript 1.1+
Nav3+, NES2+

Syntax

```
JSObject.setSlot()
```

Description

The setSlot() method is used to set the value of an array element of a JavaScript object.

Example

Listing 7.228 shows how the setSlot() method is used to set the value of the second array element to the string 0-60.

Listing 7.228   Example Using the setSlot() Method

```
import netscape.javascript.*;

public class car
{
    public car(JSObject jsCar)
    {
        // Set the value of array element 2.
        jsCar.getSlot(2,"0-60");
    }
}
```

JSObject.toString()

JavaScript 1.1+
Nav3+, NES2+

Syntax

```
JSObject.toString()
```

Description

The toString() method is used to obtain the string representation of the JSObject.

Example

Listing 7.229 shows how the toString() method is used to get the string representation of the *win* object.

Listing 7.229   Example Using the toString() Method

```
public void display() {
    win = JSObject.getWindow(this);
    win.eval("alert(win.toString() )" );

}
```

label

JavaScript 1.2+, JScript 1.0+
Nav4+, NES3+, IE3+

Syntax

```
label:

    code;
```

Description

The `label` keyword provides an identifier that can be used with `break` or `continue` to indicate where a program should continue execution. You can associate a block of JavaScript statements with each other using a label. When a label is called using `break` or `continue`, *code* is executed.

Example

Listing 7.230 shows an example of the `label` statement in conjunction with `break`.

Listing 7.230 Example of `label`

```
<html>
<body>
<script type="text/javascript" language="JavaScript">
<!--
// Define a label called doSomething.
doSomething:
   var x = 2+2;
   var y = 5*5;
   document.write("The value of 2+2 is: " + x + "<br>");


   // Define another label called doSomeMore.
   doSomeMore:
      for(i=0; i<5; i++){
         document.write("Ths value of i is: " + i + "<br>");
         if(i==2){
            break doSomeMore;
         }
      }
      document.write("I did some more." + "<br>");

   document.write("The value of 5 x 5 is: " + y + "<br>");
// -->
</script>

</body>
</html>
```

long

JavaScript 1.2+
Nav4+, NES3+

Syntax

Reserved Keyword

Description

The `long` keyword has not been implemented in server-side JavaScript to date. It has been reserved for future use.

Example

This keyword has not been implemented; therefore, no example is provided.

Math()

JavaScript 1.0+, ECMAScript 1E+, JScript 1.0+
Nav2+, NES2+, IE3+, Opera3+

Syntax

```
Core JavaScript Object
```

Description

The `Math` object is a built-in object containing properties and methods used for mathematical computation. It is a predefined JavaScript object and can be accessed without the use of a constructor or calling method. All `Math` properties and methods are static. Table 7.39 shows the different methods and properties of the `Math` object.

Table 7.39   *Properties and Methods of the* `Math` *Object*

Type	Item	Description
Property	ceil	Returns the smallest integer greater than or equal to a number
	E	Returns the value for Euler's constant
	LN10	Returns the natural logarithm of 10
	LN2	Returns the natural logarithm of 2
	LOG10E	Returnsthe base 10 logarithm of E
	LOG2E	Returns the base 2 logarithm of E
	PI	Returns the value of PI
	SQRT1_2	Returns the square root of 1/2
	SQRT2	Returns the square root of 2
Method	abs()	Returns the absolute value of a number
	acos()	Returns the arccosine of a number
	asin()	Returns the arcsine of a number
	atan()	Returnsthe arctangent of a number
	atan2()	Returns the arctangent of the quotient of its parameters
	cos()	Returns the cosine of a number
	exp()	Returns E^x, where x is a number
	floor()	Returns the largest integer less than or equal to a number
	log()	Returns the natural logarithm (base E) of a number

Type	Item	Description
	max()	Returns the larger of two arguments
	min()	Returns the smaller of two arguments
	pow()	Returns base to the exponent power, base^{exp}
	random()	Returns a random number between 0 and 1
	round()	Rounds a number to its nearest integer
	sin()	Returns the sine of a number
	sqrt()	Returns the square root of a number
	tan()	Returns the tangent of a number
	toSource()	Creates a copy of an object
	toString()	Returns a string representation of an object
	unwatch()	Removes a watchpoint
	watch()	Sets a watchpoint

Example

Listing 7.231 shows how to create a new Math object.

Listing 7.231 Example of Creating a Math Object

```
<html>
<body>
<title>Example of creating a Math object</title>
<script type="text/javascript" language="JavaScript">
<!--
// Create a new Math object.
var newMathObject = Math.E;
// -->
</script>

</body>
</html>
```

Math.abs()

JavaScript 1.0+, ECMAScript 1E+, JScript 1.0+
Nav2+, NES2+, IE3+, Opera3+

Syntax

math.abs (*num*)

Description

The abs() method of the Math object is used to calculate the absolute value of *num* compared to the Math object on which it is invoked.

Example

Listing 7.232 shows how to use the abs() method and what it returns.

Listing 7.232   Example of the abs() **Method**

```
<html>
<body>
<script type="text/javascript" language="JavaScript">
<!--
// Function calculates the absolute value of the input number.
function doMath(){
    var inputNum=document.form1.input.value;
    var result = Math.abs(inputNum);
    document.form1.answer.value = result;
}
// -->
</script>

<form name="form1">
This example calculates the absolute value of the number entered.
<br><br>
Enter Number:
<input type="text" name="input" size="10">
<input type="button" value="Calculate" onClick='doMath()'>
<br>
Answer:
<input type="text" name="answer" size="10">
</form>

</body>
</html>
```

Math.acos()

JavaScript 1.0+, ECMAScript 1E+, JScript 1.0+
Nav2+, NES2+, IE3+, Opera3+

Syntax

math.acos(num)

Description

The acos() method of the Math object is used to calculate the arccosine of a number.
The return value is between 0 and PI and is measured in radians. If the return value is
outside this range, 0 is returned.

Example

Listing 7.233 shows how the acos() method is used and what values can be returned.

Listing 7.233   Example of How to Use acos()

```
<html>
<body>
```

```
<script type="text/javascript" language="JavaScript">
<!--
// Function calculates the arccosine of the input number.
function doMath(){
    var inputNum=document.form1.input.value;
    var result = Math.acos(inputNum);
    document.form1.answer.value = result;
}
// -->
</script>

<form name="form1">
This example calculates the arccosine of the number entered.
<br><br>
Enter Number:
<input type="text" name="input" size=10>
<input type="button" value="Calculate" onClick='doMath()'>
<br>
The arccosine is:
<input type="text" name="answer" size=10>
</form>

</body>
</html>
```

Math.asin()

JavaScript 1.0+, ECMAScript 1E+, JScript 1.0+
Nav2+, NES2+, IE3+, Opera3+

Syntax

math.asin (num)

Description

The asin() method of the Math object calculates and returns the arcsine of a number. The return value is –PI/2 and PI/2 in radians. If the return value is not within this range, 0 is returned.

Example

Listing 7.234 shows how the asin() method is used.

Listing 7.234   Example of asin()

```
<html>
<body>
<script type="text/javascript" language="JavaScript">
<!--
// Function calculates the arcsine of the input number.
function doMath(){
```

Listing 7.234   Continued

```
    var inputNum=document.form1.input.value;
    var result = Math.asin(inputNum);
    document.form1.answer.value = result;
}
// -->
</script>

<form name="form1">
This example calculates the arcsine of the entered number.
<br><br>
Enter Number:
<input type="text" name="input" size="10">
<input type="button" value="Calculate" onClick='doMath()'>
<br>
The arcsine is:
<input type="text" name="answer" size="10">
</form>

</body>
</html>
```

Math.atan()

JavaScript 1.0+, ECMAScript 1E+, JScript 1.0+
Nav2+, NES2+, IE3+, Opera3+

Syntax

*math.*atan *(num)*

Description

The atan()method of the Math object is used to calculate the arctangent of a number.
The return value is a numeric value between –PI/2 and PI/2 radians.

Example

Listing 7.235 shows how the atan() method is used to calculate the arctangent of a
number.

Listing 7.235   Example of the atan() **Method**

```
<html>
<body>
<script type="text/javascript" language="JavaScript">
<!--
// Function calculates the arctangent of the input number.
function doMath(){
    var inputNum=document.form1.input.value;
    var result = Math.atan(inputNum);
```

```
    document.form1.answer.value = result;
}
// -->
</script>

<form name="form1">
This example calculates the arctangent of the input number.
<br><br>
Enter Number:
<input type="text" name="input" size="10">
<input type="button" value="Calculate" onClick='doMath()'>
<br>
The arctan is:
<input type="text" name="answer" size="10">
</form>

</body>
</html>
```

Math.atan2()

JavaScript 1.0+, ECMAScript 1E+, JScript 3.0+
Nav2+, NES2+, IE4+

Syntax

math.atan2*(num1, num2)*

Description

The atan2() method of the Math object is used to calculate the arctangent of the quotient of its parameters. It returns a numeric value between –PI and PI representing the angle theta of an (x, y) point.

Example

Listing 7.236 shows an example of how the atan2() method is used. The two inputs are taken and stored in variables, inputNum1 and inputNum2. The atan2() method is then called using the user input, and the result is stored in the variable result.

Listing 7.236   Example of the atan2() **Method**

```
<html>
<body>
<script type="text/javascript" language="JavaScript">
<!--
// Function calculates the arctangent of the
// quotient of the two arguments.
function doMath(){
    var inputNum1=document.form1.input1.value;
    var inputNum2=document.form1.input2.value;
```

Listing 7.236   Continued

```
    var result = Math.atan2(inputNum1, inputNum2);
    document.form1.answer.value = result;
}
// -->
</script>

<form name="form1">
Enter First Number:
<input type="text" name="input1" size="10">
<br>
Enter Second Number:
<input type="Text" name="input2" size="10">
<br><br>
<input type="button" value="Calculate" onClick='doMath()'>
<br>
Answer:
<input type="text" name="answer" size="10">
</form>

</body>
</html>
```

Math.ceil()

JavaScript 1.0+, ECMAScript 1E+, JScript 1.0+
Nav2+, NES2+, IE3+, Opera3+

Syntax

math.ceil (num)

Description

The ceil() method of the Math object is used to calculate the smallest integer that is greater than or equal to the number passed in as a parameter. This is similar to getting the ceiling of a number.

Example

Listing 7.237 shows how the ceil() method is used to get the smallest integer, which is greater than or equal to the number input by the user.

Listing 7.237   Example of the ceil() Method

```
<html>
<body>
<title>Example of the ceil() method</title>
<script type="text/javascript" language="JavaScript">
<!--
// Function calculates the ceiling integer.
```

```
// Takes input and passes it to the ceil method.
function doMath(){
    var inputNum=document.form1.input.value;
    var result = Math.ceil(inputNum);
    document.form1.answer.value = result;
}
// -->
</script>

<form name="form1">
This example calculates ceiling of the entered number.
<br><br>
Enter First Number:
<input type="text" name="input" size="10">
<input type="button" value="Calculate" onClick='doMath()'>
<br>
The ceil output is:
<input type="text" name="answer" size="10">
</form>

</body>
</html>
```

Math.cos()

JavaScript 1.0+, ECMAScript 1E+, JScript 1.0+
Nav2+, NES2+, IE3+, Opera3+

Syntax

math.cos (num)

Description

The cos() method of the Math object is used to calculate the cosine of a number. It returns a numeric value between −1 and 1, representing the cosine of an angle.

Example

Listing 7.238 shows how the cos() method is used to get the cosine of the number input by the user.

Listing 7.238   Example of the cos() Method

```
<html>
<body>

<script type="text/javascript" language="JavaScript">
<!--
// Function calculates the cosine of the input number
// takes the input from the user and passes the value to
// the cos() method which calculates the cosine value.
```

Listing 7.238   Continued

```
function doMath(){
    var inputNum=document.form1.input.value;
    var result = Math.cos(inputNum);
    document.form1.answer.value = result;
}
// -->
</script>

<form name="form1">
This example calculates the cosine of the entered number.
<br><br>
Enter First Number:
<input type="text" name="input" size="10">
<input type="button" value="Calculate" onClick='doMath()'>
<br>
The cosine is:
<input type="text" name="answer" size="10">
</form>

</body>
</html>
```

Math.E

JavaScript 1.0+, ECMAScript 1E+, JScript 1.0+
Nav2+, NES2+, IE3+, Opera3+

Syntax

math.E

Description

The E property of the Math object is used to get the value of Euler's constant. This is approximately 2.718.

Example

Listing 7.239 shows how the E property is used.

Listing 7.239   Example of the E Property

```
<html>
<body>

<script type="text/javascript" language="JavaScript">
<!--
// function to return Euler's constant
function doMath(){
    var result = Math.E;
    document.form1.answer.value = result;
```

```
}
// -->
</script>

<form name="form1">
Click on the button to get Euler's constant.
<br><br>
Euler's constant is:
<input type="text" name="answer" size="20">
<input type="button" value="Calculate" onClick='doMath()'>
<br>
</form>

</body>
</html>
```

Math.exp()

JavaScript 1.0+, ECMAScript 1E+, JScript 1.0+
Nav2+, NES2+, IE3+, Opera3+

Syntax

*math.*exp(*num*)

Description

The exp() method of the Math object is used to calculate an exponent in which the base is Euler's constant (the base of the natural logarithms).

Example

Listing 7.240 shows how the exp() method is used to calculate an exponential value using the number input by the user.

Listing 7.240 Example of the exp() Method

```
<html>
<body>

<script type="text/javascript" language="JavaScript">
<!--
// Function doMath calculates exponential value.
function doMath(){
    var inputNum=document.form1.input.value;
    var result = Math.exp(inputNum);
    document.form1.answer.value = result;
}
// -->
</script>

<form name="form1">
Enter First Number:
```

Listing 7.240   Continued

```
<input type="text" name="input" size="10">
<input type="button" value="Calculate" onClick='doMath()'>
<br>
The exponent is:
<input type="text" name="answer" size="10">
</form>

</body>
</html>
```

Math.floor()

JavaScript 1.0+, ECMAScript 1E+, JScript 1.0+
Nav2+, NES2+, IE3+, Opera3+

Syntax

math.floor (num)

Description

The floor() method of the Math object is used to get the largest integer number, which is equivalent to or less than the number passed as the parameter.

Example

Listing 7.241 shows how the floor() method is used.

Listing 7.241   Example of the floor() Method

```
<html>
<body>

<script type="text/javascript" language="JavaScript">
<!--
// Function calculates the floor of the input number.
function doMath(){
    var inputNum=document.form1.input.value;
    var result = Math.floor(inputNum);
    document.form1.answer.value = result;
}
// -->
</script>

<form name="form1">
This example calculates the floor of the number entered.
<br><br>
Enter First Number:
<input type="text" name="input" size="10">
<input type="button" value="Calculate" onClick='doMath()'>
<br>
```

```
The floor is:
<input type="text" name="answer" size="10">
</form>

</body>
</html>
```

Math.LN10

JavaScript 1.0+, ECMAScript 1E+, JScript 1.0+
Nav2+, NES2+, IE3+, Opera3+

Syntax

math.LN10

Description

The LN10 property of the Math object is used to get the natural logarithm of 10. This is approximately equal to 2.302.

Example

Listing 7.242 shows how the LN10 property is used. When the user clicks the button, the doMath function is called, which calculates the natural logarithm of 10 and displays the result in the input box.

Listing 7.242 Example of the LN10 Property

```
<html>
<body>

<script type="text/javascript" language="JavaScript">
<!--
// Function gets the natural log of 10.
function doMath(){
    var result = Math.LN10;
    document.form1.answer.value = result;
}
// -->
</script>

<form name="form1">
The Natural Logarithm of 10 is:
<input type="text" name="answer" size="20">
<input type="button" value="Calculate" onClick='doMath()'>
<br>
</form>

</body>
</html>
```

Math.LN2

JavaScript 1.0+, ECMAScript 1E+, JScript 1.0+
Nav2+, NES2+, IE3+, Opera3+

Syntax

*math.*LN2

Description

The LN2 property of the Math object is used to get the natural logarithm of 2. This is approximately equal to 0.693.

Example

Listing 7.243 shows how the LN2 property is used to get the natural logarithm of 2.

Listing 7.243   Example of the* LN2 *Property

```
<html>
<body>

<script type="text/javascript" language="JavaScript">
<!--
// Function gets the natural log of 2.
function doMath(){
    var result = Math.LN2;
    document.form1.answer.value = result;
}
// -->
</script>

<form name="form1">
The Natural Logarithm of 2 is:
<input type="text" name="answer" size="20">
<input type="button" value="Calculate" onClick='doMath()'>
<br>
</form>

</body>
</html>
```

Math.log()

JavaScript 1.0+, ECMAScript 1E+, JScript 1.0+
Nav2+, NES2+, IE3+, Opera3+

Syntax

*math.*log*(num)*

Description

The log() method of the Math object is used to calculate the natural logarithm (base E) of a number.

Example

Listing 7.244 shows how the log() method is used.

Listing 7.244   Example of the log() Method

```
<html>
<body>

<script type="text/javascript" language="JavaScript">
<!--

// Calculates the log of the input and displays the result.
function doMath(){
    var inputNum=document.form1.input.value;
    var result = Math.log(inputNum);
    document.form1.answer.value = result;
}
// -->
</script>

<form name="form1">
This example calculates the natural log of the number entered.
<br><br>
Enter First Number:
<input type="text" name="input" size="15">
<input type="button" value="Calculate" onClick='doMath()'>
<br>
The log is:
<input type="text" name="answer" size="10">
</form>

</body>
</html>
```

Math.LOG10E

JavaScript 1.0+, ECMAScript 1E+, JScript 1.0+
Nav2+, NES2+, IE3+, Opera3+

Syntax

math.LOG10E

Description

The LOG10E property of the Math object calculates the base 10 logarithm of Euler's constant. The return value is approximately 0.434.

Example

Listing 7.245 shows how the LOG10E property is used. When the user chooses the Calculate button, the doMath function is executed, which calculates the base 10 logarithm of Euler's constant and outputs the result in the text box.

Listing 7.245 Example of the LOG10E Property

```
<html>
<body>

<script type="text/javascript" language="JavaScript">
<!--
// Function gets the LOG10E value and displays the result.
function doMath(){
    var result = Math.LOG10E;
    document.form1.answer.value = result;
}
// -->
</script>

<form name="form1">
The Base 10 logarithm of Euler's constant is:
<input type="text" name="answer" size="20">
<input type="button" value="Calculate" onClick='doMath()'>
<br>
</form>

</body>
</html>
```

Math.LOG2E

JavaScript 1.0+, ECMAScript 1E+, JScript 1.0+
Nav2+, NES2+, IE3+, Opera3+

Syntax

math.LOG2E

Description

The LOG2E property of the Math object calculates the base 2 logarithm of Euler's constant. The return value is approximately 1.442.

Example

Listing 7.246 shows how the LOG2E property is used.

Listing 7.246   Example of the 1OG2E *Property*

```
<html>
<body>

<script type="text/javascript" language="JavaScript">
<!--
// Function calculates the LOG2E and display the result.
function doMath(){
    var result = Math.LOG2E;
    document.form1.answer.value = result;
}
// -->
</script>

<form name="form1">
The Base 2 logarithm of Euler's constant is:
<input type="text" name="answer" size="20">
<input type="button" value="Calculate" onClick='doMath()'>
<br>
</form>

</body>
</html>
```

Math.max()

JavaScript 1.0+, ECMAScript 1E+, JScript 1.0+
Nav2+, NES2+, IE3+, Opera3+

Syntax

math.max(num1, num2)

Description

The max() method of the Math object gets the maximum number of the two parameters passed to it. The larger value is returned as the result.

Example

Listing 7.247 shows how the max() method is used to get the larger of two values.

Listing 7.247   Example of the max() *Method*

```
<html>
<body>
```

Listing 7.247   Continued

```
<script type="text/javascript" language="JavaScript">
<!--
// Function returns the maximum of two arguments.
function doMath(){
    var inputNum1=document.form1.input1.value;
    var inputNum2=document.form1.input2.value;
    var result = Math.max(inputNum1, inputNum2);
    document.form1.answer.value = result;
}
// -->
</script>

<form name="form1">
This example takes the two numbers entered and determines which is
the larger number.
<br><br>
Enter First Number:
<input type="text" name="input1" size="10">
<br>
Enter Second Number:
<input type="text" name="input2" size="10">
<input type="button" value="Show Max number" onClick='doMath()'>
<br>
The Maximum number is:
<input type="text" name="answer" size="10">
</form>

</body>
</html>
```

Math.min()

JavaScript 1.0+, ECMAScript 1E+, JScript 1.0+
Nav2+, NES2+, IE3+, Opera3+

Syntax

math.min(num1, num2)

Description

The min() method of the Math object gets the minimum number of the two number
parameters passed to it. The smaller value is returned as the result.

Example

Listing 7.248 shows how to use the Math.min() method.

Listing 7.248 **Example of the** `min()` **Method**

```
<html>
<body>

<script type="text/javascript" language="JavaScript">
<!--
// Function returns the minimum of two arguments.
function doMath(){
    var inputNum1=document.form1.input1.value;
    var inputNum2=document.form1.input2.value;
    var result = Math.min(inputNum1, inputNum2);
    document.form1.answer.value = result;
}
// -->
</script>

<form name="form1">
This example takes the two numbers entered and determind which is
the smaller number.
<br><br>
Enter First Number:
<input type="text" name="input1" size="10">
<br>
Enter Second Number:
<input type="text" name="input2" size="10">
<input type="button" value="Show Min number" onClick='doMath()'>
<br>
The Minimum number is:
<input type="text" name="answer" size="10">
</form>

</body>
</html>
```

Math.PI

JavaScript 1.0+, ECMAScript 1E+, JScript 1.0+
Nav2+, NES2+, IE3+, Opera3+

Syntax

math.PI

Description

The PI property of the Math object is used to get the constant PI. This is approximately
3.14159.

Example

Listing 7.249 shows how the PI property is used. When the user clicks the Calculate button, the doMath function is called, which calculates the value of PI and returns the result to the text box.

Listing 7.249   Example of the PI Property

```html
<html>
<body>

<script type="text/javascript" language="JavaScript">
<!--
// Function returns the value of PI.
function doMath(){
    var result = Math.PI;
    document.form1.answer.value = result;
}
// -->
</script>

<form name="form1">
The Approximate value of PI is:
<input type="text" name="answer" size="20">
<input type="button" value="Calculate" onClick='doMath()'>
<br>
</form>

</body>
</html>
```

Math.pow()

JavaScript 1.0+, ECMAScript 1E+, JScript 1.0+
Nav2+, NES2+, IE3+, Opera3+

Syntax

math.pow(*num1, num2*)

Description

The pow() method of the Math object is used to calculate an exponent power.

Example

Listing 7.250 shows how the pow() method is used.

Listing 7.250   Example of the pow() Method

```html
<html>
<body>
```

```
<script type="text/javascript" language="JavaScript">
<!--
// Function takes two numbers and calculates the
// exponential power.
function doMath(){
    var inputNum1=document.form1.input1.value;
    var inputNum2=document.form1.input2.value;
    var result = Math.pow(inputNum1, inputNum2);
    document.form1.answer.value = result;
}
// -->
</script>

<form name="form1">
Enter Base number:
<input type="text" name="input1" size="10">
<br>
Enter exponent to be raised to:
<input type="text" name="input2" size="10">
<input type="button" value="Calculate" onClick='doMath()'>
<br>
The result is:
<input type="text" name="answer" size="10">
</form>

</body>
</html>
```

Math.random()

JavaScript 1.1+, ECMAScript 1E+, JScript 1.0+
Nav3+, NES2+, IE3+, Opera3+

Syntax

*math.*random(*num*)

Description

The random() method of the Math object is used to obtain a random number between
the values 0 and 1.

Example

Listing 7.251 shows how the random() method is used to calculate random numbers.

Listing 7.251   Example of the random() Method

```
<html>
<body>
```

Listing 7.251   *Continued*

```
<script type="text/javascript" language="JavaScript">
<!--
// Function generates a random number between 0 & 1.
function doMath(){
    var result = Math.random();
    document.form1.answer.value = result;
}
// -->
</script>

<form name="form1">
The random number is:
<input type="text" name="answer" size="20">
<input type="button" value="Calculate" onClick='doMath()'>
<br>
</form>

</body>
</html>
```

Math.round()

JavaScript 1.0+, ECMAScript 1E+, JScript 1.0+
Nav2+, NES2+, IE3+, Opera3+

Syntax

*math.*round*(num)*

Description

The round() method of the Math object is used to round a number to its nearest integer value. If the fractional portion of the number is .5 or greater, the result is rounded to the next highest integer. If the fractional portion of number is less than .5, the result is rounded to the next lowest integer.

Example

Listing 7.252 shows how the round() method is used.

Listing 7.252   *Example of the* round() *Method*

```
<html>
<body>

<script type="text/javascript" language="JavaScript">
<!--
// Function rounds input number to nearest integer.
function doMath(){
    var inputNum1=document.form1.input1.value;
```

```
        var result = Math.round(inputNum1);
        document.form1.answer.value = result;
}
// -->
</script>

<form name="form1">
Enter Number:
<input type="text" name="input1" size="10">
<input type="button" value="Round" onClick='doMath()'>
<br>
The rounded value is:
<input type="text" name="answer" size="10">
</form>

</body>
</html>
```

Math.sin()

JavaScript 1.0+, ECMAScript 1E+, JScript 1.0+
Nav2+, NES2+, IE3+, Opera3+

Syntax

math.sin (num)

Description

The sin() method of the Math object is used to calculate the sine of a number. It returns a numeric value between −1 and 1.

Example

Listing 7.253 shows how the sin() method is used.

Listing 7.253   Example of the sin() Method

```
<html>
<body>

<script type="text/javascript" language="JavaScript">
<!--
// Function calculates the sine of input number.
function doMath(){
        var inputNum1=document.form1.input1.value;
        var result = Math.sin(inputNum1);
        document.form1.answer.value = result;
}
// -->
</script>
```

Listing 7.253   Continued

```
<form name="form1">
Enter Number:
<input type="text" name="input1" size="10">
<input type="button" value="Calculate" onClick='doMath()'>
<br>
The sine is:
<input type="text" name="answer" size="20">
</form>

</body>
</html>
```

Math.sqrt()

JavaScript 1.0+, ECMAScript 1E+, JScript 1.0+
Nav2+, NES2+, IE3+, Opera3+

Syntax

math.sqrt *(num)*

Description

The sqrt() method of the Math object is used to calculate the square root of a number. If the return value is outside the required range, sqrt() returns 0.

Example

Listing 7.254 shows how the sqrt() method is used.

Listing 7.254   Example of the sqrt() Method

```
<html>
<body>

<script type="text/javascript" language="JavaScript">
<!--
// Function calculates the square root of input number.
function doMath(){
    var inputNum1=document.form1.input1.value;
    var result = Math.sqrt(inputNum1);
    document.form1.answer.value = result;
}
// -->
</script>

<form name="form1">
Enter Number:
<input type="text" name="input1" size="10">
<input type="button" value="Calculate" onClick='doMath()'>
```

```
<br>
The square root is:
<input type="text" name="answer" size="20">
</form>

</body>
</html>
```

Math.SQRT1_2

JavaScript 1.0+, ECMAScript 1E+, JScript 1.0+
Nav2+, NES2+, IE3+, Opera3+

Syntax

*math.*SQRT1_2

Description

The SQRT1_2 property of the Math object returns the square root of one half, which is approximately 0.707.

Example

Listing 7.255 shows how SQRT1_2 can be used. The function, doMath, returns the square root of 1/2 to the text box on the page.

Listing 7.255   Example of the SQRT1_2 **Property**

```
<html>
<body>

<script type="text/javascript" language="JavaScript">
<!--
// Function returns the square root of 1/2.
function doMath(){
    var result = Math.SQRT1_2;
    document.form1.answer.value = result;
}
// -->
</script>

<form name="form1">
The square root of 1/2 is:
<input type="text" name="answer" size="20">
<input type="button" value="Calculate" onClick='doMath()'>
<br>
</form>

</body>
</html>
```

Math.SQRT2

JavaScript 1.0+, ECMAScript 1E+, JScript 1.0+
Nav2+, NES2+, IE3+, Opera3+

Syntax

math.SQRT2

Description

The SQRT2 property of the Math object returns the value of the square root of 2. This is approximately equal to 1.414.

Example

Listing 7.256 shows how the SQRT2 property is used. The function, doMath, returns the square root of 2 to the text box on the page.

Listing 7.256   *Example of the* SQRT2 *Property*

```
<html>
<body>

<script type="text/javascript" language="JavaScript">
<!--
// Function returns the square root of 2.
function doMath(){
    var result = Math.SQRT2;
    document.form1.answer.value = result;
}
// -->
</script>

<form name="form1">
The square root of 2 is:
<input type="text" name="answer" size="20">
<input type="button" value="Calculate" onClick='doMath()'>
<br>
</form>

</body>
</html>
```

Math.tan()

JavaScript 1.0+, ECMAScript 1E+, JScript 1.0+
Nav2+, NES2+, IE3+, Opera3+

Syntax

math.tan *(num)*

Description

The tan() method of the Math object is to calculate the tangent of a number. It returns a value representing the tangent of an angle.

Example

Listing 7.257 shows how the tan() method is used.

Listing 7.257   *Example of the* tan() *Method*

```
<html>
<body>

<script type="text/javascript" language="JavaScript">
<!--
// Function returns the tangent of input number.
function doMath(){
    var inputNum1=document.form1.input1.value;
    var result = Math.tan(inputNum1);
    document.form1.answer.value = result;
}
// -->
</script>

<form name="form1">
This example calculates the tangent of the entered number.
<br><br>
Enter Number:
<input type="text" name="input1" size="10">
<input type="button" value="Calculate" onClick='doMath()'>
<br>
The tangent is:
<input type="text" name="answer" size="20">
</form>

</body>
</html>
```

Math.toSource()

> JavaScript 1.3+
> Nav4.06+

Syntax

math.toSource()

Description

The toSource()method of the Math object is used to create a copy of the object. It returns a string representation of an object, which can be passed to the eval() method to create a copy of the object.

Example

Listing 7.258 shows how the toSource() method is used to make a copy of the Math object.

Listing 7.258   Example of the toSource() **Method**

```html
<html>
<body>

<script type="text/javascript" language="JavaScript">
<!--
// Function makes copy of math object.
function copy(){
    var result = Math.toSource(Math.E);
    document.form1.answer.value = result;
}
// -->
</script>

<form name="form1">
Click on the button to create a copy of a Math object.
<br><br>
<input type="button" value="Copy" onClick='copy()'>
<br>
The result of toSource is:
<input type="text" name="answer" size="20">
</form>

</body>
</html>
```

Math.toString()

JavaScript 1.0+, JScript 3.0+
Nav2+, NES2+, IE4+

Syntax

math.toString()

Description

The toString() method of the Math object returns a string value representing the object.

Example

Listing 7.259 shows how the toString() method is used to get a string value representing the Math object.

Listing 7.259   Example of the toString() *Method*

```
<html>
<body>

<script type="text/javascript" language="JavaScript">
<!--
// Function returns string representation of math object.
function copy(){
    var result = Math.toString(Math.sqrt(45));
    document.form1.answer.value = result;
}
// -->
</script>

<form name="form1">
<input type="button" value="Get String" onClick='copy()'>
<br>
The result of toString is:
<input type="text" name="answer" size="20">
</form>

</body>
</html>
```

Math.unwatch()

> JavaScript 1.2+
> Nav4+, NES3+

Syntax

math.unwatch (prop)

Description

The unwatch() method of the Math object is used to turn off the watch on a particular property specified by *prop*. It is inherited from the Object object; however it cannot be used because math properties are read-only.

Example

All math properties are read-only; therefore, no example can be provided.

Math.watch()

> JavaScript 1.2+
> Nav4+, NES3+

Syntax

math.watch(prop, handler)

Description

The watch() method of the Math object will watch for an assignment to a specific property, *prop*. When an assignment is made, a specified *handler* will be called to perform a user-defined function. It is inherited from the Object object; however, it cannot be used because math properties are read-only.

Example

Math properties are read-only; therefore, no example is provided.

NaN

JavaScript 1.3+, JScript 1.0+
Nav4.06+, IE3+

Syntax

NaN

Description

The NaN object represents an object that is not equal to any number, including itself. NaN stands for *Not a Number*.

Example

Listing 7.260 shows how the NaN object is used within a comparison.

Listing 7.260   *Example Using the* NaN *Object*

```
<script type="text/javascript" language="JavaScript">
<!--
// Check to see if "a" is a number or not.
if ("a" != NaN){
    document.write("This is not a number");
}
// -->
</script>
```

native

JavaScript 1.2+
Nav4+, NES3+

Syntax

Reserved Keyword

Description

The native keyword has not been implemented in server-side JavaScript to date. It has been reserved for future use.

Example

This keyword has not been implemented, therefore no example is provided.

netscape

JavaScript 1.1+
Nav3+, NES2+, Opera3+

Syntax

```
netscape
```

Description

The `netscape` object allows you to access any class within the package `netscape.*`. It is shorter and works the same way as using the `packages.netscape` property.

Example

Listing 7.261 shows how the `netscape` property can be used to determine whether the current browser supports the `netscape` package.

Listing 7.261   Example Using the netscape *Object*

```
<html>
<body>
<script type="text/javascript" language="JavaScript">
<!--

// Check to see if the netscape package exists.
if (netscape){
   document.write ("This browser has the netscape package");
}
else{
    document.write ("This browser does not have the netscape package");
}

// -->
</script>

</body>
</html>
```

new

JavaScript 1.0+, JScript 1.0+
Nav2+, NES2+, IE3+, Opera3+

Syntax

```
new
```

Description

The new operator is used to create a new object.

Example

Listing 7.262 shows how new is used to create a new Array object.

Listing 7.262   *Example of* new

```
<html>
<body>

<script type="text/javascript" language="JavaScript">
<!--

// Creates a new array object with the name myArray.
var myArray = new Array();

// -->
</script>

</body>
</html>
```

null

JavaScript 1.2+, JScript 3.0+, ECMAScript 1.0+
Nav4+, NES3+, IE4+

Syntax

```
Reserved Keyword
```

Description

The null keyword has not been implemented in server-side JavaScript to date. It has been reserved for future use.

Example

This keyword has not been implemented; therefore, no example is provided.

Number()

JavaScript 1.2+, ECMAScript 1.0+
Nav4+, NES3+, IE5+

Syntax

```
Number (obj)
```

Description

The `Number()` method takes an object, *obj*, as input and converts it to a number. If the object is a string that is not a well-formed numeric literal, `NaN` is returned.

Example

Listing 7.263 shows an example of the `Number()` method. A new `Date` object is created and converted to a number.

Listing 7.263   Example `Number()` *Method*

```
<html>

<script type="text/javascript" language="JavaScript">
<!--
// Create a Date object.
var myStr = new Date();

// Convert the Date to a Number object and display.
document.write("The Number is: " + Number(myStr));

// -->
</script>

</html>
```

Number()

JavaScript 1.1+, ECMAScript 1E+, JScript 1.0+
Nav3+, NES2+, IE3+, Opera3+

Syntax

```
var variable = new Number(value)
```

Description

The `Number()` object represents numeric value types. You can create a `Number()` object by specifying a value in the parameter for the number constructor. Table 7.40 shows the different methods and properties of the `Number()` object.

Table 7.40   Properties and Methods of the `Number()` *Object*

Type	Item	Description
Property	`constructor`	Specifies the function that creates the object's prototype.
	`MAX_VALUE`	Specifies the largest value a number can have.
	`MIN_VALUE`	Specifies the smallest value a number can have without being equal to 0.
	`NaN`	Stands for *Not a Number*. Represents a value that is not equal to any numeric value.

Table 7.40   *Continued*

Type	Item	Description
	`NEGATIVE_INFINITY`	A special value that represents a negative infinity value.
	`POSITIVE_INFINITY`	A special value that represents a positive infinity value.
	`prototype`	Represents the prototype for the number class.
Method	`toExponential()`	Returns a string in exponential notation.
	`toFixed()`	Returns a fixed-length string representation of the number object.
	`toLocaleString()`	Returns a string representation of the number object in the host's Locale form.
	`toPrecision()`	Returns a string representation of the number object in an exponential format with a user specified number of digits.
	`toSource()`	Returns a string representation of the number object.
	`toString()`	Returns a string representing the specified number object.
	`unwatch()`	Removes a watchpoint on a specified property.
	`valueOf()`	Returns the primitive value of a number object as a number data type.
	`watch()`	Sets a watch point on a specified property.

Example

Listing 7.264 shows how a new `Number` object is created.

Listing 7.264   *Example of the* Number *Constructor*

```
<html>
<body>

<script type="text/javascript" language="JavaScript">
<!--
// Creates a new number object.

var aNum = new Number(3);
// -->
</script>

</body>
</html>
```

Number.constructor

JavaScript 1.1+, ECMAScript 1E+, JScript 2.0+
Nav3+, NES2+, IE4+

Syntax

```
Number.constructor
```

Description

The constructor property of the Number object specifies the function that creates the object.

Example

Listing 7.265 shows an example of the constructor property.

Listing 7.265 *Example Number* constructor *Property*

```
<html>

<script type="text/javascript" language="JavaScript">
<!--

// Create a new number object using the constructor property.
num = new Number(3)
if(num.constructor == Number){
    document.write("Object is created");
}
// -->
</script>

</html>
```

Number.MAX_VALUE

JavaScript 1.1+, ECMAScript 1E+, JScript 2.0+
Nav3+, NES2+, IE3+, Opera3+

Syntax

```
Number.MAX_VALUE
```

Description

The MAX_VALUE property of the Number object is used to get the maximum representable value for a number. This is approximately: 1.79E+308.

Example

Listing 7.266 shows how the MAX_VALUE property is used.

Listing 7.266 *Example of the* MAX_VALUE *Property*

```
<html>
<body>
```

Listing 7.266 Continued

```
<script type="text/javascript" language="JavaScript">
<!--
// Checks to see if the number is a MAX_VALUE.

if((9999*9999) != Number.MAX_VALUE){
    document.write("The number is not greater than the maximum value");
}
// -->
</script>

</body>
</html>
```

Number.MIN_VALUE

JavaScript 1.1+, ECMAScript 1E+, JScript 2.0+
Nav3+, NES2+, IE3+, Opera3+

Syntax

```
Number.MIN_VALUE
```

Description

The MIN_VALUE property of the Number object is used to get the minimum possible numeric value known to JavaScript. This is approximately: 2.22E–308.

Example

Listing 7.267 shows how the MIN_VALUE property is used.

Listing 7.267 Example of MIN_VALUE

```
<html>
<body>

<script type="text/javascript" language="JavaScript">
<!--
// Checks to see if the number is equal to the MIN_VALUE.

if((0.00000002) != Number.MIN_VALUE){
    document.write("The number is not the minimum value");
}
// -->
</script>

</body>
</html>
```

Number.NaN

JavaScript 1.1+, ECMAScript 1E+, JScript 2.0+
Nav3+, NES2+, IE3+, Opera3+

Syntax

```
Number.NaN
```

Description

The `NaN` property of the `Number` object represents a value that is not equal to any numeric value.

Example

Listing 7.268 shows how to use the `NaN` property. An integer constant, 123, is compared to the `NaN` constant to see whether it is a numeric value.

Listing 7.268   Example of the* NaN *Property

```
<html>
<body>

<script type="text/javascript" language="JavaScript">
<!--
// Checks to see if 123 is a number or not.

if(123 == Number.NaN){
     document.write("This is not a number");
}
// -->
</script>

</body>
</html>
```

Number.NEGATIVE_INFINITY

JavaScript 1.1+, ECMAScript 1E+, JScript 2.0+
Nav3+, NES2+, IE3+, Opera3+

Syntax

```
Number.NEGATIVE_INFINITY
```

Description

The `NEGATIVE_INFINITY` property of the `Number` object represents a negative infinity number. It is returned when a calculation returns a negative number greater than the largest negative number in JavaScript.

Example

Listing 7.269 shows how the NEGATIVE_INFINITY property is used. The sqrt() method is used on a number and the result is compared to NEGATIVE_INFINITY.

Listing 7.269   **Example of** NEGATIVE_INFINITY

```
<html>
<body>

<script type="text/javascript" language="JavaScript">
<!--
// Performs a square root calculation to obtain a negative result
// and then checks against the NEGATIVE_INFINITY value.

if((Math.sqrt(-2)) != Number.NEGATIVE_INFINITY_){
    document.write("This is not equal to NEGATIVE_INFINITY");
}
else{
    document.write("This is equal to NEGATIVE_INFINITY");
}

// -->
</script>

</body>
</html>
```

Number.POSITIVE_INFINITY
JavaScript 1.1+, ECMAScript 1E+, JScript 2.0+
Nav3+, NES2+, IE3+, Opera3+

Syntax

```
Number.POSITIVE_INFINITY
```

Description

The POSITIVE_INFINITY property of the Number object represents a positive infinity number. It is returned when a calculation returns a positive number greater than the largest number in JavaScript.

Example

Listing 7.270 shows how the POSITIVE_INFINITY property is used.

Listing 7.270   **Example of** POSITIVE_INFINITY

```
<html>
<body>
```

```
<script type="text/javascript" language="JavaScript">
<!--
// Performs some math computation and then checks the
// result against the POSITIVE_INFINITY value.
if((Math.exp(999)) != Number.POSITIVE_INFINITY_){
    document.write("This is less than POSITIVE INFINITY");
}
else{
    document.write('This is greater than POSITIVE_INFINITY");
}

// -->
</script>

</body>
</html>
```

Number.prototype
JavaScript 1.1+, ECMAScript 1E+, JScript 2.0+
Nav3+, NES2+, IE3+, Opera3+

Syntax

Number.prototype.*property*

Number.prototype.*method*

Description

The prototype property of the Number object allows you to add properties or methods to all instances of this class.

Example

Listing 7.271 shows how the prototype property is used.

Listing 7.271   Example of prototype

```
<html>
<body>

<script type="text/javascript" language="JavaScript">
<!--

// Creates a new Number property myProp.
var myProp = new Number();

// Sample function multiplies number by 3.
function triple(num){
```

Listing 7.271 **Continued**

```
    var result;
    result = (num * 3);
    return result;
}

// Add the prototype property to the number object.
Number.prototype.calc3 = triple;

document.write("Example demonstrates the prototype property for the number
object." + "<br><br>");
document.write("150 tripled is: " + myProp.calc3(150) + "<br>");
// -->
</script>

</body>
</html>
```

Number.toExponential()
JavaScript 1.3+, ECMAScript 3E+
Nav6+, IE5.5+

Syntax
number.toExponential()

Description
The toExponential()method of the Number object is used to get an exponential representation of the Number object.

Example
Listing 7.272 shows how the toExponential() method is used.

Listing 7.272 **Example of the** toExponential() **Method**

```
<script type="text/javascript" language="JavaScript">
<!--

var abc = 51000;
// Convert the number to Exponential form and display.
document.write("The variable in exponential form is: " + abc.toExponential() );

// -->
</script>
```

Number.toFixed()

JavaScript 1.4+, ECMAScript 3E+
Nav6+, IE5.5+

Syntax

number.toFixed(num)

Description

The toFixed() method of the Number object is used to get a fixed-point string representation of the Number object. The *num* parameter represents the number of digits after the decimal point.

Example

Listing 7.273 shows how the toFixed() method is used to get the fixed form of the standard Number object.

Listing 7.273   *Example of the* toFixed() *Method*

```
<script type="text/javascript" language="JavaScript">
<!--

var standard = 888000.4325;
// Convert the number to a fixed form and display.
document.write("Fixed Form is: " + standard.toFixed(0) );

// -->
</script>
```

Number.toLocaleString()

JavaScript 1.4+, ECMAScript 3E+, JScript 1.0+
Nav6+, IE5.5+, Opera5+

Syntax

number.toLocaleString()

Description

The toLocaleString()method of the Number object is used to get a string value that represents the Number object. The value will be formatted according to the conventions of the host environment's current locale.

Example

Listing 7.274 shows how the toLocaleString() method is used to display the string value of myNum.

Listing 7.274 *Example of the* `toLocaleString()` *Method*

```
<script type="text/javascript" language="JavaScript">
<!--

var myNum = 123456789;
// Get the string value and display.
document.write("The Locale String is: " + myNum.toLocaleString() );

// -->
</script>
```

Number.toPrecision()

JavaScript 1.4+, ECMAScript 3E+
Nav6+, IE5.5+

Syntax

number.toPrecision(num)

Description

The `toPrecision()`method of the `Number` object returns a string representation of the number in the format of one digit before the significand's decimal point and *num-1* digits after the diginificand's decimal point.

Example

Listing 7.275 shows how the `toPrecision()` method is used.

Listing 7.275 *Example of the* `toPrecision()` *Method*

```
<script type="text/javascript" language="JavaScript">
<!--

var myNum = 123456789.4444;
// Return the result of the toPrecision() method on myNum.
document.write("The Precision String is: " + myNum.toPrecision(2) );

// -->
</script>
```

Number.toSource()

JavaScript 1.3+, ECMAScript 1E+
Nav4.06+

Syntax

number.toSource()

Description

The toSource()method of the Number object is used to get a string representation of the Number object.

Example

Listing 7.276 shows how the toSource() method is used.

Listing 7.276 **Example of the** toSource() **Method**

```
<script type="text/javascript" language="JavaScript">
<!--
// Creates a new number object and then gets the string
// representation of that object.
var aNum = Number(21);
document.write(aNum.toSource());
// -->
</script>
```

Number.toString()

> JavaScript 1.1+, ECMAScript 1E+, JScript 1.0+
> Nav3+, NES2+, IE3+, Opera3+

Syntax

number.toString()

Description

The toString() method of the Number object is used to get a string representation of the Number object.

Example

Listing 7.277 shows how the toString() method is used.

Listing 7.277 **Example of the** toString() **Method**

```
<script type="text/javascript" language="JavaScript">
<!--
var aNum = Number(21);
// Return the string representation of aNum.
document.write("The string value for 21 is: " + "<b>"
➥+ aNum.toString() + "</b>");
// -->
</script>
```

Number.unwatch()

> JavaScript 1.1+, JScript 3.0+
> Nav3+, NES2+, IE4+

Syntax

number.unwatch(prop)

Description

The unwatch() method of the Number object will remove a watch point on a property set by the watch() method.

Example

Listing 7.278 shows an example for the unwatch() method.

Listing 7.278   Example of unwatch() **Method**

```
<html>

<script type="text/javascript" language="JavaScript">
<!--
function alertme(id,oldValue,newValue)
{
  document.writeln("myNum." + id + " changed from " + oldValue
+ " to " + newValue + "<br>")
  return newValue;
}

// Create a new Number object.
var myNum = new Number(10);

// Create a new property p.
Number.prototype.p = 1;
myNum.watch("p",alertme);

myNum.p = 2;
// Remove the watchpoint.
myNum.unwatch("p");
myNum.p = 3;
myNum.p = 4;

// Set the watchpoint.
myNum.watch("p",alertme);
myNum.p = 5;

// -->
</script>

</html>
```

Number.valueOf()

JavaScript 1.1+, JScript 2.0+
Nav3+, NES2+, IE4+

Syntax

*number.*valueOf()

Description

The valueOf() method of the Number object is used to get the primitive value of a Number object as a number data type.

Example

Listing 7.279 shows an example for the valueOf() method. A Number object is created and set to myNum. The document then outputs the result of performing a valueOf function on the number.

Listing 7.279   Example of the Number.valueOf() **Method**

```
<html>
<body>

<script type="text/javascript" language="JavaScript">
<!--

// Create a new number object.
myNum = new Number(24)

// Output the valueOf result.
document.write("The value of myNum is: " + myNum.valueOf());

// -->
</script>

</body>
</html>
```

Number.watch()

JavaScript 1.2+
Nav4+, NES3+

Syntax

*number.*watch(prop, handler)

Description

The watch() method of the Number object will watch for an assignment to a specific property, *prop.* When an assignment is made, a specified *handler* will be called to perform a user-defined operation.

Example

Listing 7.280 shows an example for the watch() method.

Listing 7.280 **Example of the** watch() *Method*

```
<html>
<body>

<script type="text/javascript" language="JavaScript">
<!--
// Function to alert user that p has changed.
function alertme(id,oldValue,newValue)
{
  document.writeln("myNum." + id + " changed from " + oldValue
➥+ " to " + newValue + "<br>")
  return newValue;
}

var myNum= new Number(10);
// Create a new property p.
Number.prototype.p = 1;

// Set the watchpoint on p.
myNum.watch("p",alertme);

myNum.p = 15;
// -->
</script>

</body>
</html>
```

Object()

JavaScript 1.1+, ECMAScript 1E+, JScript1.0+
Nav3+, NES2+, IE3+, Opera3+

Syntax

```
var variable = new Object(string)
```

Description

The Object() object is a primitive data type from which all JavaScript objects are derived. Table 7.41 shows the different properties and methods of the Object() object.

Table 7.41 **Properties/Methods of the** Object() *Object*

Type	Item	Description
Property	constructor	Creates an Object
	prototype	Creates a new property for a specific object
Method	eval()	Evaluates a string of JavaScript code for the specified object

Type	Item	Description
	toSource()	Returns a string representation for the object
	toString()	Converts the object to its string representation
	unwatch()	Removes a watchpoint for the object
	valueOf()	Returns the value of the specific object
	watch()	Adds a watchpoint to the object property

Example

Listing 7.281 shows how the Object object is used.

Listing 7.281   Example of the Object *Object*

```
<html>
<body>

<script type="text/javascript" language="JavaScript">
<!--
// Create an Object.
var myObj = new Object(foo);
document.write(Object foo created);
// -->
</script>

</body>
</html>
```

Object.constructor

JavaScript 1.1+, ECMAScript 1E+, JScript 3.0+
Nav3+, NES2+, IE4+

Syntax

```
object.constructor
```

Description

The constructor property of the Object object specifies the function that creates the object.

Example

Listing 7.282 shows an example of the constructor property.

Listing 7.282   Example Object constructor *Property*

```
<html>
<body>

<script type="text/javascript" language="JavaScript">
<!--
```

Listing 7.282 Continued

```
// Create a new number object using the constructor property.
num = new Number(3)
if(num.constructor == Number){
    document.write("Object is created");
}
// -->
</script>

</body>
</html>
```

Object.eval()

JavaScript 1.1+, ECMAScript 1E+, JScript 3.0+
Nav3+, NES2+, IE4+

Syntax

object.eval (*string*)

Description

The eval() method of the Object object evaluates a *string* of JavaScript code in reference to this object. Note: In version 1.4 and later, the eval() method is deprecated and can no longer be called directly for the Object object. To use eval() in versions 1.4 and 1.5, you must use the top-level *eval()* function.

Example

Listing 7.283 shows how the eval() method is used. Two variables are declared and set. A statement multiplying the two variables together is passed to the eval() method to be evaluated.

Listing 7.283 Example of the eval() **Method**

```
<html>
<body>

<script type="text/javascript" language="JavaScript">
<!--

var x = 9;
var y = 8;

// Display the result of x*y.
document.write("The result of x * y is: " + eval(x * y));
// -->
</script>

</body>
</html>
```

Object.prototype
JavaScript 1.1+, ECMAScript 1E+, JScript 2.0+
Nav3+, NES2+, IE4+

Syntax
```
object.prototype.property
```
```
object.prototype.method
```

Description
The `prototype` property of the `Object` object allows the addition of properties or methods to the `Object` class.

Example
Listing 7.284 shows how the `prototype` property is used.

Listing 7.284   Example of the `prototype` Property
```
<html>
<body>

<script type="text/javascript" language="JavaScript">
<!--
Object.prototype.newProperty = 2;
// Display the value of the newProperty.
document.write(document.object.newProperty.value);
// -->
</script>

</body>
</html>
```

Object.toSource()
JavaScript 1.3+
Nav4.06+

Syntax
```
object.toSource()
```

Description
The `toSource()` method is used to get a string representation of the object.

Example
Listing 7.285 shows how the `toSource()` is used.

Listing 7.285   Example of the toSource() **Method**

```
<html>
<body>

<script type="text/javascript" language="JavaScript">
<!--
// Creates a new number object and then gets the string
// representation of that object.
var aNum = Number(21);
document.write(aNum.toSource());
// -->
</script>

</body>
</html>
```

Object.toString()

JavaScript 1.1+, ECMAScript 1E+, JScript 2.0+
Nav3+, NES2+, IE4+, Opera3+

Syntax

object.toString()

Description

The toString() method is used to get a string representation of the Number object.

Example

Listing 7.286 shows how the toString() method is used.

Listing 7.286   Example of the toString() **Method**

```
<html>
<body>

<script type="text/javascript" language="JavaScript">
<!--
// Creates a number object.
var aNum = Number(21);

// Converts the number object to a string and outputs to document.
document.write(aNum.toString());
// -->
</script>

</body>
</html>
```

Object.unwatch()
JavaScript 1.2+
Nav4+, NES3+

Syntax
object.unwatch (*prop*)

Description
The unwatch() method of the Object object allows you to remove a watchpoint set on a property with the watch() method. This method takes the property, *prop*, as a parameter.

Example
Listing 7.287 shows how the unwatch() object is used. A temporary variable, tmp, is created and initialized. It is then set to be watched by invoking the watch() method. If any changes occur to the tmp variable, the inform function is called. After a change is made to the variable, unwatch() is called to turn off watch operations on the variable. After watch operations are disabled, the variable can be changed without notification.

Listing 7.287   Example of the unwatch() Method

```
<html>
<body>

<script type="text/javascript" language="JavaScript">
<!--
// Function informs the user when the tmp variable is changed.
function inform(){
    document.write("Tmp variable changed from 1 to 3");
}

// Declare a tmp variable.
var tmp = 1;

// Watch the tmp variable for any changes.
watch("tmp",inform);
tmp=3;

// Turn off watch on the tmp variable.
unwatch("tmp");
tmp=7;
// -->
</script>

</body>
</html>
```

Object.valueOf()

JavaScript 1.1+, ECMAScript 1E+, JScript 3.0+
Nav3+, NES2+, IE4+, Opera3+

Syntax

```
object.valueOf()
```

Description

The valueOf()method for the Object object is used to obtain the value of the specified object.

Example

Listing 7.288 shows how the valueOf() method is used.

Listing 7.288   Example of the valueOf() Method

```
<html>
<body>

<script type="text/javascript" language="JavaScript">
<!--

// Declare an age variable which contains a Number object.
var age = Number(30);

// Calculate the valueOf the variable and output to the document.
document.write(age.valueOf());
// -->
</script>

</body>
</html>
```

Object.watch()

JavaScript 1.2+
Nav4+, NES3+

Syntax

```
object.watch(prop, function)
```

Description

The watch() method of the Object object is used to watch for the event in which a property gets assigned a value. When the assignment is made, a user-defined function is executed. The method itself takes the property to watch, *prop*, and the function to call, *func*, when the event occurs.

Example

Listing 7.289 shows how the watch() method is used.

Listing 7.289   *Example of the* watch() *Method*

```
<html>
<body>
<title>Example of the watch method</title>
<script type="text/javascript" language="JavaScript">
<!--

// Function informs the user when the tmp variable is changed.
function inform(){
    document.write("Tmp variable changed from 1 to 3");
}

// Declare a tmp variable and initialize.
var tmp = 1;

// Turn on watch operations on the variable. If the tmp
// variable is changed, then the inform function is run.
watch("tmp",inform);

// Change the tmp variable.
tmp=3;
// -->
</script>

</body>
</html>
```

package

> JavaScript 1.2+
> Nav4+, NES3+

Syntax

Reserved Keyword

Description

The package keyword has not been implemented in server-side JavaScript to date. It has been reserved for future use.

Example

This keyword has not been implemented; therefore, no example is provided.

Packages

JavaScript 1.1+
Nav3+, NES2+

Syntax

Packages.*packagename*

Description

The Packages object is a built-in object that provides access to various Java packages within the browser. Each property of the Packages object refers to a JavaPackage object containing references to specific classes. Table 7.42 shows the default packages included in the Packages object.

Table 7.42   Properties of the Packages **Object**

Package	Description
classname	Refers to fully qualified name of Java class in package
java	Refers to the core Java classes
netscape	Refers to a set of Netscape classes
sun	Refers to the core Sun classes

Example

Listing 7.290 shows how the Packages object is used. The user is provided with an input text box. When something is entered in the input box and the button clicked, the input is sent to the Java Console using the Java classes package.

Listing 7.290   Example of the Packages **Object**

```
<html>
<body>
<script type="text/javascript" language="JavaScript">
<!--

// Function takes the users input and writes it out to
// the Java Console
function writeOut(input){
    Packages.java.lang.System.out.println(input);
}
// -->
</script>

<form name="form1">
This script takes the text input and writes it out to the Java Console
using the Java package.
<br><br>
Input:
```

```
<input type="text" size="40" name="txt">
<br><br>
<input type="button" value="Write Out Text" name="button1"
➥ onClick='writeOut(document.form1.txt.value)'>
<br>
</form>

</body>
</html>
```

Packages.className
> JavaScript 1.1+
> Nav3+, NES2+

Syntax

Packages.*className*

Description

The className property of the Packages object is used to access classes in packages other than netscape, sun, or java. Just specify the fully qualified name of the package you want to access for *className*.

Example

Listing 7.291 shows an example for accessing a fictitious class using the className property.

Listing 7.291 **Example of** Packages.className

```
<html>
<body>
<script type="text/javascript" language="JavaScript">
<!--

// Access the class: myClass.
myName = new Packages.myClass.Car()

// -->
</script>

</body>
</html>
```

Packages.java
> JavaScript 1.1+
> Nav3+, NES2+

Syntax

```
Packages.java.className.methodName
```

Description

The java sub-package of the Packages object refers to the JavaPackage containing the core Java class library. This sub-package is used for several things, but most notably for adding security to LiveConnect and accessing the Java Console.

Example

Listing 7.292 shows an example for the java sub-package. It is used to write text to the Java Console.

Listing 7.292   Example of the Packages.java Sub-package

```html
<html>
<body>
<script type="text/javascript" language="JavaScript">
<!--

// Use the Java sub-package to write text to the Java Console.
Packages.java.lang.System.out.println("Hello World!");

// -->
</script>

</body>
</html>
```

Packages.netscape

JavaScript 1.1+
Nav3+, NES2+

Syntax

```
Packages.netscape.className.methodName
```

Description

The netscape sub-package of the Packages object refers to the JavaPackage containing the netscape package. This sub-package is used by Java applets to access JavaScript code via LiveConnect. The package itself has two classes: plugin and javascript.

Example

Use of this package occurs within the code of a Java applet, and not JavaScript code. However, Listing 7.293 shows an example of calling the netscape package directly to verify it is implemented in the operating browser.

Listing 7.293 *Example of Accessing the* netscape *Package*

```
<html>
<body>
<script type="text/javascript" language="JavaScript">
<!--

// Call the package to see if it exists.
if(Packages.netscape){
  document.write("This browser has LiveConnect!");
}else{
  document.write("This browser does not have LiveConnect!");
}
// -->
</script>

</body>
</html>
```

Packages.sun

JavaScript 1.1+
Nav3+, NES2+

Syntax

Packages.sun.*className.methodName*

Description

The sun sub-package of the Packages object refers to the JavaPackage for the sun property. This sub-package is used for several things, but most notably for adding security to LiveConnect.

Example

Use of this package occurs within the code of a Java applet, and not JavaScript code. However, Listing 7.294 shows an example of calling the sun package directly to verify it is implemented in the operating browser.

Listing 7.294 *Example of Accessing the* sun *Package*

```
<html>
<body>
<script type="text/javascript" language="JavaScript">
<!--

// Call the package to see if it exists.
if(Packages.sun){
  document.write("This browser has LiveConnect!");
}else{
  document.write("This browser does not have LiveConnect!");
```

Listing 7.294 Continued

```
}
// -->
</script>

</body>
</html>
```

parseFloat()

JavaScript 1.0+, ECMAScript 1E+, JScript 1.0+
Nav2+, NES2+, IE3+, Opera3+

Syntax

```
paraseFloat (string)
```

Description

The parseFloat() function is used to convert a string to a number.

Example

Listing 7.295 shows how the parseFloat() is used. In the example, parseFloat() is called with two different strings. The first string, which contains numeric characters, is converted into a number without any problem. The second string, which contains alphabetic characters, is unable to be converted into a number.

Listing 7.295 Example of the parseFloat() Method

```
<html>
<body>

<script type="text/javascript" language="JavaScript">
<!--
// Convert the "1245.31" string to a number.
document.write("The string 1245.31 converted is"
+ parseFloat("1245.31") + "<br>");

// Try to convert the string "test" to a number.
// If not possible, then print error.
if( isNaN(parseFloat("test")) ){
   document.write("Cannot convert test string to a number.");
}
// -->
</script>

</body>
</html>
```

parseInt()

JavaScript 1.0+, ECMAScript 1E+, JScript 1.0+
Nav2+, NES2+, IE3+, Opera3+

Syntax

```
parseInt(string, radix)

parseInt(string)
```

Description

The parseInt() method is used to convert a string to an integer. It can take *string* input with an optional *radix* input. The *radix* input represents the base of the number in the string.

Example

Listing 7.296 shows how parseInt() is used to parse a string. A few different examples are shown for different types of strings.

Listing 7.296   Example of the parseInt() **Method**

```
<html>
<body>
<script type="text/javascript" language="JavaScript">
<!--

// Converts the "859" string to an integer.
document.write("The string 859 converted to an integer is: ");
document.write(parseInt("859") + "<br>");

// Converts a binary string into an integer.
document.write("The binary string 101101 converted to an integer is: ");
document.write(parseInt("101101", 2) + "<br>");

// Converts a hexidecimal string into an integer.
document.write("The hexidecimal string FA832B converted to an integer is: ");
document.write(parseInt("FA832B", 16) + "<br>");

// -->
</script>

</body>
</html>
```

private

JavaScript 1.2+
Nav4+, NES3+

Syntax

```
Reserved Keyword
```

Description

The private keyword has not been implemented in server-side JavaScript to date. It has been reserved for future use.

Example

This keyword has not been implemented; therefore, no example is provided.

protected

> JavaScript 1.2
> Nav4+, NES3+

Syntax

```
Reserved Keyword
```

Description

The protected keyword has not been implemented in server-side JavaScript to date. It has been reserved for future use.

Example

This keyword has not been implemented; therefore, no example is provided.

public

> JavaScript 1.2+
> Nav4+, NES3+

Syntax

```
Reserved Keyword
```

Description

The public keyword has not been implemented in server-side JavaScript to date. It has been reserved for future use.

Example

This keyword has not been implemented; therefore, no example is provided.

RegExp()

> JavaScript 1.2+, JScript 3.0+
> Nav4+, NES3+, IE4+

Syntax

```
var variable = new RegExp(pattern, flags)
```

Description

The RegExp() object represents a regular expression that is used for pattern matching. The creation of the object takes *pattern* and *flags* parameters. The *pattern* is a valid regular expression. The *flags* are either or both g (global) and i (ignore case). Table 7.43 displays the properties and methods of the RegExp() object.

Table 7.43   *Properties and Methods of the* RegExp() *Object*

Type	Item	Description
Property	RegExp,$*	Represents multiline
	RegExp.$&	Represents lastmatch
	RegExp.$_	Represents input
	RegExp.$`	Represents leftContext
	RegExp.$'	Represents rightContext
	RegExp.$+	Represents lastParen
	RegExp.$1,$2,...$9	Represents substring of matches
	constructor	Creates the object
	global	Specifies whether to check the expressions against all possible matches
	ignoreCase	Whether case is ignored during a string search
	input	String that is matched
	lastIndex	Specifies the index at which to start matching the next string
	lastMatch	Last matched characters
	lastParen	The last parenthesized substring match
	leftContext	The substring preceding the most recent match
	multiline	Specifies whether to search on multiple lines
	prototype	Represents the prototype for the RegExp object
	rightContext	The substring following the most recent match
	source	The string pattern
Method	compile()	Compiles a regular expression
	exec()	Executes the search for a match in a specified string
	test()	Tests for a string match
	toString()	Returns a string representation of the object
	unwatch()	Removes a watch point on the object
	valueOf()	Returns the primitive value of the object
	watch()	Sets a watchpoint on the object

Example

Listing 7.297 shows how to use the RegExp object. The user is given an input field, which is used to input a Social Security Number (SSN). Once entered, the Validate button is clicked, which checks whether the input is valid. This is performed by using a RegExp object for the SSN.

Listing 7.297   Example of the RegExp Object

```
<html>
<body>

<script type="text/javascript" language="JavaScript">
<!--
// Function checks to see if the ssn is valid.
function isSSN(str){

   // Define a RegExp object which checks for either
   // a 9 digit input or an input in the form:
   // xxx-xx-xxxx
   var regexp = /^(\d{9}|\d{3}-\d{2}-\d{4})$/;
   return regexp.test(str);
}

// Checks the SSN input.
function checkInput(){
  var valid = true;
  var ssn = document.form1.ssn.value;
  if (!isSSN (ssn)){
      window.alert("Invalid SSN: " + ssn);
      valid = false;
  }
  else{
    alert(ssn + " is a valid SSN");
  }
}

// -->
</script>

<form name="form1">
Enter your SSN:
<input type="text" size="15" name="ssn">
<br><br>
<input type="button" value="Validate SSN" onClick='checkInput()'>
<br>
</form>
</body>
</html>
```

RegExp,$*

JavaScript 1.2+
Nav4+, NES3+, IE4+

Syntax

```
RegExp, $*
```

Description

The `RegExp,$*` property reflects a `multiline` string search. This is a Boolean, read-only value that reflects whether strings should be searched across multiple lines. This is the same as using the `multiline` property.

Example

Listing 7.298 shows how to use `RegExp,$*` for pattern matching.

Listing 7.298   Example of `RegExp,$*`

```
<html>

<script type="text/javascript" language="JavaScript">
<!--
// Function checks for the "the" expression.  However, if
// multiple lines are read, an alert box is displayed
// indicating so.
function getinfo(){

var myPat = new RegExp("the", "i");
var str = document.form1.mytext.value;
myArray = myPat.exec(str);

    alert("RegExp.$* is: " + RegExp["$*"]);
}
// -->
</script>

<body>
<form name="form1">
When the text in the text box is changed, and the document is clicked,
an alert box will be displayed showing the value of RegExp.$*.
<br><br>
<textarea name="mytext" cols="60" rows="8" onChange='getinfo()'>
This is a sample textarea containing some dummy text for
testing purposes. The text in this box will be used to
demonstrate how the multiline property is used. If multiple lines are
read, then RegExp.$* will be true.
</textarea>
```

Listing 7.298   Continued

```
<br>
</form>

</body>
</html>
```

RegExp.$&

JavaScript 1.2+, JScript 3.0+
Nav4+, NES3+, IE4+

Syntax

```
RegExp.$&
```

Description

The RegExp.$& property represents the last matched characters. This is the same as using the lastMatch property.

Example

Listing 7.299 shows how RegExp.$& is used.

Listing 7.299   Example of RegExp.$&

```
<html>
<body>

<script type="text/javascript" language="JavaScript">
<!--
// Define a pattern to search for.
var pat = new RegExp("test", "gi");
str = "Testing Testing 123";
myArray = pat.exec(str);

// Once pattern is found, display message.
document.write("Pattern found: " + myArray[0] +
            ". the last match expression ($&) is: " + RegExp["$&"]);
// -->
</script>

</body>
</html>
```

RegExp,$_

JavaScript 1.2+
Nav4+, NES3+, IE4+

Syntax

```
RegExp,$_
```

Description

The `RegExp,$_` property represents the input to which a string is matched. This is the same as using the `input` property.

Example

Listing 7.300 shows how to use the `RegExp,$_` property.

Listing 7.300 ***Example of*** `RegExp,$_`

```
<html>
<body>

<script type="text/javascript" language="JavaScript">
<!--
// Function creates a new regular expression and
// then executes it against the text in the textbox.
// Outputs an alert message indicating the value
// of the RegExp.input property.
function getinput(){

var myPat = new RegExp("the", "i");
var str = document.form1.mytext.value;
myArray = myPat.exec(str);

    alert("The RegExp$ is: " + RegExp["$_"]);
}
// -->
</script>

<form name="form1">
When the text in the text box below is changed, an alert message
will appear showing the value of the input.
<br><br>
Enter some Text:
<input type="text" name="mytext" size="40" onChange='getinput()'>
<br>
</form>

</body>
</html>
```

RegExp.$`

JavaScript 1.2+
Nav4+, NES3+, IE4+

Syntax

```
RegExp.$`
```

Description

The `RegExp.$`` property represents the substring preceding the most recent pattern match. This is the same as using the `leftContext` property.

Example

Listing 7.301 shows how to use `RegExp.$``.

Listing 7.301   Example of `RegExp.$``

```
<html>
<body>

<script type="text/javascript" language="JavaScript">
<!--
// Define a regular expression pattern and match globally.
pat = /is*/g;

// Create a string object.
var str = "I know where the fish is tonight.";

// Create an array to hold the results.
myArray = pat.exec(str);

document.write("Check for the substring " + "<i>" + "is" + "</i>");
document.write("preceeding most recent pattern match");
document.write("In the string: " + "<b>");
document.write("I know where the fish is tonight" + "</b><br><br>");
document.write("The RegExp. $` is: " + RegExp["$`"]);

// -->
</script>

</body>
</html>
```

RegExp.$'

> JavaScript 1.2+
> Nav4+, NES3+, IE4+

Syntax

```
RegExp.$'
```

Description

The `RegExp.$'` property represents the substring following the most recent pattern match. This is the same as using the `rightContext` property.

Example

Listing 7.302 shows how to use `RegExp.$'`.

Listing 7.302   *Example of* `RegExp.$'`

```
<html>
<body>

<script type="text/javascript" language="JavaScript">
<!--
// Define a regular expression pattern and match globally.
pat = /be*/gi;

// Create a string object.
var str = "Eat Drink and be Merry.";

// Create an array to hold the results.
myArray = pat.exec(str);

document.write("Check for the substring " + "<i>" + "be" + "</i>");
document.write("following the most recent pattern match");
document.write("In the string: " + "<b>" +
               "Eat Drink and be Merry" + "</b><br><br>");
document.write("The RegExp$' is: " + RegExp["$'"]);

// -->
</script>

</body>
</html>
```

RegExp.$+

JavaScript 1.2+, JScript 3.0+
Nav4+, NES3+, IE4+

Syntax

`RegExp.$+`

Description

The `RegExp.$+` property represents the last parenthesized substring pattern match. This is the same as using the `lastParen` property.

Example

Listing 7.303 shows how RegExp.$+ is used.

Listing 7.303   Example of RegExp.$+

```
<html>
<body>

<script type="text/javascript" language="JavaScript">
<!--
// Define a regular expression.
exp = new RegExp("(please)", "g");

// Create a string object.
str = "Will you (please) stop yelling!";
myArray = exp.exec(str);

// Inform user what the lastParen property is.
document.write("The RegExp.$+is: " + "<b>"
              + RegExp["$+"]+ "</b>");

// -->
</script>

</body>
</html>
```

RegExp.$1,$2,..$9

JavaScript 1.2+, JScript 1.0+
Nav4+, NES3+, IE4+

Syntax

```
RegExp.$1,$2,..$9
```

Description

The RegExp.$1,$2,..$9 property represents parenthesized substring matches.

Example

Listing 7.304 shows how RegExp.$1,$2,..$9 is used. The user will enter his phone number in the input text box and, when the button is clicked, the swap function swaps the last four digits in the phone number with the first three.

Listing 7.304   Example of RegExp.$1,$2,..$9

```
<html>


<script type="text/javascript" language="JavaScript">
```

```
<!--
// Function takes the input and swaps the last 4 digits with the
// first three digits.
function swap(){
re = /(\w+)\D(\w+)/;
str = document.form1.text1.value;
newstr=str.replace(re, "$2, $1");
document.form1.text2.value = newstr;
}
// -->
</script>

<body>
<form name="form1">
Enter your 7 digit phone number in the form xxx-xxxx
<br><br><br>
Phone Number (7 digits):<input type="text" name="text1" size="10">
<br><br>
<input type="button" value="Swap" onClick='swap()'>
<br><br><br>
Output: <input type="text" name="text2" size="10">
</form>

</body>
</html>
```

RegExp.constructor()

JavaScript 1.1+, JScript 3.0+
Nav3+, NES2+, IE4+, Opera5+

Syntax

regexp.constructor

Description

The constructor property of the RegExp object specifies the function that creates the object.

Example

Listing 7.305 shows how the constructor property is used to create a RegExp object.

Listing 7.305   *Example of the* constructor *Property*

```
<html>
<body>

<script type="text/javascript" language="JavaScript">
<!--
```

Listing 7.305   Continued

```
// Create a new RegExp object using the constructor property.
myExp = new RegExp("the")
if(myExp.constructor == RegExp){
    document.write("Object is created");
}
// -->
</script>

</body>
</html>
```

RegExp.compile()

JavaScript 1.2+
Nav4+, NES3+, IE4+

Syntax

regexp.compile(*pattern*, *flag*)

Description

The compile() method of the RegExp object compiles a regular expression object. The creation of the object takes *pattern* and *flags* parameters. The *pattern* is a valid regular expression. The *flags* are either or both g (global) and i (ignore case).

Example

Listing 7.306 shows how to use the compile() method. A pattern is created using the RegExp constructor. It is then compiled using the compile() method, and the result is displayed in the text area.

Listing 7.306   Example of the compile() *Method*

```
<html>


<script type="text/javascript" language="JavaScript">
<!--
var myPat = new RegExp("jane", "i");
var newPat = myPat.compile(myPat);

// function displays the result of the compiled pattern.
function getinfo(){
    document.form1.text1.value = newPat;
}
// -->
</script>
<body>
```

```
<form name="form1">
Click the button below to get the pattern for the following
command: new RegExp("jane", "i");
<br><br><br>
Compiled Pattern: <input type="text" name="text1" size="30">
<br><br>
<input type="button" value="Get Pattern" onClick='getinfo()'>
</form>

</body>
</html>
```

RegExp.exec()
JavaScript 1.2+
Nav4+, NES3+, IE4+

Syntax

regexp.exec (*string*)

Description

The exec() method of the RegExp object executes the search for a match in a specified string. The results are returned in an array. The *string* passed contains the string the regular expression is trying to match in.

Example

In Listing 7.307, you see how the exec() method is used. A regular expression is defined and executed on the string using the exec() method.

Listing 7.307   Example of the exec() Method

```
<html>
<body>

<script type="text/javascript" language="JavaScript">
<!--
// Checks for the pattern "xyz" in str. If found, then
// output written to document indicating that it was found and
// displays the index it was found in the string.

myRe=/xyz*/g;
str = "abcxyzdefhij"
myArray = myRe.exec(str);

document.writeln("Found " + myArray[0] + " in the pattern: " + "<b>" +
                 "abcxyzdefhij " + "</b>" + " at index " +
                 (myRe.lastIndex - 3));
```

Listing 7.307   Continued

```
// -->
</script>
</body>
</html>
```

RegExp.global

> JavaScript 1.2+
> Nav4+, NES3+, IE4+

Syntax

regexp.global

Description

The `global` property of the `RegExp` object specifies whether the g flag is used with the regular expression. If so, a global pattern match will be performed.

Example

Listing 7.308 shows how the `global` property is used. A new `RegExp` object is created specifying the `global` option. When the script is loaded, the expression is checked and the value of the `global` property is printed out.

Listing 7.308   Example of the global *Property*

```
<html>
<body>

<script type="text/javascript" language="JavaScript">
<!--
// Defines a regular expression on the pattern "if"
// with the global flag set.
var myPat = new RegExp("if", "g");

// Define a string.
var str = "What if Angela is wondering about gifs?";

// Store results of exec into myArray.
myArray = myPat.exec(str);

document.write("The value of RegExp.global is: " + "<b>"
               + myPat.global + "</b>");
// -->
</script>

</body>
</html>
```

RegExp.ignoreCase
JavaScript 1.2+
Nav4+, NES3+, IE4+

Syntax
`regexp.ignoreCase`

Description
The `ignoreCase` property of the `RegExp` object is a flag that informs the user whether case is to be ignored during pattern matching.

Example
Listing 7.309 shows how `ignoreCase` is used. A new `RegExp` object is created specifying the `ignoreCase` option. When the script is loaded, the expression is checked and according to the value of the `ignoreCase` property, an appropriate message is displayed.

Listing 7.309   Example of `ignoreCase`

```
<html>
<body>

<script type="text/javascript" language="JavaScript">
<!--
// Defines a regular expression on the pattern "and"
// with the ignore case flag set.
var myPat = new RegExp("and", "i");

// Define a string.
var str = "Would Missy and Livvy like some Candy?";

// Store results of exec into myArray.
myArray = myPat.exec(str);

if (myPat.ignoreCase == true){
    document.write("The " + "<i>" + "ignoreCase" + "</i>" + " option WAS
used");
}
else{
    document.write("The " + "<i>" + "ignoreCase" + "</i>" + " was NOT used");
}

// -->
</script>

</body>
</html>
```

RegExp.input

JavaScript 1.2+, JScript 3.0+
Nav4+, NES3+, IE4+

Syntax

regexp.input

Description

The input property of the RegExp object represents the string on which the pattern matching is performed.

Example

Listing 7.310 shows how to use the input property.

Listing 7.310 Example of the input Property

```
<html>
<body>

<script type="text/javascript" language="JavaScript">
<!--
// Function creates a new regular expression and
// then executes it against the text in the textbox.
// Outputs an alert message indicating the value
// of the RegExp.input property.
function getinput(){

var myPat = new RegExp("the", "i");
var str = document.form1.mytext.value;
myArray = myPat.exec(str);

    alert("The RegExp.input is: " + RegExp.input);
}

// -->
</script>

<form name="form1">
When the text in the text box below is changed, an alert message
will appear showing the value of the input.
<br><br>
Enter some Text:
<input type="text" name="mytext" size="40" onChange='getinput()'>
<br>
</form>

</body>
</html>
```

RegExp.lastIndex

JavaScript 1.2+, JScript 3.0+
Nav4+, NES3+, IE4+

Syntax

regexp.lastIndex

Description

The lastIndex property of the RegExp object is used to get the index of where the next match begins.

Example

Listing 7.311 shows how the lastIndex property is used. A regular expression for "is" is created and checked against the string. When found, results are written to the document.

Listing 7.311   *Example of* lastIndex

```
<html>
<body>

<script type="text/javascript" language="JavaScript">
<!--
</script>

// Creates a regular expression for "is".
exp=/is*/g;
str = "This is just a sample sentence.";
myArray = exp.exec(str);

document.write("Found: " + myArray[0] +
             ". Next match starts at index: " + exp.lastIndex);
// -->
</script>
</body>
</html>
```

RegExp.lastMatch

JavaScript 1.2+, JScript 5.5+
Nav4+, NES3+, IE4+

Syntax

regexp.lastMatch

Description

The lastMatch property of the RegExp object represents the last matched characters.

Example

Listing 7.312 shows how the `lastMatch` property is used. A `RegExp` object is created to look for the string `"test"` within the `str` variable. Upon loading the document, the `lastMatch` property will display the last pattern to be matched.

Listing 7.312   Example of the `lastMatch` Property

```
<html>
<body>

<script type="text/javascript" language="JavaScript">
<!--
// Define a pattern to search for.
var pat = new RegExp("test", "gi");
str = "Testing Testing 123";
myArray = pat.exec(str);

// Once pattern is found, display message.
document.write("Pattern found: " + myArray[0] +
            ". the last match expression is: " + RegExp.lastMatch);
// -->
</script>

</body>
</html>
```

RegExp.lastParen
JavaScript 1.2+, JScript 5.5+
Nav4+, NES3+, IE4+

Syntax

regexp.lastParen

Description

The `lastParen` property of the `RegExp` object represents the last parenthesized substring match. It returns a string value for the last parenthesized substring.

Example

Listing 7.313 shows how the `lastParen` property is used.

Listing 7.313   Example of the `lastParen` Property

```
<html>
<body>

<script type="text/javascript" language="JavaScript">
<!--
```

```
// Define a regular expression.
exp = new RegExp("(please)", "g");

// Create a string object.
str = "Will you (please) stop yelling!";
myArray = exp.exec(str);

// Inform user what the lastParen property is.
document.write("The RegExp.lastParen is: " + "<b>"
              + RegExp.lastParen + "</b>");

// -->
</script>

</body>
</html>
```

RegExp.leftContext

JavaScript 1.2+, JScript 5.5+
Nav4+, NES3+, IE4+

Syntax

regexp.leftContext

Description

The leftContext property of the RegExp object represents the substring preceding the most recent pattern match.

Example

Listing 7.314 shows how the leftContext property is used. A RegExp pattern is used to get all the contents of the string before the is pattern.

Listing 7.314   Example of the leftContext Property

```
<html>
<body>

<script type="text/javascript" language="JavaScript">
<!--
// Define a regular expression pattern and match globally.
pat = /is*/g;

// Create a string object.
var str = "I know where the fish is tonight.";

// Create an array to hold the results.
myArray = pat.exec(str);
```

Listing 7.314   Continued

```
document.write("In the string: " + "<b>" +
              "I know where the fish is tonight" + "</b><br><br>");
document.write("The RegExp.leftContext is: " + RegExp.leftContext);
// -->
</script>

</body>
</html>
```

RegExp.multiline
JavaScript 1.2+
Nav4+, NES3+, IE4+

Syntax

regexp.multiline

Description

The multiline property of the RegExp object is used to determine whether pattern matching should be performed across multiple lines.

Example

Listing 7.315 shows how multiline is used.

Listing 7.315   Example of multiline

```
<html>
<body>

<script type="text/javascript" language="JavaScript">
<!--
// Function creates a new regular expression and
// then executes it against the text in the textarea.
// Outputs an alert message indicating the boolean value
// of the RegExp.multiline property.
function getinfo(){

var myPat = new RegExp("the", "i");
var str = document.form1.mytext.value;
myArray = myPat.exec(str);

   alert("RegExp.multiline is: " + RegExp.multiline);
}

// -->
</script>
```

```
<form name="form1">
When the text in the text box is changed, and the document is clicked,
an alert box will be displayed showing the value of RegExp.multiline.
<br><br>
<textarea name="mytext" cols="60" rows="8" onChange='getinfo()'>
This is a sample textarea containing some dummy text for
testing purposes. The text in this box will be used to
demonstrate how the multiline property is used. If multiple lines are
read, then RegExp.multiline will be true.
</textarea>
<br>
</form>

</body>
</html>
```

RegExp.prototype

JavaScript 1.1+
Nav3+, NES2+, Opera4+

Syntax

regexp.prototype.*property*

regexp.prototype.*method*

Description

The prototype property of the RegExp object allows you to add properties or methods to all instances of this class. After properties or methods have been added, any future instances of the object will contain the newly created prototype property.

Example

Listing 7.316 shows how the prototype property is used to create a new property named *myProp*. Then the property is assigned a value and displayed.

Listing 7.316   *Example of the* prototype *Property for* RegExp *Object*

```
<html>
<body>

<script type="text/javascript" language="JavaScript">
<!--

// Create a new property called myProp.
RegExp.myProp = null;

// Create a new RegExp object that contains the new property.
var myExp = new RegExp("now");
myExp.myProp = "nothing special";
```

Listing 7.316 Continued

```
document.write("The value of myProp is: " + myExp.myProp);
// -->
</script>

</body>
</html>
```

RegExp.rightContext
JavaScript 1.2+, JScript 5.5+
Nav4+, NES3+, IE4+

Syntax

regexp.rightContext

Description

The `rightContext` property of the `RegExp` object represents the substring following the most recent pattern match.

Example

Listing 7.317 shows how the `rightContext` property is used. A pattern is defined so that all the contents of the string that appear after the be pattern will be displayed.

Listing 7.317 Example of `rightContext`

```
<html>
<body>

<script type="text/javascript" language="JavaScript">
<!--
// Define a regular expression pattern and match globally.
pat = /be*/gi;

// Create a string object.
var str = "Eat Drink and be Merry.";

// Create an array to hold the results.
myArray = pat.exec(str);

document.write("In the string: " + "<b>" +
               "Eat Drink and be Merry" + "</b><br><br>");
document.write("The RegExp.rightContext is: " + RegExp.rightContext);

// -->
</script>

</body>
</html>
```

RegExp.source
JavaScript 1.2+
Nav4+, NES3+, IE4+

Syntax
`regexp.source`

Description
The `source` property of the `RegExp` object represents the text of the pattern being used for pattern matching.

Example:
Listing 7.318 shows how the `source` property can be used to get the pattern being matched.

Listing 7.318   Example of the source Property

```
<html>
<body>

<script type="text/javascript" language="JavaScript">
<!--

// Create a new RegExp object.
exp = new RegExp("am", "g");

// Create a string.
str = "This is just a sample sentence.";

myArray = exp.exec(str);

document.write("The source is: " + "<b>" + exp.source + "</b>");
// -->
</script>

</body>
</html>
```

RegExp.test()
JavaScript 1.2+
Nav4+, NES3+, IE4+

Syntax
`regexp.test()`

Description

The test() method of the RegExp object is used to test for a pattern match in a string. Returns boolean value true or false.

Example

Listing 7.319 shows how the test() method is used.

Listing 7.319   Example of the test() Method

```
<html>
<body>

<script type="text/javascript" language="JavaScript">
<!--
// Create a new regular expression.
myExp = new RegExp("hope", "g");

// Define a string object.
str = "I hope everything is going well.";

// Test to see if the regular expression exists in the string.
if(myExp.test(str)){
   document.write("The test found \"hope\" in the string: "
                 + "<b>" + " I hope everything is going well" + "</b>");
}

// -->
</script>

</body>
</html>
```

RegExp.toSource()

JavaScript 1.3+, ECMAScript 1E+
Nav4.06+

Syntax

regexp.toSource()

Description

The toSource() method of the Number object is used to get a string representation of the Number object.

Example

Listing 7.320 shows how the toSource() method is used.

Listing 7.320 **Example of the** toSource() **Method**

```
<html>
<body>

<script type="text/javascript" language="JavaScript">
<!--
// Creates a new RegExp object and then gets the string
// representation of that object.
var myExp = RegExp("the");
document.write(myExp.toSource());
// -->
</script>

</body>
</html>
```

RegExp.toString()

JavaScript 1.1+, ECMAScript 1E+
Nav3+, NES2+, IE4+, Opera3+

Syntax

regexp.toString()

Description

The toString() method of the RegExp object is used to get a string representation of the RegExp object.

Example

Listing 7.321 shows how the toString() method is used.

Listing 7.321 **Example of the** toString() **Method**

```
<html>
<body>

<script type="text/javascript" language="JavaScript">
<!--
// Create a new RegExp object.
var myExp = RegExp("and");

// Display the string representation of myExp.
document.write("The RegExp toString output is: " + "<b>" + myExp.toString() +
"</b>");
// -->
</script>

</body>
</html>
```

RegExp.unwatch()

JavaScript 1.2+
Nav4+, NES3+

Syntax

*regexp.*unwatch(prop)

Description

The unwatch() method of the RegExp object will remove a watch point on a property set by the watch() method.

Example

Listing 7.322 shows an example for the unwatch() method. A property is created using the prototype() method. Then a watch point is placed on the newly created property and a message is displayed when the watch point is hit. When the unwatch() method is called, the watch point is removed.

Listing 7.322 *Example of the* unwatch() *Method*

```
<html>
<body>

<script "type="text/javascript" language="JavaScript">
<!--

function alertme(id,oldValue,newValue)
{
  document.writeln("myExp." + id + " changed from " + "<b>" + oldValue +
➡"</b>"+ " to " + "<b>" + newValue + "</b><br>")
  return newValue;
}

myExp = new RegExp("and");

// Create new property p.
RegExp.prototype.p = "the";

// Set the watchpoint on p.
myExp.watch("p",alertme);

myExp.p = "or";
// Remove the watchpoint on p.
myExp.unwatch("p");
myExp.p = "cat";
myExp.p = "dog";
```

```
// Set the watchpoint on p again.
myExp.watch("p",alertme);
myExp.p = "cow";

// -->
</script>
</body>
</html>
```

RegExp.valueOf()

JavaScript 1.1+
Nav3+, NES2+, IE4+

Syntax

regexp.valueOf()

Description

The valueOf()method of the RegExp object is used to get the primitive value of a RegExp object as a number data type.

Example

Listing 7.323 shows an example for the valueOf() method. A RegExp object is created and set to myExp. The document then outputs the result of performing a valueOf function on the RegExp object.

Listing 7.323   Example of the RegExp.valueOf() **Method**

```
<html>
<body>

<script type="text/javascript" language="JavaScript">
<!--

// Create a new number object.
myExp = new RegExp("or");

// Output the valueOf result.
document.write("The value of myExp is: " + myExp.valueOf());

// -->
</script>

</body>
</html>
```

RegExp.watch()
JavaScript 1.2+
Nav4+, NES3+

Syntax

`regexp.watch(prop, handler)`

Description

The `watch()` method of the `RegExp` object will watch for an assignment to a specific property. When an assignment is made, a specified handler will be called to perform a user-defined operation.

Example

Listing 7.324 shows an example for the `watch()` method. A new property is created using the `prototype` method. Then a watch point is set on the newly created property. When an assignment is made, the `alertme` function will be called to display a message.

Listing 7.324 *Example of the* watch() *Method*

```
<html>
<body>

<script type="text/javascript" language="JavaScript">
<!--

function alertme(id,oldValue,newValue)
{
  document.writeln("myExp." + id + " changed from " + "<b>" +
➥oldValue + "</b>"+ " to " + "<b>" + newValue + "</b><br>")
  return newValue;
}

myExp = new RegExp("and");

// Create a new property p.
RegExp.prototype.p = "the";

// Set a watchpoint on p.
myExp.watch("p",alertme);

myExp.p = "or";

// -->
</script> type="text

</body>
</html>
```

return

JavaScript 1.0+, JScript 1.0+
Nav2+, NES2+, IE3+, Opera3+

Syntax

```
return
```

Description

The return keyword will exit the existing function and return a value.

Example

Listing 7.325 shows an example of using the return statement to return the value of the processing from the function.

Listing 7.325   Example of return

```
<html>
<body>

<script type="text/javascript" language="JavaScript">
<!--
//Function to get the value of 4 times 3.
function getValue(){
    var myValue = 4*3;
    return myValue;
}

// Function calls getValue() and fills the tmp input box element
// with the value returned.
function fill(){
    var x = getValue();
    document.form1.tmp.value = x;
}
// -->
</script>

<form name="form1">
Value: <input type="text" Name="tmp" Size="5">
<br>
<br>
<input type="button" name="get" value="Get Returned Value" onClick='fill()'>
<br>
<br>
</form>

</body>
</html>
```

ScriptEngine
JScript 2.0+

Syntax
```
ScriptEngine()
```

Description
The `ScriptEngine()`function has three possible return values: `JScript`, `VBScript`, and VBA. When implemented in JavaScript scripts, this function returns `JScript`.

Example
Listing 7.326 prints the complete version information for the Internet Explorer browser interpreting the script. In addition to the `ScriptEngine` property, it also uses other Internet Explorer specific functions.

Listing 7.326   Using the `ScriptEngine` Function to Retrieve Information About the Version of the Scripting Engine in an Internet Explorer Browser

```
<script type="text/jscript">
<!--

// Write the scripting engine type.
document.write(ScriptEngine());

// Write the "major" version value to the page.
document.write(" " + ScriptEngineMajorVersion() + ".");

// Write the "minor" version value to the page.
document.write(ScriptEngineMinorVersion());

// Write the build number to the page.
document.write(" build " + ScriptEngineBuildVersion());

//-->
</script>
```

ScriptEngineBuildVersion
JScript 2.0+

Syntax
```
ScriptEngineBuildVersion
```

Description
The `ScriptEngineBuildVersion()` function contains the actual build number of the scripting engine contained on the user's machine.

Example

Listing 7.327 prints the build number of the scripting engine interpreting the script.

Listing 7.327   Using the ScriptEngineBuildVersion **Function to Retrieve the Build Number of the Scripting Engine in an Internet Explorer Browser**

```
<script type="text/jscript">
<!--

// Write the build number to the page
document.write("Build " + ScriptEngineBuildVersion());

//-->
</script>
```

ScriptEngineMajorVersion
JScript 2.0+

Syntax

```
ScriptEngineMajorVersion()
```

Description

The ScriptEngineMajorVersion() function contains the actual major version number of the scripting engine contained on the user's machine.

Example

Listing 7.328 prints the major version number of the scripting engine interpreting the script.

Listing 7.328   Using the ScriptEngineMajorVersion **Function to Retrieve the Major Version Number of the Scripting Engine in an Internet Explorer Browser**

```
<script type="text/jscript">
<!--

// Write the build number to the page
document.write("Major Version: " + ScriptEngineMajorVersion());

//-->
</script>
```

ScriptEngineMinorVersion
JScript 2.0+

Syntax

```
ScriptEngineMinorVersion()
```

Description

The `ScriptEngineMinorVersion()` function contains the actual minor version number of the scripting engine contained on the user's machine.

Example

Listing 7.329 prints the minor version number of the scripting engine interpreting the script.

Listing 7.329   Using the `ScriptEngineMinorVersion` Function to Retrieve the Minor Version Number of the Scripting Engine in an Internet Explorer Browser

```
<script type="text/jscript">
<!--

// Write the build number to the page.
document.write("Minor Version: " + ScriptEngineMinorVersion());

//-->
</script>
```

short

JavaScript 1.2+
Nav4+, NES3+

Syntax

```
Reserved Keyword
```

Description

The `short` keyword has not been implemented in JavaScript to date. It has been reserved for future use.

Example

This keyword has not been implemented; therefore, no example is provided.

static

JavaScript 1.2+
Nav4+, NES3+,

Syntax

```
Reserved Keyword
```

Description

The `static` keyword has not been implemented in JavaScript to date. It has been reserved for future use.

Example

This keyword has not been implemented; therefore, no example is provided.

String (Function)

JavaScript 1.2+, JScript 3.0+, ECMAScript 1E+
Nav4+, NES3+, IE4+, Opera4+

Syntax

```
String (var)
```

Description

The `String()` function is a top-level function, which is often of the `Global` object. It converts the value of any *var* into a readable string.

Example

In Listing 7.330, we will create an instance of the `Date` object, and then use the `String()` function to write out a readable string version of the date.

Listing 7.330   Using the `String()` Function

```
<script type="text/javascript" language="JavaScript1.2">
<!--

// Create an instance of Date object.
myDate = new Date (430057843027);

// writes Thu Aug 18 07:30:43 EST 1983
document.write(String(myDate));

//-->
</script>
```

String (Object)

JavaScript 1.0+, JScript 1.0+, ECMAScript 1E+
Nav2+, NES2+, IE3+, Opera3+

Syntax

```
var variable = new String(string)   JavaScript1.1+

"string"
```

Description

The String object is one of the core JavaScript objects. Instances are created when a program constructs an instance using the new keyword and passing it the String object. In JavaScript 1.0, instances were also created when programmers quoted characters in their script. Table 7.44 lists the properties and methods used by this object.

Table 7.44 **Properties and Methods Used by the String Object**

Type	Item	Description
Method	anchor()	Creates an instance of the <a> tag with the name attribute set to the string passed to the method.
	big()	Converts the string into an instance of the <big> tag.
	blink()	Converts the string into an instance of the <blink> tag.
	bold()	Converts the string into an instance of the <b> tag.
	charAt()	Returns the character at the index passed to the method.
	charCodeAt()	Returns the ISO-Latin-1 number of the character at the index passed to the method.
	concat()	Concatenates the two strings passed to return a new string. This method was added in JavaScript 1.2.
	fixed()	Converts the string into an instance of the <tt>, fixed pitch font tag.
	fontcolor()	Sets the color attribute of an instance of the <font> tag.
	fontsize()	Sets the size attribute of an instance of the <font> tag.
	fromCharCode()	Returns the string value of the ISO-Latin-1 number passed to the method.
	indexOf()	Returns the index of the first occurrence of the string passed to the method within an instance of a String object.
	italics()	Converts the string into an instance of the <i> tag.
	lastIndexOf()	Returns the index of the last occurrence of the string passed to the method within an instance of a String object.
	link()	Converts the string into an instance of the <a> tag and sets the href attribute with the URL that is passed to the method.

Type	Item	Description
	`match()`	Returns an array containing the matches found based on the regular expression passed to the method. This method was added in JavaScript 1.2.
	`replace()`	Performs a search and replace, using the regular expression and replace string passed to the method, on the instance of a `String` that calls it. This method was added in JavaScript 1.2.
	`search()`	Returns the index location of the match found in the string passed to the method. A –1 is returned if the string is not found. This method was added in JavaScript 1.2.
	`slice()`	Returns the string between the beginning and ending index passed to the method. If a negative number is passed, the index is referenced from the end of the string passed. This method was added in JavaScript 1.2.
	`small()`	Converts the string into an instance of the `<small>` tag.
	`split()`	Returns the string split into segments defined by the string and instance limit passed to the method. This method was added in JavaScript 1.1.
	`strike()`	Converts the string into an instance of the `<strike>` tag.
	`sub()`	Converts the string into an instance of the `<sub>` tag.
	`substr()`	Returns the string beginning with the indexed location and number of characters to return. If a negative number is passed, the index is referenced from the end of the string passed. This method was added in JavaScript 1.2.
	`substring()`	Returns the string between the beginning and ending index passed to the method.
	`sup()`	Converts the string into an instance of the `<sup>` tag.
	`toLocaleLowerCase()`	Converts all the characters in the string to lowercase according to the host machine's current locale. This method was added in JavaScript 1.5.

Table 7.44   Continued

Type	Item	Description
	`toLocaleUpperCase()`	Converts all the characters in the string to uppercase according to the host machine's current locale. This method was added in JavaScript 1.5.
	`toLowerCase()`	Converts all the characters in the string to lowercase.
	`toSource()`	Returns the string representation of the `String` passed. This method was added in JavaScript 1.3.
	`toString()`	Returns the characters passed as type string. This method was added in JavaScript 1.3.
	`toUpperCase()`	Converts all the characters in the string to uppercase.
	`unwatch()`	Turns off the watch for a particular property.
	`watch()`	Turns on the watch for a particular property.
Property	`length`	Returns the length of the string.
	`prototype`	Provides the ability for a programmer to add properties to instances of the `string` object. This property was added in JavaScript 1.1.

Example

Listing 7.331 displays the use of some of the `String` properties and methods. It contains a single button. After the user clicks the button, a second window is opened. Various methods are called by a string instance created in the script. The results of such are displayed in the pop-up window.

Listing 7.331   Examples of an Instance of the `String` *Object*

```
<html>
<head>
  <title>Examples of the String Object</title>
<script type="text/javascript" language="JavaScript1.1">
<!--

// Define the openWin function called by pressing the button.
function openWin(){

  // Open a window to store the results and create a new String object.
  var myWin = open("", "","width=450,height=200");
  var myString = new String("Hello, World!");

  // Call various methods on this instance and write their results to the
  // window.
  myWin.document.write("Original String, " + myString);
```

```
myWin.document.write(" has " + myString.length + " characters.<br>");
myWin.document.write("Big: " + myString.big() + "<br>");
myWin.document.write("Small: " + myString.small() + "<br>");
myWin.document.write("Blinking: " + myString.blink() + "<br>");
myWin.document.write("Italics: " + myString.italics() + "<br>");
myWin.document.write("Convert to Lower: " + myString.toLowerCase());
myWin.document.write("<br>");
myWin.document.write("Convert to Upper: " + myString.toUpperCase());
myWin.document.write("<br>");

// Close the stream to the window.
myWin.document.close();
}
//-->
</script>
</head>
<body>
<form name="myForm">
  <input type="button" value="Click to Process" name="myButton"
        onClick="openWin()">
</form>
</body>
 </html>
```

String.anchor()

JavaScript 1.0+, JScript 1.0+
Nav2+, NES2+, IE3+, Opera3+

Syntax

string.anchor(*name*)

Description

The anchor() method will convert the string it is called on to an instance of the <a> tag, setting the name attribute to the *name* that is passed.

Example

Listing 7.332 creates an instance of the String object and uses the document.write() method to write the tag to the page. The results of running this script will be the following:

```
<a name="HELLO">Hello, World!</a>
```

Listing 7.332 *Using the* anchor() *Method of the* String *Object*
```
<script type="text/javascript" language="JavaScript1.1">
<!--
```

Listing 7.332 *Continued*

```
// Create an instance of the String object.
var myString = new String("Hello, World!");

// Write the string to the page after invoking the anchor() method on it.
document.write(myString.anchor("HELLO"));

// Close the stream to the window.
document.close();

//-->
</script>
```

String.big()

JavaScript 1.0+, JScript 1.0+
Nav2+, NES2+, IE3+, Opera3+

Syntax

string.big()

Description

The big() method will convert the string it is called on to an instance of the <big> tag.

Example

Listing 7.333 creates an instance of the String object and uses the document.write() method to write the tag to the page. The results of running this script will be the following:

```
<big>Hello, World!</big>
```

Listing 7.333 *Using the* big() *Method of the* String *Object*

```
<script type="text/javascript" language="JavaScript1.1">
<!--

// Create an instance of the String object.
var myString = new String("Hello, World!");

// Write the string to the page after invoking the big() method on it.
document.write(myString.big());

// Close the stream to the window.
document.close();

//-->
</script>
```

String.blink()

JavaScript 1.0+
Nav2+, NES2+

Syntax

string.blink()

Description

The blink() method will convert the string it is called on to an instance of the <blink>
tag. This method is only supported in Netscape Navigator because it is the only browser
that has an implementation of the <blink> tag.

Example

Listing 7.334 creates an instance of the String object and uses the document.write()
method to write the tag to the page. The results of running this script will be the following:

```
<blink>Hello, World!</blink>
```

Listing 7.334 **Using the** blink() *Method of the* String *Object*

```
<script type="text/javascript" language="JavaScript1.1">
<!--

// Create an instance of the String object.
var myString = new String("Hello, World!");

// Write the string to the page after invoking the blink() method on it.
document.write(myString.blink());

// Close the stream to the window.
document.close();

//-->
</script>
```

String.bold()

JavaScript 1.0+, JScript 1.0+
Nav2+, NES2+, IE3+, Opera3+

Syntax

string.bold()

Description

The bold() method will convert the string it is called on to an instance of the <bold>
tag.

Example

Listing 7.335 creates an instance of the String object and uses the document.write() method to write the tag to the page. The results of running this script will be the following:

```
<bold>Hello, World!</bold>
```

Listing 7.335 Using the bold() ***Method of the*** String ***Object***

```
<script type="text/javascript" language="JavaScript1.1">
<!--

// Create an instance of the String object.
var myString = new String("Hello, World!");

// Write the string to the page after invoking the bold() method on it.
document.write(myString.bold());

// Close the stream to the window.
document.close();

//-->
</script>
```

String.charAt()

JavaScript 1.0+, JScript 1.0+, ECMAScript 1E+
Nav2+, NES2+, IE3+, Opera3+

Syntax

string.charAt(*num*)

Description

The charAt() method of an instance of the String object returns the character located at the indexed, *num*, position passed. This indexing is done from left to right starting with the 0 (zero) position. If the *num* passed is not a valid index in the string, −1 is returned.

Example

Listing 7.336 creates an instance of a String object. When the page is loaded, the user is prompted for an index number. After entering the index number and clicking OK, the character at that indexed location is written to the document. Notice that there is also a check to see whether the character at that location is a space.

Listing 7.336 Using the charAt() ***Method to Retrieve a Character at a User-specified Location in a String***

```
<html>
<head>
```

```
   <title>Using the String.charAt() method</title>
</head>
<body>
<script type="text/javascript" language="JavaScript1.1">
<!--

// Create an instance of the String object.
var myString = new String("Here is a short sentence.");

// Prompt the user for a number.
var myIndex = prompt("Please enter a number", "");

// Store the character at that location in a variable.
var myChar = myString.charAt(myIndex);

// Write the character to the page, but check to see if it
// is a space first.
document.write('<b>The string you searched through was: </b>' + myString);
document.write('<br>The ' + myIndex + ' character in this string is ');

if (myChar == " "){
  document.write('&lt;space&gt;');
}else{
  document.write(myChar);
}

// Close the stream to the window.
myWin.document.close();

//-->
</script>
</body>
</html>
```

String.charCodeAt()
JavaScript 1.0+, JScript 1.0+, ECMAScript 1E+
Nav2+, NES2+, IE3+, Opera3+

Syntax
string.charCodeAt(*num*)

Description
The charCodeAt() method of an instance of the String object returns the ISO-Latin-1 number of the character located at the indexed, *num*, position passed. This indexing is done from left to right starting with the 0 (zero) position. If the *num* passed is not a valid index in the string, −1 is returned.

Example

Listing 7.337 creates an instance of a `String` object. When the page is loaded, the user is then prompted for an index number. After entering the index number and clicking OK, the ISO-Latin-1 number of the character at that indexed location is written to the document. Notice that there is also a check to see whether the character at that location is a space.

Listing 7.337 Using the `charCodeAt()` Method to Retrieve a Character at a User-specified Location in a String

```html
<html>
<head>
  <title>Using the String.charCodeAt() method</title>
</head>
<body>
<script type="text/javascript" language="JavaScript1.1">
<!--

// Create an instance of the String object.
var myString = new String("Here is a short sentence.");

// Prompt the user for a number.
var myIndex = prompt("Please enter a number", "");

// Store the character code at that location in a variable.
var myCharCode = myString.charCodeAt(myIndex);
var myChar = myString.charAt(myIndex);

// Write the character code to the page.
document.write('<b>The string you searched through was: </b>' + myString);
document.write('<br>The ' + myIndex + ' character in this string is ');

// Check to see if it is a space.
if (myChar == " "){
  document.write('&lt;space&gt;');
}else{
  document.write(myChar);
}

// Write the character code.
document.write(' and its ISO-Latin-1 code is ' + myCharCode);

// Close the stream to the window.
myWin.document.close();

//-->
</script>
</body>
</html>
```

String.concat()
JavaScript 1.2+, JScript 3.0+
Nav4+, NES3+, IE4+

Syntax
`string.concat(string2)`

Description
The concat() method of an instance of the String object concatenates the string in *string2* to the end of *string* to return a new string.

Example
Listing 7.338 creates two instances of the String object and uses the concat() method to concatenate them to create a new string. The string is then displayed in an alert box.

Listing 7.338   *Using the* concat() *Method to Concatenate Two Strings*

```
<script type="text/javascript" language="JavaScript1.2">
<!--

// Create 2 instances of the String object and concatenate
// them together.
var myString1 = new String("Hello, ");
var myString2 = new String("World!");
var myConcatString = myString1.concat(myString2);

// Popup an alert box showing the concatenation.
alert(myConcatString);

//-->
</script>
```

String.constructor
JavaScript 1.1+, JScript 3.0+, ECMAScript 1E+
Nav3+, NES2+, IE4+, Opera3+

Syntax
`string.constructor`

Description
The constructor property of the String object specifies the function that creates the object.

Example
Listing 7.339 shows an example of the constructor property, which is used to check the type of variable.

Listing 7.339 *Example of the* constructor *Property*

```
<script type="text/javascript" language="JavaScript1.1">
<!--

// Create an instance of the String object.
var myString = new String("Hello, World!");

if(myString.constructor == String){
    document.write("Object created");
}

//-->
</script>
```

String.fixed()

JavaScript 1.0+, JScript 1.0+
Nav2+, NES2+, IE3+, Opera3+

Syntax

```
string.fixed()
```

Description

The fixed() method will convert the string it is called on to an instance of the <tt> tag.

Example

Listing 7.340 creates an instance of the String object and uses the document.write() method to write the tag to the page. The results of running this script will be the following:

```
<tt>Hello, World!</tt>
```

Listing 7.340 *Using the* fixed() *Method of the* String *Object*

```
<script type="text/javascript" language="JavaScript1.1">
<!--

// Create an instance of the String object.
var myString = new String("Hello, World!");

// Write the string to the page after invoking the fixed() method on it.
document.write(myString.fixed());

// Close the stream to the window.
document.close();

//-->
</script>
```

String.fontcolor()

JavaScript 1.0+, JScript 1.0+
Nav2+, NES2+, IE3+, Opera3+

Syntax

```
string.fontcolor (hexnum)
string.fontcolor(color)
```

Description

The `fontcolor()` method sets the `color` attribute of an instance of the `<font>` tag, which it creates. This attribute can either be passed as the hexadecimal equivalent of the color or the actual string that represents that color.

Example

Listing 7.341 creates an instance of the `String` object and uses the `document.write()` method to write two instances of the tag to the page. The results of running this script will be the following:

```
Hex usage: <font color="#FF0000">Hello, World!</font>
<br>Color usage: <font color="blue">Hello, World!</font>
```

Listing 7.341   Using the `fontcolor()` **Method of the** String **Object**

```
<script type="text/javascript" language="JavaScript1.1">
<!--

// Create an instance of the String object.
var myString = new String("Hello, World!");

// Write the string twice to the page after invoking the
// fontcolor() method on them.
document.write("Hex usage: " + myString.fontcolor('FF0000'));
document.write("<br>Color usage: " + myString.fontcolor('blue'));

// Close the stream to the window.
document.close();

//-->
</script>
```

String.fontsize()

JavaScript 1.0+, JScript 1.0+
Nav2+, NES2+, IE3+, Opera3+

Syntax

```
string.fontsize(num)
string.fontsize(string2)
```

Description

The `fontsize()` method sets the `size` attribute of an instance of the `<font>` tag, which it creates. This attribute can be a number between 1 and 7. If you pass the method the number in the form of a string, the size displayed is relative to the `<basefont>` tag.

Example

Listing 7.342 creates an instance of the `String` object and uses the `document.write()` method to write two instances of the tag to the page. The results of running this script will be the following:

```
Hex usage: <font size="6">Hello, World!</font>
<br>Color usage: <font size="-2">Hello, World!</font>
```

Listing 7.342   Using the `fontsize()` Method of the `String` Object

```
<script type="text/javascript" language="JavaScript1.1">
<!--

// Create an instance of the String object.
var myString = new String("Hello, World!");

// Write the string twice to the page after invoking the
// fontsize() method on them.
document.write("Size=6: " + myString.fontsize(6));
document.write("<br>Size=-2: " + myString.fontsize('-2'));

// Close the stream to the window.
document.close();

//-->
</script>
```

String.fromCharCode()
JavaScript 1.2+, JScript 3.0+, ECMAScript 1E+
Nav4+, NES3+, IE4+

Syntax

```
String.fromCharCode(num1,  num2, ..., numN)
String.fromCharCode(keyevent.which)
```

Description

The `fromCharCode()` method of the `String` object returns the characters that correspond to the ISO-Latin-1 numbers (*num1*, *num2*, ..., *numN*) position passed. You can also pass the method a key event and use the `which` property to determine which key has been pressed. The possible key events are `KeyDown`, `KeyPress`, and `KeyUp`.

As you can see in the syntax definition, this is a method of the actual String object and not an instance of this object. Because of this, you might want to store the results generated by this method into a variable for future processing.

Example

Listing 7.343 invokes the fromCharCode() method on the numbers 88, 89, and 90. The results of this processing are then written to the user's page.

Listing 7.343   Using the fromCharCode() **Method to Determine the Characters of the ISO-Latin-1 Numbers Passed**

```
<script type="text/javascript" language="JavaScript1.2">
<!--

// Invoke the fromCharCode() method and store the results in
// a variable.
var myString = String.fromCharCode(88,89,90);

// Write the results to the page.
document.write("These numbers evaluate to: " + myString);

// Close the stream to the page.
document.close();

//-->
</script>
```

String.indexOf()

JavaScript 1.0+, JScript 1.0+, ECMAScript 1E+
Nav2+, NES2+, IE3+, Opera3+

Syntax

```
string.indexOf(string, num)
string.indexOf(string)
```

Description

The indexOf() method of an instance of the String object returns the indexed start position of the *string* passed. Additionally, you can specify an index, defined by *num* in the syntax definition, to start your search for the string specified. This method is the same as the String.lastIndexOf() method, but it starts at the beginning of the string.

Example

Listing 7.344 creates a simple instance of the String object. This instance is then passed to the indexOf() method on two occasions with the result written to the user's page. The first occasion looks for a space in the string, which returns 6. The second occasion starts the search at the fourth position, so it returns the location of the letter "l" in the word "world".

Listing 7.344 Using the `indexOf()` **Method to Find the Location of a Character in a String**

```
<script type="text/javascript" language="JavaScript1.1">
<!--

// Create an instance of the String object.
var myString = new String("Hello, World!");

// Look for the first instance of a space.
document.write(myString.indexOf(" ") + '<br>');

// By specifying an indexed location to start looking you
// can return the indexed location of the third instance of
// the letter 'l'.
document.write(myString.indexOf("l", 4));

// Close the stream to the page.
document.close();

//-->
</script>
```

String.italics()

> JavaScript 1.0+, JScript 1.0+
> Nav2+, NES2+, IE3+, Opera3+

Syntax

string.italics()

Description

The `italics()` method will convert the string it is called on to an instance of the `<i>` tag.

Example

Listing 7.345 creates an instance of the `String` object and uses the `document.write()` method to write the tag to the page. The results of running this script will be the following:

```
<i>Hello, World!</i>
```

Listing 7.345 Using the `italics()` **Method of the** `String` **Object**

```
<script type="text/javascript" language="JavaScript1.1">
<!--

// Create an instance of the String object.
var myString = new String("Hello, World!");
```

```
// Write the string to the page after invoking the italics() method on it.
document.write(myString.italics());

// Close the stream to the window.
document.close();

//-->
</script>
```

String.lastIndexOf()

JavaScript 1.0+, JScript 1.0+, ECMAScript 1E+
Nav2+, NES2+, IE3+, Opera3+

Syntax

```
string.lastIndexOf(string, num)
string.lastIndexOf(string)
```

Description

The lastIndexOf() method of an instance of the String object returns the indexed start position of the *string* passed, starting from the right and going left. Additionally, you can specify an index, defined by num in the syntax definition, to start your search for the string specified. This method is the same as the String.indexOf() method, but it starts at the end of the string.

Example

Listing 7.346 creates a simple instance of the String object. This instance is then passed to the lastIndexOf() method on two occasions with the result written to the user's page. The first occasion looks for the last occurrence of the letter e in the string, which returns 16. The second occasion starts the search at the third position, so it returns the location of the first l in the word "Hello".

Listing 7.346 *Using the* lastIndexOf() *Method to Find the Location of a Character in a String*

```
<script type="text/javascript" language="JavaScript1.1">
<!--

// Create an instance of the String object.
var myString = new String("Hello World, here I am!");

// Look for the last instance of the letter 'e'.
document.write(myString.lastIndexOf("e") + '<br>');

// By specifying an indexed location to start looking, you
// can return the indexed location of the first instance of
// the letter 'l'.
document.write(myString.lastIndexOf("l", 3));
```

Listing 7.346 Continued

```
// Close the stream to the page
document.close();

//-->
</script>
```

String.length

JavaScript 1.0+, JScript 1.0+, ECMAScript 1E+
Nav2+, NES2+, IE3+, Opera3+

Syntax

string.length

Description

The length property of an instance of the String object returns the total length of the string.

Example

Listing 7.347 creates three instances of the String object. The length property of each of these instances is accessed and written to the user's page.

Listing 7.347 Accessing the length Property of an Instance of the
String *Object*

```
<script type="text/javascript" language="JavaScript1.1">
<!--

// Create an instance of the String object.
var myString1 = new String("Hello, World");
var myString2 = new String("Here is a longer string");
var myString3 = new String("Here is an even longer string");

// Write the lengths of these strings to the user's page.
document.write(myString1 + ": is " + myString1.length);
document.write(" characters long.<br>");
document.write(myString2 + ": is " + myString2.length);
document.write(" characters long.<br>");
document.write(myString3 + ": is " + myString3.length);
document.write(" characters long.<br>");

// Close the stream to the page.
document.close();

//-->
</script>
```

String.link()

JavaScript 1.0+, JScript 1.0+
Nav2+, NES2+, IE3+, Opera3+

Syntax

`string.link(URL)`

Description

The `link()` method will convert the string it is called on to an instance of the `<a>` tag, setting the `href` attribute to the URL that is passed.

Example

Listing 7.348 creates an instance of the `String` object and uses the `document.write()` method to write the tag to the page. The results of running this script will be the following:

```
<a href="http://www.purejavascript.com">The online book!</a>
```

Listing 7.348   Using the `link()` ***Method of the*** `String` ***Object***

```
<script type="text/javascript" language="JavaScript1.1">
<!--

// Create an instance of the String object.
var myString = new String("The online book!");

// Write the string to the page after invoking the link() method on it.
document.write(myString.link('http://www.purejavascript.com'));

// Close the stream to the window.
document.close();

//-->
</script>
```

String.localeCompare()

JavaScript 1.5+, ECMAScript 3E+
Nav6

Syntax

`string.localeCompare (string2)`

Description

The `localeCompare()` method of an instance of the `String` object compares *string* against *string2*. The resulting numerical value, which can be negative, zero, or positive, orders the strings in a sort order specified by the system default locale.

Example

In Listing 7.349, two strings are created and the `localeCompare()` method is called to compare them.

Listing 7.349   *Using the* `localeCompare()` *Method*

```
<script type="text/javascript" language="JavaScript1.5">
<!--

// Define two strings.
myString = new String("hello")
myString2 = new String("world")

// Returns -15 in Netscape 6.
document.write(myString.localeCompare(myString2));

//-->
</script>
```

String.match()

JavaScript 1.2+, JScript 3.0+
Nav4+, NES3+, IE4+

Syntax

string.match (*regexpression*)

Description

The `match()` method of an instance of the `String` object searches the string in which it is invoked for the regular expression passed to the method. The *regexpression* is made up of a pattern and flags that dictate what is to be matched. The method returns an array containing the matches found in the string.

TIP

See the reference entry for `RegExp` for a list of the patterns and flags that can be used to create a regular expression.

Example

Listing 7.350 creates an instance of the `String` object and tries to match instances that contain a space followed by some characters. If any matches were returned into the array, they are written to the user's page one at a time.

Listing 7.350   *Using the* `match()` *Method to Match Regular Expressions in a String*

```
<script type="text/javascript" language="JavaScript1.2">
<!--
```

```
// Create an instance of the String object and load it with a name.
var myString = new String("Mr. R. Allen Wyke");

// Match occurrences of a space followed by characters.
var myRegExp = /\s\w*/g;
var answerArray = myString.match(myRegExp);

// Check to see if there were any matches found.
if(answerArray == null){
  document.write('No matches were found');
}else{
  document.write('The following matches were found: <br>');

  // Write the contents of the array to the page. This will put
  // R, Allen, and Wyke each on a separate line.
  for(var i = 0; i < answerArray.length; i++){
    document.write(answerArray[i] + '<br>');
  }
}

// Close the stream to the window.
document.close();

//-->
</script>
```

String.prototype

JavaScript 1.1+, ECMAScript 1E+, JScript 3.0+
Nav3+, NES2+, IE4+, Opera3+

Syntax

```
String.prototype.property
String.prototype.method
```

Description

The prototype property of the String object allows a programmer to add properties or methods to a core JavaScript object.

Example

Listing 7.351 creates two instances of the String object. Then it prototypes a new property, type, and a new method, verify(). In the script, the type property is assigned to the string instances and then they are checked using the verify() method. The results of the validation are then written to the user's page.

Listing 7.351   Using the prototype *Property to Create New Properties and Methods of the* String *Object*

```
<script type="text/javascript" language="JavaScript1.1">
<!--

// Define the method that we prototyped.
function myVerify(){

  // Check to see if the type property we added is set to "Name".
  // If it is, then return true. If not, then return false.
  if(this.type != "Name"){
    return false;
  }else{
    return true;
  }
}


// Create a new property and method of the String object.
String.prototype.type = null;
String.prototype.verify = myVerify;

// Create two instances of the String object and load it with a name.
var myString1 = new String("Mr. R. Allen Wyke");
var myString2 = new String("Mr. Robert J. Wyke");

// Using the prototype we defined, assign the type property to Name
// for the first string and to "Title" for the second.
myString1.type = "Name";
myString2.type = "Title";

// Check each of the types of the strings to see if they are valid.
if(myString1.verify()){
  document.write(myString1 + " has a valid type of " + myString1.type);
}else{
  document.write(myString1 + " has an invalid type of " + myString1.type);
}

document.write('<br>');

if(myString2.verify()){
  document.write(myString2 + " has a valid type of " + myString2.type);
}else{
  document.write(myString2 + " has an invalid type of " + myString2.type);
}

// Close the stream to the window
//document.close();

//-->
</script>
```

String.replace()
JavaScript 1.2+, JScript 3.0+
Nav4+, NES3+, IE4+

Syntax
`string.replace(regexpression, replacestring)`

Description
The `replace()` method of an instance of the `String` object searches the string in which it is invoked for the regular expression passed to the method. The `regexpression` is made up of a pattern and flags that dictate what is to be matched. If and when a match is found, the method returns a new string with that match supplanted with the replacement string passed to the method.

TIP

See the reference entry for `RegExp` for a list of the patterns and flags that can be used to create a regular expression.

Example
Listing 7.352 creates an instance of the `String` object. This instance is then searched through to see whether any occurrence of the word `"Wyke"` is found. If so, it is replaced with `"White"`.

Listing 7.352 Using the `replace()` Method to Replace Regular Expression Matches in a String

```
<script type="text/javascript" language="JavaScript1.2">
<!--

// Create an instance of the String object and load it with a name.
var myString = new String("Mr. R. Allen Wyke");

// Search for "Wyke" and replace it with "White".
var myRegExp = /Wyke/g;
var newString = myString.replace(myRegExp, "White");

// Write the results to the page.
document.write('Notice the last name in the original string, ' + myString);
document.write(', was replaced and is now '+ newString);

// Close the stream to the window.
document.close();

//-->
</script>
```

String.search()

JavaScript 1.2+, JScript 3.0+
Nav4+, NES3+, IE4+

Syntax

string.search (*regexpression*)

Description

The search() method of an instance of the String object searches the string in which it is invoked for the regular expression passed to the method. The *regexpression* is made up of a pattern and flags that dictate what is to be matched. The method returns the indexed start location of the string if it is found and –1 if the string does not contain a regular expression match.

TIP

See the reference entry for RegExp for a list of the patterns and flags that can be used to create a regular expression.

Example

Listing 7.353 creates an instance of the String object, which is searched for the first instance of a space. If a match is found, the indexed start position is returned. The results of running this script are written to the user's page.

Listing 7.353 Using the search() ***Method to Search Regular Expressions in a String***

```
<script type="text/javascript" language="JavaScript1.2">
<!--

// Create an instance of the String object and load it with a name.
var myString = new String("Mr. R. Allen Wyke");

// Find the first occurrences of a space.
var myRegExp = /\s/;
var answerIdx = myString.search(myRegExp);

// Check to see if there were any matches found.
if(answerIdx == -1){
  document.write('No matches were found');
}else{
  document.write('Your search string was found starting at: ' + answerIdx);
}

// Close the stream to the window.
document.close();
```

```
//-->
</script>
```

String.slice()

JavaScript 1.0+, JScript 1.0+
Nav2+, NES2+, IE3+, Opera3+

Syntax

```
string.slice(num1, num2)
string.slice(num)
```

Description

The slice() method of an instance of the String object returns the characters in the string between the indexed positions *num1* and *num2* in which the method is invoked. The string itself is zero based, so the first character is in position 0. It is also possible to pass *num2* as a negative number. In this scenario, the string counts from the end of the string to end the slice.

As the syntax definition states, it is also possible to pass a single index location to the method. In this implementation, the method will not stop at a position and will return all characters until the end of the string.

Example

Listing 7.354 creates an instance of the String object. The slice() method is invoked on this string and asked to return the first seven characters of the string. The results of running this script are written to the user's page.

Listing 7.354   Using the slice() *Method to Return Seven Characters in a String*

```
<script type="text/javascript" language="JavaScript1.1">
<!--

// Create an instance of the String object and load it with a name.
var myString = new String("Mr. R. Allen Wyke");

// Grab the first 7 characters of the string.
var mySlice = myString.slice(0,6);

// Write the results to the page.
document.write('The first 7 characters of our string, ' + myString);
document.write(', are: ' + mySlice);

// Close the stream to the window.
document.close();

//-->
</script>
```

String.small()

JavaScript 1.0+, JScript 1.0+
Nav2+, NES2+, IE3+, Opera3+

Syntax

string.small()

Description:

The small() method will convert the string it is called on to an instance of the <small> tag.

Example

Listing 7.355 creates an instance of the String object and uses the document.write() method to write the tag to the page. The results of running this script will be the following:

```
<small>Hello, World!</small>
```

Listing 7.355 ***Using the*** small() ***Method of the*** String ***Object***

```
<script type="text/javascript" language="JavaScript1.1">
<!--

// Create an instance of the String object.
var myString = new String("Hello, World!");

// Write the string to the page after invoking the small() method on it.
document.write(myString.small());

// Close the stream to the window.
document.close();

//-->
</script>
```

String.split()

JavaScript 1.1+, JScript 1.0+, ECMAScript 1E+
Nav3+, NES2+, IE3+, Opera3+

Syntax

string.split(*separator*, *num*)
string.split(*separator*)
string.split(*regexpression*, *num*)
string.split(*regexpression*)

Description

The split() method of an instance of the String object splits the string in which it is invoked into separate strings based on the *regexpression* or *separator* passed to the method. If a regular expression is passed, it is made up of a pattern and flags that dictate what is to be matched. The *separator* is a string or character that is matched to perform the separation.

NOTE

If the language attribute of the <script> tag is set to "JavaScript1.2" when using the second syntactical definition and the separator is a space, consecutive spaces are treated differently. In JavaScript 1.1, each space would be split and returned as part of the results. So if there were an instance of three consecutive spaces, two of the spaces would be returned in the array. Specifying JavaScript 1.2 tells the interpreter to treat the three spaces as a single space, so you are able to perform proper splits.

The method returns an array containing each of the segments found in the string.

TIP

See the reference entry for RegExp for a list of the patterns and flags that can be used to create a regular expression.

Example

Listing 7.356 creates an instance of the String object. This instance is then split, looking for a space as the separator, using each of the syntactical definitions. The results are then written to the user's page.

Listing 7.356 Using the split() *Method to Split the String Passed into Separate Strings*

```
<script type="text/javascript" language="JavaScript1.2">
<!--

// Define a function to handle writing the results.
function genResults(arrayName, testName){
  document.write('<b>Currently Evaluating: ' + testName + '</b><hr>');

  // Check to see if there were any spaces found.
  if(arrayName == null){
    document.write('No matches were found');
  }else{

    // Write the contents of the array to the page. This will put
    // R, Allen, and Wyke each on a separate line.
    for(var i = 0; i < arrayName.length; i++){
      document.write('[' + i + ']: ' + arrayName[i] + '<br>');
```

Listing 7.356 Continued

```
      }
    }
    document.write('<p>');
}

// Create an instance of the String object and load it with a name.
var myString = new String("Mr. R. Allen Wyke");

// Define a regular expression and a separator. Both are set to
// split on a single space.
var myRegExp = /\s/g;
var mySeparator = " ";

genResults(myString.split(mySeparator), "Separator Only");
genResults(myString.split(mySeparator, 2), "Separator With Limit of 2");
genResults(myString.split(myRegExp), "Regular Expression Only");
genResults(myString.split(myRegExp, 3), "Regular Expression With Limit of 3");

// Close the stream to the window.
document.close();

//-->
</script>
```

String.strike()

> JavaScript 1.0+, JScript 1.0+
> Nav2+, NES2+, IE3+, Opera3+

Syntax

string.strike()

Description

The strike() method will convert the string it is called on to an instance of the <strike> tag.

Example

Listing 7.357 creates an instance of the String object and uses the document.write() method to write the tag to the page. The results of running this script will be the following:

```
<strike>Hello, World!</strike>
```

Listing 7.357 Using the strike() Method of the String Object

```
<script type="text/javascript" language="JavaScript1.1">
<!--
```

```
// Create an instance of the String object.
var myString = new String("Hello, World!");

// Write the string to the page after invoking the strike() method on it.
document.write(myString.strike());

// Close the stream to the window.
document.close();

//-->
  </script>
```

String.sub()

JavaScript 1.0+, JScript 1.0+
Nav2+, NES2+, IE3+, Opera3+

Syntax

string.sub()

Description

The sub() method will convert the string it is called on to an instance of the <sub> tag.

Example

Listing 7.358 creates an instance of the String object and uses the document.write() method to write the tag to the page. The results of running this script will be the following:

```
<sub>Hello, World!</sub>
```

Listing 7.358   **Using the** sub() **Method of the** String **Object**

```
<script type="text/javascript" language="JavaScript1.1">
<!--

// Create an instance of the String object.
var myString = new String("Hello, World!");

// Write the string to the page after invoking the sub() method on it.
document.write(myString.sub());

// Close the stream to the window.
document.close();

//-->
</script>
```

String.substr()

JavaScript 1.0+, JScript 1.0+
Nav2+, NES2+, IE3+, Opera3+

Syntax

```
string.substr(num1, num2)
string.substr (num)
```

Description

The substr() method of an instance of the String object returns the characters in the string, starting with the indexed position *num1* and counting to *num2* characters. The string itself is zero based, so the first character is in position 0. It is also possible to pass *num1* as a negative number. In this scenario, the string starts from the end of the string to begin the substring extraction.

As the syntax definition states, it is also possible to pass a single index location to the method. In this implementation, the method will not stop at a position and will return all characters until the end of the string.

Example

Listing 7.359 creates an instance of the String object. The substr() method is invoked on this string and asked to return the first six characters of the string. The results of running this script are written to the user's page.

Listing 7.359   Using the substr() Method to Return Seven Characters in a String

```
<script type="text/javascript" language="JavaScript1.1">
<!--

// Create an instance of the String object and load it with a name.
var myString = new String("Mr. R. Allen Wyke");

// Grab the first 7 characters of the string.
var mySubString = myString.substr(0,6);

// Write the results to the page.
document.write('The first 6 characters of our string, ' + myString);
document.write(', are: ' + mySubString);

// Close the stream to the window.
document.close();

//-->
</script>
```

String.substring()

JavaScript 1.0+, JScript 1.0+
Nav2+, NES2+, IE3+, Opera3+

Syntax

```
string.substring(num1, num2)
string.substring(num)
```

Description

The substring() method of an instance of the String object returns the characters in the string, starting with the indexed position *num1* and ending with the character before *num2*. The string itself is zero based, so the first character is in position 0.

If you pass *num1* as a negative number, it will be treated as 0. Likewise if you pass *num2* as a value greater than the String.length property, it will be treated as String.length. And finally, if *num1* equals *num2*, an empty string is returned.

As the syntax definition states, it is also possible to pass a single index location to the method. In this implementation, the method will not stop at a position and will return all characters until the end of the string.

NOTE

If the language attribute of the <script> tag is set to "JavaScript1.2" and a Navigator 4 browser is interpreting the script, a runtime out of memory error will be produced if num1 is greater than num2. Without this attribute set, the method returns a substring beginning with num2 and ending with num1 −1.

Example

Listing 7.360 creates an instance of the String object. The substring() method is invoked on this string and asked to return the first 10 characters of the string. The results of running this script are written to the user's page.

Listing 7.360   Using the substring() Method to Return 11 Characters in a String

```
<script type="text/javascript" language="JavaScript1.1">
<!--

// Create an instance of the String object and load it with a name.
var myString = new String("Mr. R. Allen Wyke");

// Grab the first 11 characters of the string.
var mySubString = myString.substring(0,10);

// Write the results to the page.
document.write('The first 10 characters of our string, ' + myString);
document.write(', are: ' + mySubString);
```

Listing 7.360   Continued

```
// Close the stream to the window.
document.close();

//-->
</script>
```

String.sup()

JavaScript 1.0+, JScript 1.0+
Nav2+, NES2+, IE3+, Opera3+

Syntax

string.sup()

Description

The sup() method will convert the string it is called on to an instance of the <sup> tag.

Example

Listing 7.361 creates an instance of the String object and uses the document.write() method to write the tag to the page. The results of running this script will be the following:

```
<sup>Hello, World!</sup>
```

Listing 7.361   Using the sup() *Method of the* String *Object*

```
<script type="text/javascript" language="JavaScript1.1">
<!--

// Create an instance of the String object.
var myString = new String("Hello, World!");

// Write the string to the page after invoking the sup() method on it.
document.write(myString.sup());

// Close the stream to the window.
document.close();

//-->
</script>
```

String.toLocaleLowerCase()

JavaScript 1.5+, JScript 5.5+, ECMAScript 3E+
Nav6+, IE5.5+

Syntax

string.toLocaleLowerCase()

Description

The `toLocaleLowerCase()` method of an instance of a `String` object converts the characters in that string to all lowercase values. This is often used when a programmer tries to evaluate a string a user has entered and does not care about case. This method differs from the `toLowerCase()` method by yielding its result to the host environment's current locale.

Example

Listing 7.362 pops up a prompt box and asks the user to enter various case text. After the user clicks OK, the lowercase version of the string is written to the page.

Listing 7.362   Using the `toLocaleLowerCase()` ***Method of the*** `String`
Object to Convert a String Entered by a User to Lowercase

```
<script type="text/javascript" language="JavaScript1.5">
<!--

// Create an instance of the String object.
var myString = new String(prompt("Please enter some various case text", ""));

// Convert the text to lowercase and write it to the page.
document.write(myString.toLocaleLowerCase());

// Close the stream to the window.
document.close();

//-->
</script>
```

String.toLocaleUpperCase()

JavaScript 1.5+, JScript 5.5+, ECMAScript 3E+
Nav6+, IE5.5+

Syntax

string`.toLocaleUpperCase()`

Description

The `toLocaleUpperCase()` method of an instance of a `String` object converts the characters in that string to all uppercase values. This is often used when a programmer is trying to evaluate a string a user has entered, and case is not an issue. This method differs from the `toUpperCase()` method by yielding its result to the host environment's current locale.

Example

Listing 7.363 pops up a prompt box and asks the user to enter various case text. After the user clicks OK, the uppercase version of the string is written to the page.

Listing 7.363   Using the `toLocaleUpperCase()` *Method of the* `String` *Object to Convert a String Entered by a User to Uppercase*

```
<script type="text/javascript" language="JavaScript1.1">
<!--

// Create an instance of the String object.
var myString = new String(prompt("Please enter some various case text", ""));

// Convert the text to uppercase and write it to the page.
document.write(myString.toLocaleUpperCase());

// Close the stream to the window.
document.close();

//-->
</script>
```

String.toLowerCase()

JavaScript 1.0+, JScript 1.0+, ECMAScript 1E+
Nav2+, NES2+, IE3+, Opera3+

Syntax

string.toLowerCase()

Description

The `toLowerCase()` method of an instance of a `String` object converts the characters in that string to all lowercase values. This is often used when a programmer tries to evaluate a string a user has entered and does not care about case.

Example

Listing 7.364 pops up a prompt box and asks the user to enter various case text. After the user clicks OK, the lowercase version of the string is written to the page.

Listing 7.364   Using the `toLowerCase()` *Method of the* `String` *Object to Convert a String Entered by a User to Lowercase*

```
<script type="text/javascript" language="JavaScript1.1">
<!--

// Create an instance of the String object.
var myString = new String(prompt("Please enter some various case text", ""));

// Convert the text to lowercase and write it to the page.
document.write(myString.toLowerCase());

// Close the stream to the window.
document.close();
```

```
//-->
</script>
```

String.toSource()

JavaScript 1.3+, JScript 3.0+, ECMAScript 2E+
Nav4.06+, IE4+

Syntax

```
string.toSource()
String.toSource()
```

Description

The toSource() method of the String object will return something similar to the following:

```
function String() { [native code] }
```

If it is invoked on an instance of the String object, it will contain the source of the instance you created.

Example

Listing 7.365 creates an instance of the String object. The toSource() method is then applied to the instance and the results are written to the page. A second document.write() method writes the results of applying the method to the core object.

The result of this application of the method should be something similar to the following:

```
(new String("Hello, World!"))
```

Listing 7.365   Using the toSource() *Method of the* String *Object to Obtain the Source of the Object or an Instance of It*

```
<script type="text/javascript" language="JavaScript1.3">
<!--

// Create an instance of the String object.
var myString = new String("Hello, World!");

// Apply the toSource() method to the instance and the core String
// object.
document.write(myString.toSource() + '<br>');
document.write(String.toSource());

// Close the stream to the window.
document.close();

//-->
</script>
```

String.toString()
JavaScript 1.1+, JScript1.0+, ECMAScript 1E+
Nav3+, NES2+, IE3+

Syntax
```
string.toString()
String.toString()
```

Description
The toString() method of the String object, if invoked on the core String object, will return the object type or the name of the constructor that created the object. This will be something similar to the following:

```
function String() { [native code] }
```

If it is invoked on an instance of the String object, it will contain the source string of the instance you created.

Example
Listing 7.366 creates an instance of the String object. The toString() method is then applied to the instance and the results are written to the page. A second document.write() method writes the results of applying the method to the core object.

The result of this application of the method should be something similar to the following:

```
Hello, World!
```

Listing 7.366   Using the toString() **Method of the** String **Object to Obtain the Source of the Object or an Instance of It**

```
<script type="text/javascript" language="JavaScript1.3">
<!--

// Create an instance of the String object.
var myString = new String("Hello, World!");

// Apply the toString() method to the instance and the core String
// object.
document.write(myString.toString() + '<br>');
document.write(String.toString());

// Close the stream to the window.
document.close();

//-->
</script>
```

String.toUpperCase()

JavaScript 1.0+, JScript 1.0+, ECMAScript 1E+
Nav2+, NES2+, IE3+, Opera3+

Syntax

```
string.toUpperCase ()
```

Description

The toUpperCase() method of an instance of a String object converts the characters in that string to all uppercase values. This is often used when a programmer is trying to evaluate a string a user has entered, and case is not an issue.

Example

Listing 7.367 pops up a prompt box and asks the user to enter various case text. After the user clicks OK, the uppercase version of the string is written to the page.

Listing 7.367   Using the toUpperCase() ***Method of the*** String ***Object to Convert a String Entered by a User to Uppercase***

```
<script type="text/javascript" language="JavaScript1.1">
<!--

// Create an instance of the String object.
var myString = new String(prompt("Please enter some various case text", ""));

// Convert the text to uppercase and write it to the page.
document.write(myString.toUpperCase());

// Close the stream to the window.
document.close();

//-->
</script>
```

String.unwatch()

JavaScript 1.2+
Nav4+, NES3+

Syntax

```
string.unwatch (property)
```

Description

The unwatch() method of the String object, is used to turn off the watch on a particular property specified by *property*.

Example

Listing 7.368 shows how the unwatch() method is used to stop watching the user-defined property *p*.

Listing 7.368   *Example of* unwatch() *Method of the Array Object*

```
<script type="text/javascript">
<!--

// Create a function to handle watch.
function alertme(id, oldValue, newValue){
  document.writeln("ID (" + id + ") changed from " + oldValue + " to ");
  document.writeln(newValue + "<br>");
  return newValue;
}

// Create instance of string.
var myString = new String();

// Create property for string.
String.prototype.p = 1;

// Watch property value.
myString.watch("p", alertme);

// Change value.
myString.p = 2;

// Turn off watch.
myString.unwatch("p");
myString.p = 3;

// -->
</script>
```

String.valueOf()

JavaScript 1.1+, JScript 3.0+, ECMAScript 1E+
Nav3+, NES2+, IE4+, Opera3+

Syntax

string.valueOf()

Description

The valueOf() method returns the primitive value of the object. In terms of an instance of a String object, this method returns the string itself.

Example

In Listing 7.369, an instance of the String object is created. Because the valueOf() method returns the actual value of the string, "Here is some random text" is written to the user's page.

Listing 7.369 Using the valueOf() **Method to Return the Value of the** String() **Instance**

```
<script type="text/javascript" language="JavaScript1.1">
<!--

// Create an instance of the String object.
var myString = new String("Here is some random text.");

// Write the value of the string to the page.
document.write('The value of my string instance is: ' + myString.valueOf());

// Close the stream to the window.
document.close();

//-->
</script>
```

String.watch()

JavaScript 1.2+
Nav4+, NES3+

Syntax

string.watch(*property*)

Description

The watch() method of the String object, is used to turn on the watch on a particular property specified by *property*.

Example

Listing 7.370 shows how the watch() method is used to start watching the user-defined property *p*.

Listing 7.370 Example of watch() **Method of the Array Object**

```
<script type="text/javascript">
<!--

// Create a function to handle watch.
function alertme(id, oldValue, newValue){
```

Listing 7.370   Continued

```
document.writeln("ID (" + id + ") changed from " + oldValue + " to ");
document.writeln(newValue + "<br>");
return newValue;
}

// Create instance of string.
var myString = new String();

// Create property for string.
String.prototype.p = 1;

// Watch property value.
myString.watch("p", alertme);

// Change value.
myString.p = 2;

// -->
</script>
```

sun

> JavaScript 1.1+
> Nav3+, NES2+

Syntax

sun

Description

The sun object allows you to access any class within the package sun.*. It is shorter and works the same way as using the Packages.sun property.

Example

Listing 7.371 shows how the sun property can be used to determine whether the current browser supports the sun package if Java is installed.

Listing 7.371   Example Using the sun Object

```
<script type="text/javascript" language="JavaScript1.1">
<!--

// Checks to see if the sun Java package is installed.
if(sun){
  document.write ("This browser has the sun package");
}else{
  document.write ("This browser does not have the sun package");
}
```

```
// -->
</script>
```

super

JavaScript 1.3+
Nav4.06+, NES3+,

Syntax

```
Reserved Keyword
```

Description

The super keyword was reserved for future use but has not currently been implemented.

Example

No example can be provided because super has not been implemented.

switch

JavaScript 1.2+, JScript 3.0+
Nav4+, NES3+, IE4+

Syntax

```
switch(expression){
  case label1:
    code;
    break;
  case label2:
    code;
    break;
  case labelN:
    code;
    break;
  default:
    code;
}
```

Description

The switch statement allows you to process the *expression* passed by matching it with a label—from *label1* to *labelN*. If there is a match, the code following that label is executed. If the *expression* passed does not match a label, the default section is executed. Note that you can have as many labels as you deem necessary in your script.

Example

Listing 7.372 has a text field and a button. Users are asked to enter a day of the week into the field. When they press the button, a function is called that contains a switch, which verifies they entered a correct day. If so, an alert box pops up and tells users what part of the week they entered.

Listing 7.372   *Using a* switch *Statement to Process Data*

```html
<html>
<head>
  <title>Using the switch statement</title>
<script type="text/javascript" language="JavaScript1.1">
<!--

// Display an alert box that contains the value of the
// submit button.
function verifyDay(form){

  // Read the text entered in a variable and convert it to uppercase.
  var myEntry = form.day.value.toUpperCase();

  // Define what you return.
  var firstPart = "You have entered a day at the beginning of the week";
  var endPart = "You have entered a day at the end of the week";
  var weekEnd = "You have entered a weekend day";

  // Use a switch statement to perform your processing.
  switch(myEntry){
    case "MONDAY" :
      alert(firstPart);
      break;
    case "TUESDAY" :
      alert(firstPart);
      break;
    case "WEDNESDAY" :
      alert('You have entered a "hump" day');
      break;
    case "THURSDAY" :
      alert(endPart);
      break;
    case "FRIDAY" :
      alert(endPart);
      break;
    case "SATURDAY" :
      alert(weekEnd);
      break;
    case "SUNDAY" :
      alert(weekEnd);
      break;
    default :
      alert('You have entered an invalid day');
  }
}
```

```
//-->
</script>
</head>
<body>
<form name="myForm">
<b>Please enter a day of the week:</b><br>
  <input type="text" value="" name="day">
  <input type="button" value="Verify" name="myButton"
        onClick='verifyDay(this.form)'>
</form>
</body>
</html>
```

synchronized

JavaScript 1.2+, JScript3.0+
Nav4+, NES3+, IE4+

Syntax

```
Reserved Keyword
```

Description

The synchronized keyword has not been implemented in JavaScript to date. It has been reserved for future use.

Example

This keyword has not been implemented; therefore, no example is provided.

this

JavaScript 1.0+, JScript 1.0+
Nav2+, NES2+, IE2+, Opera3+

Syntax

```
this
this.property
```

Description

The this keyword is used to refer to the current object and is often used to pass entire objects, such as those contained in Form instances, to functions and methods specified in scripts.

Example

Listing 7.373 contains a text box, a text area, and a button. When the user clicks the button, an onClick event handler passes the form's information, using the this keyword, to a function defined in the <head> of the document. The function opens a second, smaller window and writes several properties of the form to the page.

Listing 7.373 Using** this **to Pass All Form Data to a Function

```
<html>
<head>
  <title>Using this in passing form information</title>
<script type="text/javascript">
<!--

function displayInfo(form){

  // Open a window to store the results.
  var myWin = open("", "","width=450,height=200");

  // Write the text boxes properties to the window.
  myWin.document.write("The defaultValue of the text box is: ");
  myWin.document.write(form.myText.defaultValue);
  myWin.document.write("<br>The name of the text area is: ");
  myWin.document.write(form.myTextArea.name);
  myWin.document.write("<br>The value of the button is: ");
  myWin.document.write(form.myButton.value);

  // Close the stream to the window.
  myWin.document.close();
}
//-->
</script>
</head>
<body>
<form name="myForm">
  <textarea name="myTextArea" rows=2 cols=50>
    Here is some text in my text area.
  </textarea>
  <br>
  <input type="text" value="Change Me?" name="myText">
  <br>
  <input type="button" value="Display Information" name="myButton"
         onClick='displayInfo(this.form)'>
</form>
</body>
</html>
```

Listing 7.374 creates a `vehicle` object that has three properties: number of doors, color, and the type of vehicle. The `this` keyword is used to associate these properties with the object when it is referenced in other scripts. Further down in the example, an instance of the `vehicle` object is created and its properties are written to the page.

Listing 7.374 Using** this **to Internally Reference Properties of a User-defined Object

```
<html>
<head>
```

```
   <title>Using this in object creation</title>
<script type="text/javascript">
<!--

// Create vehicle object.
function vehicle(nDoors, sColor, sType){

   // Define the characteristics of the vehicle and associate
   // them with a new instance using the "this" keyword.
   this.doors = nDoors;
   this.color = sColor;
   this.type = sType;
}

//-->
</script>
</head>
<body>
<script type="text/javascript">
<!--

// Create an instance of the vehicle.
var myVehicle = new vehicle(4, "red", "Toyota");

// Call the properties of your object using the dot convention
// found throughout JavaScript.
document.writeln("I have created a " + myVehicle.type);
document.writeln(" that is " + myVehicle.color);
document.writeln(" and has " + myVehicle.doors + " doors.");
//-->
</script>
</body>
</html>
```

throw

JavaScript 1.4+, JScript 5.0+, ECMAScript 3E+
Nav6+, NES3+, IE5+

Syntax

throw *exception*

Description

The throw element of the JavaScript language was a reserved keyword in the
JavaScript 1.3 and JScript 3.0 languages and in the Netscape Enterprise server 3
environment. Netscape 6 and Internet Explorer 5 were the first browsers to implement
the keyword. It is used to generate an error condition handled by a try..catch
statement or to pass errors found in these statements to higher-level handlers.

Example

Listing 7.375 contains a text box and button. The user is asked to insert a numeric value into the text box and press the button. When this is done, the onClick event handler of the button calls a function to check whether the entered text was numeric. If it is not, the myErrorHandler function is called to handle the error. The myErrorHandler function contains a try..catch statement that allows the programmer to define what happens on an incorrect entry. In this example, an alert box is displayed containing an error code and message.

Listing 7.375   *This Example Uses* throw *in a* try..catch *Statement*

```html
<html>
<head>
  <title>Using throw in a try..catch statement</title>
<script type="text/javascript" language="JavaScript1.5">
<!--

// Declare a function to handle errors.
function myErrorHandler(data){
  try{
    // Check to see if the value passed is "string" or "NaN"
    // then "throw" the appropriate error.
    if(data == "string"){
      throw "E0";
    }else{
      throw "E1";
    }
  }catch(e){

    // If the error thrown was "E0" then return the following.
    if(e == "E0"){
      return("Error (" + e + "): Entry must be numeric.");
    }else{

      // Pass off to a higher level handler.
      return("Error (" + e + "): Entry must be numeric.");
    }
  }
}

// This function reads in the form data and calls the appropriate error.
function processData(form){

  // Check to see if a number was passed.
  if(isNaN(parseInt(form.myText.value))){
    alert(myErrorHandler("string"));
  }else{
```

```
      alert("You have correctly entered a number");
   }
}
//-->
</script>
</head>
<body>
<form name="myForm">
   Please enter a number:
   <input type="text" size="10" value="" name="myText">
   <input type="button" value="Process" name="myButton"
           onClick='processData(this.form)'>
</form>
</body>
</html>
```

throws

JavaScript 1.2+
Nav4, NES3+

Syntax

Reserved Keyword

Description

The throws keyword has not been implemented in JavaScript to date. It has been reserved for future use.

Example

This keyword has not been implemented; therefore, no example is provided.

transient

JavaScript 1.2+
Nav4+, NES3+

Syntax

Reserved Keyword

Description

The transient keyword has not been implemented in JavaScript to date. It has been reserved for future use.

Example

This keyword has not been implemented; therefore, no example is provided.

true

JavaScript 1.2+
Nav4+, NES3+

Syntax

```
Reserved Keyword
```

Description

The true keyword has not been implemented in JavaScript to date. It has been reserved for future use.

Example

This keyword has not been implemented; therefore, no example is provided.

try...catch...finally

JScript 5.0+, JavaScript 1.4, ECMAScript 3E+
Nav6+, NES3+, IE5+

Syntax

```
try{
    statement1
    throw exception;
}catch(exception if expression){
    statement2
    throw exception;
}catch(exception){
    statement3
    throw exception;
}finally{
    statement4
    throw exception;
}
```

Description

The try...catch...finally statement of the JavaScript language contained the try, catch, and finally reserve keywords in the JavaScript 1.3 and JScript 3.0 languages and in the Netscape Enterprise server 3 environments. Internet Explorer 5 and Netscape 6 were the first browsers to implement this feature.

This statement, of which both catch and finally elements are optional and can contain additional nested try...catch...finally statements, can be used to handle all or some of the errors that can occur in a script. If an error is not handled by the statement, it is passed on so other statements can handle the error. If there are no other statements to handle the error, it is passed to the browser to handle. This usually means a pop-up dialog box to the user or writing the information to a hidden error dialog.

As soon as an error occurs, the value thrown is passed to the `catch` clause via *exception*. If the error cannot be handled, another `throw` statement is used to pass the error to a higher-level (or next in line) handler if one has been defined.

statement1 is initially where an error can occur. If an `if` statement is used in the `catch` clause, *exception* is only caught if *expression* is true, at which time *statement2* is used to handle the error. If it is not handled, *statement3* will be evaluated to handle the exception. As mentioned, if no block can handle the exception, it is passed back to the browser. The `finally` block, which is optional, is executed before this is done.

> **NOTE**
>
> The ability to have multiple `catch` clauses is an extension within the Netscape 6 environment.

Example

Listing 7.376 contains a text box and button. The user is asked to insert a numeric value into the text box and click the button. When this is done, the `onClick` event handler of the button calls a function to check whether the entered text was numeric. If it is not, the `myErrorHandler` function is called to handle the error. The `myErrorHandler` function contains a `try...catch...finally` statement that allows the programmer to define what happens on an incorrect entry. In this example, an `alert` box is displayed containing an error code and message; and a second alert box is popped up, within the `finally` block, to signal the end of the error processing.

Two levels of error handling are contained in this example to demonstrate nested usage.

Listing 7.376   *This Example Uses a* `try...catch...finally` *Statement to Handle an Incorrect Entry*

```
<html>
<head>
<script type="text/javascript" language="JavaScript1.5">
<!--

// Declare a function to handle errors.
function myErrorHandler(data){
  try{
    try{
      // Check to see if the value passed is "string" or "NaN"
      // then "throw" the appropriate error.
      if(data == "string"){
        throw "E0";
      }else{
        throw "E1";
      }
    }catch(e){

      // If the error thrown was "E0" then return the following.
      if(e == "E0"){
```

Listing 7.376 Continued

```
      return("Error (" + e + "): Entry must be numeric.");
    }else{

      // Pass off to a higher level handler.
      throw e;
    }
  }

  // This is the higher level handler for demonstration purposes.
  }catch(e){
    return("Error (" + e + "): Entry was invalid.");
  }finally{
    alert("Error processing complete!");
  }
}

// This function reads in the form data and calls the appropriate error.
function processData(form){

  // Check to see if a number was passed.
  if(isNaN(parseInt(form.myText.value))){
    alert(myErrorHandler("string"));
  }else{
    alert("You have correctly entered a number");
  }
}
//-->
</script>
</head>
<body>
<form name="myForm">
  Please enter a number:
  <input type="text" size="10" value="" name="myText">
  <input type="button" value="Process" name="myButton"
        onClick='processData(this.form)'>
</form>
</body>
</html>
```

typeof

JavaScript 1.1+, JScript 1.0+
Nav3+, NES2+, IE3+, Opera3+

Syntax

```
typeof (variable)
```

Description

The typeof unary operator is used to determine the type of the variable passed to it. The return values of this operator are boolean, number, object, string, or undefined.

NOTE

Because undefined was not fully implemented until JavaScript 1.3 and JScript 3.0, many supporting browsers return null when passing a variable that has not been defined.

Example

Listing 7.377 creates boolean, number, object, string, and undefined variable instances, and then uses the typeof operator to write their types to the page.

Listing 7.377   This Example Uses the typeof ***Unary Operator to Return the Types for Four Different Variables***

```
<html>
<head>
  <title>Using typeof to determine the type of variables
  </title>
<script type="text/javascript" language="JavaScript1.1">
<!--

// Declare 4 variables of different types.
var bMyVar = true;
var nMyVar = 35;
var sMyVar = "This is a string";
var uMyVar;

//-->
</script>
</head>
<body>
<script type="text/javascript" language="JavaScript1.1">
<!--

// Declare 4 variables of different types.
document.writeln("bMyVar = " + typeof(bMyVar));
document.writeln("<br>nMyVar = " + typeof(nMyVar));
document.writeln("<br>sMyVar = " + typeof(sMyVar));
document.writeln("<br>uMyVar = " + typeof(uMyVar));

//-->
</script>
</body>
</html>
```

undefined

JavaScript 1.3+, JScript 5.0+, ECMAScript 1E+
Nav4.06+, IE5+

Syntax

```
undefined
```

Description

The undefined property is a primitive value of the Global object. It is returned by variables that have not had values assigned to them. It is also returned by methods if the variable being evaluated is not assigned a value. Browsers not supporting this property return null on the undefined variables.

NOTE

ECMAScript 1st Edition only defines undefined as a primitive value, and does not define it as a property of the Global object.

Example

Listing 7.378 creates the variable myVariable, and then checks to see whether it is undefined in an if statement. Note that Opera 3 and later browsers, even though they do not officially support this property, return null but evaluate the if statement in this example as true.

Listing 7.378   Testing a Variable to See Whether It Is undefined

```
<script type="text/javascript" language="JavaScript1.3">
<!--

// Create a variable.
var myVariable;

// Evaluate the variable in an if statement and write its
// value to the page.
if(myVariable == undefined){
  document.write("This variable is undefined at the moment");
}else{
  document.write("This variables value is: " + myVariable);
}
//-->
</script>
```

unescape()

JavaScript 1.0+, JScript 1.0+, ECMAScript 1E+
Nav2+, NES2+, IE3+, Opera3+

Syntax

```
unescape (string)
```

Description

The unescape() method takes a hexadecimal value and returns the ISO-Latin-1 ASCII equivalent. This method performs the opposite operation of the escape() method and is commonly used to escape user-entered data before form submission.

Example

Listing 7.379 declares a local variable, escapedVal, and passes it to the unescape() method. The result, "@", is then written to the page.

Listing 7.379   Using the unescape() *Method to Convert a Hexadecimal Value to Its ASCII Equivalent*

```
<script type="text/javascript">
<!--

// Create a variable.
var escapedVal = "%40";

// Evaluate the variable and place the value in a variable.
var unescapedVal = unescape(escapedVal);

document.write('The <I>escapedVal</I> value (' + escapedVal + ") ");
document.write("evaluates to " + unescapedVal);

//-->
</script>
```

var

> JavaScript 1.0+, JScript 1.0+, ECMAScript 1E+
> Nav2+, NES2+, IE3+, Opera3+

Syntax

```
var variable
var variable = value
```

Description

The var keyword is used to declare variables within a script. If it is used in a function, the scope of the variable is confined to that function. If used outside of a function, it is not limited and can be accessed anywhere on the page.

Example

Listing 7.380 declares the variable, myVar, in three different locations. It is declared once at a global level, once within a function where it is the returned value, and once in a function where it is written to the page.

Listing 7.380   This Example Shows Using the var *Keyword in Three Different Instances*

```
<html>
<head>
  <title>Examples of the var Keyword</title>
<script type="text/javascript">
<!--

// Declare a global variable.
var myVar = "Global";

// Declare a variable of the same name in this function
// and return it.
function myFunc(){
  var myVar = "Function";
  return myVar;
}

// Declare a variable of the same name in a second function
// and write it to the page.
function mySecFunc(){
  var myVar = "Second Function";
  document.write("<br>The value of myVar when called by mySecFunc() is: ");
  document.write(myVar);
}
//-->
</script>
</head>
<body>
<script type="text/javascript">
<!--

// Write the value of the global variable.
document.write("The value of myVar when called is: " + myVar)

// Write the value returned by the function.
document.write("<br>The value of myVar when called by myFunc() is: ");
document.write(myFunc());

// Call the second function to write its results.
mySecFunc();

//-->
</script>
</body>
</html>
```

VBArray

JScript 3.0+

Syntax

```
var variable = new VBArray(vbarray)
```

Description

The VBArray object provides access to Visual Basic safeArrays. These arrays are often written on the same HTML page and are written in VBScript. Table 7.45 lists the methods of the VBArray object.

Table 7.45   Methods of the VBArray Object

Method	Description
dimensions()	Returns the number of dimensions in the array
getItem()	Returns the item at a specified location
lbound()	Returns the lowest index value of the dimension in the array
toArray()	Returns a JScript array from the VBArray passed
ubound()	Returns the highest index value of the dimension in the array

Example

Listing 7.381 calls a VBScript function from a JScript new operator to create a Visual Basic safe array. The function itself writes the contents of this two-dimensional array to the user's page.

Listing 7.381   Creating a VBArray

```
<script type="text/vbscript">

' Define the VB Array
Function myVBArray()
  ' Define variables for 2-D array positioning
  Dim i
  Dim j

  ' Define variable to hold incremented values to put into
  ' array and assign it an initial value of 1
  Dim k
  k = 1

  ' Create a 2-D array
  Dim myArray(1, 1)

  ' Iterate through 2-D array and put incremented value in
  For i = 0 To 1
    For j = 0 To 1
      myArray(j, i) = k
```

Listing 7.381   Continued

```
    ' Write the value to the screen
    document.writeln(k)
    k = k + 1
  Next
  document.writeln("<br>")
Next


  ' Return the array to the calling function
  myVBArray = myArray
End Function

</script>
<script type="text/jscript">
<!--

// Create a new instance of VBArray
var myArray = new VBArray(myVBArray());

//-->
</script>
```

VBArray.dimensions()
JScript 3.0+

Syntax

vbarray.dimensions()

Description

The dimensions() method of an instance of a VBArray returns the number of dimensions of the array.

Example

Listing 7.382 calls a VBScript function from a JScript new operator to create a Visual Basic safe array. The array itself writes the contents of this two-dimensional array to the user's page. An alert box is also invoked that contains the number of dimensions of the array.

Listing 7.382   Viewing the Number of Dimensions of a VBArray Object

```
<script type="text/vbscript">

' Define the VB Array
Function myVBArray()

  ' Define variables for 2-D array positioning
  Dim i
  Dim j
```

```
' Define variable to hold incremented values to put into
' array and assign it an initial value of 1
Dim k
k = 1

' Create a 2-D array
Dim myArray(1, 1)
' Iterate through 2-D array and put incremented value in
For i = 0 To 1
  For j = 0 To 1
    myArray(j, i) = k

    ' Write the value to the screen
    document.writeln(k)
    k = k + 1
  Next
  document.writeln("<br>")
Next
' Return the array to the calling function
myVBArray = myArray
End Function

</script>
<script type="text/jscript">
<!--

// Create a new instance of VBArray.
var myArray = new VBArray(myVBArray());
alert(myArray.dimensions());

//-->
</script>
```

VBArray.getItem()
JScript 3.0+

Syntax

vbarray.getItem(*index*)
vbarray.getItem(*indexA*, *indexB*, ..., *indexN*)

Description

The getItem() method of an instance of a VBArray returns the value at the *index*
passed. If the array is multidimensional, you pass the necessary coordinates to access
the location you want.

Example

Listing 7.383 calls a VBScript function from a JScript new operator to create a Visual
Basic safe array. The array itself writes the contents of this two-dimensional array to

the user's page. An alert box is also invoked that contains the value in the second column of the second row.

Listing 7.383   Using the getItem() Method

```vbscript
<script type="text/vbscript">
' Define the VB Array
Function myVBArray()

  ' Define variables for 2-D array positioning
  Dim i
  Dim j

  ' Define variable to hold incremented values to put into
  ' array and assign it an initial value of 1
  Dim k
  k = 1
  ' Create a 2-D array
  Dim myArray(1, 1)

  ' Iterate through 2-D array and put incremented value in
  For i = 0 To 1
    For j = 0 To 1
      myArray(j, i) = k

      ' Write the value to the screen
      document.writeln(k)
      k = k + 1
    Next
    document.writeln("<br>")
  Next

  ' Return the array to the calling function
  myVBArray = myArray
End Function

</script>
<script type="text/jscript">
<!--

// Create a new instance of VBArray.
var myArray = new VBArray(myVBArray());
alert(myArray.getItem(1,1));

//-->
</script>
```

VBArray.lbound()

JScript 3.0+

Syntax

```
vbarray.lbound(dimension)
vbarray.lbound()
```

Description

The lbound() method of an instance of a VBArray returns the lowest index value in the *dimension* passed. If no *dimension* is passed, the method defaults to using 1.

Example

Listing 7.384 calls a VBScript function from a JScript new operator to create a Visual Basic safe array. The array itself writes the contents of this two-dimensional array to the user's page. An alert box is also invoked that contains the lowest index number used in the second dimension.

Listing 7.384   Using the lbound() Method

```vbscript
<script type="text/vbscript">

' Define the VB Array
Function myVBArray()

  ' Define variables for 2-D array positioning
  Dim i
  Dim j

  ' Define variable to hold incremented values to put into
  ' array and assign it an initial value of 1
  Dim k
  k = 1
  ' Create a 2-D array
  Dim myArray(1, 1)
  ' Iterate through 2-D array and put incremented value in
  For i = 0 To 1
    For j = 0 To 1
      myArray(j, i) = k

      ' Write the value to the screen
      document.writeln(k)
      k = k + 1
    Next
    document.writeln("<br>")
  Next
```

Listing 7.384 *Continued*

```
  ' Return the array to the calling function
  myVBArray = myArray
End Function


</script>
<script type="text/jscript">
<!--

// Create a new instance of VBArray.
var myArray = new VBArray(myVBArray());
alert(myArray.lbound(2));


//-->
</script>
```

VBArray.toArray()

JScript 3.0+

Syntax

vbarray.toArray()

Description

The toArray() method of an instance of a VBArray returns a valid JScript array from a VBArray.

Example

Listing 7.385 calls a VBScript function from a JScript new operator to create a Visual Basic safe array. The array itself writes the contents of this two-dimensional array to the user's page. The array is then converted into a valid JScript array and an alert box is invoked to display a value in this array.

Listing 7.385 *Using the* toArray() *Method*

```
<script type="text/vbscript">

' Define the VB Array
Function myVBArray()

  ' Define variables for 2-D array positioning
  Dim i
  Dim j

  ' Define variable to hold incremented values to put into
  ' array and assign it an initial value of 1
  Dim k
  k = 1
```

```
' Create a 2-D array
Dim myArray(1, 1
' Iterate through 2-D array and put incremented value in
For i = 0 To 1
  For j = 0 To 1
    myArray(j, i) = k

    ' Write the value to the screen
    document.writeln(k)
    k = k + 1
  Next
  document.writeln("<br>")
Next

  ' Return the array to the calling function
  myVBArray = myArray
End Function

</script>
<script type="text/jscript">
<!--

// Create a new instance of VBArray.
var myArray = new VBArray(myVBArray());

// Convert the VBArray to a JScript Array.
var myJSArray = myArray.toArray();

// Display the second column, first row value
alert(myJSArray[0,1]);

//-->
</script>
```

VBArray.ubound()

JScript 3.0+

Syntax

vbarray.ubound(*dimension*)

Description

The ubound() method of an instance of a VBArray returns the highest index value in the *dimension* passed.

Example

Listing 7.386 calls a VBScript function from a JScript new operator to create a Visual Basic safe array. The array itself writes the contents of this two-dimensional array to the user's page. An alert box is also invoked that contains the highest index number used in the second dimension.

Listing 7.386   *Using the* ubound() *Method*

```vbscript
<script type="text/vbscript">

' Define the VB Array
Function myVBArray()

  ' Define variables for 2-D array positioning
  Dim i
  Dim j

  ' Define variable to hold incremented values to put into
  ' array and assign it an initial value of 1
  Dim k
  k = 1
  ' Create a 2-D array
  Dim myArray(1, 1)
  ' Iterate through 2-D array and put incremented value in
  For i = 0 To 1
    For j = 0 To 1
      myArray(j, i) = k

      ' Write the value to the screen
      document.writeln(k)
      k = k + 1
    Next
    document.writeln("<br>")
  Next

  ' Return the array to the calling function
  myVBArray = myArray
End Function

</script>
<script type="text/jscript">
<!--

// Create a new instance of VBArray.
var myArray = new VBArray(myVBArray());
alert(myArray.ubound(2));

//-->
</script>
```

void

JavaScript 1.1+, JScript 1.0+, ECMAScript 1E+
Nav3+, NES2+, IE3+

Syntax

```
void(expression)
void expression
```

Description

The void operator is used to evaluate an expression without returning a value. This operator returns undefined and is commonly used in place of the onClick event handler because of various bugs in early Unix Navigator browsers. Note that Opera browsers do not support this operator.

Example

In Listing 7.387, the void operator is used to keep an <a> link on a page from clicking through anywhere while still invoking the function specified.

Listing 7.387 *Using the* void *Operator to Call a Function*

```
<html>
<head>
  <title>Examples of the void Operator</title>
<script type="text/javascript">
<!--

// Define a function to be called by clicking the link.
function myFunc(){
  alert("You clicked the link!");
}

//-->
</script>
</head>
<body>
<a HREF="javascript:void(myFunc())">Click here to call the function</A>
</body>
</html>
```

volatile

JavaScript 1.2+
Nav4+, NES3+

Syntax

```
Reserved Keyword
```

Description

The `volatile` keyword has not been implemented in JavaScript to date. It has been reserved for future use.

Example

This keyword has not been implemented; therefore, no example is provided.

while

JavaScript 1.0+, JScript 1.0+, ECMAScript 1E+
Nav2+, NES2+, IE3+, Opera3+

Syntax

```
while(condition){
  code;
}
```

Description

The `while` conditional statement evaluates the `condition` passed and executes the code within the block until the condition is no longer met. This is often used to evaluate the value of variables, and then perform tasks as well as to iterate through lines in a file when implemented on the server-side.

Example

Listing 7.388 defines a number and then asks the user for a second number. The user is continually asked for the second number until a number lower than the defined number is entered.

Listing 7.388   *Using the* while *Statement to Check the Value Passed In*

```
<html>
<head>
  <title>Using while</title>
</head>
<body>
<script type="text/javascript">
<!--

// Define the number to compare against and ask the user for a guess.
var indexNum = 30;
var guess = parseInt(prompt("Please enter a number.", ""));

// As long as the user puts in a higher number, keep prompting.
while(guess >= indexNum){
  guess = parseInt(prompt("Try again. Guess lower!", ""));
}
```

```
// Once the user guesses a number lower than the indexed number
// write the following to the screen.
document.write('You have guessed a number lower than the index number. ');
document.write('You guessed ' + guess + ' and the index was ');
document.write(indexNum + '.');

// Close the stream to the browser.
document.close();

//-->
</script>
</body>
</html>
```

with

JavaScript 1.0+, JScript 1.0+, ECMAScript 1E+
Nav2+, NES2+, IE3+, Opera3+

Syntax

```
with(object){
  code;
}
```

Description

The with statement takes an *object* and refers to all the properties, methods, and events of that object within the code without directly referencing the object itself. This allows you to use these characteristics of an object, such as the Math object, without specifically referencing the object.

Example

Listing 7.389 creates a variable, and then assigns it and the methods called on it, as a Math object. Because the with statement is used, you do not have to reference the methods via the instance of this object.

Listing 7.389   Using the with Statement

```
<script type="text/javascript">
<!--

// Define the variables we are going to use.
var myNum = 25;
var myE, mySin, mySqrt;

// Use a with statement to use the methods of the Math object.
with (Math) {
```

Listing 7.389   Continued

```
  myE = E;
  mySqrt = sqrt(myNum)
  mySin = sin(PI/myNum)
}

//-->
</script>
```

CHAPTER 8

Client-Side

This chapter contains all the items and elements making up the JavaScript language in browsers. As with the other chapters in this section of the book, each entry includes the version, browser support, syntax, a description, an example, as well as many other details.

JavaScript objects are in alphabetical order to provide you with quick, easy access. The methods, properties, functions, and event handlers of every object appear alphabetically after the respective parent object using the simple dot notation used in all the reference chapters.

NOTE

Throughout this chapter, the following abbreviations will be used to show browser support for each entry. Each abbreviation is followed by the browser version when the entry was first supported and a plus sign (+)if the browser continues to support the entry today:

NES = Netscape Enterprise Server

Nav = Netscape Communicator

IE = Microsoft's Internet Explorer

Opera = Opera

Anchor

JavaScript 1.2+, JScript 3.0+
Nav4+, IE4+, Opera5+

Syntax

```
document. anchors
```

Description

An instance of the Anchor object is created with each instance of the <a> tag with the name attribute (or id attribute) set. An *anchor* itself is a point in an HTML document that can be reached by using a hypertext link. The hypertext link that references an anchor can appear within the same document as the anchor or in a completely different Web page. In either case, anchors allow access to specific parts of Web pages rather than always displaying the top of a document when a Web page is loaded in a browser. For an anchor to act like an anchor, the name attribute (or id attribute) must be set for hyperlinks to reference the anchor's position in the document.

In HTML, the <a> tag is usually accompanied by an href attribute that contains a hypertext link. This is the complete opposite of the definition of an anchor because when the href is used in conjunction with the <a> tag, it is a link rather than an anchor. In fact, JavaScript uses the Link object to access the anchor tag when the tag is used as a link.

Table 8.1 lists the properties and methods available from the Anchor object.

Table 8.1   Properties and Methods Used by the Anchor **Object**

Type	Item	Description
Property	name	A name that provides access to the anchor from a link.
	text	The text that appears between the <a> and </a> tags.
	x	The x coordinate of the anchor.
	y	The y coordinate of the anchor.
Method	unwatch()	This method removes a watch point.
	watch()	This method sets a watch point.

Example

Listing 8.1 demonstrates how anchors are created and used in HTML documents by creating a dictionary of fruit. The heading for each letter of the dictionary is designated as an anchor. At the bottom of the document, some properties of the anchors are accessed using JavaScript.

Listing 8.1   Creating Anchors in a Document

```
<html>

<center>
<h1><u>Fruit Dictionary</u></h1>

Pick a letter:
<a href="#A">A</a>|<a href="#B">B</a>|<a href="#C">C</a>
</center>

<br><a name="A"><h4>The Letter A</h4></a>
Apple = A round, juicy fruit that comes in red, yellow, and green.<br>
Apricot = A round yellow-orange fruit.<br>

<br><a name="B"><h4>The Letter B</h4></a>
Banana = A long, yellow, curved fruit with a soft core.<br>
Blackberry = A black, tart fruit from a prickly bush.<br>
Blueberry = A small, round, blue berry that grows on a bush.<br>

<br><a name="C"><h4>The Letter C</h4></a>
Cantaloupe = A large orange melon with hard outer surface.<br>
Coconut = A large round fruit with a hard, fuzzy outer surface.<br>

<script type="text/javascript" language="JavaScript">
<!--
document.write("<br>The Anchor Properties:<br>");

// Display the values of the properties associated with each anchor.
for(var counter=0; counter<document.anchors.length; counter++)
{
  document.write("anchors[",counter,"].name=");
  document.write(document.anchors[counter].name,"<br>");
  document.write("anchors[",counter,"].text=");
  document.write(document.anchors[counter].text,"<br>");
  document.write("anchors[",counter,"].x=");
  document.write(document.anchors[counter].x,"<br>");
  document.write("anchors[",counter,"].y=");
  document.write(document.anchors[counter].y,"<br>");
}

// -->
</script>

</html>
```

Anchor.name
JavaScript 1.2+, JScript 3.0+
Nav4+, IE4+, Opera5+

Syntax

```
document. anchors[num].name
```

Description

The name property holds the name of the anchor and is the way hyperlinks reference the anchor's position. This property is originally set by the name attribute in the <a> tag.

Example

Listing 8.2 creates a dictionary of fruit where the heading for each letter of the dictionary is designated as an anchor. At the bottom of the document, the name property of each anchor is used to create the hyperlink text and reference each anchor.

Listing 8.2 *Accessing the* name *Property of the* Anchor *Object*

```
<html>

<center>
<h1><u>Fruit Dictionary</u></h1>

Pick a letter:
<a href="#A">A</a>|<a href="#B">B</a>|<a href="#C">C</a>
</center>

<br><a name="A"><h4>The Letter A</h4></a>
Apple = A round, juicy fruit that comes in red, yellow, and green.<br>
Apricot = A round yellow-orange fruit.<br>

<br><a name="B"><h4>The Letter B</h4></a>
Banana = A long, yellow, curved fruit with a soft core.<br>
Blackberry = A black, tart fruit from a prickly bush.<br>
Blueberry = A small, round, blue berry that grows on a bush.<br>

<br><a name="C"><h4>The Letter C</h4></a>
Cantaloupe = A large orange melon with hard outer surface.<br>
Coconut = A large round fruit with a hard, fuzzy outer surface.<br>

<script type="text/javascript" language="JavaScript">
<!--
document.write("<br>Pick a letter:");

// Create a link for each anchor using the Anchor object.
for(var counter=0; counter<document.anchors.length; counter++)
{
```

```
document.write("<a href='#",document.anchors[counter].name,"'>");
document.write(document.anchors[counter].name,"</a>|");
}

// -->
</script>

</html>
```

Anchor.text

JavaScript 1.2-1.4
Nav4-4.5

Syntax

```
document. anchors[num].text
```

Description

The text property contains the text that appears between the <a> and </a> tags. If other HTML tags appear within these two anchor tags, the text property might not contain all the text between the anchor tags.

Example

Listing 8.3 creates a dictionary of fruit where the heading for each letter of the dictionary is designated as an anchor. At the bottom of the document, the text property of the anchors is used to create hyperlink text that points to each anchor.

Listing 8.3   Accessing the text Property of the Anchor Object

```
<html>

<center>
<h1><u>Fruit Dictionary</u></h1>

Pick a letter:
<a href="#A">A</a>|<a href="#B">B</a>|<a href="#C">C</a>
</center>

<br><a name="A"><h4>The Letter A</h4></a>
Apple = A round, juicy fruit that comes in red, yellow, and green.<br>
Apricot = A round yellow-orange fruit.<br>

<br><a name="B"><h4>The Letter B</h4></a>
Banana = A long, yellow, curved fruit with a soft core.<br>
Blackberry = A black, tart fruit from a prickly bush.<br>
Blueberry = A small, round, blue berry that grows on a bush.<br>
```

Listing 8.3   Continued

```
<br><a name="C"><h4>The Letter C</h4></a>
Cantaloupe = A large orange melon with hard outer surface.<br>
Coconut = A large round fruit with a hard, fuzzy outer surface.<br>

<script type="text/javascript" language="JavaScript">
<!--
document.write("<br>Pick a letter:<br>");

// Create a link for each anchor using the Anchor object.
for(var counter=0; counter<document.anchors.length; counter++)
{
  document.write("<a href='#",document.anchors[counter].name,"'>");
  document.write(document.anchors[counter].text,"</a><br>");
}

// -->
</script>

</html>
```

Anchor.unwatch()

JavaScript 1.2+
Nav4+, NES3+

Syntax

```
document.anchors[num].unwatch(property)
```

Description

The unwatch() method of the Anchor object is used to turn off the watch for a particular property specified by *property*.

Example

Listing 8.4 shows how the unwatch() method is used to stop watching the *name* property of the Anchor object after its name has changed to "juice".

Listing 8.4   Example of the unwatch() Method of the Anchor Object

```
<html>
<a name="oranges">Oranges</a> are orange.<br>
<a name="apples">Apples</a> are red.<br><br>

<script type="text/javascript" language="JavaScript">
<!--
function alertme(id,oldValue,newValue)
{
```

```
  document.write(id + " changed from " + oldValue + " to ");
  document.write(newValue + "<br>");
  return newValue;
}

// Start watch.
document.anchors[0].watch("name",alertme);

document.write("Original anchor name: " + document.anchors[0].name + "<br>");

// Change anchor name associated with oranges.
document.anchors[0].name = "juice";

// End watch.
document.anchors[0].unwatch("name");

document.write("New anchor name: " + document.anchors[0].name + "<br>");

// Change anchor name associated with oranges.
document.anchors[0].name = "orange juice";

document.write("Final anchor name: " + document.anchors[0].name);
// -->
</script>
</html>
```

Anchor.watch()

JavaScript 1.2+
Nav4+, NES3+

Syntax

```
document.anchors[num].watch(property,function)
```

Description

The watch() method of the Anchor object is used to turn on the watch for a particular property specified by *property*. Any time the specified property is changed after the watch() method has been called, the specified function is called.

Example

Listing 8.5 shows how the watch() method is used to start watching the *name* property of the Anchor object.

Listing 8.5   Example of the watch() *Method of the* Anchor *Object*

```html
<html>
<a name="oranges">Oranges</a> are orange.<br>
<a name="apples">Apples</a> are red.<br><br>

<script type="text/javascript" language="JavaScript">
<!--
function alertme(id,oldValue,newValue)
{
  document.write(id + " changed from " + oldValue + " to ");
  document.write(newValue + "<br>");
  return newValue;
}

// Start watch.
document.anchors[0].watch("name",alertme);

document.write("Original anchor name: " + document.anchors[0].name + "<br>");

// Change anchor name associated with oranges.
document.anchors[0].name = "juice";

document.write("New anchor name: " + document.anchors[0].name + "<br>");
// -->
</script>
</html>
```

Anchor.x

> JavaScript 1.2-1.4
> Nav4-4.5

Syntax

`document. anchors[num].x`

Description

The x property contains the x coordinate of the anchor, in pixels, from the left edge of the document to the anchor.

Example

Listing 8.6 creates a single anchor out of a header at the top of the document. The x property is used to display the horizontal position of the Anchor object on the bottom of the page.

Listing 8.6   Accessing the x *Property of the* Anchor *Object*

```html
<html>

<center><a name="A"><h4>Apple</h4></a></center>
```

A round, juicy fruit that comes in red, yellow, and green.

```
<script type="text/javascript" language="JavaScript">
<!--

// Display the x property of the anchor.
document.write("The x property is equal to ",document.anchors[0].x);

// -->
</script>

</html>
```

Anchor.y

JavaScript 1.2-1.4
Nav4-4.5

Syntax

document. anchors[*num*].y

Description

The y property contains the y coordinate of the anchor, in pixels, from the top edge of the document to the anchor.

Example

Listing 8.7 creates a single anchor out of a header at the top of the document. The y property is used to display the vertical position of the Anchor object on the bottom of the page.

Listing 8.7   Accessing the y Property of the Anchor Object

```
<html>

<center><a name="B"><h4>Banana</h4></a></center>
A long, yellow, curved fruit with a soft core.<br>

<script type="text/javascript" language="JavaScript">
<!--

// Display the y property of the anchor.
document.write("The y property is equal to ",document.anchors[0].y);

// -->
</script>

</html>
```

Applet
JavaScript 1.1+, JScript 3.0+
Nav3+, IE4+

Syntax

Core client-side JavaScript object.

Description

In JavaScript, applets embedded in HTML Web pages are represented by the `Applet` object. This object, which is created with each instance of the `<applet>` tag in a document, allows access to the public fields and methods of the applet through JavaScript properties and methods. Table 8.2 lists the properties and methods used by the `Applet` object.

Table 8.2   Properties and Methods of the `Applet` Object

Type	Description
Property	All the public fields in a Java applet are accessed as properties of the `Applet` object in JavaScript.
Method	All the public methods in a Java applet are accessed as methods of the `Applet` object in JavaScript.

Example

Assume, for the sake of the example code in Listing 8.8, that you have a calculator applet that you want to embed in an HTML document. Also assume that this applet has a method called `add()`, which adds two numbers and returns the result. If you wanted to access this method from within JavaScript, you would begin by defining the applet using `<applet>` tags. Then the JavaScript code would pass the numbers 2 and 5 into the `add()` method, using dot notation, and the result of 7 would be returned and displayed in the browser.

NOTE

This example will not work unless you have an applet called `calculator` that has a function called `add()`.

Listing 8.8   Accessing the Method of an `Applet` Object

```
<html>

<applet name="calculator" code="calculator.class" width=50 height=50></applet>

<script type="text/javascript" language="JavaScript">
<!--
```

```
// Use the calculator applet to add two numbers.
document.write("2+5=",calculator.add(2,5);      // 7 is returned

// -->
</script>
</html>
```

Area

JavaScript 1.1+, JScript 1.0+
Nav3+, IE3+, Opera3+

Syntax

Core client-side JavaScript object.

Description

An instance of the Area object is created with each occurrence of the <area> tag within an HTML document. In HTML documents, the <area> tag is used in conjunction with the <map> tag to define an area within a picture that will act as a hyperlink. Because the Area object is a hyperlink, it is equivalent to the Link object in JavaScript. In fact, the Area object is stored in the same array where Link objects are stored. Table 8.3 lists the properties, methods, and event handlers of the Area object.

Table 8.3   Properties, Methods, and Event Handlers Used by the Area
Object

Type	Item	Description
Properties	hash	The portion of the URL that is the anchor, including the # symbol.
	host	The hostname (IP address) and port specified in the URL.
	hostname	The hostname specified within the URL.
	href	The entire URL.
	pathname	The path of the file specified in the URL beginning with the / symbol.
	port	The port specified in the URL.
	protocol	The protocol specified in the URL, including the ending colon (:).
	search	The search part of the URL, including the beginning question mark (?).
	target	The name of the target window in which the URL should be displayed.
Methods	handleEvent()	This method calls the event handler associated with this event.
	unwatch()	This method removes a watch point.
	watch()	This method sets a watch point.

Table 8.3   Continued

Type	Item	Description
Event Handlers	onDblClick	This event handler is invoked when the mouse is double-clicked while in the region defined by the Area object.
	onMouseOut	This event handler is invoked when the mouse moves outside the region defined by the Area object.
	onMouseOver	This event handler is invoked when the mouse moves into the region defined by the Area object.

Example

Listing 8.9 creates a paint store Web page complete with a box of colors that contains hyperlinks to bogus color sites. The hyperlinks are created over the graphic using the <map>, <img>, and <area> tags. When the mouse is moved over an area, the properties associated with that area are displayed in the text fields at the bottom of the screen. Figure 8.1 shows what happens when the mouse pointer is placed in the green box.

Listing 8.9   Creating Areas and Accessing Their Properties

```
<html>
<body>

<h2>The Paint Store</h2>

Select one of the 4 colors to find out more about the colors we carry.<br>

<map name="colorMap">
  <area name="redArea"
        coords="1,1,48,48"
        href="http://www.red.com:1234/red.html?query=red#RED"
        target="_top"
        onMouseOver="overBox(0)"
        onMouseOut="clearBox()">
  <area name="greenArea"
        coords="51,1,99,49"
        href="http://www.green.com:5678/green.html?query=green#GREEN"
        target="_top"
        onMouseOver="overBox(1)"
        onMouseOut="clearBox()">
  <area name="yellowArea"
        coords="1,51,51,99"
        href="http://www.yellow.com:9876/yellow.html?query=yellow#YELLOW"
        target="_top"
        onMouseOver="overBox(2)"
        onMouseOut="clearBox()">
```

```
      <area name="blueArea"
            coords="51,51,99,99"
            href="http://www.blue.com:5432/blue.html?query=blue#BLUE"
            target="_top"
            onMouseOver="overBox(3)"
            onMouseOut="clearBox()">
</map>
<img src="box4.gif" align="top"
     height="100"  width="100" usemap="#colorMap">

<br><br><b><u>AREA Properties</u></b>

<form name="myForm">
  hash=<input name="tHash" type="textarea"><br>
  host=<input name="tHost" type="textarea"><br>
  hostname=<input name="tHostName" type="textarea"><br>
  href=<input name="tHref" type="textarea"><br>
  pathname<input name="tPathName" type="textarea"><br>
  port=<input name="tPort" type="textarea"><br>
  protocol=<input name="tProtocol" type="textarea"><br>
  search=<input name="tSearch" type="textarea"><br>
  target=<input name="tTarget" type="textarea"><br>
</form>


<script type="text/javascript" language="JavaScript">
<!--

// Fill in the text area fields.
function overBox(num)
{
  document.myForm.tHash.value = document.links[num].hash;
  document.myForm.tHost.value = document.links[num].host;
  document.myForm.tHostName.value = document.links[num].hostname;
  document.myForm.tHref.value = document.links[num].href;
  document.myForm.tPathName.value = document.links[num].pathname;
  document.myForm.tPort.value = document.links[num].port;
  document.myForm.tProtocol.value = document.links[num].protocol;
  document.myForm.tSearch.value = document.links[num].search;
  document.myForm.tTarget.value = document.links[num].target;
}

// Clear text in the text area fields.
function clearBox()
{
  document.myForm.tHash.value = "";
  document.myForm.tHost.value = "";
  document.myForm.tHostName.value = "";
```

Listing 8.9   Continued

```
  document.myForm.tHref.value = "";
  document.myForm.tPathName.value = "";
  document.myForm.tPort.value = "";
  document.myForm.tProtocol.value = "";
  document.myForm.tSearch.value = "";
  document.myForm.tTarget.value = "";
}
// -->
</script>

</body>
</html>
```

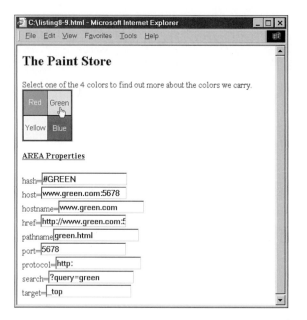

Figure 8.1

Accessing an area's properties.

Area.handleEvent()

JavaScript 1.2+

Nav4+

Syntax

```
document. links[num].handleEvent(event)
```

Description

The handleEvent() method invokes the event handler, specified by the *event* argument, that is associated with link specified by the *num* argument. The method returns the value associated with the specified *event* argument.

Example

Listing 8.10 creates a Web page for learning more about the toppings used on a pizza. When an area is clicked, the user is taken to a place within the document to learn more about the pizza topping. The handleEvent() method is used to pass all the mouse events from the first area (represented by peppers) to the event handlers of the second area (represented by onion). Normally, you would want to display a special notice when the mouse moves over the pepper area, but the handleEvent() method is used to make the pepper area do the same thing as the onion area. Notice that "onion" is placed in the text box when the mouse is moved over either of the two defined areas, thanks to the handleEvent() method.

Listing 8.10   Passing Events to Other Area Objects to be Handled

```html
<html>
<body>

<center><h1><u>
Learn more about the toppings we use on our pizza
</u></h1></center>

<h3>Choose a pizza topping from the pictures to learn more.</h3>

<map name="toppingsMap">
  <area name="peppers"
        coords="1,1,48,48"
        href="#PEPPERS"
        target="_top"
        onMouseOver="fillTextField(event)"
        onMouseOut="fillTextField(event)"><br>
  <area name="onion"
        coords="51,1,99,49"
        href="#ONION"
        target="_top"
        onMouseOver="document.pizzaForm.textbox.value='onion'"
        onMouseOut="document.pizzaForm.textbox.value=''">
</map>
<img src="toppingsBox.gif"
     align="top"
     height="50"
     width="100"
     usemap="#toppingsMap">
```

Listing 8.10   Continued

```
<br>
<form name="pizzaForm">
  <input type="text"
         name="textbox">
</form>

<script type="text/javascript" language="JavaScript">
<!--

// This function passes event to another Area object to handle.
function fillTextField(event)
{
  // Pass event to 2nd area link.
  document.links[1].handleEvent(event);
}

// -->
</script>

<a name="PEPPERS"><h3>The peppers we use:</h3></a>
<ul>
  <li>Yellow</li>
  <li>Red</li>
  <li>Green</li>
</ul>

<a name="ONION"><h3>The onions we use:</h3></a>
<ul>
  <li>Mild</li>
  <li>Hot</li>
</ul>

</body>
</html>
```

Area.hash

JavaScript 1.1+, JScript 1.0+
Nav3+, IE3+, Opera3+

Syntax

```
document. links[num].hash
```

Description

The hash property associated with an Area object contains the anchor specified in the URL including the leading hash symbol (#).

Example

Listing 8.11 creates a truck parts page that allows users to find model numbers of parts by clicking a picture of the part. When the user selects a part, she is presented with an alert window that contains the value of the hash property for the selected link. In this example the value displayed will be one of the following strings: "#SPARKPLUGS", "#TIRES", "#HEADLIGHTS", and "#FUSES". After the alert window is closed, the browser moves to the portion of the document specified by the hash property.

Listing 8.11   Displaying the hash Property of the Area Object

```
<html>
<body>

<center><h1><u>Wild Bill's Truck Parts</u></h1></center>

<h3>Select a part from the picture.</h3>

<map name="partsMap">
  <area name="sparkPlug"
        coords="1,1,48,48"
        href="#SPARKPLUGS"
        target="_top"
        onClick="alert(document.links[0].hash)">
  <area name="tires"
        coords="51,1,99,49"
        href="#TIRES"
        target="_top"
        onClick="alert(document.links[1].hash)">
  <area name="headlights"
        coords="1,51,51,99"
        href="#HEADLIGHTS"
        target="_top"
        onClick="alert(document.links[2].hash)">
  <area name="fuses"
        coords="51,51,99,99"
        href="#FUSES"
        target="_top"
        onClick="alert(document.links[3].hash)">
</map>
<img src="partsBox.gif"
     align="top"
     height="100"
     width="100"
     usemap="#partsMap">

<br>
```

Listing 8.11   Continued

```
<a name="SPARKPLUGS"><h3>Spark Plugs</h3></a>
<ul>
  <li>SP93654</li>
  <li>SP34710</li>
  <li>SP19374</li>
</ul>

<a name="TIRES"><h3>Tires</h3></a>
<ul>
  <li>Mud Stompers</li>
  <li>Low Riders</li>
  <li>Standard</li>
</ul>
<a name="HEADLIGHTS"><h3>Headlights</h3></a>
<ul>
  <li>Night Vision bulbs</li>
  <li>Standard</li>
</ul>

<a name="FUSES"><h3>Fuses</h3></a>
<ul>
  <li>Red</li>
  <li>Yellow</li>
  <li>Green</li>
  <li>Blue</li>
</ul>

</body>
</html>
```

Area.host

> JavaScript 1.1+, JScript 1.0+
> Nav3+, IE3+, Opera3+

Syntax

```
document. links[num].host
```

Description

The host property associated with an Area object contains the hostname and port that is specified in the URL separated by a colon (:).

Example

Listing 8.12 creates a truck parts page that allows users to find model numbers of parts by clicking a picture of the part. When the user selects a part, she is presented with an alert window that contains the string "www.wildbillstruckparts.com:4000", which is the value of the host property for the selected link. After the alert window is closed, the browser will attempt to load the specified file located on the fictitious Web site.

Listing 8.12 Displaying the host *Property of the* Area *Object*

```
<html>
<body>

<center><h1><u>Wild Bill's Truck Parts</u></h1>

<h3>Select a part from the picture.</h3>

<map name="partsMap">
  <area name="sparkPlug"
        coords="1,1,48,48"
        href="http://www.wildbillstruckparts.com:4000/sparkplugs.html"
        target="_top"
        onClick="alert(document.links[0].host)">
  <area name="tires"
        coords="51,1,99,49"
        href="http://www.wildbillstruckparts.com:4000/tires.html"
        target="_top"
        onClick="alert(document.links[1].host)">
  <area name="headlights"
        coords="1,51,51,99"
        href="http://www.wildbillstruckparts.com:4000/headlights.html"
        target="_top"
        onClick="alert(document.links[2].host)">
  <area name="fuses"
        coords="51,51,99,99"
        href="http://www.wildbillstruckparts.com:4000/fuses.html"
        target="_top"
        onClick="alert(document.links[3].host)">
</map>
<img src="partsBox.gif"
     align="top"
     height="100"
     width="100"
     usemap="#partsMap">

</center>

</body>
</html>
```

Area.hostname

JavaScript 1.1+, JScript 1.0+
Nav3+, IE3+

Syntax

document. links[*num*].hostname

Description

The hostname property associated with the Area object contains just the hostname that is specified in the URL.

Example

Listing 8.13 creates a truck parts page that allows users to find model numbers of parts by clicking a picture of the part. When the user selects a part, she is presented with an alert window that contains the string "www.wildbillstruckparts.com", which is the value of the hostname property for the selected link. After the alert window is closed, the browser will attempt to load the file located on the fictitious Web site.

Listing 8.13   Displaying the hostname **Property of the** Area **Object**

```
<html>
<body>

<center><h1><u>Wild Bill's Truck Parts</u></h1>

<h3>Select a part from the picture.</h3>

<map name="partsMap">
  <area name="sparkPlug"
        coords="1,1,48,48"
        href="http://www.wildbillstruckparts.com:4000/sparkplugs.html"
        target="_top"
        onClick="alert(document.links[0].hostname)">
  <area name="tires"
        coords="51,1,99,49"
        href="http://www.wildbillstruckparts.com:4000/tires.html"
        target="_top"
        onClick="alert(document.links[1].hostname)">
  <area name="headlights"
        coords="1,51,51,99"
        href="http://www.wildbillstruckparts.com:4000/headlights.html"
        target="_top"
        onClick="alert(document.links[2].hostname)">
  <area name="fuses"
        coords="51,51,99,99"
        href="http://www.wildbillstruckparts.com:4000/fuses.html"
        target="_top"
        onClick="alert(document.links[3].hostname)">
```

```
</map>
<img src="partsBox.gif"
     align="top"
     height="100"
     width="100"
     usemap="#partsMap">

</center>

</body>
</html>
```

Area.href

JavaScript 1.1+, JScript 1.0+
Nav3+, IE3+, Opera3+

Syntax

```
document.links[num].href
```

Description

The href property associated with the Area property contains the entire URL specified by the href attribute of the <area> tag. This property is a read/write string.

Example

In Listing 8.14, a sports car picture site is created. Selecting your location determines from which site a large picture of the sports car is retrieved. This is accomplished by modifying the href property to link to a completely different site based on the user's choice of cars.

Listing 8.14 *Modifying the* href *Property of the* Area *Object*

```
<html>
<body>

<center><h1><u>Sports Car Pictures</u></h1></center>

<h3>Step 1: Choose a car.</h3>

<form name="question">
<input name="carType"
       type="radio"
       checked
       onClick="updateLinks('LAMBORGHINI')">Lamborghini<br>
<input name="carType"
       type="radio"
       onClick="updateLinks('FERRARI')">Ferrari
```

Listing 8.14   Continued

```
</form>

<h3>Step 2: Click on the picture to see the car.</h3>

<map name="carMap">
  <area name="car"
        coords="1,1,48,48"
        href="http://www.cars.com:5678/cars.html?query=fast#LAMBORGHINI"
        target="_top">
</map>
<img src="cars.gif" align="top"
     height="50"   width="50" usemap="#carMap">

<br>

<script type="text/javascript" language="JavaScript">
<!--

// update the picture host links based on the radio box settings
function updateLinks(car)
{
  // Set to Lamborghini site
  if(car=="LAMBORGHINI")
    document.links[0].href="http://www.cars.com:5678/cars.html
➥?query=fast#LAMBORGHINI";

  // Set to Ferrari site
  if(car=="FERRARI")
document.links[0].href="http://www.sportscars.com:2020/fastcars.html?
➥query=fast#FERRARI";
}

// -->
</script>

</body>
</html>
```

Area.onDblClick

JavaScript 1.2+, JScript 1.0+
Nav4+, IE3+

Syntax

```
onDblClick="command"
```

Description

The onDblClick event handler associated with the Area object is invoked when the user double-clicks the mouse pointer while in the region defined by the <area> tag.

Example

Listing 8.15 creates a clothing site with a picture of a shirt. Double-clicking the shirt displays a message about red shirts, thanks to the onDblClick event handler.

Listing 8.15   *Using the* onDblClick *Property of the* Area *Object*

```html
<html>
<body>

<h2>The Clothes Site</h2>

<map name="clothesMap">
  <area name="redShirt"
        coords="1,1,48,48"
        target="_top"
        onDblClick="alert('You must like red shirts.')">
</map>
<img src="clothes.gif" align="top"
     height="100"   width="100" usemap="#clothesMap">

</body>
</html>
```

Area.onMouseOut

JavaScript 1.1+, JScript 1.0+
Nav3+, IE3+, Opera3+

Syntax

```
onMouseOut="command"
```

Description

The onMouseOut event handler associated with the Area object is invoked when the user moves the mouse pointer into the region defined by the <area> tag.

Example

Listing 8.16 creates a clothing site with a picture of a shirt. Clicking the shirt graphic takes you to a site about red shirts. If the mouse is moved out of the region, an alert box posts a message to the screen, thanks to the onMouseOut event handler.

Listing 8.16   *Using the* onMouseOut *Property of the* Area *Object*

```html
<html>
<body>
```

Listing 8.16   Continued

```
<h2>The Clothes Site</h2>

<map name="clothesMap">
  <area name="redShirt"
        coords="1,1,48,48"
        href="http://www.clothes.com/redShirts.html"
        target="_top"
        onMouseOut="alert('You did not want to go the red shirt site?')">
</map>
<img src="clothes.gif" align="top"
     height="100"   width="100" usemap="#clothesMap">

</body>
</html>
```

Area.onMouseOver

JavaScript 1.1+, JScript 1.0+
Nav3+, IE3+, Opera3+

Syntax

```
onMouseOver="command"
```

Description

The onMouseOver event handler is invoked when the user moves the mouse pointer over the region defined by the <area> tag.

Example

Listing 8.17 creates a clothing site with a picture of a shirt. Clicking the shirt graphic takes you to a site about red shirts. Simply moving the mouse over the region causes an alert box to be posted alerting the user that a mouseover event occurred.

Listing 8.17   Using the onMouseOver **Property of the** Area **Object**

```
<html>
<body>

<h2>The Clothes Page</h2>

Click on the sales tag to see the clothes that are on sale:<br>

<map name="clothesMap">
  <area name="sale"
        coords="1,1,100,100"
        href="http://www.clothes.com/specials.html"
        target="_top"
        onMouseOver="alert('An onMouseOver event occured.')">
```

```
</map>
<img src="sale.gif" align="top"
    height="100"   width="100" usemap="#clothesMap">

</body>
</html>
```

Area.pathname
JavaScript 1.1+, JScript 1.0+
Nav3+, IE3+, Opera3+

Syntax
`document.links[num].pathname`

Description
The `pathname` property contains the path of the file specified in the URL, including the leading slash (/).

Example
Listing 8.18 creates a truck parts page that allows users to find model numbers of parts by clicking a picture of the part. When the user selects a part, she is presented with an alert window that contains the value of the `pathname` property for the selected link. After the alert window is closed, the browser attempts to load the specified file.

Listing 8.18 **Displaying the** `pathname` **Property of an** Area **Object**

```
<html>
<body>

<center><h1><u>Wild Bill's Truck Parts</u></h1></center>

<h3>Select a part from the picture.</h3>

<map name="partsMap">
  <area name="sparkPlug"
        coords="1,1,48,48"
        href="sparkplugs.html"
        target="_top"
        onClick="alert(document.links[0].pathname)">
  <area name="tires"
        coords="51,1,99,49"
        href="tires.html"
        target="_top"
        onClick="alert(document.links[1].pathname)">
  <area name="headlights"
        coords="1,51,51,99"
        href="headlights.html"
```

Listing 8.18   Continued

```
        target="_top"
        onClick="alert(document.links[2].pathname)">
  <area name="fuses"
        coords="51,51,99,99"
        href="fuses.html"
        target="_top"
        onClick="alert(document.links[3].pathname)">
</map>
<img src="partsBox.gif"
     align="top"
     height="100"
     width="100"
     usemap="#partsMap">

</center>

</body>
</html>
```

Area.port

JavaScript 1.1+, JScript 1.0+
Nav3+, IE3+

Syntax

```
document.links[num].port
```

Description

The port property contains just the port specified in the URL.

Example

Listing 8.19 creates a truck parts page that allows users to find model numbers of parts by clicking a picture of the part. When the user selects a part, she is presented with an alert window that contains the string "4000", which is the value of the port property for the selected link. After the alert window is closed, the browser will attempt to load the specified Web site.

Listing 8.19   Displaying the port Property of an Area Object

```
<html>
<body>

<center><h1><u>Wild Bill's Truck Parts</u></h1>

<h3>Select a part from the picture.</h3>
```

```
<map name="partsMap">
  <area name="sparkPlug"
        coords="1,1,48,48"
        href="http://www.wildbillstruckparts.com:4000/sparkplugs.html"
        target="_top"
        onClick="alert(document.links[0].port)">
  <area name="tires"
        coords="51,1,99,49"
        href="http://www.wildbillstruckparts.com:4000/tires.html"
        target="_top"
        onClick="alert(document.links[1].port)">
  <area name="headlights"
        coords="1,51,51,99"
        href="http://www.wildbillstruckparts.com:4000/headlights.html"
        target="_top"
        onClick="alert(document.links[2].port)">
  <area name="fuses"
        coords="51,51,99,99"
        href="http://www.wildbillstruckparts.com:4000/fuses.html"
        target="_top"
        onClick="alert(document.links[3].port)">
</map>
<img src="partsBox.gif"
     align="top"
     height="100"
     width="100"
     usemap="#partsMap">

</center>

</body>
</html>
```

Area.protocol

JavaScript 1.1+, JScript 1.0+
Nav3+, IE3+

Syntax

document.links[*num*]. protocol

Description

The protocol property contains the protocol (http:, file:, ftp:, and so on) specified in the URL, including the ending colon (:).

Example

In Listing 8.20, the protocol property containing http: is displayed below the area link.

Listing 8.20   Accessing the protocol *Property of an* Area *Object*

```
<html>

<h2>The Color Page</h2>

<map name="colorMap">
  <area name="greenArea"
        coords="1,1,48,48"
        href="http://www.green.com:5678/green.html?query=green#GREEN"
        target="_top">
</map>
<img src="box4.gif" align="top"
     height="100"   width="100" usemap="#colorMap">

<script>
<!--

// Display the protocol associated with the area
document.write("protocol = ",document.links[0].protocol);

// -->
</script>
</html>
```

Area.search

JavaScript 1.1+, JScript 1.0+
Nav3+, IE3+

Syntax

```
document.links[num]. search
```

Description

The search property contains the search string specified in the URL, including the
leading question mark (?).

Example

Listing 8.21 creates a truck parts page that allows users to find model numbers of parts
by clicking a picture of the part. When the user selects a part, she is presented with an
alert window that contains the value of the search property for the selected link. In this
example, the value displayed will be one of the following strings: "?sparkplugs",
"?tires", "?headlights", or "?fuses". After the alert window is closed, the browser
attempts to load the fictitious page.

Listing 8.21   Displaying the search *Property of an* Area *Object*

```
<html>
<body>
```

```
<center><h1><u>Wild Bill's Truck Parts</u></h1>

<h3>Select a part from the picture.</h3>

<map name="partsMap">
  <area name="sparkPlug"
        coords="1,1,48,48"
        href="parts.html?sparkplugs"
        target="_top"
        onClick="alert(document.links[0].search)">
  <area name="tires"
        coords="51,1,99,49"
        href="parts.html?tires.html"
        target="_top"
        onClick="alert(document.links[1].search)">
  <area name="headlights"
        coords="1,51,51,99"
        href="parts.html?headlights.html"
        target="_top"
        onClick="alert(document.links[2].search)">
  <area name="fuses"
        coords="51,51,99,99"
        href="parts.html?fuses.html"
        target="_top"
        onClick="alert(document.links[3].search)">
</map>
<img src="partsBox.gif"
     align="top"
     height="100"
     width="100"
     usemap="#partsMap">

</center>

</body>
</html>
```

Area.target

JavaScript 1.1+, JScript 1.0+
Nav3+, IE3+, Opera3+

Syntax

document.links[*num*]. target

Description

The target property contains the name of the target window or frame in which the URL should be displayed. This property is a read/write string.

Example

In Listing 8.22, a truck parts site is created that allows the user to find out what parts the store carries. The target of the spark plugs and tires link is modified to make the information appear in a new browser window. Figure 8.2 shows the result of selecting the sparkplug image.

Listing 8.22 *Modifying the* target *Property of an* Area *Object*

```
<html>
<body>

<center><h1><u>Wild Bill's Truck Parts</u></h1></center>

<h3>Choose Part from Pictures.</h3>

<map name="partsMap">
  <area name="sparkPlug"
        coords="1,1,48,48"
        href="#SPARKPLUGS"
        target="_top">
  <area name="tires"
        coords="51,1,99,49"
        href="#TIRES"
        target="_top">
  <area name="headlights"
        coords="1,51,51,99"
        href="#HEADLIGHTS"
        target="_top">
  <area name="fuses"
        coords="51,51,99,99"
        href="#FUSES"
        target="_top">
</map>
<img src="partsBox.gif" align="top"
     height="100"   width="100" usemap="#partsMap">

<br>

<script type="text/javascript" language="JavaScript">
<!--
```

```
// Make the result of the sparkplugs and tires appear in a new window.
document.links[0].target="_blank";        // sparkplugs
document.links[1].target="_blank";        // tires

// -->
</script>

<a name="SPARKPLUGS"><h3>Truck Spark Plugs</h3></a>
<ul>
  <li>SP93654</li>
  <li>SP34710</li>
  <li>SP19374</li>
</ul>

<a name="TIRES"><h3>Truck Tires</h3></a>
<ul>
  <li>Mud Stompers</li>
  <li>Low Riders</li>
  <li>Standard</li>
</ul>

<a name="HEADLIGHTS"><h3>Truck Headlights</h3></a>
<ul>
  <li>Night Vision bulbs</li>
  <li>Standard</li>
</ul>

<a name="FUSES"><h3>Truck Fuses</h3></a>
<ul>
  <li>Red</li>
  <li>Yellow</li>
  <li>Green</li>
  <li>Blue</li>
</ul>

</body>
</html>
```

Figure 8.2

A new window opens as a result of clicking the spark plug image.

Area.unwatch()

JavaScript 1.2+
Nav4+, NES3+

Syntax

```
document.links[num]. unwatch(property)
```

Description

The unwatch() method of the Area object is used to turn off the watch for a particular property specified by *property*.

Example

Listing 8.23 shows how the unwatch() method is used to stop watching the *href* property of the Area object after its name has changed to "http://www.toys.com ".

Listing 8.23   Example of the unwatch() ***Method of the*** Area ***Object***

```
<html>

<h2>The Department Store</h2>

Select a department<br>
```

```
<map name="storeMap">
  <area name="toyArea"
        coords="1,1,100,50"
        href="toys.html"
        target="_top"
  <area name="clothesArea"
        coords="1,50,100,100"
        href="clothes.html"
        target="_top"
</map>
<img src="menu.gif" align="top"
     height="100"   width="100" usemap="#storeMap">
<br><br>

<script type="text/javascript" language="JavaScript">
<!--
function alertme(id,oldValue,newValue)
{
  document.write(id + " changed from " + oldValue + " to ");
  document.write(newValue + "<br>");
  return newValue;
}

// Start watch
document.links[0].watch("href",alertme);

document.write("Original toy department href: ");
document.write(document.links[0].href + "<br>");

// Change href
document.links[0].href = "http://www.toys.com";

document.write("New toy department href: " + document.links[0].href + "<br>");

// Stop watch
document.links[0].unwatch("href",alertme);

// Change href again
document.links[0].href = "http://www.toysrus.com";

document.write("Final toy department href: ");
document.write(document.links[0].href + "<br>");
// -->
</script>
</html>
```

Area.watch()

JavaScript 1.2+
Nav4+, NES3+

Syntax

```
document.links[num]. watch(property,function)
```

Description

The watch() method of the Area object is used to turn on the watch for a particular property specified by *property*. Any time the specified property is changed after the watch() method has been called, the specified function is called.

Example

Listing 8.24 shows how the watch() method is used to start watching the *href* property of the Area object.

Listing 8.24 Example of watch() **Method of the** Area **Object**

```
<html>

<h2>The Department Store</h2>

Select a department<br>

<map name="storeMap">
  <area name="toyArea"
        coords="1,1,100,50"
        href="toys.html"
        target="_top"
  <area name="clothesArea"
        coords="1,50,100,100"
        href="clothes.html"
        target="_top"
</map>
<img src="menu.gif" align="top"
     height="100"  width="100" usemap="#storeMap">
<br><br>

<script type="text/javascript" language="JavaScript">
<!--
function alertme(id,oldValue,newValue)
{
  document.write(id + " changed from " + oldValue + " to ");
  document.write(newValue + "<br>");
  return newValue;
}
```

```
// Start watch
document.links[0].watch("href",alertme);

document.write("Original toy department href: ");
document.write(document.links[0].href + "<br>");

// Change href
document.links[0].href = "http://www.toys.com";

document.write("New toy department href: " + document.links[0].href + "<br>");

// -->
</script>
</html>
```

Button

JavaScript 1.0+, JScript 1.0+
Nav2+, IE3+, Opera3+

Syntax

Core client-side JavaScript object.

Description

The Button object represents a graphical button that the user can click to initiate an action. Buttons are created as part of a form by using the <input> tag with the type attribute set to "button" in an HTML document. Once created, buttons can be accessed in JavaScript as an element of a form using dot notation. The arguments, properties, methods, and event handlers for the Button object are listed in Table 8.4.

Table 8.4 Arguments, Properties, Methods, and Event Handlers Associated with the Button Object

Type	Item	Description
Argument	string	The string to appear in the graphical representation of a button.
	num	An index number that allows access to buttons through a form's elements list.
Property	form	This property returns the form object of a button.
	name	The string that is specified in the name attribute of the HTML <input> tag.
	type	The string that is specified in the type attribute of the HTML <input> tag. This string is always "button" for the Button object.

Table 8.4   Continued

Type	Item	Description
	`value`	The string that appears in the graphical representation of a button.
Method	`blur()`	This method removes focus from a button.
	`click()`	This method calls the button's `onClick` event handler.
	`focus()`	This method applies focus to a button.
	`handleEvent()`	This method passes an event to the appropriate event handler associated with a button.
	`unwatch()`	This method removes a watch point.
	`watch()`	This method sets a watch point.
Event Handler	`onBlur`	The handler invoked when focus is removed from a button.
	`onClick`	The handler invoked when the left mouse button is clicked.
	`onFocus`	The handler invoked when focus is applied to a button.
	`onMouseDown`	The handler invoked when the left mouse button is clicked to select a button.
	`onMouseUp`	The handler invoked when the left mouse button is released from clicking a button.

Example

In Listing 8.25, a button is created by using the `<input>` tag. When the button is clicked, the button's name is displayed in the adjacent text box.

Listing 8.25   Creating a Button and Displaying Its Name

```
<html>

<h2>The Button's NAME Property</h2>

<form name="myForm">
  <input type="button"
         value="Press here to see the name of this button"
         name="myBigButton"
         onClick="displayButtonName()">
  <input type="text"
         name="textBox">
</form>

<script type="text/javascript" language="JavaScript">
<!--
```

```
// This function displays the button's name in the textbox.
function displayButtonName()
{
  // Display button name in textbox.
  document.myForm.textBox.value=document.myForm.myBigButton.name;
}

// -->
</script>

</html>
```

Button.blur()

JavaScript 1.1+, JScript 1.0+
Nav3+, IE3+

Syntax

document.*form*.*button*.blur()

Description

The blur() method removes the focus from a button.

CAUTION

In the Unix versions of Navigator 2 and Navigator 3, the blur() method does not work for buttons.

Example

In Listing 8.26, two buttons are created by using the <input> tag to demonstrate focus. The first button retains focus after being clicked, but the second button loses focus as soon as it is clicked due to the use of the blur() method. There are not a lot of uses for this method, but it is provided for your use all the same.

Listing 8.26   Removing Focus from a Button with the blur() Method

```
<html>

<h2>The Button Focus Game</h2>

Click both buttons. Notice that the second button does not
hold its focus after being clicked.

<form name="myForm">
  <input type="button"
         value="I hold my focus after a click"
         name="button1"><br>
```

Listing 8.26   Continued

```
  <input type="button"
         value="I cannot hold my focus after a click"
         name="button2"
         onClick="removeFocus()">
</form>

<script type="text/javascript" language="JavaScript">
<!--

// This function takes the focus off of button2.
function removeFocus()
{
  // Remove the focus from button2.
  document.myForm.button2.blur();
}

// -->
</script>

</html>
```

Button.click()

JavaScript 1.0+, JScript 1.0+
Nav2+, IE3+

Syntax

document.*form.button.* click()

Description

The click() method simulates the click event.

Example

In Listing 8.27, two buttons are created by using the <input> tag. The first button displays an alert box when it is clicked. When the second button is clicked, it causes the first button's onClick event handler to be activated, displaying the alert box associated with the first button.

Listing 8.27   Simulating a click Event with the click() Method

```
<html>

<form name="myForm">
  <input type="button"
         value="Display alert box"
         name="button1"
         onClick="alert('You clicked the first button.')"><br>
```

```
  <input type="button"
         value="Call on button 1"
         name="button2"
         onClick="clickFirstButton()">
</form>

<script type="text/javascript" language="JavaScript">
<!--

// This function activates the first button's onClick handler.
function clickFirstButton()
{
  // Click first button
  document.myForm.button1.click();
}

// -->
</script>

</html>
```

Button.focus()

JavaScript 1.1+, JScript 1.0+
Nav3+, IE3+

Syntax

```
document. form.button.focus()
```

Description

The focus() method applies focus to the button without invoking the button's onFocus event handler.

CAUTION

In the Unix versions of Navigator 2 and Navigator 3, the focus() method does not work for buttons.

Example

In Listing 8.28, two buttons are created to demonstrate focus. Choosing the second button causes the focus to shift to the first button instead of the focus staying on the second button, thanks to the focus() method.

Listing 8.28   Shifting the Focus to a Button Using the `focus()` ***Method***

```
<html>

<h2>The Button Focus Game</h2>

Click both buttons. Notice that when the second button is clicked
focus is shifted to the first button.

<form name="myForm">
  <input type="button"
         value="I hold my focus after a click"
         name="button1"><br>
  <input type="button"
         value="I shift my focus when clicked"
         name="button2"
         onClick="moveFocus()">
</form>

<script type="text/javascript" language="JavaScript">
<!--

// This function puts button1 in focus.
function moveFocus()
{
  // Give button1 the focus.
  document.myForm.button1.focus();
}

// -->
</script>

</html>
```

Button.form

> JavaScript 1.0+, JScript 1.0+
> Nav2+, IE3+, Opera3+

Syntax

document. *form.button.*form

Description

The `form` property provides access to the button's parent `Form` object.

Example

Listing 8.29 proves that the button's `form` property contains the parent form object by evaluating the `if` statement to `true`. The sentence `"myButton's form property is equal to myForm object"` is displayed in the browser.

```
    document.myForm.doorsButton.handleEvent(event);
    document.myForm.engineButton.handleEvent(event);
    document.myForm.transmissionButton.handleEvent(event);
}

// -->
</script>

</html>
```

Button.name

JavaScript 1.0+, JScript 1.0+
Nav2+, IE3+, Opera3+

Syntax

```
document. name.button.name
```

Description

The name property provides access to the name attribute of the button as specified by the <input> tag. This property is a read-only string.

Example

In Listing 8.31, a button is created. When the button is clicked, the button's name property is displayed.

Listing 8.31   Accessing a Button's Name with the name *Property*

```
<html>

<form name="myForm">
  <input type="button"
         value="Big Button"
         name="myButton"
         onClick="displayMessage()">
</form>

<script type="text/javascript" language="JavaScript">
<!--

// This function displays an alert box the contains the name of the button.
function displayMessage()
{
  // Create a string with name of button.
  var alertString = String("You pressed the button named ");
  alertString += document.myForm.myButton.name;
```

Listing 8.31   Continued

```
  // Create alert box.
  alert(alertString);
}

// -->
</script>

</html>
```

Button.onBlur

JavaScript 1.1+, JScript 1.0+
Nav3+, IE3+

Syntax

```
onBlur="command"
```

Description

The onBlur event handler is defined in an <input> tag and specifies what to do when the button loses focus.

Example

The code in Listing 8.32 uses the onBlur event handler to display an alert box any time the button loses focus.

Listing 8.32   Use the onBlur Event Handler to Display an Alert Box When the Button Loses Focus

```
<html>

<form name="myForm">
  <input type="button"
         value="Big Button"
         name="myButton"
         onBlur="alert('Blur event occurred')">
</form>

</html>
```

Button.onClick

JavaScript 1.0+, JScript 1.0+
Nav2+, IE3+, Opera5+

Syntax

```
onClick="command"
```

Description

The onClick event handler is defined in an <input> tag and specifies what to do when the button is clicked.

Example

The code in Listing 8.33 uses the onClick event handler to display an alert box any time the button is clicked.

Listing 8.33   Use the onClick ***Event Handler to Display an Alert Box When the Button Is Clicked***

```
<html>

<form name="myForm">
  <input type="button"
         value="Big Button"
         name="myButton"
         onClick="alert('Click event occurred')">
</form>

</html>
```

Button.onFocus

JavaScript 1.1+, JScript 1.0+
Nav3+, IE3+

Syntax

onFocus="*command*"

Description

The onFocus event handler is defined in an <input> tag and specifies what to do when the button gains focus.

Example

The code in Listing 8.34 uses the onFocus event handler to display an alert box any time the button gains focus.

Listing 8.34   Use the onFocus ***Event Handler to Display an Alert Box When the Button Gains Focus***

```
<html>

<form name="myForm">
  <input type="button"
         value="Big Button"
         name="myButton"
         onFocus="alert('Focus event occured')">
```

Listing 8.34   Continued

```
</form>

</html>
```

Button.onMouseDown

JavaScript 1.0+, JScript 1.0+
Nav2+, IE3+

Syntax

```
onMouseDown="command"
```

Description

The onMouseDown event handler is defined in an <input> tag and specifies what to do when the left mouse button is clicked.

Example

The code in Listing 8.35 uses the onMouseDown event handler to display an alert box any time the button is clicked.

Listing 8.35   Use the onMouseDown Event Handler to Display an Alert Box When the Button Is Clicked

```
<html>

<form name="myForm">
  <input type="button"
        value="Big Button"
        name="myButton"
        onMouseDown="alert('MouseDown event occured')">
</form>

</html>
```

Button.onMouseUp

JavaScript 1.0+, JScript 1.0+
Nav2+, IE3+

Syntax

```
onMouseUp="command"
```

Description

The onMouseUp event handler is defined in an <input> tag and specifies what to do when the left mouse button is released while over the button.

Example

The code in Listing 8.36 uses the `onMouseUp` event handler to display an alert box any time the left mouse button is released while over the button.

Listing 8.36   Use the `onMouseUp` Event Handler to Display an Alert Box When the Mouse Button Is Released over the Button

```
<html>

<form name="myForm">
  <input type="button"
         value="Big Button"
         name="myButton"
         onMouseUp="alert('MouseUp event occured')">
</form>

</html>
```

Button.type

> JavaScript 1.1+, JScript 1.0+
> Nav3+, IE3+, Opera3+

Syntax

`document.`*`form`*`.`*`button`*`.type`

Description

The `type` property provides access to the `type` attribute of the button. This property is a read-only string that always contains `"button"`.

Example

Listing 8.37 creates buttons that relate to various math problems. The `type` property is used to determine the number of buttons on the page. This number is then used in the instructions that are displayed on the bottom of the page.

Listing 8.37   Accessing a Button's `type` Property

```
<html>

<h2>The Math Page</h2>

<form name="mathForm">
  <input type="button"
         name="4plus2"
         value="(4 + 2)"
         onClick="document.mathForm.answer.value='(4 + 2) = 6'">
  <input type="button"
         name="4minus2"
```

Listing 8.37   Continued

```
          value="(4 - 2)"
          onClick="document.mathForm.answer.value='(4 - 2) = 2'"><hr>
  Answer:
  <input type="text"
         name="answer">
</form>

<script type="text/javascript" language="JavaScript">
<!--

// Create a counter to count the number of buttons in mathForm.
var buttonCount = 0;

// Loop through all the elements of mathForm.
for(var x=0; x<document.mathForm.length; x++)
{
  // Is element a button?
  if(document.mathForm.elements[x].type=="button")
    buttonCount++;        // Increment buttonCount
}

// Display the number of buttons in the mathForm.
document.write("Please select one of the ",buttonCount);   // 2 buttons
document.write(" buttons above to find out the answer to the math problem.");

// -->
</script>

</html>
```

Button.unwatch()

JavaScript 1.2
Nav4, NES3+

Syntax

document.*form*.*button*.unwatch(*property*)

Description

The unwatch() method of the Button object is used to turn off the watch for a particular property specified by *property*.

Example

Listing 8.38 shows how the unwatch() method is used to stop watching the *value* property of the Button object after its name has changed to "Blue".

CAUTION

A bug associated with the `watch()` and `unwatch()` methods prevents the actual text in the button from getting redrawn even though the button's *value* property does get changed.

Listing 8.38   *Example of the* `unwatch()` *Method of the* Button *Object*

```
<html>

<form name="colorForm">
<input type="button" name="colorButton" value="Red">
</form>

<script type="text/javascript" language="JavaScript">
<!--

function alertme(id,oldValue,newValue)
{
  document.write(id + " changed from " + oldValue + " to ");
  document.write(newValue + "<br>");
  return newValue;
}

// Start watch
document.colorForm.colorButton.watch("value",alertme);

document.write("Original button value: ");
document.write(document.colorForm.colorButton.value + "<br>");

// Change button text
document.colorForm.colorButton.value = "Blue";

document.write("New button value: ");
document.write(document.colorForm.colorButton.value + "<br>");

// Stop watch
document.colorForm.colorButton.unwatch("value");

// Change button text
document.colorForm.colorButton.value = "Green";

document.write("Final button value: ");
document.write(document.colorForm.colorButton.value + "<br>");

// -->
</script>
</html>
```

Button.value

JavaScript 1.0+, JScript 1.0+
Nav2+, IE3+, Opera3+

Syntax

document.*form.button.*value

Description

The value property provides access to the value attribute of the button. This property
is a read-only string that is displayed in the graphical button.

Example

Listing 8.39 uses the value property to customize the text in a button. To modify the
button value, enter your name into the text field and then click the Customize the
Button button. The button at the bottom of the document will no longer contain just the
word "Press".

Listing 8.39   *Modifying Text in a Button Using the* value *Property*

```
<html>

<h2>Customize the Button</h2>

<form name="myForm">
  Please enter your name:
  <input type="text"
         name="nameBox">
  <input type="button"
         name="customizeTheButton"
         value="Customize the button"
         onClick="customizeButton()"><br>
  <input type="button"
         name="theButton"
         value="Press                "
         onClick="displayAlert()">
</form>

<script type="text/javascript" language="JavaScript">
<!--

// This function customizes the button.
function customizeButton()
{
  // Create a string using the name entered in text box.
  var aString = document.myForm.nameBox.value;
  aString += " press this button!";
```

```
  // Change the value displayed in the button.
  document.myForm.theButton.value=aString;
}

// This function creates an alert box.
function displayAlert()
{
  // Create an alert box.
  alert("You pressed the button.");
}

// -->
</script>

</html>
```

Button.watch()

JavaScript 1.2+
Nav4+, NES3+

Syntax

document.*form*.*button*.watch(*property,function*)

Description

The watch() method of the Button object is used to turn on the watch for a particular property specified by *property*. Any time the specified property is changed after the watch() method has been called, the specified function is called.

Example

Listing 8.40 shows how the watch() method is used to start watching the *value* property of the Button object.

CAUTION

A bug associated with the watch() and unwatch() methods prevents the actual text in the button from getting redrawn even though the button's *value* property does get changed.

Listing 8.40 **Example of the** watch() **Method of the** Button **Object**

```
<html>

<form name="colorForm">
<input type="button" name="colorButton" value="Red">
</form>
```

Listing 8.40 Continued

```
<script type="text/javascript" language="JavaScript">
<!--

function alertme(id,oldValue,newValue)
{
  document.write(id + " changed from " + oldValue + " to ");
  document.write(newValue + "<br>");
  return newValue;
}

// Start watch
document.colorForm.colorButton.watch("value",alertme);

document.write("Original button value: ");
document.write(document.colorForm.colorButton.value + "<br>");

// Change button text
document.colorForm.colorButton.value = "Blue";

document.write("New button value: ");
document.write(document.colorForm.colorButton.value + "<br>");

// -->
</script>
</html>
```

Checkbox

> JavaScript 1.0+, JScript 1.0+
> Nav2+, IE3+, Opera3+

Syntax

Core client-side JavaScript object.

Description

The `Checkbox` object represents a graphical check box that the user can click to toggle the check on or off. Check boxes are created as part of a form by using the `<input>` tag with the `type` attribute set to `checkbox` in an HTML document. Once created, check boxes can be accessed in JavaScript as an element of a form using dot notation. Check boxes can also be grouped together under the same name and accessed as an array by using brackets. The arguments, properties, methods, and event handlers of the `Checkbox` object are listed in Table 8.5

Table 8.5   *Arguments, Properties, Methods, and Event Handlers Associated with the* Checkbox *Object*

Type	Item	Description
Argument	num1	An index number that allows access to check boxes through a form's element list.
	num2	An index number that allows access to individual check boxes that are grouped together under the same name.
Property	checked	A boolean value that determines whether the check box is checked.
	defaultChecked	A boolean value that holds the initial state of the check box. This value is set with the checked attribute.
	form	This property returns the Form object of the check box.
	name	The string that is specified in the name attribute of the HTML <input> tag.
	type	The string that is specified in the type attribute of the HTML <input> tag. This string is always "checkbox" for the Checkbox object.
	value	The value returned when the form is submitted.
Method	blur()	This method removes focus from the check box.
	click()	This method calls the check box's onClick event handler.
	focus()	This method applies focus to this check box.
	handleEvent()	This method passes an event to the appropriate event handler associated with the check box.
	unwatch()	This method removes a watch point.
	watch()	This method sets a watch point.
Event Handler	onBlur	The handler invoked when focus is removed from the check box.
	onClick	The handler invoked when the check box is selected.
	onFocus	The handler invoked when focus is applied to the check box.

Example

Listing 8.41 creates a hamburger order page. Check boxes are used to select toppings for the hamburger. When the Submit Order button is clicked, an alert box is displayed with the selected toppings.

Listing 8.41 Creating Check Boxes and Accessing Some of Their Properties

```html
<html>

<h2>Hamburger Order</h2>

Step 1: Please select the toppings you would like on your hamburger:<br>

<form name="orderForm">
  Lettuce
  <input type="checkbox"
         value="lettuce"
         name="lettuceCB"><br>
  Cheese
  <input type="checkbox"
         value="cheese"
         name="cheeseCB"><br>
  Tomato
  <input type="checkbox"
         value="tomato"
         name="tomatoCB"><br>
  Step 2:
  <input type="button"
         value="Submit Order"
         name="orderButton"
         onClick="submitOrder()">
</form>

<script type="text/javascript" language="JavaScript">
<!--

// This function creates an alert box to display which toppings were selected.
function submitOrder()
{
  // Create a string to display in the alert box
  var alertString = String("Order: Hamburger ");
  if(document.orderForm.lettuceCB.checked == true)
    alertString += " with lettuce ";        // Add lettuce to string
  if(document.orderForm.cheeseCB.checked == true)
    alertString += "with cheese ";          // Add cheese to string
  if(document.orderForm.tomatoCB.checked == true)
    alertString += "with tomato ";          // Add tomato to string

  // Create alert box
  alert(alertString);
}
```

```
// -->
</script>

</html>
```

Checkbox.blur()

JavaScript 1.1+, JScript 3.0+
Nav3+, IE4+

Syntax

```
document.form.checkbox.blur()
```

Description

The blur() method removes the focus from a check box.

CAUTION

> In the Unix versions of Navigator 2 and Navigator 3, the blur() method does not
> work for check boxes.

Example

In Listing 8.42, two check boxes are created by using the <input> tag. The first check
box retains focus after being clicked, but the second check box loses focus as soon as
it is clicked because of the use of the blur() method. Do not be surprised if you do not
see a difference between the check boxes in this example. In some browsers, you will
not be able to detect the difference between a check box that is focused versus one that
is not focused. For this reason, you will probably find very little use for this method.

Listing 8.42   Removing Focus from a Check Box with the blur() Method

```
<html>

<h2>The Checkbox Focus Test</h2>

Click both check boxes. Notice that the second check box does not
hold its focus after being clicked.

<form name="myForm">
  I hold my focus after a click
  <input type="checkbox"
         name="checkBox1"><br>
  I cannot hold my focus after a click
  <input type="checkbox"
         name="checkBox2"
         onClick="removeFocus()">
```

Listing 8.42   Continued

```
</form>

<script type="text/javascript" language="JavaScript">
<!--

// This function takes the focus off of checkBox2.
function removeFocus()
{
  // Remove the focus from checkBox2
  document.myForm.checkBox2.blur();
}

// -->
</script>

</html>
```

Checkbox.checked

JavaScript 1.0+, JScript 3.0+
Nav2+, IE4+, Opera3+

Syntax

```
document.form.checkbox.checked
```

Description

The checked property holds the current state of a check box. Because this property is a read/write Boolean, the state of the check box can be altered by changing this property.

Example

In Listing 8.43, the user is asked to select the door style wanted on her new car. When the order is submitted, the checked property of each check box is analyzed to determine whether two different door styles were selected or none at all. If two styles were selected, the check boxes are reset by altering the checked property.

Listing 8.43   Modifying the checked **Property of a Check Box**

```
<html>

<h2>Car Purchase Sheet</h2>

Step1: Please select the door style you want on your new car:<br>

<form name="orderForm">
  <input type="checkbox"
         name="door4">4 doors<br>
```

```
  <input type="checkbox"
         name="door2">2 doors<br>
  Step 2:
  <input type="button"
         value="Submit Order"
         name="orderButton"
         onClick="submitOrder()">
</form>

<script type="text/javascript" language="JavaScript">
<!--

// This function creates a box alerting what door styles were selected.
function submitOrder()
{
  // Check for duplicate door selections
  if((document.orderForm.door4.checked == true) &&
     (document.orderForm.door2.checked == true))
  {
    // Create alert box.
    alert("You selected two different door the  styles. Reselect door style.");

    // Uncheck check boxes for door styles.
    document.orderForm.door4.checked = false;
    document.orderForm.door2.checked = false;
  }
  // Check for no door selection.
  else if((document.orderForm.door4.checked == false) &&
          (document.orderForm.door2.checked == false))
  {
    // Create alert box.
    alert("You did not select a door style! Please select a door style.");
  }
  // Display the car order
  else
  {
    // Create a string to display in alert box.
    var alertString = String("Order: Car with ");
    if(document.orderForm.door4.checked == true)
      alertString += "4 doors.";        // Add 4 doors to string
    if(document.orderForm.door2.checked == true)
      alertString += "2 doors.";        // Add 2 door to string

    // Create alert box.
    alert(alertString);
  }
}
```

Listing 8.43 *Continued*

```
// -->
</script>

</html>
```

Checkbox.click()

JavaScript 1.1+, JScript 3.0+
Nav3+, IE4+, Opera5+

Syntax

```
document.form.checkbox.click()
```

Description

The `click()` method simulates the `click` event. The clicked property is adjusted accordingly when this method is used.

Example

In Listing 8.44, the user can select options for her new car. If the user selects the Alloy Wheel option, she is told that alloy wheels are great. If the Sports package is selected, a message is posted to let the user know that alloy wheels come with the sports package. In addition to this message, the message about allow wheels being great is displayed and the Alloy Wheels options is checked, thanks to the `click()` method.

Listing 8.44 *Using the Check Box's* `click()` *Method*

```
<html>

<h2>Car Purchase Sheet</h2>

Step1: Please select options for your new car:<br>

<form name="orderForm">
  <input type="checkbox"
        name="alloy"
        onClick="alert('Alloy wheels look great!')">Alloy Wheels
  <br>
  <input type="checkbox"
        name="sporty"
        onClick="displayNote()">Sports Package<br>
  Step 2:
  <input type="button"
        value="Submit Order"
        name="orderButton"
        onClick="alert('Your order has been submitted')">
</form>
```

```
<script type="text/javascript" language="JavaScript">
<!--

//This function calls on another click handler
function displayNote()
{
  if(!document.orderForm.alloy.checked)
  {
    //Alert user that allow wheels come with the sports package
    alert("Alloy wheels come with the sports package");

    //Display the alloy wheel note using click() method.
    document.orderForm.alloy.click();
  }
}
// -->
</script>

</html>
```

Checkbox.defaultChecked

JavaScript 1.0+, JScript 3.0+
Nav2+, IE4+

Syntax

document.*form*.*checkbox*.defaultChecked

Description

The defaultChecked property holds the initial state of a check box as defined by the checked attribute of the <input> tag. Because this property only holds the initial state of the check box, it is a read-only boolean value.

Example

In Listing 8.45, the defaultChecked property is used to reset the car door check boxes to their initial state.

Listing 8.45   Resetting Check Boxes with the defaultChecked Property

```
<html>

<h2>Car Purchase Sheet</h2>

Step1: Please select the door style you want on your new car:<br>

<form name="orderForm">
  <input type="checkbox"
         name="door4">4 doors<br>
```

Listing 8.45 Continued

```
  <input type="checkbox"
         name="door2"
         checked>2 doors<br>
  Step 2:
  <input type="button"
         value="Submit Order"
         name="orderButton"
         onClick="alert('Your order has been submitted')">
  <input type="button"
         value="Reset Checkboxes"
         name="resetButton"
         onClick="resetCheckboxes()">
</form>

<script type="text/javascript" language="JavaScript">
<!--

// This function resets the check boxes back to their initial state
function resetCheckboxes()
{
  // Access initial state with the defaultChecked property.
  document.orderForm.door4.checked = document.orderForm.door4.defaultChecked;
  document.orderForm.door2.checked = document.orderForm.door2.defaultChecked;
}

// -->
</script>

</html>
```

Checkbox.focus()

JavaScript 1.0+, JScript 3.0+
Nav2+, IE4+

Syntax

```
document.form.checkbox.focus()
```

Description

The focus() method applies focus to a check box without invoking the check box's
onFocus event handler.

CAUTION

In the Unix versions of Navigator 2 and Navigator 3, the focus() method does not
work for check boxes.

Example

In Listing 8.46, two check boxes are created by using the `<input>` tag. Click the Option 1 check box and then the Option 2 check box. Finally, click the Move Focus button to move the focus back to the first check box. Do not be surprised if you do not see a difference in the check boxes in this example. In some browsers, you will not be able to detect the difference between a check box that is focused versus one that is not focused. For this reason, you will probably find very little use for this method.

Listing 8.46   *Applying Focus to a Check Box Using the* `focus()` *Method*

```
<html>

<h2>The Checkbox Focus Test</h2>

Click both checkboxes and then click the button to return focus to
the first checkbox.

<form name="myForm">
  <input type="checkbox"
         name="checkBox1">Option 1<br>
  <input type="checkbox"
         name="checkBox2">Option 2<br>
  <input type="button"
         name="focusButton"
         value="Move Focus"
         onClick="moveFocus()">
</form>

<script type="text/javascript" language="JavaScript">
<!--

// This function moves the focus to checkBox1.
function moveFocus()
{
  // Move the focus to from checkBox1
  document.myForm.checkBox1.focus();
}

// -->
</script>

</html>
```

Checkbox.form
> JavaScript 1.0+, JScript 3.0+
> Nav2+, IE4+, Opera3+

Syntax

`document.form.checkbox.form`

Description

The form property provides access to a check box's parent Form object.

Example

The code in Listing 8.47 proves that the check box's form property contains the parent Form object by evaluating the if statement to true.

Listing 8.47   Accessing a Check Box's Parent with the form ***Property***

```
<html>

<form name="myForm">
  <input type="checkbox"
         value="YES"
         name="myCheckBox"
         checked>
</form>

<script type="text/javascript" language="JavaScript">
<!--

// Does the parent of the myCheckBox equal myForm?
if(document.myForm.myCheckBox.form == document.myForm)
  alert("myCheckBox's form property is equal to myForm object");
else
  alert("myCheckBox's form property is NOT equal to myForm object");

// -->
</script>

</html>
```

Checkbox.handleEvent()
        JavaScript 1.2-1.3
        Nav4-4.5

Syntax

```
document.form.checkbox.handleEvent(event)
```

Description

The handleEvent() method provides a way to invoke a check box's event handler, even though the event never happened. The *event* argument specifies the Event object associated with the event handler that is to be invoked.

Example

In Listing 8.48, the user is asked to select the engine wanted in her new car. If the user selects the V6 engine, she is alerted that the V6 has lots of power. If the 4-cylinder engine is selected, a message is posted to encourage the user to consider the V6. The click event is passed to the first check box via the handleEvent() method. This causes the message about more power to be displayed.

*Listing 8.48 **Passing Events to a Check Box with the** handleEvent()*
Method

```
<html>

<h2>Car Purchase Sheet</h2>

Step1: Please select the engine style you want on your new car:<br>

<form name="orderForm">
  <input type="checkbox"
         name="v6"
         onClick="alert('The V6 has lots of power!')">V6<br>
  <input type="checkbox"
         name="cylinder4"
         onClick="displayNote(event)">4 Cylinder<br>
  Step 2:
  <input type="button"
         value="Submit Order"
         name="orderButton"
         onClick="alert('Your order has been submitted')">
</form>

<script type="text/javascript" language="JavaScript">
<!--

// This function passes the click event along to another check box
// using the check box's handleEvent method.
function displayNote(event)
{
  // Display note about V6 engine
  alert("Have you considered the V6 engine?");

  // Pass event along to first V6 check box.
  document.orderForm.v6.handleEvent(event);
}

// -->
</script>

</html>
```

Checkbox.name

JavaScript 1.0+, JScript 3.0+
Nav2+, IE4+, Opera3+

Syntax

document.*form.checkbox*.name

Description

The name property provides access to the name attribute of the check box. This property is a read-only string.

Example

Listing 8.49 uses the name property of the check boxes to display what engine type was selected.

Listing 8.49   Display the Name of the Check Box with the name **Property**

```
<html>

<h2>Truck Purchase Sheet</h2>

Step1: Please select the engine style you want on your new truck:<br>

<form name="orderForm">
  <input type="checkbox"
         name="V6"
         onClick="duplicateCheck(V6,V8)">V6<br>
  <input type="checkbox"
         name="V8"
         onClick="duplicateCheck(V8,V6)">V8<br>
  Step 2:
  <input type="button"
         value="Submit Order"
         name="orderButton"
         onClick="submitOrder()">
</form>

<script type="text/javascript" language="JavaScript">
<!--

//This function uses the name property to let the user
//know what options were selected.
function submitOrder()
{
  //Create a string to be displayed in the alert box
  var alertString = String("You have selected a ");
```

```
  //Determine what type of engine was selected.
  if(document.orderForm.V6.checked == true)
  {
    alertString += document.orderForm.V6.name;  //Display V6
    alertString += " truck.";
    alert(alertString);
  }
  else if(document.orderForm.V8.checked == true)
  {
    alertString += document.orderForm.V8.name;  //Display V8
    alertString += " truck.";
    alert(alertString);
  }
  else
    alert("You have not selected an engine type!");  //No Engine
}


//This function removes the check from the other
//checkbox if both checkboxes are about to be selected.
function duplicateCheck(theCheckBox,otherCheckBox)
{
  //Determine if both boxes are checked
  if(theCheckBox.checked && otherCheckBox.checked)
    otherCheckBox.checked = 0;
}


// -->
</script>

</html>
```

Checkbox.onBlur

JavaScript 1.1+, JScript 3.0+
Nav3+, IE4+

Syntax

```
onBlur="command"
```

Description

The onBlur event handler is defined in an <input> tag and specifies what to do when a check box loses focus.

Example

The code in Listing 8.50 uses the onBlur event handler to display a message alerting the customer that the peppers she is ordering on her pizza are hot.

Listing 8.50 Use the onBlur *Event Handler to Display an Alert Box When the Check Box Loses Focus*

```
<html>

<h2>Pizza Machine</h2>

Step 1: Please select your pizza toppings:<br>

<form name="orderForm">
  <input type="checkbox"
         name="peppers"
         onBlur="pepperAlert()">Peppers<br>
  <input type="checkbox"
         name="sausage">Sausage<br>
  Step 2:
  <input type="button"
         value="Order Pizza"
         name="orderButton"
         onClick="alert('Your pizza has been ordered.')">
</form>

<script type="text/javascript" language="JavaScript">
<!--

// This function alerts the customer that peppers are hot!
function pepperAlert()
{
  // If peppers are selected then display alert.
  if(document.orderForm.peppers.checked == true)
  {
    // Create alert box.
    alert("These are extremely hot peppers.");
  }
}

// -->
</script>

</html>
```

Checkbox.onClick

> JavaScript 1.1+, JScript 3.0+
> Nav3+, IE4+, Opera5+

Syntax

```
onClick="command"
```

Description

The onClick event handler is defined in an <input> tag and specifies what to do when a check box is clicked.

Example

The code in Listing 8.51 uses the onClick event handler to display a message alerting the customer that sausage goes well with peppers.

Listing 8.51 **Use the** onClick ***Event Handler to Display a Message***

```html
<html>

<h2>Pizza Machine</h2>

Step 1: Please select your pizza toppings:<br>

<form name="orderForm">
  <input type="checkbox"
         name="peppers"
         onClick="recommendSausage()">Peppers<br>
  <input type="checkbox"
         name="sausage">Sausage<br>
  Step 2:
  <input type="button"
         value="Order Pizza"
         name="orderButton"
         onClick="alert('Your pizza has been ordered.')">
</form>

<script type="text/javascript" language="JavaScript">
<!--

// This function recommends that the customer consider ordering sausage.
function recommendSausage()
{
  // If peppers are selected, display alert.
  if(document.orderForm.peppers.checked == true)
  {
    // Create alert box
    alert("Sausage goes well with peppers.");
  }
}

// Display the event handler associated with onClick.
document.write("The pepper checkbox onClick event handler: ");
document.write(document.orderForm.peppers.onclick);
```

Listing 8.51   Continued

```
// -->
</script>

</html>
```

Checkbox.onFocus

JavaScript 1.1+, JScript 3.0+
Nav3+, IE4+

Syntax

```
onFocus="command"
```

Description

The onFocus event handler is defined in an <input> tag and specifies what to do when a check box gains focus.

Example

The code in Listing 8.52 uses the onFocus event handler to automatically select extra cheese when the customer selects sausage.

Listing 8.52   Using the onFocus *Event Handler to Select Extra Cheese*

```
<html>

<h2>Pizza Machine</h2>

Step1: Please select your pizza toppings:<br>

<form name="orderForm">
  <input type="checkbox"
        name="peppers">Peppers<br>
  <input type="checkbox"
        name="sausage"
        onFocus="chooseExtraCheese()">Sausage<br>
  <input type="checkbox"
        name="cheese">Extra Cheese<br>
  Step 2:
  <input type="button"
        value="Order Pizza"
        name="orderButton"
        onClick="alert('Your pizza has been ordered.')">
</form>

<script type="text/javascript" language="JavaScript">
<!--
```

```
// This function chooses the extra cheese checkbox.
function chooseExtraCheese()
{
  // If sausage is selected, select extra cheese.
  if(document.orderForm.sausage.checked == false)
  {
    // select extra cheese
    document.orderForm.cheese.checked = true;
  }
}

// -->
</script>

</html>
```

Checkbox.type

JavaScript 1.1+, JScript 3.0+
Nav3+, IE4+, Opera3+

Syntax

document.*form*.*checkbox*.type

Description

The type property provides access to the type attribute of the check box. This property is a read-only string that always contains "checkbox".

Example

Listing 8.53 instructs the customer to select only two toppings (check boxes) of all those offered. To determine the number of toppings, the type property of the check box is used to determine how many check boxes are in orderForm. The program finds four check boxes that represent the possible pizza toppings.

Listing 8.53   Accessing a Check Box's type Property

```
<html>
<h2>Pizza Machine</h2>

Step 1: Please select your pizza toppings:<br>

<form name="orderForm">
  <input type="checkbox"
         name="peppers">Peppers<br>
  <input type="checkbox"
         name="sausage">Sausage<br>
  <input type="checkbox"
         name="onion">Onion<br>
```

Listing 8.53   Continued

```
  <input type="checkbox"
         name="bacon">Bacon<br>
  Step 2:
  <input type="button"
         value="Order Pizza"
         name="orderButton"
         onClick="alert('Your pizza has been ordered.')">
</form>

<script type="text/javascript" language="JavaScript">
<!--

// Initialize a counter to zero.
var counter = 0;

// Count the number of check boxes in orderForm.
for(var x=0; x<document.orderForm.length; x++)
{
  // Is element a check box?
  if(document.orderForm.elements[x].type == "checkbox")
  {
    // Increment the counter.
    counter++;
  }
}

// Display the topping instructions.
document.write("Please select no more than 2 of the ");
document.write(counter," possible toppings.");    // Insert 4

// -->
</script>

</html>
```

Checkbox.unwatch()
JavaScript 1.2+
Nav4+, NES3+

Syntax

```
document.form.checkbox.unwatch(property)
```

Description

The unwatch() method of the Checkbox object is used to turn off the watch for a particular property specified by *property*.

Example

Listing 8.54 shows how the unwatch() method is used to stop watching the *value* property of the Checkbox object after its value has changed to "Blue".

Listing 8.54   *Example of the* unwatch() *Method of the* Checkbox *Object*

```
<html>

<form name="myForm">
<input type="checkbox" name="myCheckbox" value="Red">
</form>

<script type="text/javascript" language="JavaScript">
<!--

function alertme(id,oldValue,newValue)
{
  document.write(id + " changed from " + oldValue + " to ");
  document.write(newValue + "<br>");
  return newValue;
}

// Start watch
document.myForm.myCheckbox.watch("value",alertme);

document.write("Original checkbox value: ");
document.write(document.myForm.myCheckbox.value + "<br>");

// Change checkbox value
document.myForm.myCheckbox.value = "Blue";

document.write("New checkbox value: ");
document.write(document.myForm.myCheckbox.value + "<br>");

// Stop watch
document.myForm.myCheckbox.unwatch("value");

// Change checkbox value
document.myForm.myCheckbox.value = "Green";

document.write("Final checkbox value: ");
document.write(document.myForm.myCheckbox.value + "<br>");

// -->
</script>
</html>
```

Checkbox.value

JavaScript 1.0+, JScript 3.0+
Nav2+, IE4+, Opera3+

Syntax

document.*form.checkbox.*value

Description

The value property provides access to value attribute of the check box. This property is a read/write value that is sent to the server when the form is submitted.

Example

Listing 8.55 uses the value property of each check box to create instructions for the customer on how to order her custom pizza.

Listing 8.55   Accessing a Check Box's value Property

```
<html>

<h2>Pizza Machine</h2>

Step1: Please select your pizza toppings:<br>

<form name="orderForm">
  <input type="checkbox"
         name="onion"
         value="hot onion">Onion<br>
  <input type="checkbox"
         name="bacon"
         value="spicy bacon">Bacon<br>
  Step 2:
  <input type="button"
         value="Order Pizza"
         name="orderButton"
         onClick="alert('Your pizza has been ordered.')">
</form>

<script type="text/javascript" language="JavaScript">
<!--

// Display instructions using the check box value property.
document.write("Please select either ");
document.write(document.orderForm.onion.value);   // Insert hot onion
document.write(" or ",document.orderForm.bacon.value);  // Insert spicy bacon
document.write(" on your custom pizza!");
```

```
// -->
</script>

</html>
```

Checkbox.watch()

JavaScript 1.2+
Nav4+, NES3+

Syntax

```
document.form.checkbox.watch(property,function)
```

Description

The watch() method of the Checkbox object is used to turn on the watch for a particular property specified by *property*. Any time the specified property is changed after the watch() method has been called, the specified function is called.

Example

Listing 8.56 shows how the watch() method is used to start watching the *value* property of the Checkbox object.

Listing 8.56 **Example of the** watch() **Method of the** Checkbox **Object**

```
<html>

<form name="myForm">
<input type="checkbox" name="myCheckbox" value="Red">
</form>

<script type="text/javascript" language="JavaScript">
<!--

function alertme(id,oldValue,newValue)
{
  document.write(id + " changed from " + oldValue + " to ");
  document.write(newValue + "<br>");
  return newValue;
}

// Start watch
document.myForm.myCheckbox.watch("value",alertme);

document.write("Original checkbox value: ");
document.write(document.myForm.myCheckbox.value + "<br>");
```

Listing 8.56   Continued

```
// Change checkbox value
document.myForm.myCheckbox.value = "Blue";

document.write("New checkbox value: ");
document.write(document.myForm.myCheckbox.value + "<br>");
// -->
</script>
</html>
```

Document

>JavaScript 1.0+, ECMAScript 1.0+, JScript 1.0+
>Nav2+, IE3+, Opera3+

Syntax

Core client-side JavaScript object.

Description

The Document object represents a Web page that is displayed in a browser window, frame, or layer. An instance is created with each document that is loaded by the browser. This object has many properties and methods that vary greatly between JavaScript and JScript. Table 8.6 lists all the properties, methods, and event handlers associated with the Document object.

Table 8.6   Properties, Methods, and Event Handlers Associated with the Document ***Object***

Type	Item	Description
Property	alinkColor	Color of activated link.
	all	Array of all HTML tags in the document.
	anchors	Array of Anchor objects.
	applets	Array of Applet objects.
	bgcolor	Background color of document.
	classes	Style sheet classes array.
	cookie	Cookie associated with document.
	domain	Domain of document.
	embeds	Array of embedded objects.
	fgcolor	Color of text in document.
	forms	Array of Form objects.
	ids	Style sheet IDs array.
	images	Array of Image objects.
	lastModified	Date when document was last modified.
	layers	Array of Layer objects.
	linkColor	Color of links.
	links	Array of Link objects.
	plugins	Array of embedded objects.

Type	Item	Description
	referrer	URL of document to which the current document was linked.
	tags	Style sheet tag array.
	title	Title of document.
	URL	URL of current document.
	vlinkColor	Color of visited links.
Method	captureEvents()	This method captures events to be handled by a document.
	close()	This method closes output stream to a document.
	contextual()	This method applies styles to selected HTML elements.
	getSelection()	This method returns the selected text.
	open()	This method opens an output stream to a document.
	releaseEvents()	This method releases events captured by a document.
	routeEvent()	This method routes captured events to other objects.
	unwatch()	This method removes a watch point.
	watch()	This method sets a watch point.
	write()	This method appends text to a document.
	writeln()	This method appends text and a newline character to a document.
Event Handler	onClick	Handler for click events.
	onDblClick	Handler for double-click events.
	onKeyDown	Handler for KeyDown events.
	onKeyPress	Handler for KeyPress events.
	onKeyUp	Handler for KeyUp events.
	onLoad	Handler that is used when Document has finished loading.
	onMouseDown	Handler for MouseDown events.
	onMouseUp	Handler for MouseUp events.
	onUnLoad	Handler that is used when Document unloaded from window.

document.alinkColor

JavaScript 1.0+, JScript 1.0+
Nav2+, IE3+

Syntax

```
document.alinkColor
```

Description

The `alinkColor` property specifies the color of activated links. A link is considered activated between the time the mouse button is clicked and released over a link. The color is expressed as a string in hexadecimal digits or as one of the HTML standard color names. The hexadecimal form is made up of six digits that follow the pattern "RRGGBB."

Example

The sample code in Listing 8.57 sets the activated link's color to green for all links on the page, even if they are placed before the <script> tags.

Listing 8.57   *Setting the Document* `alinkColor` *Property*

```
<html>

<a href="myGreenPage.html">The Green Site</a><br>

<script type="text/javascript" language="JavaScript">
<!--

// Set the activated links color to green.
document.alinkColor="00ff00";

// -->
</script>

<a href="myGreenGrassPage.html">The Green Grass Page</a>

</html>
```

document.all

JScript 3.0+
IE4+

Syntax

`document.all[index]`

Description

The `document.all` property is an array of all the HTML elements that are in the document. The elements appear in the array in the order in which they were created. Table 8.7 lists the methods associated with `document.all` array.

Table 8.7   **Methods Associated with the** `document.all` **Array**

Methods	Description
`item()`	Returns an HTML element based on the element's name.
`tags()`	Returns an array of elements that have the specified tag.

Example

Listing 8.58 uses the `document.all` property array and array notation (brackets) to access the *Paint* anchor, which happens to be the fourth HTML element on the page. Using dot notation, the name of the anchor is used to create a link to the top of the page.

Listing 8.58   **Using** `document.all`

```
<html>

<a name="Paint"><h2><u>Paint Colors</u></h2></a>
Red<br>
Green<br>
Blue<br>
Orange<br>
<br>

<script type="text/javascript" language="JavaScript">
<!--

// Create a link using the name associated with the Paint anchor (4th element).
document.write("<a href='#",document.all[4].name,"'>");   // Insert "Paint"
document.write(document.all[4].name,"</a>");              // Insert "Paint"

// -->
</script>

</html>
```

document.all.item()

> JScript 3.0+
> IE4+

Syntax

`document.all.item(name)`

Description

The `item()` method provides a way to retrieve an HTML element out of the `document.all` array without having to know its position in the array. Instead of using an index position, the `item()` method allows you to just pass in the name of the element as specified by the `name` or `id` attribute of HTML tags. Normally, the method returns the element, but, if more than one element is found with the same name, an array of elements is returned.

Example

Listing 8.59 uses the item() method to access the *Paint* anchor. Using dot notation, the name of the anchor is used to create a link to the top of the page.

Listing 8.59   Using the item() *Method to Find a Particular HTML Element*

```
<html name="top">

<a name="Paint"><h2><u>Paint Colors</u></h2></a>
Red<br>
Green<br>
Blue<br>
Orange<br>
<br>

<script type="text/javascript" language="JavaScript">
<!--

// Create a link using the name associated with HTML element 4.
document.write("<a href='#")                 // Create first part of link tag
document.write(document.all.item("Paint").name,"'>");   // Insert "Paint"
document.write(document.all.item("Paint").name,"</a>"); // Insert "Paint"

// -->
</script>

</html>
```

document.all.tags()

> JScript 3.0+
>
> IE4+

Syntax

```
document.all.tags(tag)
```

Description

The tags() method provides a way to retrieve all HTML elements of a particular tag type from the document.all array. The method returns an array of elements.

Example

Listing 8.60 uses the tags() method to create an array of all the anchor tags in the document. Using dot notation, the name of the first anchor in the temporary array is used to create a link to the top of the page.

Listing 8.60   Using the tags() *Method to Find HTML Elements with a Particular Tag*

```html
<html>

<a name="Paint"><h2><u>Paint Colors</u></h2></a>
Red<br>
Green<br>
Blue<br>
Orange<br>
<br>

<script type="text/javascript" language="JavaScript">
<!--

// Get all the anchor tags.
var arrayOfAnchors = document.all.tags("a");

// Create a link using name of the first element in the arrayOfAnchors.
document.write("<a href='#",arrayOfAnchors[0].name,"'>");   // Insert "Paint"
document.write(arrayOfAnchors[0].name,"</a>");              // Insert "Paint"

// -->
</script>

</html>
```

document.anchors

JavaScript 1.2+, JScript 3.0+
Nav4+, IE4+, Opera5+

Syntax

```
document.anchors
document.anchors[index]
```

Description

The anchors property is an array that contains all the Anchor objects that appear within the HTML document when using the <a name="*string*"> tag. The anchors property has one property of its own, called length, which contains the number of Anchor objects in the array. The *index* number ranges from zero to the length of the array minus one. See "Anchor," earlier in the chapter, for a detailed explanation of all the properties associated with anchors.

CAUTION

Although hyperlinks are created using the <a> tag, they are not accessible through the anchors array. Hyperlinks are stored in the document's links array.

Example

Listing 8.61 demonstrates how to access anchor names using the document's `anchors` array.

Listing 8.61   *Accessing Anchor Names Using the* anchors *Array*

```
<html>

<a name="A"><h4>The Letter A</h4></a>
apple<br>
alligator<br>

<a name="B"><h4>The Letter B</h4></a>
baby.<br>
basketball<br>
banana<br>

<script type="text/javascript" language="JavaScript">
<!--

document.write("Anchor Names:<br>");        // Title

// Set up a loop to display the name of each anchor in document.
for(var x=0; x<=document.anchors.length; x++)
{
  // Display the name of each anchor.
  document.write(document.anchors[x].name,"<br>");
}

// -->
</script>

</html>
```

document.anchors.length

JavaScript 1.2+, JScript 3.0+
Nav4+, IE4+, Opera5+

Syntax

```
document.anchors.length
```

Description

The `length` property contains the number of `Anchor` objects that are in the document.

Example

Listing 8.62 uses the anchor `length` property to loop through all the anchors in the document. During each pass through the loop, a link to each anchor in the document is created.

Listing 8.62   Using the Anchor `length` *Property to Create Hyperlinks*

```
<html>

<center><h1><u>The Music Instrument Page</u></h1></center>

<br><a name="Trumpet"><h4>Trumpet</h4></a>
The trumpet is a brass instrument that can create bright, loud tones.  The
trumpet has 3 valves for changing the tone being played.<br>

<br><a name="Guitar"><h4>Guitar</h4></a>
The guitar is a stringed instrument that has a hollow wooden body with a long
wooden neck.  Most guitars have 6 strings each tuned to a different tone.
By pressing different combinations of strings chords can be created.<br>

<br><a name="Piano"><h4>Piano</h4></a>
The piano has one of the largest tonal ranges of any instrument.  Tones
are created by pressing keys which are attached to small wood hammers that
hit strings tuned to specific tones.<br>

<script type="text/javascript" language="JavaScript">
<!--
document.write("<br>Pick an instrument:<br>");

// Create a link for each anchor using the
// Anchor object and the length property
for(var counter=0; counter<=document.anchors.length; counter++)
{
  document.write("<a href='#",document.anchors[counter].name,"'>");
  document.write(document.anchors[counter].text,"</a><br>");
}

// -->
</script>

</html>
```

document.applets

JavaScript 1.1+, JScript 1.0+
Nav3+, IE3+

Syntax

```
document.applets
document.applets[index]
```

Description

The `applets` property is an array that contains all the `Applet` objects that appear within the HTML document from using the `<applet>` tag. The `applet` property has one property of its own, called `length`, which contains the number of `Applet` objects in the array. The *index* number ranges from zero to the length of the array minus one. See "Applet," earlier in this chapter, for a detailed explanation of all the properties associated with applets.

Example

Listing 8.63 includes two fictitious calculator applets that are embedded in the HTML document. Using the applets array, the names of the calculators are displayed on the screen.

Listing 8.63   Accessing Applets with the applets Array

```
<html>

<applet name="Home Calculator"
        code="homeCalculator.class"
        width=50
        height=50
        mayscript></applet>
<applet name="Office Calculator"
        code="officeCalculator.class"
        width=50
        height=50
        mayscript></applet>

Special thanks goes to the individuals who
provided us with the following calculators:<br>

<script type="text/javascript" language="JavaScript">
<!--

// Display the names of the calculator applets.
document.write(document.applets[0].name,"<br>");
document.write(document.applets[1].name);

// -->
</script>
</html>
```

document.applets.length

> JavaScript 1.1+, JScript 3.0+
> Nav3+, IE4+

Syntax

```
document.applets.length
```

Description

The length property contains the number of Applet objects that are in a document.

Example

Listing 8.64 uses the `length` property to display the number of applets in a HTML document.

Listing 8.64 Accessing the Number of Applets in a Document with the `length` *Property*

```
<html>

<h2>The Applets Page</h2>

<applet name="myAddApplet"
        code="add.class"
        width=50
        height=50
        mayscript></applet>
<applet name="mySubtractApplet"
        code="subtract.class"
        width=50
        height=50
        mayscript></applet>

<script type="text/javascript" language="JavaScript">
<!--

// Tell the user how many applets are currently available.
document.write("There are currently ",document.applets.length);
document.write(" applets available on this page.  Check back as");
document.write(" new applets are added daily.");
// -->
</script>

</html>
```

document.bgColor

JavaScript 1.0+, JScript 1.0+
Nav2+, IE3+, Opera3+

Syntax

```
document.bgColor
```

Description

The `bgColor` property specifies the background color of the HTML document. The color is expressed as a string in hexadecimal digits or as one of the HTML standard color names. The hexadecimal form is made up of six digits that follow the pattern "RRGGBB." The color of the background can also be set with `bgcolor` attribute of the `<body>` tag.

Example

Listing 8.65 changes the document's background color based on which button is chosen.

Listing 8.65   Modifying the Document bgColor Property

```
<html>

<form>
<input type="button"
       value="Yellow"
       name="Yellow"
       onClick="changeBG('yellow')">
<input type="button"
       value="Green"
       name="Green"
       onClick="changeBG('green')">
<input type="text"
       name="color">
</form>

<script type="text/javascript" language="JavaScript">
<!--

// This function changes the background color and fills in the text box.
function changeBG(color)
{
  document.bgColor=color;                // Change background color
  document.myForm.color.value=color;     // Display the color
}

// -->
</script>

</html>
```

document.captureEvents()

> JavaScript 1.2+
> Nav4+

Syntax

```
document.captureEvents(eventMask)
```

Description

The captureEvents() method specifies the type of events that should be passed to the document rather than to the object for which they were intended. The eventMask argument(s) specifies what events to capture. The following list shows all the possible event masks. Multiple events can be captured by using the bitwise OR (|) operator:

- Event.ABORT
- Event.BLUR
- Event.CHANGE
- Event.CLICK
- Event.DBCLICK
- Event.DRAGDROP
- Event.ERROR
- Event.FOCUS
- Event.KEYDOWN
- Event.KEYPRESS
- Event.KEYUP
- Event.LOAD
- Event.MOUSEDOWN
- Event.MOUSEMOVE
- Event.MOUSEOUT
- Event.MOUSEOVER
- Event.MOUSEUP
- Event.MOVE
- Event.RESET
- Event.RESIZE
- Event.SELECT
- Event.SUBMIT
- Event. UNLOAD

Example

Listing 8.66 attempts to change the background color from yellow to purple when the mouse button is clicked and released. Before the Event.MOUSEDOWN and Event.MOUSEUP events can be handled by the button, they are intercepted by Document's captureEvent() method and routed to special functions that change the background colors to red and blue.

Listing 8.66   Capture Events with the captureEvent() Method

```
<html>

Normally the button below would toggle the background color between
yellow and purple but since the mouseup and mousedown events are captured
and handled by the document the events are never allowed to reach the button
level.

<form>
<input type="button"
       value="Yellow/Purple"
       onMouseDown="document.bgColor='yellow'"
       onMouseUp="document.bgColor='purple'">
</form>
```

Listing 8.66   Continued

```
<script>
<!--

// Intercept all mouseup and mousedown events and handle them
// by document event handlers.  This will cause the button event handlers
// to be intercepted.
document.captureEvents(Event.MOUSEDOWN | Event.MOUSEUP);

// Define event handlers within document to handle the mousedown
// and mouseup events.
document.onmousedown = function(event){document.bgColor='red'};
document.onmouseup = function(event){document.bgColor='blue'};

// -->
</script>

</html>
```

document.classes

JavaScript 1.2-1.3
Nav4-4.5

Syntax

```
document.classes.className.tagName.style
```

Description

The `classes` property is an associative array that contains classes associated with Netscape style sheets. Using dot notation, *className* specifies the `class` attribute and associated HTML tag (*tagName*) for which the *style* is applied. When *tagName* is set to `all`, the *style* is applied to all tags with a `class` attribute of *className*. The style sheet classes are created within `<style>` or `<script>` using JavaScript or HTML. The style specified can be any one of the style properties or methods shown in Table 8.8. For more information on any of the properties, see the `Style` object entries in this chapter.

NOTE

When creating a class, make sure that the declaration appears before the new class is used because many HTML objects cannot be changed after they have been created in the document.

NOTE

If JavaScript dot notation is used when creating a new class within `<style>` tags, `document` does not have to be specified.

Table 8.8 *Properties and Methods of the* `Style` *Object that Can Be Used with the* `classes` *Property*

Type	Item	Description
Property	align	Alignment of element within its parent
	backgroundColor	Background color of element
	backgroundImage	Background image of element
	borderBottomWidth	Width of bottom border of element
	borderColor	Color of border of element
	borderLeftWidth	Width of left border of element
	borderRightWidth	Width of right border of element
	borderStyle	Style of border that surrounds element
	borderTopWidth	Width of top border of element
	clear	Sides of element where floating elements are not allowed
	color	Foreground color of element
	display	Element to be displayed
	fontFamily	Font the element should use
	fontSize	Size of fonts used by element
	fontStyle	Font style used by element
	fontWeight	Font weight used by element
	lineHeight	Distance between two lines that are next to each other
	listStyleType	Format of list items elements
	marginBottom	Distance between bottom border of an element and top margin border of another element
	marginLeft	Distance between left border of an element and right margin border of another element
	marginRight	Distance between right border of an element and left margin border of another element
	marginTop	Distance between top border of an element and bottom margin border of another element
	paddingBottom	Distance between bottom border of element and its content
	paddingLeft	Distance between left border of element and its content
	paddingRight	Distance between right border of element and its content
	paddingTop	Distance between top border of element and its content
	textAlign	Alignment of text within element
	textDecoration	Type of decoration added to text
	textIndent	Indenting should appear before text

Table 8.8   Continued

Type	Item	Description
	`textTransform`	Transformation that should be applied to text
	`verticalAlign`	Vertical alignment of element
	`whiteSpace`	How whitespace should be handled within element
	`width`	Width of element
Method	`borderWidths()`	Width of border surrounding element
	`margins()`	Margin distance between border of an element and border of adjacent elements
	`paddings()`	Distance between borders of element and its content

Example

Listing 8.67 demonstrates three different ways to create style sheet classes using JavaScript and HTML within <style> and <script> tags. Notice how the order in which the classes are declared and used ultimately affects the style result.

Listing 8.67   Creating New Style Sheet Classes

```
<html>

<style type="text/css">
  all.TEXTFORMAT {font-style: italic;}
</style>

<p CLASS=TEXTFORMAT>After first STYLE tag.<p>

<style type="text/javascript">
  classes.TEXTFORMAT.all.fontWeight = "bold";
</style>

<p class=TEXTFORMAT>After second STYLE tag.<p>

<script>
<!--
document.classes.TEXTFORMAT.all.textDecoration = "underline";
// -->
</script>

<p class=TEXTFORMAT>After SCRIPT tag.<p>

</html>
```

document.close()

JavaScript 1.0+, JScript 1.0+
Nav2+, IE3+, Opera3+

Syntax

```
document.close()
```

Description

The `close()` method closes the output stream to the document. Any output that has not been written prior to calling the method will be displayed.

CAUTION

The implementation of the `close()` method varies greatly between browsers and their versions. In some browsers, output continues to be streamed after calling the `close()` method, so it is best to avoid using this method if possible. If you must use this function, test it carefully on all the browsers you intended to support.

Example

Listing 8.68 uses the `close()` method to close the output stream to a document.

Listing 8.68   Close Document Output Stream with the `close()` Method

```
<html>

<script type="text/javascript" language="JavaScript">
<!--

// Write some text to the screen and then close the document.
document.write("This line is a long line that should wrap around the ");
document.write("browser.  If it does not wrap around the screen then ");
document.write("resize your browser window so that it does wrap and ");
document.write("reexecute this code.<br>");


// Close document and write all lines that are currently in the buffer.
document.close();

// Write another paragraph.
document.write("If the paragraph above wrapped around the browser then ");
document.write("you will notice that this paragraph was only written after ");
document.write("the close method was called.");

// Create an alert box so you can see where the close operation takes place.
alert("Press to continue");
```

Listing 8.68   Continued

```
// -->
</script>

</html>
```

document.contextual()

JavaScript 1.2-1.4
Nav4

Syntax

```
document.contextual(context1,...,[contextN], style)
```

Description

The `contextual()` method provides a way to apply a style to HTML elements based on the context of the HTML elements. For example it is possible to specify that the color of text within an `<i>` tag that appears in an `<h2>` tag is set to green. The final argument passed to the method is the `style` to be to effected. The `context` arguments can also be used to specify other styles in which the final style should exist in order to be effected.

Example

The code in Listing 8.69 uses the `contextual()` method to make all italic text that appears within 2nd level header tags green.

Listing 8.69   Making All Italic Text Green with the `contextual()` *Method*

```
<html>

<script type="text/javascript" language="JavaScript">
document.contextual(document.tags.h2, document.tags.i).color="green";
</script>

<h2>This word is <i>Green</i></h2>

</html>
```

document.cookie

JavaScript 1.0+, JScript 1.0+
Nav2+, IE3+

Syntax

```
document.cookie
```

Description

The `cookie` property provides the ability to read and write cookies. A cookie represents a small amount of data that a Web browser stores to allow information to be shared among Web pages.

Example

Listing 8.70 creates a cookie and then reads back the result.

Listing 8.70   Create a Cookie and Read It Back Using the `cookie` ***Property***

```
<html>

<script>
<!--

// Create a cookie.
document.cookie = "temperature=75";

// Display the contents of the cookie.
document.write("The cookie contains: ",document.cookie);

// -->
</script>

</html>
```

document.domain

JavaScript 1.1+, JScript 1.0+
Nav3+, IE3+, Opera3+

Syntax

`document.domain`

Description

The `domain` property initially contains the hostname of the server from which the document was loaded. The document is allowed to change the value to the domain minus the subdomain. For example, if a Web page originated from *www.example.com*, the document could change this to *example.com*. The reason this is allowed is so different pages that come from various servers within the same Web site can share properties. The restrictive quality of this property keeps unrelated documents from wrongfully seeing the data each document might have collected.

Example

No example is provided because the document would have to originate from a server that has a domain name for this property not to be empty.

document.embeds
JavaScript 1.1+, JScript 1.0+
Nav3+, IE3+, Opera3+

Syntax
```
document.embeds
document.embeds[index]
```

Description
The embeds property is an array that contains all the embedded objects and plug-ins that appear within the HTML document when using the <embed> tag. The embeds property has one property of its own, called length, which contains the number of items in the array. The index number ranges from zero to the length minus one.

> **NOTE**
>
> The embeds array property accesses the same data as the document.plugins array property.

Example
Listing 8.71 uses the length property to display the number of embedded objects in a HTML document.

Listing 8.71   List the Number of Embedded Objects Using the embeds Property

```html
<html>

<h2>Learn your shapes</h2>

<h2>A Circle</h2>
<embed src="circle.gif">

<h2>A Square</h2>
<embed src="square.gif">

<script type="text/javascript" language="JavaScript">
<!--

// Display the length of the embeds array.
document.write(document.embeds.length," embedded objects.");

// -->
</script>

</html>
```

document.embeds.length

JavaScript 1.1+, JScript 1.0+
Nav3+, IE3+, Opera3+

Syntax

```
document.embeds.length
```

Description

The length property contains the number of objects that are in the embeds[] array.

Example

Listing 8.72 uses the length property to display the number of embedded objects in an HTML document.

Listing 8.72 List the Number of Embedded Objects Using the length Property

```html
<html>

<h2>A Circle</h2>
<embed src="circle.gif">

<h2>A Square</h2>
<embed src="square.gif">

<script type="text/javascript" language="JavaScript">
<!--

// Display the length of the embeds array.
document.write(document.embeds.length," embedded objects.");

// -->
</script>

</html>
```

document.fgColor

JavaScript 1.0+, JScript 1.0+
Nav2+, IE3+, Opera3+

Syntax

```
document.fgColor
```

Description

The fgColor property specifies the default text color of all the text that appears in a Web document. This is equivalent to assigning the color to the text attribute in the <body> tag. The color is expressed as a string in hexadecimal digits or as one of the

HTML standard color names. The hexadecimal form is made up of six digits that follow the pattern "RRGGBB."

Example

Listing 8.73 sets the default color of all the text on the page to blue.

Listing 8.73   Set the Text Color with the `fgColor` Property

```
<html>

<script type="text/javascript" language="JavaScript">
<!--

// Set the text color to blue.
document.fgColor="0000ff";

// -->
</script>

<body>
The color of all text on this page is blue.
</body>

</html>
```

document.*formName*

JavaScript 1.1+, JScript 1.0+
Nav3+, IE3+, Opera3+

Syntax

`document.formName`

Description

The `formName` property is actually the name of any form that exists in the HTML document. By simply placing the name of a particular form after the word `document.`, you gain access to the specified form object. It is also possible to access forms using the `forms` property and array notation. See the `document.forms` entry in this chapter for more information.

Example

Listing 8.74 accesses the action of each form by simply specifying its name using the `document` object and dot notation.

Listing 8.74   Accesses Form Actions Using Forms' Names

```
<html>

<form name="Form1" action="green">
  <input type="button"
```

```
            value="Green"
            onClick = "document.bgColor='green'">
</form>
<form name="Form2" action="blue">
   <input type="button"
            value="Blue"
            onClick = "document.bgColor='blue'">
</form>

<script type="text/javascript" language="JavaScript">

// Display the action of each of the form objects.
document.write("The action associated with the Form1 object is ");
document.write(document.Form1.action, "<br>");
document.write("The action associated with the Form2 object is ");
document.write(document.Form2.action);

</script>
</html>
```

document.forms

JavaScript 1.1+, JScript 1.0+
Nav3+, IE3+, Opera3+

Syntax

```
document.forms
document.forms[index]
```

Description

The forms property is an array that contains all the forms that exist within the HTML document from using the `<form>` tag. The forms property has one property of its own, called length, which contains the number of items in the array. The *index* number ranges from zero to the length minus one.

Example

Listing 8.75 accesses the names of each form using the forms[] array.

Listing 8.75   Access Form Names Using the forms Array

```
<html>

<form name="Form1">
   <input type="button"
            value="Green"
            onClick = "document.bgColor='green'">
</form>
```

Listing 8.75 *Continued*

```
<form name="Form2">
  <input type="button"
         value="Blue"
         onClick = "document.bgColor='blue'">
</form>

<script type="text/javascript" language="JavaScript">
<!--

// Display the name of the form objects.
for(i=0;i<document.forms.length;i++)
{
  document.write("The name of form object ",(i+1));
  document.write(" is <i><b>",document.forms[i].name,"</b></i><br>");
}

// -->
</script>

</html>
```

document.forms.length

> JavaScript 1.0+, JScript 1.0+
> Nav2+, IE3+, Opera3+

Syntax

```
document.forms.length
```

Description

The `length` property contains the number of Form objects that are in the `forms[]` array.

Example

Listing 8.76 uses the `length` property to display the number of Form objects in the document.

Listing 8.76 *Access the Number of Forms in the Document with the* `length` *Property*

```
<html>

<form name="Form1">
  <input type="button"
         value="Green"
         onClick = "document.bgColor='green'">
</form>
<form name="Form2">
```

```
  <input type="button"
         value="Blue"
         onClick = "document.bgColor='blue'">
</form>

<script type="text/javascript" language="JavaScript">
<!--

// How many items in forms[] array?
document.write(document.forms.length," Form objects in document.");

// -->
</script>

</html>
```

document.getSelection()
JavaScript 1.2+
Nav4+

Syntax
```
document.getSelection()
```

Description
The getSelection() method returns the text that is selected within the HTML document.

Example
Listing 8.77 uses the getSelection() method to display all captured text in a text box. The result of selecting "JavaScript is Great!" from the text is shown in Figure 8.3.

Listing 8.77   Displaying the Selected Text
```
<html>

The following text area will display any text that you
select within the Web page.  Try selecting the phrase
"JavaScript is Great!" with the mouse.<br><br>

<form name="Form1">
  <input type="text"
         name="TextArea">
</form>

<script type="text/javascript" language="JavaScript">
<!--
```

Listing 8.77   *Continued*

```
// Fill in textarea when mouse button is released.
document.captureEvents(Event.MOUSEUP);
document.onmouseup = function(event){document.Form1.TextArea.value =
➥document.getSelection()};

// -->
</script>

</html>
```

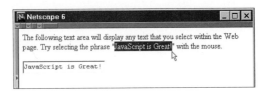

Figure 8.3

Selecting a portion of text and displaying it in a text box.

document.handleEvent()

JavaScript 1.2-1.3
Nav4-4.5

Syntax

```
document.handleEvent(event)
```

Description

The handleEvent() method provides a way to invoke a document's event handler, even though the event never happened. The *event* argument specifies the Event object associated with the event handler that is to be invoked.

Example

In Listing 8.78, an event handler is designated to handle all document Click events. When the user selects the button labeled 9, the clickHandler() method is used to route the event to the document's event handler.

Listing 8.78   *Pass Events to Document with the* handleEvent() *Method*

```
<html>

<h2>Math Quiz</h2>

What is 6+3?
```

```
<form name="answerForm">
  <input type="button"
         value="   8   "
         name="answer8"
         onClick="alert('Incorrect. Try again.')">
  <input type="button"
         value="   9   "
         name="answer9"
         onClick="document.handleEvent(event)">
</form>

<script type="text/javascript" language="JavaScript">
<!--

// Function designated to handle click events.
function clickHandler(event)
{
  // Display an alert box.
  alert("A click event occured within the document.");
}

// Register the Click event with the document event handler.
document.onClick = clickHandler;

// -->
</script>

</html>
```

document.ids

JavaScript 1.2-1.3
Nav4-4.5

Syntax

`document.ids.`*idName*`.style`

Description

The `ids` property is an associative array that contains IDs associated with Netscape style sheets. Using dot notation, *idName* specifies an ID associated with a style. The style sheet IDs are created within the <style> or <script> tags using JavaScript or HTML. The *style* specified can be any one of the style properties or methods shown in Table 8.9. For more information on any of the properties, see the Style object entries in this chapter.

NOTE

When creating an ID, make sure that the declaration appears before the new ID is used because many HTML objects cannot be changed after they have been created in the document.

NOTE

If JavaScript dot notation is used when creating a new ID within `<style>` tags, `document` does not have to be specified.

Table 8.9   Properties and Methods of the `Style` Object that Can Be Used with the `ids` Property

Type	Item	Description
Property	`align`	Alignment of element within its parent
	`backgroundColor`	Background color of element
	`backgroundImage`	Background image of element
	`borderBottomWidth`	Width of bottom border of element
	`borderColor`	Color of border of element
	`borderLeftWidth`	Width of left border of element
	`borderRightWidth`	Width of right border of element
	`borderStyle`	Style of border that surrounds element
	`borderTopWidth`	Width of top border of element
	`clear`	Sides of element where floating elements are not allowed
	`color`	Foreground color of element
	`display`	Element to be displayed
	`fontFamily`	Font the element should use
	`fontSize`	Size of fonts used by element
	`fontStyle`	Font style used by element
	`fontWeight`	Font weight used by element
	`lineHeight`	Distance between two lines that are next to each other
	`listStyleType`	Format of list items elements
	`marginBottom`	Distance between bottom border of an element and top margin border of another element
	`marginLeft`	Distance between left border of an element and right margin border of another element
	`marginRight`	Distance between right border of an element and left margin border of another element
	`marginTop`	Distance between top border of an element and bottom margin border of another element

Type	Item	Description
	`paddingBottom`	Distance between bottom border of element and its content
	`paddingLeft`	Distance between left border of element and its content
	`paddingRight`	Distance between right border of element and its content
	`paddingTop`	Distance between top border of element and its content
	`textAlign`	Alignment of text within element
	`textDecoration`	Type of decoration added to text
	`textIndent`	Indenting that should appear before text
	`textTransform`	Transformation that should be applied to text
	`verticalAlign`	Vertical alignment of element
	`whiteSpace`	How whitespace should be handled within element
	`width`	Width of element
Method	`borderWidths()`	Width of border that surrounds element
	`margins()`	Margin distance between border of an element and margin border of adjacent elements
	`paddings()`	Distance between borders of element and its content

Example

Listing 8.79 demonstrates three different ways to create style sheet IDs using JavaScript and HTML within `<style>` and `<script>` tags. Notice how the order in which the IDs are declared and used ultimately affects the style result.

Listing 8.79   Creating Style Sheet IDs

```
<html>

<style type="text/css">
  #TEXTFORMAT {font-style: italic;}
</style>

<p id=TEXTFORMAT>After first STYLE tag.<p>

<style type="text/javascript">
  ids.TEXTFORMAT.fontWeight = "bold";
</style>

<p id=TEXTFORMAT>After second STYLE tag.<p>
```

Listing 8.79   Continued

```
<script>
<!--
document.ids.TEXTFORMAT.textDecoration = "underline";
// -->
</script>

<p id=TEXTFORMAT>After SCRIPT tag.<p>

</html>
```

document.images

JavaScript 1.1+, JScript 1.0+
Nav3+, IE3+, Opera3+

Syntax

```
document.images
document.images[index]
```

Description

The `images` property is an array that contains all the objects that appear within the HTML document from using the `<img>` tag. The `images` property has one property of its own, called `length`, which contains the number of items in the array. The *index* number ranges from zero to the length of the array minus one.

Example

The code in Listing 8.80 accesses the source of each image using the `images` array.

Listing 8.80   Accessing Images with the `images` **Array**

```
<html>

<h2>A Circle</h2>
<img src="circle.gif">

<h2>A Square</h2>
<img src="square.gif"><br>

<script type="text/javascript" language="JavaScript">
<!--

// Display the source of the image objects.
for(i=0;i<document.images.length;i++)
{
```

```
    document.write("The source of image object ",(i+1));
    document.write(" is <i><b>",document.images[i].src,"</b></i><br>");
}

// -->
</script>

</html>
```

document.images.length

JavaScript 1.1+, JScript 1.0+
Nav3+, IE3+, Opera 5+

Syntax

```
document.images.length
```

Description

The length property contains the number of objects that are in the images[] array.

Example

The code in Listing 8.81 uses the length property to display the number of images in the HTML document.

Listing 8.81   Display the Number of Images in Document Using the length Property

```
<html>

<h2>A Circle</h2>
<img src="circle.gif">

<h2>A Square</h2>
<img src="square.gif"><br>

<script type="text/javascript" language="JavaScript">
<!--

// Display the length of the images array.
document.write(document.images.length," image objects.");

// -->
</script>

</html>
```

document.lastModified

JavaScript 1.0+, JScript 3.0+
Nav2+, IE3+, Opera3+

Syntax

```
document.lastModified
```

Description

The lastModified property contains the date and time the document was last modified on the server. This property can be very useful when dealing with documents that contain information that is very date-specific. Be careful when using this date because Web servers are not required to provide this timestamp. If the timestamp is not provided, JavaScript will set the lastModified property to midnight, January 1, 1970 (GMT).

Example

The code in Listing 8.82 lists limited discount prices on clothing, starting with when the document was last modified.

Listing 8.82   Display Prices Based on the lastModified Property

```html
<html>
<center>
<h2>LIMITED TIME SALE ON CLOTHING</h2>

<script type="text/javascript" language="JavaScript">
<!--
document.write("Starting ",document.lastModified," the following ");
document.write("clothing items will be on sale for one week ");
document.write("so order now!<br>");
// -->
</script>

<table border=ON>
  <tr>
    <th>Item</th>
    <th>Retail Price</th>
    <th>Sale Price</th>
  </tr>
  <tr>
    <td>T-shirt</td>
    <td>$20.00</td>
    <td><font color="RED">$10.99</font></td>
  </tr>
  <tr>
    <td>Jeans</td>
    <td>$60.00</td>
    <td><font color="RED">$30.99</font></td>
  </tr>
```

```
   <tr>
     <td>Hats</td>
     <td>$25.00</td>
     <td><font color="RED">$15.00</font></td>
   </tr>
 </table>
 </center>

 </html>
```

document.layers

JavaScript 1.2-1.4
Nav4-4.7

Syntax

```
document.layers
document.layers[index]
```

Description

The `layers` property is an array that contains all the objects that appear within the HTML document from using the `<layer>` tag. The `layers` property has one property of its own, called `length`, which contains the number of items in the array. The `index` number ranges from zero to the length.

CAUTION

The `layers` property is no longer supported as of JavaScript 1.5, so this property is not available in Netscape 6.

Example

The code in Listing 8.83 creates two layers and then displays their names at the bottom of the page using the `layers[]` array.

Listing 8.83 Accessing the Layer **Objects Using the** layers[] **Array**

```
<html>

<layer name="Layer1"
       PAGEX=50
       PAGEY=50
       width=100
       height=100
 bgcolor="blue">Layer 1</layer>
<layer name="Layer2"
       PAGEX=150
       PAGEY=150
```

Listing 8.83   Continued

```
     width=100
     height=100
 bgcolor="red">Layer 2</layer>

<script type="text/javascript" language="JavaScript">
<!--

// Display the name of the layer objects.
for(i=0;i<document.layers.length;i++)
{
  document.write("The name of layer object ",(i+1));
  document.write(" is <i><b>",document.layers[i].name,"</b></i><br>");
}

// -->
</script>

</html>
```

document.layers.length
JavaScript 1.2-1.4
Nav4-4.7

Syntax
`document.layers.length`

Description
The `length` property contains the number of objects that are in the `layers[]` array.

CAUTION

The `length` property associated with the `layers[]` array is no longer supported as of JavaScript 1.5, so this property is not available in Netscape 6.

Example
Listing 8.84 creates two layers and then displays the number of layers on the bottom of the page using the `length` property.

Listing 8.84   Display the Number of Layers in the Document Using the `length` *Property*

```
<html>

<layer name="Layer1"
       pagex=50
       pagey=50
```

```
        width=100
        height=100
 bgcolor="blue">Layer 1</layer>
<layer name="Layer2"
        pagex=150
        pagey=150
        width=100
        height=100
 bgcolor="red">Layer 2</layer>

<script type="text/javascript" language="JavaScript">
<!--

// Display the length of the layers array.
document.write(document.layers.length," layer objects.");

// -->
</script>

</html>
```

document.linkColor

JavaScript 1.0+, ECMAScript 1.0+, JScript 1.0+
Nav2+, IE3+

Syntax

```
document.linkColor
```

Description

The linkColor property specifies the color of unvisited links. The color is expressed as a string in hexadecimal digits or as one of the HTML standard color names. The hexadecimal form is made up of six digits that follow the pattern "RRGGBB."

Example

Listing 8.85 sets all the unvisited links on the page to the color green.

Listing 8.85   Setting Link Colors with the linkColor *Property*

```
<html>

<a href="myGreenPage.html">The Green Site</a><br>

<script type="text/javascript" language="JavaScript">
<!--
```

Listing 8.85   Continued

```
// Set the unvisited links color to green.
document.linkColor="00ff00";

// -->
</script>

<a href="myGreenGrassPage.html">The Green Grass Page</a>

</html>
```

document.links

JavaScript 1.0+, JScript 1.0+
Nav2+, IE3+, Opera3+

Syntax

```
document.links
document.links[index]
```

Description

The links property is an array that contains all the Link objects that appear within the HTML document from using the `<a href="source">` tag. The links property has one property of its own, called length, which contains the number of Link objects in the array. The index number ranges from zero to the length minus one. See the Link object earlier in this chapter for a detailed explanation of all the properties associated with links.

CAUTION

Although anchors are created using the `<a>` tag, they are not accessible through the links array. Anchors are stored in the document's anchors array.

Example

Listing 8.86 displays the URL of each link using the links[] array.

Listing 8.86   Display the URL of each Link in the Document using the link *array*

```
<html>

<a href="EmployeeList.html">The Employee List Page</a><br>
<a href="EmployeeBenefits.html">The Employee Benefits Page</a><br>

<script type="text/javascript" language="JavaScript">
<!--
```

```
// Display the URL of the link objects.
for(i=0;i<document.links.length;i++)
{
  document.write("The URL of link object ",(i+1));
  document.write(" is <i><b>",document.links[i].href,"</b></i><br>");
}

// -->
</script>

</html>
```

document.links.length

JavaScript 1.0+, JScript 1.0+
Nav2+, IE3+, Opera3+

Syntax

```
document.links.length
```

Description

The `length` property contains the number of `Link` objects that are in the `document.links` array.

Example

Listing 8.87 uses the `length` property to display the number of links in the HTML document.

Listing 8.87   Display the Number of Links in the Document Using the `length` **Property**

```
<html>

<a href="EmployeeList.html">The Employee List Page</a><br>
<a href="EmployeeBenefits.html">The Employee Benefits Page</a><br>

<script type="text/javascript" language="JavaScript">
<!--

// Display the length of the links array.
document.write(document.links.length," links.");

// -->
</script>

</html>
```

document.onClick

JavaScript1.0+, JScript 1.0-3.0
Nav2+, IE3-4

Syntax

```
document.onClick
```

Description

The onClick event handler specifies what should happen when the mouse is clicked within the Document object.

Example

In Listing 8.88, the script in the <head> of the document specifies a function to handle all Click events in the document. To be able to do this, the document's captureEvents() method is used to capture all events of type Event.CLICK. When the page itself is clicked, Document's event handler generates an alert box notifying the user of the event.

Listing 8.88   Handle the Click *Event with the* onClick *Event Handler*

```html
<html>
<head>
<script type="text/javascript" language="JavaScript1.2">
<!--

// Tell the browser you want to intercept ALL click events
// on the page and then define a function to handle them.
document.captureEvents(Event.CLICK);
document.onClick = myClickHandler;

// Define the myClickHandler function to handle click events
function myClickHandler(e){
  alert("The document was clicked!");
}

// -->
</script>
</head>
<body>
Any time you click anywhere within this document you will
get a message alerting you that a Click event has taken place.
</body>
</html>
```

document.onDblClick

JavaScript1.0+, JScript 1.0-3.0
Nav2+, IE3-4

Syntax

```
document.onDblClick
```

Description

The `onDblClick` event handler specifies what should happen when the mouse is double-clicked within the `Document` object.

Example

In Listing 8.89, the script in the `<head>` of the document specifies a function to handle all `DblClick` events in the document. To be able to do this, the document's `captureEvents()` method is used to capture all events of type `Event.DBLCLICK`. When the page itself is double-clicked, `Document`'s event handler generates an alert box notifying the user of the event.

Listing 8.89 ***Handle the*** `DblClick` ***Event with the*** `onDblClick` ***Event Handler***

```html
<html>
<head>

<script type="text/javascript" language="JavaScript1.2">
<!--

// Tell the browser you want to intercept ALL DblClick events
// on the page and then define a function to handle them.
document.captureEvents(Event.DBLCLICK);
document.onDblClick = myDblClickHandler;

// Define the myDblClickHandler function to handle DblClick events.
function myDblClickHandler(e){
  alert("The document was double clicked!");
}

// -->
</script>
</head>
<body>
Any time you double-click anywhere within this document, you will
get a message alerting you that a DblClick event has taken place.
</body>
</html>
```

document.onKeyDown
JavaScript1.0+, JScript 1.0-3.0
Nav2+, IE3-4

Syntax

```
document.onKeyDown
```

Description

The onKeyDown event handler specifies what should happen when any key is pressed when the Document object is in focus.

Example

In Listing 8.90, the script in the <head> of the document specifies a function to handle all KeyDown events in the document. To be able to do this, the document's captureEvents() method is used to capture all events of type Event.KEYDOWN. When any key is pressed within the page, the document's event handler generates an alert box notifying the user of the event.

Listing 8.90   **Handle the** KeyDown **Event with the** onKeyDown **Event Handler**

```
<html>
<head>

<script type="text/javascript" language="JavaScript1.2">
<!--

// Tell the browser you want to intercept ALL key down events
// on the page and then define a function to handle them.
document.captureEvents(Event.KEYDOWN);
document.onKeyDown = myKeyDownHandler;

// Define the myKeyDownHandler function to handle
// key down events.
function myKeyDownHandler(e){
  alert("A key down event took place within the document!");
}

// -->
</script>
</head>
<body>
Anytime you press a key within this document, you will
get a message alerting you that a KeyDown event has taken place.
</body>
</html>
```

document.onKeyPress

JavaScript1.0+, JScript 1.0-3.0
Nav2+, IE3-4

Syntax

```
document.onKeyPress
```

Description

The onKeyPress event handler specifies what should happen when any key is pressed when the Document object is in focus.

Example

In Listing 8.91, the script in the <head> of the document specifies a function to handle all KeyPress events in the document. To be able to do this, the document's captureEvents() method is used to capture all events of type Event.KEYPRESS. When any key is pressed within the page, the document's event handler generates an alert box notifying the user of the event.

Listing 8.91 **Handle the** KeyPress **Event with the** onKeyPress **Event Handler**

```
<html>
<head>

<script type="text/javascript" language="JavaScript1.2">
<!--

// Tell the browser you want to intercept ALL key press events
// on the page and then define a function to handle them.
document.captureEvents(Event.KEYPRESS);
document.onKeyPress = myKeyPressHandler;

// Define the myKeyPressHandler function to handle
// key press events.
function myKeyPressHandler(e){
  alert("A key press event took place within the document!");
}

// -->
</script>
</head>
<body>
Anytime you press a key within this document, you will
get a message alerting you that a KeyPress event has taken place.
</body>
</html>
```

document.onKeyUp

JavaScript1.0+, JScript 1.0-3.0
Nav2+, IE3-4

Syntax

```
document.onKeyUp
```

Description

The onKeyUp event handler specifies what should happen when any key is pressed and then released when the Document object is in focus.

Example

In Listing 8.92, the script in the <head> of the document specifies a function to handle all KeyUp events in the document. To be able to do this, the document's captureEvents() method is used to capture all events of type Event.KEYUP. When any key is pressed and then released within the page, the document's event handler generates an alert box notifying the user of the event.

Listing 8.92   *Handle the* KeyUp *Event with the* onKeyUp *Event Handler*

```
<html>
<head>

<script type="text/javascript" language="JavaScript1.2">
<!--

// Tell the browser you want to intercept ALL key up events
// on the page and then define a function to handle them.
document.captureEvents(Event.KEYUP);
document.onKeyUp = myKeyUpHandler;

// Define the myKeyUpHandler function to handle
// key up events.
function myKeyUpHandler(e){
  alert("A key up event took place within the document!");
}

// -->
</script>
</head>
<body>
Anytime you press a key and release it within this document, you will
get a message alerting you that a KeyUp event has taken place.
</body>
</html>
```

document.onLoad

JavaScript1.0+, JScript 1.0+
Nav2+, IE3+

Syntax

onLoad="*command*"

Description

The onLoad event handler of the Document object is fired when the page has finished loading in that particular window instance. This event handler actually belongs to the Window object but is accessible through the Document object.

> **NOTE**
>
> The onLoad event in the <body> of a document that is loaded in a frame will fire before an event loaded in the <frameset> tag that loaded the document.

Example

The sample of code in Listing 8.93 pops up an alert box when the page has finished loading using the onLoad event handler.

Listing 8.93   Handle the Load **Event with the** onLoad **Event Handler**

```
<html>
<body onLoad='alert("The document has completely loaded.")'>
<h2>The document.onLoad entry</h2>
</body>
</html>
```

document.onMouseDown

JavaScript1.0+, JScript 1.0-3.0
Nav2+, IE3-4

Syntax

document.onMouseDown

Description

The onMouseDown event handler specifies what should happen when the mouse button is clicked within the Document object.

Example

In Listing 8.94, the script in the <head> of the document specifies a function to handle all MouseDown events in the document. To be able to do this, the document's captureEvents() method is used to capture all events of type Event.MOUSEDOWN. When the mouse button is clicked within the page, the document's event handler generates an alert box notifying the user of the event.

Listing 8.94 *Handle the* MouseDown *Event with the* onMouseDown *Event Handler*

```
<html>
<head>

<script type="text/javascript" language="JavaScript1.2">
<!--

// Tell the browser you want to intercept ALL mouse
// down events on the page and then define a function
// to handle them.
document.captureEvents(Event.MOUSEDOWN);
document.onMouseDown = myMouseDownHandler;

// Define the myMouseDownHandler function to handle
// mouse down events.
function myMouseDownHandler(e){
  alert("A mouse down event took place within the document!");
}

// -->
</script>
</head>
<body>
Anytime you press the mouse button down within this document, you will
get a message alerting you that a MouseDown event has taken place.
</body>
</html>
```

document.onMouseUp

JavaScript1.0+, JScript 1.0-3.0
Nav2+, IE3-4

Syntax

document.onMouseUp

Description

The onMouseUp event handler specifies what should happen when the mouse button is clicked and then released within the Document object.

Example

In Listing 8.95, the script in the <head> of the document specifies a function to handle all MouseUp events in the document. To be able to do this, the document's captureEvents() method is used to capture all events of type Event.MOUSEUP. When the mouse button is clicked and then released within the page, the document's event handler generates an alert box notifying the user of the event.

Listing 8.95 Handle the MouseUp ***Event with the*** onMouseUp ***Event Handler***

```
<html>
<head>

<script type="text/javascript" language="JavaScript1.2">
<!--

// Tell the browser you want to intercept ALL mouse
// up events on the page and then define a function
// to handle them.
document.captureEvents(Event.MOUSEUP);
document.onMouseUp = myMouseUpHandler;

// Define the myMouseUpHandler function to handle
// mouse up events.
function myMouseUpHandler(e){
  alert("A mouse up event took place within the document!");
}

// -->
</script>
</head>
<body>
Anytime you press the mouse button and then release it within this
Document, you will get a message alerting you that a MouseUp
event has taken place.
</body>
</html>
```

document.onUnLoad

JavaScript 1.0+, JScript 1.0+
Nav2+, IE3+, Opera3+

Syntax

onUnLoad="*command*"

Description

The onUnLoad event handler of a Document object is fired when the page is unloaded in that particular window instance. This occurs when the user leaves the page for another page. This event handler actually belongs to the Window object but is accessible through the Document object. See Window.onUnLoad, later in this chapter, for more information.

NOTE

The onUnLoad event handler in the <body> of a document that is loaded in a frame will fire before an event loaded in the <frameset> tag that loaded the document.

Example

The code in Listing 8.96 pops up an alert box when the user clicks the bogus link to leave the current HTML page, thanks to the onUnLoad event handler.

Listing 8.96   Handle the UnLoad ***Event with the*** onUnLoad ***Event Handler***

```
<html>
<body onUnLoad='alert("Please do not leave!")'>
<a href="nextpage.html">Press this link to go to the next page.</a>
</body>
</html>
```

document.open()
JavaScript1.0+, JScript 1.0+
Nav2+, IE3+, Opera3+

Syntax

```
document.open()
document.open(mimetype)
```

Description

The open() method of the Document object clears the current document and opens a stream for new data to be placed in the document. This method accepts one argument, *mimetype*, that specifies what type of data will be written to the document. The argument can be one of the following standard mimetypes: text/html, text/plain, image/gif, image/jpeg, or image/x-bitmap.

Example

Listing 8.97 opens a document with the open() method and then writes text to the document.

Listing 8.97   Open a Document with the open() ***Method***

```
<script type="text/javascript" language="JavaScript">
<!--

document.open()
document.write("Stream text to document");
document.close()

// -->
</script>
```

document.plugins

JavaScript 1.1+, JScript 1.0+
Nav3+, IE3+, Opera3+

Syntax

```
document.plugins
document.plugins[index]
```

Description

The `plugins` property is an array that contains all the embedded objects and plug-ins that appear within the HTML document from using the `<embed>` tag. The `plugins` property has one property of its own, called `length`, which contains the number of items in the array. The *index* number ranges from zero to the `length` minus one.

NOTE

The `plugins[]` array property accesses the same data as the `document.embeds[]` array property.

Example

Listing 8.98 uses the `length` property to display the number of embedded objects in the HTML document.

Listing 8.98   Display the Number of Plug-ins Using the `plugins` **Property**

```
<html>

<h2>Learn Shapes</h2>

<h2>A Circle</h2>
<embed src="circle.gif">

<h2>A Square</h2>
<embed src="square.gif">

<script type="text/javascript" language="JavaScript">
<!--

// Display the length of the plugins array.
document.write(document.plugins.length," embedded objects.");

// -->
</script>

</html>
```

document.plugins.length

JavaScript 1.1+, JScript 1.0+
Nav3+, IE3+

Syntax

```
document.plugins.length
```

Description

The `length` property contains the number of objects that are in the `plugins[]` array.

Example

Listing 8.99 uses the `length` property to display the number of embedded objects in the HTML document.

Listing 8.99 *Display the Number of Plug-ins in the Document using the* `length` *property*

```
<html>

<h2>A Circle</h2>
<embed src="circle.gif">

<h2>A Square</h2>
<embed src="square.gif">

<script type="text/javascript" language="JavaScript">
<!--

// Display the length of the plugins array.
document.write(document.plugins.length," embedded objects.");

// -->
</script>

</html>>
```

document.referrer

JavaScript 1.0+, JScript 3.0+
Nav2+, IE4+

Syntax

```
document.referrer
```

Description

The `referrer` property contains the URL of the document that was used to reach the current document. If the URL was typed directly in to the browser's location field, this property will be empty.

Example

In Listing 8.100, the `referrer` property is used to create a link back to the previous document from within the current document in the example.

Listing 8.100   Create a Link Back to the Calling Document Using the `referrer` *Property*

```
<script type="text/javascript" language="JavaScript">
<!--

// Create a link back to the referring document.
document.write("<a href='",document.referrer,"'>Go back</a>");

// -->
</script>
```

document.releaseEvents()

JavaScript1.2-1.3
Nav4-4.5

Syntax

```
document.releaseEvents(event)
document.releaseEvents(event1 | event2 | eventN)
```

Description

The `releaseEvents()` method of the `Document` object releases all previously captured events of the event type passed. These events can be captured with the `Document.captureEvents()` method. The following events can be released:

- Event.ABORT
- Event.BLUR
- Event.CHANGE
- Event.CLICK
- Event.DBLCLICK
- Event.DRAGDROP
- Event.ERROR
- Event.FOCUS
- Event.KEYDOWN
- Event.KEYPRESS
- Event.KEYUP
- Event.LOAD
- Event.MOUSEDOWN
- Event.MOUSEMOVE
- Event.MOUSEOUT
- Event.MOUSEOVER
- Event.MOUSEUP

- Event.MOVE
- Event.RESET
- Event.RESIZE
- Event.SELECT
- Event.SUBMIT
- Event. UNLOAD

After one of these events has been captured, you can define a function to replace the built-in method for handling the event. Use the releaseEvents() method to free the event after a capture.

Example

Listing 8.101 has a single text box and a button. The script in the <head> of the document specifies a function to handle all Click events in the document. To be able to do this, the captureEvents() method had to be used to capture all events of type Event.CLICK. When the page itself is clicked, a counter, which is displayed in the text box, is incremented.

When the mouse button is clicked, the MouseDown event is fired, the Event.CLICK is released, and the counter no longer increments when the page is clicked.

Listing 8.101 ***Using the*** releaseEvents() ***Method to Stop Capturing Specific Events***

```
<html>
<head>

<script type="text/javascript" language="JavaScript1.2">
<!--

// Define a click counter variable.
var counter = 0;

// Tell the browser you want to intercept ALL click events
// on the page. Then define a function to handle them.
document.captureEvents(Event.CLICK);
document.onClick = myClickHandler;

// Define the myClickHandler function to handle click events.
function myClickHandler(e){
  // Pass all click events to the onClick event of the text box.
  document.myForm.myText.handleEvent(e);
}

// Function is called by onClick of text box. Displays the number
// of clicks that have occurred.
function changeText(){
  document.myForm.myText.value = counter++;
}
```

```
// Releases the click event capturing
function releaseClick(){
  document.releaseEvents(Event.CLICK);
  document.onClick="";
}

// -->
</script>
</head>
<body>
<form name="myForm">
  <input type=TEXT size=2 value="" name="myText" onClick="changeText()">
  <input type=BUTTON value="Release Event" onMouseDown="releaseClick()">
</form>
</body>
</html>
```

document.routeEvent()

JavaScript1.2+
Nav4+

Syntax

```
document.routeEvent(event)
```

Description

The routeEvent() method of the Document object passes all previously captured events of the event type passed through their normal event processes. The events that can be passed are as follows:

- Event.ABORT
- Event.BLUR
- Event.CHANGE
- Event.CLICK
- Event.DBLCLICK
- Event.DRAGDROP
- Event.ERROR
- Event.FOCUS
- Event.KEYDOWN
- Event.KEYPRESS
- Event.KEYUP
- Event.LOAD
- Event.MOUSEDOWN
- Event.MOUSEMOVE
- Event.MOUSEOUT
- Event.MOUSEOVER
- Event.MOUSEUP

- Event.MOVE
- Event.RESET
- Event.RESIZE
- Event.SELECT
- Event.SUBMIT
- Event. UNLOAD

After one of these events has been captured using the Document.captureEvents() method, you can define a function to replace the built-in method for handling the event. Use the releaseEvents() method to free the event after a capture, and use routeEvent() to allow normal processing to take place.

Example

Listing 8.102 has a single text box and a link. The script in the <head> of the document specifies a function to handle all Click events in the window. To be able to do this, the captureEvents() method had to be used to capture all events of type Event.CLICK. When the page itself is clicked, a counter, which is displayed in the text box, is incremented.

When the link is clicked, the MouseDown event is fired, the Event.CLICK is routed through its normal means, and the counter no longer increments when the page is clicked.

Listing 8.102   Using the routeEvent() **Method to Continue Routing a Captured Event**

```
<html>
<head>

<script type="text/javascript" language="JavaScript1.2">
<!--

// Define a click counter variable.
var counter = 0;

// Tell the browser you want to intercept ALL click events
// on the page. Then define a function to handle them.
document.captureEvents(Event.CLICK);
document.onClick = myClickHandler;

// Define the myClickHandler function to handle click events.
function myClickHandler(e){
  // Pass all click events to the onClick event of the text box.
  document.myForm.myText.handleEvent(e);
}

// Function is called by onClick of text box. Displays the number
// of clicks that have occurred.
```

```
function changeText(){
  document.myForm.myText.value = counter++;
}

// Releases the click event capturing
function releaseClick(){
  document.routeEvent(Event.CLICK);
}

// -->
</script>
</head>
<body>
<form name="myForm">
  <input type="TEXT" size="2" value="" name="myText" onClick="changeText()">
  <a href="http://www.purejavascript.com"
     onMouseDown="window.routeEvent(Event.CLICK)">Click Here!</a>
</form>
</body>
</html>
```

document.tags

> JavaScript 1.2+
> Nav4+

Syntax

document.tags.*tagName*.*style*

Description

The `tags` property is an associative array that contains tags associated with Netscape style sheets. Using dot notation, *tagName* specifies a tag associated with a style. The style sheet tags are created within the `<style>` or `<script>` tags using JavaScript or HTML. The *style* specified can be any one of the style properties or methods shown in Table 8.10. For more information on any of the properties, see the `Style` object entries in this chapter.

NOTE

When creating a tag, make sure that the declaration appears before the new tag is used because many HTML objects cannot be changed after they have been created in the document.

NOTE

If JavaScript dot notation is used when creating a new tag within `<style>` tags, document does not have to be specified.

Table 8.10   Properties and Methods of the Style *Object that Can Be Used with the* tags *Property*

Type	Item	Description
Property	align	Alignment of element within its parent
	backgroundColor	Background color of element
	backgroundImage	Background image of element
	borderBottomWidth	Width of bottom border of element
	borderColor	Color of border of element
	borderLeftWidth	Width of left border of element
	borderRightWidth	Width of right border of element
	borderStyle	Style of border that surrounds element
	borderTopWidth	Width of top border of element
	clear	Sides of element where floating elements are not allowed
	color	Foreground color of element
	display	Element to be displayed
	fontFamily	Font the element should use
	fontSize	Size of fonts used by element
	fontStyle	Font style used by element
	fontWeight	Font weight used by element
	lineHeight	Distance between two lines that are next to each other
	listStyleType	Format of list items elements
	marginBottom	Distance between bottom border of an element and top margin border of another element
	marginLeft	Distance between left border of an element and right margin border of another element
	marginRight	Distance between right border of an element and left margin border of another element
	marginTop	Distance between top border of an element and bottom margin border of another element
	paddingBottom	Distance between bottom border of element and its content
	paddingLeft	Distance between left border of element and its content
	paddingRight	Distance between right border of element and its content
	paddingTop	Distance between top border of element and its content
	textAlign	Alignment of text within element
	textDecoration	Type of decoration added to text
	textIndent	Indenting that should appear before text

Type	Item	Description
	`textTransform`	Transformation that should be applied to text
	`verticalAlign`	Vertical alignment of element
	`whiteSpace`	How whitespace should be handled within element
	width	Width of element
Method	`borderWidths()`	Width of border that surrounding element
	`margins()`	Margin distance between border of an element and border of adjacent elements
	`paddings()`	Distance between borders of element and its content

Example

Listing 8.103 demonstrates three different ways to create style sheet tags using JavaScript and HTML within <style> and <script> tags. Notice that the order in which the tags are declared and used ultimately affects the style result.

Listing 8.103   Creating New Style Sheet Tags

```
<html>

<style type="text/css">
  P {font-style: italic;}
</style>

<p>After first STYLE tag.<p>

<style type="text/javascript">
  tags.P.fontWeight = "bold";
</style>

<p>After second STYLE tag.<p>

<script>
<!--
document.tags.P.textDecoration = "underline";
// -->
</script>

<p>After SCRIPT tag.<p>

</html>
```

document.title

JavaScript 1.0+, JScript 1.0+
Nav2+, IE3+, Opera3+

Syntax

```
document.title
```

Description

The `title` property is a read-only string that specifies the title of the document. This property is commonly set with the `<title>` tag.

Example

In Listing 8.104, the title of the Web page is written to the screen using the `title` property.

Listing 8.104 Accessing the `title` Property of a Document

```
<html>
<head><title>My Web Page</title></head>

<script>
<!--

// Output the title of the document.
document.write("The title of this page is <i>");
document.write(document.title,"</i>");

// -->
</script>
```

document.unwatch()

JavaScript 1.2+
Nav4+, NES3+

Syntax

```
document.unwatch(property)
```

Description

The `unwatch()` method of the `Document` object is used to turn off the watch for a particular property specified by `property`.

Example

Listing 8.105 shows how the `unwatch()` method is used to stop watching the `fgColor` property of the `Document` object after its value has changed to `"Blue"`.

CAUTION

A bug associated with the watch() and unwatch() methods prevents the actual text color from changing in the browser even though the document's *fgColor* property does get changed.

Listing 8.105 **Example of the** unwatch() **Method of the** Document **Object**

```
<html>
<b>What color is this text?</b><br><br>

<script type="text/javascript" language="JavaScript">
<!--

function alertme(id,oldValue,newValue)
{
  document.write(id + " changed from " + oldValue + " to ");
  document.write(newValue + "<br>");
  return newValue;
}

// Start watch
document.watch("fgColor",alertme);

document.write("Original text color: " + document.fgColor + "<br>");

// Change text color
document.fgColor = "Blue";

document.write("New text color: " + document.fgColor + "<br>");

// Stop watch
document.unwatch("fgColor");

// Change text color
document.fgColor = "Red";

document.write("Final text color: " + document.fgColor + "<br>");

// -->
</script>
</html>
```

document.URL
JavaScript 1.1+, JScript 1.0+
Nav3+, IE3+, Opera3+

Syntax
```
document.URL
```

Description
The URL property specifies the URL of the document. This property is read-only.

Example
Listing 8.106 uses the URL property to write the document's URL to the screen.

Listing 8.106   Accessing a Document's URL Property
```
<html>

<script>
<!--

// Output the URL of the document.
document.write("The URL of this page is -->",document.URL);

// -->
</script>

</html>
```

document.vlinkColor
JavaScript 1.0+, JScript 1.0+
Nav2+, IE3+

Syntax
```
document.vlinkColor
```

Description
The vlinkColor property specifies the color of visited links. The color is expressed as a string in hexadecimal digits or as one of the HTML standard color names. The hexadecimal form is made up of six digits that follow the pattern "RRGGBB."

Example
Listing 8.107 sets the visited links color to green for all links on the page, that you have visited, only if they are placed before the <script> tags.

Listing 8.107 **Setting the Visited Links Color with the** vLinkColor **Property**

```
<html>

<a href="myGreenPage.html">The Green Site</a><br>

<script type="text/javascript" language="JavaScript">
<!--

// Set the visited links color to green.
document.vlinkColor="00ff00";

// -->
</script>

<a href="myGreenGrassPage.html">The Green Grass Page</a>

</html>
```

document.watch()

JavaScript 1.2+
Nav4+, NES3+

Syntax

```
document.watch(property,function)
```

Description

The watch() method of the Document object is used to turn on the watch for a particular property specified by *property*. Any time the specified property is changed after the watch() method has been called, the specified function is called.

Example

Listing 8.108 shows how the watch() method is used to start watching the *fgColor* property of the Document object.

CAUTION

A bug associated with the watch() and unwatch() methods prevents the actual text color from changing in the browser even though the document's *fgColor* property does get changed.

Listing 8.108 **Example of the** watch() **Method of the** Document **Object**

```
<html>
<b>What color is this text?</b><br><br>
```

Listing 8.108 Continued

```
<script type="text/javascript" language="JavaScript">
<!--

function alertme(id,oldValue,newValue)
{
  document.write(id + " changed from " + oldValue + " to ");
  document.write(newValue + "<br>");
  return newValue;
}

// Start watch
document.watch("fgColor",alertme);

document.write("Original text color: " + document.fgColor + "<br>");

// Change text color
document.fgColor = "Blue";

document.write("Final text color: " + document.fgColor + "<br>");

// -->
</script>
</html>
```

document.write()
JavaScript 1.0+, JScript 1.0+
Nav2+, IE3+, Opera3+

Syntax

```
document.write(value,....)
```

Description

The write() method appends the comma-separated argument(s) (*value*) to the document as a string. If any of the arguments are not strings, they are converted to strings before being appended to the document.

Example

Listing 8.109 writes some text, as well as the value of a property, to the current document using the write() method.

Listing 8.109   Displaying Text in a Document Using the `write()` *Method*

```
<html>
<head><title>Movies</title></head>

<script type="text/javascript" language="JavaScript">
<!--

// Write data to the current document.
document.write("The title of this web page is called <u>");
document.write(document.title,"</u>");

// -->
</script>

</html>
```

document.writeln()

JavaScript 1.0+, JScript 1.0+
Nav2+, IE3+, Opera3+

Syntax

```
document.writeln(value,....)
```

Description

The `writeln()` method appends the comma-separated argument(s) (*value*) to the document as a string. Unlike the `write()` method, the `writeln()` method appends a newline character to the document after the last argument has been written. If any of the arguments are not strings, they are converted to strings before being appended to the document.

Example

Listing 8.110 writes some text, as well as the value of a property, to the current document using the `writeln()` method. The <pre> tag is used to make the newline character, which was created by the `writeln()` method, appear in the Web page.

Listing 8.110   Displaying Text on a Line in a Document Using the `writeln()` *Method*

```
<html>
<head><title>Movies</title></head>

<script type="text/javascript" language="JavaScript">
<!--
```

Listing 8.110 Continued

```
// Write data to the current document.
document.writeln("<pre>The title of this web page is called <u>");
document.writeln(document.title,"</u></pre>");


// -->
</script>

</html>
```

Embed

JavaScript 1.0+, JScript 3.0+
Nav2+, IE4+, Opera3+

Syntax

Core client-side JavaScript object.

Description

The Embed object references any object that is embedded within a Web page using the HTML <embed> tag. It is inherited from the document object. Embed is typically used for audio and video files, but can be used for any type of embedded file. Embedded objects are referenced by either the embeds array or by name.

Example

Listing 8.111 shows an example of how an embedded midi file can be referenced using the embeds array.

When this HTML code is loaded in a browser, the AUTOSTART option for the <embed> tag will start playing the midi file automatically. The stopsong() function calls the stop method, which is part of browser audio plug-in, to stop playing the midi file.

Listing 8.111 **Accessing an Embedded Object by the** embeds **Array**

```
<html>

<body>
<script "type="text/javascript" language="JavaScript">
<!--
// function stops the playing of the midi song.
function stopsong(){
    document.embeds[0].stop();
}
// -->
</script>

<embed src="phantom.mid" name="phantom" width="100" height="50"
➡ autostart="true">
<br>
<form>
Click on the stop button to stop playing the midi file.
<input type="button" value="stop" onCLick='stopsong()'>
</form>

</body>
</html>
```

Event

JavaScript 1.2+, JScript 1.0+
Nav4+, IE3+

Syntax

Core client-side JavaScript object.

Description

The Event object is a built-in object that handles the passing of properties to an event handler. The available properties are shown in Table 8.11.

Table 8.11 **Properties of the** Event *Object*

Type	Item	Description
Property	data	Array of URLs for dragged and dropped objects
	height	Height of the window
	layerX	Horizontal cursor position within a layer
	layerY	Vertical cursor position within a layer
	modifiers	Bit mask representing modifier keys
	pageX	Horizontal cursor position within a Web page
	pageY	Vertical cursor position within a Web page
	screenX	Horizontal cursor position within a computer screen
	screenY	Vertical cursor position within a computer screen
	target	Object for captured events
	type	Type of event
	which	The mouse button that is pressed
	width	Width of window
Method	unwatch()	Removes a watchpoint set in an event
	watch()	Adds a watchpoint to an event property

In addition to the Event properties, events exist that get handled. The available events are shown in Table 8.12.

Table 8.12 **Handled Events**

Events	Description
ABORT	Loading of Web page is interrupted by user.
BLUR	Focus is removed from the object.
CHANGE	Contents or setting for document object are changed.
CLICK	Mouse button is clicked once.
DBLCLICK	Mouse button is clicked twice.
DRAGDROP	Object is dragged and dropped.
ERROR	Error occurred during loading.
FOCUS	Focus is applied to an object.
KEYDOWN	A key is pressed down.

Events	Description
KEYPRESS	A key is pressed.
KEYUP	A key is released after being pressed down.
LOAD	Load the document within a browser.
MOUSEDOWN	The left mouse button is pressed down.
MOUSEMOVE	The mouse cursor is moved.
MOUSEOUT	The mouse cursor is moved away from a specific object.
MOUSEOVER	The mouse cursor is moved over a specific object.
MOUSEUP	The pressed mouse button is released.
MOVE	Object is moved on the screen.
RESET	Reset button is pressed.
RESIZE	Window or frame has been resized.
SELECT	Document object is selected.
SUBMIT	Submit button is pressed.
UNLOAD	Document is unloaded from the browser.

Example

Without using the Event properties, Event is used only as an argument to functions for event capturing. An example of this is shown in Listing 8.112. The example captures all KEYPRESS and DBLCLICK events for the Window object and captures SUBMIT events for the document. After the events are captured, they are passed to event handlers that perform specific functions on them. In two of the event handlers, event properties are returned.

Listing 8.112   Use of Event Keyword

```
<html>

<body>

<script type="text/javascript" language="JavaScript">
<!--

// Sets up the document to capture multiple events.
window.captureEvents(Event.KEYPRESS | Event.DBLCLICK);
document.captureEvents(Event.SUBMIT);

// Function handles the KEYPRESS event.
function handlePress(evnt){
    alert("You pressed a key down. The event it triggered was: " + evnt.type);
    return true;
}
```

Listing 8.112   Continued

```
// Function handles the DBLCLICK event.
function handleDblClick(evnt){
    alert("You double clicked at location: " + evnt.pageX + "," + evnt.pageY);
    return(true);
}


// Function handles the SUBMIT event.
function handleSubmit(evnt){
    alert("You clicked on the submit button");
}


// This registers the :
//      handlePress function as the event handler for the KEYPRESS event
//      handleDblClick as the event handler for the DBLCLICK event
//      handleSubmit as the event handler for the SUBMIT event
window.onKeyPress = handlePress;
window.onDblClick = handleDblClick;
document.onSubmit = handleSubmit;


// -->
</script>


This example shows a number of different things.
<br><br>
<ul>
<li>How to capture multiple events</li>
<li>How to process those events using the event handlers</li>
<li>How to access properties of the <b>event</b> object</li>
</ul>
<br><br><br>
When you click on the submit button, it triggers the <b>SUBMIT</b>
event which displays an alert box.
<br><br>
If you double click somewhere in the page, it triggers the
<b>DBLCLICK</b> event which displays an alert box showing the
coordinates of where you double clicked.
<br><br>
When a key is pressed down in the browser, the <b>KEYPRESS</b>
event is triggered and an alert box is displayed indicating the type of event.
<br><br><br>
<form>
<input type="submit" value="Submit" onSubmit=''>
</form>

</body>
</html>
```

event.data

JavaScript 1.2+
Nav4+

Syntax

`event.data`

Description

The `data` property of the `Event` object references an array of strings for events of objects that have been dragged and dropped. Each string in the array contains a URL representing the dropped object. The `data` property can be read-only if the script has the `UniversalBrowserRead` privilege.

Example

Listing 8.113 shows an example of how the `data` property can be used to determine the URL of objects that have been dragged and dropped. The example captures all `DRAGDROP` events and passes them to a function called `handleDragDrop()`. The function extracts the data property from the event and outputs it.

Listing 8.113   Accessing the `event.data` **Property**

```
<html>

<body>


<script type="text/javascript" language="JavaScript">
<!--
// Sets up the window to capture DRAGDROP events.
window.captureEvents(Event.DRAGDROP);

// function that handles the specific event. The evnt parameter refers to
// the event object.
function handleDragDrop(evnt){

   // Request the Universal Browser Read privilege.
  netscape.security.PrivilegeManager.enablePrivilege("UniversalBrowserRead");

   // Declare a temporary array to hold the URL data from the event.data
   // property.
   tmp = new Array();
   tmp = evnt.data;

   // Informs the user of the URL for the dragged and dropped object.
   alert("The URL for the dragdrop object is: " + tmp);
   return true;
}
```

Listing 8.113   Continued

```
// This registers the handleDragDrop function as the event handler for the
// DRAGDROP event.
window.onDragDrop = handleDragDrop;

// -->
</script>

This example requires the use of <b>UniversalBrowserRead</b> privilege.
<br><br>
Simply drag and drop an object, gif image, folder, file, etc. to the browser
and an alert box will appear indicating the URL path for the object.
</body>
</html>
```

event.height
JavaScript 1.2+
Nav4+

Syntax

event.height

Description

The height property of the Event object controls the height of a window or frame during the RESIZE event.

Example

Listing 8.114 shows how the height property can be accessed when an event such as RESIZE occurs. The RESIZE event means that the corresponding window or frame has changed size, thereby changing the height property.

Listing 8.114   Accessing event.height *Property*

```
<html>

<body>

<script type="text/javascript" language="JavaScript">
<!--
// Sets up the window to capture RESIZE events.
window.captureEvents(Event.RESIZE);

// function that changes the size of the window.
function changeSize(){
    window.resizeTo(300,400);
}
```

```
// function that handles the specific event. The evnt parameter refers to
// the event object.
function handle(evnt){
    alert("A RESIZE event has occurred. The new height of the window is: "
➡ + evnt.height);
    return true;
}

// This registers the handle function as the event handler for the
// RESIZE event.
window.onResize = handle;

// -->
</script>

<form name="form1">
Click button to change the window size:
<input type="button" value="Resize window" onClick = 'changeSize()'>
</form>
</body>
</html>
```

event.layerX

JavaScript 1.2+
Nav4+

Syntax

event.layerX

Description

The layerX property of the Event object controls the horizontal (x coordinate) positioning within the layer in which the event occurred.

Example

Listing 8.115 shows an example of a function that is listening for a RESIZE event. When one occurs, a variable stores the new x-coordinate position of the window in the layerX property. In the example, when the user resizes the window, an alert box appears informing her of the new X value.

Listing 8.115   Accessing the layerX *Property of the* event *Object*

```
<html>

<body>
<script type="text/javascript" language="JavaScript">
<!--
```

Listing 8.115   Continued

```
// Sets up the window to capture RESIZE events.
window.captureEvents(Event.RESIZE);

// function that changes the size of the window.
function changeSize(){
    window.resizeTo(300,400);
}

// function that handles the specific event. The evnt parameter refers to
// the event object.
function handle(evnt){
    alert("The new width (X value) after the resize is: " + evnt.layerX);
    return true;
}

// This registers the handle function as the event handler for the
// RESIZE event.
window.onResize = handle;
// -->
</script>

<form name="form1">
Click button to resize:
<input type="Button" value="Resize Window" onClick='changeSize()'>
</form>
</body>
</html>
```

event.layerY

> JavaScript 1.2+
>
> Nav4+

Syntax

event.layerY

Description

The layerY property of the Event object controls the vertical (y coordinate) position-ing within the layer in which the event occurred. When a window or frame is resized, the new value for the vertical coordinate is stored in the layerY property.

Example

Listing 8.116 shows an example of how the layerY property is used. When a RESIZE event occurs, it invokes the event handler that displays an alert box indicating the new Y value. The Y value is obtained from the layerY property of the event object.

Listing 8.116   Example of How to Change the `layerY` *Property*

```
<html>

<body>
<script type="text/javascript" language="JavaScript">
<!--

// Sets up the window to capture RESIZE events.
window.captureEvents(Event.RESIZE);

// function that changes the size of the window.
function changeSize(){
    window.resizeTo(200,350);
}

// function that handles the specific event. The evnt parameter refers to
// the event object.
function handle(evnt){
    alert("The new height (Y value) of the window object after the resize is: "
➡+
 evnt.layerY);
    return true;
}

// This registers the handle function as the event handler for the
// RESIZE event.
window.onResize = handle;
// -->
</script>

<form name="form1">
Click button to resize:

<input type="Button" value="Resize Window" onClick='changeSize()'>
</form>
</body>
</html>
```

event.modifiers

> JavaScript 1.2+
> Nav4+

Syntax

event.modifiers

Description

The `modifiers` property of the `Event` object refers to any keyboard modifier that occurs during an event. Modifiers are in the form of a bitmask object and might consist of the following values: `ALT_MASK`, `CONTROL_MASK`, `META_MASK`, and `SHIFT_MASK`.

Example

Listing 8.117 shows how the `modifiers` property can be accessed when some sort of modifier, such as a mouse or keyboard event, has occurred. The `KEYPRESS` event is captured and the `modifiers` property checked to see which type of key was pressed. If a match is found, a message is sent to the user so indicating.

Listing 8.117   Accessing the `modifiers` *Property*

```
<html>

<body>
<script type="text/javascript" language="JavaScript">
<!--
// Sets up the window to capture KEYPRESS events.
document.captureEvents(Event.KEYPRESS);

// function that handles the KEYPRESS event.
// It checks the event.modifiers property to see
// what button was pressed.
//
// The available values are:
//          META_MASK = 0
//          CONTROL_MASK = 2
//          ALT_MASK = 3
//          SHIFT_MASK = 4
function handlePress(evnt){

    if(evnt.modifiers == "0"){
        alert("The Meta key was pressed");
    }

    if(evnt.modifiers == "2"){
       alert("The Ctrl key was pressed");
    }

    if(evnt.modifiers == "4"){
       alert("The Shift key was pressed");
     }
    return true;
}
```

```
// This registers the handlePress function as the event handler for the
// KEYPRESS event.
document.onKeyPress = handlePress;
// -->
</script>
```

```
This example demonstrates the modifiers property of the event object.
<br><br>
The modifier checks for pressing of the <b>Meta</b> key.
<br><br>
If you press the "<b>Ctrl</b>" key the modifiers property indicates so.
<br><br>
By pressing the "<b>Shift</b>" key, you trigger an event which checks
for the SHIFT_MASK modifier.
<br><br>
</body>
</html>
```

To access a specific modifier value, simply reference it using the Event object. Listing 8.118 shows how to access the ALT_MASK modifier.

Listing 8.118   Accessing a Specific Modifier Value

```
Event.ALT_MASK
```

event.pageX

> JavaScript 1.2+
> Nav4+

Syntax

event.pageX

Description

The pageX property of the Event object controls the horizontal (x coordinate) positioning within a Web page in which the event occurred.

Example

Listing 8.119 shows an example of how you can find the x-coordinate positioning of where the click event occurred within the browser. Simply click in the browser window and an alert box will appear indicating the x-coordinate value of where the mouse was clicked.

Listing 8.119   *Example of Using the* pageX *Property*

```
<html>

<body>

<script type="text/javascript" language="JavaScript">
<!--

// Sets up the window to capture CLICK events.
window.captureEvents(Event.CLICK);

// function that handles the specific event. The evnt parameter refers to
// the event object.
function handle(evnt){
  alert("The X coordinate of where the click event occurred is: "
➥ + evnt.pageX);
    return true;
}

// This registers the handle function as the event handler for the
// CLICK event.
window.onClick = handle;

// -->
</script>

<form>
This example shows you how to access the <b>pageX</b>
property of the <i>event</i> object.  As you click in the
web browser, an alert box will pop up indicating the value of
the X-coordinate of where you clicked.
</form>

</body>
</html>
```

event.pageY

JavaScript 1.2+
Nav4+

Syntax

event.pageY

Description

The pageY propertyof the Event object controls the vertical (y coordinate) positioning within the Web page in which the event occurred.

Example

Listing 8.120 shows an example of how to determine the y-coordinate cursor positioning by using the pageY event property. The JavaScript code listens for a CLICK event to occur. When this happens, it calls the handle() function that is defined to handle any captured click events. The handle() function simply pops up an alert box indicating the y-coordinate value of where the click occurred.

Listing 8.120   Example of Using the pageY **Event Property**

```
<html>

<body>

<script type="text/javascript" language="JavaScript">
<!--

// Sets up the window to capture CLICK events.
window.captureEvents(Event.CLICK);

// function that handles the specific event. The evnt parameter refers to
// the event object.
function handle(evnt){
  alert("The Y coordinate of where the click event occurred is: "
➥+ evnt.pageY);
    return true;
}

// This registers the handle function as the event handler for the
// CLICK event.
window.onClick = handle;

// -->
</script>

This example shows you how to access the <b>pageY</b> property of the
<i>event</i> object.  As you click in the web browser, an alert box will
pop up indicating the value of the Y-coordinate of where you clicked.

</body>
</html>
```

event.screenX

JavaScript 1.2+, JScript 3.0+
Nav4+, IE4+

Syntax

event.screenX

Description

The screenX property of the event object controls the horizontal (x coordinate) positioning within the computer screen in which the event occurred.

Example

Listing 8.121 shows an example of how to determine the x coordinate of the cursor relative to the screen of where the click event occurred. The code captures the CLICK event. When captured, control is passed to the handle() function, which determines the x-coordinate position using the screenX property.

Listing 8.121   Using the screenX **Property**

```
<html>

<body>

<script type="text/javascript" language="JavaScript">
<!--

// Sets up the window to capture CLICK events.
window.captureEvents(Event.CLICK);

// function that handles the specific event. The evnt parameter refers to
// the event object.
function handle(evnt){
  alert("The X coordinate relative to the computer screen of where the
➡ click occurred is: " + evnt.screenX);
    return true;
}

// This registers the handle function as the event handler for the
// CLICK event.
window.onClick = handle;

// -->
</script>

This example shows you how to access the <b>screenX</b>
property of the <i>event</i> object.  As you click in
the web browser, an alert box will pop up indicating
the value of the X-coordinate (relative to the computer screen)
of where you clicked.

</body>
</html>
```

event.screenY

JavaScript 1.2+, JScript 3.0+
Nav4+, IE4+

Syntax

event.screenY

Description

The screenY property of the Event object controls the vertical (y coordinate) positioning within the computer screen in which the event occurred.

Example

Listing 8.122 shows an example of how to determine the y coordinate of the cursor
positioning relative to the computer screen when the CLICK event occurs. The code captures the CLICK event. When captured, control is passed to the handle() function,
which determines the y-coordinate position using the screenY property.

Listing 8.122   Accessing the** screenY **Property of the** Event **Object

```
<html>

<body>

<script type="text/javascript" language="JavaScript">
<!--

// sets up the window to capture CLICK events
window.captureEvents(Event.CLICK);

// function that handles the specific event. The evnt parameter refers to
// the event object.
function handle(evnt){
  alert("The Y coordinate relative to the computer screen of where the
➥ click occurred is: " + evnt.screenY);
    return true;
}

// This registers the handle function as the event handler for the
// CLICK event.
window.onClick = handle;

// -->
</script>

This example shows you how to access the <b>screenY</b>
property of the <i>event</i> object.  As you click in
the web browser, an alert box will pop up indicating
```

Listing 8.122   Continued

```
the value of the Y-coordinate (relative to the computer screen)
of where you clicked.
```

```
</body>
</html>
```

event.target

JavaScript 1.2+
Nav4+

Syntax

event.target

Description

The target property of the Event object refers to the object on which the event takes place.

Example

Listing 8.123 shows an example of how the target property can be used to determine to which object an event occurred. In the HTML document, there are three buttons. When the button is clicked, a JavaScript function catches the click event and, using the target property, tells the user which button was clicked.

Listing 8.123   Accessing the target Property

```html
<html>

<body>
<script type="text/javascript" language="JavaScript">
<!--
// Informs the user which mouse button was pressed.
function whichButton(evnt){
    window.captureEvents(evnt.CLICK);
    alert("The button you pressed was:" + evnt.target.value);
}
// -->
</script>

<form name="form1">
Choose a button and click on it.
<br><br>
<input type="button" value="Button1" name="Button1"
➥ onClick = whichButton(event)>
<input type="button" value="Button2" name="Button2"
➥ onClick = whichButton(event)>
```

```
<input type="button" value="Button3" name="Button3"
➥ onClick = whichButton(event)>
</form>

</body>
</html>
```

event.type

JavaScript 1.2+, JScript 3.0+
Nav4+, IE4+

Syntax

event.type

Description

The type property of the Event object refers to the type of event that occurred. The value assigned to type is a string representing the name of the event. See Table 8.12 for the valid event types.

Example

Listing 8.124 shows how the type property can be used to figure out what type of event is being set. This example checks for a few different events. When an event is detected, a message is displayed in the message box indicating to the user which type of event occurred. This example can be expanded to include many different events.

Listing 8.124   Accessing the type Property

```
<html>

<body>

<form>
<script type="text/javascript" language="JavaScript">
<!--

// Sets up the window to capture multiple events.
document.captureEvents(Event.CLICK|Event.KEYPRESS|Event.MOUSEDOWN);

// function that handles the specific event. The evnt parameter refers to
// the event object.
function handle(evnt){

//alert(evnt.type)
    if(evnt.type == "click"){
        document.form1.msg.value += "The click event occurred.\n"
    }
```

Listing 8.124   Continued

```
    if(evnt.type == "mousedown"){
        document.form1.msg.value += "The mousedown event occurred.\n"
    }

    if(evnt.type == "keypress"){
        document.form1.msg.value += "The keypress event occurred.\n"
    }

    return true;
}

// This registers the handle function as the event handler for the
// multiple events.
document.onKeyPress = handle;
document.onClick = handle;
document.onMouseDown = handle;


// -->
</script>

<form name="form1">
This page demonstrates a few different events. Upon events occurring,
a message will be displayed in the textarea indicating which event occurred.
<br><br><br>
<ul>
<li><input type="Button" value="Click Me"></li>
<br><br>
<li>
Dummy text area.
<input type="text" size="20">
<br>
Click mouse in text field.
<br><br>
</li>

<br><br>
<b>Message output:</b>
<textarea name="msg" rows="10" cols="60"></textarea>
<br><br>
<input type="reset" value="Clear">
</form>

</body>
</html>
```

event.unwatch()

JavaScript 1.2+
Nav4+

Syntax

event.unwatch(*prop*)

Description

The unwatch() method of the Event object is used to remove a watchpoint set on a property by the unwatch() method. It takes one parameter, *prop*, which is the property to unwatch.

Example

Listing 8.125 shows how the unwatch() method is used to turn off the watchpoint set on the height property of the event object. When the resize button is clicked, the RESIZE event is captured. The event handler then alerts the user that the window size has changed and sets the watchpoint. A new value is then assigned to the height property, the watchpoint removed, and the result is displayed in the browser.

Listing 8.125   *Using the* unwatch() *Method*

```
<html>
<body>

<script type="text/javascript" language="JavaScript">
<!--
// Sets up the window to capture RESIZE events.
window.captureEvents(Event.RESIZE);

// function that changes the size of the window.
function changeSize(){
    window.resizeTo(300,400);
}


function alertme(id,oldValue,newValue)
{
   document.writeln(id + " changed from " + "<b>" + oldValue + "</b>"
➥ + " to " + "<b>" + newValue + "</b><br>")
   return newValue;
}


// function that handles the specific event. The evnt parameter refers to
// the event object.
function handle(evnt){
    alert("A RESIZE event has occurred. The new height of the window is: "
➥ + evnt.height);
```

Listing 8.125   Continued

```
function setWatch(){
   myProp = evnt.height;
   watch("myProp",alertme);
   myProp = 200;
   unwatch("myProp");
   myProp = 100;
   }

   setWatch();
   return true;
}

// This registers the handle function as the event handler for the
// RESIZE event.
window.onResize = handle;

// -->
</script>

<form name="form1">
Click button to change the window size:
<input type="button" value="Resize window" onClick = 'changeSize()'>
</form>
</body>
</html>
```

event.watch()

JavaScript 1.2+
Nav4+

Syntax

event.watch(*prop,handler*)

Description

The watch() method of the Event object is used to watch for changes to Event properties. When one of the properties, *prop,* is assigned a value, a *handler* is used to call a
user-defined function.

Example

Listing 8.126 shows how the watch() method is used to see when the height property
of the event object has changed. When the resize button is clicked, the RESIZE event
is captured. The event handler then alerts the user that the window size has changed
and sets the watchpoint. A new value is then assigned to the height property and then
is displayed in the browser.

Listing 8.126 Using the `watch()` *Method of the Event*

```
<html>
<script type="text/javascript" language="JavaScript">
<!--
// Sets up the window to capture RESIZE events.
window.captureEvents(Event.RESIZE);

// function that changes the size of the window.
function changeSize(){
    window.resizeTo(300,400);
}

function alertme(id,oldValue,newValue)
{
   document.writeln(id + " changed from " + "<b>" +
➥oldValue + "</b>"+ " to " + "<b>" + newValue + "</b><br>")
   return newValue;
}


// function that handles the specific event. The evnt parameter refers to
// the event object.
function handle(evnt){
  alert("A RESIZE event has occurred. The new height of the window is: "
➥ + evnt.height);

   function setWatch(){
     myProp = evnt.height;
     watch("myProp",alertme);
     myProp = 200;
    }

     setWatch();
    return true;
}

// This registers the handle function as the event handler for the
// RESIZE event.
window.onResize = handle;

// -->
</script>

<form name="form1">
Click button to change the window size:
<input type="button" value="Resize window" onClick = 'changeSize()'>
</form>
</body>
</html>
```

event.which

JavaScript 1.2+
Nav4+

Syntax

event.which

Description

The which property of the Event object refers to which key or mouse button was pressed or clicked. The value returned for mouse events is a numeric value 1, 2, or 3, representing the left, middle, and right mouse buttons, respectively. The value returned for keyboard events is a character representation for the key that was pressed.

Example

Listing 8.127 shows how the which property can be used to determine which mouse button was pressed. When the user clicks the radio button, an alert box is shown informing her of the corresponding number for the mouse button clicked.

Listing 8.127 *Accessing the* which *Property of the* Event *Object*

```
<html>

<body>

<form>
This example uses the which property of the event object to determine
which mouse button is pressed.
<br><br>
<input type="radio" onClick = 'alert("Mouse button Number " + event.which
➥ + "was pressed.")'>
</form>

</body>
</html>
```

event.width

JavaScript 1.2+
Nav4+

Syntax

event.width

Description

The width property of the Event object refers to the width of a window or frame. It is set during the RESIZE event to the new width of the window or frame being resized.

Example

Listing 8.128 shows an example using the width property. The RESIZE event is captured and passed to the handle() function. This function informs the user that a RESIZE event has occurred and outputs the new width of the window.

Listing 8.128   Accessing the width Property

```
<html>

<body>

<script type="text/javascript" language="JavaScript">
<!--

// Sets up the window to capture RESIZE events.
window.captureEvents(Event.RESIZE);

// function that changes the size of the window.
function changeSize(){
    window.resizeTo(300,400);
}

// function that handles the specific event. The evnt parameter refers to
// the event object.
function handle(evnt){
    alert("A RESIZE event has occurred. The new width of the window is: "
➥ + evnt.height);
    return true;
}

// This registers the handle function as the event handler for the
// RESIZE event.
window.onResize = handle;

// -->
</script>

<form name="form1">

Click the button to resize the window:
<input type="Button" value="Resize">
</form>

</body>
</html>
```

Event.ABORT

JavaScript 1.0+, JScript 1.0+
Nav2+, IE3+, Opera3+

Syntax

Event.ABORT

Description

The ABORT property of the Event object is used by images and refers to the event in which a transfer is interrupted or aborted by a user.

Example

Listing 8.129 shows an example in which an HTML document might have a large .gif file embedded within it, but, during the document loading process, the loading of the .gif file is aborted (by clicking the Stop button in the browser). The captureEvents() method catches the ABORT event and passes it to the handleAbort() method, which handles it accordingly.

Listing 8.129   Using the ABORT Event Property

```
<html>

<body>
<script type="text/javascript" language="JavaScript">
<!--

// Sets up the window to capture ABORT events.
document.captureEvents(Event.ABORT);

// function that handles the specific event. The evnt parameter refers to
// the event object. In this case the function is handling any type of
// ABORT events.
function handleAbort(evnt){
    alert("An ABORT event has occurred.");
    return true;
}

// This registers the handle function as the event handler for the
// ABORT event.
document.onAbort = handleAbort;
// -->
</script>

This page loads the sample.gif image. Assuming this is a large image
and takes some time to load, if the user clicks the stop button on
the browser, an <b>abort</b> event will be captured.
<br><br><br>
```

```
<img src="sample.gif" width="350" height="500" onAbort=''>

</body>
</html>
```

Event.BLUR

JavaScript 1.0+, JScript 1.0+
Nav2+, IE3+, Opera3+

Syntax

```
Event.BLUR
```

Description

The BLUR property of the Event object is used by all windows, frames, and form elements when focus is removed from a particular object.

Example

Listing 8.130 shows an example in which the user wants to be alerted when the focus had been removed from the text area. A function is created to capture the BLUR event that occurs when focus is removed from an object. When the event is captured, the handlerBlur() function alerts the user of the event.

Listing 8.130 *Using the BLUR Event Property*

```
<html>

<body>

<script type="text/javascript" language="JavaScript">
<!--

// Sets up the window to capture BLUR events.
document.captureEvents(Event.BLUR);

// function that handles the specific event. The evnt parameter refers to
// the event object.
function handleBlur(evnt){
    document.form1.msg.value += "A BLUR event has occurred.\n";
    return true;
}

// This registers the handle function as the event handler for the
// BLUR event.
document.onBlur = handleBlur;
```

Listing 8.130 Continued

```
// -->
</script>

<form>
Set focus to the first text box. Then click in the second
text box to remove focus from text 1.
<br><br>
Text 1:<input type="text" size="20" onBlur=''>
<br><br>
Text 2:<input type="text" size="20">
<br><br>
<b>Message box:</b>
<textarea name="msg" rows="5" cols="50"></textarea>
</form>

</body>
</html>
```

Event.CHANGE

JavaScript 1.0+, JScript 1.0+
Nav2+, IE3+, Opera3+

Syntax

`Event.CHANGE`

Description

The CHANGE property of the Event object is used by any text-related and select-box form elements to indicate a change in the element settings.

Example

Listing 8.131 shows an example of a function checking for any occurrences of the CHANGE event. When a CHANGE event occurs, it is captured by the Document object and then passed to the handleChange() function, which alerts the user.

Listing 8.131 Accessing the CHANGE Property

```
<html>

<body>

<script type="text/javascript" language="JavaScript">
<!--

// Sets up the window to capture CHANGE event.
document.captureEvents(Event.CHANGE);
```

```
// function that handles the specific event. The evnt parameter
// refers to the event object.
function handleChange(evnt){
    alert("The text in TextBox1 has been changed");
    return true;
}

// This registers the handle function as the event handler for the
// CHANGE event.
document.onChange = handleChange;

// -->
</script>
```

This example demonstrates the change event. Initially TextBox1
is empty, however when you enter information into the textbox,
the CHANGE event occurs. This triggers an alert box to open
up informing you that the text in box 1 has been changed.
```
<br><br>
<form name="form1">
TextBox1:
<input type="text" size="20" name="text1" onChange=''>
<br><br>
TextBox2:
<input type="text" size="20" name="text2">
</form>
</body>
</html>
```

Event.CLICK

JavaScript 1.0+
Nav2+, Opera3+

Syntax

Event.CLICK

Description

The CLICK property of the Event object is used by all button objects, documents, and
links to indicate a single mouse button click.

Example

Listing 8.132 shows how the CLICK property is used to determine whether the mouse
was clicked or not. When you click the browser window, the captureEvents() method
captures the CLICK event. The event handler then alerts you that a click has been performed.

Listing 8.132 Accessing the CLICK *Property*

```
<html>

<body>
<script type="text/javascript" language="JavaScript">
<!--

// Sets up the window to capture CLICK events.
window.captureEvents(Event.CLICK);

// function that handles the specific event. The evnt parameter refers to
// the event object.
function handleClick(evnt){
    alert("A CLICK event has occurred in this window.");
    return true;
}

// This registers the handleClick function as the event handler for the
// CLICK event.
window.onClick = handleClick;

// -->
</script>

<form>
<input type="button" value="Click Here" onClick = 'handleClick(event)'>
</form>

</body>
</html>
```

Event.DBLCLICK

JavaScript 1.2+, JScript 3.0+
Nav4+, IE4+

Syntax

```
Event.DBLCLICK
```

Description

The DBLCLICK property of the Event object is used by documents and links to indicate a double mouse click.

Example

Listing 8.133 shows an example of the onDblClick event handler being used to handle the DBLCLICK event. When the user double-clicks the button or anywhere in the window, an alert box appears indicating that she double-clicked.

Listing 8.133   Accessing the DBLCLICK **event**

```
<html>

<body>


<script type="text/javascript" language="JavaScript">
<!--

// Sets up the window to capture DBLCLICK events.
window.captureEvents(Event.DBLCLICK);

// function that handles the specific event. The evnt parameter refers to
// the event object.
function handle(evnt){
    alert("A DBLCLICK event has occurred in this window.");
    return true;
}

// This registers the handle function as the event handler for the
// DBLCLICK event.
window.onDblClick = handle;

// -->
</script>

This example demonstrates the double-click event. Double-click
anywhere in the browser window and an alert box will appear
indicating that a <b>DBLCLICK</b> event has been captured.
<br><br>

<form>
<input type="button" value="Double-click me" onDblClick=''>
</form>
</body>
</html>
```

Event.DRAGDROP

JavaScript 1.2+
Nav4+

Syntax

Event.DRAGDROP

Description

The DRAGDROP property of the Event object is used by the window to indicate the
event in which an object has been dragged and dropped.

Example

Listing 8.134 shows the how the DRAGDROP event is used to check for any object that has been dragged and dropped into the browser window. If this occurs, an alert box is shown indicating that the DRAGDROP event has occurred.

Listing 8.134   Using the DragDrop *Event Handler*

```
<html>

<body>

<script type="text/javascript" language="JavaScript">
<!--

// Sets up the window to capture DRAGDROP events.
window.captureEvents(Event.DRAGDROP);

// function that handles the specific event. The evnt parameter refers to
// the event object.
function handleDragDrop(evnt){
    alert("An object has been dragged and dropped.");
    return true;
}

// This registers the handle function as the event handler for the
// DRAGDROP event.
window.onDragDrop = handleDragDrop;

// -->
</script>

This example demonstrates the dragdrop event. Drag and drop an
object in the browser window and an alert box will appear
indicating that a <b>DRAGDROP</b> event has occurred.
<br><br>

</body>
</html>
```

Event.ERROR

JavaScript 1.1+, JScript 3.0+
Nav3+, IE4+, Opera3+

Syntax

```
Event.ERROR
```

Description

The ERROR property of the Event object is used by windows and images to indicate any errors that occurred during the loading of the Web page.

Example

Listing 8.135 shows an example of how ERROR events can be handled. When an ERROR event is captured, it is passed to the handle() function, which informs the user of the error.

Listing 8.135   Accessing the ERROR Property

```
<html>

<body>

<script type="text/javascript" language="JavaScript">
<!--

// Sets up the window to capture ERROR event.
window.captureEvents(Event.ERROR);

// function that handles the specific event. The evnt parameter refers to
// the event object.
function handle(evnt){
    alert("ERROR: The image was unable to be loaded.");
    return true;
}

// This registers the handle function as the event handler for the
// ERROR event.
window.onerror = handle;
// -->
</script>

This page only contains a gif image. However since this gif doesn't
exist there will be an error loading the page. This error event will
be captured and alerted to the user.
<br><br>
<img src="nothing.gif" onerror=''>

</body>
</html>
```

Event.FOCUS

JavaScript 1.0+, JScript 1.0+
Nav2+, IE3+, Opera3+

Syntax

```
Event.FOCUS
```

Description

The FOCUS property of the Event object is used by windows, frames, and form elements to indicate when focus is applied to an object.

Example

Listing 8.136 shows an example of how the FOCUS property is used to determine when focus is set on a certain object. As you click each object, a message is displayed in the message box indicating which object has focus. The onFocus event handler handles all Event.FOCUS events by default.

Listing 8.136 *Accessing the* FOCUS *Property*

```
<html>

<body>
<script type="text/javascript" language="JavaScript">
<!--

function showMsg1(){
   document.form1.msg.value += "Focus set on Text 1.\n";
}

function showMsg2(){
   document.form1.msg.value += "Focus set on Text 2.\n";
}

function showMsg3(){
   document.form1.msg.value += "Focus set on Button 1.\n";
}

function showMsg4(){
   document.form1.msg.value += "Focus set on the Message Box.\n";
}
// -->
</script>

<form name="form1">
Set focus to an object.
<br><br>
Text 1:<input type="text" size="20" onFocus='showMsg1()'>
<br><br>
```

```
Text 2:<input type="text" size="20" onFocus='showMsg2()'>
<br><br>
Button 1:<input type="button" value="Click Me" onfocus='showMsg3()'>
<br><br>
<b>Message box:</b>
<textarea name="msg" rows="5" cols="50" onfocus='showMsg4()'></textarea>
</form>

</body>
</html>
```

Event.KEYDOWN

JavaScript 1.2+
Nav4+

Syntax

```
Event.KEYDOWN
```

Description

The KEYDOWN property of the Event object is used by documents, images, links, and text area form elements to indicate when a key is pressed by the user.

Example

Listing 8.137 shows an example of how a JavaScript function can use the KEYDOWN event to determine if a key was pressed down. When the KEYDOWN event is captured, the handle() function processes the event and informs the user that a key has been pressed down.

Listing 8.137 *Accessing the* KEYDOWN *Property*

```
<html>

<body>
<script type="text/javascript" language="JavaScript">
<!--

// Sets up the window to capture KEYDOWN events.
window.captureEvents(Event.KEYDOWN);

// function that handles the specific event. The evnt parameter refers to
// the event object.
function handle(evnt){
    document.form1.msg.value += " A key was pressed down.\n";
    return true;
}
```

Listing 8.137   Continued

```
// This registers the handle function as the event handler for the
// KEYPRESS event.
window.onKeyDown = handle;
// -->
</script>
<form name="form1">

Press a key down. When a key is pressed down, a message is displayed
in the message box indicating that the <b>KEYDOWN</b> event has occurred.
<br><br>
<b>Message box:</b>
<textarea name="msg" rows="5" cols="50"></textarea>
<br><br>
<input type="reset" value="Clear Message Box">
</form>

</body>
</html>
```

Event.KEYPRESS

JavaScript 1.2+
Nav4+

Syntax

```
Event.KEYPRESS
```

Description

The KEYPRESS property of the Event object is used by documents, images, links, and text area form elements to indicate when a key is pressed and held by the user.

Example

Listing 8.138 shows how the KEYPRESS property is used to determine when a key has been pressed. When the KEYPRESS event is captured, it is sent to the handle() function, which informs the user that a key has been pressed.

Listing 8.138   Accessing the KEYPRESS Object

```
<html>

<body>
<script type="text/javascript" language="JavaScript">
<!--

// Sets up the window to capture KEYPRESS events.
window.captureEvents(Event.KEYPRESS);
```

```
// function that handles the specific event. The evnt parameter refers to
// the event object.
function handle(evnt){
    document.form1.msg.value += " A key was pressed.\n";
    return true;
}

// This registers the handle function as the event handler for the
// KEYPRESS event.
window.onKeyPress = handle;
// -->
</script>

<form name="form1">
Press a key. When a key is pressed, a message is displayed in the message box
indicating that a key has been pressed.
<br><br>
<b>Message box:</b>
<textarea name="msg" rows="5" cols="50"></textarea>
</form>

</body>
</html>
```

Event.KEYUP

JavaScript 1.2+
Nav4+

Syntax

```
Event.KEYUP
```

Description

The KEYUP property of the Event object is used by documents, images, links, and text area form elements to indicate when a pressed key is released by the user.

Example

Listing 8.139 shows how to determine when a key has been released. The KEYUP event is captured. When this occurs, the handle() function is invoked, informing the user that a key which had been pressed down has been released.

Listing 8.139   Accessing the KEYUP Property

```
<html>

<body>
<script type="text/javascript" language="JavaScript">
```

Listing 8.139   Continued

```
<!--

// Sets up the window to capture KEYUP events.
window.captureEvents(Event.KEYUP);

// function that handles the specific event. The evnt parameter refers to
// the event object.
function handle(evnt){
    document.form1.msg.value += " A key was pressed down and let up.\n";
    return true;
}

// This registers the handle function as the event handler for the
// KEYPRESS event.
window.onKeyUp = handle;
// -->
</script>

<form name="form1">

Press a key down. When a key is pressed down and let back up, a message is
displayed in the message box indicating that the <b>KEYUP</b> event has
occurred.If you press a key down and hold it down, no message displayed.
Only when the key
is let back up is a message displayed.
<br><br>
<b>Message box:</b>
<textarea name="msg" rows="5" cols="50"></textarea>
<br><br>
<input type="reset" value="Clear Message Box">
</form>

</body>
</html>
```

Event.LOAD

JavaScript 1.0+, JScript 1.0+
Nav2+, IE3+

Syntax

```
Event.LOAD
```

Description

The LOAD property of the Event object is used by the Document object to indicate when
a page is loaded by the browser.

Example

Listing 8.140 shows an example of how to inform the user when a Web page has loaded. The LOAD event is captured. When this occurs, the handle() function is invoked, which informs the user that the page has finished being loaded.

Listing 8.140 *Example of Using the* LOAD *Event Property*

```
<html>

<body>
<script type="text/javascript" language="JavaScript">
// Sets up the window to capture LOAD events.
window.captureEvents(Event.LOAD);

// function that handles the specific event. The evnt parameter refers to
// the event object.
function handle(evnt){
    alert("The page is finished being loaded.");
    return true;
}

// This registers the handle function as the event handler for the
// LOAD event.
window.onload = handle;

// -->
</script>

This page only contains a gif image. When the page is finished loading,
a message is displayed indicating so.
<br><br>
<img src="mypic.gif" onload=''>
</body>
</html>
```

Event.MOUSEDOWN

JavaScript 1.2+, JScript 3.0+
Nav4+, IE4+

Syntax

```
Event.MOUSEDOWN
```

Description

The MOUSEDOWN property of the Event object is used by button objects, documents, and links to indicate when the mouse button is pressed by the user.

Example

Listing 8.141 shows how to use the MOUSEDOWN property to determine when the mouse has been pressed down. The onMouseDown event handler is used to catch the MOUSEDOWN event. When it is caught, an alert box is used to inform the user that the event has just occurred.

Listing 8.141   Accessing the MOUSEDOWN *Property*

```
<html>

<body>

<script type="text/javascript" language="JavaScript">
<!--

// Sets up the window to capture MOUSEDOWN events.
window.captureEvents(Event.MOUSEDOWN);

// function that handles the specific event. The evnt parameter refers to
// the event object.
function handle(evnt){
    alert("The mouse button has been pressed down.");
    return true;
}

// This registers the handle function as the event handler for the
// MOUSEDOWN event.
window.onMouseDown = handle;

// -->
</script>

This example uses the <b>MOUSEDOWN</b> event. When the mouse button
is pressed down, an alert box is shown.

</body>
</html>
```

Event.MOUSEMOVE

JavaScript 1.2+, JScript 3.0+
Nav4+, IE4+

Syntax

```
Event.MOUSEMOVE
```

Description

The MOUSEMOVE property of the Event object indicates when the mouse cursor is moved by the user.

Example

Listing 8.142 shows how the MOUSEMOVE event is used to determine when the user is moving the mouse. As the mouse cursor is moved, the coordinates are displayed in the text boxes.

Listing 8.142   Accessing the MOUSEMOVE *Property*

```
<html>

<body>
<script type="text/javascript" language="JavaScript">
<!--

// Sets up the window to capture MOUSEMOVE events.
window.captureEvents(Event.MOUSEMOVE);

// function that handles the specific event. The evnt parameter refers to
// the event object. The function sets the x and y coordinates into the text
// areas.
function handle(evnt){
    document.form1.x.value=evnt.pageX;
    document.form1.y.value=evnt.pageY;
    return true;
}

// This registers the handle function as the event handler for the
// MOUSEMOVE event.
window.onMouseMove = handle;
// -->
</script>

<form name="form1">
This example uses the <b>MOUSEMOVE</b> event. When the mouse is moved,
then the coordinates are changed.
<br><br>
Mouse x-Coordinate value:<input type="text" name="x" size="3"><br><br>
Mouse y-Coordinate value:<input type="text" name="y" size="3">
</form>
</body>
</html>
```

Event.MOUSEOUT

JavaScript 1.1+, JScript 3.0+
Nav3+, IE4+, Opera3+

Syntax

```
Event.MOUSEOUT
```

Description

The MOUSEOUT property of the Event object is used by links and document layers to indicate when the focus of the mouse cursor is moved away from an object.

Example

Listing 8.143 shows how the onMouseOut event handler is used to catch the MOUSEOUT event that occurs when the mouse cursor is removed from a HTML link.

Listing 8.143   Using the MOUSEOUT *Property*

```
<html>

<body>

<a href="http://www.microsoft.com" onMouseout = 'alert("The mouse has moved
➥ out of the area of this link")'>
Microsoft Website</a>

</body>
</html>
```

Event.MOUSEOVER
JavaScript 1.0+, JScript 1.0+
Nav2+, IE3+, Opera3+

Syntax

property of the Event object is used by links and document layers to indicate when the mouse cursor is moved over an object.

Example

Listing 8.144 shows an example of how the MOUSEOVER event property can be used to modify form element values. As the user moves the mouse cursor over the link, the MOUSEOVER event is captured and the user is alerted.

Listing 8.144   Accessing the MOUSEOVER *Property*

```
<html>


<body>

<script type="text/javascript" language="JavaScript">
<!--

// Sets up the window to capture MOUSEOVER events.
window.captureEvents(Event.MOUSEOVER);
```

```
// function that handles the specific event. The evnt parameter refers to
// the event object.
function handle(evnt){
    alert("Your mouse cursor is over the Netscape link.");
    return true;
}

// This registers the handle function as the event handler for the
// MOUSEOVER event.
window.onMouseOver = handle;

// -->
</script>

<form name="form1">
Move the mouse cursor over the link to Netscape. When you do,
it will trigger a <b>MOUSEOVER</b> event which is captured.
An alert box will then appear indicating that the mouse cursor
is over the link.
<br><br><br>
<a href="http://www.netscape.com" onMouseOver = ''>
Link to Netscape Website</a>
<br>
<br><br><br></form>

</body>
</html>
```

Event.MOUSEUP

JavaScript 1.2+, JScript 3.0+
Nav4+, IE4+

Syntax

```
Event.MOUSEUP
```

Description

The MOUSEUP property of the Event object is used by button objects, documents, and links to indicate when a mouse button is released.

Example

Listing 8.145 shows how the onMouseUp event handler is used to determine when the mouse button is released after being pressed. The user clicks the button and, when the mouse button is released, a message is displayed indicating the action.

Listing 8.145   Accessing the MOUSEUP *Property*

```
<html>

<body>

<form>
This example demonstrates the MOUSEUP event. When you click the
button and let the mouse up, an alert message is

displayed indicating that the event occurred.
<input type="button" value="Click Me"
➡onMouseup = 'alert("The Mouse button was let up")'>
</form>

</body>
</html>
```

Event.MOVE

JavaScript 1.2+
Nav4+

Syntax

```
Event.MOVE
```

Description

The MOVE property of the Event object is used by windows and frames to indicate when movement by the window or frame occurs.

Example

Listing 8.146 shows the syntax for accessing the MOVE property. When you begin to move the browser window, the MOVE event will be captured, and the coordinates for the upper-left of the window will be displayed.

Listing 8.146   Accessing the MOVE *Property*

```
<html>

<body>

<script type="text/javascript" language="JavaScript">
<!--

// Sets up the window to capture MOVE events.
window.captureEvents(Event.MOVE);

// function that handles the specific event. The evnt parameter refers to
// the event object. The function sets the x and y coordinates into the text
// areas.
```

```
function handleMove(evnt){
    document.form1.msg.value="The window has been moved to coordinates: "
➡ + evnt.screenX + "," + screenY;
    document.form1.x.value=evnt.screenX;
    document.form1.y.value=evnt.screenY;
    return true;
}


// This registers the handleMove function as the event handler for the
// MOVE event.
window.onMove = handleMove;

// -->
</script>

<form name="form1">
This example uses the <b>MOVE</b> event. When the browser window is moved,
then the coordinates are displayed and updated in the field.
<br><br>
Upper-Left Corner X-Coordinate value:
<input type="text" name="x" size="3"><br><br>
Upper-Left Corner Y-Coordinate value:
<input type="text" name="y" size="3">
<br><br><br>
Message Box:
<br>
<textarea name="msg" rows="3" cols="60"></textarea>
<br>
<input type="reset" value="Clear">
</form>

</body>
</html>
```

Event.RESET

JavaScript 1.1+, JScript 1.0+
Nav3+, IE3+, Opera3+

Syntax

```
Event.RESET
```

Description

The RESET property of the Event object is used solely by forms to indicate when the
Reset button is clicked.

Example

Listing 8.147 shows an example of how to determine if a Reset button has been pressed. When the RESET event is captured, the function handle() alerts the user that the button has been clicked.

Listing 8.147   Accessing the RESET Property

```
<html>

<body>
<script type="text/javascript" language="JavaScript">
<!--

// Sets up the window to capture RESET events.
window.captureEvents(Event.RESET);

// function that handles the specific event. The evnt parameter refers to
// the event object.
function handle(evnt){
    alert("You have clicked the Reset button");
    return true;
}

// This registers the handle function as the event handler for the
// RESET event.
window.onReset = handle;
// -->
</script>

This example demonstrates the <b>Reset</b> event.
➥Click the different buttons below. Only the Reset
➥button will trigger the submit event.
<br><br>
<form>
<br><br>
Dummy Text:<input type="text" size="20">
<br><br>
<input type="button" value="Click Button 1">
<br><br>
<input type="button" value="Click Button 2">
<br><br>
<input type="reset" value="Reset" onReset=''>
</form>
</body>
</html>
```

Event.RESIZE

JavaScript 1.2+, JScript 3.0+
Nav4+, IE4+

Syntax

```
Event.RESIZE
```

Description

The RESIZE property of the Event object is used by windows and frames to indicate the event of resizing the window or frame.

Example

Listing 8.148 shows how to determine when the window has been resized using the RESIZE event. When the RESIZE event is captured, the handle() function outputs the height and width properties of the window.

Listing 8.148   Using the RESIZE **Property**

```
<html>

<body>
<script type="text/javascript" language="JavaScript">
<!--

// Sets up the window to capture RESIZE events.
window.captureEvents(Event.RESIZE);

// function that handles the specific event. The evnt parameter refers to
// the event object.
function handle(evnt){
    alert("You have resized the window to: " + evnt.height + "x" + evnt.width);
    return true;
}

// This registers the handle function as the event handler for the
// RESIZE event.
window.onResize = handle;
// -->
</script>

<form name="form1">
Click button to resize:
<input type="Button" value="Resize" onClick=window.resizeTo(250,400)>
</form>

</body>
</html>
```

Event.SELECT

JavaScript 1.0+
Nav2+, Opera3+

Syntax

```
Event.SELECT
```

Description

The SELECT property of the Event object is used by text objects and select-box form elements to indicate when an element is selected by the user.

Example

Listing 8.149 shows how the SELECT event can be used to determine which form object has been selected. When some text in the textarea is selected, the SELECT event is invoked. The document will then capture the event and call the handleSelect() function, which informs the user that the SELECT event occurred.

Listing 8.149   Using the SELECT Property

```
<html>

<body>
<script type="text/javascript" language="JavaScript">
<!--

// Sets up the window to capture SELECT events.
document.captureEvents(Event.SELECT);

// Handles the SELECT event.
function handleSelect(evnt){

     alert("You have selected some text in the textarea");
}

// This registers the handle function as the event handler for the
// SELECT event.
document.onSelect = handleSelect;

// -->
</script>

<form name="form1">
Message:
<input type="text" size="25" name="txtbox" value="" onSelect=''>
<br><br><br>
Display text:<br>
<textarea name="msg" rows="5" cols="60" onSelect=''>
```

```
In this example we check for the SELECT event to
occur. This occurs when some text in a textarea or
textbox is selected. To see this, select some text
in this paragraph and an alert box will pop up
indicating that the select event has occurred.
</textarea>
<br><br>
</form>

</body>
</html>
```

Event.SUBMIT

JavaScript 1.0+, JScript 1.0+
Nav2+, IE3+, Opera3+

Syntax

```
Event.SUBMIT
```

Description

The SUBMIT property of the Event object is used solely by forms to indicate the clicking of the Submit button.

Example

Listing 8.150 shows an example of how JavaScript can be used to process a form when the Submit button is clicked. The Window listens for the SUBMIT event. When captured, it will call the handle() function. This function informs the user that the Submit button was clicked.

Listing 8.150   Example of Using the SUBMIT Property

```
<html>

<body>
<script type="text/javascript" language="JavaScript">
<!--

// Sets up the window to capture SUBMIT events.
window.captureEvents(Event.SUBMIT);

// function that handles the specific event. The evnt parameter refers to
// the event object.
function handle(evnt){
    alert("You have clicked the Submit button");
    return true;
}
```

Listing 8.150   Continued

```
// This registers the handle function as the event handler for the
// SUBMIT event.
window.onSubmit = handle;
// -->
</script>

This example demonstrates the submit event. Click the different buttons below.
Only the Submit button will trigger the submit event.
<br><br>
<form>
<input type="button" value="Click Me">
<br><br>
<input type="Submit" value="Submit" onsubmit=''>
<br><br>
<input type="button" value="Click on Me too">
</form>
</body>
</html>
```

Event.UNLOAD

JavaScript 1.0+, JScript 1.0+
Nav2+, IE3+, Opera3+

Syntax

```
Event.UNLOAD
```

Description

The UNLOAD property of the Event object is used by documents to indicate when a new document is loaded in a browser or when the browser window is closed.

Example

Listing 8.151 shows how the UNLOAD property can be used to find out when a browser has finished unloading a Web page. When the UNLOAD event has been captured, the handle() function is called, which informs the user that the page has been unloaded.

Listing 8.151   Accessing the UNLOAD Property

```
<html>

<body>
<script type="text/javascript" language="JavaScript">
<!--

// Sets up the window to capture UNLOAD events.
window.captureEvents(Event.UNLOAD);
```

```
// function that handles the specific event. The evnt parameter refers to
// the event object.
function handle(evnt){
    alert("The page has been unloaded.");
    return true;
}

// This registers the handle function as the event handler for the
// LOAD event.
window.onunload = handle;

// -->
</script>
```

This page only contains a gif image. When it is unloaded, an alert
message is displayed indicating so.<i> (To unload the page, simply l
oad another page or click on the browser back button.)</i>
```
<br><br>
<img src="star.gif" onunload=' '>

</body>
</html>
```

FileUpload
JavaScript 1.0+, JScript 3.0+
Nav2+, IE4+, Opera3+

Syntax
Core client-side JavaScript object.

Description
The FileUpload object represents a file upload box within an HTML form. An upload box is created by using the HTML <input> tag and specifying the type attribute as file. The FileUpload object has specific properties and methods associated with it, which are shown in Table 8.13.

Table 8.13 Properties and Methods of the FileUpload object

Type	Item	Description
Property	form	Reference form object containing the FileUpload box
	name	HTML name attribute for the FileUpload box
	onBlur	Event handler for the Blur event
	onChange	Event handler for the Change event
	onFocus	Event handler for the Focus event

Table 8.13   *Continued*

Type	Item	Description
	`type`	The HTML `type` attribute for the `FileUpload` box
	`value`	String specifying the pathname of a selected file
Method	`blur()`	Removes focus from the `FileUpload` box
	`focus()`	Sets focus on the `FileUpload` box
	`handleEvent()`	Handles specific event
	`select()`	Selects input area for the `FileUpload` box
	`unwatch()`	Removes a watchpoint from a `FileUpload` property
	`watch()`	Sets a watchpoint on a `FileUpload` property

Example

Listing 8.152 shows how an upload box is created and then how the `name` property is accessed using the `FileUpload` object.

A `FileUpload` object in the HTML page contains a Browse button that allows you to browse the computer for a file to upload. After this is chosen, normally it would be sent to a server to be uploaded. However, this example only demonstrates how to get the full pathname for the file to be uploaded.

Listing 8.152   *How the* `FileUpload` *Object Is Used*

```
<html>

<body>
<script type="text/javascript" language="JavaScript">
<!--
// Function demonstrates how to obtain property values of the
// FileUpload object.
function showname(){
    // Declare a variable to hold the name of the upload box.
    var  file = document.form1.uploadBox.value ;
     document.form1.filename.value = file ;
}
// -->
</script>

<form name="form1">
Click on browse to choose a file to send.
<br>
Click on the Send button to see the full path for the file sent.
<br><br>
File to send: <input type="file" name="uploadBox">
<br><br>
<input type="button" value="Send" name="get" onClick='showname()'>
<br><br>
<input type="text" name="filename" size="40">
```

```
</form>
</body>
</html>
```

FileUpload.blur()

JavaScript 1.1+
Nav3+, Opera3+

Syntax

`fileupload.blur()`

Description

The `blur()`method of the `FileUpload` object is used to remove focus from the `FileUpload` box.

Example

Listing 8.153 shows how the `blur()` method is used to remove focus from the upload box. When the OK button is clicked, the focus is removed from the upload box and a message is displayed.

Listing 8.153   Example of the `blur()` Method

```
<html>

<body>
<script type="text/javascript" language="JavaScript">
<!--
function showMessage(){
// Removes focus from the upload box and writes text.
    document.form1.uploadbox.blur();
    document.form1.textbox.value = "File Submitted";
}
// -->
</script>

<form name="form1">
Enter Filename:
<input type="file" name="uploadbox">
<input type="button" value="Okay" onClick=showMessage()>
<br><br>
Confirmation:
<input type="text" name="textbox">

</form>

</body>
</html>
```

FileUpload.focus()

JavaScript 1.1+, JScript 3.0+
Nav3+, IE4+, Opera3+

Syntax

`fileupload.focus()`

Description

The `focus()()`method is used to set focus to the `FileUpload` object.

Example

Listing 8.154 shows how to set the focus on the `FileUpload` object. When the user clicks the OK button, the JavaScript function `checkFile()` is called to reset the focus to the upload box and display a message.

Listing 8.154   Setting Focus to the Upload Box

```
<html>

<body>
<script type="text/javascript" language="JavaScript">
<!--
function checkFile(){
// Sets focus to the upload box.
    document.form1.uploadbox.focus();
    document.form1.textbox.value = "Verify that filename is correct";
}
// -->
</script>

<form name="form1">
Enter Filename:
<input type="file" name="uploadbox">
<input type="button" value="Okay" onClick=checkFile()>
<br><br>
Confirmation Message:
<input type="text" name="textbox" size="35">

</form>

</body>
</html>
```

FileUpload.form
JavaScript 1.0+, JScript 3.0+
Nav2+, IE4+, Opera3+

Syntax

```
fileupload.form
```

Description

The form property()of the FileUpload object is used to reference the form object that contains the FileUpload box.

Example

Listing 8.155 shows an example of how the form property can be used to extract any attributes of the form containing the FileUpload box. The page contains two boxes in which a file can be specified to be uploaded. The checkFiles() function verifies whether a file has been chosen for each upload box. If a file hasn't been chosen, the script will alert the user.

Listing 8.155   Using the FileUpload form Property

```
<html>

<body>
<script type="text/javascript" language="JavaScript">
<!--

// Function verifies whether a file has been chosen for each FileUpload box.
function checkFiles(){

    if (document.secret.file1.value == ""){
        alert("You did not enter anything for file 1");
    }
    if (document.secret.file2.value == ""){
        alert("You did not enter anything for file 2");
    }
    else {
        alert("The files are okay and will be uploaded");
    }
}
// -->
</script>

<form name="secret">

Please choose two files to upload.
<br><br>
File 1:<input type="file" name="file1">
<br><br>
```

Listing 8.155   Continued

```
File 2:<input type="file" name="file2">
<br><br>
<input type="button" value="Verify" onClick='checkFiles()'>
</form>

</body>
</html>
```

The first example shows one method of referencing the upload box. There is a second way, though. It can also be referenced by using the form `elements` array. An example of this is in Listing 8.156.

Listing 8.156   Second Method of Referencing a `FileUpload` Object Using the `forms` Elements Array

```
<html>

<body>
<script type="text/javascript" language="JavaScript">
<!--
function showUploadName(){
    alert("The FileUpload box name is: " + document.secret.elements[0].name);
}
// -->
</script>

<form name="secret">
Please choose a file to be uploaded.
<br><br>
<input type="file" name="mybox" >
<br><br>
Click the button to get the name of the form containing the FileUpload box.
<br><br>
<input type="button" value="Get Form Name" onClick='showUploadName()'>
</form>

</body>
</html>
```

FileUpload.handleEvent()

JavaScript 1.2+

Nav4+

Syntax

fileupload.handleEvent(*event*)

Description

The handleEvent()method of the FileUpload object invokes the event handler for the specific event.

Example

Listing 8.157 shows how the handleEvent() method is used to handle all CHANGE events. When the user chooses or enters a filename in the FileUpload box and then changes the information, the CHANGE event occurs and is captured. The handleChange function processes the CHANGE event and passes it to the handleEvent() method of the upload box. So the event handler for the upload box will handle all CHANGE events.

Listing 8.157 Using the handleEvent() *Method*

```html
<html>

<body>

<script type="text/javascript" language="JavaScript">
<!--

// Sets up the window to capture CHANGE events.
window.captureEvents(Event.CHANGE);

// function that handles the specific event. The evnt parameter refers to
// the event object.
function handleChange(evnt){
    window.document.uploadbox.handleEvent(evnt);
}

function displayText(){
    document.form1.msg.value += "Change made to object\n";
}

// This registers the handle function as the event handler for the
// CHANGE event.
window.onChange = handleChange;
// -->
</script>


Choose a file:
<br>
<form name="form1">
<input type="file" size="40" name="uploadbox" onChange='displayText()'>
<br><br>
<textarea name="msg" rows="10" cols="50"></textarea>
```

Listing 8.157   Continued

```
</form>

</body>
</html>
```

FileUpload.name
JavaScript 1.0+
Nav2+, Opera3+

Syntax

```
fileupload.name
```

Description

The name property of the FileUpload object represents the name attribute of the HTML <input> tag that creates the FileUpload box. This allows you to reference a FileUpload object directly by name.

Example

Listing 8.158 shows how the name of the upload box is used to access its properties. The function getname() uses the form object and the name of the upload box to access the name property.

Listing 8.158   Accessing the FileUpload Object by Name

```
<html>

<body>
<script type="text/javascript" language="JavaScript">
<!--

// Function alerts the user to what the name of the upload box is.
function getname(){
    var boxname = document.form1.myUploadbox.name;
    alert("The name of the FileUpload box is: " + boxname);
}
// -->
</script>

<form name="form1">
Click on the button below to get the name of the upload box.
<br><br>
<input type="file" name="myUploadbox">
<br><br>
```

```
<input type="button" value="Get Name" onClick='getname()'>
</form>

</form>
</html>
```

FileUpload.onBlur

JavaScript 1.1+
Nav3+, Opera3+

Syntax

onBlur="*command*"

Description

The onBlur event handler is an event handler for the FileUpload object that notifies you when the focus is removed from an upload box.

Example

Listing 8.159 shows how the onBlur event handler is used to detect when the focus is removed from the specified upload box. The user chooses a file from the FileUpload box and then clicks the text box that removes the focus from the FileUpload box, causing the Blur event to be thrown.

Listing 8.159   Example of the FileUpload onBlur **Method**

```
<html>

<body>
<script type="text/javascript" language="JavaScript">
<!--
function inform(){
     document.form1.msg.value="File submitted and focus removed from
➥FileUpload object";
}

// -->
</script>

<form name="form1">
Please choose a file to upload to the server.
<br><br>
<input type="file" onBlur= 'inform()'>
<br><br>
Click on the text box.
<br><br>
```

Listing 8.159   Continued

```
Message:
<input type="text" name="msg" size="50">
</form>

</body>
</html>
```

FileUpload.onChange
JavaScript 1.1+
Nav3+, Opera3+

Syntax

```
onChange="command"
```

Description

The onChange event handler of the FileUpload object is an event handler that notifies you when the upload box information has been changed.

Example

Listing 8.160 uses the onChange event handler to check for a user entering information into an upload box. When the filename entered has been changed, the onChange event handler is triggered and a message is displayed in the text box.

Listing 8.160   Example of the onChange Event Handler

```
<html>

<body>
<script type="text/javascript" language="JavaScript">
<!--
// function that informs the user that the filename in the FileUpload box
// has been changed.
function inform(){
    document.form1.msg.value = "Filename has been changed";
}

// -->
</script>

<form name="form1">

Please choose a file.
<input type="file" name="uploadbox" size="35" onChange='inform()'>
<br><br>
```

```
Message:
<input type="text" name="msg" size="40">
</form>

</body>
</html>
```

FileUpload.onFocus

JavaScript 1.1+
Nav3+, Opera3+

Syntax

```
onFocus="command"
```

Description

The onFocus event handler of the FileUpload object notifies you when the focus is set on the upload box.

Example

In Listing 8.161, the onFocus event handler is used to notify the user when the focus is moved to the upload box. If the user sets the focus to the FileUpload box, a message is displayed. If the user removes the focus from the FileUpload box, another message is displayed.

Listing 8.161   Example of the onFocus Event Handler

```
<html>

<body>
<script type="text/javascript" language="JavaScript">
<!--
// function that displays a message whenever focus is set on the FileUpload
// box.
function showMsg1(){
    document.form1.msg.value = "Focus on the FileUpload box\n";
}

// Function displays a message when focus is removed from the FileUpload box.
function showMsg2(){
    document.form1.msg.value = "Focus removed from FileUpload box\n";
}

// -->
</script>
<form name="form1">
```

Listing 8.161   Continued

```
Click in the FileUpload box to set focus to it.
<br><br>
<input type="file" name="uploadbox" onFocus = 'showMsg1()'>
<br><br>
Click on the button to remove focus from the FileUpload box.
<br>
<input type="button" value="Click here" onClick='showMsg2()'>
<br><br>
<textarea name="msg" rows="5" cols="50"></textarea>
</form>

</body>
</html>
```

FileUpload.select()

JavaScript 1.0+
Nav2+, Opera3+

Syntax

fileupload.select()

Description

The select() method of the FileUpload box is used to select the input area of the upload field.

Example

Listing 8.162 shows an example of how the select() method is used to select the input text box of the FileUpload box.

Listing 8.162   Using the select() Method of the FileUpload Object

```
<html>

<body>
<script type="text/javascript" language="JavaScript">
<!--
function enterName(){
// Selects the input area of upload box when button is clicked.
    document.form1.uploadbox.select();
}
// -->
</script>

<form name="form1">
<input type="file" name="uploadbox">
<br><br>
```

```
<input type="button"  value="Go to Filename Box" onClick=enterName()>

</body>
</html>
```

FileUpload.type
JavaScript 1.1+
Nav3+, Opera3+

Syntax

`fileupload.type`

Description

The type propertyof the FileUpload object represents the type attribute of the HTML <input> tag used to create the upload box.

Example

Listing 8.163 shows how to access the type property. When the user clicks the Get Type button, an alert box appears indicating the type of input.

Listing 8.163   Accessing the FileUpload Type Property

```
<html>

<body>
<script type="text/javascript" language="JavaScript">
<!--
// Function informs the user what type of input the first element is.
function getType(){
     var mytype = document.form1.uploadbox.type;

     alert("The input box type is: " + mytype);
}
// -->
</script>

<form name="form1">
<input type="file" name="webfile">
<br><br>
Interested in finding out what type of input box is above?
Click on the button below.
<br>
<input type="button" value="Get Type" onClick='getType()'>
</form>
</body>
</html>
```

FileUpload.unwatch()

JavaScript 1.2+
Nav4+

Syntax

fileupload.unwatch(*prop*)

Description

The unwatch()method of the FileUpload object is used to remove a watchpoint set on a property by the watch() method. It takes one parameter, *prop*, which is the property to unwatch.

Example

Listing 8.164 shows how the unwatch() method is used to disable the watchpoint set on the name property.

Listing 8.164   *Using the* unwatch() *Method of the* FileUpload *Object*

```
<html>
<script type="text/javascript"  language="JavaScript">
<!--

function alertme(id,oldValue,newValue)
{
  document.writeln(id + " changed from " + "<b>" + oldValue +
➥"</b>"+ " to " + "<b>" + newValue + "</b><br>")
  return newValue;
}

function setWatch(){
  myProp = document.form1.uploadbox.name;
  watch("myProp",alertme);
  myProp = "yahoo";
  unwatch("myProp");
  myProp = "ebay";
}

// -->
</script>
<body>

<form name="form1">
Please select a file.
<input type="file" name="uploadbox">
<br><br>
Click on the button to change the FileUpload name property
<br>
```

```
<input type="button" value="Click Here" onClick='setWatch()'>
</form>

</body>
</html>
```

FileUpload.value

JavaScript 1.0+
Nav2+, Opera3+

Syntax

fileupload.value

Description

The value property of the FileUpload object specifies either the filename of the file selected or input by the user.

Example

Listing 8.165 shows how to access the value property. The form object is used in conjunction with the upload box name to get the value attribute of the FileUpload box.

Listing 8.165 *Accessing the* FileUpload *Value Property*

```
<html>

<body>
<script type=text/javascript" language="JavaScript">
<!--
function showFile(){
    var input = document.form1.uploadbox.value;
    alert("The filename entered is: " + input);
}
// -->
</script>

<form name="form1">
Please select a file.
<input type="file" name="uploadbox">
<br><br>
Click on the button to see the value of the FileUpload object.
<br>
<input type="button" value="Submit" onClick=showFile()>
</form>

</body>
</html>
```

FileUpload.watch()

JavaScript 1.2+

Nav4+

Syntax

`fileupload.watch(prop, handler)`

Description

The `watch()` method of the `FileUpload` object is used to watch for changes to `FileUpload` properties. When one of the properties, *prop*, is assigned a value, a *handler* is used to call a user-defined function.

Example

Listing 8.166 shows how the `watch()` method is used to set a watchpoint on the `name` property. When the upload box name is changed, the `alertme` function is called to display the change to the user.

Listing 8.166 Using the** watch() **Method of the** FileUpload **Object

```
<html>
<script type="text/javascript"  language="JavaScript">
<!--

function alertme(id,oldValue,newValue)
{
  document.writeln(id + " changed from " + "<b>" + oldValue +
➡ "</b>"+ " to " + "<b>" + newValue + "</b><br>")
  return newValue;
}

function setWatch(){
  myProp = document.form1.uploadbox.name;
  watch("myProp",alertme);
  myProp = "yahoo";
  myProp = "ebay";
}

// -->
</script>
<body>

<form name="form1">
Please select a file.
<input type="file" name="uploadbox">
<br><br>
Click on the button to change the FileUpload name property
<br>
```

```
<input type="button" value="Click Here" onClick='setWatch()'>
</form>

</body>
</html>
```

Form

JavaScript 1.0+, JScript 1.0+
Nav2+, IE3+, Opera3+

Syntax

Core client-side JavaScript object.

Description

The Form object represents an HTML property created by the `<form>` tag. The Form object can be used to access all the properties of the specified form. Forms can be referenced either by the `forms` array or directly by name. Table 8.14 shows the different Form methods and properties.

Table 8.14 Properties and Methods of the Form *Object*

Type	Item	Description
Property	action	HTML `action` attribute of the Form object
	elements	Array reflecting elements within a form
	elements.length	Length of the elements array
	encoding	HTML enctype attribute of the Form object
	length	Number of elements within a form
	method	HTML `method` attribute of the Form object
	name	HTML `name` attribute of the Form object
	onReset	Event handler for the Reset button
	onSubmit	Event handler for the Submit button
	target	HTML `target` attribute of the Form object
Method	handleEvent()	Handles a specific event
	reset()	Resets form elements
	submit()	Submit for data
	unwatch()	Removes a watchpoint on a Form propert
	watch()	Sets a watchpoint on a Form property

Example

Listing 8.167 uses the method of accessing the Form object directly by name.

Listing 8.167 **Accessing the** Form **Object by Name**

```
<html>

<body>
<script type="text/javascript" language="JavaScript">
<!--
// Function shows the name entered by the user to verify that
// the information is correct.
function checkName(){


    var firstName = document.formEx.first.value;
    var lastName = document.formEx.last.value;
    alert("The name you entered is: " + firstName + " " + lastName);
}
// -->
</script>

<form name="formEx">
First Name:
<input type="text" name="first" size="20">
Last Name:
<input type="text" name="last" size="25">
<br><br>
Click the button to check that the information is correct.
<br>
<input type="button" value="verify" name="check" onClick='checkName()'>
</form>
</body>
</html>
```

Listing 8.168 accesses the Form object by using the forms array. The form simply contains one text box. Clicking the button shows an alert box containing the name of the form. Because it is the first form in the document, it is index 0 in the forms array.

Listing 8.168 **Using the** forms **Array**

```
<html>

<body>
<script type="text/javascript" language="JavaScript">
<!--
function showFormName(){
    var name = document.forms[0].name;

    alert("The name of the form is: " + name);
}
```

```
// -->
</script>

<form name="form1">
This text box belongs to a form.
<input type="text" name="street">
<br><br>
Click on the button to get the name of the form.
<br>
<input type="button" value="Get Form name" onClick='showFormName()'>
</form>

<form name="form2">
This is the second form in the document. It contains a FileUpload object.
<input type="file" name="uploadbox" size="25">
</form>
</body>
</html>
```

Form.action

JavaScript 1.0+, JScript 1.0+
Nav2+, IE3+, Opera3+

Syntax

form.action

Description

The action property represents the action attribute of the HTML <form> tag. It is typically the URL to which the form is being submitted.

Example

Listing 8.169 shows one method of how to use the Form object to access the action property of the HTML form. The action property specifies the server and program to which the form is submitted.

Listing 8.169 *Accessing the Action Value of the* Form *Object*

```
<html>

<body>
<script type="text/javascript" language="JavaScript">
<!--
function getAction(){
    var actionValue = document.form1.action;
document.form1.msg.value =
        "Your form was submitted to the following URL:\n " + actionValue;
```

Listing 8.169   Continued

```
}
// -->
</script>

<form name="form1" action="http://www.test.org/cgi-bin/process.pl">
Enter your street address:
<input type="text" name="address" size="40">
<br><br>
<input type="button" value="Submit" onClick='getAction()'>
<br><br><br>
<textarea name="msg" rows="5" cols="62"></textarea>
</form>
</body>
</html>
```

Form.elements

JavaScript 1.0+, JScript 1.0+
Nav2+, IE3+, Opera3+

Syntax

form.elements

Description

The elements property of the Form object represents the elements array, which is used to access each element within a form. The order of the form elements in the elements array is the order in which they appear in the HTML source.

Example

Listing 8.170 shows how to access form elements using the elements array. Because it is accessing the first element in the form, the index 0 is used. The second element in the form can be accessed with elements[1].

Listing 8.170   Accessing Form Elements

```
<html>

<body>
<script type="text/javascript" language="JavaScript">
<!--
function getName(){
    var textName = document.form1.elements[0].name;
    alert("The textbox name is: " + textName);
}
   // -->
</script>

<form name="form1">
```

```
This is a blank input textbox. Click on the button below to get
the name of the textbox.
<br>
<input type="text" name="textbox1" size=25>
<br><br>
<input type="button" value="Get Name" onClick = 'getName()'>
</form>
</body>
</html>
```

Form.elements.length

JavaScript 1.0+, JScript 1.0+
Nav2+, IE3+, Opera3+

Syntax

form.elements.length

Description

The elements.length property of the Form object specifies the number of items in the elements array. Each item in the array refers to an object in the HTML form.

Example

Listing 8.171 shows how to use the elements.length property. When the user clicks the Get Elements button, an alert box is displayed indicating the number of elements in the form.

Listing 8.171   *Using the* elements.length *Property*

```
<html>

<body>
<script type="text/javascript" language="JavaScript">
<!--
// function uses the elements.length property to get the number
// of elements in the form.
function getNum(){
    var numOfElements = document.form1.elements.length;
alert("The number of elements in this document are:" + numOfElements);
}
// -->
</script>

<form name="form1">
Dummy text box:
<input type="text" name="textbox1" size="25">
<br>
```

Listing 8.171   Continued

```
<input type="button" value="Dummy Button">
<input type="text" size="20" name="Sample">
<br><br>
Click on the button to get the number of elements in this form.
<input type="button" value="Get Elements" onClick='getNum()'>
</form>
</body>
</html>
```

Form.encoding

JavaScript 1.0+, JScript 1.0+
Nav2+, IE3+, Opera3+

Syntax

form.encoding

Description

The encoding property of the Form object represents the type of encoding used by the form. It can be specified in the HTML <form> tag as the enctype attribute.

NOTE

Setting the encoding property will override the HTML enctype attribute.

Example

In Listing 8.172, the encoding property of the Form object is used to get the type of encoding being used by the form.

Listing 8.172   Accessing Form Encoding Property

```
<html>

<body>
<script type="text/javascript" language="JavaScript">
<!--
// This function returns the encoding type for the specified form.
function getEncoding(){
    var encodingType = document.form1.encoding;
    return encodingType;
}
// -->
</script>

<form name="form1" action="post" enctype="application/x-www-form-urlencoded">
```

```
<input type="button" value="Get Encoding" onClick='getEncoding()'>
</form>
</body>
</html>
```

Form.handleEvent()

JavaScript 1.2+, JScript 1.0+
Nav4+, IE3+

Syntax

form.handleEvent(*event*)

Description

The handleEvent() method of the Form property invokes the handler for the specified event. It takes one parameter, which is the event to be handled.

Example

In Listing 8.173, the handleEvent() method is being used to handle the event being passed. The script captures the CLICK event. When this occurs, the handleMyClick() function calls the handleEvent() method to handle the CLICK event.

Listing 8.173 *Using the* handleEvent() *Method*

```
<html>

<body>
<script type="text/javascript" language="JavaScript">
<!--

// Sets up the document to capture CLICK events.
document.captureEvents(Event.CLICK);

// function that handles the specific event. The evnt parameter refers to
// the event object.
function handleMyClick(evnt){
    window.document.button1.handleEvent(evnt);
}

function displayMsg(){
    document.form1.msg.value += "Click event occurred.\n";
}

// This registers the handle function as the event handler for the
// CLICK event.
document.onClick = handleMyClick;
```

Listing 8.173   Continued

```
// -->
</script>


<form name="form1">
<input type="button" value="Click on Me" name="button1" onClick='displayMsg()'>
<br><br>
<textarea name="msg" rows="10" cols="50" onClick='displayMsg()'></textarea>
</form>

</body>
</html>
```

Form.length

JavaScript 1.0+, JScript 1.0+
Nav2+, IE3+, Opera3+

Syntax

form.length

Description

The length property of the Form object represents the number of elements within a form.

NOTE

This property works the same as the elements.length property.

Example

Listing 8.174 shows an example of how the length property is used to determine the number of elements in the document. The showNumElements() function informs the user of the form length, which represents the number of form elements.

Listing 8.174   Using the Form.length *Property*

```
<html>

<body>
<script type="text/javascript" language="JavaScript">
<!--
// function displays an alert box indicating the number of elements
// in the form.
function showNumElements(){
    alert("There are " + document.form1.length +
➥ " elements in this document");
}
```

```
// -->
</script>

<form name="form1">
Enter First Name:
<input type="text" size="15"><br>
Enter Last Name:
<input type="text" size="20"><br>
Enter address:
<input type="text" size="40"><br><br>
<input type="button" value="Submit" onClick='showNumElements()'>
</form>

</body>
</html>
```

Form.method

JavaScript 1.0+, JScript 1.0+
Nav2+, IE3+, Opera3+

Syntax

form.method

Description

The method property of the Form object represents the type of submission, GET or POST, being used by the form.

Example

In Listing 8.175, the method property is used to get the type of method being used by the form. The informMethod() function alerts the user of the method, GET or POST, being used by the form.

Listing 8.175   Accessing the method Property

```
<html>

<body>
<script type="text/javascript" language="JavaScript">
<!--

function informMethod(){
alert("The form method is:" + document.form1.method);
}
// -->
</script>
```

Listing 8.175 *Continued*

```
<form name="form1" method="get">

First Name:<input type=text" name="first" size="15">
Last Name:<input type=text" name="last" size="25">
<br>
City:<input type=text" name="city" size="20">
State:<input type=text" name="state" size="2" maxlength="2">
Zip:<input type=text" name="zip" size="5" maxlength="5">
<br><br>
Click the button to see what type of Method is used for submission.
<input type="button" value="Click Here" onClick='informMethod()'>
</form>
</body>
</html>
```

Form.name

JavaScript 1.0+, JScript 1.0+
Nav2+, IE3+, Opera3+

Syntax

form.name

Description

The name property of the Form object represents the name of the form as specified in the HTML <form> tag.

Example

Listing 8.176 shows how the name property is used to get the HTML name attribute of the form. The showName function uses the Form object to access the name attribute of the form.

Listing 8.176 *Accessing the* name *Property*

```
<html>

<body>
<script type="text/javascript" language="JavaScript">
<!--
function showName(){
// Alert box tells what the name of the form is
alert("Form Name is: " + document.form1.name);
}
// -->
</script>

<form name ="form1" >
```

```
Dummy input text box.
<input type= "text" size="15">
<br><br>
Click on the button to get the name of the form
<input type="button" value="click me" onclick='showName()'>

</form>
</body>
</html>
```

Form.onReset

JavaScript 1.1+, JScript 1.0+
Nav3+, IE3+, Opera3+

Syntax

onReset="*command*"

Description

The onReset method of the Form object executes JavaScript code when a reset event occurs.

Example

Listing 8.177 demonstrates the use of the onReset event handler. The JavaScript function checks to see if the Reset button has been clicked. If so, all the text values are reset to a specified value.

Listing 8.177   Using the onReset Event Handler

```
<html>

<body>
<script type="text/javascript" language="JavaScript">
<!--
// Function displays a message when the onReset event handler determines that
// the reset button has been pressed.
function showMsg(){
    document.form2.msg.value = "You have cleared the Entry Fields.";
}
// -->
</script>

<form name="form1" onReset='showMsg()'>
Entry 1:<input type= "text" name="text1" sizesize="20"><br>
Entry 2:<input type= "text" name="text2" sizesize="20"><br>
Entry 3:<input type= "text" name="text3" sizesize="20"><br>
<input type="reset" value="reset" name="Reset"
```

Listing 8.177   Continued

```
</form>

<form name="form2">
Message:<input type="text" name="msg" size="50">
<br><br>
</form>
</body>
</html>
```

Form.onSubmit

JavaScript 1.0+, JScript 1.0+
Nav2+, IE3+, Opera3+

Syntax

```
onSubmit="command"
```

Description

The onSubmit method of the Form property executes JavaScript code when a submit event occurs.

Example

Listing 8.178 shows how the onSubmit event handler is used for a Form object. A user would enter her comments in the text area provided. When finished, she clicks the Submit button to submit the form. Using the onSubmit event handler, you can display a thank you note when the user has submitted her comments.

Listing 8.178   Using the onSubmit() **Form Method**

```
<html>

<body>

<script type="text/javascript" language="JavaScript">
<!--
//Function displays a confirmation message when a form is submitted.
function confirm(){
    alert("Your comments have been submitted. Thank you.");
}
// -->
</script>

<form name="form1" onSubmit = 'confirm()'
<b>Enter Comments:</b>
<br>
<textarea name="comments" rows="5" cols="60"></textarea>
<br><br>
```

```
<input type = "submit" Value="Submit Comments">
</form>
</body>
</html>
```

Form.reset()

JavaScript 1.1+, JScript 1.0+
Nav3+, IE3+, Opera3+

Syntax

form.reset()

Description

The reset method of the Form object resets all the form elements to their default values. It operates the same as a mouse click on a Reset button for the calling form.

Example

Listing 8.179 shows how the reset method is used to reset a form. When the Reset button is clicked, all values in the form object are reset (text boxes are cleared of their values).

Listing 8.179   Accessing the reset() **Method**

```
<html>

<body>
<script type="text/javascript" language="JavaScript">
<!--
function resetForm(form){
    document.form1.reset(form);
}
// -->
</script>

<form name="form1">
Field 1:<input type="text" size="20" name="text1"><br>
Field 2:<input type="text" size="20" name="text2"><br>
Field 3:<input type="text" size="20" name="text3"><br>
<input type="button" name="reset" value="reset" onClick='resetForm(this.form)'>
</form>

</body>
</html>
```

Form.submit()

JavaScript 1.0+, JScript 1.0+
Nav2+, IE3+, Opera3+

Syntax

```
form.submit()
```

Description

The submit() method of the Form object is used to submit a form. It operates the same as if a Submit button was clicked.

Example

Listing 8.180 shows how you would submit a form using the submit() method. The form is submitted to the value specified in the action attribute of the HTML <form> tag. In this specific example, a made up script processes the form.

Listing 8.180 Accessing the submit() Method

```
<html>

<body>
<script type="text/javascript" language="JavaScript">
<!--
// Function submits a form to a server specified in the <form> tag
function submitForm(form){
    document.form1.submit(form);
}
// -->
</script>

<form name= "form1" method="post"
➥ action="http://www.myserver.com/cgi-bin/test.pl">
This is a sample form
<br><br>
Name:<input type="text" size="40" name="name">
<br>
Age:<input type="text" size="3" name="age">
<br>
Phone Number:<input type="text" size="10" name="phone">
<br><br>
<input type= "button" value="Submit" onclick = 'submitForm(this.form)'>
</form>
</body>
</html>
```

Form.target

JavaScript 1.0+, JScript 1.0+
Nav2+, IE3+, Opera3+

Syntax

form.target

Description

The target property of the Form object represents the target window or frame in which the form results will be displayed. This can also reflect the target attribute of the HTML <form> tag. Valid target attributes are: _blank, _parent, _self, and _top.

Example

In Listing 8.181, a sample form is created for submission. When the Submit button is clicked, the show() function is called to inform the user whether the target property has been specified or not.

Listing 8.181 Displaying Results Using the target Property

```
<html>

<body>
<script type="text/javascript" language="JavaScript">
<!--
function show(){

var tar = document.form1.target;

    if(tar == "_self"){
      alert("The target for this form submission is this window");
    }
    else{
      alert("The target has not been specifically specified");
    }
}
// -->
</script>

<form name="form1" action="post" target="_self">
First Name:<input type="text" size="15" name="first">
Last Name:<input type="text" size="20" name="last">
<br>
Street:<input type="text" size="40" name="street">
<br>
City:<input type="text" size="15" name="city">
State:<input type="text" size="2" name="st">
Zip:<input type="text" size="5" name="zip">
```

Listing 8.181   Continued

```
<br><br><br>
<input type="button" value="submit" onClick='show()'>
</form>

</body>
</html>
```

Form.unwatch()

JavaScript 1.2+
Nav4+

Syntax

form.unwatch(*prop*)

Description

The unwatch() method of the Form object is used to remove a watchpoint set on a property by the watch() method. It takes one parameter, *prop*, which is the property to unwatch.

Example

Listing 8.182 shows how the unwatch() method is used to disable the watchpoint on the form name.

Listing 8.182   Using the unwatch() Method of the Form Object

```
<html>
<script type="text/javascript"  language="JavaScript">
<!--

function alertme(id,oldValue,newValue)
{
  document.writeln(id + " changed from " + "<b>" + oldValue +
➥"</b>"+ " to " + "<b>" + newValue + "</b><br>")
  return newValue;
}

function setWatch(){
  myProp = document.forms[0].name;
  watch("myProp",alertme);
  myProp = "red_form";
  unwatch("myProp");
  myProp = "blue_form";
}

// -->
</script>
<body>
```

```
<form name="form1">
<input type="button" value="Click Here" onClick='setWatch()'>
</form>

</body>
</html>
```

Form.watch()

JavaScript 1.2+
Nav4+

Syntax

form.watch(*prop, handler*)

Description

The watch() method of the Form object is used to watch for changes to Form properties. When one of the properties, *prop,* is assigned a value, a *handler* is used to call a user defined function.

Example

Listing 8.183 shows how the watch() method is set on the form name property. When the button is clicked, the watchpoint is set and then the property is changed. Each time it is changed, the alertme function is called to display the changes.

Listing 8.183   *Using the* watch() *Method of the* Form *Object*

```
<html>
<script type="text/javascript"  language="JavaScript">
<!--

function alertme(id,oldValue,newValue)
{
  document.writeln(id + " changed from " + "<b>" + oldValue +
➥"</b>"+ " to " + "<b>" + newValue + "</b><br>")
  return newValue;
}

function setWatch(){
  myProp = document.forms[0].name;
  watch("myProp",alertme);
  myProp = "red_form";
  myProp = "blue_form";
}

// -->
</script>
<body>
```

Listing 8.183   Continued

```
<form name="form1">
<input type="button" value="Click Here" onClick='setWatch()'>
</form>

</body>
</html>
```

Frame

JavaScript 1.0+, JScript 1.0+
Nav2+, IE3+, Opera3+

Syntax

Core client-side JavaScript object.

Description

A window can display multiple, independently scrollable frames on a single screen, each with its own distinct URL. The Frame object, which has an instance created with each occurrence of the <frame> tag, is a convenience for thinking about the objects that make up these frames. However, JavaScript actually represents a frame using a Window object. Every Frame object is a Window object, and has all the methods and properties of a Window object. Table 8.15 shows the available methods and properties of Frames.

NOTE

> The majority of examples for the Frame object assume that top.html and bottom.html files exist. Some examples also only display the JavaScript code that would be contained in a document.

Table 8.15   Properties and Methods of the Frame Object

Type	Item	Description
Property	document	Current document loaded within the frame
	frames	Array containing references to the child frames
	length	Length of the frames array
	name	HTML name attribute of the Frame object
	onBlur	Event handler for the blur event
	onFocus	Event handler for the focus event
	onMove	Event handler for the move event
	onResize	Event handler for the resize event
	parent	Main window or frame from which child frames are created
	self	Refers to the current frame
	top	Browser window that executes script
	window	Refers to the current window or frame

Type	Item	Description
Method	blur()	Removes focus from the frame
	clearInterval()	Cancels a repeated execution
	clearTimeout()	Cancels any delayed execution
	focus()	Applies focus to the frame
	print()	Invokes the print dialog box
	setInterval()	Sets a function schedule for repeated execution
	setTimeout()	Sets a function schedule for delayed execution
	unwatch()	Removes a watchpoint on a Frame property
	watch()	Sets a watchpoint on a Frame property

Example

Listing 8.184 shows the code to create an HTML frame and access its properties. This example assumes that the files top.html and bottom.html already exist.

Listing 8.184   Frame *Example*

```
<html>


<script type="text/javascript" language="JavaScript">
<!--

//Function returns the name of the frame
function getName(){
    var frameName = document.window.frame.name;
    return frameName;
}
// -->
</script>

<frameset rows="100,*">
<frame src="top.html" name="upper">
<frame src="bottom.html" name="bottom" scrolling="yes">
</frameset>

</html>
```

Frame.blur()
JavaScript 1.1+, JScript 1.0+
Nav3+, IE3+, Opera3+

Syntax

```
frame.blur()
```

Description

The blur() method of the Frame object removes focus from the frame.

Example

Listing 8.185 uses the blur() method to remove focus from the frame.

Listing 8.185   *Example of the* blur() *Method*

```
<html>


<script type="text/javascript" language="JavaScript">
<!--
function removeFocus(){
     document.upper.blur()
}
// -->
</script>

<frameset rows="100,*">
<frame src="top.html" name="upper" onDblClick='removeFocus()'>
<frame src="bottom.html" name="bottom" scrolling="yes">
</frameset>

 </html>
```

Frame.clearInterval()

JavaScript 1.2+, JScript 1.0+
Nav4+, IE3+

Syntax

```
frame.clearInterval()
```

Description

The clearInterval() method of the Frame object is used to cancel a repeated execution.

Example

Listing 8.186 shows the syntax for accessing the clearInterval() method. For a more detailed example, see window.clearInterval().

Listing 8.186   *Example of the* clearInterval() *Method*

```
<script type="text/javascript" language="JavaScript">
<!--
function cancel(){
     framename.clearInterval();
```

```
}
// -->
 </script>
```

Frame.clearTimeout()

JavaScript 1.0+, JScript 1.0+
Nav2+, IE3+, Opera3+

Syntax

`frame.clearTimeout()`

Description

The `clearTimeout()` method of the `Frame` object is used to cancel a delayed execution. For a more detailed example, see `window.clearTimeout()`.

Example

Listing 8.187 shows the syntax for accessing the `clearTimeout()` method.

Listing 8.187   Accessing the `clearTimeout()` ***Method***

```
<script type="text/javascript" language="JavaScript">
<!--
function stop(){
    framename.clearTimeout();
}
// -->
 </script>
```

Frame.document

JavaScript 1.0+, JScript 1.0+
Nav2+, IE3+, Opera3+

Syntax

`frame.document`

Description

The `document` property of the `Frame` object contains information about the current document. The `document` property is created by the HTML `<body>` tag and is available in every `Frame` or `Window` object. The `document` property is used to access other aspects of the HTML document.

Example

Listing 8.188 shows how the `document` property can be used to access document elements within a specific frame. For a more detailed example, see `window.document`.

Listing 8.188 **Accessing the** document **Property**

```
<script type="text/javascript" language="JavaScript">
<!--
function getName(){
    var name = framename.document.elements[1].name;
}
// -->
</script>
```

Frame.focus()

> JavaScript 1.1+, JScript 1.0+
> Nav3+, IE3+, Opera3+

Syntax

```
frame.focus()
```

Description

The focus() method of the Frame object is used to set the focus to a specific frame.

Example

Listing 8.189 shows the syntax for using the focus() method. When the document is loaded, the focus is automatically set to the bottom frame.

Listing 8.189 **Accessing the** focus() **Method**

```
<html>


<script type="text/javascript" language="JavaScript">
<!--
//Set initial focus to bottom frame.
document.bottom.focus;
// -->
</script>

<frameset rows="80, *">
<frame name=top src=top.html>
<frame name=bottom src=bottom.html>
</frameset>

</html>
```

Frame.frames

> JavaScript 1.0+, JScript 1.0+
> Nav2+, IE3+, Opera3+

Syntax

```
frame.frames[num]
```

Description

The `frames` property of the `Frame` object represents an array that stores child frame objects. Array entries of the child frame can be referenced either by index number or by the name assigned from the `name` attribute.

Example

In Listing 8.190, the `frames` array is used to access the length of the child frame.

Listing 8.190   Example Using the `frames` *Property*

```
<script type="text/javascript" language="JavaScript">
<!--
function getFrameLength(){
    var childLength = document.frames["firstChild"].length;
}
// -->
 </script>
```

Frame.length

JavaScript 1.0+, ECMAScript 1.0+, JScript 1.0+
Nav2+, IE3+, Opera3+

Syntax

```
frame.length
```

Description

The `length` property of the `frames` object represents the length of the `frames` array, which is the number of child frames.

Example

Listing 8.191 shows a simple function call that uses the `length` property to set a variable for the number of child frames.

Listing 8.191   Example Using the `length` *Property*

```
<script type="text/javascript" language="JavaScript">
<!--
function getLength(){
    var numOfChildFrames = window.frameName.length;
}
// -->
</script>
```

Frame.name

JavaScript 1.0+, JScript 1.0+
Nav2+, IE3+, Opera3+

Syntax

```
frame.name
```

Description

The `name` property of the `Frame` object represents the name given to a frame as speci-fied from the `name` attribute of the HTML `<frame>` tag.

Example

In Listing 8.192, the `name` property is used to inform the user of the active frame.

Listing 8.192 Example of the name **Property**

```
<script type="text/javascript" language="JavaScript">
<!--
function activeFrame(){
    var frameName = window.myframe.name;
    alert("The active frame is: " + frameName);
}
// -->
</script>
```

Frame.onBlur

JavaScript 1.1+, JScript 1.0+
Nav3+, IE3+, Opera3+

Syntax

```
onBlur="command"
```

Description

The `onBlur` event handler specifies what happens when the focus has been removed from a frame.

Example

In Listing 8.193, the `onBlur` event handler is used to change the color of the upper frame when the focus is set on it.

Listing 8.193 Using the onBlur **Event Handler**

```
<html>


<script type="text/javascript" language="JavaScript">
```

```
<!--
function change(){
    frames[0].onblur=new Function("document.bgColor='green'")
}
// -->
</script>

<frameset rows="50%,*" onload='change()'>
<frame name="topFrame" src="top.html">
<frame name="bottomFrame" src=bottom.html>
</frameset>

</html>
```

Frame.onFocus

JavaScript 1.1+, JScript 1.0+
Nav3+, IE3+, Opera3+

Syntax

```
onFocus="command"
```

Description

The onFocus event handler is used to specify when the focus is brought to a frame. The user can set the focus either by pressing the mouse button or by using the Tab key.

Example

The syntax for accessing the onFocus event handler is shown in Listing 8.194. When the focus is set on the top frame, an alert box is displayed.

Listing 8.194   Syntax for the onFocus Event Handler

```
<html>


<frameset rows="80, *">
<frame src="top.html" name="top" onFocus='alert("You are now in the top
frame")'>
<frame src="bottom.html" name="bottom">
</frameset>

 </html>
```

Frame.onMove

JavaScript 1.2+, ECMAScript 1.0+, JScript 1.0+
Nav4+, IE3+

Syntax

```
onMove="command"
```

Description

The onMove frame event handler is used to specify what happens when a move event occurs within a frame.

Example

Listing 8.195 shows the onMove event handler being used to inform the user when the frame is being moved.

Listing 8.195   Example of the onMove **Event Handler**

```
<html>


<frameset rows="80, *" onMove='alert("You are now moving the frame")'>
<frame src="top.html" name="top" >
<frame src="bottom.html" name="bottom">
</frameset>

</html>
```

Frame.onResize

JavaScript 1.2+, ECMAScript 1.0+
Nav4+

Syntax

```
onResize="command"
```

Description

The onResize frame event handler is used to specify when a frame has been resized.

Example

Listing 8.196 shows how you would use the onResize event handler to check for when a frame has been resized.

Listing 8.196   Syntax of the onResize **Event Handler**

```
<html>


<frameset rows="80, *">
```

```
<frame src="top.html" name="top" >
<frame src="bottom.html" name="bottom"
➡ onResize='alert("You are resizing the bottom frame")'>
</frameset>

</html>
```

Frame.parent

JavaScript 1.0+, JScript 1.0+
Nav2+, IE3+, Opera3+

Syntax

frame.parent

Description

The parent property of the Frame object specifies the frame containing the current frame.

Example

Listing 8.197 shows a small example of how the name of the Frame parent can be accessed.

Listing 8.197   Example of the Frame.parent ***Property***

```
<script type="text/javascript" language="JavaScript">
<!--
function getParent(){
     var parentName = parent.frameName.name;
}
// -->
 </script>
```

Frame.print()

JavaScript 1.2+, JScript 1.0+
Nav4+, IE3+

Syntax

frame.print(*options*)

Description

The print method of the Frame object is used to send the document output of a particular frame to a printer. This works the same as executing the Print command from a browser menu.

Example

Listing 8.198 shows an example of the `print` method. Using the `onClick` event handler, the `print()` method is executed when the bottom frame is clicked.

Listing 8.198 *Example of the* `print()` *Method*

```
<html>



<frameset rows="80, *">
<frame src="top.html" name="top" >
<frame src="bottom.html" name="bottom" onClick='document.window.bottom.
➥print()'>
</frameset>


</html>
```

Frame.self

> JavaScript 1.0+, JScript 1.0+
> Nav2+, IE3+, Opera3+

Syntax

```
frame.self
```

Description

The `self` property of the `Frame` object is used as a keyword to reference the current frame.

Example

Listing 8.199 shows an example of the `self` property being used to get the name for the current frame.

Listing 8.199 *Syntax for the* `self` *Property*

```
<script type="text/javascript" language="JavaScript">
<!--
function getName(){
    var name=window.frame.self.name;
}
// -->
</script>
```

Frame.setInterval()

> JavaScript 1.2+, JScript 1.0+
> Nav4+, IE3+

Syntax

```
frame.setInterval(exp,num)
```

Description

The setInterval() method of the Frame object is used to schedule a function for repeated execution. It takes two parameters. The first parameter, *exp*, is the expression being executed. The second parameter, *num*, is the time in milliseconds that elapses before the expression is executed again. The function being executed is stopped by calling the clearInterval() method.

Example

Listing 8.200 shows a simple example of a setInterval() method call. For a more detailed example, see window.setInterval.

Listing 8.200 ***Example of the*** setInterval() ***Method Call***

```
<script type="text/javascript" language="JavaScript">
<!--
Frame.setInterval(document.write('Begin writing", 50);
 // -->
</script>
```

Frame.setTimeout()

JavaScript 1.0+, JScript 1.0+
Nav2+, IE3+, Opera3+

Syntax

```
frame.setTimeout(str,num)
```

Description

The setTimeout() method of the Frame object is used to schedule a function for delayed execution. The method accepts two parameters. The first parameter, *str*, is the function or expression being evaluated. The second parameter, *num*, is a numeric value specifying the millisecond units that elapse before the function or expression is executed.

Example

Listing 8.201 shows a example of the setTimeout() method being used to delay the printing of text.

Listing 8.201 ***Example of the*** setTimeout() ***Method***

```
<html>


<script type="text/javascript" language="JavaScript">
<!--
```

Listing 8.201   Continued

```
document.bottom.setTimeout(document.bottom.print("Keep on running"), 500);
// -->
</script>

<frameset rows="100,*">
<frame src="top.html" name="upper">
<frame src="bottom.html" name="bottom" scrolling="yes">
</frameset>

</html>
```

Frame.top

JavaScript 1.0+, JScript 1.0+
Nav2+, IE3+, Opera3+

Syntax

```
frame.top
```

Description

The `top` property of the `Frame` object specifies the top-most browser window containing frames.

Example

Listing 8.202 shows an example of how the `top` property is used to get the name of the top frame.

Listing 8.202   Example of the `top` Property

```
<script type="text/javascript" language="JavaScript">
<!--

var topBrowserName = myframe.document.top.name;
alert("The name of the topmost browser is: " + topBrowser);
// -->
 </script>
```

Frame.unwatch()

JavaScript 1.2+
Nav4+

Syntax

```
frame.unwatch(prop)
```

Description

The `unwatch()` method of the `Frame` object is used to remove a watchpoint set on a property by the `watch()` method. It takes one parameter, *prop*, which is the property to unwatch.

Example

Listing 8.203 shows how the `unwatch()` method is used to remove the watchpoint set on the frame name. The *setWatch* method sets the watchpoint on the frame name initially. When the name is changed, the *alertme* function is called. The watchpoint is then removed using the `unwatch()` method.

Listing 8.203   Using the `unwatch()` **Method of the** `Frame` **Object**

```
<script type="text/javascript" language="JavaScript">
<!--

// Alert user when watch property changed.
function alertme(id,oldValue,newValue)
{
  document.writeln(id + " changed from " + "<b>" + oldValue +
➥"</b>"+ " to " + "<b>" + newValue + "</b><br>")
  return newValue;
}

// Set the watchpoint on the frame name.
function setWatch(){
  myProp = document.frameName.name;
  watch("myProp",alertme);
  myProp = "bugs";
  unwatch("myProp");
  myProp = "daffy";
}

// -->
</script>
```

Frame.watch()

JavaScript 1.2+
Nav4+

Syntax

`frame.watch(prop, handler)`

Description

The `watch()` method of the `Frame` object is used to watch for changes to `Frame` properties. When one of the properties, *prop,* is assigned a value, a *handler* is used to call a user-defined function.

Example

Listing 8.204 shows how the watch() method is used to set a watchpoint on the frame name. The *setWatch* method sets the watchpoint on the frame name initially. When the name is changed, the *alertme* function is called.

Listing 8.204   *Using the* watch() *Method*

```
<script type="text/javascript" language="JavaScript">
<!--

// Alert user when watch property has been changed.
function alertme(id,oldValue,newValue)
{
  document.writeln(id + " changed from " + "<b>" + oldValue +
➥"</b>"+ " to " + "<b>" + newValue + "</b><br>")
  return newValue;
}

// Set the watchpoint on the frame name.
function setWatch(){
  myProp = document.frameName.name;
  watch("myProp",alertme);
  myProp = "bugs";
}

// -->
</script>
```

Frame.window
JavaScript 1.0+, JScript 1.0+
Nav2+, IE3+, Opera3+

Syntax

```
frame.window
```

Description

The window property of the Frame object is used to reference the current frame. This works the same as using the self property.

Example

Listing 8.205 shows an example of the syntax of the window property.

Listing 8.205   *Syntax for the* window *Property*

```
<html>


<script type="text/javascript" language="JavaScript">
```

```
<!--
//Sets focus to the upper frame.
document.upper.window.focus();
// -->
</script>

<frameset rows="100,*">
<frame src="top.html" name="upper">
<frame src="bottom.html" name="bottom">
</frameset>

</html>
```

Hidden

JavaScript 1.0+, JScript 1.0+
Nav2+, IE3+, Opera3+

Syntax

Core client-side JavaScript object.

Description

The Hidden object is created using the HTML <input> tag. Specifying the type parameter of the <input> tag as hidden creates the Hidden object. It is a text object that is not visible in an HTML form. The Hidden object is primarily used for passing name/value pairs from a form. Table 8.16 shows the properties of the Hidden object.

Table 8.16 **Properties and Methods of the** Hidden *Object*

Type	Item	Description
Property	form	Specifies the form containing the Hidden object.
	name	Refers to the name of the Hidden object.
	type	Refers to the HTML type attribute of the Hidden object.
	value	Refers to the HTML value attribute of the Hidden object.
Method	unwatch()	Removes a watchpoint on a Hidden property.
	watch()	Sets a watchpoint on a Hidden property.

Example

Listing 8.206 shows how a Hidden object is created and how some of its properties are accessed.

Listing 8.206   Creating a Hidden Object

```
<html>

<body>
<form name="form1">
<input type="hidden" name="hide1" value="Test">
<p>
<input type="button" value="Get Hidden Attributes"
   onClick='alert("The Hidden object Name is: " + form1.hide1.name +
➡ " The Hidden Type is: " + form1.hide1.type + " The Hidden Value is: "
➡ + form1.hide1.value)'>
</form>

</body>
</html>
```

Hidden.form

JavaScript 1.0+, JScript 1.0+
Nav2+, IE3+, Opera3+

Syntax

hidden.form

Description

The form property of the Hidden object is used to reference the form containing the Hidden object.

Example

Listing 8.207 shows how the form property is used to store the name of the form.

Listing 8.207   Example of the form Property

```
<html>

<body>
<form name="form1">
Form name:<input type="hidden" name="hide1" value="Test">
<p>
<input type="button" value="Form Name"
   onClick="this.form.hide1.value=this.form.name">
</form>

</body>
</html>
```

Hidden.name

JavaScript 1.0+, JScript 1.0+
Nav2+, IE3+, Opera3+

Syntax

hidden.name

Description

The name property of the Hidden object is used to get the name of the Hidden object. This is the HTML name attribute for the Hidden object.

Example

Listing 8.208 shows an example of how the name property is used. The form object is used to access the name property.

Listing 8.208   Example of the name *Property*

```
<html>

<body>
<form name="form1">
Form name:<input type="hidden" name="hide1" value="Test">
<p>
<input type="button" value="Hidden Name"
   onClick='alert("The Hidden object name is: " + form1.hide1.name)'>
</form>

</body>
</html>
```

Hidden.type

JavaScript 1.1+, JScript 3.0+
Nav3+, IE4+, Opera3+

Syntax

hidden.type

Description

The type property of the Hidden object specifies the hidden type. For all Hidden objects, the type value is Hidden.

Example

Listing 8.209 shows an example of how the type property is used to get the hidden type. The form object is used to access the type property.

Listing 8.209   Example of the type **Property**

```
<html>

<body>
<form name="form1">
Form name:<input type="hidden" name="hide1" value="Test">
<p>
<input type="button" value="Hidden Type"
    onClick='alert("The Hidden object type is: " + form1.hide1.type)'>
</form>

</body>
</html>
```

Hidden.unwatch()

JavaScript 1.2+
Nav4+

Syntax

hidden.unwatch(*prop*)

Description

The unwatch() method of the Hidden object is used to remove a watchpoint set on a property by the watch() method. It takes one parameter, which is the property to unwatch.

Example

Listing 8.210 shows how the unwatch() method is used to turn off the watch point set on the Hidden object value.

Listing 8.210   Using the unwatch() **Method of the** Hidden **Object**

```
<html>
<script type="text/javascript"  language="JavaScript">
<!--

function alertme(id,oldValue,newValue)
{
  document.writeln(id + " changed from " + "<b>" + oldValue +
➡"</b>"+ " to " + "<b>" + newValue + "</b><br>")
  return newValue;
}

function setWatch(){
  myProp = document.form1.hide1.value;
  watch("myProp",alertme);
  myProp = "joe";
```

```
      unwatch("myProp");
      myProp = "jane";
}

// -->
</script>
<body>
<form name="form1">
Hidden Input<input type="hidden" name="hide1" value="Test">
<p>
<input type="button" value="Click Here" onClick='setWatch()'>
</form>

</body>
</html>
```

Hidden.value

JavaScript 1.0+, JScript 1.0+
Nav2+, IE3+, Opera3+

Syntax

hidden.value

Description

The value property of the hidden object reflects the HTML value attribute of the Hidden object.

Example

Listing 8.211 shows how the value property of the Hidden object is used. The onClick event handler is used to display an alert box to the user indicating the value of the Hidden object.

Listing 8.211 *Using the* value *Property of the* Hidden *Object*

```
<html>

<body>
<form name="form1">
Form name:<input type="hidden" name="hide1" value="Test">
<p>
<input type="button" value="Get Hidden Value"
     onClick='alert("The Hidden object value is: " + form1.hide1.value)'>
</form>

</body>
</html>
```

Hidden.watch()

JavaScript 1.2+
Nav4+

Syntax

hidden.watch(*prop, handler*)

Description

The watch() method of the Hidden object is used to watch for changes to Hidden properties. When one of the properties, *prop,* is assigned a value, a *handler* is used to call a user-defined function.

Example

Listing 8.212 shows how the watch() method is used to check for assignments to the hidden object value. If an assignment is made, the alertme function is called to notify the user.

Listing 8.212 Using the* watch() *Method of the* Hidden *Object

```
<html>
<script type="text/javascript"  language="JavaScript">
<!--

function alertme(id,oldValue,newValue)
{
  document.writeln(id + " changed from " + "<b>" + oldValue + "</b>"
➥+ " to " + "<b>" + newValue + "</b><br>")
  return newValue;
}

function setWatch(){
  myProp = document.form1.hide1.value;
  watch("myProp",alertme);
  myProp = "joe";
  myProp = "jane";
}

// -->
</script>
<body>
<form name="form1">
Hidden Input<input type="hidden" name="hide1" value="Test">
<p>
<input type="button" value="Click Here" onClick='setWatch()'>
</form>

</body>
</html>
```

History

JavaScript 1.0+, ECMAScript 1.0+, JScript 1.0+
Nav2+, IE3+, Opera3+

Syntax

Core client-side JavaScript object.

Description

The `History` object is a predefined JavaScript object that allows you to navigate through the history of Web sites that a browser has displayed. The browser stores a history of visited URLs in a list, which the `History` object references. Table 8.17 shows the methods and properties of the `History` object.

Table 8.17   Properties and Methods of the `History` **Object**

Type	Item	Description
Property	`current`	Refers to the current URL in the history list
	`length`	Returns the number of entries in the history list
	`next`	Refers to the next URL in the history list
	`previous`	Refers to the previous URL in the history list
Method	`back()`	Loads the URL for the previously visited Web site
	`forward()`	Loads the next URL in the history list
	`go()`	Loads a URL from the history list
	`unwatch()`	Removes a watchpoint on a `History` property
	`watch()`	Sets a watchpoint on a `History` property

Example

Listing 8.213 shows an example of how the `History` object is used. A `for` loop is used to loop through the history list and outputs the Web site entries in the list.

Listing 8.213   Example of the `History` **Object**

```
<html>

<body>
<script type="text/javascript" language="JavaScript">
<!--
// code loops though the history list and outputs a history list
// of web sites visited.
for (i=0; i<history.length; i++){
document.writeln(window.history.previous);
}
//-- End Hide>
</script>

</body>
</html>
```

History.back()

JavaScript 1.0+, ECMAScript 1.0+, JScript 1.0+
Nav2+, IE3+, Opera3+

Syntax

```
history.back()
```

Description

The back() method of the History object is used to load the URL for the previously visited Web site.

Example

Listing 8.214 shows an example of how a JavaScript button can use the back() method to simulate the browser's back functionality.

Listing 8.214   Example of the back() Method

```
<html>

<body>

<form name="form1">
Click on the button to go back to the previous page.
<input type="button" value="Go Back" onClick='window.history.back()'>
</form>

</body>
</html>
```

History.current

JavaScript 1.1+, ECMAScript 1.0+, JScript 3.0+
Nav3+, IE4+

Syntax

```
history.current
```

Description

The current property of the History object contains a string that specifies the complete URL of the current history entry.

NOTE

In Navigator 4 and higher, getting the current value requires the
UniversalBrowserRead privilege.

Example

Listing 8.215 shows an example of how the current property is used. For this example, the UniversalBrowserRead privilege must be set. When this is done, the onClick event handler alerts the user of the History current property.

Listing 8.215 Example of the current *Property*

```
<html>

<body>

<script type="text/javascript" language="JavaScript">
<!--

// Request the Universal Browser Read privilege.
netscape.security.PrivilegeManager.enablePrivilege("UniversalBrowserRead");

// -->
</script>

<form name="form1">
<input type="button" value="Get Current"
➥ onClick='alert(window.history.current)'>
</form>

</body>
</html>
```

History.forward()

JavaScript 1.0+, ECMAScript 1.0+, JScript 1.0+
Nav2+, IE3+, Opera3+

Syntax

```
history.forward()
```

Description

The forward() method of the History object is used to load the URL for the next Web site in the history list.

Example

Listing 8.216 shows an example of how the forward() method is used to simulate the forward functionality of the browser.

Listing 8.216 **Example of the** forward() **Method**

```
<html>

<body>

<form name="form1">
Click on the button to go to the forward browser page.
<input type="button" value="Go Forward" onClick='window.history.forward()'>
</form>

</body>
</html>
```

History.go()

JavaScript 1.0+, ECMAScript 1.0+, JScript 1.0+
Nav2+, IE3+, Opera3+

Syntax

history.go(*num*)

Description

The go() method of the History object loads a URL from the history list.

Example

Listing 8.217 shows how the go() method can be used to navigate to another Web site in the history list.

Listing 8.217 **Example of the** History go() **Method**

```
<html>

<body>

<form name="form1">
Click on the button to go back 2 pages.
<input type="button" value="Go" onClick='window.history.go(-2)'>
</form>

</body>
</html>
```

History.length

JavaScript 1.0+, ECMAScript 1.0+, JScript 1.0+
Nav2+, IE3+, Opera3+

Syntax

history.length

Description

The length property of the History object is used to get the number of URLs in the history list.

Example

Listing 8.218 shows an example of how the length property is used to determine how many URLs are in the history list.

Listing 8.218   *Example of the* length *Property*

```
<html>

<body>

<script type="text/javascript" language="JavaScript">
<!--
//Write the number of elements in the history list.
var numOfURL = window.history.length;
document.write("The number of URL's in the history list is: " + numOfURL);
// -->
</script>

</body>
</html>
```

History.next

JavaScript 1.1+, ECMAScript 1.0+, JScript 3.0+
Nav3+, IE4+

Syntax

```
history.next
```

Description

The next property of the History object is used to get the URL for the next entry in the history list.

NOTE

In Navigator 4 and later, getting the next value requires the UniversalBrowserRead privilege.

Example

Listing 8.219 shows an example of how the next property is used to get the next URL in the history list. If nothing is displayed for the nextURL, you are at the end of the history list.

Listing 8.219 **Example of the** next **Property**

```
<html>

<body>

<script type="text/javascript" language="JavaScript">
<!--
// Request the Universal Browser Read privilege.
netscape.security.PrivilegeManager.enablePrivilege("UniversalBrowserRead");

//Get the next URL in the history list.
var nextURL = window.history.next;
document.write("The next URL in the history list is: " + nextURL);
// -- >
</script>

</body>
</html>
```

History.previous

JavaScript 1.1+, ECMAScript 1.0+, JScript 3.0+
Nav3+, IE4+

Syntax

```
history.previous
```

Description

The previous property of the History object is used to get the URL for the previous entry in the history list.

NOTE

In Navigator 4 and later, getting the previous value requires the UniversalBrowserRead privilege.

Example

Listing 8.220 shows an example of how the previous property is used to get the previous URL in the history list.

Listing 8.220 **Example of the** previous **Property**

```
<html>

<body>
<script type="text/javascript" language="JavaScript">
<!--
```

```
// Request the Universal Browser Read privilege.
netscape.security.PrivilegeManager.enablePrivilege("UniversalBrowserRead");
// -->
</script>

<form name="form1">
<input type="button" value="Get Previous"
➥ onClick='alert(window.history.previous)'>
</form>

</body>
</html>
```

History.unwatch()

JavaScript 1.2+
Nav4+, NES3+

Syntax

*history.*unwatch(*prop*)

Description

The unwatch() method of the History object is used to remove a watchpoint set on a property by the watch() method. It takes one parameter, which is the property to unwatch.

Example

Listing 8.221 shows how the unwatch() method is used to remove the watchpoint set on the History object.

Listing 8.221 *Using the* unwatch() *Method on the* History *Object*

```
<html>

<script type="text/javascript"  language="JavaScript">
<!--

function alertme(id,oldValue,newValue)
{
  document.writeln(id + " changed from " + "<b>" + oldValue +
➥"</b>"+ " to " + "<b>" + newValue + "</b><br>")
  return newValue;
}

function setWatch(){
  myRes = window.history.previous;
  watch("myRes",alertme);
```

Listing 8.221   Continued

```
  myRes = "something";
  unwatch("myRes");
  myRes = "otherthing";
}

// -->
</script>

<body>
<form name="form1">
<input type="button" value="Get Previous" onClick='setWatch()'>
</form>
</body>
</html>
```

History.watch()

JavaScript 1.2+
Nav4+, NES3+

Syntax

history.watch(*prop, handler*)

Description

The watch() method of the History object is used to watch for changes to History properties. When one of the properties, *prop,* is assigned a value, a *handler* is used to call a user-defined function.

Example

Listing 8.222 shows how the watch() method is used to watch for changes to the history property.

Listing 8.222   Using the watch() **Method on the** History **Object**

```
<html>
<script type="text/javascript"  language="JavaScript">
<!--

function alertme(id,oldValue,newValue)
{
  document.writeln(id + " changed from " + "<b>" + oldValue +
➥"</b>"+ " to " + "<b>" + newValue + "</b><br>")
  return newValue;
}

function setWatch(){
  myRes = window.history.previous;
  watch("myRes",alertme);
```

```
  myRes = "something";
  myRes = "otherthing";
}

// -->
</script>

<body>

<form name="form1">
<input type="button" value="Get Previous" onClick='setWatch()'>
</form></body>
</html>
```

Image

JavaScript 1.1+, JScript 1.0+
Nav3+, IE3+, Opera3+

Syntax

Core client-side JavaScript object.

Description

The Image object represents an image that was created with the <img> tag. Images can be downloaded and cached dynamically by using the Image() constructor, but they cannot be displayed using the constructor. The constructor takes two optional arguments, width and height. The argument *width* specifies the width of the image in pixels, whereas the argument *height* specifies the height of the image in pixels. If these arguments are larger than the actual image, the image will be stretched to these dimensions. You have probably noticed that there is no argument specifying the image to load. The image to load is specified using dot notation and the src property after the image constructor has been called. Table 8.18 lists all the properties, methods, and events associated with Image object.

Table 8.18   Properties, Methods, and Events Associated with the Image *Object*

Type	Item	Description
Property	border	Width of the border around an image.
	complete	Has the image finished loading?
	height	Height of the image.
	hspace	Padding on left and right of the image.
	lowsrc	Alternate image for low-resolution displays.
	name	Name of the image.
	src	URL of the image.

Table 8.18 *Continued*

Type	Item	Description
	`vspace`	Padding on top and bottom of the image.
	`width`	Width of the image.
Method	`handleEvent()`	Invokes an images event handler.
	`unwatch()`	Removes a watchpoint on an **Image** property.
	`watch()`	Sets a watchpoint on an **Image** property.
Event	`onAbort`	Handler when the image load is aborted.
	`onError`	Handler when an error occurs while loading the image.
	`onKeyDown`	Handler for **KeyDown** events within the image.
	`onKeyPress`	Handler for **KeyPress** events within the image.
	`onKeyUp`	Handler for **KeyUp** events within the image.
	`onLoad`	Handler when the image is finished loading.

Example

Listing 8.223 demonstrates how to use the <img> tag and the Image() constructor to alternate images in a document.

Listing 8.223 *Example of the* Image *Object*

```
<html>

<script type="text/javascript" language="JavaScript">
<!--

//Alternate flag
alternate=0;

//Create an Image object and preload image.
circle = new Image();
circle.src = "circle.gif";
square = new Image();
square.src = "square.gif";

function changeImage()
{
  if(alternate==0)
  {
    document.magic.src=circle.src;
    alternate=1;
  }
  else
  {
    document.magic.src=square.src;
```

```
    alternate=0;
  }
}

// -->
</script>

<center>
<h2>Magic Trick</h2>

<form>
<input type="button"
       value="Change Image"
       onClick="changeImage()">
</form>

<img name="magic" src="square.gif">
</center>

</html>
```

Image.border
JavaScript 1.1+, JScript 1.0+
Nav3+, IE3+, Opera3+

Syntax
image.border

Description
The border property of the Image object specifies the width of the border around an image in pixels. This property can only be set by the border attribute of the <img> tag.

Example
Listing 8.224 shows how the border property is used.

Listing 8.224 *Example of the* border *Property*
```
<html>

<img name="circle"
     src="circle.gif"
     border=10>
<br>

<script type="text/javascript" language="JavaScript">
<!--
```

Listing 8.224   *Continued*

```
//Display width of border.
document.write("The image has a border width of ");
document.write(document.circle.border," pixels.");


// -->
</script>

</html>
```

Image.complete

JavaScript 1.1+, JScript 1.0+
Nav3+, IE3+, Opera3+

Syntax

image.complete

Description

The complete property of the Image object is a boolean value that specifies if an image has finished loading. After an image has completely loaded, the property is changed to false. If the load is aborted or an error occurs during the loading process, the property will be set to true.

Example

Listing 8.225 displays a message based on the value of the complete property.

Listing 8.225   *Example of the* complete *Property*

```
<html>

<img name="circle" src="circle.gif">
<br>

<script type="text/javascript" language="JavaScript">
<!--

//Display message about loading progress of image.
if(document.circle.complete == true)
  document.write("The image has finished loading.");
else
  document.write("The image has not finished loading.");

// -->
</script>

</html>
```

Image.handleEvent()

JavaScript 1.2+,
Nav4+

Syntax

image.handleEvent(*event*)

Description

The handleEvent() method provides a way to invoke an image's event handler, even though the event never happened. The *event* argument associated with this method can be any of the events handled by the Image object.

Example

Listing 8.226 shows how to force an image to handle a KEYDOWN event.

Listing 8.226   *The* handleEvent() *Method*

```
<img name="circle" src="circle.gif" onKeyDOwn="alert('Key pressed')">

<script type="text/javascript" language="JavaScript">
<!--
document.circle.handleEvent(Event.KEYDOWN);
// -->
</script>
```

Image.height

JavaScript 1.1+, JScript 1.0+
Nav3+, IE3+, Opera3+

Syntax

image.height

Description

The height property of the Image object specifies the height of the image in pixels. This property can only be set by the height attribute of the <img> tag.

Example

Listing 8.227 displays the value of the height property.

Listing 8.227   *Example of the* height *Property*

```
<html>

<img name="circle"
    src="circle.gif"
    height="200">
```

Listing 8.227   Continued

```
<br>

<script type="text/javascript" language="JavaScript">
<!--

//Display the height of the image
document.write("The height of the image is ");
document.write(document.circle.height, " pixels.");

// -->
</script>

</html>
```

Image.hspace

JavaScript 1.1+, JScript 1.0+
Nav3+, IE3+, Opera3+

Syntax

image.hspace

Description

The hspace property of the Image object specifies the number of extra pixels that should appear on the left and right of the image. This property can only be set by the hspace attribute of the <img> tag.

Example

Listing 8.228 demonstrates the hspace property. When the code sample is loaded, the JavaScript code will write to the screen the value of the Image hspace property.

Listing 8.228   Example of the hspace Property

```
<html>

Text to left of image.
<img name="circle" src="circle.gif" HSPACE=100>
Text to right of image.<br>

<script type="text/javascript" language="JavaScript">
<!--

//Display value of hspace property
document.write("The hspace property of the image is ");
document.write(document.circle.hspace);
```

```
// -->
</script>

</html>
```

Image.lowsrc

JavaScript 1.1+, JScript 1.0+
Nav3+, IE3+, Opera3+

Syntax

image.lowsrc

Description

The lowsrc property of the Image object specifies the URL of an alternate image to use on low-resolution displays. This property can only be set by the lowsrc attribute of the <img> tag.

Example

Listing 8.229 displays the URL of the low-resolution image. When the code sample is loaded into a browser, the JavaScript code will output the value of the lowsrc property.

Listing 8.229   Example of the lowsrc **Property**

```
<html>

<img name="circle"
     src="circle.gif"
     LOWsrc="circle_low.gif">
<br>

<script type="text/javascript" language="JavaScript">
<!--

//Display the low resolution image
document.write("The URL of the low resolution image is ");
document.write("<i><b>",document.circle.lowsrc,"</b></i>");

// -->
</script>

</html>
```

Image.name

JavaScript 1.1+, JScript 1.0+
Nav3+, IE3+, Opera3+

Syntax

image.name

Description

The name property of the Image object specifies the name of the image. This property can only be set by the name attribute of the <img> tag.

Example

Listing 8.230 displays the name of the image. When the code sample is loaded into a browser, the JavaScript code will output the value of the name property.

Listing 8.230   *Example using the* name *Property*

```
<html>

<img name="circle" src="circle.gif">
<br>

<script type="text/javascript" language="JavaScript">
<!--

//Display name of image
document.write("The name of the image is <i>");
document.write(document.circle.name,"</i>");

// -->
</script>

</html>
```

Image.onAbort

JavaScript 1.1+, JScript 1.0+
Nav3+, IE3+

Syntax

onAbort="*command*"

Description

TheonAbort event defines a handler when the loading of the image is aborted.

Example

Listing 8.231 creates an alert box when the loading of the image is aborted.

Listing 8.231   Example of the onAbort *Event*

```
<img name="circle"
     src="circle.gif"
     onAbort="alert('This image did not finish loading!')">
```

Image.onError

JavaScript 1.1+, JScript 3.0+
Nav3+, IE4+

Syntax

onError="*command*"

Description

The onError event handler is triggered when an error occurs while loading the image.

Example

Listing 8.232 creates an alert box if an error occurs while loading the image.

Listing 8.232   Example of the onError *Event Handler*

```
<img name="circle"
     src="circle.gif"
     onError="alert('An error occurred while this image was loading!')">
```

Image.onKeyDown

JavaScript 1.2+, JScript 3.0+
Nav4+, IE4+

Syntax

onKeyDown="*command*"

Description

The onKeyDown event handler is triggered when a key is pressed down while the image is selected.

Example

Listing 8.233 defines an event handler for the onKeyDown event within an image.

Listing 8.233   Example of the onKeyDown *Event*

```
<input type="image" name="circle"src="circle.gif"
➥   onKeyDown="alert('An ONKEYDOWN event occurred!')">
```

Image.onKeyPress

JavaScript 1.2+, JScript 3.0+
Nav4+, IE4+

Syntax

onKeyPress="*command*"

Description

The onKeyPress event defines a handler when a key is pressed down while the image is selected.

Example

Listing 8.234 defines an event handler for the onKeyPress event within an image.

Listing 8.234   Example of the onKeyPress **Event Handler**

```
<input type="image" name="circle" src="circle.gif"
➥ onKeyPress="alert('An ONKEYPRESS event occurred!')">
```

Image.onKeyUp

JavaScript 1.2+, JScript 3.0+
Nav4+, IE4+

Syntax

onKeyUp="*command*"

Description

The onKeyUp event defines a handler when a key is pressed and then released while the image is selected.

Example

Listing 8.235 defines an event handler for the onKeyUp event within an image.

Listing 8.235   Example of the onKeyUp **Event**

```
<input type="image" name="circle"src="circle.gif"
➥ onKeyUp="alert('An ONKEYUP event occurred!')">
```

Image.onLoad

JavaScript 1.1+, JScript 1.0+
Nav3+, IE3+

Syntax

onLoad="*command*"

Description

The onLoad event handler defines what should happen once the image has finished loading.

Example

Listing 8.236 displays a message once the image has finished loading.

Listing 8.236   Example of the onLoad Event Handler

```
<img name="circle"
    src="circle.gif"
    onLoad="alert('This image has finished loading!')">
```

Image.src

JavaScript 1.1+, JScript 1.0+
Nav3+, IE3+, Opera3+

Syntax

image.src

Description

The src property of the Image object specifies the URL of the image. This property can only be set by the src attribute of the <img> tag.

Example

Listing 8.237 displays the URL of the image.

Listing 8.237   Example of the src Property

```
<html>

<img name="circle" src="circle.gif"><br>

<script type="text/javascript" language="JavaScript">
<!--

//Display the URL of the image
document.write("The URL of the image is ");
document.write("<i><b>",document.circle.src,"</b></i>");

// -->
</script>

</html>
```

Image.unwatch()

JavaScript 1.2+
Nav4+, NES3+

Syntax

*image.*unwatch(*prop*)

Description

The unwatch() method of the Image object is used to remove a watchpoint set on a property by the watch() method. It takes one parameter, which is the property to unwatch.

Example

Listing 8.238 shows how the unwatch() method is used to remove the watchpoint set on myImg.

Listing 8.238 Using the unwatch() *Method on the* Image *Object*

```
<html>
<img src="myhome.jpg" name="myhome">
<br><br>

<script type="text/javascript"  language="JavaScript">
<!--

// Function which is run when the value of myImg is changed.
// It alerts the user of the changes.
function alertme(id,oldValue,newValue)
{
  document.writeln(id + " changed from " + "<b>" + oldValue +
➥"</b>"+ " to " + "<b>" + newValue + "</b><br>")
  return newValue;
}

  myImg = document.myhome.name;
  watch("myImg",alertme);
  myImg = "Yourhome";
  unwatch("myImg");
  myImg = "theirhome";

// -->
</script>
</html>
```

Image.vspace

JavaScript 1.1+, JScript 1.0+
Nav3+, IE3+, Opera3+

Syntax

image.vspace

Description

The vspace property of the Image object specifies the number of extra pixels that should appear on the top and bottom of the image. This property can only be set by the vspace attribute of the <img> tag.

Example

Listing 8.239 demonstrates the vspace property. When the code sample is loaded into a browser, the JavaScript code will output the value of the vspace property.

Listing 8.239   Example of the vspace Property

```
<html>

Text at top of image.<br>
<img name="circle" src="circle.gif" VSPACE=100><br>
Text at bottom of image.<br>

<script type="text/javascript" language="JavaScript">
<!--

//Display value of vspace property
document.write("The vspace property of the image is ");
document.write(document.circle.vspace);

// -->
</script>

</html>
```

Image.watch()

JavaScript 1.2+
Nav4+, NES3+

Syntax

image.watch(*prop, handler*)

Description

The watch() method of the Image object is used to watch for changes to Image properties. When one of the properties, *prop,* is assigned a value, a *handler* is used to call a user-defined function.

Example

Listing 8.240 shows how the watch() method is used to determine when the name property has been modified.

Listing 8.240   Using the watch() Method of the Image Object

```
<html>
<img src="myhome.jpg" name="myhome">
<br><br>

<script type="text/javascript"  language="JavaScript">
<!--

function alertme(id,oldValue,newValue)
{
  document.writeln(id + " changed from " + "<b>" +
➥oldValue + "</b>"+ " to " + "<b>" + newValue + "</b><br>")
  return newValue;
}

  myImg = document.myhome.name;
  watch("myImg",alertme);
  myImg = "Yourhome";
  myImg = "theirhome";

// -->
</script>
</html>
```

Image.width

> JavaScript 1.1+, JScript 1.0+
> Nav3+, IE3+, Opera3+

Syntax

image.width

Description

The width property of the Image object specifies the width of the image in pixels. This property can only be set by the width attribute of the <img> tag.

Example

Listing 8.241 displays the value of the width property.

Listing 8.241   Example of the width *Property*

```
<html>

<img name="circle"
    src="circle.gif"
    width=150>
<br>

<script type="text/javascript" language="JavaScript">
<!--

//Display width of image
document.write("The width of the image is ");
document.write(document.circle.width, " pixels.");

// -->
</script>

</html>
```

Layer

>JavaScript 1.2+
>Nav4+

Syntax

Core client-side JavaScript object.

Description

The Layer object represents an object that contains a single document. A document can contain multiple layers, and thereby contain multiple documents. Layers are useful for displaying graphics which overlay each other within a browser. The Layer object has specific properties and methods associated with it, as shown in Table 8.19.

Table 8.19   Properties and Methods of the Layer *Object*

Type	Item	Description
Property	above	Specifies the layer above
	background	Refers to the background image of the layer
	below	Specifies the layer below
	bgColor	Refers to the background color of the layer
	clip.bottom	Refers to the bottom of the layer's clipping area
	clip.height	Refers to the height of the layer's clipping area
	clip.left	Refers to the left of the layer's clipping area
	clip.right	Refers to the right of the layer's clipping area
	clip.top	Refers to the top of the layer's clipping area
	clip.width	Refers to the width of the layer's clipping area

Table 8.19   Continued

Type	Item	Description
	document	The document object that contains the layer
	left	The x coordinate of the layer
	name	Refers to the name of the layer
	onBlur	Event handler when focus is removed from the layer
	onFocus	Event handler when focus is set to a layer
	onLoad	Event handler when a document is loaded in a layer
	onMouseOut	Event handler when the mouse cursor is removed from a layer's area
	onMouseOver	Event handler when the mouse cursor is moved over a layer's area
	pageX	The x coordinate relative to the document
	pageY	The y coordinate relative to the document
	parentLayer	The containing layer
	siblingAbove	The layer above in the zIndex
	siblingBelow	The layer below in the zIndex
	src	The source URL for the layer
	top	The y coordinate of the layer
	visibility	Specifies the visibility state of the layer
	zIndex	The relative z-order of this layer with respect to its siblings
Method	captureEvents()	Specifies the event types to capture
	handleEvent()	Invokes handler for specified event
	load()	Loads a new URL
	moveAbove()	Moves the layer above another layer
	moveBelow()	Moves the layer below another layer
	moveBy()	Moves the layer to a specified position
	moveTo()	Moves the top-left corner of the window to the specified screen coordinates
	moveToAbsolute()	Changes the layer position to the specified pixel coordinates within the page
	releaseEvents()	Sets the layer to release captured events of the specified type
	resizeBy()	Resizes the layer by the specified height and width values
	resizeTo()	Resizes the layer to have the specified height and width values
	routeEvent()	Passes a captured event along the normal event hierarchy
	unwatch()	Removes a watchpoint on a **Layer** property
	watch()	Sets a watchpoint on a **Layer** property

Example

Listing 8.242 creates a layer. When the mouse cursor is moved over the Layer object, an alert message is displayed informing which layer the cursor was moved over.

Listing 8.242   Example of the Layer ***Object***

```
<html>

<body>
<layer id="layer1" width="150" height="200" bgcolor="yellow" top="170"
left="200" visibility="show" onMouseOut='alert("This is layer 1")'>
<center>Layer 1</center>
</layer>

<layer id="layer2" width="150" height="160" bgcolor="green" top="100"
left="70" visibility="show" onMouseOut='alert("This is layer 2")'>
<center>Layer 2</center>
</layer>

</body>
</html>
```

Layer.above

>
> JavaScript 1.2+
>
> Nav4+

Syntax

layer.above

Description

The above property of the Layer object refers to the layer immediately above the layer in the zIndex. If this does not exist, the value is null.

Example

Listing 8.243 shows how the above property is used. Two layers are created and when the Get Above button is clicked, an alert box is displayed with the value of the above attribute.

Listing 8.243   Example of the above ***Property***

```
<html>

<body>

<layer id="layer1" width="200" height="200" bgcolor="yellow" top="170"
left="200" visibility="show">
<center>Layer 1</center>
</layer>
```

Listing 8.243   Continued

```
<layer ID="layer2" width="150" height="160" bgcolor="green" top="100"
left="70" visibility="show">
<center>Layer 2</center>
</layer>

<form name="form1">
<input type="button" value="Get Above" onClick='alert(document.layers.above)'>
</form>

</body>
</html>
```

Layer.background

JavaScript 1.2+
Nav4+

Syntax

layer.background

Description

The background property of the Layer object refers to the background attribute of the
<layer> tag. The background images for the layer object can be changed by setting the
background.src property.

Example

Listing 8.244 shows an example of how to change the layer background image. Two
layers are created and when the Change Background button is clicked, the change()
function is called. The change() function sets the background property of layer1 to
water.gif.

Listing 8.244   Example of the background **Property**

```
<html>

<body>

<script type="text/javascript" language="JavaScript">
<!--
function change(){
    document.layer1.background.src = "water.gif";
}
// -->
</script>

<layer id="layer1" width="200" height="200" bgcolor="yellow" top="170"
left="200" visibility="show">
```

```
<center>Layer 1</center>
</layer>

<layer id="layer2" width="150" height="160" bgcolor="green" top="100"
left="70" visibility="show">
<center>Layer 2</center>
</layer>

<form name="form1">
<input type="button" value="Change Background" onClick='change()'>
</form>


</body>
</html>
```

Layer.below

JavaScript 1.2+

Nav4+

Syntax

layer.below

Description

The below property of the Layer object specifies the layer object immediately below the layer in the zIndex. If this does not exist, the below value is null.

Example

Listing 8.245 shows an example of the below property. Two layers are created using the <layer> tag. When the Get Below button is clicked, an alert box is displayed showing the value of the below property.

Listing 8.245   *Example of the* below *Property*

```
<html>

<body>

<layer id="layer1" width="200" height="200" bgcolor="yellow" top="170"
left="200" visibility="show">
<center>Layer 1</center>
</layer>

<layer id="layer2" width="150" height="160" bgcolor="green" top="100"
left="70" visibility="show">
```

Listing 8.245   Continued

```
<center>Layer 2</center>
</layer>

<form name="form1">
<input type="button" value="Get Below" onClick='alert(document.layers.below)'>
</form>

</body>
</html>
```

Layer.bgColor

JavaScript 1.2+
Nav4+

Syntax

```
layer.bgColor
```

Description

The `bgColor` property of the `Layer` object represents the `bgcolor` attribute of the `<layer>` tag. The background color for the `Layer` object can be changed by setting the `bgColor.src` property. The color can only be changed if the `background` property is not set.

Example

Listing 8.246 shows how the `bgColor` property is used to change the background colors of the layer's objects.

Listing 8.246   Example of the `bgColor` *Property*

```
<html>

<body>

<script type="text/javascript" language="JavaScript">
<!--

// function changes the color of layer1
function change1(){
    document.layer1.bgColor = "#FF00FA";
}

// function changes the color of Layer2
function change2(){
    document.layer2.bgColor="orange";
}
```

```
// -->
</script>

<layer id="layer1" width="200" height="200" bgcolor="yellow" top="170"
left="200" visibility="show">
<center>Layer 1</center>
</layer>

<layer id="layer2" width="150" height="160" bgcolor="green" top="100"
left="70" visibility="show">
<center>Layer 2</center>
</layer>

<form name="form1">
<input type="button" value="Change Layer 1 Background" onClick='change1()'>
<br><br>
<input type="button" value="Change Layer 2 Background" onClick='change2()'>
</form>

</body>
</html>
```

Layer.captureEvents()

JavaScript 1.2+
Nav4+

Syntax

layer.captureEvents(*event.type*)

Description

The captureEvents() method of the Layer object is used to handle all events of a specific type.

Example

Listing 8.247 shows how the captureEvents() method is used. The captureEvents() method is used for layer2 to listen for the RESIZE event. When this occurs, the resize2() function is called, which displays a message to the user.

Listing 8.247   Example of the captureEvents() *Method*

```
<html>

<body>

<script type="text/javascript" language="JavaScript">
<!--
```

Listing 8.247 Continued

```
document.layer2.captureEvents(Event.RESIZE);

// function resizes layer2 and upon the resize event alerts the
// user that the layer was resized.
function resize2(){
    document.layer2.resizeTo(300,100);
    onResize=alert("Layer2 has been resized.");
}
// -->
</script>

<layer id="layer1" width="200" height="200" bgcolor="yellow" top="170"
left="200" visibility="show">
<center>Layer 1</center>
</layer>

<layer id="layer2" width="150" height="160" bgcolor=green" top="100"
left="70" visibility="show">
<center>Layer 2</center>
</layer>

<form>
Click the button to resize Layer 2
<br>
<input type="button" value="Resize Layer2" onClick='resize2()'>
</form>
</body>
</html>
```

Layer.clip.bottom

JavaScript 1.2+

Nav4+

Syntax

`layer.clip.bottom`

Description

The `clip.bottom` property of the Layer object refers to the bottom of the layer's clipping area.

Example

Listing 8.248 shows an example of how `clip.bottom` is used. Two layers are created using the `<layer>` tag. When the button is clicked, the `clip1` function is called, which clips the bottom of `layer1` by 100 pixels.

Listing 8.248 *Example of the* `clip.bottom` *Property*

```html
<html>

<body>

<script type="text/javascript" language="JavaScript">
<!--

// function clips the bottom of layer 1 by 100 pixels
function clip1(){
    document.layer1.clip.bottom = 100;
}
// -->
</script>

<layer id="layer1" width="200" height="200" bgcolor="yellow" top="170"
left="200" visibility="show">
<center>Layer 1</center>
</layer>

<layer id="layer2" width="150" height="160" bgcolor="green" top="100"
left="70" visibility="show">
<center>Layer 2</center>
</layer>

<form name="form1">
<input type="button" value="Clip bottom of Layer 1" onClick='clip1()'>
</form>

</body>
</html>
```

Layer.clip.height

JavaScript 1.2+
Nav4+

Syntax

`layer.clip.height`

Description

The `clip.height` property of the `Layer` object refers to the height of the layer's clipping area.

Example

Listing 8.249 shows how the `clip.height` property is used. Two layers are created using the `<layer>` tag. When the button is clicked, the `clip1()` function is called, which clips the height of `layer1` by 75 pixels.

Listing 8.249   Example of the `clip.height` Property

```
<html>

<body>

<script type="text/javascript" language="JavaScript">
<!--

// function clips the height of layer 1 by 75 pixels
function clip1(){
     document.layer1.clip.height = 75;
}
// -->
</script>

<layer id="layer1" width="200" height="200" bgcolor="yellow" top="170"
left="200" visibility="show">
<center>Layer 1</center>
</layer>

<layer id="layer2" width="150" height="160" bgcolor="green" top="100"
left="70" visibility="show">
<center>Layer 2</center>
</layer>

<form name="form1">
<input type="button" value="Clip Height of Layer 1" onClick='clip1()'>
</form>

</body>
</html>
```

Layer.clip.left

JavaScript 1.2+
Nav4+

Syntax

`layer.clip.left`

Description

The `clip.left` property of the `Layer` object represents the left of the layer's clipping area.

Example

Listing 8.250 shows how the `clip.left` property is used. Two layers are created using the `<layer>` tag. When the button is clicked, the `clip1()` function is called, which clips the left side of `layer1` by 90 pixels.

Listing 8.250   Example of the `clip.left` *Property*

```
<html>

<body>

<script type="text/javascript" language="JavaScript">
<!--

// function clips the left side of layer1 by 90 pixels
function clip1(){
     document.layer1.clip.left = 90;
}
// -->
</script>

<layer id="layer1" width="200" height="200" bgcolor="yellow" top="170"
left="200" visibility="show">
<center>Layer 1</center>
</layer>

<layer id="layer2" width="150" height="160" bgcolor="green" top="100"
left="70" visibility="show">
<center>Layer 2</center>
</layer>

<form name="form1">
<input type="button" value="Clip Left of Layer 1" onClick='clip1()'>
</form>

</body>
</html>
```

Layer.clip.right

JavaScript 1.2+
Nav4+

Syntax

`layer.clip.right`

Description

The `clip.right` property of the `Layer` object represents the right of the layer's clipping area.

Example

Listing 8.251 shows how the `clip.right` property is used to shorten the right side of the layer. Two layers are created using the `<layer>` tag. When the button is clicked, the `clip1()` function is called, which clips the right side of `layer1` by 110 pixels.

Listing 8.251 **Example of the** `clip.right` **Property**

```html
<html>

<body>

<script type="text/javascript" language="JavaScript">
<!--

// function clips the right side of layer1 by 110 pixels
function clip1(){
    document.layer1.clip.right = 110;
}
// -->
</script>

<layer id="layer1" width="200" height="200" bgcolor="yellow" top="170"
left="200" visibility="show">
<center>Layer 1</center>
</layer>

<layer id="layer2" width="150" height="160" bgcolor="green" top="100"
left="70" visibility="show">
<center>Layer 2</center>
</layer>

<form name="form1">
<input type="button" value="Clip Right of Layer 1" onClick='clip1()'>
</form>

</body>
</html>
```

Layer.clip.top

JavaScript 1.2+
Nav4+

Syntax

`layer.clip.top`

Description

The `clip.top` property of the `Layer` object represents the top part of the layer's clipping area.

Example

Listing 8.252 uses the `clip.top` property to shorten the height of the layer. Two layers are created using the `<layer>` tag. When the button is clicked, the `clip1()` function is called, which clips the top of `layer1` by 88 pixels.

Listing 8.252 Example of the `clip.top` Property

```
<html>

<body>

<script type="text/javascript" language="JavaScript">
<!--

// function clips the top of layer 1 by 88 pixels.
function clip1(){
    document.layer1.clip.top = 88;
}
// -->
</script>

<layer id="layer1" width="200" height="200" bgcolor="yellow" top="170"
left="200" visibility="show">
<center>Layer 1</center>
</layer>

<layer id="layer2" width="150" height="160" bgcolor="green" top="100"
left="70" visibility="show">
<center>Layer 2</center>
</layer>

<form name="form1">
<input type="button" value="Clip Top of Layer 1" onClick='clip1()'>
</form>

</body>
</html>
```

Layer.clip.width

>JavaScript 1.2+
>Nav4+

Syntax

`layer.clip.width`

Description

The `clip.width` property of the `Layer` object represents the width of the layer's clipping area.

Example

Listing 8.253 shows how the `clip.width` property is used to shorten the width of the layer. Two layers are created using the `<layer>` tag. When the button is clicked, the `clip1()` function is called, which clips the width of `layer1` by 60 pixels.

Listing 8.253   Example of the `clip.width` *Property*

```
<html>

<body>

<script type="text/javascript" language="JavaScript">
<!--

// function changes the width of Layer 1
function clip1(){
    document.layer1.clip.width = 60;
}
// -->
</script>

<layer id="layer1" width="200" height="200" bgcolor="yellow" top="170"
left="200" visibility="show">
<center>Layer 1</center>
</layer>

<layer id="layer2" width="150" height="160" bgcolor="green" top="100"
left="70" visibility="show">
<center>Layer 2</center>
</layer>

<form name="form1">
<input type="button" value="Clip Width of Layer 1" onClick='clip1()'>
</form>

</body>
</html>
```

Layer.document

JavaScript 1.2+
Nav4+

Syntax

`layer`.document

Description

The `document` property of the `Layer` object references the `Document` object contained in the layer.

Example

Listing 8.254 shows how the `document` property is used. When the button is clicked, the `getInfo()` function is called. This displays the name of the document in `layer1`.

Listing 8.254 **Example of the** document *Property*

```
<html>

<body>

<script type="text/javascript" language="JavaScript">
<!--

// function displays an alert box indicating the name of Layer 1 document
function getInfo(){
    alert("The name of Layer 1's document is: " +
➡ document.layer1.document.name);
}
// -->
</script>

<layer id="layer1" width="200" height="200" bgcolor="yellow" top="170"
left="200" visibility="show">
<center>Layer 1</center>
</layer>

<layer id="layer2" width="150" height="160" bgcolor="green" top="100"
left="70" visibility="show">
<center>Layer 2</center>
</layer>

<form name="form1">
<input type="button" value="Get Layer1 document info" onClick='getInfo()'>
</form>

</body>
</html>
```

Layer.handleEvent()

JavaScript 1.2+
Nav4+

Syntax

layer.handleEvent(*event*)

Description

The handleEvent method of the Layer object determines what type of event occurred and passes the event to the object's appropriate event handler.

Example

Listing 8.255 shows how to use the handleEvent method. The document is set up to capture any FOCUS events. When one occurs, it is sent to the handle() function, which passes it to the default handler for `layer2` object. This calls the `displayMsg()` function for any FOCUS events that occur.

Listing 8.255   *Example of the* `handleEvent()` *Method*

```html
<html>

<body>

<script type="text/javascript" language="JavaScript">
<!--

// sets up the document to capture FOCUS events
document.captureEvents(Event.FOCUS);

// function that handles the specific event. The evnt parameter refers to
// the event object.
function handle(evnt){
    window.document.layer2.handleEvent(evnt);
}

function displayMsg(){
    alert("Focus event occurred.");
}

// This registers the handle function as the event handler for the
// FOCUS event.
document.onFocus = handle;
// -->
</script>

<layer id="layer1" width="200" height="200" bgcolor="yellow" top="170"
left="200" visibility="show">
<center>Layer 1</center>
</layer>

<layer id="layer2" width="150" height="160" bgcolor="green" top=100
left="70" visibility="show" onFocus='displayMsg()'>
<center>Layer 2</center>
</layer>

<form name="form1">
<input type="button" value="Get Layer1 document info" onClick='getInfo()'>
</form>

</body>
</html>
```

Layer.left

JavaScript 1.2+
Nav4+

Syntax

```
layer.left
```

Description

The left property of the Layer object represents the x-coordinate position of the layer within the document. Changing this property can move the layer left or right.

Example

Listing 8.256 shows how the left property is used to move the layer from left to right across the screen. When the button is clicked, the move() function is called, which moves layer1 to the left by 60 pixels.

Listing 8.256 Example of the left Property

```html
<html>

<body>

<script type="text/javascript" language="JavaScript">
<!--

// function moves Layer 1 to the left
function move(){
    document.layer1.left = document.layer1.left + 60;
}
// -->
</script>

<layer id="layer1" width="200" height="200" bgcolor="yellow" top="170"
left="200" visibility="show">
<center>Layer 1</center>
</layer>

<layer id="layer2" width="150" height="160" bgcolor="green" top="100"
left="70" visibility="show">
<center>Layer 2</center>
</layer>

<form name="form1">
<input type="button" value="Move layer 1" onClick='move()'>
</form>

</body>
</html>
```

Layer.load()

JavaScript 1.2+
Nav4+

Syntax

```
layer.load(src, width)
```

Description

The `load()` method of the `Layer` object is used to load a new document in the layer. As described in the syntactical definition, this method takes the URL of the source of the layer and the width.

Example

Listing 8.257 shows how to use the `load()` method. When the button is clicked, the `onClick` event handler loads the `tmp.html` file.

Listing 8.257   Example of the `load()` ***Method***

```
<html>
<body>

<layer id="layer1" width="200" height="200" bgcolor="yellow" top="170"
left="200" visibility="show">
<center>Layer 1</center>
</layer>

<layer id="layer2" width="150" height="160" bgcolor="green" top="100"
left="70" visibility="show">
<center>Layer 2</center>
</layer>

<form name="form1">
<input type="button" value="Load Layer 2"
➡ onClick='document.layer2.load("tmp.html", 400)'>
</form>

</body>
</html>
```

Layer.moveAbove()

JavaScript 1.2+
Nav4+

Syntax

```
layer.moveAbove(layername)
```

Description

The moveAbove() method of the Layer object is used to move the current layer above another specified layer. The parameter, *layername*, is the Layer object that gets moved back.

Example

Listing 8.258 an example of how the moveAbove() method is used. When the button is clicked, the onClick event handler handles the CLICK event and moves Layer1 above Layer2.

Listing 8.258 Example of the moveAbove() ***Method***

```
<html>

<body>

<layer id="layer1" width="200" height="200" bgcolor="yellow" top="170"
left="150" visibility="show">
<center>Layer 1</center>
</layer>

<layer id="layer2" width="150" height="160" bgcolor="green" top="100"
left="70" visibility="show">
<center>Layer 2</center>
</layer>

<form name="form1">
<input type="button" value="Move layer 1 above layer 2"
onClick='document.layer1.moveAbove(document.layer2)'>
</form>

</body>
</html>
```

Layer.moveBelow()

JavaScript 1.2+
Nav4+

Syntax

layer.moveBelow(*layername*)

Description

The moveBelow() method of the Layer object is used to move a Layer object below another specified layer. The function takes a single parameter, *layername*, representing the Layer object that gets moved forward.

Example

Listing 8.259 shows how the moveBelow() method is used to move Layer2 below Layer1.

Listing 8.259 **Example of the** moveBelow() **Method**

```
<html>
<body>

<layer id="layer1" width="200" height="200" bgcolor="yellow" top="170"
left="150" visibility="show">
<center>Layer 1</center>
</layer>

<layer id="layer2" width="150" height="160" bgcolor="green" top="100"
left="70" visibility="show">
<center>Layer 2</center>
</layer>

<form name="form1">
<input type="button" value="Move layer 2 below layer 1"
onClick='document.layer2.moveBelow(document.layer1)'>
</form>

</body>
</html>
```

Layer.moveBy()

JavaScript 1.2+
Nav4+

Syntax

```
layer.moveBy(x,y)
```

Description

The moveBy() method of the Layer object moves the layer object to the right and down from its current position. The method takes two parameters, x and y. The x parameter refers to the number of pixels the layer is moved to the right. The y parameter refers to the number of pixels the layer is moved down.

Example

Listing 8.260 shows how the moveBy() method is used. When the button is clicked, the onClick event handler uses the moveBy method to move layer2 50 pixels to the right and 30 pixels down.

Listing 8.260 **Example of the** moveBy() **Method**

```html
<html>

<body>

<layer id="layer1" width="200" height="200" bgcolor="yellow" top="170"
left="150" visibility="show">
<center>Layer 1</center>
</layer>

<layer id="layer2" width="150" height="160" bgcolor="green" top="100"
left="70" visibility="show">
<center>Layer 2</center>
</layer>

<form name="form1">
<input type="button" value="Move layer 2"
➡ onClick='document.layer2.moveBy(50,30)'>
</form>

</body>
</html>
```

Layer.moveTo()

JavaScript1.2+
Nav4+

Syntax

```
Layer.moveTo(x,y)
```

Description

The moveTo() method of the Layer object moves the top-left corner of the Layer object to the specified screen coordinates. The *x* parameter refers to an integer representing the top edge of the window in screen coordinates. The *y* parameter refers to an integer representing the left edge of the window in screen coordinates.

Example

Listing 8.261 shows how the moveTo() method is used. Two layers are created using the <layer> tag. When the button is clicked, the onClick event handler for layer2 invokes the moveTo method, which moves the layer to the screen coordinates 100, 200.

Listing 8.261 **Example of the** moveTo() **Method**

```html
<html>
<body>

<layer id="layer1" width="200" height="200" BGCOLOR="yellow" top="170"
left="150" visibility="show">
```

Listing 8.261   Continued

```
<center>Layer 1</center>
</layer>

<layer id="layer2" width="150" height="160" BGCOLOR="green" top="100"
left="70" visibility="show">
<center>Layer 2</center>
</layer>

<form name="form1">
<input type="button" value="Move layer 2"
➥ onClick='document.layer2.moveTo(100,200)'>
</form>

</body>
</html>
```

Layer.moveToAbsolute()

JavaScript 1.2+
Nav4+

Syntax

```
layer.moveToAbsolute(x,y)
```

Description

The moveToAbsolute() method of the Layer object moves the upper-left corner of the layer to the specified position. This position is relative to the top-level document. The method takes two parameters, x and y. The x parameter refers to the number of pixels the layer is moved to the right. The y parameter refers to the number of pixels the layer is moved down.

Example

Listing 8.262 an example of how the moveToAbsolute() method is used. When the button is clicked, the upper-left corner of the second layer is moved to position 350x 400y.

Listing 8.262   Example of the moveToAbsolute() Method

```
<html>
<body>

<layer id="layer1" width="200" height="200" bgcolor="yellow" top="170"
left="150" visibility="show">
<center>Layer 1</center>
</layer>
```

```
<layer id="layer2" width="150" height="160" bgcolor="green" top="100"
left="70" visibility="show">
<center>Layer 2</center>
</layer>

<form name="form1">
<input type="button" value="Move layer 2"
onClick='document.layer2.moveToAbsolute(350,400)'>
</form>

</body>
</html>
```

Layer.name

JavaScript 1.2+
Nav4+

Syntax

layer.name

Description

The name property of the Layer object refers to the name or ID attribute of the <layer> tag.

Example

Listing 8.263 shows how to access the layer's name.

Listing 8.263   Example of the name *Property*

```
<html>
<body>

<layer id="Tarzan" width="200" height="200" bgcolor="yellow" top="170"
left="250" visibility="show">
<center>Layer 1</center>
</layer>

<layer id="Jane" width="150" height="160" bgcolor="green" top="100"
left="70" visibility="show">
<center>Layer 2</center>
</layer>

<form name="form1">
<input type="button" value="Get Layer 1 Name"
onClick='alert("The name of this layer is: " + document.layer1.name)'>
<br><br><br>
```

Listing 8.263   Continued

```
<input type="button" value="Get Layer 2 Name"
onClick='alert("The name of this layer is: " + document.layer2.name)'>
</form>

</body>
</html> >
```

Layer.onBlur

JavaScript 1.2+
Nav4+

Syntax

```
onBlur="command"
```

Description

The onBlur event handler of the Layer object handles the event when the focus is removed from the Layer object.

Example

Listing 8.264 shows how the onBlur event handler is used. When focus is removed from layer1, the onBlur event handler calls the showMsg() function.

Listing 8.264   Example of the onBlur Event Handler

```
<html>
<body>

<script type="text/javascript" language="JavaScript">
<!--
function showMsg(){
    document.form1.text1.value = "Focus was removed from Layer 1";
}
// -->
</script>

<layer id="layer1" width=200 height=200 bgcolor="yellow" top="170"
left="200" visibility="show"onBlur='showMsg()'>
<center>Layer 1</center>
</layer>

<layer id="layer2" width=150 height=160 bgcolor="green" top="100"
left="70" visibility="show">
<center>Layer 2</center>
</layer>
```

```
<form name="form1">
Click on Layer 1 and the click on Layer 2.
<br><br>
<input type="text" name="text1" size="40">
</form>

</body>
</html>
```

Layer.onFocus
JavaScript 1.2+
Nav4+

Syntax
onFocus="*command*"

Description
The onFocus event handler for the Layer object notifies you when the focus is set on a layer object.

Example
Listing 8.265 shows how the onFocus event handler is used to detect when focus is set on Layer 1.

Listing 8.265   *Example of the* onFocus *Event Handler*

```
<html>
<body>

<script type="text/javascript" language="JavaScript">
<!--
function showMsg(){
    document.form1.text1.value = "Focus set on Layer 1";
}
// -->
</script>

<layer id="layer1" width="200" height="200" bgcolor="yellow" top="170"
left="200" visibility="show"onFocus='showMsg()'>
<center>Layer 1</center>
</layer>

<layer id="layer2" width="150" height="160" bgcolor="green" top="100"
left="70" visibility="show">
<center>Layer 2</center>
</layer>
```

Listing 8.265   Continued

```
<form name="form1">
Click on Layer 2 and then click on layer 1.
<br><br>
<input type="text" name="text1" size="40">
</form>

</body>
</html>
```

Layer.onLoad

JavaScript 1.2+
Nav4+

Syntax

```
onLoad="command"
```

Description

The onLoad property of the Layer object is an event handler that notifies you when the layer's contents are being loaded.

Example

Listing 8.266 shows how the onLoad event handler is used.

Listing 8.266   Example of the onLoad Event Handler

```
<html>

<body>

<script type="text/javascript" language="JavaScript">
<!--
function showMsg(){
    document.form1.text1.value = "Layer contents being loaded";
}
// -->
</script>

<layer id="layer1" width="200" height="200" bgcolor="yellow" top="170"
left="200" visibility="show"onLoad='showMsg()'>
<center>Layer 1</center>
</layer>

<layer id="layer2" width="150" height="160" bgcolor="green" top="100"
left="70"visibility="show">
<center>Layer 2</center>
</layer>
```

```
<form name="form1">
<input type="text" name="text1" size="40">
<br><br>
<input type="button" value="Load Layer 1"
➥ onClick='document.layer1.load("tmp.html",300)'>
</form>

</body>
</html>
```

Layer.onMouseOut

JavaScript 1.2+
Nav4+

Syntax

onMouseOut="*command*"

Description

The onMouseOut property of the Layer object is an event handler that notifies you when the mouse cursor has moved out of the layer region.

Example

Listing 8.267 shows how the onMouseOut event handler is used. When the the mouse cursor is moved over Layer 1 and then is moved out of the Layer 1 region, the event handler invokes the showMsg1() function to alert the user.

Listing 8.267 ***Example of the*** onMouseOut ***Event Handler***

```
<html>

<body>

<script type="text/javascript" language="JavaScript">
<!--
function showMsg1(){
    document.form1.text1.value = "Mouse Moved out of Layer 1 area.";
}
// -->
</script>

<layer id="layer1" width="200" height="200" bgcolor="yellow" top="170"
left="200" visibility="show"onMouseOut='showMsg1()'>
<center>Layer 1</center>
</layer>
```

Listing 8.267 Continued
```
<layer id="layer2" width="150" height="160" bgcolor="green" top="100"
left="70" visibility="show">
<center>Layer 2</center>
</layer>

<form name="form1">
<input type="text" name="text1" size="40">
<br><br>
</form>

</body>
</html>
```

Layer.onMouseOver
JavaScript 1.2+
Nav4+

Syntax
onMouseOver="*command*"

Description
The onMouseOver event handler of the Layer object handles the events when the mouse cursor is moved over the layer area.

Example
Listing 8.268 shows an example of the onMouseOver event handler. When the mouse cursor is moved over Layer 2, the event handler invokes the showMsg1() function to alert the user.

Listing 8.268 Example of the onMouseOver Event Handler
```
<html>
<body>

<script type="text/javascript" language="JavaScript">
<!--

// function displays a message everytime the mouse is moved over Layer 2
function showMsg1(){
    document.form1.text1.value = "Mouse Moved over Layer 2 area.";
}
// -->
</script>

<layer id="layer1" width="200" height="200" bgcolor="yellow" top="170"
left="200" visibility="show">
```

```
<center>Layer 1</center>
</layer>

<layer id="layer2" width="150" height="160" bgcolor="green" top="100"
left="70" visibility="show" onMouseOver='showMsg1()'>
<center>Layer 2</center>
</layer>

<form name="form1">
<input type="text" name="text1" size="40">
<br><br>
</form>

</body>
</html>
```

Layer.pageX

JavaScript 1.2+
Nav4+

Syntax

layer.pageX

Description

The pageX property of the Layer object represents the x-coordinate position of the
layer relative to the top-level document.

Example

Listing 8.269 shows how to use the pageX property. When the button is clicked, the
value of the pageX property is displayed.

Listing 8.269   *Example of the* pageX *Property*

```
<html>
<body>

<script type="text/javascript" language="JavaScript">
<!--

// function increases the size of Layer 1 pageX property
function size(){
    document.layer1.pageX = document.layer1.pageX +20;
}
// -->
</script>
```

Listing 8.269 **Continued**

```
<layer id="layer1" width="200" height="200" bgcolor="yellow" top="170"
left="200" visibility="show">
<center>Layer 1</center>
</layer>

<layer id="layer2" width="150" height="160" bgcolor="green" top="100"
left="70" visibility="show">
<center>Layer 2</center>
</layer>

<form name="form1">
<input type="button" value="Change Layer 1 X-coordinate" onClick=size()>
</form>

</body>
</html>
```

Layer.pageY

JavaScript 1.2+
Nav4+

Syntax

```
layer.pageY
```

Description

The pageY property of the Layer object represents the y-coordinate position of the layer relative to the top-level document.

Example

Listing 8.270 shows how to manipulate the pageY property. When the button is clicked, the size function is called, which adds 20 pixels to the pageY attribute of layer1.

Listing 8.270 **Example of the** pageY **Property**

```
<html>

<body>

<script type="text/javascript" language="JavaScript">
<!--

// function changes the value of the PageY attribute
function size(){
    document.layer1.pageY = document.layer1.pageY +20;
}
```

```
// -->
</script>

<layer id="layer1" width="200" height="200" bgcolor="yellow" top="170"
left="200" visibility="show">
<center>Layer 1</center>
</layer>

<layer id="layer2" width=150 height=160 bgcolor="green" top="100"
left="70" visibility="show">
<center>Layer 2</center>
</layer>

<form name="form1">
<input type="button" value="Change Layer 1 Y-coordinate" onClick='size()'>
</form>

</body>
</html>
```

Layer.parentLayer

JavaScript 1.2+

Nav4+

Syntax

layer.parentLayer

Description

The parentLayer property of the Layer object represents the window or Layer object that contains the current Layer object.

Example

Listing 8.271 shows how to use the parentLayer. The function getname() gets and returns the name of the parent layer.

Listing 8.271 *Example of the* parentLayer *Property*

```
<html>

<body>

<script type="text/javascript" language="JavaScript">
<!--
```

Listing 8.271   Continued

```
// function gets the name of the parent layer
function getname(){
    document.form1.text1.value = document.layer1.parentLayer.name;
}
// -->
</script>

<layer id="layer1" width="200" height="200" bgcolor="yellow" top="170"
left="200" visibility="show">
<center>Layer 1</center>
</layer>

<layer id="layer2" width=150 height=160 bgcolor="green" top="100"
left="70" visibility="show"'>
<center>Layer 2</center>
</layer>

<form name="form1">
<input type="button" value="Get Layer 1 parent name" onClick='getname()'>
<br><br>
<input type="text" name="text1" size="40">
</form>

</body>
</html>
```

Layer.releaseEvents()

JavaScript 1.2+
Nav4+

Syntax

`layer.releaseEvents(event)`

Description

The `releaseEvents()` method of the `Layer` object specifies that the `Layer` object should no longer capture events of the specified type.

Example

Listing 8.272 is an example of how the `releaseEvents()` method is used. When the FOCUS event is captured, it is handled by the `handle()` method. After this is done, executing the event is released using the `releaseEvents()` method.

Listing 8.272   Example of the releaseEvents() *Method*

```
<html>

<body>

<script type="text/javascript" language="JavaScript">
<!--
// sets up the document to capture FOCUS events
document.captureEvents(Event.FOCUS);

// function that handles the specific event. The evnt parameter refers to
// the event object.
function handle(evnt){
   alert("The layer got a FOCUS event and calls releaseEvents");
   return true;
}

function releaseFocus(){
    document.layer2.releaseEvents(Event.FOCUS);
}

// This registers the handle function as the event handler for the
// FOCUS event.
document.onFocus = handle;

// -->
</script>

<layer id="layer1" width="200" height="200" bgcolor="yellow" top="170"
left="200" visibility="show">
<center>Layer 1</center>
</layer>

<layer id="layer1" width="150" height="160" bgcolor=green" top="100"
left="70" visibility="show">
<center>Layer 2</center>
</layer>

</body>
</html>
```

Layer.resizeBy()

JavaScript 1.2+

Nav4+

Syntax

*layer.*resizeBy(*x,y*)

Description

The resizeBy() method of the Layer object resizes the layer by a relative size. The *x* parameter refers to the number of pixels the layer width is increased. The *y* parameter refers to the number of pixels the layer height is increased.

Example

Listing 8.273 shows how to resize a Layer object. When the button is clicked, the onClick event handler executes the resizeBy() method to resize layer2.

Listing 8.273 **Example of the** resizeBy() **Method**

```
<html>

<body>

<layer id="layer1" width="200" height="200" bgcolor="yellow" top="170"
left="200' visibility="show">
<center>Layer 1</center>
</layer>

<layer id="layer2" width="150" height="160" bgcolor="green" top="100"
left="70" visibility="show">
<center>Layer 2</center>
</layer>

<form name="form1">
<input type="button" value="Resize Layer 2"
➥ onClick='document.layer2.resizeBy(30, 50)'>
<br>
</form>

</body>
</html>
```

Layer.resizeTo()

JavaScript 1.2+
Nav4+

Syntax

```
layer.resizeTo(x,y)
```

Description

The resizeTo() method of the Layer object resizes the Layer object to the specified value. The *x* parameter refers to the number of pixels by which the layer width is increased. The *y* parameter refers to the number of pixels by which the layer height is increased.

Example

Listing 8.274 shows how to resize a layer. When the button is clicked, the onClick event handler uses the resizeTo() method to resize layer2.

Listing 8.274   Example of the resizeTo() **Method**

```html
<html>

<body>

<layer id="layer1" width="200" height="200" bgcolor="yellow" top="170"
left="200" visibility="show">
<center>Layer 1</center>
</layer>

<layer id="layer2" width="150" height="160" bgcolor="green" top="100"
left="70" visibility="show">
<center>Layer 2</center>
</layer>

<form name="form1">
<input type="button" value="Resize Layer 2"
➥ onClick='document.layer2.resizeTo(100, 300)'>
<br>
</form>

</body>
</html>
```

Layer.routeEvent()

> JavaScript 1.2+
>
> Nav4+

Syntax

layer.routeEvent(*event*)

Description

The routeEvent() method of the Layer object reroutes a captured event to another event handler. The method takes a single parameter representing the event to be routed.

Example

Listing 8.275 shows an example of the routeEvent() method. When the focus event occurs, it is captured and the event is rerouted.

Listing 8.275   Example of the routeEvent() **Method**

```html
<html>

<body>

<script type="text/javascript" language="JavaScript">
<!--

// sets up the document to capture FOCUS events
document.captureEvents(Event.FOCUS);

// function that handles the specific event. The evnt parameter refers to
// the event object.
function handle(evnt){
   alert("The layer got a FOCUS event and executes routeEvent");
   document.routeEvent(evnt);
   alert("Event has been routed");
   return true;
}

// This registers the handle function as the event handler for the
// FOCUS event.
document.onFocus = handle;

// -->
</script>

<layer id="layer1" width="200" height="200" bgcolor="yellow" top="170"
left="200" visibility="show">
<center>Layer 1</center>
</layer>

<layer id="layer2" width="150" height="160" bgcolor="green" top="100"
left="70" visibility="show">
<center>Layer 2</center>
</layer>

</body>
</html>
```

Layer.siblingAbove

JavaScript 1.2+
Nav4+

Syntax

layer.siblingAbove

Description

The `siblingAbove` property of the `Layer` object refers to the sibling layer immediately above the current layer in the zIndex. If this doesn't exist, `null` is returned.

NOTE

> Any child of a parent layer is considered a sibling.

Example

Listing 8.276 shows how to get the `siblingAbove` property value. When the button is clicked, the `siblingAbove` value is displayed.

Listing 8.276 **Example of the** `siblingAbove` **Property**

```
<html>

<body>


<layer id="layer1" width="200" height="200" bgcolor="yellow" top="170"
left="200" visibility="show">
<center>Layer 1</center>
</layer>

<layer id="layer1" width="150" height="160" bgcolor="green" top="100"
left="70" visibility="show">
<center>Layer 2</center>
</layer>

<form name="form1">
<input type="button" value="Get Sibling Above Layer 1"
onClick='alert(document.layer1.siblingAbove)'>
<br>
</form>

</body>
</html>
```

Layer.siblingBelow

JavaScript 1.2+
Nav4+

Syntax

`layer.siblingBelow`

Description

The `siblingBelow` property of the `Layer` object refers to the sibling layer immediately below the current layer in the zIndex. If this doesn't exist, `null` is returned.

Example

Listing 8.277 shows the `siblingBelow` property. When the button is clicked, the `siblingBelow` value is displayed.

Listing 8.277   Example of the `siblingBelow` *Property*

```
<html>

<body>

<layer id="layer1" width="200" height="200" bgcolor="yellow" top="170"
left="200" visibility="show">
<center>Layer 1</center>
</layer>

<layer id="layer1" width="150" height="160" bgcolor="green" top="100"
left="70" visibility="show">
<center>Layer 2</center>
</layer>

<form name="form1">
<input type="button" value="Get Sibling Above Layer 1"
onClick='alert(document.layer1.siblingBelow)'>
<br>
</form>

</body>
</html>
```

Layer.src

> JavaScript 1.2+
> Nav4+

Syntax

`layer.src`

Description

The `src` property of the `Layer` object represents the source URL of a particular layer.

Example

Listing 8.278 shows how the `src` property is used. When the button is clicked, the `src` property is displayed.

Listing 8.278   Example of the src *Property*

```
<html>

<body>

<layer id="layer1" width="200" height="200" bgcolor="yellow" top="170"
left="200" visibility="show">
<center>Layer 1</center>
</layer>

<layer id="layer2" width="150" height="160" bgcolor="green" top="100"
left="70" visibility="show">
<center>Layer 2</center>
</layer>

<form name="form1">
<input type="button" value="Get Layer 1 src"
➥onClick='alert(document.layer1.src)'>
</form>

</body>
</html>
```

Layer.top

JavaScript 1.2+
Nav4+

Syntax

layer.top

Description

The top property of the Layer object represents the y-coordinate position of the layer relative to the top-level document. Increasing or decreasing this value can move the Layer object up or down.

Example

Listing 8.279 uses the top property to move the layer up. When the button is clicked, the move() function is executed, which will move the layer up by 10 pixels.

Listing 8.279   Example of the top *Property*

```
<html>

<body>

<script type="text/javascript" language="JavaScript">
<!--
```

Listing 8.279   *Continued*

```
function move(){
     document.layer1.top = document.layer1.top - 10;
}
// -->
</script>

<layer id="layer1" width="200" height="200" bgcolor="yellow" top="170"
left="200" visibility="show">
<center>Layer 1</center>
</layer>

<layer id="layer2" width="150" height="160" bgcolor="green" top="100"
left="70" visibility="show">
<center>Layer 2</center>
</layer>

<form name="form1">
<input type="button" value="Move layer 1 Up" onClick='move()'>
</form>

</body>
</html>
```

Layer.unwatch()

> JavaScript 1.2+
> Nav4+

Syntax

layer.unwatch(*prop*)

Description

The unwatch() method of the Layer object is used to remove a watchpoint set on a property by the watch() method. It takes one parameter, which is the property to unwatch.

Example

Listing 8.280 shows how the unwatch() method is used to disable the watchpoint set on the name property of the Layer object.

Listing 8.280   *Using the* unwatch() *Method of the* Layer *Object*

```
<html>
<script type="text/javascript" language="JavaScript">
<!--

function alertme(id,oldValue,newValue)
{
```

```
  document.writeln(id + " changed from " + "<b>" + oldValue +
➡"</b>"+ " to " + "<b>" + newValue + "</b><br>")
  return newValue;
}

function setWatch(){
  myProp = document.layers.name;
  watch("myProp",alertme);
  myProp = "red_layer";
  unwatch("myProp");
  myProp = "blue_layer";
}

// -->
</script>
<body>

<layer id="layer1" width="200" height="200"  bgcolor="yellow" top="170"
left="200" visibility="show">
<center>Layer 1</center>
</layer>

<layer ID="layer2" width="150" height="160"  bgcolor="green" top="100"
left="70" visibility="show">
<center>Layer 2</center>
</layer>

<form name="form1">
<input type="button" value="Enable/Disable watchpoint" onClick='setWatch()'>
</form>

</body>
</html>
```

Layer.visibility

JavaScript 1.2+
Nav4+

Syntax

layer.visibility

Description

The visibility property of the Layer object controls whether the layer is displayed or hidden. Valid values for this property are: hide, show, and inherit. This property also represents the HTML visibility attribute of the <layer> tag.

Example

Listing 8.281 shows how the visibility property is used to hide a Layer object.

Listing 8.281   Example of the visibility Property

```
<html>

<body>

<script type="text/javascript" language="JavaScript">
<!--
function hide(){
    document.layer2.visibility =" hide";
}
// -->
</script>

<layer id="layer1" width="200" height="200" bgcolor="yellow" top="170"
left="200" visibility="show">
<center>Layer 1</center>
</layer>

<layer id="layer2" width="150" height="160" bgcolor="green" top="100"
left="70" visibility="show">
<center>Layer 2</center>
</layer>

<form name="form1">
<input type="button" value="Hide Layer 2" onClick='hide()'>
</form>

</body>
</html>
```

Layer.watch()

JavaScript 1.2+
Nav4+

Syntax

`layer.watch(prop, handler)`

Description

The watch() method of the Layer object is used to watch for changes to Layer properties. When one of the properties, *prop*, is assigned a value, a *handler* is used to call a user-defined function.

Example

Listing 8.282 shows how the `watch()` method is used to set a watchpoint on the `name` property. When the name is changed, the *alertme* function is called to display the changes to the browser.

Listing 8.282   Using the `watch()` ***Method of the*** Layer ***Object***

```
<html>
<script type="text/javascript" language="JavaScript">
<!--

function alertme(id,oldValue,newValue)
{
  document.writeln(id + " changed from " + "<b>" + oldValue +
➥"</b>"+ " to " + "<b>" + newValue + "</b><br>")
  return newValue;
}

function setWatch(){
  myProp = document.layers.name;
  watch("myProp",alertme);
  myProp = "red_layer";
  myProp = "blue_layer";
}

// -->
</script>
<body>

<layer id="layer1" width="200" height="200" bgcolor="yellow" top="170"
left="200" visibility="show">
<center>Layer 1</center>
</layer>

<layer ID="layer2" width="150" height="160" bgcolor="green" top="100"
left="70" visibility="show">
<center>Layer 2</center>
</layer>

<form name="form1">
<input type="button" value="Enable watchpoint" onClick='setWatch()'>
</form>

</body>
</html>
```

Layer.zIndex

JavaScript 1.2+
Nav4+

Syntax

```
layer.zIndex
```

Description

The `zIndex` property of the `Layer` object represents the stacking order of the layers.

Example

Listing 8.283 shows an example of the `zIndex` property. When the button is clicked, an alert box is displayed showing the value of `zIndex`.

Listing 8.283   Example of the `zIndex` Property

```
<html>

<body>

<layer id="layer1" width="200" height="200" bgcolor="yellow" top="170"
left="200" visibility="show">
<center>Layer 1</center>
</layer>

<layer id="layer2" width="150" height="160" bgcolor="green" top="100"
left="70" visibility="show">
<center>Layer 2</center>
</layer>

<form name="form1">
<input type="button" value="Get Layer 2 zIndex"
➥ onClick='alert(document.layer2.zIndex)'>
</form>

</body>
</html>
```

Link

JavaScript 1.0+, JScript 1.0+
Nav2+, IE3+, Opera3+

Syntax

Core client-side JavaScript object.

Description

The Link object represents an HTML hypertext link. This can be an image, text, or predefined area within the Web page. All HTML links are stored in a links[] array. The Link object has specific properties and methods associated with it, as shown in Table 8.20.

Table 8.20 Properties and Methods of the Link Object

Type	Item	Description
Property	handleEvent	Event Handler
	hash	Represents an anchor name in the URL for the link, which begins with the # character
	host	Represents the host portion of the URL associated with a link
	hostname	Represents the hostname portion of the URL associated with a link
	href	Represents the complete URL associated with a link
	onClick	Event handler for mouse click events
	onDblClick	Event handler for double mouse click events
	onKeyDown	Event handler for pressing a key down on a Link object
	onKeyPress	Event handler for pressing a key on the Link object
	onKeyUp	Event handler for releasing a key on the Link object
	onMouseDown	Event handler for pressing the mouse button down on the link
	onMouseOut	Event handler for moving the mouse cursor away from the link
	onMouseOver	Event handler for moving the mouse cursor over the link
	onMouseUp	Event handler for releasing the mouse button on thelink
	pathname	Represents the pathname portion of the link URL
	port	Represents the port portion of the link URL
	protocol	Specifies the protocol portion of the link URL
	search	Represents the query portion of the link URL
	target	Represents the name of the Window object in which the link is displayed
	text	The text used to create the link
Method	unwatch()	Removes a watchpoint on a Link property
	watch()	Sets a watchpoint on a Link property

Example

Listing 8.284 shows how to use the Link object. When the link is clicked, the text of the link is displayed.

Listing 8.284   Example of the Link *Object*

```
<html>

<body>

Click on the link to go to the site.
<br><br>
<a href="http://www.samspublishing.com"
onClick='alert("Go to:" + document.links[0].text)'> Sams Publishing</a>

</body>
</html>
```

Link.handleEvent()

> JavaScript 1.2+
> Nav4+

Syntax

link.handleEvent(*event*)

Description

The handleEvent() method invokes the event handler for the Link object.

Example

Listing 8.285 shows how to access the handleEvent() method. All click events are handled by the first link in the document.

Listing 8.285   Example of the handleEvent() *Method*

```
<html>

<body>

<script type="text/javascript" language="JavaScript">
<!--
// sets up the document to capture CLICK events
document.captureEvents(Event.CLICK);

// function that handles the specific event. The evnt parameter refers to
// the event object.
function handle(evnt){
    document.form1.links[0].handleEvent(Event.CLICK);
}

function displayMsg(){
    alert("Click event occurred.");
}
```

```
// This registers the handle function as the event handler for the
// CLICK event.
document.onClick = handle;

// -->
</script>

<form name="form1">
<a href="http://www.samspublishing.com:80/foo?something#foobar"
onClick='displayMsg()'>
http://www.samspublishing.com:80/foo?something#foobar</a>
<br>
</form>

</body>
</html>
```

Link.hash
JavaScript 1.0+
Nav2+, Opera3+

Syntax
link.hash

Description
The hash property represents a portion of the currently displayed URL.

Example
Listing 8.286 shows an example of how the hash property is used. When the button is clicked, the showHash() function displays the value of the hash property for the link.

Listing 8.286   Example of the hash Property

```
<html>

<body>

<script type="text/javascript" language="JavaScript">
<!--
// function shows the hash value of the link
function showHash(){
    document.form1.text1.value = document.links[0].hash;
}
// -->
</script>
```

Listing 8.286   Continued

```
Click the button to see the hash for the URL
<form name="form1">
<a href="http://www.samspublishing.com:80/foo?something#foobar">
http://www.samspublishing.com:80/foo?something#foobar</a>
<br><br>
Hash value: <input type="text" name="text1" size="20">
<br>
<input type="button" name="hash" value="Get hash value" onClick='showHash()'>
<br><br>
</form>

</body>
</html>
```

Link.host

JavaScript 1.0+, JScript 1.0+
Nav2+, IE3+, Opera3+

Syntax

link.host

Description

The host property represents the host portion of the URL.

Example

Listing 8.287 shows how to use the host property. When the button is clicked, the showHost() function is called to show the value of the host property.

Listing 8.287   Example of the host Property

```
<html>

<body>

<script type="text/javascript" language="JavaScript">
<!--
// function shows the host value
function showHost(){
    document.form1.text1.value = document.links[0].host;
}
// -->
</script>

Click the button to see the host for the URL
<form name="form1">
<a href="http://www.samspublishing.com:80/foo?something#foobar">
```

```
http://www.samspublishing.com:80/foo?something#foobar</a>
<br><br>
Host value: <input type="text" name="text1" size="20">
<br><br>
<input type="button" name="host" value="Get Host Value" onClick='showHost()'>
<br>
</form>

</body>
</html>
```

Link.hostname

JavaScript 1.0+, JScript 1.0+
Nav2+, IE3+, Opera3+

Syntax

link.hostnamename

Description

The hostname property of the Link object represents the hostname portion of the link's URL.

Example

Listing 8.288 shows an example of how the hostname property is used. When the button is clicked, the showHostname() function is called, which displays the value of the hostname property for the link.

Listing 8.288 ***Example of the*** hostname ***Property***

```
<html>

<body>

<script type="text/javascript" language="JavaScript">
<!--

// displays the hostname for the URL
function showHostname(){
    document.form1.text1.value = document.links[0].hostname;
}
// -->
</script>

Click the button to see the hostname for the URL
<form name="form1">
<a href="http://www.samspublishing.com:80/foo?something#foobar">
http://www.samspublishing.com:80/foo?something#foobar</a>
```

Listing 8.288   Continued

```
<br><br>
Host value: <input type="text" name="text1" size="20">
<br><br>
<input type="button" name="host" value="Get Hostname Value"
➥ onClick='showHostname()'>
<br>
</form>

</body>
</html>
```

Link.href

JavaScript 1.0+, JScript 1.0+
Nav2+, IE3+, Opera3+

Syntax

link.href

Description

The href property of the Link object represents the whole URL for the link.

Example

Listing 8.289 shows how to use the href property. When the button is clicked, the showhref() function displays the value of the href property of the link.

Listing 8.289   Example of the href Property

```
<html>

<body>

<script type="text/javascript" language="JavaScript">
<!--

// displays the value of the href property in the text box.
function showhref(){
     document.form1.text1.value = document.links[0].href;
}
// -->
</script>

Click the button to see the href property for the URL
<form name="form1">
<a href="http://www.samspublishing.com:80/foo?something#foobar">
http://www.samspublishing.com:80/foo?something#foobar</a>
<br><br>
```

```
Host value: <input type="text" name="text1" size="45">
<br><br>
<input type="button" name="href" value="Get href Value" onClick='showhref()'>
<br>
</form>

</body>
</html>
```

Link.onClick

JavaScript 1.0+, JScript 1.0+
Nav2+, IE3+, Opera3+

Syntax

onClick="*command*"

Description

The onClick event handler for the Link object is used to handle the event when the mouse cursor is clicked on the link.

Example

Listing 8.290 shows how to determine a mouse click using the onClick event handler.

Listing 8.290   Example of the onClick Event Handler

```
<html>

<body>

Click the link.
<form name="form1">
<a href="http://www.samspublishing.com:80/foo?something#foobar"
➥ onClick='alert("You clicked the link")'>
http://www.samspublishing.com:80/foo?something#foobar</a>
<br><br>
</form>

</body>
</html>
```

Link.onDblClick

JavaScript 1.2+, JScript 1.0+
Nav4+, IE3+

Syntax

onDblClick="*command*"

Description

The onDblClick event handler of the Link object is used to handle the event when the mouse cursor is double-clicked on the link.

Example

Listing 8.291 shows how to use the onDblClick event handler. When the link is double-clicked, the event handler alerts the user indicating that the double-click action occurred.

Listing 8.291   Example of the** onDblClick **Event Handler

```
<html>

<body>

Click the link.
<form name="form1">
<a href="http://www.samspublishing.com:80/foo?something#foobar"
onDblClick='alert("You double-clicked the link")'>
http://www.samspublishing.com:80/foo?something#foobar</a>
<br><br>
</form>

</body>
</html>
```

Link.onKeyDown

JavaScript 1.2+, JScript 1.0+
Nav4+, IE3+

Syntax

onKeyDown="*command*"

Description

The onKeyDown event handler for the Link object is used to handle the event when a key is pressed down while the focus is on the link.

Example

Listing 8.292 shows how the onKeyDown event handler operates. When a key is pressed down, the event handler alerts the user about the action that occurred.

Listing 8.292   Example of the** onKeyDown **Event Handler

```
<html>

<body>

Click the link.
```

```
<form name="form1">
<a href="http://www.samspublishing.com:80/foo?something#foobar"
onKeyDown='alert("You pressed the key DOWN on the link")'>
http://www.samspublishing.com:80/foo?something#foobar</a>
<br><br>
</form>

</body>
</html>
```

Link.onKeyPress

JavaScript 1.2+, JScript 1.0+
Nav4+, IE3+

Syntax

onKeyPress="*command*"

Description

The onKeyPress event handler for the Link object is used to handle the event if a key is pressed when the focus is set on the link.

Example

Listing 8.293 shows how the onKeyPress event handler is used. The onKeyPress event handler is invoked any time a key is pressed on the link.

Listing 8.293   Example of the onKeyPress **Event Handler**

```
<html>

<body>

Click the link.
<form name="form1">
<a href="http://www.samspublishing.com:80/foo?something#foobar"
onKeyPress='alert("You pressed the key on the link")'>
http://www.samspublishing.com:80/foo?something#foobar</a>
<br><br>
</form>

</body>
</html>
```

Link.onKeyUp

JavaScript 1.2+, JScript 1.0+
Nav4+, IE3+

Syntax

onKeyUp="*command*"

Description

The onKeyUp event handler for the Link object is used to handle events in which a key is pressed and then released.

Example

Listing 8.294 shows an example of how the onKeyUp event handler is used. The onKeyUp event handler is invoked any time a key is pressed and released on the link.

Listing 8.294 Example of the onKeyUp **Event Handler**

```
<html>

<body>

Highlight the link, press a key and let it up.
<form name="form1">
<a href="http://www.samspublishing.com:80/foo?something#foobar"
onKeyUp='alert("You let the key up")'>
http://www.samspublishing.com:80/foo?something#foobar</a>
<br><br>
</form>

</body>
</html>
```

Link.onMouseDown

JavaScript 1.2+, JScript 1.0+
Nav4+, IE3+

Syntax

onMouseDown="*command*"

Description

The onMouseDown event handler of the Link object is used to handle the event when the mouse button is pressed down while the mouse pointer is over the link.

Example

Listing 8.295 shows how the onMouseDown event handler is used. The onMouseDown event handler is invoked any time the mouse button is pressed down while the cursor is on the link.

Listing 8.295 **Example of the** onMouseDown **Event Handler**

```
<html>

<body>

Click the mouse button while the cursor is on the link.
<form name="form1">
<a href="http://www.samspublishing.com:80/foo?something#foobar"
onMouseDown='alert("The mouse button was pressed DOWN.")'>
http://www.samspublishing.com:80/foo?something#foobar</a>
<br><br>
</form>

</body>
</html>
```

Link.onMouseOut

JavaScript 1.1+, JScript 1.0+
Nav3+, IE3+, Opera3+

Syntax

onMouseOut="*command*"

Description

The onMouseOut event handler of the Link object is used to handle the event when the mouse cursor is moved away from the link.

Example

Listing 8.296 shows how the onMouseOut event handler is used.

Listing 8.296 **Example of the** onMouseOut **Event Handler**

```
<html>

<body>

<script type="text/javascript" language="JavaScript">
<!--
// displays message when the MouseEvent occurs.
function showMsg(){
    document.form1.text1.value = "The Mouse cursor was removed from the link";
}
// -->
</script>
```

Listing 8.296   Continued

```
Click the mouse button while the cursor is on the link.
<form name="form1">
<a href="http://www.samspublishing.com:80/foo?something#foobar"
onMouseOut='showMsg()'>
http://www.samspublishing.com:80/foo?something#foobar</a>
<br><br>
<input type="text" name="text1" size="50">
</form>

</body>
</html>
```

Link.onMouseOver

JavaScript 1.0+, JScript 1.0+
Nav2+, IE3+, Opera3+

Syntax

```
onMouseOver="command"
```

Description

The onMouseOver event handler of the Link object handles the event when the mouse cursor is moved over the HTML link.

Example

Listing 8.297 shows how the onMouseOver event handler is used to display a message when the mouse cursor is moved over the link.

Listing 8.297   Example of the onMouseOver Event Handler

```
<html>

<body>

<script type="text/javascript" language="JavaScript">
<!--
// sets the text in the textbox to display the message.
function showMsg(){
    document.form1.text1.value = "The Mouse cursor was moved over the link";
}

// -->
</script>

Move the mouse cursor over the link.
<form name="form1">
<a href="http://www.samspublishing.com:80/foo?something#foobar"
onMouseOver='showMsg()'>
```

```
http://www.samspublishing.com:80/foo?something#foobar</a>
<br><br>
<input type="text" name="text1" size="50">
</form>

</body>
</html>
```

Link.onMouseUp

JavaScript 1.2+, JScript 1.0+
Nav4+, IE3+

Syntax

onMouseUp="*command*"

Description

The onMouseUp event handler for the Link object is used to handle the event when the mouse button is pressed on the link and then released.

Example

Listing 8.298 shows how the onMouseUp event handler is used.

Listing 8.298   Example of the onMouseUp *Event Handler*

```
<html>

<body>

Click the mouse button while the cursor is on the link.
<form name="form1">
<a href="http://www.samspublishing.com:80/foo?something#foobar"
onMouseUp='alert("The Mouse button was let up")'>
http://www.samspublishing.com:80/foo?something#foobar</a>
<br><br>
<input type="text" name="text1" size=50>
</form>

</body>
</html>
```

Link.pathname

JavaScript 1.0+, JScript 1.0+
Nav2+, IE3+, Opera3+

Syntax

link.pathname

Description

The pathname property of the Link object represents the pathname portion of the link URL.

Example

Listing 8.299 shows how the pathname property is used. When the button is clicked, the showpathname function is executed. This displays the pathname for the link.

Listing 8.299   Example of the pathname *Property*

```
<html>

<body>

<script type="text/javascript" language="JavaScript">
<!--

// displays the pathname for the specified URL
function showpathname(){
     document.form1.text1.value = document.links[0].pathname;
}
// -->
</script>

Click the button to see the pathname for the URL
<form name="form1">
<a href="http://www.samspublishing.com:80/tmp/foo.html?something#foobar">
http://www.a.com:80/tmp/foo.html?something#foobar</a>
<br><br>
Pathname value: <input type="text" name="text1" size="20">
<br><br>
<input type="button" name="path" value="Get Pathname Value"
➥ onClick='showpathname()'>
<br>
</form>

</body>
</html>
```

Link.port

JavaScript 1.0+, JScript 1.0+
Nav2+, IE3+, Opera3+

Syntax

link.port

Description

The `port` property of the `Link` object represents the port number in the URL. This is not always present in all URLs.

Example

Listing 8.300 shows how to obtain the `port` number if available. When the button is clicked, the port number for the link is displayed.

Listing 8.300   Accessing the `port` *Number*

```
<html>

<body>

<script type="text/javascript" language="JavaScript">
<!--

// displays the port number of the URL
function showport(){
     document.form1.text1.value = document.links[0].port;
}
// -->
</script>

Click the button to see the port number for the URL
<form name="form1">
<a href="http://www.samspublishing.com:80/foo?something#foobar">
http://www.samspublishing.com:80/foo?something#foobar</a>
<br><br>
Port value: <input type="text" name="text1" size="20">
<br><br>
<input type="button" name="port" value="Get Port Number" onClick='showport()'>
<br>
</form>

</body>
</html>
```

Link.protocol

JavaScript 1.0+, JScript 1.0+
Nav2+, IE3+, Opera3+

Syntax

`link.protocol`

Description

The `protocol` property of the `Link` object represents the protocol being used in the current Web browser. This is the first piece of text in the URL.

Example

Listing 8.301 shows how you can get the protocol type being used. When the button is clicked, the protocol for the link is displayed.

Listing 8.301   Example of the protocol *Property*

```
<html>

<body>

<script type="text/javascript" language="JavaScript">
<!--

// displays the type of protocol being used for the URL
function showproto(){
     document.form1.text1.value = document.links[0].protocol;
}
// -->
</script>

Click the button to see the protocol used for the URL
<form name="form1">
<a href="http://www.samspublishing.com:80/foo?something#foobar">
http://www.samspublishing.com:80/foo?something#foobar</a>
<br><br>
Protocol value: <input type="text" name="text1" size="20">
<br><br>
<input type="button" name="proto" value="Get Protocol" onClick='showproto()'>
<br>
</form>

</body>
</html>
```

Link.search

JavaScript 1.0+, JScript 1.0+
Nav2+, IE3+, Opera3+

Syntax

link.search

Description

The search property of the Link object represents the query portion of the URL (if available). This includes the leading question mark (?).

Example

Listing 8.302 shows how the search property can be determined. When the button is clicked, the showsearch() function displays the search value of the link.

Listing 8.302   Example of the search *Property*

```
<html>

<body>

<script type="text/javascript" language="JavaScript">
<!--

// display the information being queried
function showsearch(){
    document.form1.text1.value = document.links[0].search;
}
// -->
</script>

Click the button to see the search portion of the URL
<form name="form1">
<a href="http://www.samspublishing.com:80/foo?something#foobar">
http://www.samspublishing.com:80/foo?something#foobar</a>
<br><br>
Search value: <input type="text" name="text1" size="20">
<br><br>
<input type="button" name="search" value="Get Search portion"
➥ onClick='showsearch()'>
<br>
</form>

</body>
</html>
```

Link.target

> JavaScript 1.0+, JScript 1.0+
> Nav2+, IE3+, Opera3+

Syntax

link.target

Description

The target property of the Link object represents the name of the window in which the URL is to be displayed.

Example

Listing 8.303 shows how the target property is used. When the button is clicked, the showtarget() function displays the target value of the link.

Listing 8.303   Example of the target *Property*

```
<html>

<body>

<script type="text/javascript" language="JavaScript">
<!--

// displays the name of the window in which the link will be displayed.
function showtarget(){
    document.form1.text1.value = document.links[0].target;
}
// -->
</script>

Click the button to see the target of the URL
<form name="form1">
<a href="http://www.samspublishing.com:80/foo?something#foobar">
http://www.samspublishing.com:80/foo?something#foobar</a>
<br><br>
Target value: <input type="text" name="text1" size="20">
<br><br>
<input type="button" name="tar" value="Get Target" onClick='showtarget()'>
<br>
</form>

</body>
</html>
```

Link.text

JavaScript 1.2+
Nav4+

Syntax

link.text

Description

The text property of the Link object is used to get the text value of the link.

Example

Listing 8.304 shows how to use the text property. When the button is clicked, the showtext function displays the text value of the link.

Listing 8.304   Example of the text *Property*

```
<html>

<body>
```

```
<script type="text/javascript" language="JavaScript">
<!--
// function to display the value of the text property
function showtext(){
    document.form1.text1.value = document.links[0].text;
}
// -->
</script>

Click the button to see the text value of the link.
<form name="form1">
<a href="http://www.samspublishing.com:80/foo?something#foobar">
Link to Something</a>
<br><br>
Text value: <input type="text" name="text1" size="50">
<br><br>
<input type="button" name="txt" value="Get Text Value" onClick='showtext()'>
<br>
</form>

</body>
</html>
```

Link.unwatch()

JavaScript 1.2+
Nav4+, NES3+

Syntax

link.unwatch(*prop*)

Description

The unwatch() method of the Link object will remove a watchpoint on a property, *prop*, set by the watch() method.

Example

Listing 8.305 shows how the unwatch() method is used to disable the alert when the href property has been changed.

Listing 8.305   Using the unwatch() *Method for the* Link *Object*

```
<html>
<script type="text/javascript" a language="JavaScript">
<!--

function alertme(id,oldValue,newValue)
{
```

Listing 8.305   Continued

```
  document.writeln(id + " changed from " + "<b>" + oldValue + "</b>"+
➥" to " + "<b>" + newValue + "</b><br>")
  return newValue;
}

  myLink = document.links.href;
  watch("myLink",alertme);
  myLink = "http://www.bmw.com";
  unwatch("myLink");
  myLink = "http://www.amazon.com";
  watch("myLink",alertme);
  myLink = "http://www.buy.com";


// -->
</script>

<body>
<form name="form1">
<a href="http://www.samspublishing.com:80/foo?something#foobar">
➥Link to Something</a>
</form>

</body>
</html>
```

Link.watch()

JavaScript 1.2+
Nav4+

Syntax

```
watch(prop, handler)
```

Description

The watch() method of the Link object is used to watch for changes to Link properties. When one of the properties, *prop,* is assigned a value, a *handler* is used to call a user-defined function.

Example

Listing 8.306 shows how the watch() method is used to determine when the href property of the link has changed.

Listing 8.306   Using the watch() Method on the Link Object

```
<html>
<script type="text/javascript" language="JavaScript">
```

```
<!--

function alertme(id,oldValue,newValue)
{
  document.writeln(id + " changed from " + "<b>" + oldValue + "</b>"+ " to " +
➥"<b>" + newValue + "</b><br>")
  return newValue;
}

  myLink = document.links.href;
  watch("myLink",alertme);
  myLink = "http://www.bmw.com";
  myLink = "http://www.amazon.com";


// -->
</script>

<body>
<form name="form1">
<a href="http://www.samspublishing.com:80/foo?something#foobar">
➥Link to Something</a>
</form>

</body>
</html>
```

Location

JavaScript 1.0+, JScript 1.0+
Nav2+, IE3+, Opera3+

Syntax

Core client-side JavaScript object.

Description

The Location object represents the current Web address displayed in the browser. The Location object has specific properties and methods associated with it, as shown in Table 8.21.

Table 8.21 *Properties and Methods of the* Location *Object*

Type	Item	Description
Property	hash	Represents an anchor name in the URL that begins with the # character
	host	Represents the hostname and port number of the URL
	hostname	Represents the hostname part of the URL

Table 8.21 **Continued**

Type	Item	Description
	`href`	Represents the complete URL
	`pathname`	Represents the pathname part of the URL
	`port`	Represents the port part of the URL
	`protocol`	Represents the protocol part of the URL
	`search`	The search part of the URL, including the ?
Method	`reload()`	Reloads the current URL
	`replace()`	Loads a new Web page in the current browser
	`unwatch()`	Removes a watchpoint on the `Location` property
	`watch()`	Sets a watchpoint on the `Location` property

Example

Listing 8.307 shows how to access the `Location` object.

Listing 8.307 **Example of the** `Location` **Object**

```
<html>

<body>

<form name="form1">
Click the button to get the current location value.
<br><br><br>
<input type="button" name="getLoc" value="Get Location"
onClick='alert("The current location is: " + document.location)'>
<br>
</form>

</body>
</html>
```

Location.hash

JavaScript 1.0+, JScript 1.0+
Nav2+, IE3+, Opera3+

Syntax

`location.hash`

Description

The `hash` property of the `Location` object refers to the anchor portion of the URL, including the hash symbol (#).

In the following fictitious Web address:

```
http://www.samspublishing.com:80/foo?something#foobar
```

the hash value would be the #foobar portion.

Example

Listing 8.308 shows an example of how to get the hash value.

Listing 8.308   Example of the hash Property

```
<html>

<body>

<script type="text/javascript" language="JavaScript">
<!--

// displays the anchor portion of the URL
function show(){
      document.form1.text1.value=document.location.hash;
}
// -->
</script>

<form name="form1">
Click the button to get the current location.hash
➥value of the following address:
<br>
http://www.samspublishing.com:80/foo?something#foobar
<br><br>
Location.hash value: <input type="text" name="text1" size="20">
<br>
<input type="button" name="getLoc"
➥ value="Get hash value" onClick='show()'>
<br>
</form>

</body>
</html>
```

Location.host

JavaScript 1.0+, JScript 1.0+
Nav2+, IE3+, Opera3+

Syntax

```
location.host
```

Description

The host property of the Location object represents the host portion of the URL. This is composed of the hostname and the port number (if available).

In the following fictitious Web address:

```
http://www.samspublishing.com:80/foo?something#foobar
```

the host value would be the www.samspublishing.com:80 portion.

Example

Listing 8.309 shows the how the host property is used.

Listing 8.309   Example of the host Property

```html
<html>

<body>

<script type="text/javascript" language="JavaScript">
<!--

// shows the host part of the URL
function show(){
     document.form1.text1.value=document.location.host
}
// -->
</script>

<form name="form1">
Click the button to get the current location.host value of
the following address:
<br>
http://www.samspublishing.com:80/foo?something#foobar
<br><br>
Location.host value: <input type="text" name="text1" size=20>
<br>
<input type="button" name="getLoc" value="Get host" onClick='show()'>
<br>
</form>

</body>
</html>
```

Location.hostname
JavaScript 1.0+, JScript 1.0+
Nav2+, IE3+, Opera3+

Syntax

```
location.hostname
```

Description

The hostname property of the Location object represents the hostname portion of the URL.

In the following fictitious Web address:

```
http://www.samspublishing.com:80/foo?something#foobar
```

the hostname value would be the www.samspublishing.com portion.

Example

Listing 8.310 shows an example of how the hostname property is used. When the button is clicked, the show() function is called, which displays the value of hostname in the text box.

Listing 8.310   *Example of the* hostname *Property*

```
<html>

<body>

<script type="text/javascript" language="JavaScript">
<!--

// displays the hostname of the URL
function show(){
    document.form1.text1.value=document.location.hostname;
}
// -->
</script>

<form name="form1">
Click the button to get the current location.hostname
➥value of the following address:
<br>
http://www.samspublishing.com:80/foo?something#foobar
<br><br>
Location.hostname value: <input type="text" name="text1" size="20">
<br>
<input type="button" name="gethost"
➥value="Get hostname" onClick='show()'>
```

Listing 8.310   Continued

```
<br>
</form>

</body>
</html>
```

Location.href

JavaScript 1.0+, JScript 1.0+
Nav2+, IE3+, Opera3+

Syntax

```
location.href
```

Description

The href property of the Location object represents the entire URL string for the current page displayed in the browser.

In the following fictitious Web address:

```
http://www.samspublishing.com:80/foo?something#foobar
```

the href value would be the entire URL address.

Example

An example of how to get the href value is shown in Listing 8.311.

Listing 8.311   Example of the href Property

```
<html>

<body>

<script type="text/javascript" language="JavaScript">
<!--
function show(){
    document.location.href ="http://www.samspublishing.com:80/
    ➡foo?something#foobar";
}
// -->
</script>

<form name="form1">
Click the button to set the current location.href
➡value of the following address:
<br>
http://www.samspublishing.com:80/foo?something#foobar
<br><br>
```

```
Location.href value: <input type="text" name="text1" size="20">
<br>
<input type="button" name="sethref" value="Set href" onClick='show()'>
<br>
</form>

</body>
</html>
```

Location.pathname

JavaScript 1.0+, JScript 1.0+
Nav2+, IE3+, Opera3+

Syntax

```
location.pathname
```

Description

The pathname property of the Location object represents the pathname portion of the URL.

In the following fictitious Web address:

```
http://www.samspublishing.com:80/foo?something#foobar
```

the pathname value would be the /foo portion.

Example

Listing 8.312 shows an example of how to get the pathname.

Listing 8.312 *Example of the* pathname *Property*

```
<html>

<body>

<script type="text/javascript" language="JavaScript">
<!--
// function to display the pathname value
function show(){
    document.form1.text1.value=document.location.pathname;
}
// -->
</script>

<form name="form1">
Click the button to get the current location.pathname
➥value of the following address:
```

Listing 8.312   Continued

```
<br>
http://www.samspublishing.com:80/foo?something#foobar
<br><br>
Location.pathname value: <input type="text" name="text1" size="20">
<br>
<input type="button" name="getLoc" value="Get pathname" onClick='show()'>
<br>
</form>

</body>
</html>
```

Location.port

JavaScript 1.0+, JScript 1.0+
Nav2+, IE3+, Opera3+

Syntax

```
location.port
```

Description

The `port` property of the `Location` object represents the port portion of the URL. This normally follows the hostname, but is not always available.

In the following fictitious Web address:

```
http://www.samspublishing.com:80/foo?something#foobar
```

the port value would be the `80` portion.

Example

Listing 8.313 shows how to get the `port` number.

Listing 8.313   Example of the `port` Property

```
<html>

<body>

<script type="text/javascript" language="JavaScript">
<!--
// Function to display the port value
function show(){
    document.form1.text1.value=document.location.port;
}
// -->
</script>
```

```
<form name="form1">
Click the button to get the current location.port
➥value of the following address:
<br>
http://www.samspublishing.com:80/foo?something#foobar
<br><br>
Location.port value: <input type="text" name="text1" size="20">
<br>
<input type="button" name="getport" value="Get port"
➥onClick='show()'>
<br>
</form>

</body>
</html>
```

Location.protocol

JavaScript 1.0+, JScript 1.0+
Nav2+, IE3+, Opera3+

Syntax

```
location.protocol
```

Description

The protocol property of the Location object represents the protocol portion of the URL. This is located in the beginning of the URL address (the text before ://).

In the following fictitious Web address:

```
http://www.samspublishing.com:80/foo?something#foobar
```

the protocol value would be the http portion.

Example

The protocol property is used in Listing 8.314.

Listing 8.314   Example of the protocol Property

```
<html>

<body>

<script type="text/javascript" language="JavaScript">
<!--
// Function to display the protocol value
function show(){
    document.form1.text1.value=document.location.protocol;
}
```

Listing 8.314 Continued

```
// -->
</script>

<form name="form1">
Click the button to get the current location.protocol
➥value of the following address:
<br>
http://www.samspublishing.com:80/foo?something#foobar
<br><br>
Location.protocol value: <input type="text" name="text1" size="20">
<br>
<input type="button" name="getproto" value="Get protocol"
➥onClick='show()'>
<br>
</form>

</body>
</html>
```

Location.reload()

JavaScript 1.1+, JScript 3.0+
Nav3+, IE4+, Opera3+

Syntax

```
location.reload()
```

Description

The reload() method is used to reload the current page displayed in the browser.

Example

Listing 8.315 shows an example of how the reload() method is used.

Listing 8.315 Example of the reload() Method

```
<html>

<body>

<form name="form1">
Click the button to reload the current page.
<br><br>
Location.hash value: <input type="text" name="text1" size="20">
<br>
<input type="button" name="load" value="Reload page"
➥ onClick='document.location.reload()'>
<br>
</form>
```

```
</body>
</html>
```

Location.replace()

JavaScript 1.1+, JScript 3.0+
Nav3+, IE4+, Opera3+

Syntax

```
location.replace(URL)
```

Description

The replace() method is used to load a new page, specified by *URL*, in the current browser window. The new page replaces the previous page's position in the history list.

Example

Listing 8.316 shows the replace() method being used to load the new Web site.

Listing 8.316   Example of the replace() Method

```
<html>

<body>

<form name="form1">
Click the button to load the new page: http://www.samspublishing.com
<br>
<br>
<input type="button" name="load" value="Load new page"
onClick='document.location.replace("http://www.samspublishing.com")'>
<br>
</form>

</body>
</html>
```

Location.search

JavaScript 1.0+, JScript 1.0+
Nav2+, IE3+, Opera3+

Syntax

```
location.search
```

Description

The search property of the Location object represents the query portion of the URL, including the preceding question mark.

In the following fictitious Web address:

```
http://www.samspublishing.com:80/foo?something#foobar
```

the search value would be the ?something portion.

Example

Listing 8.317 shows how to use the search property. When the button is clicked, the show function displays the value of the search property in the text box.

Listing 8.317   Example of the search Property

```
<html>

<body>

<script type="text/javascript" language="JavaScript">
<!--
// function displays the search property value
function show(){
     document.form1.text1.value=document.location.search;
}
// -->
</script>

<form name="form1">
Click the button to get the current location.search
➥value of the following address:
<br>
http://www.samspublishing.com:80/foo?something#foobar
<br><br>
Location.search value: <input type="text" name="text1" size="20">
<br>
<input type="button" name="getsearch" value="Get search"
➥onClick='show()'>
<br>
</form>

</body>
</html>
```

Location.unwatch()
JavaScript 1.2+
Nav4+

Syntax

location.unwatch(*prop*)

Description

The unwatch() method of the Location object is used to remove a watchpoint set on a property by the watch() method. It takes one parameter, which is the property to unwatch.

Example

Listing 8.318 shows how the unwatch() method is used to disable the watchpoint on the location host property.

Listing 8.318   Using the unwatch() ***Method of the*** Location ***Object***

```
<html>
<script type="text/javascript" language="JavaScript">
<!--

function alertme(id,oldValue,newValue)
{
  document.writeln(id + " changed from " + "<b>" + oldValue
➥ + "</b>"+ " to " + "<b>" + newValue + "</b><br>")
  return newValue;
}

function setWatch(){
  myProp = document.location.host;
  watch("myProp",alertme);
  myProp = "amazon";
  unwatch("myProp");
  myProp = "google";
}

// -->
</script>
<body>
<form name="form1">
Click the button to get the current location.host
value of the following address:
<br>
http://www.samspublishing.com:80/foo?something#foobar
<br><br>
Location.host value: <input type="text" name="text1" size="20">
<br>
<input type="button" name="gethost" value="set watch" onClick='setWatch()'>
<br>
</form>

</body>
</html>
```

Location.watch()
JavaScript 1.2+
Nav4+

Syntax
```
watch(prop, handler)
```

Description
The watch() method of the Location object is used to watch for changes to Location properties. When one of the properties, *prop,* is assigned a value, a *handler* is used to call a user-defined function.

Example
Listing 8.319 shows how the watch() method is used to determine when the port value has been altered.

Listing 8.319   Using the watch **Method of the** Location **Object.**
```
<html>
<head>
<title>Using the watch method of the Location object</title>
<script type="text/javascript" language="JavaScript1.2">
<!--

// Function to change the value of the Location port
function changeValue(){

    origPort = document.location.port;
    newPort = document.form1.myNewPort.value;
    watch( origPort, informChange(newPort) );
    origPort = newPort;

}


// Function to invoke an alert box from the watch method
function informChange(val){
    alert("The Port value has been changed to: " + val);
}

// -->
</script>
</head>
<body>

<form name="form1">
Click the button to get the current location.port
value of the following address:
<br>
```

```
http://www.samspublishing.com:80/foo?something#foobar
<br><br>
Enter New Location.port value: <input type="text" name="myNewPort" size="20">
<br>
<input type="button" name="port" value="Change port" onClick='changeValue()'>
<br>
</form>

</body>
</html>
```

MimeType

JavaScript 1.1+

Nav3+

Syntax

Core client-side JavaScript object.

Description

The `MimeType` object is a predefined JavaScript object that you access through the `mimeTypes` array of the `Navigator` or `Plugin` object. MIME stands for multipart Internet mail extensions. Table 8.22 shows the different methods and properties of the `MimeType` object.

Table 8.22   Properties and Methods of the `MimeType` Object

Type	Item	Description
Property	description	Returns a description of a `MimeType`
	enabledPlugin	Returns a plug-in for a specific `MimeType`
	suffixes	Returns a file extension for a `MimeType`
	type	Returns a string representation of a `MimeType`
Method	unwatch()	Removes a watchpoint on a `MimeType` property
	watch()	Sets a watchpoint on a `MimeType` property

Example

Listing 8.320 shows an example of accessing a `MimeType` though the `mimeTypes` array. It prints out a few `mimeTypes` to the browser window.

Listing 8.320   Example of `MimeType`

```
<html>

<body>
<script type="text/javascript" language="JavaScript">
<!--
```

Listing 8.320   Continued

```
// function prints the first three MimeTypes
 for (i=0; i < 3; i++) {
   document.writeln(navigator.mimeTypes[i].type);
   document.writeln(navigator.mimeTypes[i].description);
   document.writeln(navigator.mimeTypes[i].suffixes);
   //document.writln("<br>");
}
// -->
</script>

</body>
</html>
```

MimeType.description

JavaScript 1.1+
Nav3+

Syntax

```
mimetype.description
```

Description

The `description` property of the `MimeType` object is used to obtain a description of the data type described by the `MimeType` object.

Example

Listing 8.321 shows an example of how the `description` property is used. A `for` loop is used to output the suffixes of the first three `MimeTypes`.

Listing 8.321   Accessing the `description` Property

```
<html>

<body>

<script type="text/javascript" language="JavaScript">
<!--
// function prints the suffixes for the first three MimeTypes
 for (i=0; i < 3; i++) {
   document.write("MimeType description " + i + " : ");
   document.writeln(navigator.mimeTypes[i].description);
   document.write("<br>");
}
// -->
</script>

</body>
</html>
```

MimeType.enabledPlugin

JavaScript 1.1+
Nav3+

Syntax

mimetype.enabledPlugin

Description

The enabledPlugin property of the MimeType object is used to determine which plug-in is configured for a specific MIME type.

Example

Listing 8.322 shows how the enabledPlugin property is used. A for loop is used to output the first three enabledPlugin values.

Listing 8.322   Accessing the enabledPlugin *Property*

```
<html>

<body>

<script type="text/javascript" language="JavaScript">
<!--

// loop through and output enabledPlugin values
 for (i=0; i < 3; i++) {
    document.write("MimeType enabledPlugin " + i + " : ");
    document.writeln(navigator.mimeTypes[i].enabledPlugin);
    document.write("<br>");
}
// -->
</script>

</body>
</html>
```

MimeType.suffixes

JavaScript 1.1+
Nav3+

Syntax

mimetype.suffixes

Description

Thesuffixes property of the MimeType object is used to obtain a string listing the possible file suffixes or filename extensions for the MIME type.

Example

Listing 8.323 shows an example of how the suffixes property is used. A for loop is used to output the first three suffix values.

Listing 8.323   Accessing the suffixes Property

```
<html>

<body>

<script type="text/javascript" language="JavaScript">
<!--
// function prints the suffixes for the first three MimeTypes
 for (i=0; i < 3; i++) {
    document.write("MimeType suffix " + i + " : ");
    document.writeln(navigator.mimeTypes[i].suffixes);
    document.write("<br>");
}
// -->
</script>

</body>
</html>
```

MimeType.type

JavaScript 1.1+
Nav3+

Syntax

mimetype.type

Description

The type property of the MimeType object is used to obtain a string specifying the name of the MIME type.

Example

Listing 8.324 shows how the type property is used. A for loop is used to output the first three MIME types.

Listing 8.324   Example of the type Property

```
<html>

<body>

<script type="text/javascript" language="JavaScript">
<!--
```

```
// function prints the types for the first 3 MimeTypes
 for (i=0; i < 3; i++) {
    document.write("MimeType type " + i + " :");
    document.writeln(navigator.mimeTypes[i].type);
    document.write("<br>");
}
// -->
</script>

</body>
</html>
```

MimeType.unwatch()

JavaScript 1.2+
Nav4+

Syntax

```
unwatch(prop)
```

Description

The unwatch() method of the MimeType object is used to remove a watchpoint on a property set by the watch() method. It takes a single parameter, *prop*, which specifies the property on which to remove the watchpoint.

Example

All MimeType properties are read-only, hence no example is provided.

MimeType.watch()

JavaScript 1.2+
Nav4+

Syntax

```
watch(prop, handler)
```

Description

The watch() method of the MimeType object is used to watch for changes to MimeType properties. When one of the properties, *prop*, is assigned a value, a *handler* is used to call a user-defined function.

Example

All MimeType properties are read-only, hence no example is provided.

navigator

JavaScript 1.0+
Nav2+, Opera3+

Syntax

Core client-side JavaScript object.

Description

The `navigator` object is a built-in object that is used to obtain information related to the Navigator browser. Table 8.23 shows the different methods and properties of the `navigator` object.

Table 8.23 **Properties and Methods of the** `navigator` *Object*

Type	Item	Description
Property	appCodeName	Represents the code name of the browser
	appName	Refers to the official browser name
	appVersion	Refers to the version information of the browser
	language	Refers to the language of the browser
	mimeTypes	Refers to an array of `MimeType` objects that contains all the MIME types that the browser supports
	platform	A string representing the platform on which the browser is running
	plugins	Refers to an array of `Plugin` objects that contains all the plug-ins installed in the browser
	userAgent	String that represents the user-agent header
Method	javaEnabled()	Function that tests to see that Java is supported in the browser
	plugins.refresh()	Checks for any newly installed plug-ins
	preference()	Allows reading and setting of various user preferences in the browser
	taintEnabled()	Tests to see whether data-tainting is enabled
	unwatch()	Removes a watchpoint on a `navigator` property
	watch()	Sets a watchpoint on a `navigator` property

Example

Listing 8.325 shows an example for the `navigator` object.

Listing 8.325   Example of the navigator **Object**

```
<html>

<body>

<script type="text/javascript" language="JavaScript">
<!--
// Output the navigator appName property
document.write(navigator.appName);
// -->
</script>

</body>
</html>
```

navigator.appCodeName

JavaScript 1.0+
Nav2+, Opera3+

Syntax

```
navigator.appCodeName
```

Description

The appCodeName property of the navigator object refers to the internal code name of the browser.

Example

Listing 8.326 shows an example of how the appCodeName property is used.

Listing 8.326   Example of the appCodeName **Property**

```
<html>

<body>

<script type="text/javascript" language="JavaScript">
<!--
// Output the navigate appCodeName property
document.write(navigator.appCodeName);
// -->
</script>

</body>
</html>
```

navigator.appName

JavaScript 1.0+
Nav2+, Opera3+

Syntax

```
navigator.appName
```

Description

The appName property of the navigator object refers to the browser name.

Example

Listing 8.327 shows an example of how the appName property is used.

Listing 8.327   Example of the appName Property

```
<html>

<body>

<script type="text/javascript" language="JavaScript">
<!--
// output the appName property
document.write(navigator.appName);
// -->
</script>

</body>
</html>
```

navigator.appVersion

JavaScript 1.0+
Nav2+, Opera3+

Syntax

```
navigator.appVersion
```

Description

The appVersion property of the navigator object is used to get the browser version. The returned property contains the browser version, platform on which the browser is running, and the country (either international or domestic).

Example

Listing 8.328 shows an example of how the appVersion property is used.

Listing 8.328   Example of the `appVersion` *Property*

```
<html>

<body>

<script type="text/javascript" language="JavaScript">
<!--
// output the appVersion property
document.write(navigator.appVersion);
// -->
</script>

</body>
</html>
```

navigator.javaEnabled()

JavaScript 1.1+
Nav3+, Opera3+

Syntax

```
navigator.javaEnabled()
```

Description

The `javaEnabled()` method is used to test whether the browser supports Java.

Example

Listing 8.329 shows an example of how the `javaEnabled()` method is used. A check is made to determine whether Java is enabled on the browser. If so, a message is output indicating that to be the case.

Listing 8.329   Example of the `javaEnabled()` *Method*

```
<html>

<body>

<script type="text/javascript" language="JavaScript">
<!--

// check to determine if Java is enabled on the browser.
// If so then output a message.
if (navigator.javaEnabled()){
    document.write("This browser supports Java");
}
```

Listing 8.329   Continued

```
// -->
</script>

</body>
</html>
```

navigator.language
JavaScript 1.2+
Nav4+

Syntax

```
navigator.language
```

Description

The `language` property of the `navigator` object is used to determine what language the browser supports. The return value is a string.

Example

Listing 8.330 shows an example of how the `language` property is used.

Listing 8.330   Example of the `language` Property

```
<html>

<body>

<script type="text/javascript" language="JavaScript">
<!--
// output the navigator language property
    document.write(navigator.language);
// -->
</script>

</body>
</html>
```

navigator.mimeTypes
JavaScript 1.1+
Nav3+, Opera3+

Syntax

```
navigator.mimeTypes
```

Description

The mimeTypes property of the navigator object is used to obtain a list of all the MIME types supported by the browser. The returned object is an array containing all supported MIME types. The mimetypes array contains all the properties of the Array object.

Example

Listing 8.331 shows an example of how the mimeTypes property is used.

Listing 8.331   Example of the mimeTypes *Property*

```
<html>

<body>

<script type="text/javascript" language="JavaScript">
<!--
// output the navigator mimeTypes length property
    document.write(navigator.mimeTypes.length);
// -->
</script>

</body>
</html>
```

navigator.platform

JavaScript 1.2+
Nav4+

Syntax

```
navigator.platform
```

Description

The platform property of the navigator object returns a string representing the platform on which the browser is running. Valid platform values are: Win32, Win16, Mac68k, MacPPCa.

Example

Listing 8.332 shows an example of how the platform property is used.

Listing 8.332   Example of the platform *Property*

```
<html>

<body>
```

Listing 8.332   Continued

```
<script type="text/javascript" language="JavaScript">
<!--
// output the navigator platform property
    document.write(navigator.platform);
// -->
</script>

</body>
</html>
```

navigator.plugins
JavaScript 1.1+
Nav3+

Syntax

```
navigator.plugins[num]
```

Description

The plugins property of the navigator object returns an array of the Plugins object representing all the plug-ins installed on a particular browser. These can be accessed by the indexed *num* passed.

Example

Listing 8.333 shows an example of how the plugins property is used. A loop is used to output a list of all the plug-ins for the browser.

Listing 8.333   Example of the plugins Property

```
<html>

<body>

<script type="text/javascript" language="JavaScript">
<!--
var plugLength = navigator.plugins.length

// loop through and output all the plugins
// present in the browser
for(i=0; i<plugLength; i++){
    document.write(navigator.plugins[i].name);
}
// -->
</script>

</body>
</html>
```

navigator.plugins.refresh()

JavaScript 1.1+
Nav3+

Syntax

```
navigator.plugins.refresh()
```

Description

The `plugins.refresh()` method of the `navigator` object is used to check for any new plug-ins installed on the browser.

Example

Listing 8.334 shows an example of how the `plugins.refresh()` method is used. When the document is loaded, the `plugins.refresh()` method.

Listing 8.334 **Example of the** `plugins.refresh()` **Method**

```html
<html>

<body>

<script type="text/javascript" language="JavaScript">
<!--
    document.write(navigator.plugins.refresh());
// -->
</script>

</body>
</html>
```

navigator.preference()

JavaScript 1.2+
Nav4+, Opera3+

Syntax

```
navigator.preference(name)
```

```
navigator.preference(name, value)
```

Description

The `preference()` method of the `navigator` object is used to read or set any user preferences in the browser. For security reasons, reading a preference with the `preference()` method requires the `UniversalPreferencesRead` privilege. Setting a preference with this method requires the `UniversalPreferencesWrite` privilege.

Example

Listing 8.335 shows an example of how the `preference()` method can be used to set a preference.

Listing 8.335 **Example of the** `preference()` **Method**

```html
<html>

<body>

<script type="text/javascript" language="JavaScript">
<!--
// This disables Java support in the browser
navigator.preference(security.enable_java, false);
// -->
</script>

</body>
</html>
```

navigator.taintEnabled()

JavaScript 1.1+
Nav3

Syntax

```
navigator.taintEnabled()
```

Description

The `taintEnabled()` method of the `navigator` specifies whether data tainting is enabled.

NOTE

This method is removed in Navigator 4 and later releases.

Example

Listing 8.336 shows an example of how the `taintEnabled()` method is used.

Listing 8.336 **Example of the** `taintEnabled()` **Method**

```html
<html>

<body>

<script type="text/javascript" language="JavaScript">
<!--
```

```
// determine if tainting is enabled in the browser
if(navigator.taintEnabled()){
    document.write("Data tainting is enabled");
}
else{
    document.write("There is no data tainting");
}
// -->
</script>

</body>
</html>
```

navigator.userAgent

JavaScript 1.0+
Nav2+, Opera3+

Syntax

```
navigator.userAgent
```

Description

The `userAgent` property of the `navigator` object returns a string identifying the browser. This value is often sent to servers during HTTP data requests.

Example

Listing 8.337 shows an example of how the `userAgent` property is used.

Listing 8.337 *Example of the* userAgent *Property*

```
<html>

<body>

<script type="text/javascript" language="JavaScript">
<!--
//Returns the userAgent property of the browser

document.write(navigator.userAgent);
// -->
</script>

</body>
</html>
```

navigator.unwatch()

JavaScript 1.2+
Nav4+

Syntax

`unwatch(prop)`

Description

The `unwatch()` method of the navigator object is used to remove a watchpoint on a property set by the `watch()` method. It takes a single parameter, *prop*, which specifies the property on which to remove the watchpoint.

Example

All `navigator` properties are read-only, hence no example is provided.

navigator.watch()

JavaScript 1.2+
Nav4+

Syntax

`watch(prop, handler)`

Description

The `watch()` method of the `navigator` object is used to watch for changes to navigator properties. When one of the properties, *prop*, is assigned a value, a *handler* is used to call a user-defined function.

Example

All `navigator` properties are read-only, hence no example is provided.

Option

JavaScript 1.0+, JScript 1.0+
Nav2+, IE3+

Syntax

Core client-side JavaScript object.

Description

The `Option` object is used to reference a property of an HTML select list. An `Option` object can be created by using the option constructor and specifying the appropriate values. Table 8.24 shows the different properties and methods of the `Option` object.

Table 8.24   **Properties and Methods of the** Option **Object**

Type	Item	Description
Property	defaultSelected	Refers to the option that is selected by default from the select box
	selected	Refers to the selected value of the select box
	text	Refers to the text for the option
	value	Refers to the value that is returned to when the option is selected
Method	unwatch()	Removes a watchpoint on an Option property
	watch()	Sets a watchpoint on an Option property

Example

Listing 8.338 shows an example of how a select list is populated.

Listing 8.338   **Example of the** Option **Object**

```html
<html>

<body>

<script>
<script type="text/javascript" language="JavaScript">
<!--
// function adds the options to the select list.
function add(myForm) {

   var option0 = new Option("Joe", "person1");
   var option1 = new Option("Jane", "person2");
   var option2 = new Option("Mark", "person3");
   var option3 = new Option("Melissa", "person4");

   for (var i=0; i < 4; i++) {
      eval("myForm.people.options[i]=option" + i)
}

   history.go(0)
}
// -->
</script>

<form>
<select name="people" multiple></select><p>
<input type="button" value="Add People" onClick="add(this.form)">
</form>
</body></html>
```

Option.defaultSelected

JavaScript 1.1+, JScript 1.0+
Nav3+, IE3+

Syntax

option.defaultSelected

Description

The defaultSelected property of the Option object specifies the initial option selection of the select list.

Example

Listing 8.339 shows an example of how the defaultSelected property is used. The check function checks for the default selected option.

Listing 8.339 **Example of the** defaultSelected **Property**

```
<html>

<body>


<script type="text/javascript" language="JavaScript">
<!--
// function checks the form to see what is the default selected.
function check(myForm){
    for (var i = 0; i < document.form1.myList.length; i++) {
        if (document.form1.myList.options[i].defaultSelected == true) {
            alert("The default value is: 2");
        }
    }
}
// -->
</script>

<form name=form1>
<select name="myList" multiple>
<option value=1>One
<option value=2 selected>Two
<option value=3>Three
<option value=4>Four
</select><p>
<input type="button" value="Get Default Value" onClick='check(this.form)'>
</form>

</body>
</html>
```

Option.selected

JavaScript 1.2+
Nav4+

Syntax

option.selected

Description

The selected property of the Option object specifies the current selected option of the
select list.

Example

Listing 8.340 shows an example of how the selected property is used. The check
function checks to see what the selected property is.

Listing 8.340   Example of the selected *Property*

```
<html>

<body>


<script type="text/javascript" language="JavaScript">
<!--
// function checks the forms to see what the selected property is
function check(myForm){
    for (var i = 0; i < document.form1.myList.length; i++) {
        if (document.form1.myList.options[i].selected == true) {
            alert("The selected value is: "
➥+ document.form1.myList.options[i].value);
        }
    }
}
// -->
</script>

<form name=form1>
<select name="myList" multiple>
<option value=1>One
<option value=2>Two
<option value=3>Three
<option value=4>Four
</select><p>
<input type="button" value="Get Value" onClick='check(this.form)'>
</form>

</body>
</html>
```

Option.text

JavaScript 1.0+, JScript 1.0+
Nav2+, IE3+

Syntax

option.text

Description

The text property of the Option object specifies the text for the selected option of the select list.

Example

Listing 8.341 shows an example of how the text property is used. The check function determines what the text is for the selected value.

Listing 8.341   Example of the text **Property**

```
<html>

<body>


<script type="text/javascript" language="JavaScript">
<!--
// function check the form to see what the selected value's text is
function check(myForm){
    for (var i = 0; i < document.form1.myList.length; i++) {
        if (document.form1.myList.options[i].selected == true) {
            alert("The selected text value is: "
➥+ document.form1.myList.options[i].text);
        }
    }
}
// -->
</script>

<form name=form1>
<select name="myList" multiple>
<option value=1>One
<option value=2>Two
<option value=3>Three
<option value=4>Four
</select><p>
<input type="button" value="Get Text Value" onClick='check(this.form)'>
</form>

</body>
</html>
```

Option.unwatch()

JavaScript 1.2+
Nav4+

Syntax

option.unwatch(*prop*)

Description

The unwatch() method of the Option object will remove a watchpoint on a property, *prop*, set by the watch() method.

Example

Listing 8.342 shows how the unwatch() method is used to remove the watchpoint set on the Option value. When the submit button is clicked, the setWatch() method is called, which sets the watchpoint and then changes the Option value. This causes the alertme function to be executed, which displays the results of the change to the browser.

Listing 8.342   Using the unwatch() **Method of** Option

```
<html>
<script type="text/javascript" language="JavaScript">
<!--

function alertme(id,oldValue,newValue)
{
  document.writeln(id + " changed from " + "<b>" + oldValue +
➥"</b>"+ " to " + "<b>" + newValue + "</b><br>")
  return newValue;
}

function setWatch(){
  myProp = document.form.myList.value;
  watch("myProp",alertme);
  myProp = 6;
  myProp = 9;
}

// -->
</script>

<body>

<form name="form">
<select name="myList" multiple>
<option value=1>One
<option value=2 selected>Two
```

Listing 8.342   Continued

```
<option value=3>Three
</select>
<br>

<input type="button" value="submit" onClick='setWatch()'>
</form>

</body>
</html>
```

Option.value

JavaScript 1.0+, JScript 1.0+
Nav2+, IE3+

Syntax

option.value

Description

The value property of the Option object specifies the value that is returned to the server when the option is selected and the form is submitted.

Example

Listing 8.343 shows an example of how the value property is used. The function getValue gets the value of the selected option.

Listing 8.343   Example of the value Property

```
<html>

<body>

<script>
<script type="text/javascript" language="JavaScript">
<!--
// Function gets the value of the selected option
function getValue(myForm){
   for (var i = 0; i < document.form1.myList.length; i++) {
      if (document.form1.myList.options[i].selected == true) {
         alert("The selected value is: "
➥+ document.form1.myList.options[i].value);
      }
   }
}
// -->
</script>
```

```
<form name="form1">
<select name="myList" multiple>
<option value=1>One
<option value=2>Two
<option value=3>Three
<option value=4>Four
</select><p>
<input type="button" value="Get Value" onClick='getValue(this.form)'>
</form>

</body>
</html>
```

Option.watch()

JavaScript 1.2+
Nav4+

Syntax

```
watch(prop, handler)
```

Description

The watch() method of the Option object is used to watch for changes to Option properties. When one of the properties, *prop*, is assigned a value, a *handler* is used to call a user-defined function.

Example

Listing 8.344 shows how the watch() method is used to monitor when the value property of the Option object is modified.

Listing 8.344 ***Using the*** watch() ***method of the*** Option ***Object***

```
<html>
<head>
<script type="text/javascript" language="JavaScript">
<!--

function alertme(id,oldValue,newValue)
{
  document.writeln(id + " changed from " + "<b>" + oldValue +
➥"</b>"+ " to " + "<b>" + newValue + "</b><br>")
  return newValue;
}

function setWatch(){
  myProp = document.form.myList.value;
  watch("myProp",alertme);
```

Listing 8.344   Continued

```
  myProp = 6;
  myProp = 9;
}
// -->
</script>

</head>
<body>

<form name="form">
<select name="myList" multiple>
<option value=1>One
<option value=2 selected>Two
<option value=3>Three
</select>
<br>

<input type="button" value="submit" onClick='setWatch()'a
```

Password

JavaScript 1.0+, JScript 1.0+
Nav2+, IE3+, Opera3+

Syntax

Core client-side JavaScript object.

Description

The Password object refers to the HTML element created with the `<input>` tag, setting the type to specify password. It operates similarly to a standard HTML text input box because input is entered into the box. Instead of displaying the input in `cleartext`, input is displayed using the * symbol. Table 8.25 shows the different methods and properties of the Password object.

Table 8.25   Properties, Methods and Events of the Password Object

Type	Item	Description
Property	defaultValue	Refers to the value attribute of the HTML password box
	form	Refers to the form that contains the password box
	name	Refers to the name attribute of the HTML password box
	type	Refers to the type attribute of the HTML password box
	value	Refers to the current contents of the password box
Method	blur()	Removes focus from the password box

Type	Item	Description
	focus()	Sets focus to the password box
	handleEvent()	Invokes the event handler
	select()	Selects the text entered in the password box
	unwatch()	Removes a watchpoint on a **Password** property
	watch()	Sets a watchpoint on a **Password** property
Event	onBlur	Event handler used when the focus is removed from the password box
	onFocus	Event handler used when the focus is put on the password box

Example

Listing 8.345 shows an example of how the **Password** object is used to read the value entered in a password box.

Listing 8.345 *Example of the* Password *Object*

```
<html>

<body>

<form name="form1">
<input type="PASSWORD" Name="pass" size="10">
<br>
<input type="BUTTON" value="Show Password"
➥ onClick='alert(document.form1.pass.value)'>
</form>

</body>
</html>
```

Password.blur()

JavaScript 1.0+, JScript 1.0+
Nav2+, IE3+, Opera3+

Syntax

password.blur()

Description

The blur method for the **Password** object is used to remove the focus from the password box.

Example

Listing 8.346 shows an example of how the focus is removed from the password box.

Listing 8.346   Example of the `blur()` **Method**

```
<html>

<body>

<script type="text/javascript" language="JavaScript">
<!--
// function that shifts focus when the button is clicked
function shift(){
    document.form1.pass.blur();
    document.form1.txt.value="Get Focus";
}
// -->
</script>

<form name="form1">
<input type="PASSWORD" Name="pass" size="10">
<br>
<input type="Text" name="txt" size="10">
<br>
<input type="BUTTON" value="Show Password" onClick='shift()'>
</form>

</body>
</html>
```

Password.defaultValue

JavaScript 1.0+, JScript 1.0+
Nav2+, IE3+

Syntax

password.`defaultValue`

Description

The `defaultValue` property of the `Password` object is used to get the HTML value attribute of the password box.

Example

Listing 8.347 shows an example of how the `defaultValue` is used to get the password value.

Listing 8.347   Example of the `defaultValue` **Property**

```
<html>

<body>

<form name="form1">
```

```
<input type="PASSWORD" Name="pass" size="10" value="pass123">
<br>
<input type="BUTTON" value="Show Password"
➥ onClick='alert(document.form1.pass.defaultValue)'>
</form>

</body>
</html>
```

Password.focus()

JavaScript 1.0+, JScript 1.0+
Nav2+, IE3+, Opera3+

Syntax

*password.*focus()

Description

The focus() method of the Password object sets the focus to the password box.

Example

Listing 8.348 shows an example of how the focus() method is used to move the focus back to the password box.

Listing 8.348   Example of the focus() Method

```
<html>

<body>

<form name="form1">
<input type="PASSWORD" Name="pass" size="10">
<br>
<input type="BUTTON" value="Show Password"
➥ onClick='document.form1.pass.focus()'>
</form>

</body>
</html>
```

Password.form

JavaScript 1.0+, JScript 1.0+
Nav2+, IE3+, Opera3+

Syntax

*password.*form

Description

The `form` property of the `Password` object is used to access the `Form` object in which the password box resides.

Example

Listing 8.349 shows an example of how the `form` property is used to get the form name.

Listing 8.349   Example of the `form` Property

```
<html>

<body>

<form name="form1">
<input type="PASSWORD" Name="pass" size="10">
<br>
<input type="BUTTON" value="Show Formname"
➡ onClick='alert(document.form1.pass.form.name)'>
</form>

</body>
</html>
```

Password.handleEvent()

> JavaScript 1.2+, JScript 1.0+
> Nav4+, IE3+, Opera3+

Syntax

password.handleEvent(*event*)

Description

The `handleEvent()` method of the `Password` object is used to handle events of the type of *event* passed.

Example

Listing 8.350 shows an example of how the `handleEvent()` method is used to handle the `Click` event when the button is clicked.

Listing 8.350   Example of the `handleEvent()` Method

```
<html>

<body>

<script type="text/javascript" language="JavaScript">
<!--
```

```
// sets up the document to capture CHANGE events
document.captureEvents(Event.CHANGE);

// function that handles the specific event. The evnt parameter refers to
// the event object.
function handleChange(evnt){
    window.document.pass.handleEvent(evnt);
}

function showMsg(){
    alert("Password Changed.");
}

// This registers the handle function as the event handler for the
// CHANGE event.
document.onChange = handleChange;
// -->
</script>

<form name="form1">

Enter password:
<input type="PASSWORD" name="pass" size="15" onChange='showMsg()'>
</form>

</body>
</html>
```

Password.name

JavaScript 1.0+, JScript 1.0+
Nav2+, IE3+, Opera3+

Syntax

password.name

Description

The name property of the Password object is used to get the HTML name attribute of
the password box.

Example

Listing 8.351 shows an example of how the name property is used. When the button is
clicked, an alert box is displayed showing the password object name.

Listing 8.351 *Example of the* name *Property*

```
<html>

<body>

<form name="form1">
<input type="PASSWORD" Name="pass" size="10">
<br>
<input type="BUTTON" value="Show Formname"
➥ onClick='alert(document.form1.pass.name)'>
</form>

</body>
</html>
```

Password.onBlur

JavaScript 1.0+, JScript 1.0+
Nav2+, IE3+, Opera3+

Syntax

onBlur="*command*"

Description

The onBlur event handler of the Password object is used to handle the event that occurs when the focus is removed from the password box.

Example

Listing 8.352 shows an example of how the onBlur event handler is used. When the focus is removed from the Password object, the setTxt() function is called to display a message in the text box.

Listing 8.352 *Example of the* onBlur *Event Handler*

```
<html>

<body>

<script type="text/javascript" language="JavaScript">
<!--
// function that sets the text value
function setTxt(){
    document.form1.txt.value="setup";
}
// -->
</script>
```

```
<form name="form1">
<input type="PASSWORD" Name="pass" size="10" onBlur='setTxt()'>
<br>
<input type="Text" name="txt" size="10" >
</form>

</body>
</html>
```

Password.onFocus

> JavaScript 1.0+, JScript 1.0+
> Nav2+, IE3+, Opera3+

Syntax

onFocus="*command*"

Description

The onFocus event handler of the Password object is used to handle the Focus event for the password box.

Example

Listing 8.353 shows an example of the onFocus event handler.

Listing 8.353   *Example of the* onFocus *Event Handler*

```
<html>

<body>

<script type="text/javascript" language="JavaScript">
<!--
// sets a message in the text box
function set(){
    document.form1.pass.value="aha123";
}
// -->
</script>

<form name="form1">
<input type="PASSWORD" Name="pass" size="10" onFocus='set()'>
<br>
<input type="BUTTON" value="Show Formname" >
</form>

</body>
</html>
```

Password.select()

JavaScript 1.0+, JScript 1.0+
Nav2+, IE3+, Opera3+

Syntax

```
password.select()
```

Description

The select() method of the Password object is used to select the value entered into
the password box. The selected value is highlighted.

Example

Listing 8.354 shows an example of how the password value can be selected.

Listing 8.354   Example of the select() Method

```
<html>

<body>

<form name="form1">
<input type="PASSWORD" Name="pass" size="10">
<br>
<input type="BUTTON" value="Select Password"
➡onClick='document.form1.pass.select()'>
</form>

</body>
</html>
```

Password.type

JavaScript 1.1+, JScript 1.0+
Nav3+, IE3+, Opera3+

Syntax

```
password.type
```

Description

The type property of the Password object is used to get the HTML type attribute associated with the password box. For the Password object, this value is always password.

Example

Listing 8.355 shows an example of how the type property is used. When the button is
clicked, an alert box is displayed, showing the value of the type property.

Listing 8.355   Example of the type **Property**

```html
<html>

<body>

<form name="form1">
<input type="PASSWORD" Name="pass" size="10">
<br>
<input type="BUTTON" value="Get Type"
➥ onClick='alert(document.form1.pass.type)'>
</form>

</body>
</html>
```

Password.unwatch()

JavaScript 1.2+
Nav4+, NES3+

Syntax

*password.*unwatch(*prop*)

Description

The unwatch() method of the Password object will remove a watchpoint on a property, *prop*, set by the watch() method.

Example

Listing 8.356 shows how the unwatch() method is used to turn off the watchpoint set on the Password value.

Listing 8.356   Using the unwatch() **Method for** Password

```html
<html>
<script type="text/javascript" language="JavaScript">
<!--

function alertme(id,oldValue,newValue)
{
  document.writeln(id + " changed from " + "<b>" + oldValue +
➥"</b>"+ " to " + "<b>" + newValue + "</b><br>")
  return newValue;
}

function setWatch(){
  myPass = document.form1.pass.value;
  watch("myPass",alertme);
  myPass = "abc123";
```

Listing 8.356   Continued

```
  unwatch("myPass");
  myPass = "purejs2";
}


// -->
</script>

<form name="form1">
Enter Password <input type="PASSWORD" Name="pass" size="10">
<br>
<input type="BUTTON" value="Submit" onClick='setWatch()'>
</form>

</body>
</html>
```

Password.value

> JavaScript 1.0+, JScript 1.0+
> Nav2+, IE3+, Opera3+

Syntax

password.`value`

Description

The `value` property of the `Password` object is used to get the value entered in the password box.

Example

Listing 8.357 shows an example of how the `value` property is used.

Listing 8.357   Example of the `value` **Property**

```
<html>

<body>

<form name="form1">
<input type="PASSWORD" Name="pass" size="10">
<br>
<input type="BUTTON" value="Get Value"
➥ onClick='alert(document.form1.pass.value)'>
</form>

</body>
</html>
```

Password.watch()

JavaScript 1.2+
Nav4+, NES3+

Syntax

```
watch(prop, handler)
```

Description

The watch() method of the Password object is used to watch for changes to Password properties. When one of the properties, *prop,* is assigned a value, a *handler* is used to call a user-defined function.

Example

Listing 8.358 shows how the watch() method is used to inform the user that the password value has changed within the changeValue() function.

Listing 8.358   Using the watch() ***Method on the*** Password ***Object***

```
<html>
<script type="text/javascript" language="JavaScript">
<!--

function alertme(id,oldValue,newValue)
{
  document.writeln(id + " changed from " + "<b>" + oldValue + "</b>"+
➡" to " + "<b>" + newValue + "</b><br>")
  return newValue;
}

function setWatch(){
  myPass = document.form1.pass.value;
  watch("myPass",alertme);
  myPass = "abc123";
}


// -->
</script>

<form name="form1">
Enter Password <input type="PASSWORD" Name="pass" size="10">
<br>
<input type="BUTTON" value="Submit" onClick='setWatch()'>
</form>

</body>
</html>
```

Plugin

JavaScript 1.1+, JScript 1.0+
Nav3+, IE3+, Opera3+

Syntax

Core client-side JavaScript object.

Description

The Plugin object is used to obtain plug-in information from the browser. The Plugin object contains an array of elements containing the MIME types handled by each plug-in. Table 8.26 shows the different properties and methods of the Plugin object.

Table 8.26   Properties and Methods of the Plugin *Object*

Type	Item	Description
Property	description	Refers to a description of the plug-in
	filename	Refers to the filename of a plug-in program
	length	Refers to the number of MIME types supported
	name	Refers to the plug-in name
Method	unwatch()	Removes a watchpoint on a Plugin property
	watch()	Sets a watchpoint on a Plugin property

Example

Listing 8.359 shows an example in which all the browser's plug-ins are printed to the document.

Listing 8.359   Example Using the Plugin *Object*

```
<html>

<body>

<script type="text/javascript" language="JavaScript">
<!--
// function that prints all the browser plug-ins
for(i=0; i<navigator.plugins.length; i++){
    document.write(navigator.plugins[i].description);
}
// -->
</script>

</body>
</html>
```

Plugin.description

JavaScript 1.1+, JScript 1.0+
Nav3+, IE3+, Opera3+

Syntax

plugin.description

Description

The description property of the Plugin object is used to obtain a description of the
browser plug-ins.

Example

Listing 8.360 shows an example of how the description property is used.

Listing 8.360   Example of the description Property

```
<html>

<body>

<script type="text/javascript" language="JavaScript">
<!--
// print the description for the first plug-in
    document.write(navigator.plugins[0].description);

// -->
</script>

</body>
</html> >
```

Plugin.filename

JavaScript 1.1+, JScript 1.0+
Nav3+, IE3+, Opera3+

Syntax

plugin.filename

Description

The filename property of the Plugin object is used to get the path and filename for a
plug-in.

Example

Listing 8.361 shows an example of how the filename property is used.

Listing 8.361   Example of the `filename` *Property*

```
<html>

<body>

<script type="text/javascript" language="JavaScript">
<!--
// print the filename for the first browser plug-in
    document.write(navigator.plugins[0].filename);

// -->
</script>

</body>
</html>
```

Plugin.length
JavaScript 1.1+, JScript 1.0+
Nav3+, IE3+, Opera3+

Syntax

plugin.length

Description

The `length` property of the `Plugin` object determines the number of MIME data types the plug-in can support.

Example

Listing 8.362 shows an example of how the `length` property is used.

Listing 8.362   Example of the `length` *Property*

```
<html>

<body>

<script type="text/javascript" language="JavaScript">
<!--
// print the number of browser plug-ins
    document.write(navigator.plugins.length);

// -->
</script>

</body>
</html>
```

Plugin.name

JavaScript 1.1+, JScript 1.0+
Nav3+, IE3+, Opera3+

Syntax

plugin.name

Description

The name property of the Plugin object is used to get the plug-in's name.

Example

Listing 8.363 shows an example of how the name property is used.

Listing 8.363   Example of the name **Property**

```
<html>

<body>

<script type="text/javascript" language="JavaScript">
<!--
// print the name of the first browser plug-in
    document.write(navigator.plugins[0].name);

// -->
</script>

</body>
</html>
```

Plugin.unwatch()

JavaScript 1.2+
Nav4+

Syntax

unwatch(prop)

Description

The unwatch() method of the Plugin object is used to disable a watch on a Plugin property. Specify the property, *prop*, to disable.

Example

All Plugin properties are read-only, hence no example is provided.

Plugin.watch()

JavaScript 1.2+
Nav4+

Syntax

```
watch(prop, handler)
```

Description

The watch() method of the Plugin object is used to watch for changes to Plugin properties. When one of the properties, *prop,* is assigned a value, a *handler* is used to call a user-defined function.

Example

All Plugin properties are read-only, hence no example is provided.

Radio

JavaScript 1.0+, JScript 1.0+
Nav2+, IE3+, Opera3+

Syntax

Core client-side JavaScript object.

Description

The Radio object represents a check box within an HTML form. A check box is created using the HTML <input> tag and specifying the type attribute as radio. The Radio object has specific properties and methods associated with it, as shown in Table 8.27.

Table 8.27   Properties, Methods, and Events of the Radio **Object**

Type	Item	Description
Property	checked	Specifies whether a button is checked or unchecked
	defaultChecked	Refers to the checked attribute of the HTML <input> tag
	form	Refers to the Form object that contains the Radio object
	name	Refers to the name attribute of the HTML <input> tag
	type	Refers to the type attribute of the HTML <input> tag
	value	Refers to the value attribute of the HTML <input> tag
Method	blur()	Removes focus from the Radio object
	click()	Simulates a mouse click on the button

Type	Item	Description
	focus()	Sets the focus to a button
	handleEvent()	Invokes the default handler for the specified event
	unwatch()	Removes a watchpoint on a Radio property
	watch()	Sets a watchpoint on a Radio property
Event	onBlur	Event handler for the Blur event
	onClick	Event handler for the Click event
	onFocus	Event handler for the Focus event

Example

Listing 8.364 shows how a check box is created and then how the name property is accessed using the Radio object.

Listing 8.364   Example of the Radio Object

```
<html>

<body>

<form name="form1">
<input type="radio" name=button1
➡onClick='alert(document.form1.button1.name)'>Box 1
<br>
<input type="radio" name="button2">Box 2
<br>
</form>

</body>
</html>
```

Radio.blur()

JavaScript 1.0+, JScript 1.0+
Nav2+, IE3+, Opera3+

Syntax

radio.blur()

Description

The blur() method of the Radio object is used to remove the focus from the check box.

Example

Listing 8.365 shows how the `blur()` method is used to remove focus from the radio button. When the Remove Focus button is clicked, the focus is removed from the radio button and a text message is displayed.

Listing 8.365   Example of the `blur()` Method

```
<html>

<body>

<script type="text/javascript" language="JavaScript">
<!--

// function removes focus from the button
function change(){
document.form1.button1.blur();
document.form1.text1.value="Focus removed from button";
}
// -->
</script>

<form name="form1">
<input type="radio" name="button1" CHECKED>Box 1
<br>
<input type="radio" name="button2">Box 2
<br>
<input type="button" value="Remove Focus" onClick='change()'>
<br>
<input type="text" name="text1" size="15">
</form>

</body>
</html>
```

Radio.checked

JavaScript 1.0+, JScript 1.0+
Nav2+, IE3+, Opera3+

Syntax

`radio.checked`

Description

The `checked` property of the `Radio` object is a boolean value used to determine whether a radio button is in a checked or unchecked state.

Example

Listing 8.366 shows an example of how to determine whether the radio button is checked by using the `checked` property.

Listing 8.366   Example of the `checked` *Property*

```
<html>

<body>

<script type="text/javascript" language="JavaScript">
<!--

// function looks to see if button 1 is checked and displays
// an appropriate alert message.
function checkButton(){
if(document.form1.button1.checked == true){
    alert("Box1 is checked");
}
else if(document.form1.button2.checked == true){
    alert("Box 2 is checked");
}
}
// -->
</script>

<form name="form1">
<input type="radio" name="button1">Box 1
<br>
<input type="radio" name="button2" CHECKED>Box 2
<br>
< INPUT type="button" value="Get Checked" onClick='checkButton()'>
</form>

</body>
</html>
```

Radio.click()

JavaScript 1.0+, JScript 1.0+
Nav2+, IE3+, Opera3+

Syntax

radio.click()

Description

The `click()` property of the `Radio` object is used to simulate a mouse click on the radio button.

Example

Listing 8.367 shows an example of how the click() property is used.

Listing 8.367   Example of the click() Property

```
<html>

<body>

By pressing the "Simulate Click" button below,  box 2 becomes checked
because a simulated mouse click is performed.
<form name="form1">
<input type="radio" name="button1" CHECKED>Box 1
<br>
<input type="radio" name="button2">Box 2
<br>
<input type="button" value="Simulate Click"
➥ onClick='document.form1.button2.click()'>
</form>

</body>
</html>
```

Radio.defaultChecked

JavaScript 1.0+, JScript 1.0+
Nav2+, IE3+, Opera3+

Syntax

radio.defaultChecked

Description

The defaultChecked property of the Radio object is a boolean value that reports which radio buttons contain the HTML checked attribute. If the checked attribute is contained in the Radio object, true is returned. Otherwise, false is returned.

Example

Listing 8.368 shows how the defaultChecked property is used to find out which box is checked by default.

Listing 8.368   Example of the defaultChecked Property

```
<html>

<body>

<script type="text/javascript" language="JavaScript">
<!--
function checkBox(){
```

```
if(document.form1.button1.defaultChecked == true){
    alert("Box1 is checked by default");
}
else if(document.form1.button2.defaultChecked == true){
    alert("Box 2 is checked by default");
}
}
// -->
</script>

<form name="form1">
<input type="radio" name="button1">Box 1
<br>
<input type="radio" name="button2" CHECKED>Box 2
<br><br>
<input type="button" value="Get Default" onClick='checkBox()'>
</form>

</body>
</html>
```

Radio.focus()

JavaScript 1.0+, JScript 1.0+
Nav2+, IE3+, Opera3+

Syntax

radio.focus()

Description

The focus() method of the Radio object sets the focus to the radio button.

Example

Listing 8.369 shows how the focus() method is used.

Listing 8.369   Example of the focus() Method

```
<html>

<body>

<form name="form1">
<input type="radio" name="button1">Box 1
<br>
<input type="radio" name="button2">Box 2
<br><br>
<input type="button" value="Set Focus to Box 1"
➥ onClick='document.form1.button1.focus()'>
```

Listing 8.369   Continued
```
</form>

</body>
</html>
```

Radio.form

JavaScript 1.0+, JScript 1.0+
Nav2+, IE3+, Opera3+

Syntax

radio.form

Description

The form property of the Radio object is used to reference the Form object that contains the Radio box.

Example

Listing 8.370 shows an example of how the form property can be used to get the name of the form that contains the Radio object.

Listing 8.370   Example of the form Property
```
<html>

<body>

<form name="form1">
<input type="radio" name="button1">Box 1
<br>
<input type="radio" name="button2">Box 2
<br><br>
<input type="button" value="Get Form Name"
  onClick='alert("The form name is: " + document.form1.button1.form.name)'>
</form>

</body>
</html>
```

Radio.handleEvent()

JavaScript 1.0+, JScript 1.0+
Nav2+, IE3+, Opera3+

Syntax

radio.handleEvent(*event*)

Description

The `handleEvent()` method of the `Radio` object invokes the event handler for the specific event.

Example

Listing 8.371 shows how the `handleEvent()` method is used to capture all CLICK events and pass them to the `but1` object event handler.

Listing 8.371   Using the `handleEvent()` **Method**

```html
<html>

<body>

<script type="text/javascript" language="JavaScript">
<!--
// sets up the document to capture CLICK events
document.captureEvents(Event.CLICK);

// function that handles the specific event. The evnt parameter refers to
// the event object.
function handleClick(evnt){
    window.document.but1.handleEvent(evnt);
}

function showMsg(){
    alert("Button clicked.");
}

// This registers the handle function as the event handler for the
// CLICK event.
document.onClick = handleClick;
// -->
</script>

<form name="form1">
<input type="radio" name="but1" onClick='showMsg()'>Choice 1
<br>
<input type="radio" name="but1" onClick='showMsg()'>Choice 2
<br>
</form>

</body>
</html>
```

Radio.name

JavaScript 1.0+, JScript 1.0+
Nav2+, IE3+, Opera3+

Syntax

`radio.name`

Description

The `name` property of the `Radio` object represents the `name` attribute of the HTML `<input>` tag that creates the `Radio` button. This allows you to reference a `Radio` object directly by name.

Example

Listing 8.372 shows how the name of the `Radio` button is used to access its properties.

Listing 8.372 **Accessing the** `Radio` **Button by Name**

```
<html>

<body>

<form name="form1">
<input type="radio" name="myButton">Box 1
<br><br>
<input type="button" value="Get Name"
➥onClick='alert("The name of the button is: " +
document.form1.myButton.name)'>

</form>

</body>
</html>
```

Radio.onBlur

JavaScript 1.0+, JScript 1.0+
Nav2+, IE3+, Opera3+

Syntax

`onBlur="command"`

Description

The `onBlur` property is an event handler for the `Radio` object that notifies you when the focus is removed from a radio button.

Example

Listing 8.373 shows how the `onBlur` event handler is used to detect when the focus is removed from the specified radio button.

Listing 8.373   Example of the onBlur Event Handler

```
<html>

<body>

<script type="text/javascript" language="JavaScript">
<!--
function showChange(){
    document.form1.text1.value = "Focus removed from Radio Button";
}
// -->
</script>


<form name="form1">
Click the radio button first, then click in the text area.
<br><br>
<input type="radio" name="button1" onBlur='showChange()'>Box 1
<br>
Click the text box
<input type="text" name="text1" size="40">
<br>
</form>

</body>
</html>
```

Radio.onClick

JavaScript 1.0+, JScript 1.0+
Nav2+, IE3+, Opera3+

Syntax

```
onClick="command"
```

Description

The onClick property of the Radio object is an event handler that notifies you when the mouse has been clicked on the button.

Example

Listing 8.374 uses the onClick event handler to check for a mouse click event.

Listing 8.374   Example of the onClick Event Handler

```
<html>

<body>

<form name="form1">
```

Listing 8.374   Continued

```
<input type="radio" name="button1"
➥onClick='alert("This mouse was clicked on this object")'>Box 1
<br>
</form>

</body>
</html>
```

Radio.onFocus()

JavaScript 1.0+, JScript 1.0+
Nav2+, IE3+, Opera3+

Syntax

```
onFocus="command"
```

Description

The onFocus event handler of the Radio object is an event handler that notifies you when the focus is set on the radio button.

Example

In Listing 8.375, the onFocus event handler notifies the user with a text message when the focus is set on the radio button.

Listing 8.375   Example of the onFocus Event Handler

```
<html>

<body>

<script type="text/javascript" language="JavaScript">
<!--

// function sets the focus to box 1
function showFocus(){
    document.form1.text1.value = "Focus set on Box 1";
}
// -->
</script>

<form name="form1">
Click on the radio button
<br><br>
<input type="radio" name="button1" onFocus='showFocus()'>Box 1
<br><br>
<input type="text" name="text1" size="40">
```

```
</form>

</body>
</html>
```

Radio.type

JavaScript 1.0+, JScript 1.0+
Nav2+, IE3+, Opera3+

Syntax

`radio.type`

Description

The `type` property of the `Radio` button represents the button's `type` HTML attribute. For this object, it is always `radio`.

Example

Listing 8.376 shows an example of the `type` property.

Listing 8.376   Example of the `type` Property

```
<html>

<body>

<form name="form1">
<input type="radio" name="button1">Box 1
<br><br>
<input type="button" value="Get Button Type"
onClick='alert("The button type is: " + document.form1.button1.type)'>
</form>

</body>
</html>
```

Radio.unwatch()

JavaScript 1.2+
Nav4+, NES3+

Syntax

`radio.unwatch(prop)`

Description

The `unwatch()` method of the `Radio` object will remove a watchpoint on a property, `prop`, set by the `watch()` method.

Example

Listing 8.377 shows how the unwatch() method is used to turn off the watchpoint on the myRadio object.

Listing 8.377   Using the unwatch() **Method**

```
<html>
<script type="text/javascript" language="JavaScript">
<!--

function alertme(id,oldValue,newValue)
{
  document.writeln(id + " changed from " + "<b>" + oldValue +
➥ "</b>"+ " to " + "<b>" + newValue + "</b><br>")
  return newValue;
}

function setWatch(){
  myRadio = document.form1.button1.value;
  watch("myRadio",alertme);
  myRadio = 4;
  unwatch("myRadio");
  myRadio = 6;
}

// -->
</script>

<body>
<form name="form1">
<input type="radio" name="button1" value="1">Box 1
<br><br>
<input type="button" value="Get Button Value" onClick='setWatch()'>
</form>

</body>
</html>
```

Radio.value

JavaScript 1.0+, JScript 1.0+
Nav2+, IE3+, Opera3+

Syntax

radio.value

Description

The value property of the Radio object represents the value attribute of the HTML <input> tag used to create the radio button.

Example

Listing 8.378 shows how to access the value property.

Listing 8.378   Example of the value *Property*

```
<html>

<body>

<form name="form1">
<input type="radio" name="button1" value="1">Box 1
<br><br>
<input type="button" value="Get Button Value"
onClick='alert("The button value is: " + document.form1.button1.value)'>
</form>

</body>
</html>
```

Radio.watch()

JavaScript 1.2+
Nav4+, NES3+

Syntax

radio.watch(*prop, handler*)

Description

The watch() method of the Radio object is used to watch for changes to Radio properties. When one of the properties, *prop,* is assigned a value, a *handler* is used to call a user-defined function.

Example

Listing 8.379 shows how the watch() method is used to track when the value of the Radio button has been changed.

Listing 8.379   Using the watch() *Method on the* Radio *Value Property*

```
<html>
<script type="text/javascript" language="JavaScript">
<!--

function alertme(id,oldValue,newValue)
{
  document.writeln(id + " changed from " + "<b>" + oldValue +
"</b>"+ " to " + "<b>" + newValue + "a")
  return newValue;
}
```

Listing 8.379 *Continued*

```
function setWatch(){
  myRadio = document.form1.button1.value;
  watch("myRadio",alertme);
  myRadio = "4";
  myRadio = "6";
}

// -->
</script>

<body>
<form name="form1">
<input type="radio" name="button1" value="1">Box 1
<br><br>
<input type="button" value="Get Button Value" onClick='setWatch()'>
</form>

</body>
</html>
```

Reset

JavaScript 1.2+, JScript 1.0+
Nav4+, IE3+

Syntax

Core client-side JavaScript object.

Description

The Reset object represents a Reset button within an HTML form. The button is created using the HTML <input> tag and specifying the type attribute as reset. Reset buttons are used for form submissions. The Reset object has specific properties and methods associated with it, as shown in Table 8.28.

Table 8.28   *Properties, Methods, and Events of the* Reset *Object*

Type	Item	Description
Property	form	Specifies the form name that contains the Reset button
	name	HTML name attribute for the Reset button
	type	HTML type attribute for the Reset button
	value	HTML value attribute for the Reset button
Method	blur()	Removes focus from the Reset button
	click()	Simulates a mouse click on a Reset button
	focus()	Sets the focus to the Reset button
	handleEvent()	Invokes the event handler

Type	Item	Description
	unwatch()	Removes a watchpoint on a Reset property
	watch()	Sets a watchpoint on a Reset property
Event	onBlur	Event handler for the Blur event
	onClick	Event handler for the Click event
	onFocus	Event handler for the Focus event

Example

Listing 8.380 shows the syntax for using the Reset object.

Listing 8.380   Example of the Reset Object

```
<html>

<body>

<form name="form1">
Click the Reset button to reset the form.
<br><br><br>
Enter Name: <input type="text" Name="name" Size="15">
<br>
Enter Phone: <input type="text" Name="phone" Size="10">
<br><br>
<input type="reset" name="resetbutton" value="Reset">
<br>
<br>
</form>

</body>
</html>
```

Reset.blur()

JavaScript 1.0+, JScript 1.0+
Nav2+, IE3+, Opera3+

Syntax

reset.blur()

Description

The blur() method of the Reset object is used to remove the focus from the Reset button.

Example

Listing 8.381 shows an example of how the blur() method is used.

Listing 8.381   Example of the `blur()` **Method**

```
<html>

<body>

<script type="text/javascript" language="JavaScript">
<!--

// displays a message when focus is removed from the reset button
function showMsg(){
    document.form1.msg.value="Focus removed from the Reset button.";
}
// -->
</script>

<form name="form1">
Enter Name: <input type="text" Name="name" Size="15">
<br>
Enter Phone: <input type="text" Name="phone" Size="10">
<br>
Message: <input type="text" Name="msg" Size="40">
<br>
<input type="reset" name="resetbutton" value="Reset" onBlur='showMsg()'>
<br>
<br>
</form>

</body>
</html>
```

Reset.click()

JavaScript 1.0+, JScript 1.0+
Nav2+, IE3+, Opera3+

Syntax

`reset.click()`

Description

The `click()` method of the `Reset` object is used to simulate a mouse click on the Reset button.

Example

Listing 8.382 shows how the `click()` method is used.

Listing 8.382   Example of the `click()` *Method*

```
<html>

<body>

<script type="text/javascript" language="JavaScript">
<!--
function clickReset(){
     document.form1.resetbutton.click();
}

function inform(){
     alert("The Reset button was clicked");
 }
// -->
</script>

<form name="form1">
Enter Name: <input type="text" Name="name" Size="15">
<br>
Enter Phone: <input type="text" Name="phone" Size="10">
<br><br>
<input type="reset" name="resetbutton" value="Reset" onClick='inform()'>
<br>
<br>
<input type="button" value="Simulate Click" onClick='clickReset()'>
</form>

</body>
</html>
```

Reset.focus()

JavaScript 1.1+, JScript 1.0+
Nav3+, IE3+, Opera3+

Syntax

`reset.focus()`

Description

The focus() method of the Reset object is used to set the focus to the Reset button.

Example

Listing 8.383 shows an example of how the focus() method is used.

Listing 8.383   Accessing the focus() **Method**

```
<html>

<body>

<script type="text/javascript" language="JavaScript">
<!--
function focusReset(){
    document.form1.resetbutton.focus();
}
// -->
</script>

<form name="form1">
Enter Name: <input type="text" Name="name" Size="15">
<br>
Enter Phone: <input type="text" Name="phone" Size="10">
<br><br>
<input type="reset" name="resetbutton" value="Reset">
<br>
<br>
<input type="button" value="Set Focus to Reset" onClick='focusReset()'>
<br>
</form>

</body>
</html>
```

Reset.form

JavaScript 1.0+, JScript 1.0+
Nav2+, IE3+, Opera3+

Syntax

reset.form

Description

The form property of the Reset object is used to obtain the name of the form that contains the Reset button.

Example

Listing 8.384 shows an example of how to get the form name.

Listing 8.384   Example of Using the form **Property**

```
<html>

<body>
```

```
<form name="form1">
Enter Name: <input type="text" Name="name" Size="15">
<br>
Enter Phone: <input type="text" Name="phone" Size="10">
<br><br>
<input type="reset" name="resetbutton" value="Reset"
onClick='alert("The form name is: " + document.form1.resetbutton.form.name)'>
<br>
<br>
</form>

</body>
</html>
```

Reset.handleEvent()

JavaScript 1.0+, JScript 1.0+
Nav2+, IE3+, Opera3+

Syntax

reset.handleEvent(*event*)

Description

The handleEvent() method of the Reset object invokes the event handler for the object.

Example

Listing 8.385 shows an example of how the handleEvent() method is used.

Listing 8.385   Example of the handleEvent() Method

```
<html>

<body>

<script type="text/javascript" language="JavaScript">
<!--
// sets up the document to capture CLICK events
document.captureEvents(Event.CLICK);

// function that handles the specific event. The evnt parameter refers to
// the event object.
function handleMyClick(evnt){
    window.document.resetbutton.handleEvent(evnt);
}
```

Listing 8.385   Continued

```
function showMsg(){
    alert("Form has been reset");
}

// This registers the handle function as the event handler for the
// CLICK event.
document.onClick = handleMyClick;
// -->
</script>

<form name="form1">
Enter Name: <input type="text" Name="name" Size="15">
<br>
Enter Phone: <input type="text" Name="phone" Size="10">
<br><br>
<input type="reset" name="resetbutton" value="Reset" onClick='showMsg()'>
<br>
<br>
</form>

</body>
</html>
```

Reset.name

JavaScript 1.0+, JScript 1.0+
Nav2+, IE3+, Opera3+

Syntax

reset.name

Description

The name property of the Reset object represents the name given to a Reset button as specified from the name attribute of the HTML <input type="reset"> tag.

Example

In Listing 8.386, the name property is used to inform the user of the active frame.

Listing 8.386   Example of the name Property

```
<html>

<body>

<form name="form1">
Enter Name: <input type="text" Name="name" Size="15">
<br>
```

```
Enter Phone: <input type="text" Name="phone" Size="10">
<br><br>
<input type="reset" name="resetbutton" value="Reset"
onClick='alert("The reset button name is: " +
➥document.form1.resetbutton.name)'>
<br>
<br>
</form>

</body>
</html>
```

Reset.onBlur
JavaScript 1.1+, JScript 1.0+
Nav3+, IE3+, Opera3+

Syntax
onBlur="*command*"

Description
The onBlur event handler for the Reset object is an event handler that specifies when the focus has been removed from the Reset button.

Example
In Listing 8.387, the onBlur event handler is used.

Listing 8.387   Using the onBlur *Event Handler*

```
<html>

<body>

<script type="text/javascript" language="JavaScript">
<!--
function setMsg(){
    document.form1.text1.value = "Focus was removed from the reset object";
}
// -->
</script>

<form name="form1">
Click the reset button and then click in a text area.
<br><br>
Enter Name: <input type="text" Name="name" Size="15">
<br>
Enter Phone: <input type="text" Name="phone" Size="10">
<br><br>
```

Listing 8.387   Continued

```
Message: <input type="text" name="text1" size="45">
<br><br>
<input type="reset" name="resetbutton" value="Reset" onBlur='setMsg()'>
<br>
<br>
</form>

</body>
</html>
```

Reset.onClick

JavaScript 1.1+, JScript 1.0+
Nav3+, IE3+, Opera3+

Syntax

```
onClick="command"
```

Description

The onClick property is an event handler used to handle the event of a mouse click on the Reset button.

Example

Listing 8.388 shows an example of how the onClick event handler is used.

Listing 8.388   Example of the onClick Event Handler

```
<html>

<body>

<form name="form1">
Enter Name: <input type="text" Name="name" Size="15">
<br>
Enter Phone: <input type="text" Name="phone" Size="10">
<br><br>
<input type="reset" name="resetbutton" value="Reset"
➥onClick='alert("The reset button was clicked")'>
<br>
<br>
</form>

</body>
</html>
```

Reset.onFocus

JavaScript 1.2+, ECMAScript 1.0+, JScript 1.0+
Nav4+, IE3+

Syntax

onFocus="*command*"

Description

The onFocus event handler is used to specify when the focus is set on the Reset button.

Example

Listing 8.389 shows the onFocus event handler being used to inform the user when the focus is set.

Listing 8.389   Example of the onFocus **Event Handler**

```html
<html>

<body>

<script type="text/javascript" language="JavaScript">
<!--
function setMsg(){
    document.form2.text1.value = "Focus is set on the reset button.";
}
// -->
</script>

<form name="form1">
Click the reset button.
<br><br>
Enter Name: <input type="text" Name="name" Size="15">
<br>
Enter Phone: <input type="text" Name="phone" Size="10">
<br><br>
<input type="reset" name="resetbutton" value="Reset" onFocus='setMsg()'>
<br>
</form>

<form name="form2">
<br><br>
Message: <input type="text" name="text1" size="45">
</form>

</body>
</html>
```

Reset.type

JavaScript 1.2+, ECMAScript 1.0+
Nav4+

Syntax

`reset.type`

Description

The `type` property of the `Reset` object represents the HTML `type` attribute of the Reset button. In the case of a Reset button, this will always be `reset`.

Example

Listing 8.390 shows how to get the Reset button type.

Listing 8.390   Example of the `type` *Property*

```
<html>

<body>

<form name="form1">
Enter Name: <input type="text" Name="name" Size="15">
<br>
Enter Phone: <input type="text" Name="phone" Size="10">
<br><br>
<input type="reset" name="resetbutton" value="Reset"
onClick='alert("The button type is: " + document.form1.resetbutton.type)'>
<br>
<br>
</form>

</body>
</html>
```

Reset.unwatch()

JavaScript 1.2+
Nav4+, NES3+

Syntax

`reset.unwatch(prop)`

Description

The unwatch() method of the Reset object is used to remove a watchpoint set on a property by the watch() method. It takes one parameter, which is the property to unwatch.

Example

Listing 8.391 shows how the unwatch() method to turn off the watch on the Reset object value property.

Listing 8.391 ***Using the*** unwatch() ***Method on the*** Reset ***Object***

```
<html>
<script type="text/javascript" language="JavaScript">
<!--

function alertme(id,oldValue,newValue)
{
  document.writeln(id + " changed from " + "<b>" + oldValue +
➥"</b>"+ " to " + "<b>" + newValue + "</b><br>")
  return newValue;
}

function setWatch(){
  myRes = document.form1.resetbutton.value;
  watch("myRes",alertme);
  myRes = "cat";
  unwatch("myRes");
  myRes = "dog";
}

// -->
</script>

<body>
<form name="form1">
Enter Name: <input type="text" Name="name" Size="15">
<br>
<input type="reset" name="resetbutton" value="Reset" onClick='setWatch()'>
<br>
<br>
</form>
</body>
</html>
```

Reset.value

JavaScript 1.0+, JScript 1.0+
Nav2+, IE3+, Opera3+

Syntax

reset.value

Description

The value property of the Reset object represents the HTML value attribute of the
Reset button.

Example

Listing 8.392 shows how the Reset button value can be accessed.

Listing 8.392   Example of the value Property

```
<html>

<body>

<form name="form1">
Enter Name: <input type="text" Name="name" Size="15">
<br>
Enter Phone: <input type="text" Name="phone" Size="10">
<br><br>
<input type="reset" name="resetbutton" value="Reset"
onClick='alert("The button value is: " + document.form1.resetbutton.value)'>
<br>
<br>
</form>

</body>
</html>
```

Reset.watch()

JavaScript 1.2+
Nav4+, NES3+

Syntax

reset.watch(prop, handler)

Description

The watch() method of the Reset object is used to watch for changes to Reset properties. When one of the properties, *prop,* is assigned a value, a *handler* is used to call a user-defined function.

Example

Listing 8.393 shows how the watch() method is used to watch for a change to the Reset object value property. When the value is changed, the *alertme* function is called.

Listing 8.393   *Using the* watch() ***Method on the*** Reset ***Object***

```
<html>
<script type="text/javascript" language="JavaScript">
<!--

function alertme(id,oldValue,newValue)
{
  document.writeln(id + " changed from " + "<b>" + oldValue +
"</b>"+ " to " + "<b>" + newValue + "</b><br>")
  return newValue;
}

function setWatch(){
  myRes = document.form1.resetbutton.value;
  watch("myRes",alertme);
  myRes = "cat";
  myRes = "dog";
}

// -->
</script>
```

Listing 8.393   Continued

```
<body>

<form name="form1">
Enter Name: <input type="text" Name="name" Size="15">
<br>
<input type="reset" name="resetbutton" value="Reset" onClick='setWatch()'>
<br>
<br>
</form>
</body>
</html>
```

screen

JavaScript1.2+, JScript3.0+
Nav4+, IE4+

Syntax

Core client-side JavaScript object.

Description

The `screen` object provides a programmer with access to various properties of the user's screen. These properties are often accessed and used for sizing windows that various scripts open. Table 8.29 shows the properties of the `screen` object. This object only has two methods, `watch()` and `unwatch()`, which allow you to turn on and off a watch for a particular property. See their respective entries for more information.

Table 8.29   *Properties of the* screen *Object*

Item	Description
`availHeight`	Accesses the pixel height of the user's screen, minus the toolbar or any other "permanent" objects.
`availLeft`	Accesses the x coordinate of the first pixel not part of the user's toolbar or any other "permanent" objects.
`availTop`	Accesses the y coordinate of the first pixel not part of the user's toolbar or any other "permanent" objects.
`availWidth`	Accesses the pixel width of the user's screen, minus the toolbar or any other "permanent" objects.
`colorDepth`	Accesses the maximum number of colors the user's screen can display. This is in bit format.
`height`	Accesses the pixel height of the user's screen.
`pixelDepth`	Accesses the number of bits per pixel of the user's screen. Some versions of Internet Explorer do not support this property, which returns `undefined`.
`width`	Accesses the pixel width of the user's screen.

Example

Listing 8.394 has a button that, when clicked, opens a secondary window that displays all the properties of the `screen` object.

Listing 8.394   *Displaying the Properties of the* screen *Object*

```
<html>
<head>
<script language="JavaScript1.2" type="text/javascript">
<!--

// Define the openWin function called by pressing the button.
function openWin(){
```

Listing 8.394   Continued

```
// Open a window to store the results.
var myWin = open("", "","width=450,height=200");

// Write the screen properties to the window.
myWin.document.write("The availHeight is: " + screen.availHeight + "<br>");
myWin.document.write("The availWidth is: " + screen.availWidth + "<br>");
myWin.document.write("The colorDepth is: " + screen.colorDepth + "<br>");
myWin.document.write("The height is: " + screen.height + "<br>");
myWin.document.write("The pixelDepth is: " + screen.pixelDepth + "<br>");
myWin.document.write("The width is: " + screen.width + "<br>");

// Close the stream to the window.
myWin.document.close();
}
// -->
</script>
</head>
<body>
<form name="myForm">
  <input type="button" value="Click to See Screen Properties" name="myButton"
      ➥onclick="openWin()">
</form>
</body>
</html>
```

screen.availHeight

JavaScript1.2+, JScript3.0+
Nav4+, IE4+

Syntax

```
screen.availHeight
```

Description

The availHeight property of the screen object accesses the available pixel height of the user's screen. This height is minus any toolbar or any other "permanent" objects that might be on the user's screen.

Example

Listing 8.395 displays the available height of the user's screen to the page.

Listing 8.395   Accessing the availHeight **Property of the** screen **Object**

```
<script language="JavaScript1.2" type="text/javascript">
<!--
```

```
document.write("The available height of this user's screen is <b>");
document.write(screen.availHeight + '</b> pixels');

// -->
</script>
```

screen.availLeft

JavaScript1.2+
Nav4+

Syntax

```
screen.availLeft
```

Description

The availLeft property of the screen object specifies the first available x coordinate pixel not allocated to any of the user's toolbar or any other "permanent" objects that may be on the screen.

> **NOTE**
>
> If you access this property in Netscape 6, it does not consider the My Sidebar as part of the window—just the rendering portion window.

Example

Listing 8.396 displays the available left pixel of the user's screen to the page.

Listing 8.396   Accessing the `availLeft` ***Property of the*** `screen` ***Object***

```
<script language="JavaScript1.2" type="text/javascript">
<!--

document.write("The available left of this user's screen is <b>");
document.write(screen.availLeft + '</b> pixels');

// -->
</script>
```

screen.availTop

JavaScript1.2+
Nav4+

Syntax

```
screen.availTop
```

Description

The `availTop` property of the `screen` object specifies the first available y coordinate pixel not allocated to any of the user's toolbar or any other "permanent" objects that might be on the screen.

Example

Listing 8.397 displays the available top pixel of the user's screen to the page.

Listing 8.397 Accessing the `availTop` *Property of the* screen *Object*

```
<script language="JavaScript1.2" type="text/javascript">
<!--

document.write("The available top of this user's screen is <b>");
document.write(screen.availTop + '</b> pixels');

// -->
</script>
```

screen.availWidth

JavaScript1.2+, JScript3.0+
Nav4+, IE4+

Syntax

```
screen.availWidth
```

Description

The `availWidth` property of the `screen` object accesses the available pixel width of the user's screen. This width is minus any toolbar or any other "permanent" objects that may be on the user's screen.

Example

Listing 8.398 displays the available width of the user's screen to the page.

Listing 8.398 Accessing the `availWidth` *Property of the* screen *Object*

```
<script language="JavaScript1.2" type="text/javascript">
<!--

document.write("The available width of this user's screen is <b>");
document.write(screen.availWidth + '</b> pixels');

// -->
</script>
```

screen.colorDepth

JavaScript1.2+, JScript3.0+
Nav4+, IE4+

Syntax

```
screen.colorDepth
```

Description

The colorDepth property of the screen object accesses the maximum number of colors the user's screen can display. The returned value is in terms of bits.

Example

Listing 8.399 displays the color depth of the user's screen to the page.

Listing 8.399   *Accessing the* colorDepth *Property of the* screen *Object*

```
<script language="JavaScript1.2" type="text/javascript">
<!--

document.write("The color depth of this user's screen is <b>");
document.write(screen.colorDepth + '</b> bit');

// -->
</script>
```

screen.height

JavaScript1.2+, JScript3.0+
Nav4+, IE4+

Syntax

```
screen.height
```

Description

The height property of the screen object accesses the height of the user's screen in pixels.

Example

Listing 8.400 displays the height of the user's screen to the page.

Listing 8.400   *Accessing the* height *Property of the* screen *Object*

```
<script language="JavaScript1.2" type="text/javascript">
<!--

document.write("The height of this user's screen is <b>");
document.write(screen.height + '</b> pixels');
```

Listing 8.400   Continued

```
// -->
</script>
```

Screen.pixelDepth

JavaScript1.2+
Nav4+

Syntax

```
screen.pixelDepth
```

Description

The `pixelDepth` property of the `screen` object accesses the number of bits per pixel of the user's screen.

Example

Listing 8.401 displays the pixel depth of the user's screen to the page.

Listing 8.401   Accessing the `pixelDepth` Property of the `screen` Object

```
<script language="JavaScript1.2" type="text/javascript">
<!--

document.write("The pixel depth of this user's screen is <b>");
document.write(screen.pixelDepth + '</b> bit');

// -->
</script>
```

screen.unwatch()

JavaScript 1.2+
Nav4+

Syntax

```
screen.unwatch(property)
```

Description

The `unwatch()` method of the `screen` object is used to turn off the watch for a particular *property*.

Example

Listing 8.402 shows how the `unwatch()` method is used to stop watching the `height` property. If the `screen.height` property changes, such as in changing screen resolution, this function will be called.

Listing 8.402 **Example of the** unwatch() **Method**

```
<script type="text/javascript" language="JavaScript1.2">

function alertme(id, oldValue, newValue){
  document.writeln("ID (" + id + ") changed from " + oldValue + " to ");
  document.writeln(newValue + "<br>");
  return newValue;
}

screen.watch("height",alertme);
screen.unwatch("height");

</script>
```

screen.watch()

JavaScript 1.2+
Nav4+

Syntax

```
screen.watch(property, function)
```

Description

The watch() method of the screen object is used to turn on the watch for a particular property specified by *property*. Any time the specified *property* is changed after the watch() method has been called, the specified *function* is called.

Example

Listing 8.403 shows how the watch() method is used to start watching the height property. If the screen.height property changes, such as in changing screen resolution, this function will be called.

Listing 8.403 **Example of the** watch() **method**

```
<script type="text/javascript" language="JavaScript1.2">

function alertme(id, oldValue, newValue){
  document.writeln("ID (" + id + ") changed from " + oldValue + " to ");
  document.writeln(newValue + "<br>");
  return newValue;
}

screen.watch("height",alertme);

</script>
```

screen.width

JavaScript1.2+, JScript3.0+
Nav4+, IE4+

Syntax

```
screen.width
```

Description

The width property of the screen object accesses the width of the user's screen in pixels.

Example

Listing 8.404 displays the width of the user's screen to the page.

Listing 8.404   Accessing the** width **Property of the** screen **Object

```
<script language="JavaScript1.2" type="text/javascript">
<!--

document.write("The width of this user's screen is <b>");
document.write(screen.width  + '</b> pixels');

// -->
</script>
```

Select

JavaScript1.0+, JScript1.0+
Nav2+, IE3+, Opera3+

Syntax

Core client-side JavaScript object.

Description

The Select object is one of the core JavaScript objects. Instances are created by the browser when it encounters an HTML <select> tag. In the JavaScript object hierarchy, the Select object is located at window.document.Form.Select. Table 8.30 lists the properties, methods, and event handlers used by the Select object.

Table 8.30   Event Handlers, Methods, and Properties Used by the** Select **Object

Type	Item	Description
Event Handler	onBlur	Executes code when the select box loses the focus.
	onChange	Executes code when the select box has had its value modified.

Type	Item	Description
	onFocus	Executes code when the select box receives the focus.
Method	blur()	Removes the focus from the select box.
	focus()	Gives the focus to the select box.
	handleEvent()	Invokes the handler for the event specified and was added in JavaScript 1.2.
	unwatch()	Used to turn off the watch for a particular property.
	watch()	Used to turn on the watch for a particular property.
Property	form	Returns the entire form that the select box is in.
	length	Returns the number of options in the select box.
	name	Returns the name of this select box specified by the name attribute.
	options	Returns an array containing each of the items in the select box. These items are created using the <option> HTML tag. There is also a length and selectedIndex subproperty of this property.
	selectedIndex	Returns an integer specifying the indexed location of the selected option in the select box.
	type	Returns the type of this select box specified by the type attribute. For <select> instances that contain the multiple attribute, this property returns select-multiple. Instances without this attribute return select-one. Note that this property was added in JavaScript 1.1.

Example

Listing 8.405 displays the use of the Select properties. It contains a select box and a button. When the button is clicked, a second window is opened. The values of the properties of this Select object are displayed in this window.

Listing 8.405   Displaying the Properties of an Instance of a Select Object

```
<html>
<head>
<script language="JavaScript" type="text/javascript">
<!--

// Define the openWin function called by pressing the button.
function openWin(){

  // Place the reference to the select box in a variable for easier access.
  var myInstance = document.myForm.mySelect;
```

Listing 8.405   Continued

```
  // Open a window to store the results.
  var myWin = open( "", "","width=450,height=200" );

  // Write the select box's properties to the window.
  myWin.document.write("The length is: " + myInstance.length + "<br>");
  myWin.document.write("The name is: " + myInstance.name + "<br>");
  myWin.document.write("The selected option is located at position: ");
  myWin.document.write(myInstance.selectedIndex + "<br>");
  myWin.document.write("The type is: " + myInstance.type + "<br>");

  // Note that the entire form object is passed with this property.
  // This allows you to then drill down and get the value of other
  // components in the form.
  myWin.document.write("The form can be used to grab ");
  myWin.document.write("the value of the button: ");
  myWin.document.write(myInstance.form.myButton.value);

  // Close the stream to the window.
  myWin.document.close();
}
// -->
</script>
</head>
<body>
<form name="myForm">My Favorite Sport is:
  <select name="mySelect">
    <option value="BASE">Baseball</option>
    <option value="FOOT">Football</option>
    <option value="BASKET">Basketball</option>
    <option value="SOCCER">Soccer</option>
  </select>
<input type="button" value="Click to Process" name="myButton"
        onclick="openWin()">
</form>
</body>
</html>
```

Select.blur()

JavaScript1.0+, JScript1.0+,
Nav2+, IE3+, Opera3+

Syntax

select.blur()

Description

The `blur()` method of the `Select` object removes focus from the select box. This does not mean that the selected option is unselected, but rather, the focus on this option and the select box as a whole are removed. Be careful when using this method in conjunction with the `Select.focus()` method. It can lead to a focus/blur loop, where the browser blurs a focus as soon as it is done, and vice versa.

Example

Listing 8.406 has a multiple select box and a button. If the user selects any of the options in the box and then clicks the Click Here to Remove Focus button, the option and entire select box will no longer have focus.

Listing 8.406   Using the `blur()` Method to Remove Focus from the Select Box

```
<html>
<head>
<script language="JavaScript" type="text/javascript">
<!--

// Define the removeFocus function called by pressing the button.
function removeFocus(){

  // Remove focus from the select box.
  document.myForm.mySelect.blur();
}
// -->
</script>
</head>
<body>
<p>
<form name="myForm">
  <select name="mySelect" multiple>
    <option value="BASE">Baseball</option>
    <option value="FOOT">Football</option>
    <option value="BASKET">Basketball</option>
    <option value="SOCCER">Soccer</option>
  </select>
  <input type="button" value="Click Here to Remove Focus" name="myButton"
       onclick="removeFocus()">
</form>
</body>
</html>
```

Select.focus()

JavaScript1.0+, JScript1.0+
Nav2+, IE3+, Opera3+

Syntax

```
select.focus()
```

Description

The focus() method of the Select object gives the focus to the select box. Be careful when using this method in conjunction with the Select.blur() method. It can lead to a focus/blur loop, where the browser blurs a focus as soon as it is done, and vice versa.

Example

Listing 8.407 has two text boxes and two buttons. If the user clicks the first button, the cursor is set inside the first text box. If the user clicks the second text box, the cursor is set inside the second text box.

Listing 8.407   Using the focus() **Method to Place the Cursor in the Desired Select Box**

```
<html>
<head>
<script language="JavaScript" type="text/javascript">
<!--

// Define the setFocus function called by pressing the button.
function setFocus(num){

  // Determine which button was clicked and set the cursor
  // in the appropriate select box.
  if(num == 1){
    document.myForm.mySelect1.focus();
  }else if(num == 2){
    document.myForm.mySelect2.focus();
  }
}
// -->
</script>
</head>
<body>
<p>
<form name="myForm">
  <select name="mySelect1" multiple>
    <option value="BASE">Baseball</option>
    <option value="FOOT">Football</option>
    <option value="BASKET">Basketball</option>
    <option value="SOCCER">Soccer</option>
```

```
    </select>
    <input type="button" value="Click to Set Cursor" name="myButton1"
        onclick="setFocus(1)">
    <br>
    <select name="mySelect2" multiple>
      <option value="HOCK">Hockey</option>
      <option value="RUG">Rugby</option>
      <option value="GOLF">Golf</option>
      <option value="TENNIS">Tennis</option>
    </select>
    <input type="button" value="Click to Set Cursor" name="myButton2"
        onclick="setFocus(2)">
</form>
</body>
</html>
```

Select.form

JavaScript1.0+, JScript1.0+
Nav2+, IE3+, Opera3+

Syntax

select.form

Description

The form property of an instance of a Select object holds all the data of the form in which the select box is contained. This allows a developer to obtain specific information about the form in which the select box is located.

Example

Listing 8.408 has a select box and a button. When the button is clicked, three properties of the form as a whole are displayed. These properties were referenced through the form property of the select box.

Listing 8.408   Accessing a Form Via the form *Property of an Instance of a* Select *Object*

```
<html>
<head>
<script language="JavaScript" type="text/javascript">
<!--

// Define the openWin function called by pressing the button.
function openWin(){

  // Place the reference to the form property of the select box
  // in a variable for easier access.
  var formData = document.myForm.mySelect.form;
```

Listing 8.408   Continued

```
  // Open a window to display the results.
  var myWin = open("", "","width=450,height=200");

  // Write the form properties accessed through the form
  // property to the window.
  myWin.document.write("The name of the form is: " + formData.name + "<br>");
  myWin.document.write("The selectedIndex of the option is: ");
  myWin.document.write(formData.mySelect.selectedIndex + "<br>");
  myWin.document.write("The name of the button is: ");
  myWin.document.write(formData.elements[1].name + "<br>");

  // Close the stream to the window.
  myWin.document.close();
}
// -->
</script>
</head>
<body>
<form name="myForm">
  <select name="mySelect" multiple>
    <option value="BASE">Baseball</option>
    <option value="FOOT">Football</option>
    <option value="BASKET">Basketball</option>
    <option value="SOCCER">Soccer</option>
  </select>
<input type="button" value="Click to Process" name="myButton"
       onclick="openWin()">
</form>
</body>
</html>
```

Select.handleEvent()

JavaScript1.2+, JScript3.0+
Nav4+, IE4+

Syntax

select.handleEvent(*event*)

Description

The handleEvent() method of the Select object invokes the handler for the event specified. This method was added in JavaScript 1.2.

Example

Listing 8.409 has a single select box. The script tells the browser that it wants to intercept all Click events and that it wants the myClickHandler function to handle them.

Within this function, the handleEvent() method of the select box has been specified to handle the click.

When the user clicks anywhere on the page, the onClick event handler in the <select> tag calls a function to change the selection in a select box. The change increments through the four options in the box.

Listing 8.409 Using the* handleEvent() *Method of a* Select *Object to Handle All Clicks on a Page

```
<html>
<head>
<script language="JavaScript1.2" type="text/javascript">
<!--

// Define a click counter variable.
var counter = 0;

// Tell the browser you want to intercept ALL click events
// on the page. Then define a function to handle them.
window.captureEvents(Event.CLICK)
window.onClick = myClickHandler;

// Define the myClickHandler function to handle click events.
function myClickHandler(e){

  // Pass all click events to the onClick event of the select box.
  window.document.myForm.mySelect.handleEvent(e);

}

// Function is called by onClick of select box.
function changeSelect(){
  if(counter > 3){
    counter = 0;
    document.myForm.mySelect.selectedIndex = counter;
  }else{
    document.myForm.mySelect.selectedIndex = counter++;
  }
}
// -->
</script>
</head>
<body>
<form name="myForm">
  <select name="mySelect" onclick='changeSelect()'>
    <option value="BASE">Baseball</option>
    <option value="FOOT">Football</option>
    <option value="BASKET">Basketball</option>
    <option value="SOCCER">Soccer</option>
```

Listing 8.409   Continued

```
  </select>
</form>
</body>
</html>
```

Select.length

JavaScript1.0+, JScript1.0+
Nav2+, IE3+, Opera3+

Syntax

select.length

Description

The length property of an instance of a Select object returns the number of items in the select box.

Example

Listing 8.410 has a single select box and button. The length property of a Select object is displayed in an alert box when the button is clicked.

Listing 8.410   Using the length Property to Retrieve the Name of a Select Box

```
<html>
<head>
<script language="JavaScript" type="text/javascript">
<!--

// Display an alert box that contains the length of the
// select box.
function getName(){
  alert("The length of this select box is " +
        document.myForm.mySelect.length);
}
// -->
</script>
</head>
<body>
<form name="myForm">
  <select name="mySelect">
    <option value="BASE">Baseball</option>
    <option value="FOOT">Football</option>
    <option value="BASKET">Basketball</option>
    <option value="SOCCER">Soccer</option>
  </select>
```

```
  <input type="button" value="Get Name" name="myButton" onclick='getName()'>
</form>
</body>
</html>
```

Select.name

JavaScript1.0+, JScript1.0+
Nav2+, IE3+, Opera3+

Syntax

```
select.name
```

Description

The `name` property of an instance of a `Select` object returns the name of the select box. This property is often accessed via the `elements` array of a `Form` object and used to return the name of the select area. It is most useful when there are many forms on a given page, and determining the name helps you determine what function you want to perform.

Example

Listing 8.411 has a single select box and button. The `elements` array of a `Form` object is used to retrieve the name and display it in an alert box.

Listing 8.411   Using the name *Property to Retrieve the Name of a Select Box*

```
<html>
<head>
<script language="JavaScript" type="text/javascript">
<!--

// Display an alert box that contains the name of the
// select box.
function getName(){
  alert("The name of this select box is " +
        document.myForm.elements[0].name);
}
// -->
</script>
</head>
<body>
<form name="myForm">
  <select name="mySelect" multiple>
    <option value="BASE">Baseball</option>
    <option value="FOOT">Football</option>
```

Listing 8.411 Continued

```
      <option value="BASKET">Basketball</option>
      <option value="SOCCER">Soccer</option>
    </select>
    <input type="button" value="Get Name" name="myButton" onclick='getName()'>
  </form>
  </body>
  </html>
```

Select.onBlur

JavaScript1.0+, JScript1.0+,
Nav2+, IE3+, Opera3+

Syntax

```
onblur="command"
```

Description

The onBlur event handler of an instance of a Select object is fired when the focus is moved away from that particular select box. Care should be taken when using this event handler because it is possible to get into an infinite loop when using the onFocus event handler or the focus() method.

Example

Listing 8.412 contains two select boxes, one of which has the Blur event intercepted within its tag and a text box. The text box is used for a counter for the number of times the Blur event is fired.

In the script, the event is fired and the event handler calls a function that reassigns the first select box focus. The result of this is that when a user tries to click or tab away from the first select box, the counter is incremented and the focus returns. Note that this does not mean the selected item in the select box becomes unselected, but rather the first select box gains the focus.

As you will see if you run Listing 8.412, even clicking in other windows or the URL bar increments the counter.

Listing 8.412 Example of Using the onBlur Event Handler

```
<html>
<head>
<script language="JavaScript" type="text/javascript">
<!--

// Initialize a counter to show clicks.
var counter = 0;
```

```
// Set the focus on the first select box, and increment
// counter in the text box.
function comeBack(){
  document.myForm.mySelect1.focus();
  document.myForm.counter.value = counter++;
}
// -->
</script>
</head>
<body onload='comeBack()'>
<form name="myForm">
  <select name="mySelect1" multiple onblur='comeBack()'>
    <option value="BASE">Baseball</option>
    <option value="FOOT">Football</option>
    <option value="BASKET">Basketball</option>
    <option value="SOCCER">Soccer</option>
  </select>
  <br>
  <select name="mySelect2" multiple>
    <option value="HOCK">Hockey</option>
    <option value="RUG">Rugby</option>
    <option value="GOLF">Golf</option>
    <option value="TENNIS">Tennis</option>
  </select>
  <input type="text" size="2" value="" name="counter">
</form>
</body>
</html>
```

Select.onChange

JavaScript1.0+, JScript1.0+
Nav2+, IE3+, Opera3+

Syntax

onchange="*command*"

Description

The onChange event handler of an instance of a Select object is fired when the option selected in the select box is changed. Care should be taken when using this event handler because it is possible to get into an infinite loop when using other event handlers or methods that are fired when focus is placed on or away from the select box.

Example

Listing 8.413 has a single select box. If the user changes the selected option, an alert box is displayed showing the option that has been selected.

Listing 8.413 ***Using the*** onChange ***Event Handler to Display an Alert Box When an Option Is Selected in the Select Box***

```
<html>
<head>
<script language="JavaScript" type="text/javascript">
<!--

// Pop up an alert box displaying the option selected.
function changeBack(form){
  for (var i = 0; i < form.mySelect.options.length; i++) {
    if (form.mySelect.options[i].selected){
      alert("You have selected " + form.mySelect.options[i].text);
    }
  }
}
// -->
</script>
</head>
<body>
<form name="myForm">
  <select name="mySelect" onchange='changeBack(this.form)'>
    <option value="HOCK">Hockey</option>
    <option value="RUG">Rugby</option>
    <option value="GOLF">Golf</option>
    <option value="TENNIS">Tennis</option>
  </select>
</form>
</body>
</html>
```

Select.onFocus

JavaScript1.0+, JScript1.0+
Nav2+, IE3+, Opera3+

Syntax

onfocus="*command*"

Description

The onFocus event handler of an instance of a Select object is fired when the focus is set on that particular select box. Care should be taken when using this event handler because it is possible to get into an infinite loop when using the onBlur event handler or the blur() method.

Example

Listing 8.414 contains a multiple select box and a text box. The select box has an onFocus event handler within its tag that is fired every time you select an option in the box. In the script, the onFocus event handler within the <select> tag calls a function that assigns the text box focus. Each time a user clicks or tabs to the select box, the counter is incremented and the focus bar is returned to the text box.

Listing 8.414   Example of Using the onFocus **Event Handler**

```
<html>
<head>
<script language="JavaScript" type="text/javascript">
<!--

// Initialize a counter to show clicks.
var counter = 0;

// Set the focus on the counter text box, and increment
// counter.
function sendAway(){
  document.myForm.counter.focus();
  document.myForm.counter.value = counter++;
}
// -->
</script>
</head>
<body onload='sendAway()'>
<form name="myForm">
  <select name="mySelect" multiple onfocus='sendAway()'>
    <option value="HOCK">Hockey</option>
    <option value="RUG">Rugby</option>
    <option value="GOLF">Golf</option>
    <option value="TENNIS">Tennis</option>
  </select>
  <input type="text" size="2" value="" name="counter">
</form>
</body>
</html>
```

Select.options

JavaScript1.0+, JScript1.0+
Nav2+, IE3+, Opera3+

Syntax

`select.options`

Description

The `options` property of the `Select` object is an array that contains the elements of each of the options in the select box. This property is often used to retrieve properties of the options in a select box, such as the value or text.

Example

Listing 8.415 has a select box with four options in it. When an option is selected, a second window pops up. In this window, the `document.write()` method is used to write the properties of the selected option to the page.

Listing 8.415 Example of Using the `options` *Array to Retrieve the Properties of a Selected Option in a Select Box*

```
<html>
<head>
<script language="JavaScript" type="text/javascript">
<!--

// Pop up an alert box displaying the option selected.
function infoBox(form){

  // Store the passed info into a variable for easier coding.
  var myIn = form.mySelect;

  // Open a window to store the results.
  var myWin = open("", "","width=400,height=150");

  // Write the header info.
  myWin.document.write("The following is information about the ");
  myWin.document.write("option you selected");
  myWin.document.write('<hr height=1>');

  // Determine which option was selected.
  for (var i = 0; i < form.mySelect.options.length; i++) {
    if (form.mySelect.options[i].selected){

      // Write the option's properties to the window.
      myWin.document.write('<br><b>Value:</b> ' + myIn.options[i].value);
      myWin.document.write('<br><b>Text:</b> ' + myIn.options[i].text);
      myWin.document.close();
    }
  }
}
// -->
</script>
</head>
<body>
<form name="myForm">
  <select name="mySelect" onchange='infoBox(this.form)'>
    <option value="HOCK">Hockey</option>
    <option value="RUG">Rugby</option>
    <option value="GOLF">Golf</option>
    <option value="TENNIS">Tennis</option>
  </select>
```

```
</form>
</body>
</html>
```

Select.options.length

JavaScript1.0+, JScript1.0+
Nav2+, IE3+, Opera3+

Syntax

select.options.length

Description

The length property of the options array of the Select object returns the number of options in that instance of a select box.

Example

Listing 8.416 has a single select box. When the user makes a selection, the onChange event handler is used to pop up an alert box that displays the number of options in this select box.

Listing 8.416 *Accessing the* length *Property of the* options *Array of a* Select *Object*

```
<form name="myForm">
  <select name="mySelect" onchange='alert(mySelect.options.length)'>
    <option value="HOCK">Hockey</option>
    <option value="RUG">Rugby</option>
    <option value="GOLF">Golf</option>
    <option value="TENNIS">Tennis</option>
  </select>
</form>
```

Select.options.selectedIndex

JavaScript1.0+, JScript1.0+
Nav2+, IE3+, Opera3+

Syntax

select.options.selectedIndex

Description

The selectedIndex property of the options array of the Select object returns the index number of the selected option in that instance of a select box.

Example

Listing 8.417 has a single select box. When the user makes a selection, the `onChange` event handler is used to pop up an alert box that displays the index number of the selected option in this select box.

Listing 8.417 *Accessing the* `selectedIndex` *Property of the* `options` *Array of a* `Select` *Object*

```
<form name="myForm">
  <select name="mySelect" onchange='alert(mySelect.options.selectedIndex)'>
    <option value="HOCK">Hockey</option>
    <option value="RUG">Rugby</option>
    <option value="GOLF">Golf</option>
    <option value="TENNIS">Tennis</option>
  </select>
</form>
```

Select.options.value

JavaScript1.0+, JScript1.0+
Nav2+, IE3+, Opera3+

Syntax

```
select.options.value
```

Description

The `value` property of the `options` array of the `Select` object returns the value of the option that is selected in that instance of a select box.

Example

Listing 8.418 has a single select box. When the user makes a selection, the `onChange` event handler is used to pop up an alert box that displays the value of the selected option in this select box.

> **NOTE**
>
> Different browsers might fire this event at different times, so it is possible that the alert box is displayed differently.

Listing 8.418 *Accessing the* `value` *Property of the* `options` *Array of a* `Select` *Object*

```
<form name="myForm">
<select name="mySelect"
        onchange='alert(mySelect.options[selectedIndex].value)'>
    <option value="HOCK">Hockey</option>
    <option value="RUG">Rugby</option>
    <option value="GOLF">Golf</option>
```

```
      <option value="TENNIS">Tennis</option>
    </select>
</form>
```

Select.selectedIndex

JavaScript1.0+, JScript1.0+
Nav2+, IE3+, Opera3+

Syntax

`select.selectedIndex`

Description

The `selectedIndex` property of the `Select` object returns the index number of the selected option in that instance of a select box. If this property is used to access a multiple select box, it will return the index number of the first selected item.

Example

Listing 8.419 has a single select box. When the user makes a selection, the `onChange` event handler is used to pop up an alert box that displays the index number of the selected option in this select box.

Listing 8.419   *Accessing the* `selectedIndex` *Property of the* Select *Object*

```
<form name="myForm">
  <select name="mySelect" onchange='alert(mySelect.selectedIndex)'>
    <option value="HOCK">Hockey</option>
    <option value="RUG">Rugby</option>
    <option value="GOLF">Golf</option>
    <option value="TENNIS">Tennis</option>
  </select>
</form>
```

Select.type

JavaScript1.1+, JScript1.0+
Nav3+, IE3+, Opera3+

Syntax

`select.type`

Description

The `type` property of an instance of a `Select` object returns the type of the select box. This is either `select-multiple`, if the `multiple` attribute is set in the `<select>` tag, or `select-one` if it is not.

Example

Listing 8.420 has a select box and a button. When the button is clicked, an `alert` box is popped up that displays the `type` property of the select box.

Listing 8.420   Displaying the type **Property in an Alert Box**

```
<html>
<head>
<script language="JavaScript1.1" type="text/javascript">
<!--

// Display an alert box that contains the type of the
// select box.
function getType(){
  alert("The name of this text box is " +
        document.myForm.elements[0].type);
}
// -->
</script>
</head>
<body>
<form name="myForm">
  <select name="mySelect">
    <option value="HOCK">Hockey</option>
    <option value="RUG">Rugby</option>
    <option value="GOLF">Golf</option>
    <option value="TENNIS">Tennis</option>
  </select>
  <input type="button" value="Get Type" name="myButton" onclick='getType()'>
</form>
</body>
</html>
```

Select.unwatch()

> JavaScript 1.2+
> Nav4+

Syntax

```
select.unwatch(property)
```

Description

The `unwatch()` method of the `Select` object is used to turn off the watch for a particular *property*.

Example

Listing 8.421 shows how the `unwatch()` method is used to stop watching the `value` property.

Listing 8.421   Example of the unwatch() *Method*

```
<html>
<head>
  <script type="text/javascript" language="JavaScript1.2">

  function alertme(id, oldValue, newValue){
    document.writeln("ID (" + id + ") changed from " + oldValue + " to ");
    document.writeln(newValue + "<br>");
    return newValue;
  }

  function check(){
    document.myForm.mySelect.watch("value", alertme);
    document.myForm.mySelect.unwatch("value");
    document.myForm.mySelect.value="GOLF";
  }
  </script>
</head>
<body onload="check()">
<form name="myForm">
  <select name="mySelect">
    <option value="HOCK">Hockey</option>
    <option value="RUG">Rugby</option>
    <option value="GOLF">Golf</option>
    <option value="TENNIS">Tennis</option>
  </select>
</form>
</body>
</html>
```

Select.watch()

JavaScript 1.2+
Nav4+

Syntax

select.watch(*property, function*)

Description

The watch() method of the Select object is used to turn on the watch for a particular *property*. Any time the specified *property* is changed after the watch() method has been called, the specified *function* is called.

Example

Listing 8.422 shows how the watch() method is used to start watching the value property.

Listing 8.422   Example of the `watch()` *Method*

```
<html>
<head>
  <script type="text/javascript" language="JavaScript1.2">

  function alertme(id, oldValue, newValue){
    document.writeln("ID (" + id + ") changed from " + oldValue + " to ");
    document.writeln(newValue + "<br>");
    return newValue;
  }

  function check(){
    document.myForm.mySelect.watch("value", alertme);
    document.myForm.mySelect.value="GOLF";
  }
  </script>
</head>
<body onload="check()">
<form name="myForm">
  <select name="mySelect">
    <option value="HOCK">Hockey</option>
    <option value="RUG">Rugby</option>
    <option value="GOLF">Golf</option>
    <option value="TENNIS">Tennis</option>
  </select>
</form>
</body>
</html>
```

Style

JavaScript1.2,
Nav4

Syntax

Core client-side JavaScript object.

```
document.classes.className.tagName
document.ids.idName
document.tags.tagName
document.contextual(tag1, tag2)
```

Description

The `Style` object is a core client-side object within the Navigator 4 browser. Instances of this object exist and are accessible through four different methods. Three of these methods, `document.ids`, `document.classes`, and `document.tags`, represent associative arrays that contains the ids, classes, or tags, respectively, associated with the various style access options. The `document.contextual()` method, on the other hand, finds instances of *tag1* that occur within instances of *tag2*, and then creates an array filled with matching instances.

Table 8.31 contains a list of properties and methods for this object.

Table 8.31 **Properties and Methods of the** `Style` *Object*

Type	Item	Description
Method	borderWidths()	Sets border width of an HTML element.
	margins()	Sets minimal distance between the sides of an HTML element and the sides of adjacent elements.
	paddings()	Sets space to insert between the sides of an element and its content, such as text or an image.
	unwatch()	Turns off the watch for a particular property.
	watch()	Turns on the watch for a particular property.
Property	align	Sets alignment of an HTML element within its parent.
	backgroundColor	Sets solid background color for an element.
	backgroundImage	Sets background image for an HTML element.
	borderBottomWidth	Sets width of the bottom border of an HTML element.
	borderColor	Sets color of the border of an HTML element.
	borderLeftWidth	Sets width of the left border of an HTML element.
	borderRightWidth	Sets width of the right border of an HTML element.
	borderStyle	Sets style of border around a block-level HTML element.
	borderTopWidth	Sets width of the top border of an HTML element.
	clear	Sets sides of an HTML element that allow floating elements.
	color	Sets color of the text in an HTML element.
	display	Overrides the default display of an element and specifies whether it will appear in line, as a block-level element, or as a block-level list item.
	fontFamily	Sets font family, such as Helvetica or Arial, for an HTML text element.
	fontSize	Sets font size for an HTML text element.
	fontStyle	Sets style of the font of an HTML element.
	fontWeight	Sets weight of the font of an HTML element.
	lineHeight	Sets distance between the baselines of two adjacent lines of block-level type.
	listStyleType	Sets style of bullet displayed for list items.

Table 8.31 **Continued**

Type	Item	Description
	marginBottom	Sets minimum distance between the bottom of an HTML element and the top of an adjacent element.
	marginLeft	Sets minimum distance between the left side of an HTML element and the right side of an adjacent element.
	marginRight	Sets minimum distance between the right side of an HTML element and the left side of an adjacent element.
	marginTop	Sets minimum distance between the top of an HTML element and the bottom of an adjacent element.
	paddingBottom	Sets space to insert between the bottom of an element and its content, such as text or an image.
	paddingLeft	Sets space to insert between the left side of an element and its content, such as text or an image.
	paddingRight	Sets space to insert between the right side of an element and its content, such as text or an image.
	paddingTop	Sets space to insert between the top of an element and its content, such as text or an image.
	textAlign	Sets alignment of an HTML block-level text element.
	textDecoration	Sets special effects, such as blinking, strike-outs, and underlines, added to an HTML text element.
	textIndent	Sets length of indentation appearing before the first formatted line of a block-level HTML text element.
	textTransform	Sets case of an HTML text element.
	whiteSpace	Sets whether whitespace within an HTML element should be collapsed.
	width	Sets width of a block-level HTML element.

NOTE

Navigator 4 is the only browser that supports this object, which was deprecated in Netscape 6. You should only use it if you are scripting HTML or XHTML documents that require backward compatibility with Navigator 4.

Example

Listing 8.423 demonstrates three different ways to use document.ids to control the style result.

Listing 8.423 *Using the* Style *Object*

```
<html>

<style type="text/css">
  #TEXTFORMAT {font-style: italic;}
</style>

<p id="TEXTFORMAT">After first STYLE tag.<p>

<style type="text/javascript">
  ids.TEXTFORMAT.fontWeight = "bold";
</style>

<p id="TEXTFORMAT">After second STYLE tag.<p>

<script type="text/javascript" language="JavaScript">
<!--
document.ids.TEXTFORMAT.textDecoration = "underline";
document.classes.no-under.a.textDecoration = "none";
// -->
</script>

<p id="TEXTFORMAT">After SCRIPT tag.<p>
<a href="http://www.purejavascript.com" class="no-under">No underline</a>

</html>
```

Style.align

> JavaScript1.2
> Nav4

Syntax

*style.name.*align

Description

The align property specifies the alignment of an element within its parent as associated with *name*. Because *style* can be created using the document.classes, document.ids, document.tags, or document.contextual() methods, you should check the entries for these items for more information on the exact syntax.

The align property can be assigned one of the following values: left, right, or none.

> **NOTE**
>
> The `align` property is referred to as `float` when using CSS syntax. JavaScript could not use the word "float" because it is a reserved word.

Example

Listing 8.424 uses the `align` property to align a paragraph to the right of its parent, the document.

Listing 8.424   Aligning Right with the `align` *Property*

```
<html>

<script type="text/javascript" language="JavaScript">
<!--

//Create a style sheet id that aligns right.
document.ids.RIGHT.align = "right";

// -->
</script>

<p id="RIGHT">Send me to the right!</p>

<p>Where am I?</p>

</html>
```

Style.backgroundColor

JavaScript1.2
Nav4

Syntax

`style.name.backgroundColor`

Description

The `backgroundColor` property specifies the background color as associated with *name*. Because `style` can be created using the `document.classes`, `document.ids`, `document.tags`, or `document.contextual()` methods, you should check the entries for these items for more information on the exact syntax.

Example

Listing 8.425 uses the `backgroundColor` property to make the background color around an anchor red.

Listing 8.425   Setting the Background Color with the backgroundColor
Property

```
<html>

<script type="text/javascript" language="JavaScript">
<!--

//Create a style sheet id that contains the background color
document.ids.BG.backgroundColor = "red";

// -->
</script>

<a id="BG" name="THIS">This</a> is an anchor that uses
styles from the BG id.

</html>
```

Style.backgroundImage

JavaScript1.2
Nav4

Syntax

*style.name.*backgroundImage

Description

The backgroundImage property specifies the background image of an element as associated with *name*. Because *style* can be created using the document.classes, docu-
ment.ids, document.tags, or document.contextual() methods, you should check
the entries for these items for more information on the exact syntax.

Example

The code in Listing 8.426 makes the image logo.gif the background for the header
text.

Listing 8.426   Setting the Background Image with the backgroundImage
Property

```
<html>

<script type="text/javascript" language="JavaScript">
<!--

//Create a style sheet id that uses an image as a background
document.ids.BGI.backgroundImage = "logo.gif";
```

Listing 8.426   Continued

```
// -->
</script>

<h2 id="BGI">Look at my background image!</h2>

</html>
```

Style.borderBottomWidth

JavaScript1.2
Nav4

Syntax

`style.name.borderBottomWidth`

Description

The `borderBottomWidth` property specifies the width of the bottom border of an element as associated with *name*. Because *style* can be created using the `document.classes`, `document.ids`, `document.tags`, or `document.contextual()` methods, you should check the entries for these items for more information on the exact syntax.

Example

Listing 8.427 uses the `borderBottomWidth` property to set the size of bottom border that surrounds a text header. Notice that only the bottom portion of the border is shown.

Listing 8.427   Setting the Bottom Border Width with the
borderBottomWidth **Property**

```
<html>

<script type="text/javascript" language="JavaScript">
<!--

//Create a style sheet id that creates a bottom border
document.ids.BBW.borderBottomWidth = "10";

// -->
</script>

<h2 id="BBW">This text has a bottom border</h2>

</html>
```

Style.borderColor

JavaScript1.2
Nav4

Syntax

```
style.name.borderColor
```

Description

The borderColor property specifies the color of the border of an element as associated with *name*. Because *style* can be created using the document.classes, document.ids, document.tags, or document.contextual() methods, you should check the entries for these items for more information on the exact syntax.

Example

Listing 8.428 uses the borderColor property to set the color of the border that surrounds a text header to blue.

Listing 8.428 *Setting the Border Color with the* borderColor *Property*

```
<html>

<script type="text/javascript" language="JavaScript">
<!--

//Create a style sheet id that creates a left border
document.ids.a.borderWidths(10);
document.ids.a.borderColor = "blue";

// -->
</script>

<h2 id="a">This text has a blue border</h2>

</html>
```

Style.borderLeftWidth

JavaScript1.2
Nav4

Syntax

```
style.name.borderLeftWidth
```

Description

The borderLeftWidth property specifies the width of the left border of an element as associated with *name*. Because *style* can be created using the document.classes, document.ids, document.tags, or document.contextual() methods, you should check the entries for these items for more information on the exact syntax.

Example

Listing 8.429 uses the `borderLeftWidth` property to set the size of the left border that surrounds a text header. Notice that only the left portion of the border is shown.

Listing 8.429   Setting the Left Border Width with the `borderLeftWidth` Property

```
<html>

<script type="text/javascript" language="JavaScript">
<!--

//Create a style sheet id that creates a left border
document.ids.BLW.borderLeftWidth = "10";

// -->
</script>

<h2 id="BLW">This text has a left border</h2>

</html>
```

Style.borderRightWidth

JavaScript1.2
Nav4

Syntax

style.name.`borderRightWidth`

Description

The `borderRightWidth` property specifies the width of the right border of an element as associated with *name*. Because *style* can be created using the `document.classes`, `document.ids`, `document.tags`, or `document.contextual()` methods, you should check the entries for these items for more information on the exact syntax.

Example

Listing 8.430 uses the `borderRightWidth` property to set the size of right border that surrounds a text header. Notice that only the right portion of the border is shown.

Listing 8.430   Setting the Right Border Width with the `borderRightWidth` Property

```
<html>

<script type="text/javascript" language="JavaScript">
<!--
```

```
//Create a style sheet id that creates a right border.
document.ids.BRW.borderRightWidth = "10";

// -->
</script>

<h2 id="BRW">This text has a right border</h2>

</html>
```

Style.borderStyle

JavaScript1.2
Nav4

Syntax

*style.name.*borderStyle

Description

The borderStyle property specifies the style of the border that surrounds an element as associated with *name*. Because *style* can be created using the document.classes, document.ids, document.tags, or document.contextual() methods, you should check the entries for these items for more information on the exact syntax.

The borderStyle property can be assigned one of the following values: none, solid, double, inset, outset, groove, and ridge.

Example

Listing 8.431 uses the borderStyle property to set the border around a text header to a double line.

Listing 8.431   Setting the Border Style with the borderStyle *Property*

```
<html>

<script type="text/javascript" language="JavaScript">
<!--

//Create a style sheet id that creates a double border.
document.ids.a.borderWidths(10);
document.ids.a.borderColor = "red";
document.ids.a.borderStyle = "double";

// -->
</script>

<h2 id="a">This text has a double border</h2>

</html>
```

Style.borderTopWidth

JavaScript1.2
Nav4

Syntax

style.name.borderTopWidth

Description

The borderTopWidth property specifies the width of the top border of an element as associated with *name*. Because *style* can be created using the document.classes, document.ids, document.tags, or document.contextual() methods, you should check the entries for these items for more information on the exact syntax.

Example

Listing 8.432 uses the borderTopWidth property to set the size of top border that surrounds a text header. Notice that only the top portion of the border is shown.

Listing 8.432   Setting the Top Border Width with the borderTopWidth **Property**

```
<html>

<script type="text/javascript" language="JavaScript">
<!--

//Create a style sheet id that creates a top border.
document.ids.BTW.borderTopWidth = "10";

// -->
</script>

<h2 id="BTW">This text has a top border</h2>

</html>
```

Style.borderWidths()

JavaScript1.2
Nav4

Syntax

style.borderWidths(*top, right, bottom, left*)
style.borderWidths(*top-bottom, right-left*)
style.borderWidths(*all*)

Description

The borderWidths() method specifies the width of the border that surrounds an element as associated with *style*. Because *style* can be created using the document.classes, document.ids, document.tags, or document.contextual() methods, you should check the entries for these items for more information on the exact syntax.

Setting border widths is equivalent to setting the borderBottomWidth, borderLeftWidth, borderRightWidth, and borderTopWidth properties. Table 8.32 lists all the arguments associated with the borderWidths() method.

Table 8.32   Arguments Associated with the borderWidths() **Method**

Item	Description
top	Width of the top border
right	Width of the right border
left	Width of the left border
bottom	Width of the bottom border
top-bottom	Width of both the top and bottom border
left-right	Width of both the left and right border
all	Width of all four sides of the border

Example

Listing 8.433 uses the borderWidths() method to set the width of the border that surrounds a text header.

Listing 8.433   Setting All the Border Widths with the borderWidths() **Method**

```
<html>

<script type="text/javascript" language="JavaScript">
<!--

//Create a style sheet id that creates a border.
document.ids.a.borderWidths(5,10,15,20);

// -->
</script>

<h2 id="a">This text has a border</h2>

</html>
```

Style.clear

JavaScript1.2
Nav4

Syntax

```
style.clear
```

Description

The clear property specifies the sides of an element where floating elements (elements that define the align property) are not allowed. Using dot notation, this property is associated with style. Because style can be created using the document.classes, document.ids, document.tags, or document.contextual() methods, you should check the entries for these items for more information on the exact syntax.

The clear property can be assigned one of the following values: left, right, both, and none.

Example

Listing 8.434 uses the clear property to prevent floating elements from being on either side.

Listing 8.434   Using the clear Property

```html
<html>

<script type="text/javascript" language="JavaScript">
 <!--

  //Create style sheet classes and id that set alignments.
  document.classes.LEFT.all.align = "left";
  document.classes.LEFT.all.backgroundColor = "yellow";
  document.classes.RIGHT.all.align = "right";
  document.classes.RIGHT.all.backgroundColor = "red";
  document.ids.KEEPAWAY.clear = "both";

  // -->
</script>

<p class="LEFT">Send me to the left!</p>
<p class="RIGHT">Send me to the right!</p>
<p>I like other elements next to me!</p>

<p class="LEFT">Send me to the left!</p>
<p class="RIGHT">Send me to the right!</p>
<p id="KEEPAWAY">I don't like other elements next to me!</p>

</html>
```

Style.color

JavaScript1.2
Nav4

Syntax

`style.color`

Description

The `color` property specifies the foreground color of an element as associated with `style`. Because `style` can be created using the `document.classes`, `document.ids`, `document.tags`, or `document.contextual()` methods, you should check the entries for these items for more information on the exact syntax.

Example

Listing 8.435 uses the `color` property to set the color of various text.

Listing 8.435   Set the Color of Text Using the `color` Property

```
<html>

<script type="text/javascript" language="JavaScript">
<!--

//Create style sheet classes that define colors.
document.ids.BLUE.color = "blue";
document.ids.RED.color = "red";

// -->
</script>

<p id="BLUE">The blue boat floated on the blue ocean.</p>
<p id="RED">The red car stopped at a red stop sign.</p>

</html>
```

Style.display

JavaScript1.2
Nav4

Syntax

`style.display`

Description

The `display` property specifies an element to be displayed when associated with `style`. Because `style` can be created using the `document.classes`, `document.ids`, `document.tags`, or `document.contextual()` methods, you should check the entries for these items for more information on the exact syntax.

The display property can be assigned one of the following values: inline, block, list-item, and none.

Specifying an inline value is equivalent to using the <em> tag. The block value is the same as creating header text with the <h1>–<h6> tags. Using list-item is equivalent to using the <li> tag. If none is specified, the element is not displayed.

Example

Listing 8.436 uses the display property to create header text. block consists of a line break and resetting margins to their default values. Notice that in this example a carriage return is automatically entered before the bold tag.

Listing 8.436   Set the display Property

```
<html>

<script type="text/javascript" language="JavaScript">
<!--

//Create a style sheet id that defines a block display.
document.ids.H.display = "block";

// -->
</script>

<u id="H">A BIG HEADER</u>

Just some regular text following the Big Header.

</html>
```

Style.fontFamily
JavaScript1.2
Nav4

Syntax
style.fontFamily

Description

The fontFamily property specifies the font an element should use when associated with *style*. Because *style* can be created using the document.classes, document.ids, document.tags, or document.contextual() methods, you should check the entries for these items for more information on the exact syntax. More than one font can be specified, in case a particular font has not been loaded.

Example

Listing 8.437 uses the fontFamily property to create text with an Arial font. If that font is not available, Helvetica is used.

Listing 8.437   Set the `fontFamily` *Property*

```
<html>

<script type="text/javascript" language="JavaScript">
<!--

//Create a style sheet id that defines a font.
document.ids.F.fontFamily = "Arial, Helvetica";

// -->
</script>

<p id="F">Do you like this font?</p>

</html>
```

Style.fontSize

JavaScript1.2
Nav4

Syntax

`style.fontSize`

Description

The `fontSize` property specifies the size of fonts used by an element when associated with *name*. Because *style* can be created using the `document.classes`, `document.ids`, `document.tags`, or `document.contextual()` methods, you should check the entries for these items for more information on the exact syntax. The values that can be used to set font size can be divided into four categories, as shown in Table 8.33.

Table 8.33   Font Sizes

Category	Value
Absolute	`xx-small`
	`x-small`
	`small`
	`medium`
	`large`
	`x-large`
	`xx-large`
Relative	`smaller` (relative to font size of parent)
	`larger` (relative to font size of parent)
Length	A number followed by a unit of measurement
Percentage	The size relative to font size of parent

Example

Listing 8.438 uses absolute font sizing to define the `fontSize` property and associate with text.

Listing 8.438   Set the `fontSize` Property

```
<html>

<script type="text/javascript" language="JavaScript">
<!--

//Create a style sheet id that defines a font size.
document.ids.XXS.fontSize = "xx-small";
document.ids.XXL.fontSize = "xx-large";

// -->
</script>

<p id="XXS">Extra, extra small text</p>
<p id="XXL">Extra, extra large text</p>

</html>
```

Style.fontStyle

JavaScript1.2
Nav4

Syntax

style.fontStyle

Description

The `fontStyle` property specifies the font style used by an element when associated with *style*. Because *style* can be created using the `document.classes`, `document.ids`, `document.tags`, or `document.contextual()` methods, you should check the entries for these items for more information on the exact syntax.

The `fontStyle` property can be assigned one of the following values: `normal` or `italic`.

Example

Listing 8.439 uses the `fontStyle` property to italicize the header text.

Listing 8.439   Set the `fontStyle` Property

```
<html>

<script type="text/javascript" language="JavaScript">
```

```
<!--

//Create a style sheet id that defines a font style.
document.ids.I.fontStyle = "italic";

// -->
</script>

<h2 id="I">Italicized Heading</h2>

</html>
```

Style.fontWeight

JavaScript1.2
Nav4

Syntax

style.fontWeight

Description

The fontWeight property specifies the font weight used by an element when associated with *style*. Because *style* can be created using the document.classes, document.ids, document.tags, or document.contextual() methods, you should check the entries for these items for more information on the exact syntax.

The fontStyle property can be assigned one of the following values: normal, bold, bolder, lighter, or a number from 100 to 900.

Example

Listing 8.440 uses the fontWeight property to set different levels of weight on various text.

Listing 8.440   Set the fontWeight *Property*

```
<html>

<script type="text/javascript" language="JavaScript">
<!--

//Create a style sheet id that defines a font style.
document.ids.W1.fontWeight = 100;
document.ids.W4.fontWeight = 400;
document.ids.W9.fontWeight = 900;

// -->
</script>
```

Listing 8.440   Continued

```
<p id="W1">Font weight of 100</p>
<p id="W4">Font weight of 400</p>
<p id="W9">Font weight of 900</p>

</html>
```

Style.lineHeight

JavaScript1.2
Nav4

Syntax

style.lineHeight

Description

The lineHeight property specifies the distance between two lines that are next to each other. Using dot notation, the property is associated with *style*. Because *style* can be created using the document.classes, document.ids, document.tags, or document.contextual() methods, you should check the entries for these items for more information on the exact syntax.

Four types of values are valid for the lineHeight property: number, length, percentage, and the value normal.

When a number is given without a unit of measure, it is multiplied by the font size of the element to give the line height, while including a unit of measure after the number specifies length. A percentage is designated by including a percent sign (%) after the number to represent the line height as it relates to its parent.

Example

Listing 8.441 uses the lineHeight property to set the distance between lines. In the "D1" instance, it is set to 1 inch. In the "D2" instance, it is set to 50 point.

Listing 8.441   Set the lineHeight Property

```
<html>

<script type="text/javascript" language="JavaScript">
<!--

//Create a style sheet id that defines a line height.
document.ids.D1.lineHeight = "1in";
document.ids.D2.lineHeight = "50pt";

// -->
</script>
```

```
<p>This is the first line of text</p>
<p id="D1">This is a second line of text.</p>
<p>This is a third line of text.</p>
<p id="D2">This is a fourth line of text.</p>
<p>This is a fifth line of text.</p>

</html>
```

Style.listStyleType

JavaScript1.2
Nav4

Syntax

*style.*listStyleType

Description

The listStyleType property specifies the format of list items elements that are associated with *style*. Because *style* can be created using the document.classes, docu-
ment.ids, document.tags, or document.contextual() methods, you should check
the entries for these items for more information on the exact syntax.

Nine types of values are valid for the listStyleType property: disc, circle, square,
decimal, lower-roman, upper-roman, lower-alpha, upper-alpha, and none.

NOTE

The listStyleType property is only valid if the element also has the display
property set to list-item.

Example

Listing 8.442 uses the listStyleType property to format a list of items.

Listing 8.442   Set the listStyleType *Property*

```
<html>

<script type="text/javascript" language="JavaScript">
<!--

//Create a style sheet class and id that define a list format.
document.classes.LIST.all.display = "list-item";
document.ids.FORMAT.listStyleType = "upper-roman";

// -->
</script>
```

Listing 8.442 Continued

```
<h2>Presentation Outline</h2>

<ol class="LIST" id="FORMAT">
  <li>Introduction</li>
  <li>Overview of new product</li>
  <li>Cost of product</li>
  <li>Conclusion</li>
</ol>

</html>
```

Style.marginBottom

JavaScript1.2
Nav4

Syntax

style.marginBottom

Description

The marginBottom property specifies the minimum distance between the bottom border of an element and the top border of another element. Dot notation is used to associate this property with *style*. Because *style* can be created using the document.classes, document.ids, document.tags, or document.contextual() methods, you should check the entries for these items for more information on the exact syntax.

Example

Listing 8.443 uses the marginBottom property to set the distance between adjacent elements.

Listing 8.443 Set the Bottom Margin with the marginBottom Property

```
<html>

<script type="text/javascript" language="JavaScript">
<!--

//Create a style sheet class and id that define the bottom margin.
document.classes.FORMAT.all.borderWidths(10);
document.ids.margin.marginBottom = 40;

// -->
</script>

<b>My margins are set automatically</b>
```

```
<b class="FORMAT" id="margin">I have a large bottom margin!</b>
<b>My margins are set automatically</b>
```

```
</html>
```

Style.marginLeft
JavaScript1.2
Nav4

Syntax
style.marginLeft

Description
The marginLeft property specifies the distance between the left border of an element and the right border of another element. Dot notation is used to associate this property with *style*. Because *style* can be created using the document.classes, document.ids, document.tags, or document.contextual() methods, you should check the entries for these items for more information on the exact syntax.

Example
Listing 8.444 uses the marginLeft property to set the distance between adjacent elements. Notice the distance between the border and the right edge of the browser window.

Listing 8.444   *Set the Left Margin with the* marginLeft *Property*

```
<html>

<script type="text/javascript" language="JavaScript">
<!--

//Create a style sheet id that defines the left margin.
document.classes.FORMAT1.all.borderWidths(10);
document.ids.margin.marginLeft = 40;
document.classes.FORMAT2.all.borderWidths(10);

// -->
</script>

<p class="FORMAT1" id="margin">I have a large left margin!</p>
<p class="FORMAT2">I have an automatic left margin</p>

</html>
```

Style.marginRight

JavaScript1.2
Nav4

Syntax

```
style.marginRight
```

Description

The `marginRight` property specifies the distance between the right border of an element and the left border of another element. Dot notation is used to associate this property with `style`. Because `style` can be created using the `document.classes`, `document.ids`, `document.tags`, or `document.contextual()` methods, you should check the entries for these items for more information on the exact syntax.

Example

Listing 8.445 uses the `marginRight` property to set the distance between adjacent elements. Notice the distance between the border and the right edge of the browser window.

Listing 8.445   Set the Right Margin with the `marginRight` **Property**

```
<html>

<script type="text/javascript" language="JavaScript">
<!--

//Create a style sheet id that defines the right margin.
document.classes.FORMAT.all.borderWidths(10);
document.ids.margin1.marginRight = 40;
document.ids.margin2.marginRight = 0;

// -->
</script>

<p class="FORMAT" id="margin1">I have a large right margin!</p>
<p class="FORMAT" id="margin2">I have no right margin</p>

</html>
```

Style.margins()

JavaScript1.2
Nav4

Syntax

```
style.margins(top, right, bottom, left)
style.margins(top-bottom, right-left)
style.margins(all)
```

Description

The margins() method specifies the margin distance between the border of an element and the border of adjacent elements. Dot notation is used to associate the property with *style*. Because *style* can be created using the document.classes, document.ids, document.tags, or document.contextual() methods, you should check the entries for these items for more information on the exact syntax.

Setting margin widths is equivalent to setting the marginBottom, marginLeft, marginRight, and marginTop properties. Table 8.34 lists all the arguments associated with the margins() method.

Table 8.34 *Arguments Associated with the* margins() *Method*

Item	Description
top	Width of the top margin
right	Width of the right margin
left	Width of the left margin
bottom	Width of the bottom margin
top-bottom	Width of both the top and bottom margins
left-right	Width of both the left and right margins
all	Width of all four margins

Example

Listing 8.446 uses the margins() method to set the margin widths around a text element.

Listing 8.446 *All Margins Set with the* margins() *Method*

```
<html>

<script type="text/javascript" language="JavaScript">
<!--

//Create a style sheet id that defines the margins.
document.classes.FORMAT.all.borderWidths(10);
document.ids.margin.margins(50);

// -->
</script>

<h2 class="FORMAT" id="margin">This text has margins set to 50</h2>

</html>
```

Style.marginTop

JavaScript1.2
Nav4

Syntax

style.marginTop

Description

The marginTop property specifies the minimum distance between the top border of an element and the bottom border of another element. Dot notation is used to associate this property with *style*. Because *style* can be created using the document.classes, document.ids, document.tags, or document.contextual() methods, you should check the entries for these items for more information on the exact syntax.

Example

Listing 8.447 uses the marginTop property to set the minimum distance between adjacent elements.

Listing 8.447 Set the Top Margin with the marginTop *Property*

```
<html>

<script type="text/javascript" language="JavaScript">
<!--

//Create a style sheet id that defines the top margin.
document.classes.FORMAT.all.borderWidths(10);
document.ids.margin.marginTop = 40;

// -->
</script>

<b>My margins are set automatically</b>
<b class="FORMAT" id="margin">I have a large top margin!</b>
<b>My margins are set automatically</b>

</html>
```

Style.paddingBottom

JavaScript1.2
Nav4

Syntax

style.paddingBottom

Description

The paddingBottom property specifies the minimum distance between the bottom border of an element and its content. Using dot notation, the property is associated with *style*. Because *style* can be created using the document.classes, document.ids, document.tags, or document.contextual() methods, you should check the entries for these items for more information on the exact syntax.

Example

Listing 8.448 uses the paddingBottom property to set the distance between a line of text and its border.

Listing 8.448   *Set the Bottom Padding with the* paddingBottom *Property*

```
<html>

<script type="text/javascript" language="JavaScript">
<!--

//Create a style sheet id that defines the bottom padding.
document.classes.FORMAT.all.borderWidths(10)
document.ids.PAD.paddingBottom = "40";

// -->
</script>

<p class="FORMAT" id="PAD">This text has extra padding on the bottom.</p>

</html>
```

Style.paddingLeft

> JavaScript1.2
> Nav4

Syntax

style.paddingLeft

Description

The paddingLeft property specifies the minimum distance between the left border of an element and its content. Using dot notation, the property is associated with *style*. Because *style* can be created using the document.classes, document.ids, document.tags, or document.contextual() methods, you should check the entries for these items for more information on the exact syntax.

Example

Listing 8.449 uses the paddingLeft property to set the distance between a line of text and its border.

Listing 8.449   Set the Left Padding with the `paddingLeft` *Property*

```
<html>

<script type="text/javascript" language="JavaScript">
<!--

//Create a style sheet id that defines the left padding.
document.classes.FORMAT.all.borderWidths(10)
document.ids.PAD.paddingLeft = "40";

// -->
</script>

<p class="FORMAT" id="PAD">This text has extra padding on the left.</p>

</html>
```

Style.paddingRight

JavaScript1.2
Nav4

Syntax

`style.paddingRight`

Description

The `paddingRight` property specifies the distance between the right border of an element and its content. Using dot notation, the property is associated with `style`. Because `style` can be created using the `document.classes`, `document.ids`, `document.tags`, or `document.contextual()` methods, you should check the entries for these items for more information on the exact syntax.

Example

Listing 8.450 uses the `paddingRight` property to set the distance between a line of text and its border.

Listing 8.450   Set the Right Padding with the `paddingRight` *Property*

```
<html>

<script type="text/javascript" language="JavaScript">
<!--

//Create a style sheet id that defines the right padding.
document.classes.FORMAT.all.borderWidths(10)
document.ids.PAD.paddingRight = "40";
```

```
// -->
</script>

<p class="FORMAT" id="PAD">This text has extra padding on the right.</p>

</html>
```

Style.paddings()

JavaScript1.2
Nav4

Syntax

style.paddings(*top, right, bottom, left*)
style.paddings(*top-bottom, right-left*)
style.paddings(*all*)

Description

The paddings() method specifies the distance between the borders of an element and its content. Using dot notation, the property is associated with *style*. Because *style* can be created using the document.classes, document.ids, document.tags, or document.contextual() methods, you should check the entries for these items for more information on the exact syntax. Setting the sizes is equivalent to setting the paddingBottom, paddingLeft, paddingRight, and paddingTop properties. Table 8.35 lists all the arguments associated with this method.

Table 8.35   Arguments Associated with the paddings() *Method*

Item	Description
top	Padding between top border and content
right	Padding between right border and content
left	Padding between left border and content
bottom	Padding between bottom border and content
top-bottom	Padding between the content and both the top and bottom borders
left-right	Padding between the content and both the left and right borders
all	Padding between content and all four sides of the border

Example

Listing 8.451 uses the paddings() method to set the distance between text and all sides of its border.

Listing 8.451   Set All Paddings with the `paddings()` *Method*

```
<html>

<script type="text/javascript" language="JavaScript">
<!--

//Create a style sheet id that defines all paddings.
document.classes.FORMAT.all.borderWidths(5);
document.ids.PAD.paddings(0,20,40,60);

// -->
</script>

<p class="FORMAT" id="PAD">This text has padding on all sides of its
border.</p>

</html>
```

Style.paddingTop

JavaScript1.2
Nav4

Syntax

style.paddingTop

Description

The `paddingTop` property specifies the distance between the left border of an element and its content. Using dot notation, the property is associated with *style*. Because *style* can be created using the `document.classes`, `document.ids`, `document.tags`, or `document.contextual()` methods, you should check the entries for these items for more information on the exact syntax.

Example

Listing 8.452 uses the `paddingTop` property to set the distance between a line of text and its border.

Listing 8.452   Set Top Padding with the `paddingTop` *Property*

```
<html>

<script type="text/javascript" language="JavaScript">
<!--

//Create a style sheet id that defines the top padding.
document.classes.FORMAT.all.borderWidths(10)
document.ids.PAD.paddingTop = "40";
```

```
// -->
</script>

<p class="FORMAT" id="PAD">This text has extra padding on the top.</p>

</html>
```

Style.textAlign

JavaScript1.2
Nav4

Syntax

style.textAlign

Description

The textAlign property specifies the alignment of text within an element as associated with *style*. Because *style* can be created using the document.classes, document.ids, document.tags, or document.contextual() methods, you should check the entries for these items for more information on the exact syntax.

Four types of values are valid for the textAlign property: left, right, center, and justify.

Example

Listing 8.453 uses the textAlign property to align the text to the right.

Listing 8.453   Set the textAlign *Property*

```
<html>

<script type="text/javascript" language="JavaScript">
<!--

//Create a style sheet id that defines the right alignment.
document.classes.FORMAT.all.borderWidths(10)
document.ids.RIGHT.textAlign = "right";

// -->
</script>

<p class="FORMAT" id="RIGHT">This text is aligned right.</p>

</html>
```

Style.textDecoration

JavaScript1.2
Nav4

Syntax

style.textDecoration

Description

The textDecoration property specifies the type of decoration that is added to text as associated with *style*. Because *style* can be created using the document.classes, document.ids, document.tags, or document.contextual() methods, you should check the entries for these items for more information on the exact syntax.

Four types of values are valid for the textDecoration property: underline, line-through, blink, and none.

Example

Listing 8.454 uses the textDecoration property to put a line through a line of text.

Listing 8.454 Set the textDecoration Property

```
<html>

<script type="text/javascript" language="JavaScript">
<!--

//Create a style sheet id that defines the text decoration.
document.ids.CROSSOUT.textDecoration = "line-through";

// -->
</script>

<p id="CROSSOUT">This text is crossed out.</p>

</html>
```

Style.textIndent

JavaScript1.2
Nav4

Syntax

style.textIndent

Description

The textIndent property specifies that the indention should appear before text as associated with *style*. Because *style* can be created using the document.classes, document.ids, document.tags, or document.contextual() methods, you should check the entries for these items for more information on the exact syntax. The property is assigned a number that represents either length or a percentage.

Example

Listing 8.455 uses the textIndent property to set the text indention to 1 inch.

Listing 8.455 *Set the* textIndent *Property*

```
<html>

<script type="text/javascript" language="JavaScript">
<!--

//Create a style sheet id that defines the text indention.
document.ids.INDENT.textIndent = "1in";

// -->
</script>

<p>This text has no indention.</p>
<p id="INDENT">This text is indented 1 inch.</p>

</html>
```

Style.textTransform

JavaScript1.2
Nav4

Syntax

*style.*textTransform

Description

The textTransform property specifies the transformation that should be applied to text as associated with *style*. Because *style* can be created using the document.classes, document.ids, document.tags, or document.contextual() methods, you should check the entries for these items for more information on the exact syntax.

Four types of values are valid for the textTransform property: capitalize, uppercase, lowercase, and none.

Example

Listing 8.456 uses the textTransform property to capitalize the first letter of every word in the sentence.

Listing 8.456   Set the textTransform **Property**

```
<html>

<script type="text/javascript" language="JavaScript">
<!--

//Create a style sheet id that defines capitalization.
document.ids.CAP.textTransform = "capitalize";

// -->
</script>

<p id="CAP">This line demonstrates the ability to capitalize words.</p>

</html>
```

Style.unwatch()

JavaScript 1.2
Nav4

Syntax

```
style.unwatch(property)
```

Description

The unwatch() method of the Style object is used to turn off the watch for a particular *property*.

Example

Listing 8.457 shows how the unwatch() method is used to stop watching the user-defined property *textTransform*.

Listing 8.457   Example of the unwatch() **method**

```
<html>
<head>
<script type="text/javascript" language="JavaScript1.2">

function alertme(id, oldValue, newValue){
  document.writeln("ID (" + id + ") changed from " + oldValue + " to ");
  document.writeln(newValue + "<br>");
  return newValue;
}

document.ids.CAP.watch("textTransform", alertme);
document.ids.CAP.textTransform = "capitalize";
document.ids.CAP.unwatch("textTransform");
document.ids.CAP.textTransform = "lowercase";
```

```
// -->
</script>
</head>
<body>
<p id="CAP">This line demonstrates the ability to capitalize words.</p>
</body>
</html>
```

Style.watch()

JavaScript1.2
Nav4

Syntax

```
style.watch(property, function)
```

Description

The watch() method of the Style object is used to turn on the watch for a particular *property*. Any time the specified *property* is changed after the watch() method has been called, the specified *function* is called.

Example

Listing 8.458 shows how the watch() method is used to start watching the user-defined property *p*.

Listing 8.458   Example of the* watch() *Method

```
<html>
<head>
<script type="text/javascript" language="JavaScript1.2">

function alertme(id, oldValue, newValue){
  document.writeln("ID (" + id + ") changed from " + oldValue + " to ");
  document.writeln(newValue + "<br>");
  return newValue;
}

document.ids.CAP.watch("textTransform", alertme);
document.ids.CAP.textTransform = "capitalize";

// -->
</script>
</head>
<body>
<p id="CAP">This line demonstrates the ability to capitalize words.</p>
</body>
</html>
```

Style.whiteSpace

JavaScript1.2
Nav4

Syntax

style.whiteSpace

Description

The whiteSpace property specifies how whitespace should be handled within an element. Using dot notation, the property can be associated with *style*. Because *style* can be created using the document.classes, document.ids, document.tags, or document.contextual() methods, you should check the entries for these items for more information on the exact syntax.

Two types of values are valid for the whiteSpace property: normal and pre.

Example

Listing 8.459 uses the whiteSpace property to make whitespace collapsed within the text element.

Listing 8.459   Set the whiteSpace *Property*

```
<html>

<script type="text/javascript" language="JavaScript">
<!--

//Create a style sheet id that defines whitespace.
document.ids.NOPRE.whiteSpace = "normal";

// -->
</script>

<p><pre>This line used the PRE tag to format whitespace.</pre></p>
<p id="NOPRE">This line should have collapsed whitespace.</p>

</html>
```

Style.width

JavaScript1.2
Nav4

Syntax

style.width

Description

The width is property of the Style object is used to specify the width of a block-level HTML element. The property itself can take a numerical length, a percentage, or the keyword auto, which tells Navigator 4 to determine the width automatically. The following shows a brief example of syntax:

```
// length
myStyle.width = 12pt;

// percentage
myStyle.width = 75%;

// automatically format
myStyle.width = auto;
```

Example

Listing 8.460 shows how we can use the width property to set the border of a <p> element to 12 point.

Listing 8.460   Using the width ***Property to Set the Border Width of an Element***

```
<html>
<head>
  <script type="text/javascript" language="JavaScript">
  <!--

    //Set the border of our <p> tag to 12 point.
    document.ids.border.width = 12pt;

  // -->
  </script>
</head>
<body>
<p id="border">This has a 12 point border.</p>
</body>
</html>
```

Submit

JavaScript1.0+, JScript1.0+
Nav2+, IE3+, Opera3+

Syntax

Core client-side JavaScript object.

Description

The Submit object is one of the core JavaScript objects. Instances are created by the browser when it encounters an HTML <input> tag with the type attribute set to submit. In the JavaScript object hierarchy, the Submit object is located at window.doc-ument.Form.Submit. Table 8.36 lists the properties, methods, and events used by the Submit object.

> **NOTE**
>
> Starting with Navigator 4, if you submit a form to a mailto: or news: protocol, the UniversalSendMail security privilege must be set.

Table 8.36   Event Handlers, Methods, and Properties Used by the Submit *Object*

Type	Item	Description
Event Handler	onBlur	Executes code when the submit button loses focus. This event handler was added in JavaScript 1.1.
	onClick	Executes code when the submit button is clicked.
	onFocus	Executes code when the submit button receives the focus. This event handler was added in JavaScript 1.1.
Method	blur()	Removes focus from the submit button. This method was added in JavaScript 1.1.
	click()	Simulates a mouse click on the submit button.
	focus()	Gives the focus to the submit button. This method was added in JavaScript 1.1.
	handleEvent()	Invokes the handler for the event specified and was added in JavaScript 1.2.
	unwatch()	Used to turn off the watch for a particular property.
	watch()	Used to turn on the watch for a particular property.
Property	form	Returns the entire form that the submit button is in.
	name	Returns the name of the submit button specified by the name attribute.
	type	Returns the type of the submit button specified by the type attribute. This property always returns sub-mit. This property was added in JavaScript 1.1.
	value	Returns the value of the submit button specified by the value attribute.

Example

Listing 8.461 displays the use of the Submit properties. It contains a select box and a submit button. When the button is clicked, a second window is opened. The values of the properties of this Submit object are displayed in this window.

Listing 8.461   Displaying the Properties of an Instance of a Submit
Object

```
<html>
<head>
<script language="JavaScript" type="text/javascript">
<!--

// Define the openWin function called by clicking the button.
function openWin(){

  // Place the reference to the Submit button in a variable for easier access.
  var myInstance = document.myForm.mySubmit;

  // Open a window to store the results.
  var myWin = open("", "","width=450,height=200");

  // Write the Submit button's properties to the window.
  myWin.document.write("The name is: " + myInstance.name + "<br>");
  myWin.document.write("The type is: " + myInstance.type + "<br>");

  // Note that the entire form object is passed with this property.
  // This allows you to then drill down and get the value of other
  // components in the form.
  myWin.document.write("The form can be used to grab the ");
  myWin.document.write("value of the button: ");
  myWin.document.write(myInstance.form.mySubmit.value);

  // Close the stream to the window.
  myWin.document.close();
}
// -->
</script>
</head>
<body>
<form name="myForm">
  <input type="text" value="Hello, World!" name="myText">
  <input type="submit" value="Click to Submit" name="mySubmit"
         onclick="openWin()">
</form>
</body>
</html>
```

Submit.blur()

JavaScript1.0+, JScript1.0+
Nav2+, IE3+, Opera3+

Syntax

submit.blur()

Description

The blur() method of the Submit object removes the focus from the submit button. Be careful when using this method in conjunction with the Submit.focus() method. It can lead to a focus/blur loop, where the browser blurs a focus as soon as it is done, and vice versa.

Example

Listing 8.462 has a text box and a submit button. If the user clicks the Click Here to Remove Focus button, the button will no longer be focused. The best way to see this is to tab to the button and then click it. When tabbing to the button, you should see that it becomes selected.

Listing 8.462   Using the blur() Method to Remove the Focus from the Submit Button

```
<html>
<head>
<script language="JavaScript" type="text/javascript">
<!--

// Define the removeFocus function called by pressing the button.
function removeFocus(){

  // Remove focus from the submit button.
  document.myForm.mySubmit.blur();
}
// -->
</script>
</head>
<body>
<form name="myForm">
  <input type="text" value="Hello, World!" name="myText">
  <input type="submit" value="Click Here to Remove Focus" name="mySubmit"
        onclick="removeFocus()">
</form>
</body>
</html>
```

Submit.click()

JavaScript1.0+, JScript1.0+
Nav2+, IE3+, Opera3+

Syntax

submit.click()

Description

The `click()` method of an instance of the `Submit` object simulates a click on the submit button. Note that if you have an `onClick` event handler assigned to this button, it will not be executed.

Example

Listing 8.463 has a text field, a submit button, and a link. If the user clicks the link, a function will be called to check whether the user entered any text. If the user did not, an alert box is displayed. If the user did enter text, the function submits the form by calling the `click()` method of the submit button.

Listing 8.463   Using the `click()` Method to Submit a Form

```html
<html>
<head>
<script language="JavaScript" type="text/javascript">
<!--

// Define the submitForm function to submit the form.
function submitForm(){

  // Check to see if some text has been entered.
  if(document.myForm.myText.value == ""){
    alert("Please enter some text first");
  }else{

    // Use the click() method to submit the form.
    document.myForm.mySubmit.click();
  }
}
// -->
</script>
</head>
<body>
<form name="myForm">
Please Enter some text and click the link.<br>
  <input type="text" value="" name="myText">
  <input type="submit" value="Submit" name="mySubmit">
</form>
<br>
<a href="javascript:submitForm()">Click here to submit the form</a>
</body>
</html>
```

Submit.focus()

JavaScript1.0+, JScript1.0+
Nav2+, IE3+, Opera3+

Syntax

```
submit.focus()
```

Description

The focus() method of the Submit object places focus on the Submit button. Be careful when using this method in conjunction with the Submit.blur() method. It can lead to a focus/blur loop, where the browser blurs a focus as soon as it is done, and vice versa.

Example

Listing 8.464 has a text box and a submit button. If the user clicks in the text box, focus is placed on the submit button.

Listing 8.464   Using the focus() Method to Set the Focus on the Submit Button

```
<html>
<head>
<script language="JavaScript" type="text/javascript">
<!--

// Define the setFocus function called by clicking in the text box.
function setFocus(){

  // Place focus on the submit button.
  document.myForm.mySubmit.focus();
}
// -->
</script>
</head>
<body>
<form name="myForm">
  <input type="text" value="Hello, World!" name="myText" onfocus="setFocus()">
  <input type="submit" value="Submit" name="mySubmit">
</form>
</body>
</html>
```

Submit.form

JavaScript1.0+, JScript1.0+
Nav2+, IE3+, Opera3+

Syntax

submit.form

Description

The `form` property of an instance of the `Submit` object provides access to all the data of the form in which the submit button is located.

Example

Listing 8.465 has a text box and a submit button. When the button is clicked, three properties of the form as a whole are displayed. These properties were referenced through the `form` property of the submit button.

Listing 8.465   Accessing a Form Via the `form` Property of an Instance of a `Submit` Object

```
<html>
<head>
<script language="JavaScript" type="text/javascript">
<!--

// Define the openWin function called by pressing the button.
function openWin(){

  // Place the reference to the form property of submit button
  // in a variable for easier access.
  var formData = document.myForm.mySubmit.form;

  // Open a window to display the results.
  var myWin = open("", "","width=450,height=200");

  // Write the form properties accessed through the form
  // property to the window.
  myWin.document.write("The name of the form is: " + formData.name + "<br>");
  myWin.document.write("The value of the text box is: ");
  myWin.document.write(formData.myText.value + "<br>");
  myWin.document.write("The name of the button is: ");
  myWin.document.write(formData.elements[1].name + "<br>");

  // Close the stream to the window.
  myWin.document.close();
}
// -->
</script>
</head>
<body>
<form name="myForm">
  <input type="text" value="Hello, World!" name="myText">
  <input type="button" value="Click to Process" name="mySubmit"
         onclick="openWin()">
```

Listing 8.465   Continued

```
</form>
</body>
</html>
```

Submit.handleEvent()

JavaScript1.2+, JScript3.0+
Nav4+, IE4+

Syntax

submit.handleEvent(*event*)

Description

The handleEvent() method of the Submit object invokes the handler for the event specified. This method was added in JavaScript 1.2.

Example

Listing 8.466 has a single text box. The script tells the browser that it wants to intercept all Click events and that it wants the myClickHandler function to handle them. Within this function, the handleEvent() method of the submit button has been specified to handle the click.

When the user clicks anywhere on the page, the onClick event handler in the <input type="submit"> tag calls a function to change the text in the text box. The change is nothing more than a simple number that is incremented, counting the number of times the page has been clicked.

Listing 8.466   Using the handleEvent() **Method of a** Submit **Object to Handle all Clicks on a Page**

```
<html>
<head>
<script language="JavaScript1.2" type="text/javascript">
<!--

// Define a click counter variable.
var counter = 0;

// Tell the browser you want to intercept ALL click events
// on the page. Then define a function to handle them.
window.captureEvents(Event.CLICK)
window.onClick = myClickHandler;

// Define the myClickHandler function to handle click events.
function myClickHandler(e){
```

```
// Pass all click events to the onClick event of the submit button.
window.document.myForm.mySubmit.handleEvent(e);

}

// Function is called by onClick of the submit button. Displays the number
// of clicks that have occurred in the text box. Note that you have to
// return false so the form is not submitted.
function changeText(){
  counter++;
  document.myForm.myText.value = counter;
  return false;
}
// -->
</script>
</head>
<body>
<form name="myForm">
  <input type="text" size="2" value="" name="myText">
  <input type="submit" value="Submit" name="mySubmit" onclick='changeText()'>
</form>
</body>
</html>
```

Submit.name

JavaScript1.0+, JScript1.0+
Nav2+, IE3+, Opera3+

Syntax

submit.name

Description

The name property of an instance of a Submit object returns the name of the submit button. This property is often accessed via the elements array of a Form object and used to return the name of the button. It is most useful when there are many forms on a given page, and determining the name helps you determine what function you want to perform.

Example

Listing 8.467 has a single text box and submit button. The elements array of a Form object is used to retrieve the name and display it in an alert box.

Listing 8.467   Using the name **Property to Retrieve the Name of a Submit Button**

```
<html>
<head>
<script language="JavaScript" type="text/javascript">
<!--

// Display an alert box that contains the name of the
// submit button.
function getName(){
  alert("The name of this submit button is " +
        document.myForm.elements[1].name);
}
// -->
</script>
</head>
<body>
<form name="myForm">
  <input type="text" value="First Box" name="myText">
  <input type="submit" value="Submit" name="mySubmit" onclick='getName()'>
</form>
</body>
</html>
```

Submit.onBlur

> JavaScript1.0+, JScript1.0+
> Nav2+, IE3+, Opera3+

Syntax

onblur="*command*"

Description

The onBlur event handler is fired when the focus is moved away from that particular submit button. Care should be taken when using this event handler because it is possible to get into an infinite loop when using the onFocus event handler or focus() method.

Example

Listing 8.468 contains two text boxes and a submit button. The button has the Blur event intercepted within its tag. The second text box is used as a counter for the number of times the onBlur event handler is fired.

In the script, the event calls a function that reassigns the submit button focus. The result of this is that when a user tries to click or tab away from the submit button box, the counter is incremented and the focus returns. As you will see if you run Listing 8.486, even clicking in other windows or the URL bar increments the counter.

Listing 8.468   Example of Using the onBlur *Event Handler*

```
<html>
<head>
<script language="JavaScript" type="text/javascript">
<!--

// Initialize a counter to show clicks.
var counter = 0;

// Set the focus on the submit button, and increment
// the counter in the text box.
function comeBack(){
  document.myForm.mySubmit.focus();
  document.myForm.counter.value = counter++;
}
// -->
</script>
</head>
<body onload='comeBack()'>
<form name="myForm">
  <input type="text" value="Text Box" name="myText">
  <input type="submit" value="Submit" name="mySubmit" onblur='comeBack()'><br>
  <input type="text" size="2" value="" name="counter">
</form>
</body>
</html>
```

Submit.onClick

> JavaScript1.0+, JScript1.0+
> Nav2+, IE3+, Opera3+

Syntax

onclick="*command*"

Description

The onClick event handler is fired when a submit button is clicked. Note that this is not fired in the instances where a single form object is in the form, such as a text box, and the user presses the Enter or Return key to submit the form.

Example

Listing 8.469 has a single text box and a button. If the user presses the submit button, the Click event is fired, calling a function that changes the text in the text box to all uppercase.

Listing 8.469   Using the onClick *Event Handler to Display the Contents of a Form Textbox Before It Is Submitted*

```
<html>
<head>
<script language="JavaScript" type="text/javascript">
<!--

// Define the setText function to change the text to uppercase.
function setText(){

  // Change the text to uppercase.
  document.myForm.myText.value = document.myForm.myText.value.toUpperCase();

}
// -->
</script>
</head>
<body>
<form name="myForm">
Please Enter some text and click the Submit Button.<br>
  <input type="text" value="Enter Text Here" name="myText">
  <input type="button" value="Submit" name="mySubmit" onclick="setText()">
</form>
</body>
</html>
```

Submit.onFocus

JavaScript1.0+, JScript1.0+
Nav2+, IE3+, Opera3+

Syntax

```
onfocus="command"
```

Description

The onFocus event handler of an instance of a Submit object is fired when focus is set to that particular submit button. Care should be taken when using this event handler because it is possible to get into an infinite loop when using the onBlur event handler or blur() method.

Example

Listing 8.470 contains two text boxes and a submit button. The submit button has the Focus event intercepted within its tag. The second text box is used for a counter for the number of times the onFocus event handler is fired.

In the script, the event calls a function that assigns the first text box focus. The result of this is that when a user tries to click or tab to the submit button, the counter is incremented and the focus is returned to the text box.

Listing 8.470   Example of Using the onFocus *Event Handler*

```
<html>
<head>
<script language="JavaScript" type="text/javascript">
<!--

// Initialize a counter to show clicks.
var counter = 0;

// Set the focus on the text box, and increment
// counter in text box.
function sendAway(){
  document.myForm.myText.focus();
  document.myForm.counter.value = counter++;
}
// -->
</script>
</head>
<body onload='sendAway()'>
<form name="myForm">
  <input type="text" value="First Box" name="myText">
  <input type="submit" value="Submit" name="mySubmit" onfocus='sendAway()'><br>
  <input type="text" size="2" value="" name="counter">
</form>
</body>
</html>
```

Submit.type

JavaScript1.1+, JScript1.0+
Nav3+, IE3+, Opera3+

Syntax

submit.type

Description

The type property of an instance of a Submit object returns the type of the text box.
This always returns submit.

Example

Listing 8.471 has a text box and a submit button. When the button is clicked, an alert
box is popped up that displays the type property of the submit button.

Listing 8.471   Displaying the type *Property in an Alert Box*

```
<html>
<head>
<script language="JavaScript1.1" type="text/javascript">
<!--
```

Listing 8.471 **Continued**

```
// Display an alert box that contains the type of the
// submit button.
function getType(){
  alert("The name of this submit button is " +
         document.myForm.elements[1].type);
}
// -->
</script>
</head>
<body>
<form name="myForm">
  <input type="text" value="First Box" name="myText">
  <input type="submit" value="Submit" name="mySubmit" onclick='getType()'>
</form>
</body>
</html>
```

Submit.unwatch()

> JavaScript 1.2+
> Nav4+

Syntax

submit.unwatch(*property*)

Description

The unwatch() method of the Submit object is used to turn off the watch for a particular *property*.

Example

Listing 8.472 shows how the unwatch() method is used to stop watching the value property.

Listing 8.472 **Example of the** unwatch() **Method**

```
<html>
<head>
  <script type="text/javascript" language="JavaScript1.2">

  // Define a function to be called when the property changes.
  function alertme(id, oldValue, newValue){
    document.writeln("ID (" + id + ") changed from " + oldValue + " to ");
    document.writeln(newValue + "<br>");
    return newValue;
  }
```

```
// Once loaded, watch the value property and then change it, and then
// turn off the watch.
function check(){
  document.myForm.mySubmit.watch("value", alertme);
  document.myForm.mySubmit.value="Send";
  document.myForm.mySubmit.unwatch("value");
}
</script>
</head>
<body onload="check()">
<form name="myForm">
  <input type="submit" name="mySubmit" value="Submit">
</form>
</body>
</html>
```

Submit.value

JavaScript1.0+, JScript1.0+
Nav2+, IE3+, Opera3+

Syntax

submit.value

Description

The value property of an instance of a Submit object returns the current value of the submit button. This value is what is displayed on the button itself.

Example

Listing 8.473 contains a text box and button. When a user clicks the submit button, an alert box pops up displaying the value of this instance.

Listing 8.473   Accessing the Value of a Submit Object

```
<html>
<head>
<script language="JavaScript1.1" type="text/javascript">
<!--

// Display an alert box that contains the value of the
// submit button.
function getValue(){
  alert("The value of this submit button is " +
        document.myForm.elements[1].value);
}
```

Listing 8.473   Continued

```
// -->
</script>
</head>
<body>
<form name="myForm">
  <input type="text" value="First Box" name="myText">
  <input type="submit" value="Submit" name="mySubmit" onclick='getValue()'>
</form>
</body>
</html>
```

Submit.watch()

JavaScript 1.2+
Nav4+

Syntax

```
submit.watch(property, function)
```

Description

The watch() method of the Submit object is used to turn on the watch for a particular *property*. Any time the specified *property* is changed after the watch() method has been called, the specified *function* is called.

Example

Listing 8.474 shows how the watch() method is used to start watching the value property.

Listing 8.474   Example of the watch() **Method**

```
<html>
<head>
  <script type="text/javascript" language="JavaScript1.2">

  // Define a function to be called when the property changes.
  function alertme(id, oldValue, newValue){
    document.writeln("ID (" + id + ") changed from " + oldValue + " to ");
    document.writeln(newValue + "<br>");
    return newValue;
  }

  // Once page is loaded, watch the value property then change it.
  function check(){
    document.myForm.mySubmit.watch("value", alertme);
    document.myForm.mySubmit.value="Send";
  }
```

```
    </script>
  </head>
  <body onload="check()">
  <form name="myForm">
    <input type="submit" name="mySubmit" value="Submit">
  </form>
  </body>
  </html>
```

taint()

JavaScript1.1
Nav3

Syntax

`taint(object)`

Description

The `taint()` method was a security measure that was only implemented in JavaScript 1.1 and that allowed a developer to keep return values from being used by and propagated to other scripts. This method does not change the data element passed to it, but rather returns a marked reference to the element.

Because `taint()` and the functionality of data tainting was removed in JavaScript 1.2, you should avoid using this method. You should use it only if you have a specific security reason for compatibility with Navigator 3 browsers. See Chapter 1, "What is JavaScript to a Programmer?" for more information on the security model that is now used in Navigator browsers.

Example

Listing 8.475 simply taints a variable that is defined in a separate window.

Listing 8.475   Use of the `taint()` *Method, Which Is No Longer Supported*

```
<script language="JavaScript1.1" type="text/javascript">
<!--

// Store the tainted variable from the second window
// in the variable taintMyVar.
var taintMyvar = taint(myWin.myVar);

// -->
</script>
```

Text

JavaScript1.0+, JScript1.0+
Nav2+, IE3+, Opera3+

Syntax

Core client-side JavaScript object.

Description

The Text object is one of the core JavaScript objects. Instances are created by the browser when it encounters an HTML <input> tag with the type attribute set to text. In the JavaScript object hierarchy, the Text object is located at window.document.Form.Text. Table 8.37 lists the properties, methods, and events used by the Text object.

Table 8.37   Event Handlers, Methods, and Properties Used by the
Text **Object**

Type	Item	Description
Event Handler	onBlur	Executes code when the text box loses the focus.
	onChange	Executes code when the text box loses the focus and has had its value modified.
	onFocus	Executes code when the text box receives the focus.
	onSelect	Executes code when a user selects some of the text within the text box.
Method	blur()	Removes the focus from the text box.
	focus()	Gives the focus to the text box.
	handleEvent()	Invokes the handler for the event specified and was added in JavaScript 1.2.
	select()	Selects the text in the text box.
	unwatch()	Used to turn off the watch for a particular property.
	watch()	Used to turn on the watch for a particular property.
Property	defaultValue	Returns the value of the text box specified by the value attribute. Note that this property is not supported by the Opera browsers.
	form	Returns the entire form the text box is in.
	name	Returns the name of the text box specified by the name attribute.
	type	Returns the type of the text box specified by the type attribute. Note that this is always text and was added in JavaScript 1.1.
	value	Returns the value that is actually displayed in the text box.

Example

Listing 8.476 displays the use of the Text properties. It contains a text box and a button. When the button is clicked, a second window is opened. The values of the properties of this Text object are displayed in the second window.

Listing 8.476 Displaying the Properties of an Instance of a Text Object

```
<html>
<head>
<script language="JavaScript" type="text/javascript">
<!--

// Define the openWin function called by pressing the button.
function openWin(){

  // Place the reference to the text box in a variable for easier access.
  var myInstance = document.myForm.myText;

  // Open a window to store the results.
  var myWin = open("", "","width=450,height=200");

  // Write the text box's properties to the window.
  myWin.document.write("The defaultValue is: " + myInstance.defaultValue);
  myWin.document.write("<br>");
  myWin.document.write("The name is: " + myInstance.name + "<br>");
  myWin.document.write("The type is: " + myInstance.type + "<br>");
  myWin.document.write("The value is: " + myInstance.value + "<br>");

  // Note that the entire form object is passed with this property.
  // This allows you to then drill down and get the value of other
  // components in the form.
  myWin.document.write("The form can be used to grab the value ");
  myWin.document.write("of the button: ");
  myWin.document.write(myInstance.form.myButton.value);

  // Close the stream to the window.
  myWin.document.close();
}
// -->
</script>
</head>
<body>
<form name="myForm">
  <input type="text" value="Hello world" name="myText">
  <input type="button" value="Click to Process" name="myButton"
         onclick="openWin()">
</form>
</body>
</html>
```

Text.blur()

JavaScript1.0+, JScript1.0+
Nav2+, IE3+, Opera3+

Syntax

```
text.blur()
```

Description

The `blur()` method of the `Text` object removes focus from the text box. Be careful when using this method in conjunction with the `Text.focus()` method. It can lead to a focus/blur loop, where the browser blurs a focus as soon as it is done, and vice versa.

Example

Listing 8.477 has a text box and a button. If the user highlights some of the text in the box and then clicks the Click Here to Remove Focus button, the text will no longer be highlighted.

Listing 8.477   Using the `blur()` Method to Remove Focus from the Text Box

```
<html>
<head>
<script language="JavaScript" type="text/javascript">
<!--

// Define the removeFocus function called by pressing the button.
function removeFocus(){

  // Remove focus from the text box.
  document.myForm.myText.blur();
}
// -->
</script>
</head>
<body>
<b>Highlight some of the text in the following text box:</b>
<p>
<form name="myForm">
  <input type="text" value="hello world" name="myText">
  <input type="button" value="Click Here to Remove Focus" name="myButton"
        onclick="removeFocus()">
</form>
</body>
</html>
```

Text.defaultValue

JavaScript1.0+, JScript1.0+
Nav2+, IE3+, Opera5+

Syntax

```
text.defaultValue
```

Description

The defaultValue property of a Text object instance contains the default value specified by the value attribute of the <input> tag. This property is often used to reset
forms to their default values after a user has entered some data.

Example

Listing 8.478 has a text box and a button. If the user edits some of the text in the box
and then clicks the Click to Reset button, the text will change back to the default value.

Listing 8.478   Using the defaultValue **Property to Set the Value of the
Text Box Back to Its Original Value**

```
<html>
<head>
<script language="JavaScript" type="text/javascript">
<!--

// Define the resetForm function called by pressing the button.
function resetForm(){

  // Set the text in the text box back to "hello world".
  document.myForm.myText.value = document.myForm.myText.defaultValue;
}
// -->
</script>
</head>
<body>
<b>Edit the text in the following text box:</b>
<p>
<form name="myForm">
  <input type="text" value="hello world" name="myText">
  <input type="button" value="Click to Reset" name="myButton"
         onclick="resetForm()">
</form>
</body>
</html>
```

Text.focus()

JavaScript1.0+, JScript1.0+
Nav2+, IE3+, Opera3+

Syntax

```
text.focus()
```

Description

The focus() method of the Text object gives focus to the text box. Be careful when using this method in conjunction with the Text.blur() method. It can lead to a focus/blur loop, where the browser blurs a focus as soon as it is done, and vice versa.

Example

Listing 8.479 has two text boxes and two buttons. If the user clicks the first button, the cursor is set inside the first text box. If the user clicks the second button, the cursor is set inside the second text box.

Listing 8.479   Using the focus() **Method to Place the Cursor in the Desired Text Box**

```
<html>
<head>
<script language="JavaScript" type="text/javascript">
<!--

// Define the setFocus function called by pressing the button.
function setFocus(num){

  // Determine which button was clicked and set the cursor
  // in the appropriate text box.
  if(num == 1){
    document.myForm.myText1.focus();
  }else if(num == 2){
    document.myForm.myText2.focus();
  }
}
// -->
</script>
</head>
<body>
<p>
<form name="myForm">
  <input type="text" value="Textbox 1" name="myText1">
  <input type="button" value="Click to Set Cursor" name="myButton1"
        onclick="setFocus(1)">
  <br>
```

```
<input type="text" value="Textbox 2" name="myText2">
<input type="button" value="Click to Set Cursor" name="myButton2"
      onclick="setFocus(2)">
</form>
</body>
</html>
```

Text.form

JavaScript1.0+, JScript1.0+
Nav2+, IE3+, Opera3+

Syntax

text.form

Description

The form property of an instance of a Text object holds all the data of the form in which the text box is contained. This allows a developer to obtain specific information about the form in which the text box is located.

Example

Listing 8.480 has a text box and a button. When the button is clicked, three properties of the form as a whole are displayed. These properties were referenced though the form property of the text box.

Listing 8.480 **Accessing a Form via the** form **Property of an Instance of a** Text **Object**

```
<html>
<head>
<script language="JavaScript" type="text/javascript">
<!--

// Define the openWin function called by pressing the button.
function openWin(){

  // Place the reference to the form property of the text box
  // in a variable for easier access.
  var formData = document.myForm.myText.form;

  // Open a window to display the results.
  var myWin = open("", "","width=450,height=200");

  // Write the form properties accessed through the form
  // property to the window.
  myWin.document.write("The name of the form is: " + formData.name + "<br>");
  myWin.document.write("The value of the text box is: ");
```

Listing 8.480   Continued

```
  myWin.document.write(formData.myText.value + "<br>");
  myWin.document.write("The name of the button is: ");
  myWin.document.write(formData.elements[1].name + "<br>");

  // Close the stream to the window.
  myWin.document.close();
}
// -->
</script>
</head>
<body>
<form name="myForm">
  <input type="text" value="Hello world" name="myText">
  <input type="button" value="Click to Process" name="myButton"
        onclick="openWin()">
</form>
</body>
</html>
```

Text.handleEvent()

> JavaScript1.2+, JScript3.0+
> Nav4+, IE4+

Syntax

text.handleEvent(*event*)

Description

The handleEvent() method of the Text object invokes the handler for the event specified. This method was added in JavaScript 1.2.

Example

Listing 8.481 has a single text box. The script tells the browser that it wants to intercept all Click events and that it wants the myClickHandler function to handle them.
Within this function, the handleEvent() method of the text box has been specified to
handle the click.

When the user clicks anywhere on the page, the onClick event handler in the <input
type="text"> tag calls a function to change the text in the text box. The change is
nothing more than a simple number that is incremented, counting the number of times
the page has been clicked.

Listing 8.481   Using the handleEvent() *Method of a* Text *Object to
Handle All Clicks on a Page*

```
<html>
<head>
```

```
<script language="JavaScript1.2" type="text/javascript">
<!--

// Define a click counter variable.
var counter = 0;

// Tell the browser you want to intercept ALL click events
// on the page. Then define a function to handle them.
window.captureEvents(Event.CLICK)
window.onClick = myClickHandler;

// Define the myClickHandler function to handle click events.
function myClickHandler(e){

  // Pass all click events to the onClick event of the text box.
  window.document.myForm.myText.handleEvent(e);

}

// Function is called by onClick of text box. Displays the number
// of clicks that have occurred.
function changeText(){
  document.myForm.myText.value = counter++;
}
// -->
</script>
</head>
<body>
<form name="myForm">
  <input type="text" size="2" value="" name="myText" onclick='changeText()'>
</form>
</body>
</html>
```

Text.name
JavaScript1.0+, JScript1.0+
Nav2+, IE3+, Opera3+

Syntax
text.name

Description
The name property of an instance of a Text object returns the name of the text box. This
property is often accessed via the elements array of a Form object and used to return
the name of the text area. It is most useful when there are many forms on a given page,
and determining the name helps you determine what function you want to perform.

Example

Listing 8.482 has a single text box and button. The elements array of a Form object is used to retrieve the name and display it in an alert box.

Listing 8.482   Using the name *Property to Retrieve the Name of a Text Box*

```
<html>
<head>
<script language="JavaScript" type="text/javascript">
<!--

// Display an alert box that contains the name of the
// text box.
function getName(){
  alert("The name of this text box is " +
        document.myForm.elements[0].name);
}
// -->
</script>
</head>
<body>
<form name="myForm">
  <input type="text" value="First Box" name="myText">
  <input type="button" value="Get Name" name="myButton" onclick='getName()'>
</form>
</body>
</html>
```

Text.onBlur

JavaScript1.0+, JScript1.0+
Nav2+, IE3+, Opera3+

Syntax

onblur="*command*"

Description

The onBlur event handler of an instance of a Text object is fired when the focus is moved away from that particular text box. Care should be taken when using this event handler because it is possible to get into an infinite loop when using the onFocus event handler or the focus() method.

Example

Listing 8.483 contains three text boxes, one of which has the onBlur event handler intercepted within its tag. The third text box is used for a counter for the number of times the onBlur event handler is fired.

In the script, the event calls a function that reassigns the first text box focus. The result of this is that when a user tries to click or tab away from the first text box, the counter is incremented and the focus returns. As you will see if you run Listing 8.499, even clicking in other windows or the URL bar increments the counter.

Listing 8.483   Example of Using the `onBlur` ***Event Handler***

```
<html>
<head>
<script language="JavaScript" type="text/javascript">
<!--

// Initialize a counter to show clicks.
var counter = 0;

// Set the focus on the first text box, and increment
// counter in last text box.
function comeBack(){
  document.myForm.myText1.focus();
  document.myForm.counter.value = counter++;
}
// -->
</script>
</head>
<body onload='comeBack()'>
<form name="myForm">
  <input type="text" value="First Box" name="myText1" onblur='comeBack()'>
  <input type="text" value="Second Box" name="myText2"><br>
  <input type="text" size="2" value="" name="counter">
</form>
</body>
</html>
```

Text.onChange

JavaScript1.0+, JScript1.0+
Nav2+, IE3+, Opera3+

Syntax

`onchange="command"`

Description

The `onChange` event handler of an instance of a `Text` object is fired when the text in the box is modified. Care should be taken when using this event handler because it is possible to get into an infinite loop when using other events or methods that are fired when focus is placed on or away from the text box.

Example

Listing 8.484 has a single text box. If the user changes the text and then shifts the focus away from the text box by clicking elsewhere or pressing Return, the default text is placed back in the text box.

Listing 8.484   Using the onChange *Event Handler to Change the Text Back to the Default*

```
<html>
<head>
<script language="JavaScript" type="text/javascript">
<!--

// Change the text back to the default if user tries to change it.
// Note that the user has to click away or hit return for this
// to change back.
function changeBack(){
  document.myForm.myText.value = document.myForm.myText.defaultValue;
}
// -->
</script>
</head>
<body>
<form name="myForm">
  <input type="text" value="Change Me?" name="myText" onchange='changeBack()'>
</form>
</body>
</html>
```

Text.onFocus

JavaScript1.0+, JScript1.0+
Nav2+, IE3+, Opera3+

Syntax

onfocus="*command*"

Description

The onFocus event handler of an instance of a Text object is fired when focus is made on that particular text box. Care should be taken when using this event handler because it is possible to get into an infinite loop when using the onBlur event handler or the blur() method.

Example

Listing 8.485 contains three text boxes, one of which has the onFocus event handler intercepted within its tag. The third text box is used for a counter for the number of times the Focus event is fired.

In the script, the event handler calls a function that assigns the second text box focus. The result of this is that when a user tries to click or tab to the first text box, the counter is incremented and the focus is returned to the second text the box.

Listing 8.485   Example of Using the onFocus ***Event Handler***

```
<html>
<head>
<script language="JavaScript" type="text/javascript">
<!--

// Initialize a counter to show clicks.
var counter = 0;

// Set the focus on the second text box, and increment
// counter in last text box.
function sendAway(){
  document.myForm.myText2.focus();
  document.myForm.counter.value = counter++;
}
// -->
</script>
</head>
<body onload='sendAway()'>
<form name="myForm">
  <input type="text" value="First Box" name="myText1" onfocus='sendAway()'>
  <input type="text" value="Second Box" name="myText2"><br>
  <input type="text" size="2" value="" name="counter">
</form>
</body>
</html>
```

Text.onSelect

JavaScript1.0+, JScript1.0+
IE3+, Net6

Syntax

onselect="*command*"

Description

The onSelect event handler of an instance of a Text object is fired when the text in the box is highlighted. Care should be taken when using this event handler because it is possible to get into an infinite loop when using other events or methods that are fired when focus is placed on the text box.

NOTE

Note that Netscape defined this function in JavaScript 1.0; however, it was not fully implemented until Netscape 6. Opera browsers do not support this function either.

Example

Listing 8.486 has two text boxes. If the user highlights the text in the first text box, the default text of the first text box is written to the second text box.

Listing 8.486   Using the `onSelect` Event Handler to Set the Text in the Second Text Box

```
<html>
<head>
<script language="JavaScript" type="text/javascript">
<!--

// Change the text of the second text box to the default
// of the first if user highlights text in the first.
function setText(){
  document.myForm.myText2.value = document.myForm.myText1.defaultValue;
}
// -->
</script>
</head>
<body>
<form name="myForm">
  <input type="text" value="Change Me?" name="myText1" onselect='setText()'>
  <br>
  <input type="text" value="" name="myText2">
</form>
</body>
</html>
```

Text.select()

JavaScript1.0+, JScript1.0+
Nav2+, IE3+, Opera3+

Syntax

`text.select()`

Description

The `select()` method of the `Text` object selects the text in the text box. Be careful when using this method in conjunction with the `blur()` and `focus()` methods. It can lead to a focus/blur loop where the browser blurs or focuses as soon as it is has been selected, and vice versa.

Example

Listing 8.487 has a text box and a button. If the user clicks the button, the text inside the text box will be highlighted. Notice that the focus() method had to be used to tell the browser to actually highlight the text.

Listing 8.487 *Using the* select() *Method to Select the Text in a Text Box*

```
<html>
<head>
<script language="JavaScript" type="text/javascript">
<!--

// Define the selectText function called by pressing the button.
function selectText(){

  // Select the text in the box, then place focus on it.
  document.myForm.myText.select();
  document.myForm.myText.focus();
}
// -->
</script>
</head>
<body>
<form name="myForm">
  <input type="text" value="Hello world" name="myText">
  <input type="button" value="Click to Select Text" name="myButton"
        onclick="selectText()">
</form>
</body>
</html>
```

Text.type

JavaScript1.1+, JScript1.0+
Nav3+, IE3+, Opera3+

Syntax

text.type

Description

The type property of an instance of a Text object returns the type of the text box. This always returns text.

Example

Listing 8.488 has a text box and a button. When the button is clicked, an alert box is popped up that displays the type property of the text box.

Listing 8.488 *Displaying the* type *Property in an Alert Box*

```
<html>
<head>
<script language="JavaScript1.1" type="text/javascript">
<!--

// Display an alert box that contains the type of the
// text box.
function getType(){
  alert("The name of this text box is " +
        document.myForm.elements[0].type);
}
// -->
</script>
</head>
<body>
<form name="myForm">
  <input type="text" value="First Box" name="myText">
  <input type="button" value="Get Type" name="myButton" onclick='getType()'>
</form>
</body>
</html>
```

Text.unwatch()

JavaScript 1.2+
Nav4+

Syntax

text.unwatch(*property*)

Description

The unwatch() method of the text object is used to turn off the watch for a particular *property*.

Example

Listing 8.489 shows how the unwatch() method is used to stop watching the value property.

Listing 8.489 *Example of the* unwatch() *Method*

```
<html>
<head>
  <script type="text/javascript" language="JavaScript1.2">

  function alertme(id, oldValue, newValue){
    document.writeln("ID (" + id + ") changed from " + oldValue + " to ");
    document.writeln(newValue + "<br>");
```

```
      return newValue;
    }

    function check(){
      document.myForm.myItem.watch("value", alertme);
      document.myForm.myItem.unwatch("value");
      document.myForm.myItem.value="Send";
    }
    </script>
</head>
<body onload="check()">
<form name="myForm">
    <input type="text" name="myItem" value="Submit">
</form>
</body>
</html>
```

Text.value

JavaScript1.0+, JScript1.0+
Nav2+, IE3+, Opera3+

Syntax

text.value

Description

The value property of an instance of a Text object returns the current value of the text box. Note that this is not the default value that can be accessed via the Text.defaultValue property and is often used to set the value of a text box.

Example

Listing 8.490 contains a text box and button. You can edit the text in the text box and then click the Reset button to reset the text back to the default value.

Listing 8.490   Resetting the Value of a Text Box to the Default Value

```
<html>
<head>
<script language="JavaScript" type="text/javascript">
<!--

// Reset the text in the text box to its default value.
function resetText(){
  document.myForm.myText.value = document.myForm.myText.defaultValue;
}
// -->
</script>
</head>
```

Listing 8.490   Continued

```
<body>
<form name="myForm">
  <input type="text" value="First Box" name="myText">
  <input type="button" value="Reset" name="myButton" onclick='resetText()'>
</form>
</body>
</html>
```

Text.watch()

JavaScript 1.2+
Nav4+

Syntax

```
text.watch(property, function)
```

Description

The watch() method of the Text object is used to turn on the watch for a particular *property*. Any time the specified *property* is changed after the watch() method has been called, the specified *function* is called.

Example

Listing 8.491 shows how the watch() method is used to start watching the value property.

Listing 8.491   Example of the watch() Method

```
<html>
<head>
  <script type="text/javascript" language="JavaScript1.2">

  function alertme(id, oldValue, newValue){
    document.writeln("ID (" + id + ") changed from " + oldValue + " to ");
    document.writeln(newValue + "<br>");
    return newValue;
  }

  function check(){
    document.myForm.myItem.watch("value", alertme);
    document.myForm.myItem.value="Send";
  }
  </script>
</head>
<body onload="check()">
<form name="myForm">
  <input type="text" name="myItem" value="Submit">
```

```
</form>
</body>
</html>
```

Textarea

JavaScript1.0+, JScript1.0+
Nav2+, IE3+, Opera3+

Syntax

Core client-side JavaScript object.

Description

The Textarea object is one of the core JavaScript objects. Instances are created by the browser when it encounters an HTML <textarea> tag. In the JavaScript object hierarchy, the Textarea object is located at window.document.Form.Textarea. Table 8.38 lists the event handlers, methods, and properties used by the Textarea object.

Table 8.38   Event Handlers, Methods, and Properties Used by the
Textarea *Object*

Type	Item	Description
Event Handler	onBlur	Executes code when the text area loses the focus.
	onChange	Executes code when the text area loses the focus and has had its value modified.
	onFocus	Executes code when the text area receives the focus.
	onKeyDown	Executes code when a key is pressed down. This occurs before an onKeyPress event handler is triggered and was added in JavaScript 1.2.
	onKeyPress	Executes code when a key is pressed down immediately after an onKeyDown event handler is triggered. This event handler was added in JavaScript 1.2.
	onKeyUp	Executes code when a key is released. This was added in JavaScript 1.2.
	onSelect	Executes code when a user selects some of the text within the text area.
Method	blur()	Removes the focus from the text area.
	focus()	Gives the focus to the text area.
	handleEvent()	Invokes the handler for the event specified and was added in JavaScript 1.2.
	select()	Selects the text in the text area.
	unwatch()	Used to turn off the watch for a particular property.
	watch()	Used to turn on the watch for a particular property.

Table 8.38   Continued

Type	Item	Description
Property	`defaultValue`	Returns the value of the text area defined between the beginning and ending `<textarea>` tags. Note that this property is not supported by the Opera browsers.
	`form`	Returns the entire form the text area is in.
	`name`	Returns the name of this text area specified by the name attribute.
	`type`	Returns the type of this text area. Note that this is always `textarea` and was added in JavaScript 1.1.
	`value`	Returns the value that is actually displayed in the text area.

Example

Listing 8.492 displays the use of the `Textarea` properties. It contains a text area and a button. When the button is clicked, a second window is opened. The values of the properties of this `Textarea` object are displayed in this window.

Listing 8.492   Displaying the Properties of an Instance of a `Textarea` Object

```
<html>
<head>
<script language="JavaScript" type="text/javascript">
<!--

// Define the openWin function called by pressing the button.
function openWin(){

  // Place the reference to the text area in a variable for easier access.
  var myInstance = document.myForm.myTextArea;

  // Open a window to store the results
  var myWin = open("", "","width=450,height=200");

  // Write the text area's properties to the window.
  myWin.document.write("The defaultValue is: ");
  myWin.document.write(myInstance.defaultValue + "<br>");
  myWin.document.write("The name is: " + myInstance.name + "<br>");
  myWin.document.write("The type is: " + myInstance.type + "<br>");
  myWin.document.write("The value is: " + myInstance.value + "<br>");

  // Note that the entire form object is passed with this property.
  // This allows you to then drill down and get the value of other
  // components in the form.
  myWin.document.write("The form can be used to grab the ");
```

```
  myWin.document.write("value of the button: ");
  myWin.document.write(myInstance.form.myButton.value);

  // Close the stream to the window.
  myWin.document.close();
}
// -->
</script>
</head>
<body>
<form name="myForm">
  <textarea name="myTextArea" rows="6" cols="50">
  Here is some text in my text area.
  </textarea>
  <input type="button" value="Click to Process" name="myButton"
        onclick="openWin()">
</form>
</body>
</html>
```

Textarea.blur()

JavaScript1.0+, JScript1.0+
Nav2+, IE3+, Opera3+

Syntax

textarea.blur()

Description

The blur() method of the Textarea object removes the focus from the text area. Be careful when using this method in conjunction with the Textarea.focus() method. It can lead to a focus/blur loop, where the browser blurs a focus as soon as it is done, and vice versa.

Example

Listing 8.493 has a text area and a button. If the user highlights some of the text in the box and then clicks the Click Here to Remove Focus button, the text will no longer be highlighted.

Listing 8.493   *Using the* blur() *Method to Remove the Focus from the* Text Area

```
<html>
<head>
<script language="JavaScript" type="text/javascript">
<!--
```

Listing 8.493   Continued

```
// Define the removeFocus function called by pressing the button.
function removeFocus(){

  // Remove focus from the text area.
  document.myForm.myTextArea.blur();
}
// -->
</script>
</head>
<body>
<b>Highlight some of the text in the following text area:</b>
<p>
<form name="myForm">
  <textarea name="myTextArea" rows="6" cols="50">
  Here is some text in my text area.
  </textarea>
  <input type="button" value="Click Here to Remove Focus" name="myButton"
      onclick="removeFocus()">
</form>
</body>
</html>
```

Textarea.defaultValue

JavaScript1.0+, JScript1.0+
Nav2+, IE3+

Syntax

`textarea.defaultValue`

Description

The `defaultValue` property of a `Textarea` object instance contains the text between the beginning and ending `<textarea>` tags. This property is often used to reset areas to their default values after a user has modified them.

Example

Listing 8.494 has a text area and a button. If the user edits some of the text in the box and then clicks the Click to Reset button, the text will change back to the default value.

Listing 8.494   Using the `defaultValue` Property to Set the Value of the Text Area Back to Its Original Value

```
<html>
<head>
<script language="JavaScript" type="text/javascript">
<!--
```

```
// Define the resetForm function called by pressing the button.
function resetForm(){

  // Set the text in the text area back to "hello world".
  document.myForm.myTextArea.value = document.myForm.myTextArea.defaultValue;
}
// -->
</script>
</head>
<body>
<b>Edit the text in the following text box:</b>
<p>
<form name="myForm">
    <textarea name="myTextArea" rows="6" cols="50">
    Here is some text in my text area.
  </textarea>
<input type="button" value="Click to Reset" name="myButton"
       onclick="resetForm()">
</form>
</body>
</html>
```

Textarea.focus()

JavaScript1.0+, JScript1.0+
Nav2+, IE3+, Opera3+

Syntax

```
textarea.focus()
```

Description

The focus() method of the Textarea object gives the focus to the text area. Be careful when using this method in conjunction with the Textarea.blur() method. It can lead to a focus/blur loop, where the browser blurs a focus as soon as it is done, and vice versa.

Example

Listing 8.495 has two text areas and two buttons. If the user clicks the first button, the cursor is set inside the first text area. If the user clicks the second button, the cursor is set inside the second text area.

Listing 8.495   Using the focus() Method to Place the Cursor in the Desired Text Area

```
<html>
<head>
<script language="JavaScript" type="text/javascript">
```

Listing 8.495   Continued

```
<!--

// Define the setFocus function called by pressing the button.
function setFocus(num){

  // Determine which button was clicked and set the cursor
  // in the appropriate text area.
  if(num == 1){
    document.myForm.myTextArea1.focus();
  }else if(num == 2){
    document.myForm.myTextArea2.focus();
  }
}
// -->
</script>
</head>
<body>
<p>
<form name="myForm">
  <textarea name="myTextArea1" rows="2" cols="50">
  Here is the first text area.
  </textarea>
<input type="button" value="Click to Set Cursor" name="myButton1"
       onclick="setFocus(1)">
  <br>
  <textarea name="myTextArea2" rows="2" cols="50">
  Here is the second text area.
  </textarea>
  <input type="button" value="Click to Set Cursor" name="myButton2"
       onclick="setFocus(2)">
</form>
</body>
</html>
```

Textarea.form

JavaScript1.0+, JScript1.0+
Nav2+, IE3+, Opera3+

Syntax

textarea.form

Description

The form property of an instance of a Textarea object holds all the data of the form in which the text box is contained. This allows a developer to obtain specific information about the form in which the text area is located.

Example

Listing 8.496 has a text area and a button. When the button is clicked, three properties of the form as a whole are displayed. These properties were referenced through the form property of the text area.

Listing 8.496   Accessing a Form via the form Property of an Instance of a Textarea Object

```
<html>
<head>
<script language="JavaScript" type="text/javascript">
<!--

// Define the openWin function called by pressing the button.
function openWin(){

  // Place the reference to the form property of text area
  // in a variable for easier access.
  var formData = document.myForm.myTextArea.form;

  // Open a window to display the results.
  var myWin = open("", "","width=450,height=200");

  // Write the form properties accessed through the form
  // property to the window.
  myWin.document.write("The name of the form is: " + formData.name + "<br>");
  myWin.document.write("The value of the text box is: ");
  myWin.document.write(formData.myTextArea.value + "<br>");
  myWin.document.write("The name of the button is: ");
  myWin.document.write(formData.elements[1].name + "<br>");

  // Close the stream to the window.
  myWin.document.close();
}
// -->
</script>
</head>
<body>
<form name="myForm">
  <textarea name="myTextArea" rows="6" cols="50">
  Here is some text in my text area.
  </textarea>
  <input type="button" value="Click to Process" name="myButton"
         onclick="openWin()">
</form>
</body>
</html>
```

Textarea.handleEvent()

JavaScript1.2+, JScript3.0+
Nav4+, IE4+

Syntax

textarea.handleEvent(*event*)

Description

The handleEvent() method of the Textarea object invokes the handler for the event specified. This method was added in JavaScript 1.2.

Example

Listing 8.497 has a single text area. The script tells the browser that it wants to intercept all Click events and that it wants the myClickHandler function to handle them. Within this function, the handleEvent() method of the text area has been specified to handle the click.

When the user clicks anywhere on the page, the onClick event handler in the <textarea> tag calls a function to change the text in the text area. The change is nothing more than a simple number that is incremented, counting the number of times the page has been clicked.

Listing 8.497 *Using the* handleEvent() *Method of a* Textarea *Object to Handle All Clicks on a Page*

```
<html>
<head>
<script language="JavaScript1.2" type="text/javascript">
<!--

// Define a click counter variable.
var counter = 0;

// Tell the browser you want to intercept ALL click events
// on the page. Then define a function to handle them.
window.captureEvents(Event.CLICK)
window.onClick = myClickHandler;

// Define the myClickHandler function to handle click events.
function myClickHandler(e){

    // Pass all click events to the onClick event of the text area.
    window.document.myForm.myTextArea.handleEvent(e);

}
```

```
// Function is called by onClick of text box. Displays the number
// of clicks that have occurred.
function changeText(){
  document.myForm.myTextArea.value = counter++;
}
// -->
</script>
</head>
<body>
<form name="myForm">
  <textarea name="myTextArea" rows="6" cols="50" onclick='changeText()'>
  Here is some text in my text area.
  </textarea>
</form>
</body>
</html>
```

Textarea.name

JavaScript1.0+, JScript1.0+,
Nav2+, IE3+, Opera3+

Syntax

textarea.name

Description

The name property of an instance of a Textarea object returns the name of the text area.
This property is often accessed via the elements array of a Form object and used to
return the name of the text area. It is most useful when there are many forms on a given
page, and determining the name helps you determine what function you want to perform.

Example

Listing 8.498 has a text area and button. The elements array of a Form object is used
to retrieve the name and display it in an alert box.

Listing 8.498   Using the name Property to Retrieve the Name of a Text Area

```
<html>
<head>
<script language="JavaScript" type="text/javascript">
<!--

// Display an alert box that contains the name of the
// text area.
```

Listing 8.498   Continued

```
function getName(){
  alert("The name of this text area is " +
        document.myForm.elements[0].name);
}
// -->
</script>
</head>
<body>
<form name="myForm">
  <textarea name="myTextArea" rows="6" cols="50">
  Here is some text in my text area.
  </textarea>
  <input type="button" value="Get Name" name="myButton" onclick='getName()'>
</form>
</body>
</html>
```

Textarea.onBlur

JavaScript1.0+, JScript1.0+
Nav2+, IE3+, Opera3+

Syntax

onblur="*command*"

Description

The onBlur event handler of an instance of a Textarea object is fired when the focus is moved away from that particular text area. Care should be taken when using this event handler because it is possible to get into an infinite loop when using onFocus event handler or focus() method.

Example

Listing 8.499 contains three text areas, one of which has the onBlur event handler used within its tag. The third text box is used as a counter for the number of times the onBlur event handler is used.

In the script, the event calls a function that reassigns the first text area focus. The result of this is that when a user tries to click or tab away from the first text area, the counter is incremented and the focus returns. As you will see if you run Listing 8.513, even clicking in other windows or the URL bar increments the counter.

Listing 8.499   Example of Using the onBlur **Event Handler**

```
<html>
<head>
<script language="JavaScript" type="text/javascript">
```

```
<!--

// Initialize a counter to show clicks.
var counter = 0;

// Set the focus on the first text area, and increment
// the counter in last text area.
function comeBack(){
  document.myForm.myTextArea1.focus();
  document.myForm.counter.value = counter++;
}
// -->
</script>
</head>
<body onload='comeBack()'>
<form name="myForm">
  <textarea name="myTextArea1" rows="2" cols="50" onblur='comeBack()'>
    Here is some text in my text area.
  </textarea>
  <textarea name="myTextArea2" rows="2" cols="50">
  Here is some text in my text area.
  </textarea><br>
  <input type="text" size="2" value="" name="counter">
</form>
</body>
</html>
```

Textarea.onChange

JavaScript1.0+, JScript1.0+
Nav2+, IE3+, Opera3+

Syntax

```
onchange="command"
```

Description

The onChange event handler of an instance of a `Textarea` object is fired when the text in the area is modified. Care should be taken when using this event handler because it is possible to get into an infinite loop when using other events or methods that are fired when focus is placed on or away from the text area.

Example

Listing 8.500 has a single text area. If the user changes the text and then shifts the focus away from the text area by clicking elsewhere, the default text is placed back in the text area.

Listing 8.500 Using the onChange *Event Handler to Change the Text Back to the Default*

```
<html>
<head>
<script language="JavaScript" type="text/javascript">
<!--

// Change the text back to the default if user tries to change it.
// Note that the user has to click away or hit return for this
// to change back.
function changeBack(){
  document.myForm.myTextArea.value = document.myForm.myTextArea.defaultValue;
}
// -->
</script>
</head>
<body>
<form name="myForm">
  <textarea name="myTextArea" rows="2" cols="50" onchange='changeBack()'>
  Here is some text in my text area.
  </textarea>
</form>
</body>
</html>
```

Textarea.onFocus

JavaScript1.0+, JScript1.0+
Nav2+, IE3+, Opera3+

Syntax

onfocus="*command*"

Description

The onFocus event handler of an instance of a Textarea object is fired when focus is made on that particular text area. Care should be taken when using this event handler because it is possible to get into an infinite loop when using the onBlur event handler or the blur() method.

Example

Listing 8.501 contains three text boxes, one of which has the Focus event intercepted within its tag. The third text box is used for a counter for the number of times the Focus event is fired.

In the script, the event calls a function that assigns the second text box focus. The result of this is that when a user tries to click or tab to the first text box, the counter is incremented and the focus is returned to the second text box.

Listing 8.501   Example of Using the onFocus *Event Handler*

```
<html>
<head>
<script language="JavaScript" type="text/javascript">
<!--

// Initialize a counter to show clicks.
var counter = 0;

// Set the focus on the second text area, and increment
// the counter in last text area.
function sendAway(){
  document.myForm.myTextArea2.focus();
  document.myForm.counter.value = counter++;
}
// -->
</script>
</head>
<body onload='sendAway()'>
<form name="myForm">
  <textarea name="myTextArea1" rows="2" cols="50" onfocus='sendAway()'>
  Here is some text in my text area.
  </textarea>
  <textarea name="myTextArea2" rows="2" cols="50">
  Here is some text in my text area.
  </textarea>
  <br>
  <input type="text" size="2" value="" name="counter">
</form>
</body>
</html>
```

Textarea.onKeyDown

JavaScript1.2+, JScript3.0+
Nav4+, IE4+

Syntax

onkeydown="*command*"

Description

The onKeyDown event handler of an instance of a Textarea object is fired when a key is pressed down within the text area. Care should be taken when using this event handler because it is possible to get into an infinite loop when using other events or methods that are fired when the focus is placed on or away from the text area or other key-related events are used. The onKeyDown event handler is called followed by a onKeyPress event handler.

Example

Listing 8.502 has a single text area. If the user presses a key while the focus is on the text area, an `alert` box is displayed as soon as the key is pressed.

Listing 8.502   **The** onKeyDown **Event Handler Causes an Alert Box to Be Displayed**

```
<html>
<head>
<script language="JavaScript1.2" type="text/javascript">
<!--

// Pop up an alert box when the user presses a key.
function showDialog(){
  alert("A key was pressed down");
}
// -->
</script>
</head>
<body>
<form name="myForm">
  <textarea name="myTextArea" rows="2" cols="50" onkeydown='showDialog()'>
  Here is some text in my text area.
  </textarea>
</form>
</body>
</html>
```

Textarea.onKeyPress

JavaScript1.2+, JScript3.0+
Nav4+, IE4+

Syntax

onkeypress="*command*"

Description

The onKeyPress event handler of an instance of a Textarea object is fired when a key is pressed within the text area. Care should be taken when using this event handler because it is possible to get into an infinite loop when using other events or methods that are fired when the focus is placed on or away from the text area or other key-related events are used. This event is called after an onKeyDown event handler.

Example

Listing 8.503 has a single text area. If the user presses a key while the focus is on the text area, an alert box is displayed as soon as the key is pressed, showing the type of event that was fired. The first event handler is onKeyDown, which is followed by an onKeyPress event handler.

Listing 8.503   The onKeyDown *and* onKeyPress *Event Handlers Cause an Alert Box to Be Displayed*

```
<html>
<head>
<script language="JavaScript1.2" type="text/javascript">
<!--

// Pop up an alert box when the user presses a key.
function showDialog(type){
  alert("An onKey" + type + " event just occurred");
}
// -->
</script>
</head>
<body>
<form name="myForm">
  <textarea name="myTextArea" rows="2" cols="50"
          onkeydown='showDialog("Down")'
          onkeypress='showDialog("Press")'>
  Here is some text in my text area.
  </textarea>
</form>
</body>
</html>
```

Textarea.onKeyUp

> JavaScript1.2+, JScript3.0+
> Nav4+, IE4+

Syntax

onkeyup="*command*"

Description

The onKeyUp event handler of an instance of a Textarea object is fired when a key is released within the text area. Care should be taken when using this event handler because it is possible to get into an infinite loop when using other events or methods that are fired when the focus is placed on or away from the text area or other key-related events are used. The onKeyUp event handler is called after an onKeyPress event handler.

Example

Listing 8.504 has a single text area. If the user releases a key while the focus is on the text area, an alert box is displayed as soon as the key is released.

Listing 8.504   The onKeyUp *Event Handler Causes an Alert Box to Be Displayed*

```
<html>
<head>
<script language="JavaScript1.2" type="text/javascript">
<!--

// Pop up an alert box when the user releases a key.
function showDialog(){
  alert("A key was released");
}
// -->
</script>
</head>
<body>
<form name="myForm">
  <textarea name="myTextArea" rows="2" cols="50" onkeyup='showDialog()'>
  Here is some text in my text area.
  </textarea>
</form>
</body>
</html>
```

Textarea.onSelect

> JavaScript1.0+, JScript1.0+
> IE3+, Net6

Syntax

```
onselect="command"
```

Description

The onSelect event handler of an instance of a Textarea object is fired when the text in the area is highlighted. Care should be taken when using this event handler because it is possible to get into an infinite loop when using other events or methods that are fired when the focus is placed on the text area.

NOTE

> Note that Netscape defined this function in JavaScript 1.0; however, it was not fully implemented until Netscape 6 was released. Opera browsers do not support this function either.

Example

Listing 8.505 has two text areas. If the user highlights the text in the first text area, the default text of the first text area is written to the second text area.

Listing 8.505   Using the onSelect *Event Handler to Set the Text in the* **Second Text Box**

```html
<html>
<head>
<script language="JavaScript" type="text/javascript">
<!--

// Change the text of the second text area to the default
// of the first if user highlights text in the first.
function setText(){
  document.myForm.myTextArea2.value = document.myForm.myTextArea1.defaultValue;
}
// -->
</script>
</head>
<body>
<form name="myForm">
  <textarea name="myTextArea1" rows="2" cols="50" onselect='setText()'>
  Here is some text in my text area.
  </textarea>
  <br>
  <textarea name="myTextArea2" rows="2" cols="50">
  </textarea>
</form>
</body>
</html>
```

Textarea.select()

JavaScript1.0+, JScript1.0+
Nav2+, IE3+, Opera3+

Syntax

```
textarea.select()
```

Description

The select() method of the Textarea object selects the text in the text area. Be careful when using this method in conjunction with the blur() and focus() methods. It can lead to a focus/blur loop where the browser blurs or focuses as soon as it is has been selected, and vice versa.

Example

Listing 8.506 has a text area and a button. If the user clicks the button, the text inside the text area will be highlighted. Notice the focus() method had to be used to tell the browser to actually highlight the text.

Listing 8.506 *Using the* `select()` *Method to Select the Text in a Text Area*

```
<html>
<head>
<script language="JavaScript" type="text/javascript">
<!--

// Define the selectText function called by pressing the button.
function selectText(){

  // Select the text in the area, then place focus on it.
  document.myForm.myTextArea.select();
  document.myForm.myTextArea.focus();
}
// -->
</script>
</head>
<body>
<form name="myForm">
  <textarea name="myTextArea" rows="6" cols="50">
  Here is some text in my text area.
  </textarea>
  <input type="button" value="Click to Select Text" name="myButton"
         onclick="selectText()">
</form>
</body>
</html>
```

Textarea.type

JavaScript1.1+, JScript1.0+
Nav3+, IE3+, Opera3+

Syntax

textarea.type

Description

The `type` property of an instance of a `Textarea` object returns the type of the text area. This always returns `textarea`.

Example

Listing 8.507 has a text area and a button. When the button is clicked, an alert box is popped up that displays the `type` property of the text area.

Listing 8.507 *Displaying the* `type` *Property in an Alert Box*

```
<html>
<head>
```

```
<script language="JavaScript1.1" type="text/javascript">
<!--

// Display an alert box that contains the type of the
// text area.
function getType(){
  alert("The name of this text area is " +
        document.myForm.elements[0].type);
}
// -->
</script>
</head>
<body>
<form name="myForm">
  <textarea name="myTextArea" rows="6" cols="50">
  Here is some text in my text area.
  </textarea>
  <input type="button" value="Get Type" name="myButton" onclick='getType()'>
</form>
</body>
</html>
```

Textarea.unwatch()

JavaScript 1.2+
Nav4+

Syntax

textarea.unwatch(*property*)

Description

The unwatch() method of the Textarea object is used to turn off the watch for a particular *property*.

Example

Listing 8.508 shows how the unwatch() method is used to stop watching the value property.

Listing 8.508   Example of the unwatch() Method

```
<html>
<head>
  <script type="text/javascript" language="JavaScript1.2">

  // Write out a note if the value of the Textarea box changes.
  function alertme(id, oldValue, newValue){
    document.writeln("ID (" + id + ") changed from " + oldValue + " to ");
    document.writeln(newValue + "<br>");
```

Listing 8.508   Continued

```
    return newValue;
  }

  // Watch the value of the Teaxtarea box, then change it, before unwatching.
  function check(){
    document.myForm.myItem.watch("value", alertme);
    document.myForm.myItem.value="Send";
    document.myForm.myItem.unwatch("value");
  }
  </script>
</head>
<body onload="check()">
<form name="myForm">
  <textarea name="myItem" rows="3" cols="30">Submit</textarea>
</form>
</body>
</html>
```

Textarea.value

JavaScript1.0+, JScript1.0+
Nav2+, IE3+, Opera3+

Syntax

textarea.value

Description

The value property of an instance of a Textarea object returns the current value of the text area. Note that this is not the default value that can be accessed via the Textarea.defaultValue property and is often used to set the value of a text area.

Example

Listing 8.509 contains a text area and button. You can edit the text in the text area, and then click the Reset button to reset the text back to the default value.

Listing 8.509   Resetting the Value of a Text Area to the Default Value

```
<html>
<head>
<script language="JavaScript" type="text/javascript">
<!--

// Reset the text in the text area to its default value.
function resetText(){
  document.myForm.myTextArea.value = document.myForm.myTextArea.defaultValue;
}
// -->
```

```
</script>
</head>
<body>
<form name="myForm">
  <textarea name="myTextArea" rows="6" cols="50">
  Here is some text in my text area.
  </textarea>
  <input type="button" value="Reset" name="myButton" onclick='resetText()'>
</form>
</body>
</html>
```

Textarea.watch()

JavaScript 1.2+
Nav4+

Syntax

textarea.watch(*property, function*)

Description

The watch() method of the Textarea object is used to turn on the watch for a particular *property*. Any time the specified *property* is changed after the watch() method has been called, the specified *function* is called.

Example

Listing 8.510 shows how the watch() method is used to start watching the value property.

Listing 8.510   Example of the watch() **Method**

```
<html>
<head>
  <script type="text/javascript" language="JavaScript1.2">

  function alertme(id, oldValue, newValue){
    document.writeln("ID (" + id + ") changed from " + oldValue + " to ");
    document.writeln(newValue + "<br>");
    return newValue;
  }

  function check(){
    document.myForm.myItem.watch("value", alertme);
    document.myForm.myItem.value="Send";
  }
  </script>
</head>
```

Listing 8.510   Continued

```
<body onload="check()">
<form name="myForm">
  <textarea name="myItem" rows="3" cols="30" value="Submit"></textarea>
</form>
</body>
</html>
```

untaint()

> JavaScript1.1
> Nav3

Syntax

```
untaint(property)
untaint(variable)
untaint(function)
untaint(object)
```

Description

The untaint() method, a security measure that was only implemented in JavaScript 1.1, allowed a developer to allow return values to be used by and propagated to other scripts. This method does not change the data element passed to it, but rather returns an unmarked reference to the element.

Because untaint() and the functionality of data tainting was removed in JavaScript 1.2, you should avoid using this method. You should use it only if you have a specific security reason for compatibility with Navigator 3 browsers. See Chapter 1 for more information on the security model that is now used in Navigator browsers.

Example

Listing 8.511 simply untaints a variable that is defined in a separate window.

Listing 8.511   Use of the untaint() **Method, Which Is No Longer Supported**

```
<script language="JavaScript1.1" type="text/javascript">
<!--

// Store the untainted variable from the second window
// in the variable utMyVar.
var utMyvar = untaint(myWin.myVar);

// -->
</script>
```

Window

JavaScript1.0+, JScript1.0+
Nav2+, IE3+, Opera3+

Syntax

Core client-side JavaScript object.

Description

The Window object is one of the top-level JavaScript objects that are created when a <body>, <frameset>, or <frame> tag is encountered. Instances of this object can also be created by using the Window.open() method. Table 8.39 lists the properties and methods associated with the Window object.

Table 8.39 **Methods and Properties of the** Window **Object**

Type	Item	Description
Method	alert()	Displays an alert dialog box with the text string passed.
	atob()	Decodes a string that has been encoded using base-64 encoding.
	back()	Loads the previous page in place of the window instance.
	blur()	Removes the focus from a window.
	btoa()	Encodes a string using base-64 encoding.
	captureEvents()	Sets the window to capture all events of a specified type.
	clearInterval()	Clears the interval set with the setInterval method.
	clearTimeout()	Clears the timeout set with the setTimeout method.
	close()	Closes the instance of the window.
	confirm()	Displays a confirmation dialog box.
	crypto.random()	Returns a random string that's length is specified by the number of bytes passed to the method.
	crypto.signText()	Returns a string of encoded data that represents a signed object.
	disableExternalCapture()	Disables external event capturing.
	enableExternalCapture()	Enables external event capturing for the pages loaded from other servers.
	find()	Displays a Find dialog box where the user can enter text to search the current page.

Table 8.39 **Continued**

Type	Item	Description
	focus()	Assigns the focus to the specified window instance.
	forward()	Loads the next page in place of the window instance.
	handleEvent()	Invokes the handler for the event passed.
	home()	Loads the user's specified home page in place of the window instance.
	moveBy()	Moves the window by the amounts specified.
	moveTo()	Moves the window to the specified location.
	open()	Opens a new instance of a window.
	print()	Invokes the Print dialog box so that the user can print the current window.
	prompt()	Displays a prompt dialog box.
	releaseEvents()	Releases the captured events of a specified type.
	resizeBy()	Resizes the window by the specified amount.
	resizeTo()	Resizes the window to the specified size.
	routeEvent()	Passes the events of a specified type to be handled natively.
	scroll()	Scrolls the document in the window to a specified location.
	scrollBy()	Scrolls the document in the window by a specified amount.
	scrollTo()	Scrolls the document, both width and height, in the window to a specified location.
	setHotKeys()	Enables or disables hot keys in a window that does not have menus.
	setInterval()	Invokes a function or evaluates an expression every time the number of milliseconds has passed.
	setResizeable()	Specifies whether a user can resize a window.
	setTimeout()	Invokes a function or evaluates an expression when the number of milliseconds has passed.
	setZOptions()	Specifies the z-order stacking behavior of the window.

Type	Item	Description
	stop()	Stops the current window from loading other items within it.
	unwatch()	Used to turn off the watch for a particular property.
	watch()	Used to turn on the watch for a particular property.
Property	closed	Specifies whether the window instance has been closed.
	crypto	Actually a subobject of the Window object, which allows access to the browser's encryption features.
	defaultStatus	Is the default message in the window's status bar.
	document	References all the information about the document within this window. See the Document object for more information.
	frames	References all the information about the frames within this window. See the Frame object for more information.
	history	References the URLs that the user has visited.
	innerHeight	Contains the height of the display area of the current window in pixels.
	innerWidth	Contains the width of the display area of the current window in pixels.
	length	Represents the number of frames in the current window.
	location	Contains the current URL loaded into the window.
	locationbar	Reference to the browser's location bar.
	menubar	Reference to the browser's menu bar.
	name	Name of the window.
	offScreenBuffering	Specifies whether updates to a window are performed in an offscreen buffer.
	opener	Contains the name of the window from which a second window was opened.
	outerHeight	Contains the height of the outer area of the current window in pixels.
	outerWidth	Contains the width of the outer area of the current window in pixels.

Table 8.39   Continued

Type	Item	Description
	pageXOffset	Contains the x coordinate of the current window.
	pageYOffset	Contains the y coordinate of the current window.
	parent	Reference to the uppermost window that is displaying the current frame.
	personalbar	Reference to the browser's personal bar.
	screenX	Specifies the x coordinate of the left edge of the window.
	screenY	Specifies the y coordinate of the top edge of the window.
	scrollbars	Reference to the browser's scrollbars.
	self	Reference to the current window.
	status	Reference to the message in the window's status bar.
	statusbar	Reference to the browser's status bar.
	toolbar	Reference to the browser's toolbar.
	top	Reference to the uppermost window that is displaying the current frame.
	window	Reference to the current window.

Any of the methods or properties of this object can have the instance name left off if it refers to the window in which they are invoked. Setting the status property, for instance, would set the status in the current window, whereas setting myWin.status sets the status in the window named myWin. The only exception to this rule is in using the location property and the close() and open() methods, which must take the instance's name when called within an event handler.

NOTE

Each of the entries for the Window object's methods and properties in this chapter will be preceded by the Window object name in its syntax definition.

Example

Listing 8.512 contains a button. When the button is clicked, a new window instance is created using the open() method. Information is then written to the window before the stream is closed. There is also a button in the new window to close it.

Listing 8.512 *Creating a New Instance of the* Window *Object*

```html
<html>
<head>

<script language="JavaScript" type="text/javascript">
<!--

// Define the openWin() function.
function openWin(){

    // Create variables to hold the various options that can be set
    // when a new Window instance is created.
    var myBars = 'directories=no,location=no,menubar=no,status=no';
    myBars += ',titlebar=no,toolbar=no';
    var myOptions = 'scrollbars=no,width=400,height=200,resizeable=no';
    var myFeatures = myBars + ',' + myOptions;
    var myReadme = "Welcome to Pure JavaScript!\n" +
          "-----------------------------------------\n" +
        'You can enter some text here.'

    // Open the window. Give the window instance the name newDoc and
    // name the document in the window myWin.
    var newWin = open('', 'myWin', myFeatures);

    newWin.document.writeln('<form>');
    newWin.document.writeln('<table cellspacing="0" cellpadding="0"
border="1">');
    newWin.document.writeln('<tr valign="top" bgcolor="#000099"><td>');
    newWin.document.writeln('<font size="-1" color="#ffffff"><b>');
    newWin.document.writeln('  Readme</b></font>');
    newWin.document.writeln('</td></tr>');
    newWin.document.writeln('<tr valign="top"><td>');
    newWin.document.writeln('<textarea cols="45" rows="7" wrap="soft">');
    newWin.document.writeln(myReadme + '</textarea>');
    newWin.document.writeln('</td></tr>');
    newWin.document.writeln('<tr valign="bottom" align="right"');
    newWin.document.writeln(' bgcolor="#c0c0c0"><td>');
    newWin.document.writeln('<input type="button" value="Close"');
    newWin.document.writeln(' onclick="window.close()">');
    newWin.document.writeln('</td></tr>');
    newWin.document.writeln('</table></form>');
```

Listing 8.512   Continued

```
// Close the stream to the document and bring the window to the front.
newWin.document.close();
newWin.focus();
}

// -->
</script>
</head>
<body>
<form>
  <b>Click the following button to open a new window: </b>
  <input type="button" value="Open" onclick='openWin()'>
</form>
</body>
</html> >
```

window.alert()

JavaScript1.0+, JScript1.0
Nav2+, IE3+, Opera3+

Syntax

window.alert(*string*)

Description

The alert() method of the Window object displays an alert dialog box when invoked. The value of the string passed to the method is displayed in the box.

Example

Listing 8.513 pops up an alert box when the script is loaded. The result of running this script can be seen in Figure 8.4.

Listing 8.513   An Alert Box

```
<script language="JavaScript" type="text/javascript">
<!--

alert('Here is an alert dialog box.');

// -->
</script>
```

Figure 8.4

An alert box created with the `Window.alert()` *method.*

window.atob()

JavaScript1.2
Nav4

Syntax

window.atob(*data*)

Description

The atob() method of the Window object, which was only implemented in Navigator 4, is used to decode *data* that was encoded in base-64 encoding.

Example

Listing 8.514 shows how you can encode data using the btoa() method, and then decode it back using atob().

Listing 8.514   *Using the* atob() *Method to Decode Data*

```
<html>
<body>
  <script type="text/javascript" language="JavaScript1.2">
  <!--
    var myString = new String();
    myString = "Hello world";

    // Write out encoded and decoded versions of the string.
    document.write(window.btoa(myString));
    document.write(window.atob(myString));
  //-->
  </script>
</body>
</html>
```

window.back()
JavaScript1.2+, JScript3.0
Nav4+, IE4+

Syntax
`window.back()`

Description
The `back()` method of the `Window` object simulates the user clicking the Back button on the browser. It returns the browser's page or frame to the previous page or frame.

Example
Listing 8.515 has two buttons. One of the buttons takes the browser back one page and the other button takes it forward. Note that there has to be a back and forward page during your session for the button to have somewhere to go.

Listing 8.515   Using the `back()` Method

```
<html>
<body>
<form>
  <input type="button" value="Back" onclick="window.back()">
  <input type="button" value="Forward" onclick="window.forward()">
</form>
</body>
</html>
```

window.blur()
JavaScript1.0+, JScript1.0+
Nav2+, IE3+, Opera3+

Syntax
`window.blur()`

Description
The `blur()` method of the `Window` object removes the focus from the window. Be careful when using this method in conjunction with the `focus()` method of objects. It can lead to a focus/blur loop, where the browser blurs a focus as soon as it is done, and vice versa.

Example
Listing 8.516 has two buttons. When the user clicks the Open button, a second, smaller window is opened. If the Blur button is clicked, the focus is removed from the parent window and placed on the child window.

Listing 8.516   Using the `blur()` *Method to Remove the Focus from a Window*

```
<html>
<head>
<script language="JavaScript" type="text/javascript">
<!--

// Define the openWin() function
function openWin(){

  // Create variables to hold the various options that can be set
  // when a new Window instance is created.
  var myBars = 'directories=no,location=no,menubar=no,status=no';
  myBars += ',titlebar=no,toolbar=no';
  var myOptions = 'scrollbars=no,width=400,height=200,resizeable=no';
  var myFeatures = myBars + ',' + myOptions;

  // Open a child window.
  newWin = open('', 'myDoc', myFeatures);

  newWin.document.writeln('Here is the child window');

  // Close the stream to the document.
  newWin.document.close();

  // Return focus to the parent window.
  self.focus();
}

// Define the blurWin() function.
function blurWin(){

  // Blur the parent window and focus on the child.
  self.blur();
  newWin.focus();
}

// -->
</script>
</head>
<body>
<form>
  <input type="button" value="Open" onclick='openWin()'>
  <input type="button" value="Blur" onclick='blurWin()'>
</form>
</body>
</html>
```

window.btoa()

JavaScript1.2
Nav4

Syntax

`window.btoa(data)`

Description

The `btoa()` method of the `Window` object, which was only implemented in Navigator 4, is used to encode *data* in base-64 encoding.

Example

Listing 8.517 shows how you can encode data using the `btoa()` method, and then decode it an back using `atob()`.

Listing 8.517 Using the `btoa()` Method to Decode Data

```
<html>
<body>
  <script type="text/javascript" language="JavaScript1.2">
  <!--
    var myString = new String();
    myString = "Hello world";

    // Write out encoded and decoded versions of string
    document.write(window.btoa(myString));
    document.write(window.atob(myString))
  //-->
  </script>
</body>
</html>
```

window.captureEvents()

JavaScript1.2+, JScript3.0+
Nav4+, IE4+

Syntax

`window.captureEvents(event)`
`window.captureEvents(event1 | event2 | eventN)`

Description

The captureEvents() method of the Window object captures all the events of the event type passed. Because you can capture the events that are natively handled by the language itself, programmers can now define a function to handle events in a manner they want. If you have multiple events that you want to capture, separate them with the pipe (|) character. The types of events that can be captured are as follows:

- Event.ABORT
- Event.BLUR
- Event.CHANGE
- Event.CLICK
- Event.DBLCLICK
- Event.DRAGDROP
- Event.ERROR
- Event.FOCUS
- Event.KEYDOWN
- Event.KEYPRESS
- Event.KEYUP
- Event.LOAD
- Event.MOUSEDOWN
- Event.MOUSEMOVE
- Event.MOUSEOUT
- Event.MOUSEOVER
- Event.MOUSEUP
- Event.MOVE
- Event.RESET
- Event.RESIZE
- Event.SELECT
- Event.SUBMIT
- Event.UNLOAD

After an event has been captured, you can define a function to replace the built-in method for handling the event.

Example

Listing 8.518 has a single text box. The script in the <head> of the document specifies a function to handle all onClick events in the window. To be able to do this, the captureEvents() method had to be used to capture all events of type Event.CLICK. When the page itself is clicked, a counter, which is displayed in the text box, is incremented.

Listing 8.518   Capturing Events with the `Window.captureEvents()`
Method

```html
<html>
<head>
<script language="JavaScript1.2" type="text/javascript">
<!--

// Define a click counter variable.
var counter = 0;

// Tell the browser you want to intercept ALL click events
// on the page. Then define a function to handle them.
window.captureEvents(Event.CLICK)
window.onClick = myClickHandler;

// Define the myClickHandler function to handle click events.
function myClickHandler(e){

  // Pass all click events to the onClick event of the text box.
  window.document.myForm.myText.handleEvent(e);

}

// Function is called by onClick of text box. Displays the number
// of clicks that have occurred.
function changeText(){
  document.myForm.myText.value = counter++;
}
// -->
</script>
</head>
<body>
<form name="myForm">
  <input type="text" size="2" value="" name="myText" onclick='changeText()'>
</form>
</body>
</html>
```

window.clearInterval()

> JavaScript1.2+, JScript3.0+
> Nav4+, IE4+

Syntax

window.clearInterval(*interval*)

Description

The clearInterval() method of the Window object clears the interval that is passed to the method. The interval that is passed has to be previously defined using the setInterval() method.

Example

Listing 8.519 sets an interval in the <head> of the document that displays a counter in a text box on the page. An interval is set to update the counter in the text box every five seconds. There is also a button on the page that can be clicked to clear the interval and stop the counting.

Listing 8.519 *Clearing an Interval with the* clearInterval() *Method*

```
<html>
<head>
<script language="JavaScript1.2" type="text/javascript">
<!--

// Create a variable to hold a counter.
var counter = 1;

// Define a function to display the counter.
function startCounter(){
  document.myForm.myText.value = counter++;
}

// Define a function to stop the counter.
function stopCounter(){
  window.clearInterval(myInterval);
}

// Set the interval to call the function every 5 seconds.
var myInterval = window.setInterval("startCounter()", 5000)

// -->
</script>
</head>
<body onload="startCounter()">
<form name="myForm">
  <input type="text" size="2" value="" name="myText">
  <input type="button" value="Clear Interval" onclick="stopCounter()">
</form>
</body>
</html>
```

window.clearTimeout()
JavaScript1.0+, JScript1.0+
Nav2+, IE3+, Opera3+

Syntax

```
window.clearTimeout(timeout)
```

Description

The `clearTimeout()` method of the `Window` object clears the timeout passed to the method. The timeout that is passed has to be previously defined using the `setTimeout()` method.

Example

Listing 8.520 has a button and text box. By the default, the time will be displayed in the text box after five seconds. This is done using the `setTimeout()` method. If the button is clicked, a function is called that invokes the `clearTimeout()` method preventing the time time from being displayed in the text box.

Listing 8.520   Using the `clearTimeout()` Method

```
<html>
<head>
<script language="JavaScript" type="text/javascript">
<!--

// Define a function to show the time.
function showTime(){
  myTime = new Date();
  myTime = myTime.getHours() + ":" + myTime.getMinutes() + ":";
  myTime += myTime.getSeconds();
  document.myForm.myText.value = myTime;
}

// Define a function to stop the display of the time.
function stopTime(){
  window.clearTimeout(myTimeout);
}

// Set the interval to call the function after 5 seconds.
var myTimeout = window.setTimeout("showTime()", 5000)

// -->
</script>
</head>
<body>
<form name="myForm">
  <input type="text" size="2" value="" name="myText">
```

```
<input type="button" value="Clear Timeout" onclick="stopTime()">
</form>
</body>
</html>
```

window.close()

JavaScript1.0+, JScript1.0+
Nav2+, IE3+, Opera3+

Syntax

window.close()

Description

The close() method of the Window object is used to close browser windows. Even though this method was first introduced in JavaScript 1.0, there have been some changes. In the first version, this method could be used to close any window. In JavaScript 1.1, it was restricted to close only windows opened using JavaScript. In JavaScript 1.2, you must have the UniversalBrowserWrite privilege to unconditionally close a window.

Example

Listing 8.521 has a button that opens a window. Within the opened window there is a Close button. Clicking this button invokes the close() method and closes the browser window.

Listing 8.521   Using the close() *Method to Close a Window*

```
<html>
<head>

<script language="JavaScript" type="text/javascript">
<!--

// Define the openWin() function.
function openWin(){

  // Create variables to hold the various options that can be set
  // when a new Window instance is created.
  var myBars = 'directories=no,location=no,menubar=no,status=no';
  myBars += ',titlebar=no,toolbar=no';
  var myOptions = 'scrollbars=no,width=400,height=200,resizeable=no';
  var myFeatures = myBars + ',' + myOptions;
  var myReadme = "Welcome to Pure JavaScript!\n" +
      "----------------------------------------\n" +
      "Click the Close button to invoke the close() " +
      "method and close the window.";
```

Listing 8.521   Continued

```
    // Open the window. Give the window instance the name newDoc and
    // name the document in the window myDoc.
    var newWin = open('', 'myDoc', myFeatures);

    newWin.document.writeln('<form>');
    newWin.document.writeln('<table cellspacing="0" cellpadding="0"
border="1">');
    newWin.document.writeln('<tr valign="top" bgcolor="#000099"><td>');
    newWin.document.writeln('<font size="-1" color="#ffffff"><b>');
    newWin.document.writeln('  Readme</b></font>');
    newWin.document.writeln('</td></tr>');
    newWin.document.writeln('<tr valign="top"><td>');
    newWin.document.writeln('<textarea cols="45" rows="7" wrap="soft">');
    newWin.dpcument.writeln(myReadme + '</textarea>');
    newWin.document.writeln('</td></tr>');
    newWin.document.writeln('<tr valign="bottom" align="right"');
    newWin.document.writeln(' bgcolor="#c0c0c0"><td>');

    // Write the close() method on the new window. Invoke it with an onClick
    // event.
    newWin.document.writeln('<input type="button" value="Close"');
    newWin.document.writeln(' onclick="window.close()">');

    newWin.document.writeln('</td></tr>');
    newWin.document.writeln('</table></form>');

    // Close the stream to the document and bring the window to the front.
    newWin.document.close();
    newWin.focus();
}

// -->
</script>
</head>
<body>
<form>
  <b>Click the following button to open a new window: </b>
  <input type="button" value="Open" onclick='openWin()'>
</form>
</body>
</html>
```

window.closed

> JavaScript1.1+, JScript1.0+
> Nav3+, IE3+, Opera3+

Syntax

window.closed

Description

The `closed` property of the `Window` object returns a Boolean value specifying whether the window instance it is referencing is closed. If the window is still open, the property returns `false`. If it is closed, the property returns `true`.

Example

Listing 8.522 has two buttons. When the Open button is clicked, a second window is opened and focused. When the Check button is clicked, the script checks to see whether the window is still open. If it is, the text in the text area of the second window is changed. If it is not, an alert dialog box is displayed.

Listing 8.522 Using the `closed` *Property to See Whether a Window Is Still Open*

```
<html>
<head>

<script language="JavaScript1.1" type="text/javascript">
<!--

// Define the openWin() function.
function openWin(){

  // Create variables to hold the various options that can be set
  // when a new Window instance is created.
  var myBars = 'directories=no,location=no,menubar=no,status=no';
  myBars += ',titlebar=no,toolbar=no';
  var myOptions = 'scrollbars=no,width=400,height=200,resizeable=no';
  var myFeatures = myBars + ',' + myOptions;
  var myReadme = "Welcome to Pure JavaScript!\n" +
        "----------------------------------------\n" +
        "Click the Close button to invoke the close() " +
        "method and close the window."

  // Open the window. Give the window instance the name newWin and
  // name the document in the window myDoc.
  newWin = open('', 'myDoc', myFeatures);

  newWin.document.writeln('<form name="secondForm">');
  newWin.document.writeln('<table cellspacing="0" cellpadding="0"
border="1">');
  newWin.document.writeln('<tr valign="top" bgcolor="#000099"><td>');
  newWin.document.writeln('<font size="-1" color="#ffffff"><b>');
  newWin.document.writeln('  Readme</b></font>');
  newWin.document.writeln('</td></tr>');
  newWin.document.writeln('<tr valign="top"><td>');
  newWin.document.writeln('<textarea name="myTextArea" cols="45" rows="7"');
  newWin.document.writeln(' wrap="soft">' + myReadme + '</textarea>');
  newWin.document.writeln('</td></tr>');
```

Listing 8.522   Continued

```
newWin.document.writeln('<tr valign="bottom" align="right"');
newWin.document.writeln(' bgcolor="#c0c0c0"><td>');
newWin.document.writeln('<input type="button" value="Close" ');
newWin.document.writeln('onclick="window.close()">');
newWin.document.writeln('</td></tr>');
newWin.document.writeln('</table></form>');

// Close the stream to the document and bring the window to the front.
newWin.document.close();
newWin.focus();
}

function checkWin(){

// Use the closed property to see if the window has been closed.
if(newWin.closed){
    alert("Sorry, the window has been closed.");
}else{
  var myText = "This window is still opened";
  newWin.document.secondForm.myTextArea.value = myText;
  newWin.focus();
  }
}
// -->
</script>
</head>
<body>
<form>
  <input type="button" value="Open" onclick='openWin()'>
  <input type="button" value="Check" onclick='checkWin()'>
</form>
</body>
</html>
```

window.confirm()

JavaScript1.0+, JScript1.0
Nav2+, IE3+, Opera3+

Syntax

window.confirm(*string*)

Description

The confirm() method of the Window object displays a confirmation dialog box when invoked. The value of the string passed to the method is displayed in the box. This box will contain both an OK and a Cancel button. The method returns a Boolean value of true if the user clicks OK and false if the user clicks Cancel.

Example

Listing 8.523 pops up a confirmation box when the script is loaded to see whether the user wishes to proceed. After the user makes a decision, the script writes his choice to the page. The result of running this script can be seen in Figure 8.5.

Listing 8.523 A Confirm Box Using the confirm() Method

```
<script language="JavaScript" type="text/javascript">
<!--

// Ask the user if they want to proceed.
if(confirm("Are you sure you want to do this?")){
  document.write("You clicked the OK button");
}else{
  document.write("You clicked the Cancel button");
}

// Close the stream to the document.
document.close();

// -->
</script>
```

Figure 8.5

A confirmation box created with the Window.confirm() *method.*

window.crypto
JavaScript1.2
Nav4

Syntax

window.crypto.method

Description

The crypto property of the Window object is used to access the encryption functions available within Navigator 4.

Example

Listing 8.524 shows how you can use the crypto property to access the random() method within Navigator's encryption features.

Listing 8.524   Using the `crypto` **Property to Access Encryption Methods**

```
<html>
<body>
  <script type="text/javascript" language="JavaScript1.2">
  <!--
  // Writes out the encryption random number.
  document.write(crypto.random(16));
  //-->
  </script>
</body>
</html>
```

window.crypto.random()

> JavaScript1.2
> Nav4

Syntax

window.crypto.random(*num*)

Description

The `random` method of the `window.crypto` object is used to create a random number of length *num* in bytes. This method is part of the encryption functions available within the Navigator 4.

Example

Listing 8.525 shows how you can use the `crypto` property to access the `random()` method within Navigator's encryption features.

Listing 8.525   Using the `random()` **Method to Generate a Random Number**

```
<html>
<body>
  <script type="text/javascript" language="JavaScript1.2">
  <!--
  // Writes out the encryption random number.
  document.write(crypto.random(16));
  //-->
  </script>
</body>
</html>
```

window.crypto.signText()

> JavaScript1.2
> Nav4

Syntax

```
window.crypto.signText(text, style)
window.crypto.signText(text, style, authority1, ..., authorityN)
```

Description

The signText() method of the window.crypto object is used to sign *text*. Depending on the *style* of signing, which can be ask or auto, the browser might pop up a dialog with a list of possible certificates to sign the *text* with. You can optionally pass 1 or more *authority* arguments that will allow you to pass Certificate Authorities.

After the data has been encoded and sent to the server, the server will decode and verify it. If a failure occurs, one of the following codes will be returned:

- error: noMatchingCert—Specifies that the user's certificate does not match one of the passed authority arguments.
- error: userCancel—Specifies that the user cancelled the ask dialog box without submitting a certificate.
- error: internalError—Specifies that an internal error has occurred while processing the data.

Example

Listing 8.526 prompts the user for some text, and then prompts him before signing the text. After being signed, the text could then be passed to the server.

Listing 8.526   Using the signText() Method

```
<html>
<script type="text/javascript" language="JavaScript1.2">
<!--

  // Prompt for text.
  myText = window.prompt("Please enter some text", "");

  // Sign the text.
  crypto.signText(myText, ask);
//-->
</script>
</html>
```

window.defaultStatus

JavaScript1.0+, JScript1.0+
Nav2+, IE3+, Opera3+

Syntax

```
window.defaultStatus = string
```

Description

The defaultStatus property of the Window object reflects the message that is displayed in the status bar of the browser. Note that in JavaScript 1.1, this property was tainted. See Chapter 1 for more information on JavaScript security and data tainting.

Example

Listing 8.527 shows how you can set the default status to be displayed after a document has finished loading. This is done in conjunction with the onLoad event handler within the <body> tag.

Listing 8.527   Setting the Default Status of a Page

```
<body onload="window.defaultStatus='Please make a selection'">
```

window.disableExternalCapture()

JavaScript1.2+

Nav4+

Syntax

```
window.disableExternalCapture()
```

Description

The disableExternalCapture() method of the Window object disables any external event capturing set up using the enableExternalCapture() method. The functionality of this method provides the capturing of events in frames loaded from a different server. Before you can enable the capturing of these external events, you must first obtain UniversalBrowserWrite privileges. After they have been obtained and the method has been invoked, use the Window.captureEvents() method to specify the events you want to capture.

> **NOTE**
>
> For more information on privileges, JavaScript security, and signed scripts, see Chapter 1.

Example

Listing 8.528 enables external event capturing when the document loads. The document itself has a button that, when clicked, calls a function to disable the external event captures.

Listing 8.528   Disabling External Event Capturing

```
<html>
<head>
<script language="JavaScript1.2" type="text/javascript">
<!--
```

```
// Ask the user for permission to enable the UniversalBrowserWrite
// privilege.
netscape.security.PrivilegeManager.enablePrivilege("UniversalBrowserWrite");

// Enable the external capturing of events.
window.enableExternalCapture();

// Specifically capture submit events.
window.captureEvents(Event.SUBMIT);

// Define a function to turn off these external event captures.
function turnOffEvents(){
  window.disableExternalCapture();
  alert("You have sucessfully turned off external event captures");
}
// -->
</script>
</head>
<body>
<form>
  <input type="button" value="Disable External Capturing"
        onclick="turnOffEvents()">
</form>
</body>
</html>
```

window.document

JavaScript1.0+, JScript1.0+
Nav2+, IE3+, Opera3+

Syntax

Creates Instance of Document Object.

window.document.*event*
window.document.*method( )*
window.document.*property*

Description

The document property, which is a child object of the Window object, is a core JavaScript object that is created when instances of the <body> tag are encountered. The properties, methods, and events associated with this object are in Table 8.40.

Table 8.40   Event Handlers, Methods, and Properties Used by the
`Window.document` *Property*

Type	Item	Description
Event Handler	`onClick`	Executes code when the document is clicked.
	`onDblClick`	Executes code when the document is double-clicked.
	`onKeyDown`	Executes code when a key is pressed down. This occurs before an `onKeyPress` event handler and was added in JavaScript 1.2.
	`onKeyPress`	Executes code when a key is pressed down immediately after an `onKeyDown` event handler. This event handler was added in JavaScript 1.2.
	`onKeyUp`	Executes code when a key is released. This was added in JavaScript 1.2.
	`onMouseDown`	Executes code when the mouse button is pressed down.
	`onMouseUp`	Executes code when the mouse button is released.
Method	`captureEvents()`	Allows you to capture all events of the type passed in the document. Note that this method was added in JavaScript 1.2.
	`close()`	Closes the stream to the document.
	`getSelection()`	Returns the currently selected text. Note that this method was added in JavaScript 1.2.
	`handleEvent()`	Invokes the handler for the event specified and was added in JavaScript 1.2.
	`open()`	Opens a stream to the document.
	`releaseEvents()`	Releases the events that you have captured of the type passed in the document. Note that this method was added in JavaScript 1.2.
	`routeEvent()`	Passes the specified event along the normal route of execution. Note that this method was added in JavaScript 1.2.
	`write()`	Writes the string passed to the document.
	`writeln()`	Writes the string, followed by a newline character, to the document.
Property	`alinkColor`	Specifies the `alink` attribute of the `<body>` tag.
	`anchors`	Array containing each `<a>` tag in a document.
	`applets`	Array containing each `<applet>` tag in a document. Note that this property was added in JavaScript 1.1.
	`bgColor`	Specifies the `bgcolor` attribute of the `<body>` tag.

Type	Item	Description
	cookie	Specifies a cookie.
	domain	Specifies the domain that served the document. Note that this property was added in JavaScript 1.1.
	embeds	Array containing each `<embed>` tag in a document. Note that this property was added in JavaScript 1.1.
	fgColor	Specifies the `text` attribute of the `<body>` tag.
	formName	The actual name of each `<form>` in a document. Note that this property was added in JavaScript 1.1.
	forms	Array containing each `<form>` tag in a document. Note that this property was added in JavaScript 1.1.
	images	Array containing each `<img>` tag in a document. Note that this property was added in JavaScript 1.1.
	lastModified	Specifies the date the document was last changed.
	layers	Array containing each `<layer>` tag in a document. Note that this property was added in JavaScript 1.2.
	linkColor	Specifies the `link` attribute of the `<body>` tag.
	links	Array containing each `<a>` and `<area>` tag in a document.
	plugins	Array containing each plug-in in a document. Note that this property was added in JavaScript 1.1.
	referrer	Specifies the referral URL.
	title	Contains the text between the beginning `<title>` and ending `</title>` tags.
	URL	Specifies the URL of the document.
	vlinkColor	Specifies the `vlink` attribute of the `<body>` tag.

See the entries in this chapter for the `Document` object for more information on each of these events, methods, and properties.

Example

Listing 8.529 uses the `write()` method of the `document` property to write text to the user's page.

Listing 8.529 *Accessing Methods of the* document *Property*

```
<script language="JavaScript" type="text/javascript">
<!--

// Simply writes out the Hello, World! text
window.document.write("Hello, World!");

// -->
</script>
```

window.enableExternalCapture()

JavaScript1.2+
Nav4+

Syntax

window.enableExternalCapture(*event*)

Description

The enableExternalCapture() method of the Window object enables external event capturing of the event that is passed to the method. This method provides the capturing of events in frames loaded from a different server. Before you can enable the capturing of these external events, you must first obtain UniversalBrowserWrite privilege. Obtaining this privilege will send a security dialog box to the user to decide whether to accept the request.

After it has been obtained and the method has been invoked, you use the Window.captureEvents() method to specify the events you want to capture. To remove the ability to capture these events, you can invoke the Window.disableExternalCapture() method. The types of events that can be captured are as follows:

- Event.ABORT
- Event.BLUR
- Event.CHANGE
- Event.CLICK
- Event.DBLCLICK
- Event.DRAGDROP
- Event.ERROR
- Event.FOCUS
- Event.KEYDOWN
- Event.KEYPRESS
- Event.KEYUP
- Event.LOAD
- Event.MOUSEDOWN
- Event.MOUSEMOVE
- Event.MOUSEOUT

- Event.MOUSEOVER
- Event.MOUSEUP
- Event.MOVE
- Event.RESET
- Event.RESIZE
- Event.SELECT
- Event.SUBMIT
- Event.UNLOAD

NOTE

For more information on privileges, JavaScript security, and signed scripts, see Chapter 1.

Example

Listing 8.530 enables external event capturing when the document loads.

Listing 8.530   Enabling External Event Capturing

```
<script language="JavaScript1.2" type="text/javascript">
<!--

// Ask the user for permission to enable the UniversalBrowserWrite
// privilege.
netscape.security.PrivilegeManager.enablePrivilege("UniversalBrowserWrite");

// Enable the external capturing of events.
window.enableExternalCapture();

// Specifically capture submit events.
window.captureEvents(Event.SUBMIT);

// -->
</script>
```

window.find()

JavaScript1.2, JScript3.0
Nav4, IE4

Syntax

window.find()

Description

The find() method of the Window object displays a find dialog box when invoked. This allows a user to search for a string in the page from which it was invoked.

> **NOTE**
>
> This method was only supported in the version 4 browsers, and has been removed since then.

Example

Listing 8.531 has a function that pops up a Find box when it is called.

Listing 8.531 _A Find Box That Can Be Used to Search for Text in the Document_

```
<script language="JavaScript1.2" type="text/javascript">
<!--

// Displays the Find window.
function mySearch(){
  window.find();
}

// -->
</script>
```

window.focus()
JavaScript1.1+, JScript1.0+
Nav3+, IE3+, Opera3+

Syntax

```
window.focus()
```

Description

The focus() method of the Window object places focus on the window. Be careful when using this method in conjunction with the blur() method of objects. It can lead to a focus/blur loop, where the browser blurs a focus as soon as it is done, and vice versa.

Example

Listing 8.532 has a button. When the user clicks the Open button, a second, smaller window is opened, and the focus is placed back on the parent window.

Listing 8.532 _Using the_ focus() _Method to Remove Focus from a Window_

```
<html>
<head>
</head>
```

```
<script language="JavaScript" type="text/javascript">
<!--

// Define the openWin() function.
function openWin(){

  // Create variables to hold the various options that can be set
  // when a new Window instance is created.
  var myBars = 'directories=no,location=no,menubar=no,status=no';
  myBars += ',titlebar=no,toolbar=no';
  var myOptions = 'scrollbars=no,width=400,height=200,resizeable=no';
  var myFeatures = myBars + ',' + myOptions;

  // Open a child window.
  newWin = open('', 'myDoc', myFeatures);

  newWin.document.writeln('Here is the child window');

  // Close the stream to the document.
  newWin.document.close();

  // Return focus to the parent window.
  self.focus();
}

// -->
</script>
<body>
<form>
  <input type="button" value="Open" onclick='openWin()'>
</form>
</body>
</html>
```

window.forward()

JavaScript1.2+, Jscript3.0
Nav4+, IE4+

Syntax

window.forward()

Description

The forward() method of the Window object simulates the user clicking the Forward button on the browser. It returns the browser's page or frame to the next page or frame in its history.

Example

Listing 8.533 has two buttons. One of the buttons takes the browser back one page and the other button takes it forward. Note that there has to be a back and forward page during your session for the button to have somewhere to go.

Listing 8.533 *Using the* forward() *Method to Take the User to the Next Page in His History*

```
<html>
<body>
<form>
  <input type="button" value="Back" onclick="window.back()">
  <input type="button" value="Forward" onclick="window.forward()">
</form>
</body>
</html>
```

window.frames

JavaScript1.0+, JScript1.0+
Nav2+, IE3+, Opera3+

Syntax

```
window.frames["frameName"]
window.frames[num]
```

Description

The frames property of the Window object contains an array that stores each frame instance, created with the <frame> tag, in a document. Array entries of the child frame can be referenced either by index number or by the name assigned by the name attribute of the <frame> tag.

Example

Listing 8.534 uses the length property of frames array and a for loop to access the name of each frame in the window. This information is then written to the document window.

Listing 8.534 *Example of Using the* frames *Property*

```
<script language="JavaScript" type="text/javascript">
<!--

// Use a for loop to write out the name of each frame.
for(var i = 0; i <= window.frames.length; i++){
  newWin.document.write("The name of frame #" + i);
  newWin.document.write(" is " + window.frames[i].name + "<br>");
}
// -->
</script>
```

window.frames.length

JavaScript1.0+, JScript1.0+
Nav2+, IE3+, Opera3+

Syntax

```
window.frames["frameName"].length
window.frames[num].length
```

Description

The `length` sub property of the `frames` property of the `Window` object contains the number of frame instances in a document created with the `<frame>` tag.

Example

Listing 8.535 uses the `length` property of the `frames` array and a `for` loop to access the name of each frame in the window. This information is then written to the document window.

Listing 8.535   *Using the* `length` *Property*

```
<script language="JavaScript" type="text/javascript">
<!--

// Use a for loop to write out the name of each frame.
for(var i = 0; i <= window.frames.length; i++){
  newWin.document.write("The name of frame #" + i);
  newWin.document.write(" is " + window.frames[i].name + "<br>");
}
// -->
</script>
```

window.handleEvent()

JavaScript1.2+, JScript3.0+
Nav4+, IE4+

Syntax

```
window.object.handleEvent(event)
```

Description

The `handleEvent()` method of the `Window` object invokes the handler for the event specified of the specified object. This method was added in JavaScript 1.2.

Example

Listing 8.536 has a single text box. The script tells the browser that it wants to intercept all `Click` events and that it wants the `myClickHandler` function to handle them. Within this function, the `handleEvent()` method of the text box has been specified to handle the click.

When the user clicks anywhere on the page, the onClick event handler in the <input type="text"> tag calls a function to change the text in the text box. The change is nothing more than a simple number that is incremented, counting the number of times the page has been clicked.

Listing 8.536 ***Using the*** `handleEvent()` ***Method of a*** `Window` ***Object to Handle All Clicks on a Page***

```
<html>
<head>
<script language="JavaScript1.2" type="text/javascript">
<!--

// Define a click counter variable.
var counter = 0;

// Tell the browser you want to intercept ALL click events
// on the page. Then define a function to handle them.
window.captureEvents(Event.CLICK)
window.onClick = myClickHandler;

// Define the myClickHandler function to handle click events.
function myClickHandler(e){

  // Pass all click events to the onClick event of the text box.
  window.document.myForm.myText.handleEvent(e);
}

// Function is called by onClick of text box. Displays the number
// of clicks that have occurred.
function changeText(){
  document.myForm.myText.value = counter++;
}
// -->
</script>
</head>
<body>
<form name="myForm">
  <input type="text" size="2" value="" name="myText" onclick='changeText()'>
</form>
</body>
</html>
```

window.history

JavaScript1.1+, JScript1.0+
Nav3+, IE3+, Opera3+

Syntax

```
window.history[num]
window.history.method()
window.history.property
```

Description

The `history` property of the `Window` object is actually one of the core JavaScript objects. This object contains an array of the names and URLs of the pages the window has visited. A specific URL in the `history` array can be accessed by specifying the indexed location, *num*, that represents the URL about which you want to retrieve information.

Also, as defined in the syntax definition, the methods and properties of this object are also accessible for programming use. Table 8.41 has a list of each of these, followed by a description.

Table 8.41 **Methods and Properties Used by the** `Window.history` **Property**

Type	Item	Description
Method	back	References the URL that is located one page back from the current page.
	forward	References the URL that is located one page ahead of the current page.
	go	Loads the URL passed to the method. This can be in relation to the current URL or a string representing part or the whole URL you want to access.
Property	current	Reflects the current URL of the window. This property was added in JavaScript 1.1.
	length	Reflects the number of URLs in the history of the window.
	next	Reflects the next URL in the history in relation to the current URL. This property was added in JavaScript 1.1.
	previous	Reflects the last URL in the history in relation to the current URL. This property was added in JavaScript 1.1.

For more information on the `History` object and its properties and methods, see its entry in this chapter.

Example

Listing 8.537 has two buttons that allow a user to move forward and back in his history.

Listing 8.537   Using the history *Array to Access Pages Visited*

```
<html>
<body>
<form>
  <input type="button" value="Back" onclick="window.history.back()">
  <input type="button" value="Forward" onclick="window.history.forward()">
</form>
</body>
</html>
```

window.home()

JavaScript1.2+, JScript3.0
Nav4+, IE4+

Syntax

```
window.home()
```

Description

The home() method of the Window object simulates the user clicking the Home button on the browser. It takes the browser to the user's specified home page.

Example

Listing 8.538 has a single button that, when clicked, takes the browser to the user's home page.

Listing 8.538   Using the home() *Method to Go to the User's Home Page*

```
<form>
<h3>Home James!</h3>
  <input type="button" value="Home" onclick="window.home()">
</form>
```

window.innerHeight

JavaScript1.2+
Nav4+

Syntax

```
window.innerHeight
```

Description

The innerHeight property of the Window object references the pixel height of the document within the browser's frame. This does not include any of the toolbars or other "chrome" that makes up the frame itself.

Example

Listing 8.539 has a button that, when clicked, opens up a second, smaller window. The
`innerHeight` property is written to this new window.

Listing 8.539   Using the `innerHeight` Property

```
<html>
<head>
<script language="JavaScript1.2" type="text/javascript">
<!--

// Define a function to open a small window.
function openWin(){

  // Create variables to hold the various options that can be set
  // when a new Window instance is created.
  var myBars = 'directories=no,location=no,menubar=no,status=no';
  myBars += ',titlebar=no,toolbar=no';
  var myOptions = 'scrollbars=no,width=400,height=200,resizeable=no';
  var myFeatures = myBars + ',' + myOptions;

  // Open the window. Give the window instance the name newDoc and
  // name the document in the window myDoc.
  var newWin = open('', 'myDoc', myFeatures);

  // Write the window height and width properties to the new window.
  newWin.document.writeln('<h4>Properties for this Window</h4>');
  newWin.document.writeln('innerHeight: ' + newWin.innerHeight + '<br>');
  newWin.document.writeln('innerWidth: ' + newWin.innerWidth + '<br>');
  newWin.document.writeln('outerHeight: ' + newWin.outerHeight + '<br>');
  newWin.document.writeln('outerWidth: ' + newWin.outerWidth + '<br>');
  newWin.document.writeln('<form>');
  newWin.document.writeln('<input type="button" value="Close"');
  newWin.document.writeln(' onclick="window.close()">');
  newWin.document.writeln('</form>');

  // Close the stream to the document.
  newWin.document.close();

}
// -->
</script>
</head>
<body>
<form>
  <input type="button" value="Open" onclick="openWin()">
</form>
</body>
</html>
```

window.innerWidth

JavaScript1.2+
Nav4+

Syntax

```
window.innerWidth
```

Description

The `innerWidth` property of the `Window` object references the pixel width of the document within the browser's frame. This does not include any of the toolbars or other "chrome" that makes up the frame itself.

Example

Listing 8.540 has a button that, when clicked, opens up a second, smaller window. The `innerWidth` property is written to this new window.

Listing 8.540   Using the `innerWidth` *Property*

```
<html>
<head>
<script language="JavaScript1.2" type="text/javascript">
<!--

// Define a function to open a small window.
function openWin(){

  // Create variables to hold the various options that can be set
  // when a new Window instance is created.
  var myBars = 'directories=no,location=no,menubar=no,status=no';
  myBars += ',titlebar=no,toolbar=no';
  var myOptions = 'scrollbars=no,width=400,height=200,resizeable=no';
  var myFeatures = myBars + ',' + myOptions;

  // Open the window. Give the window instance the name newWin and
  // name the document in the window myDoc.
  var newWin = open('', 'myDoc', myFeatures);

  // Write the window height and width properties to the new window.
  newWin.document.writeln('<h4>Properties for this Window</h4>');
  newWin.document.writeln('innerHeight: ' + newWin.innerHeight + '<br>');
  newWin.document.writeln('innerWidth: ' + newWin.innerWidth + '<br>');
  newWin.document.writeln('outerHeight: ' + newWin.outerHeight + '<br>');
  newWin.document.writeln('outerWidth: ' + newWin.outerWidth + '<br>');
  newWin.document.writeln('<form>');
  newWin.document.writeln('<input type="button" value="Close"');
  newWin.document.writeln(' onclick="window.close()">');
  newWin.document.writeln('</form>');
```

```
    // Close the stream to the document.
    newWin.document.close();

}
// -->
</script>
</head>
<body>
<form>
    <input type="button" value="Open" onclick="openWin()">
</form>
</body>
</html>
```

window.length

JavaScript1.0+, JScript1.0+
Nav2+, IE3+, Opera3+

Syntax

window.length

Description

The length property of the Window object represents the number of frames within a window. This returns the same results as Window.frames.length.

Example

Listing 8.541 shows a function that can be used to return the number of frames in a window.

Listing 8.541 *Using the* length *Property of the* Window *Object*

```
<script language="JavaScript" type="text/javascript">
<!--

// Define a function to return the number of frames in the
// window passed.
function numFrames(win){
    return win.length;
}

// -->
</script>
```

window.location

JavaScript1.0+, JScript1.0+
Nav2+, IE3+, Opera3+

Syntax

window.location

Description

The location property of the Window object returns the current URL of the document in the window.

Example

Listing 8.542 pops up an alert box that contains the URL of the current window.

Listing 8.542 *Using the* location *Property of the* Window *Object*

```
<script language="JavaScript" type="text/javascript">
<!--

// Display the current URL in an alert box.
alert(window.location);

// -->
</script>
```

window.locationbar

JavaScript1.2+
Nav4+

Syntax

window.locationbar.*property*

Description

The locationbar property of the Window object is, to some degree, an object itself. The real use of this property is to access its visible property to determine whether the location bar is visible to the user.

> **NOTE**
>
> As of this writing, the locationbar property only has one subproperty: visible.

Example

See the example of Window.locationbar.visible for an example of using the locationbar property.

window.locationbar.visible

JavaScript1.2+
Nav4+

Syntax

```
window.locationbar.visible
```

Description

The `visible` subproperty of the `locationbar` property of the `Window` is used to determine whether the location bar is visible to the user. If it is visible, the property returns `true`. It returns `false` if the bar is not visible.

Example

Listing 8.543 determines whether several of the browser bars are displayed. In the example, you will see whether the location bar is visible by using the `visible` property.

Listing 8.543   *Using the* `visible` *Property of* `locationbar`

```
<script language="JavaScript" type="text/javascript">
<!--

// Write the browser's bar status to the page. If the value
// is true, then it is displayed.
document.writeln('<h3>Browser Chrome Status</h3>')
document.writeln('Menu Bar: ' + window.menubar.visible + '<br>');
document.writeln('Tool Bar: ' + window.toolbar.visible + '<br>');
document.writeln('Location Bar: ' + window.locationbar.visible + '<br>');
document.writeln('Personal Bar: ' + window.personalbar.visible + '<br>');
document.writeln('Scroll Bars: ' + window.scrollbars.visible + '<br>');
document.writeln('Status Bar: ' + window.statusbar.visible + '<br>');

// Close the stream to the document.
document.close();


// -->
</script>
```

window.menubar

JavaScript1.2+
Nav4+

Syntax

```
window.menubar.property
```

Description

The `menubar` property of the `Window` object is, to some degree, an object itself. The real use of this property is to access its `visible` property to determine whether the menu bar is visible to the user.

NOTE

As of this writing, the `menubar` property only has one subproperty: `visible`.

Example

See the example of `Window.menubar.visible` for an example of using the `menubar` property.

window.menubar.visible

JavaScript1.2+
Nav4+

Syntax

```
window.menubar.visible
```

Description

The `visible` subproperty of the `menubar` property of the `Window` is used to determine whether the menu bar is visible to the user. If it is visible, the property returns `true`. It returns `false` if the bar is not visible.

Example

Listing 8.544 determines whether several of the browser bars are displayed. In the example, you will see whether the menu bar is visible by using the `visible` property.

Listing 8.544   Using the `visible` *Property of* `menubar`

```
<script language="JavaScript" type="text/javascript">
<!--

// Write the browser's bar status to the page. If the value
// is true, then it is displayed.
document.writeln('<h3>Browser Chrome Status</h3>')
document.writeln('Menu Bar: ' + window.menubar.visible + '<br>');
document.writeln('Tool Bar: ' + window.toolbar.visible + '<br>');
document.writeln('Location Bar: ' + window.locationbar.visible + '<br>');
document.writeln('Personal Bar: ' + window.personalbar.visible + '<br>');
document.writeln('Scroll Bars: ' + window.scrollbars.visible + '<br>');
document.writeln('Status Bar: ' + window.statusbar.visible + '<br>');
```

```
// Close the stream to the document.
document.close();

// -->
</script>
```

window.moveBy()

JavaScript1.2+, JScript3.0+
Nav4+, IE4+

Syntax

window.moveBy(*numHorz, numVert*)

Description

The moveBy() method of the Window object moves the specified window by the number of pixels passed to the method. As shown in the syntax definition, the first numeric value passed to the method represents the number of horizontal pixels you want to move the window, whereas the second numeric value represents the vertical number of pixels.

If the numbers passed are positive, the window is moved to the right horizontally, and down vertically. Negative numbers move the window in the opposite direction.

Example

Listing 8.545 has four buttons: Up, Down, Right, and Left. If you click these buttons, the window the document is loaded in will move one pixel at a time in that direction.

Listing 8.545   Using the moveBy() ***Method to Move the Location of a Window***

```
<html>
<head>
</head>
<script language="JavaScript1.2" type="text/javascript">
<!--

// Define a function to handle the window movement.
function moveWin(dir, dist){

  // Define variables to hold the movement values.
  var myVert;
  var myHorz;

  // Determine the type of movement.
  if(dir == "vert"){
    myHorz = 0;
```

Listing 8.545 Continued

```
    myVert = dist;
  }else{
    myHorz = dist;
    myVert = 0;
  }

  // Move the window.
  window.moveBy(myHorz, myVert);
}
// -->
</script>
<body>
<form>
<table border=0>
  <tr>
    <td></td>
    <td><input type="button" value="  Up  " onclick="moveWin('vert',-1)"></td>
    <td></td>
  </tr>
  <tr>
    <td><input type="button" value=" Left " onclick="moveWin('horz',-1)"></td>
    <td></td>
    <td><input type="button" value="Right" onclick="moveWin('horz',1)"></td>
  </tr>
  <tr>
    <td></td>
    <td><input type="button" value="Down" onclick="moveWin('vert',1)"></td>
    <td></td>
  </tr>
</table>
</form>
</body>
</html>
```

window.moveTo()

JavaScript1.2+, JScript3.0+
Nav4+, IE4+

Syntax

window.moveTo(*numX, numY*)

Description

The moveTo() method of the Window object moves the specified window to the specified location passed to the method. As shown in the syntax definition, the first numeric
value passed to the method represents the x coordinate to which you want to move the
window, whereas the second numeric value represents the y coordinate.

Example

Listing 8.546 has two text fields and a button. If the user enters an integer value in each of the text fields and clicks the button, the window will move to that location.

Listing 8.546 Using the `moveTo()` *Method to Move the Location of a* Window

```
<html>
<head>
</head>
<script language="JavaScript1.2" type="text/javascript">
<!--

// Define a function to handle the window movement.
function moveWin(form){

  // Define variables to hold the movement values.
  var myX = form.X.value;
  var myY = form.Y.value;

  // Move the window.
  window.moveTo(myX, myY);
}
// -->
</script>
<body>
<form>
  <b>X-Coordinate:</b>
  <input type="text" name="X"><br>
  <b>Y-Coordinate:</b>
  <input type="text" name="Y"><br>
  <input type="button" value="Move Window" onclick="moveWin(this.form)"></td>
</form>
</body>
</html>
```

window.name

JavaScript1.0+, JScript1.0+
Nav2+, IE3+, Opera3+

Syntax

window.name

Description

The `name` property of an instance of a `Window` object returns the name of the window. This property contains the name specified when new windows are created using the `Window.open()` method. In JavaScript 1.0, this property was read only, but this was changed in JavaScript 1.1 so that you can assign a name to a window not created with the `Window.open()` method. This property was tainted in JavaScript 1.1 as well.

Example

Listing 8.547 has a button that launches a second window. The name of the window is written to it using the `name` property of the `Window` object.

Listing 8.547   Using the name **Property to Retrieve the Name of a Window**

```html
<html>
<head>
<script language="JavaScript" type="text/javascript">
<!--

// Define a function to open a small window.
function openWin(){

  // Create variables to hold the various options that can be set
  // when a new Window instance is created.
  var myBars = 'directories=no,location=no,menubar=no,status=no';
  myBars += ',titlebar=no,toolbar=no';
  var myOptions = 'scrollbars=no,width=400,height=200,resizeable=no';
  var myFeatures = myBars + ',' + myOptions;

  // Open the window. Give the window instance the name newWin and
  // name the document in the window myDoc.
  var newWin = open('', 'myDoc', myFeatures);

  // Write the window's name to the new window.
  newWin.document.writeln('This window\'s name is: ' + newWin.name + '<br>');
  newWin.document.writeln('<form>');
  newWin.document.writeln('<input type="button" value="Close"');
  newWin.document.writeln(' onclick="window.close()">');
  newWin.document.writeln('</form>');

  // Close the stream to the document.
  newWin.document.close();

}
// -->
</script>
</head>
<body>
<form>
  <input type="button" value="Open" onclick="openWin()">
</form>
</body>
</html>
```

window.offscreenBuffering

JavaScript1.2, JScript3.0+
Nav4+, IE4+

Syntax

```
window.offscreenBuffering = boolean
```

Description

The `offscreenBuffering` property of the `Window` object is used to explicitly instruct the browser whether to buffer data offscreen before displaying. Without doing this, a user's window might flicker as the page is being drawn. This property simply takes a *boolean* value of `true` or `false` to set it.

Example

Listing 8.548 shows how you can instruct the browser to not buffer data offscreen.

Listing 8.548   Using the `offscreenBuffering` ***Property***

```
<script type="text/javascript" language="JavaScript1.2">
<!--

// Disallow off screen buffering
window.offscreenBuffering = false;

//-->
</script>
```

window.onBlur

JavaScript1.0+, JScript1.0+
Nav2+, IE3+, Opera3+

Syntax

```
onblur="command"
```

Description

The `onBlur` event handler is a property of a `Window` object and is fired when the focus is moved away from that particular window instance. Care should be taken when using this event handler because it is possible to get into an infinite loop when using the `onFocus` event handler or the `focus()` method. Note that when this event handler is called within the `<body>` tag, it is overridden if a `<frame>` tag that also uses this event handler loaded the document.

NOTE

Some Navigator 3 browsers do not fully support this event handler when called in a `<frameset>` tag.

Example

Listing 8.549 has a frame set with two frames. The first frame, toc, has the onBlur event handler specified in its tag. When focus leaves this frame, the event is fired and the myBlurFunc() function will be called.

Listing 8.549   Example of Using the onBlur Event

```
<frameset cols="150,*">
  <frame name="toc"
         src="/toc.htm"
         onblur='myBlurFunc()'
         marginwidth="1" marginheight="1" scrolling="auto">
  <frame name="body"
         src="/body.htm"
         marginwidth="1" marginheight="5" scrolling="auto">
</frameset>
```

window.onDragDrop

> JavaScript1.2+
> Nav4+

Syntax

```
ondragdrop="command"
```

Description

The onDragDrop event handler of a property of a Window object is fired when the user drops an object, such as a file, on that particular window instance.

Example

In Listing 8.550, if you try to drop a new file on to the browser when this page is loaded, you will be asked to confirm this operation. If you accept, the page will load. If you cancel, the page will not load.

Listing 8.550   Example of Using the onDragDrop Event

```
<html>
<body ondragdrop='return(confirm("Are you sure you want to continue?"))'>
Try to drop an element on this page.
</body>
</html>
```

window.onError

> JavaScript1.1+, JScript1.0+
> Nav3+, IE3+, Opera3+

Syntax

```
onerror="command"
```

Description

The `onError` event handler of the `Window` object is fired when an error occurs loading the page. You might find this useful to try and reload the page, using the `reload()` method of the `Location` object.

Example

Listing 8.551 is an example of placing the `onError` event handler in the `<body>` tag. If there is an error when loading this page, an alert box will be displayed to the user.

Listing 8.551   *Example of Using the* `onError` *Event Handler*

```
<body onerror='alert("Error: There has been an error loading this page.")'>
```

window.onFocus

JavaScript1.0+, JScript1.0+
Nav2+, IE3+, Opera3+

Syntax

```
onfocus="command"
```

Description

The `onFocus` event handler of a property of a `Window` object is fired when the focus is placed on that particular window instance. Care should be taken when using this event handler because it is possible to get into an infinite loop when using `onBlur` event handler or `blur()` method. Note that when this event handler is called within the `<body>` tag, it is overridden if a `<frame>` tag that also uses this event handler loaded the document.

NOTE

Some Navigator 3 browsers do not fully support this event handler when called in a `<frameset>` tag.

Example

Listing 8.552 has a frame set with two frames. The first frame, `toc`, has the `onFocus` event handler specified in its tag. When the focus leaves this frame, the event is fired and the `myFocusFunc()` function (not shown) will be called.

Listing 8.552   *Example of Using the* `onFocus` *Event*

```
<frameset cols="150,*">
  <frame name="toc"
         src="/toc.htm"
         onfocus='myFocusFunc()'
         marginwidth="1" marginheight="1" scrolling="auto">
```

Listing 8.552 *Continued*

```
  <frame name="body"
         src="/body.htm"
         marginwidth="1" marginheight="5" scrolling="auto">
</frameset>
```

window.onLoad

JavaScript1.0+, JScript1.0+
Nav2+, IE3+, Opera3+

Syntax

```
onload="command"
```

Description

The onLoad event handler of a property of a Window object is fired when the page has finished loading in that particular window instance.

> **NOTE**
>
> The onLoad event handler in the <body> of a document that is loaded in a frame will fire before an event handler loaded in the <frameset> tag that loaded the document.

Example

Listing 8.553 pops up an alert box when the page has finished loading.

Listing 8.553 *Example of Using the* onLoad *Event*

```
<body onload='alert("The document has completely loaded.")'>
```

window.onMove

JavaScript1.2+
Nav4+

Syntax

```
onmove="command"
```

Description

The onMove event handler of a property of a Window object is fired when the window it is referenced in is moved. The user physically moving the window or a script moving it can fire this event.

Example

Listing 8.554 pops up an alert box if the user tries to move the window.

Listing 8.554   Using the onMove **Event to Display an Alert Box**

```
<body onmove='alert("Do NOT move this window!")'>
```

window.onResize

JavaScript1.2+
Nav4+

Syntax

```
onresize="command"
```

Description

The onResize event handler of a property of a Window object is fired when the window it is referenced in is resized. The user physically resizing the window or a script resizing it can fire this event.

Example

Listing 8.555 pops up an alert box if the user tries to resize the window.

Listing 8.555   Using the onResize **Event to Display an Alert Box**

```
<body onresize='alert("Do NOT resize this window!")'>
```

window.onUnload

JavaScript 1.0+, JScript 1.0+
Nav2+, IE3+, Opera3+

Syntax

```
onunload="command"
```

Description

The onUnload event handler of a property of a Window object is fired when the page is unloaded in that particular window instance. This occurs when the user leaves the page for another page.

> **NOTE**
>
> The onUnLoad event handler in the <body> of a document that is loaded in a frame will fire before an event handler loaded in the <frameset> tag that loaded the document.

Example

Listing 8.556 pops up an alert box when the user leaves the page.

Listing 8.556   Example of Using the onUnLoad *Event*

```
<body onunload='alert("Please do not leave!")'>
```

window.open()

JavaScript1.0+, JScript1.0+
Nav2+, IE3+, Opera3+

Syntax

```
window.open(pageURL, name, parameters)
```

Description

The open() method of the Window object creates a new instance of a window. It loads the *pageURL* passed to the method in a window based on the *parameters* specified. The action attribute of the <form> tag and the target attribute of the <a> tag can reference the window by the *name* passed.

Most of the *parameters* passed, which are listed without spaces and commas, are toggled on and off by setting them to yes or no. It is also possible to use 1 or 0 to turn these features on or off. Either way, you should be consistent across each of the options. Table 8.42 has the different *parameters* that can be passed and how to turn them on and off.

> **NOTE**
>
> If you place spaces in the parameter string, the options will not work. Be sure to comma separate each of these options and do not insert any spaces.

Table 8.42   Parameters That Can Be Passed When Creating a New Instance of the Window *Object Using the* open() *Method*

Parameter	Initialize With	Description
alwaysLowered	yes/no	This parameter tells the window to stay behind all other windows. This must be done in signed scripts because it is a secure feature and was implemented in JavaScript 1.2.
alwaysRaised	yes/no	This parameter tells the window to stay on top of all other windows. This must be done in signed scripts because it is a secure feature and was implemented in JavaScript 1.2.
dependent	yes/no	This parameter opens the window as a true child window of the parent window. When the parent window is closed, so is the child window. This feature was implemented in JavaScript 1.2.
directories	yes/no	Specifies whether the directory bar on Navigator 2 and 3 is visible on the new window.

Parameter	Initialize With	Description
height	pixel value	Sets the height in pixels of the window. This feature, although still existent for backward compatibility, was removed in JavaScript 1.2 and replaced with innerHeight.
hotkeys	yes/no	Disables all but the Security and Quit hotkeys in a new window with no menu bar. This feature was implemented in JavaScript 1.2.
innerHeight	pixel value	Sets the height in pixels of the document in the window. This feature was implemented in JavaScript 1.2.
innerWidth	pixel value	Sets the width in pixels of the document in the window. This feature was implemented in JavaScript 1.2.
location	yes/no	Specifies whether the location bar is visible on the new window.
menubar	yes/no	Specifies whether the menu bar is visible on the new window.
outerHeight	pixel value	Sets the height in pixels of the window, including the chrome. This feature was implemented in JavaScript 1.2.
outerWidth	pixel value	Sets the width in pixels of the window, including the chrome. This feature was implemented in JavaScript 1.2.
resizable	yes/no	Specifies whether the window can be resized.
screenX	pixel value	Sets the distance in pixels of the window from the left side of the screen. This feature was implemented in JavaScript 1.2.
screenY	pixel value	Sets the distance in pixels of the window from the top of the screen. This feature was implemented in JavaScript 1.2.
scrollbars	yes/no	Specifies whether the scrollbars are visible on the new window.
titlebar	yes/no	Specifies whether the title bar is visible on the new window.
toolbar	yes/no	Specifies whether the toolbar is visible on the new window.
width	pixel value	Sets the width in pixels of the window. This feature, although still existent for backward compatibility, was removed in JavaScript 1.2 and replaced with innerWidth.

Table 8.42 Continued

Parameter	Initialize With	Description
z-lock	yes/no	Specifies that the window is not supposed to be located above other windows when it is made active. This feature was implemented in JavaScript 1.2.

NOTE

It is possible to open windows that are not on the physical screen. However, this is a secure feature and must be in a signed script to implement.

Example

Listing 8.557 has a single button that opens a new window when clicked. As you can see in the creation of the window, various parameters are passed that define how the window should look when opened.

Listing 8.557 Using the open() *Method to Open a New Window*

```
<html>

<script language="JavaScript" type="text/javascript">
<!--

// Define the openWin() function.
function openWin(){

  // Create variables to hold the various options that can be set
  // when a new Window instance is created.
  var myBars = 'directories=no,location=no,menubar=no,status=no';
  myBars += ',titlebar=no,toolbar=no';
  var myOptions = 'scrollbars=no,width=400,height=200,resizeable=no';
  var myFeatures = myBars + ',' + myOptions;
  var myReadme = "Welcome to Pure JavaScript!\n" +
         "----------------------------------------\n" +
       'You can enter some text here.'

  // Open the window. Give the window instance the name newWin and
  // name the document in the window myDoc.
  var newWin = open('', 'myDoc', myFeatures);

  newWin.document.writeln('<form>');
  newWin.document.writeln('<table cellspacing="0" cellpadding="0"
border="1">');
  newWin.document.writeln('<tr valign="top" bgcolor="#000099"><td>');
  newWin.document.writeln('<font size="-1" color="#ffffff"><b>');
  newWin.document.writeln('  Readme</b></font>');
```

```
newWin.document.writeln('</td></tr>');
newWin.document.writeln('<tr valign="top"><td>');
newWin.document.writeln('<textarea cols="45" rows="7" wrap="soft">');
newWin.document.writeln(myReadme + '</textarea>');
newWin.document.writeln('</td></tr>');
newWin.document.writeln('<tr valign="bottom" align="right"');
newWin.document.writeln(' bgcolor="#c0c0c0"><td>');
newWin.document.writeln('<input type="button" value="Close"');
newWin.document.writeln(' onclick="window.close()">');
newWin.document.writeln('</td></tr>');
newWin.document.writeln('</table></form>');

// Close the stream to the document and bring the window to the front.
newWin.document.close();
newWin.focus();
}

// -->
</script>
<body>
<form>
  <b>Click the following button to open a new window: </b>
  <input type="button" value="Open" onclick='openWin()'>
</form>
</body>
</html>
```

window.opener

JavaScript1.1+, JScript1.0+
Nav3+, IE3+, Opera3+

Syntax

window.opener
window.opener.*method*
window.opener.*property*

Description

The opener property of the Window object corresponds to the window that opens the window from which the property was accessed. When accessed by a child window, it returns the parent window. With this property, you can then invoke methods and access properties of the Window object on the "opener" window. This property can also be set in scripts that allow the browser to clean up the reference to the parent window if it is closed before the child window. Most browsers have limits on the number of open windows they can have, and, by cleaning up these closed windows, you are able to regain the ability to open more windows if your limit has been reached. This is accomplished by setting the opener property to null.

Example

Listing 8.558 has a button that opens a second window when clicked. In the second window, there is a button that closes the parent window by referencing it via the opener property. After the close() method has been called on this window, the opener property is set to null to clean up the parent window.

Listing 8.558   *Using the* opener *Property to Return the Parent Window*

```
<html>
<head>

<script language="JavaScript" type="text/javascript">
<!--

// Define the openWin() function.
function openWin(){

  // Create variables to hold the various options that can be set
  // when a new Window instance is created.
  var myBars = 'directories=no,location=no,menubar=no,status=no';
  myBars += ',titlebar=no,toolbar=no';
  var myOptions = 'scrollbars=no,width=400,height=200,resizeable=no';
  var myFeatures = myBars + ',' + myOptions;
  var myReadme = "Welcome to Pure JavaScript!\n" +
       "----------------------------------------\n" +
       'You can enter some text here.'

  // Open the window. Give the window instance the name newWin and
  // name the document in the window myDoc.
  var newWin = open('', 'myDoc', myFeatures);

  newWin.document.writeln('<form>');
  newWin.document.writeln('<table cellspacing="0" cellpadding="0"
border="1">');
  newWin.document.writeln('<tr valign="top" bgcolor="#000099"><td>');
  newWin.document.writeln('<font size="-1" color="#ffffff"><b>');
  newWin.document.writeln('  Readme</b></font>');
  newWin.document.writeln('</td></tr>');
  newWin.document.writeln('<tr valign="top"><td>');
  newWin.document.writeln('<textarea cols="45" rows="7" wrap="soft">');
  newWin.document.writeln(myReadme + '</textarea>');
  newWin.document.writeln('</td></tr>');
  newWin.document.writeln('<tr valign="bottom" align="right" ');
  newWin.document.writeln('bgcolor="#c0c0c0"><td>');

  // Close the opener window and clean it up
  newWin.document.writeln('<input type="button" value="Close"');
  var myJS = "window.opener.close();window.opener=null"
  newWin.document.writeln('onclick="' + myJS + '">');
```

```
newWin.document.writeln('</td></tr>');
newWin.document.writeln('</table></form>');

// Close the stream to the document and bring the window to the front.
newWin.document.close();
newWin.focus();
}

// -->
</script>
</head>
<body>
<form>
  <b>Click the following button to open a new window: </b>
  <input type="button" value="Open" onclick='openWin()'>
</form>
</body>
</html>
```

window.outerHeight

JavaScript1.2+
Nav4+

Syntax

window.outerHeight

Description

The outerHeight property of the Window object references the pixel height of the browser's frame. This includes any of the toolbars or other "chrome" that makes up the frame itself.

Example

Listing 8.559 has a button that, when clicked, opens up a second, smaller window. The outerHeight property is written to this new window.

Listing 8.559   *Using the* outerHeight *Property*

```
<html>
<head>
<script language="JavaScript1.2" type="text/javascript">
<!--

// Define a function to open a small window.
function openWin(){

  // Create variables to hold the various options that can be set
```

Listing 8.559   Continued

```
// when a new Window instance is created.
var myBars = 'directories=no,location=no,menubar=no,status=no';
myBars += ',titlebar=no,toolbar=no';
var myOptions = 'scrollbars=no,width=400,height=200,resizeable=no';
var myFeatures = myBars + ',' + myOptions;

// Open the window. Give the window instance the name newWin and
// name the document in the window myDoc.
var newWin = open('', 'myDoc', myFeatures);

// Write the window height and width properties to the new window.
newWin.document.writeln('<h4>Properties for this Window</h4>');
newWin.document.writeln('innerHeight: ' + newWin.innerHeight + '<br>');
newWin.document.writeln('innerWidth: ' + newWin.innerWidth + '<br>');
newWin.document.writeln('outerHeight: ' + newWin.outerHeight + '<br>');
newWin.document.writeln('outerWidth: ' + newWin.outerWidth + '<br>');
newWin.document.writeln('<form>');
newWin.document.writeln('<input type="button" value="Close"');
newWin.document.writeln(' onclick="window.close()">');
newWin.document.writeln('</form>');

// Close the stream to the document.
newWin.document.close();

}
// -->
</script>
</head>
<body>
<form>
  <input type="button" value="Open" onclick="openWin()">
</form>
</body>
</html>
```

window.outerWidth

JavaScript1.2+
Nav4+

Syntax

window.outerWidth

Description

The outerWidth property of the Window object references the pixel width of the browser's frame. This includes any of the toolbars or other "chrome" that make up the frame itself.

Example

Listing 8.560 has a button that, when clicked, opens up a second, smaller window. The outerWidth property is written to this new window.

Listing 8.560   Using the outerWidth ***Property***

```
<html>
<head>
<script language="JavaScript1.2" type="text/javascript">
<!--

// Define a function to open a small window.
function openWin(){

    // Create variables to hold the various options that can be set
    // when a new Window instance is created.
    var myBars = 'directories=no,location=no,menubar=no,status=no';
    myBars += ',titlebar=no,toolbar=no';
    var myOptions = 'scrollbars=no,width=400,height=200,resizeable=no';
    var myFeatures = myBars + ',' + myOptions;

    // Open the window. Give the window instance the name newWin and
    // name the document in the window myDoc.
    var newWin = open('', 'myDoc', myFeatures);

    // Write the window height and width properties to the new window.
    newWin.document.writeln('<h4>Properties for this Window</h4>');
    newWin.document.writeln('innerHeight: ' + newWin.innerHeight + '<br>');
    newWin.document.writeln('innerWidth: ' + newWin.innerWidth + '<br>');
    newWin.document.writeln('outerHeight: ' + newWin.outerHeight + '<br>');
    newWin.document.writeln('outerWidth: ' + newWin.outerWidth + '<br>');
    newWin.document.writeln('<form>');
    newWin.document.writeln('<input type="button" value="Close"');
    newWin.document.writeln(' onclick="window.close()">');
    newWin.document.writeln('</form>');

    // Close the stream to the document.
    newWin.document.close();

}
// -->
</script>
</head>
<body>
<form>
  <input type="button" value="Open" onclick="openWin()">
</form>
</body>
</html>
```

window.pageXOffset
JavaScript1.2+, JScript3+
Nav4+, IE4+

Syntax
```
window.pageXOffset
```

Description
The `pageXOffset` property of the `Window` object reflects the current horizontal pixel location of the top-left corner of the document in the window. In chromeless windows, this property can be referenced if you are moving a window with the `moveTo()` method before the actual move is made to see whether the window needs to be moved. It is also useful when using the `scrollTo()` method because it returns the current location of the viewable document in relation to the whole page.

Example
Listing 8.561 has a button that, when clicked, displays the current x and y coordinates of the window.

Listing 8.561   Using the `pageXoffSet` Property to See the Current Location of the Window
```
<html>
<head>
<script language="JavaScript1.2" type="text/javascript">
<!--

// Define a function to display an alert box with the current
// window location.
function showLocation(){

  // Store the offset in variables.
  var x = self.pageXOffset;
  var y = self.pageYOffset

  // Build a string to display.
  var currX = "X-coordinate: " + x + "\n";
  var currY = "Y-coordinate: " + y;

  // Display the coordinates.
  window.alert(currX + currY);
}

// -->
</script>
</head>
<body>
```

```
<form>
  <input type="button" value="Show Location" onclick="showLocation()">
</form>
</body>
</html>
```

window.pageYOffset

JavaScript1.2+, JScript3+
Nav4+, IE4+

Syntax

window.pageYOffset

Description

The pageYOffset property of the Window object reflects the current vertical pixel location of the top-left corner of the document in the window. In chromeless windows, this property can be referenced if you are moving a window with the moveTo() method before the actual move is made to see whether the window needs to be moved. It is also useful when using the scrollTo() method because it returns the current location of the viewable document in relation to the whole page.

Example

Listing 8.562 has a button that, when clicked, displays the current x and y coordinates of the window.

Listing 8.562   Using the pageYoffSet *Property to See the Current Location of the Window*

```
<html>
<head>
<script language="JavaScript1.2" type="text/javascript">
<!--

// Define a function to display an alert box with the current
// window location.
function showLocation(){

  // Store the offset in variables.
  var x = self.pageXOffset;
  var y = self.pageYOffset

  // Build a string to display.
  var currX = "X-coordinate: " + x + "\n";
  var currY = "Y-coordinate: " + y;
```

Listing 8.562   Continued

```
  // Display the coordinates.
  window.alert(currX + currY);
}

// -->
</script>
</head>
<body>
<form>
  <input type="button" value="Show Location" onclick="showLocation()">
</form>
</body>
</html>
```

window.parent

>JavaScript1.0+, JScript1.0
>Nav2+, IE3+, Opera3+

Syntax

```
window.parent.parent[num]
window.parent.frameName
```

Description

The parent property of the Window object contains a reference to the parent window of any frames that are loaded. In the instance where Frame A loads a page with a <frameset> with Frame A.1 and A.2, the parent of the documents in A.1 and A.2 is Frame A. Frame A's parent is the top level window.

The referencing of these sibling frames can either be done using the frames array and passing an index number, or you can directly reference a frame using the name that is assigned by the name attribute of the <frame> tag.

Example

Listing 8.563 shows how to reference the parent of the third frame on a page.

Listing 8.563   Using the parent Property to Reference a Frame

```
var myFrameReference = myWin.parent.frames[2];
```

window.personalbar

>JavaScript1.2+
>Nav4+

Syntax

```
window.personalbar.property
```

Description

The `personalbar` property of the `Window` object is, to some degree, an object itself. The real use of this property is to access its `visible` property to determine whether the personal bar is visible to the user.

> **NOTE**
>
> As of this writing, the `personalbar` property only has one subproperty: `visible`.

Example

Listing 8.564 determines whether several of the browser bars are displayed. In the example, you will see whether the personal bar is visible by using the `visible` property.

Listing 8.564   *Using the* visible *Property of* personalbar

```
<script language="JavaScript" type="text/javascript">
<!--

// Write the browser's bar status to the page. If the value
// is true, then it is displayed.
document.writeln('<h3>Browser Chrome Status</h3>')
document.writeln('Menu Bar: ' + window.menubar.visible + '<br>');
document.writeln('Tool Bar: ' + window.toolbar.visible + '<br>');
document.writeln('Location Bar: ' + window.locationbar.visible + '<br>');
document.writeln('Personal Bar: ' + window.personalbar.visible + '<br>');
document.writeln('Scroll Bars: ' + window.scrollbars.visible + '<br>');
document.writeln('Status Bar: ' + window.statusbar.visible + '<br>');

// Close the stream to the document.
document.close();

// -->
</script>
```

window.personalbar.visible

JavaScript1.2+
Nav4+

Syntax

window.personalbar.visible

Description

The `visible` subproperty of the `personalbar` property of the `Window` is used to determine whether the personal bar is visible to the user. If it is visible, the property returns `true`. It returns `false` if the bar is not visible.

Example

Listing 8.565 determines whether several of the browser bars are displayed. In the example, you will see whether the personal bar is visible by using the `visible` property.

Listing 8.565   Using the `visible` Property of `personalbar`

```
<script language="JavaScript" type="text/javascript">
<!--

// Write the browser's bar status to the page. If the value
// is true, then it is displayed.
document.writeln('<h3>Browser Chrome Status</h3>')
document.writeln('Menu Bar: ' + window.menubar.visible + '<br>');
document.writeln('Tool Bar: ' + window.toolbar.visible + '<br>');
document.writeln('Location Bar: ' + window.locationbar.visible + '<br>');
document.writeln('Personal Bar: ' + window.personalbar.visible + '<br>');
document.writeln('Scroll Bars: ' + window.scrollbars.visible + '<br>');
document.writeln('Status Bar: ' + window.statusbar.visible + '<br>');

// Close the stream to the document.
document.close();

// -->
</script>
```

window.print()

JavaScript 1.2+, JScript 3.0+
Nav4+, IE4+

Syntax

```
window.print()
```

Description

The `print()` method of the `Window` object simulates the user clicking the Print button on the browser. It tells the browser to open the Print dialog box to print the current page.

Example

Listing 8.566 has a button. Clicking the button will tell the browser to open the Print dialog box to allow the user to print the current page.

Listing 8.566   Using the `print()` Method to Print the Current Page

```
<html>
<body>
<form>
```

```
    <input type="button" value="Print" onclick="window.print()">
</form>
</body>
</html>
```

window.prompt()

JavaScript1.0+, JScript1.0
Nav2+, IE3+, Opera3+

Syntax

```
window.prompt(string1, string2)
```

Description

The prompt() method of the Window object displays a prompt dialog box when invoked. The value of *string1* passed to the method is displayed in the box, and the value of *string2* is contained in the text field of the prompt dialog box. The returned value of this method is the text in the text field.

Example

Listing 8.567 pops up a prompt box when the script is loaded, asking the user for a password. If the correct password is entered, the page finishes loading. The result of running this script can be seen in Figure 8.6.

Listing 8.567   A Prompt Box Displayed Using the prompt() **Method**

```
<script language="JavaScript" type="text/javascript">
<!--

// Keep asking the user for a password until they get it right.
while(prompt('Please enter your password', 'HERE') != 'admin'){
  alert('That was an incorrect response, please try again');
}

// This is only executed if 'admin' is entered.
document.write('You have entered the correct password!');

// -->
</script>
```

Figure 8.6

An alert box created with the Window.prompt() method.

window.releaseEvents()
JavaScript1.2+, JScript3.0+
Nav4+, IE4+

Syntax
window.releaseEvents(*event*)
window.releaseEvents(*event1* | *event2* | *eventN*)

Description
The releaseEvents() method of the Window object releases all previously captured events of the event type passed. These events can be captured with the Window.captureEvents() method. The events that can be released are as follows:

- Event.ABORT
- Event.BLUR
- Event.CHANGE
- Event.CLICK
- Event.DBLCLICK
- Event.DRAGDROP
- Event.ERROR
- Event.FOCUS
- Event.KEYDOWN
- Event.KEYPRESS
- Event.KEYUP
- Event.LOAD
- Event.MOUSEDOWN
- Event.MOUSEMOVE
- Event.MOUSEOUT
- Event.MOUSEOVER
- Event.MOUSEUP
- Event.MOVE
- Event.RESET
- Event.RESIZE
- Event.SELECT
- Event.SUBMIT
- Event.UNLOAD

After one of these events has been captured, you can define a function to replace the built-in method for handling the event. Use the releaseEvents() method to free the event after a capture.

Example
Listing 8.568 has a single text box and a button. The script in the <head> of the document specifies a function to handle all onClick events in the window. To be able to do this, the captureEvents() method has to be used to capture all events of type

Event.CLICK. When the page itself is clicked, a counter, which is displayed in the text box, is incremented.

When the button is pressed down, the onMouseDown event handler is fired and the Event.CLICK is released and no longer increments the page when the page is clicked.

Listing 8.568   *Capturing Events with the* Window.releaseEvents() *Method*

```html
<html>
<head>
<script language="JavaScript1.2" type="text/javascript">
<!--

// Define a click counter variable.
var counter = 0;

// Tell the browser you want to intercept ALL click events
// on the page. Then define a function to handle them.
window.captureEvents(Event.CLICK);
window.onClick = myClickHandler;

// Define the myClickHandler function to handle click events.
function myClickHandler(e){

  // Pass all click events to the onClick event of the text box.
  window.document.myForm.myText.handleEvent(e);
}

// Function is called by onClick of text box. Displays the number
// of clicks that have occurred.
function changeText(){
  document.myForm.myText.value = counter++;
}

// Releases the click event capturing.
function releaseClick(){
  window.releaseEvents(Event.CLICK);
}

// -->
</script>
</head>
<body>
<form name="myForm">
  <input type="text" size="2" value="" name="myText" onclick='changeText()'>
  <input type="button" value="Release Event" onmousedown='releaseClick()'>
</form>
</body>
</html>
```

window.resizeBy()

JavaScript1.2+, JScript3.0+
Nav4+, IE4+

Syntax

`window.resizeBy(numHort, numVert)`

Description

The `resizeBy()` method of the `Window` object resizes the specified window by the number of pixels passed to the method. As shown in the syntax definition, the first numeric value passed to the method represents the number of vertical pixels you want to size the window by, whereas the second numeric value represents the horizontal number of pixels.

If the numbers passed are positive, the window size is increased. Negative numbers reduce the size of the window.

Example

Listing 8.569 has four buttons. Two buttons are for increasing height, and the other two are for increasing width. If you click these buttons, the window will resize 10 pixels at a time.

Listing 8.569   Using the `resizeBy()` *Method to Resize a Window*

```
<html>
<head>
<script language="JavaScript1.2" type="text/javascript">
<!--

// Define a function to handle the window resizing.
function resizeWin(dir, dist){

  // Define variables to hold the sizing values.
  var myVert;
  var myHorz;

  // Determine the type of movement.
  if(dir == "vert"){
    myHorz = 0;
    myVert = dist;
  }else{
    myHorz = dist;
    myVert = 0;
  }

  // Resize the window.
  window.resizeBy(myHorz, myVert);
}
```

```
//  -->
</script>
</head>
<body>
<form>
<table border=0>
  <tr>
    <td colspan="2">
      <input type="button" value="Expand Down"
             onclick="resizeWin('vert',10)">
    </td>
  </tr>
    <tr>
    <td>
      <input type="button" value="Retract From Right"
             onclick="resizeWin('horz',-10)">
    </td>
    <td>
      <input type="button" value="Grow Right"
             onclick="resizeWin('horz',10)">
    </td>
  </tr>
    <tr>
    <td colspan="2">
      <input type="button" value="Retrack Up"
             onclick="resizeWin('vert',-10)">
    </td>
  </tr>
</table>
</form>
</body>
</html>
```

window.resizeTo()

JavaScript1.2+, JScript3.0+
Nav4+, IE4+

Syntax

window.resizeTo(*numWidth, numHeight*)

Description

The resizeTo() method of the Window object resizes the specified window to the specified size passed to the method. As shown in the syntax definition, the first numeric value passed to the method represents the width you want to size the window to, whereas the second numeric value represents the height.

Example

Listing 8.570 has two text fields and a button. If the user enters an integer value in each of the text fields and clicks the button, the window will resize to those settings.

Listing 8.570   Using the `resizeTo()` Method to Resize the Window

```
<html>
<head>
<script language="JavaScript1.2" type="text/javascript">
<!--

// Define a function to handle the window resizing.
function resizeWin(form){

  // Define variables to hold the resize values.
  var myWidth = form.width.value;
  var myHeight = form.height.value;

  // Resize the window.
  window.resizeTo(myWidth, myHeight);
}
// -->
</script>
</head>
<body>
<form>
  <b>New Width:</b>
  <input type="text" name="width"><br>
  <b>New Height:</b>
  <input type="text" name="height"><br>
  <input type="button" value="Resize Window"
         onclick="resizeWin(this.form)"></td>
</form>
</body>
</html>
```

window.routeEvent()

JavaScript1.2+, JScript3.0+
Nav4+, IE4+

Syntax

`window.routeEvent(event)`

Description

The `routeEvent()` method of the `Window` object passes all previously captured events of the event type passed through their normal event process. The events that can be passed are as follows:

- Event.ABORT
- Event.BLUR
- Event.CHANGE
- Event.CLICK
- Event.DBLCLICK
- Event.DRAGDROP
- Event.ERROR
- Event.FOCUS
- Event.KEYDOWN
- Event.KEYPRESS
- Event.KEYUP
- Event.LOAD
- Event.MOUSEDOWN
- Event.MOUSEMOVE
- Event.MOUSEOUT
- Event.MOUSEOVER
- Event.MOUSEUP
- Event.MOVE
- Event.RESET
- Event.RESIZE
- Event.SELECT
- Event.SUBMIT
- Event.UNLOAD

After one of these events has been captured using the `Window.captureEvents()` method, you can define a function to replace the built-in method for handling the event. Use the `releaseEvents()` method to free the event after a capture, and use `routeEvent()` to allow the normal processing to take place.

Example

Listing 8.571 has a single text box and a link. The script in the `<head>` of the document specifies a function to handle all `onClick` events in the window. To be able to do this, the `captureEvents()` method has to be used to capture all events of type `Event.CLICK`. When the page itself is clicked, a counter, which is displayed in the text box, is incremented.

When the link is clicked, the `onMouseDown` event handler is fired and the `Event.CLICK` is routed through its normal means and no longer increments the page when the page is clicked.

Listing 8.571 *Capturing Events with the* `Window.routeEvent()` *Method*

```
<html>
<head>
<script language="JavaScript1.2" type="text/javascript">
<!--
```

Listing 8.571   Continued

```
// Define a click counter variable.
var counter = 0;

// Tell the browser you want to intercept ALL click events
// on the page. Then define a function to handle them.
window.captureEvents(Event.CLICK);
window.onClick = myClickHandler;

// Define the myClickHandler function to handle click events.
function myClickHandler(e){

  // Pass all click events to the onClick event of the text box.
  window.document.myForm.myText.handleEvent(e);
}

// Function is called by onClick of text box. Displays the number
// of clicks that have occurred.
function changeText(){
  document.myForm.myText.value = counter++;
}

// Releases the click event capturing.
function releaseClick(){
  window.routeEvent(Event.CLICK);
}

// -->
</script>
</head>
<body>
<form name="myForm">
  <input type="text" size="2" value="" name="myText" onclick='changeText()'>
  <a href="http://www.purejavascript.com"
     onmousedown='window.routeEvent(Event.CLICK)'>Click Here!</a>
</form>
</body>
</html>
```

window.screenX

JavaScript1.2+, JScript3.0+
Nav4+, IE4+

Syntax

window.screenX

Description

The screenX property of the Window object is used to set the x coordinate of the left edge of the window. Within Netscape browsers, the property requires the UniversalBrowserWrite privilege.

Example

Listing 8.572 simply pops up an alert box that contains the screenX property value.

Listing 8.572   Checking the screenX Property Value

```
<html>
<body>
  <script type="text/javascript" language="JavaScript1.2">
  <!--
  alert(window.screenX)
  //-->
  </script>
</body>
</html>
```

window.screenY

JavaScript1.2+, JScript3.0+
Nav4+, IE4+

Syntax

window.screenY

Description

The screenY property of the Window object is used to set the y coordinate of the left edge of the window. Within Netscape browsers, the property requires the UniversalBrowserWrite privilege.

Example

Listing 8.573 simply pops up an alert box that contains the screenY property value.

Listing 8.573   Checking the screenY Property Value

```
<html>
<body>
  <script type="text/javascript" language="JavaScript1.2">
  <!--
  alert(window.screenY)
  //-->
  </script>
</body>
</html>
```

window.scroll()

JavaScript1.1, JScript3.0
Nav3, IE3, Opera3

Syntax

window.scroll(*numX*, *numY*)

Description

The scroll() method of the Window object scrolls the specified window to the specified location passed to the method. As shown in the syntax definition, the first numeric
value passed to the method represents the x coordinate to which you want to scroll the
window, whereas the second numeric value represents the y coordinate. Note that this
method has been deprecated in JavaScript 1.2 and replaced with the scrollBy() and
scrollTo() methods.

Example

Listing 8.574 has two text fields and a button. If the user enters an integer value in each
of the text fields and clicks the button, the window will be scrolled to those settings.

Listing 8.574 Using the scroll() Method to Scroll the Window

```
<html>
<head>
<script language="JavaScript1.2" type="text/javascript">
<!--

// Define a function to handle the window scrolling.
function scrollWin(dir, dist){

  // Define variables to hold the scrolling values.
  var myVert;
  var myHorz;

  // Determine the type of scrolling.
  if(dir == "vert"){
    myHorz = 0;
    myVert = dist;
  }else{
    myHorz = dist;
    myVert = 0;
  }

  // Scroll the window.
  window.scroll(myHorz, myVert);
}
// -->
</script>
```

```
    </head>
    <body>
    <form>
    <table border=0>
      <tr>
        <td colspan="2">
          <input type="button" value="Down" onclick="scrollWin('vert',10)">
        </td>
      </tr>
      <tr>
        <td>
          <input type="button" value=" Left " onclick="scrollWin('horz',-10)">
        </td>
        <td>
          <input type="button" value="Right" onclick="scrollWin('horz',10)">
        </td>
      </tr>
      <tr>
        <td colspan="2">
          <input type="button" value=" Up " onclick="scrollWin('vert',-10)">
        </td>
      </tr>
    </table>
    </form>
    </body>
    </html>
```

window.scrollbars

JavaScript1.2+
Nav4+

Syntax

window.scrollbars.*property*

Description

The scrollbars property of the Window object is, to some degree, an object itself. The real use of this property is to access its visible property to determine whether the scrollbars are visible to the user.

NOTE

As of this writing, the scrollbars property only has one subproperty: visible.

Example

See the example of Window.scrollbars.visible for an example of using the scrollbars property.

window.scrollbars.visible

JavaScript1.2+
Nav4+

Syntax

```
window.scrollbars.visible
```

Description

The `visible` subproperty of the `scrollbars` property of the `Window` is used to determine whether the scrollbars are visible to the user. If they are visible, the property returns `true`. It returns `false` if the bars are not visible.

Example

Listing 8.575 determines whether several of the browser scrollbars are displayed. In the example, you will see whether the scrollbars are visible by using the `visible` property.

Listing 8.575 *Using the* `visible` *Property of* `scrollbars`

```
<script language="JavaScript" type="text/javascript">
<!--

// Write the browser's toolbar status to the page. If the value
// is true, then it is displayed.
document.writeln('<h3>Browser Chrome Status</h3>')
document.writeln('Menu Bar: ' + window.menubar.visible + '<br>');
document.writeln('Tool Bar: ' + window.toolbar.visible + '<br>');
document.writeln('Location Bar: ' + window.locationbar.visible + '<br>');
document.writeln('Personal Bar: ' + window.personalbar.visible + '<br>');
document.writeln('Scroll Bars: ' + window.scrollbars.visible + '<br>');
document.writeln('Status Bar: ' + window.statusbar.visible + '<br>');

// Close the stream to the document.
document.close();

// -->
</script>
```

window.scrollBy()

JavaScript1.2+, JScript3.0+
Nav4+, IE4+

Syntax

```
window.scrollBy(numHorz, numVert)
```

Description

The `scrollBy()` method of the `Window` object scrolls the specified window by the number of pixels passed to the method. As shown in the syntax definition, the first numeric value passed to the method represents the number of horizontal pixels by which you want to scroll the window, whereas the second numeric value represents the vertical number of pixels.

If the numbers passed are positive, the window is scrolled up. Negative numbers are scrolled down.

Example

Listing 8.576 has four buttons. Each of these buttons scroll the windows contents in different directions when clicked.

Listing 8.576   Using the `scrollBy()` **Method to Resize a Window**

```
<html>
<head>
<script language="JavaScript1.2" type="text/javascript">
<!--

// Define a function to handle the window scrolling.
function scrollWin(dir, dist){

  // Define variables to hold the scrolling values.
  var myVert;
  var myHorz;

  // Determine the type of scrolling.
  if(dir == "vert"){
    myHorz = 0;
    myVert = dist;
  }else{
    myHorz = dist;
    myVert = 0;
  }

  // Scroll the window.
  window.scrollBy(myHorz, myVert);
}
// -->
</script>
</head>
<body>
<form>
<table border=0>
  <tr>
    <td colspan="2">
```

Listing 8.576   Continued

```
      <input type="button" value="Down"
             onclick="scrollWin('vert',10)">
    </td>
  </tr>
  <tr>
    <td>
      <input type="button" value=" Left "
             onclick="scrollWin('horz',-10)">
    </td>
    <td>
      <input type="button" value="Right"
             onclick="scrollWin('horz',10)">
    </td>
  </tr>
  <tr>
    <td colspan="2">
      <input type="button" value="  Up  "
             onclick="scrollWin('vert',-10)">
    </td>
  </tr>
</table>
</form>
</body>
</html>
```

window.scrollTo()

JavaScript1.2+, JScript3.0+
Nav4+, IE4+

Syntax

window.scrollTo(numX, numY)

Description

The `scrollTo()` method of the `Window` object scrolls the specified window to the specified location passed to the method. As shown in the syntax definition, the first numeric value passed to the method represents the x coordinate to which you want to scroll the window, whereas the second numeric value represents the y coordinate.

Example

Listing 8.577 has two text fields and a button. If the user enters an integer value in each of the text fields and clicks the button, the window will be scrolled to those settings.

Listing 8.577   Using the `scrollTo()` *Method to Scroll the Window*

```
<html>
<head>
<script language="JavaScript1.2" type="text/javascript">
<!--

// Define a function to handle the window scrolling.
function scrollWin(form){

  // Define variables to hold the scroll values.
  var myX = form.X.value;
  var myY = form.Y.value;

  // Scroll the window.
  window.scrollTo(myX, myY);
}
// -->
</script>
</head>
<body>
<form>
  <b>X-Coordinate:</b>
  <input type="text" name="X"><br>
  <b>Y-Coordinate:</b>
  <input type="text" name="Y"><br>
  <input type="button" value="Scroll Window"
         onclick="scrollWin(this.form)"></td>
</form>
</body>
</html>
```

window.self

> JavaScript1.0+, JScript1.0
> Nav2+, IE3+, Opera3+

Syntax

window.self.method
window.self.property

Description

The `self` property of the `Window` object contains a reference to the current window. This allows you to invoke functions or call properties on the current window without any confusion when multiple windows are displayed.

Example

Listing 8.578 shows how to close the current window through the `self` reference.

Listing 8.578   Using the `self` Property to Reference the Current Window

```
<script language="JavaScript" type="text/javascript">
<!--

// Define a function to close the current window
function closeWin(){

  self.close()

// -->
</script>
```

window.setHotKeys()

JavaScript1.2
Nav4

Syntax

*window.*setHotKeys*(boolean)*

Description

The setHotKeys() method of the Window object enables or disables all hot keys within a window that do not have menus. It simply takes a *boolean* value to enable or disable this option. Passing true will enable the hot keys, whereas false will disable them.

Example

Listing 8.579 shows how you can disable hot keys for a given window.

Listing 8.579   Using the `setHotKeys()` Method

```
<script type="text/javascript" language="JavaScript1.2">
<!--
setHotKeys(false)
//-->
</script>
```

window.setInterval()

JavaScript1.2+, JScript3.0+
Nav4+, IE4+

Syntax

*window.*setInterval*(expression, milliseconds)*
*window.*setInterval*(function, milliseconds)*
*window.*setInterval*(function, milliseconds, arg1, ..., argN)*

Description

The setInterval() method of the Window object sets an interval to invoke the expression or function that is passed to the method. The expression or function is invoked after every elapse of the *milliseconds*. As shown in the syntax definition, it is possible to pass arguments to the function you want to invoke. This interval can be cleared by using the clearInterval() method.

Example

Listing 8.580 sets an interval in the <head> of the document that displays the current time in a text box on the page. The interval is set so that it only updates the time in the text box every five seconds. There is also a button on this page that allows you to clear the interval if you click it.

Listing 8.580   *Clearing an Interval with the* setInterval() *Method*

```
<html>
<head>
<script language="JavaScript1.2" type="text/javascript">
<!--

// Create a variable to hold a counter.
var counter = 1;

// Define a function to display the counter.
function startCounter(){
  document.myForm.myText.value = counter++;
}

// Define a function to stop the counter.
function stopCounter(){
  window.clearInterval(myInterval);
}

// Set the interval to call the function every 5 seconds.
var myInterval = window.setInterval("startCounter()", 5000)

// -->
</script>
</head>
<body onload="startCounter()">
<form name="myForm">
  <input type="text" size="2" value="" name="myText">
  <input type="button" value="Clear Interval" onclick="stopCounter()">
</form>
</body>
</html>
```

window.setResizable()

JavaScript1.2
Nav4

Syntax

```
window.setResizable(boolean)
```

Description

The setResizable() method of the Window object enables or disables a user's ability to resize a window. It simply takes a *boolean* value to perform this option. Passing true will enable the user to resize the window, whereas false will disable this feature.

Example

Listing 8.581 shows how you can disable the resizing of a window.

Listing 8.581   Using the setResizable() **Method**

```
<script type="text/javascript" language="JavaScript1.2">
<!--
setResizable(false)
//-->
 </script>
```

window.setTimeout()

JavaScript1.0+, JScript1.0+
Nav2+, IE3+, Opera3+

Syntax

```
window.setTimeout(expression, milliseconds)
window.setTimeout(function, milliseconds)
window.setTimeout(function, milliseconds, arg1, ..., argN)
```

Description

The setTimeout() method of the Window object sets a timeout to invoke the expression or function that is passed to the method. The expression or function is invoked after the elapse of the *milliseconds*. As shown in the syntax definition, it is possible to pass arguments to the function you want to invoke. This timeout can be cleared by using the clearTimeout() method.

Example

Listing 8.582 has a button and text box. By default, the time will be displayed in the text box after five seconds. This is done using the setTimeout() method. If the button is clicked, a function is called that invokes the clearTimeout() method, preventing the time from being displayed in the text box.

Listing 8.582   Using the setTimeout() *Method*

```
<html>
<head>
<script language="JavaScript" type="text/javascript">
<!--

// Define a function to show the time.
function showTime(){
  myTime = new Date();
  myTime = myTime.getHours() + ":" + myTime.getMinutes() + ":";
  myTime += myTime.getSeconds();
  document.myForm.myText.value = myTime;
}

// Define a function to stop the display of the time.
function stopTime(){
  window.clearTimeout(myTimeout);
}

// Set the interval to call the function after 5 seconds.
var myTimeout = window.setTimeout("showTime()", 5000)

// -->
</script>
</head>
<body>
<form name="myForm">
  <input type="text" size="2" value="" name="myText">
  <input type="button" value="Clear Timeout" onclick="stopTime()">
</form>
</body>
</html>
```

window.setZOptions()

> JavaScript1.2
> Nav4

Syntax

window.setZOptions(type)

Description

The setZOptions() method of the Window object specifies the z-order stacking behavior of a window. It takes a *type* to indicate how this stacking can occur. The following are the possible values of *type*. To set this property in Navigator, you need the UniversalBrowserWrite privilege.

- alwaysLowered—Creates new windows below other windows, whether it is active or not.
- alwaysRaised—Creates new windows on top of other windows, whether it is active or not.
- z-lock—Creates new windows that do not rise above other windows when activated.

Example

Listing 8.583 shows how you can set the z-order stacking of a window.

Listing 8.583 ***Using the*** `setZOptions()` ***Method***

```
<script type="text/javascript" language="JavaScript1.2">
<!--

// Set to lower ordering
setZOptions(alwaysLowered)

//-->
</script>
```

window.status

JavaScript1.0+, JScript1.0+
Nav2+, IE3+, Opera3+

Syntax

*window.*status = *string*

Description

The `status` property of the `Window` object allows you to specify the message that is displayed in the status bar of the browser. Note that in JavaScript 1.1, this property was tainted. See Chapter 1 for more information on JavaScript security and data tainting.

> **NOTE**
>
> When setting the `Window.status` property, be sure that your function returns `true`. This also applies when setting the property within the body of an HTML tag.

Example

Listing 8.584 shows how you can set the status in the Status Bar by rolling over a link.

Listing 8.584 **Setting the Status of a Page**

```
<a href="http://www.purejavascript.com/book"
   onMouseOver="window.status='Please Visit Our Online Book!'; return true"
   onMouseOut="window.status='Document: Done'">
   Click Here!</a>
```

window.statusbar

> JavaScript1.2+
> Nav4+

Syntax

*window.*statusbar.*property*

Description

The statusbar property of the Window object is, to some degree, an object itself. The real use of this property is to access its visible property to determine whether the status bar is visible to the user.

NOTE

As of this writing, the statusbar property only has one subproperty: visible.

Example

See the example of Window.statusbar.visible for an example of using the status-bar property.

window.statusbar.visible

> JavaScript1.2+
> Nav4+

Syntax

*window.*statusbar.visible

Description

The visible subproperty of the statusbar property of the Window is used to determine whether the status bar is visible to the user. If it is visible, the property returns true. It returns false if the bar is not visible.

Example

Listing 8.585 determines whether several of the browser bars are displayed. In the example, you will see whether the status bar is visible by using the visible property.

Listing 8.585 **Using the** visible *Property of* statusbar

```
<script language="JavaScript" type="text/javascript">
<!--

// Write the browser's bar status to the page. If the value
// is true, then it is displayed.
document.writeln('<h3>Browser Chrome Status</h3>')
document.writeln('Menu Bar: ' + window.menubar.visible + '<br>');
document.writeln('Tool Bar: ' + window.toolbar.visible + '<br>');
document.writeln('Location Bar: ' + window.locationbar.visible + '<br>');
document.writeln('Personal Bar: ' + window.personalbar.visible + '<br>');
document.writeln('Scroll Bars: ' + window.scrollbars.visible + '<br>');
document.writeln('Status Bar: ' + window.statusbar.visible + '<br>');

// Close the stream to the document.
document.close();

// -->
</script>
```

window.stop()

JavaScript1.2+, Jscript3.0
Nav4+, IE4+

Syntax

window.stop()

Description

The stop() method of the Window object simulates the user clicking the Stop button on the browser. It stops the browser from downloading and rendering the current page.

Example

Listing 8.586 has a button and an image reference to a nonexistent image. The browser will continue to try and download the image until it times out or the download is stopped. Clicking the button will stop the download.

Listing 8.586 **Using the** stop() *Method to Stop a Page from Loading*

```
<html>
<body>
<form>
  <input type="button" value="Stop" onclick="window.stop()">
</form>
<p>
  <table border="1"color= bgcolor="#FF0000">
    <tr>
      <td>
```

```
        <img src="http://www.purejavascript.com/images/fake.gif"
            width=468 height=60>
      </td>
    </tr>
  </table>
</p>
</body>
</html>
```

window.toolbar
JavaScript1.2+
Nav4+

Syntax
window.`toolbar.`*property*

Description
The `toolbar` property of the `Window` object is, to some degree, an object itself. The real use of this property is to access its `visible` property to determine whether the toolbar is visible to the user.

> **NOTE**
>
> As of this writing, the `toolbar` property only has one subproperty: `visible`.

Example
See the example of `Window.toolbar.visible` for an example of using the `toolbar` property.

window.toolbar.visible
JavaScript1.2+
Nav4+

Syntax
window.`toolbar.visible`

Description
The `visible` subproperty of the `toolbar` property of the `Window` object is used to determine whether the toolbar is visible to the user. If it is visible, the property returns `true`. It returns `false` if the bar is not visible.

Example
Listing 8.587 determines whether several of the browser bars are displayed. In the example, you will see whether the toolbar is visible by using the `visible` property.

Listing 8.587 **Using the** visible **Property of** toolbar

```
<script language="JavaScript" type="text/javascript">
<!--

// Write the browser's bar status to the page. If the value
// is true, then it is displayed.
document.writeln('<h3>Browser Chrome Status</h3>')
document.writeln('Menu Bar: ' + window.menubar.visible + '<br>');
document.writeln('Tool Bar: ' + window.toolbar.visible + '<br>');
document.writeln('Location Bar: ' + window.locationbar.visible + '<br>');
document.writeln('Personal Bar: ' + window.personalbar.visible + '<br>');
document.writeln('Scroll Bars: ' + window.scrollbars.visible + '<br>');
document.writeln('Status Bar: ' + window.statusbar.visible + '<br>');

// Close the stream to the document.
document.close();

// -->
</script>
```

window.top

JavaScript1.0+, JScript1.0
Nav2+, IE3+, Opera3+

Syntax

```
window.top.frames[num]
window.top.frameName
window.top.method
window.top.property
```

Description

The top property of the Window object contains a reference to the topmost browser window of any frames or pages that are loaded. In the instance where a Frame A loads a page with a <frameset> with Frame A.1 and A.2, the top of the documents in A.1 and A.2 is the window that actually has Frame A loaded. Frame A's top is also this window.

As shown in the syntax definition, the referencing of sibling frames can either be done using the frames array and passing an index number, or you can directly reference a frame using the name that is assigned by the name attribute of the <frame> tag. From within the current page or any of the frames, you can reference the top window and execute any methods or reference any properties that might reside there.

Example

Assuming that the page with this script lies within a <frameset>, Listing 8.588 shows how you can call a function that is defined in the topmost page.

Listing 8.588 *Using the* top *Property to Call a Function in the Top Frame*

```
<script language="JavaScript" type="text/javascript">
<!--

// Call a function in the top.
top.myFunc(myVar1, myVar2);

// -->
</script>
```

window.unwatch()

JavaScript 1.2+
Nav4+

Syntax

window.unwatch(*property*)

Description

The unwatch() method of the Window object is used to turn off the watch for a particular *property* specified by *property*.

Example

Listing 8.589 shows how the unwatch() method is used to stop watching the outerHeight property of the Window object after its value has changed.

Listing 8.589 *Example of the* unwatch() *method of the* Window *object*

```
<script type="text/javascript" language="JavaScript">
<!--

function alertme(id, oldValue, newValue){
  document.write("ID (" + id + ") changed from " + oldValue + " to ");
  document.write(newValue + "<br>");
  return newValue;
}

//Start watch.
window.watch("outerHeight", alertme);

// Change value.
window.outerHeight = 100;

// End watch.
window.unwatch("outerHeight");
```

Listing 8.589   Continued

```
// -->
</script>
```

window.watch()

JavaScript 1.2+
Nav4+

Syntax

```
window.watch(property)
```

Description

The watch() method of the Window object is used to turn on the watch for a particular *property* specified by *property*.

Example

Listing 8.590 shows how the watch() method is used to start watching the outerHeight property of the Window object after its value has changed.

Listing 8.590   Example of the watch() method of the Window object

```
<script type="text/javascript" language="JavaScript">
<!--

function alertme(id, oldValue, newValue){
  document.write("ID (" + id + ") changed from " + oldValue + " to ");
  document.write(newValue + "<br>");
  return newValue;
}

//Start watch.
window.watch("outerHeight", alertme);

// Change value.
window.outerHeight = 100;

// -->
</script>
```

window.window

JavaScript1.0+, JScript1.0
Nav2+, IE3+, Opera3+

Syntax

```
window.method
window.property
```

Description

The window property of the Window object contains a reference to the current window. This allows you to invoke functions or call properties on the current window without any confusion when multiple windows are displayed.

Example

Listing 8.591 shows how to close the current window through the window reference.

Listing 8.591   Using the window *Property to Reference the Current Window*

```
<script language="JavaScript" type="text/javascript">
<!--

// Define a function to close the current window.
function closeWin(){

  window.close()

// -->
</script>
```

CHAPTER 9

Server-Side

This chapter is a detailed reference of all the items and elements making up the server-side JavaScript language. This refers to the implementation available in the Netscape and iPlanet Web Server Enterprise Edition, which we will simply refer to as Enterprise Server (ES) from this point on, and within Microsoft's Active Server Pages (ASP) environment, which is available for their Internet Information Server (IIS) or Personal Web Server (PWS).

Because both Microsoft and Netscape have taken different approaches for their server-side implementation, be sure to check the supported environments for these entries. Additionally, be sure to read Chapter 5, "JavaScript on the Server-Side," for more information on how these implementations are used.

As in other chapters of Part III, the details of the language are covered in this chapter. Each entry includes the language version, syntax, description, and an example of each server-side–specific language element.

The chapter is in alphabetical order, by JavaScript objects, to provide you with quick, easy access to the methods, properties, functions, and event handlers of every server-side object. These appear alphabetically after the respective parent object using simple dot notation.

addClient()

ES2+

Syntax

```
addClient(URL)
```

Description

The `addClient()` function is a top-level function that is not associated with any core object. This function is used to preserve the property values of a `client` object when you generate dynamic links or use the `redirect()` function. The `addClient()` function takes a `URL` as its only parameter.

Example

This example demonstrates how you can use the `addClient()` function when dynamically building links. In Listing 9.1, a link is built by using a property of the `project` object.

Listing 9.1 Using the `addClient()` Function to Dynamically Build a Link

```
<a href='<server>addClient("/myApp/page" + project.pagenum +
".html")</server>'>
Please proceed to the next page</a>
```

In Listing 9.2, the `addClient()` function is used in conjunction with the `redirect()` function. This will send the user to the URL specified in the `addClient()` function.

Listing 9.2 Using the `addClient()` Function with the `redirect()` Function

```
<server>

// Check to see if the browser is Internet Explorer.
if(request.agent.indexOf('MSIE') != -1){
  redirect(addClient("/iepages/index.html"));

// Redirect to another page if it is not IE.
}else{
  redirect(addClient("/defaultpages/index.html"));
}
</server>
```

addResponseHeader()

ES3+

Syntax

```
addResponseHeader(key, value)
```

Description

The addResponseHeader() function is a top-level function that is not associated with any core object. This function is used to add fields and values to the HTTP header sent back to the client. Because of when the actual header is sent in relation to the body of the data, you should be sure to set these fields and values before you call the flush() or redirect() functions.

NOTE

Because the JavaScript runtime engine flushes the output buffer after 64KB of content has been generated, you should be sure to call the addResponseHeader() function before this time.

Example

Listing 9.3 shows how you can send back a dynamically built external JavaScript source file to a browser with the proper content-type header field and value.

Listing 9.3 Using the addResponseHeader() Function to Set the content-type of a File Being Sent to a Browser

```
<server>

// Add a field to the header
addResponseHeader("content-type", "application/x-javascript");

</server>
```

Application

ASP1+

Syntax

Core ASP environment object

Description

The Application object is a core ASP environment object. It is used to share information across all users of a given application, which includes all .asp files as well as any virtual directories and their subdirectories. Table 9.1 contains the methods, collections, and events of this object.

Table 9.1 Methods, Collections, and Events of the Application Object

Type	Item	Description
Collection	Contents	Contains all items added to the application through script commands.
	StaticObjects	Contains all objects added to session with the <object> tag.

Table 9.1 Continued

Type	Item	Description
Event	`Application_OnEnd`	Occurs when the application quits.
	`Application_OnStart`	Occurs before the first new session is created.
Method	`Contents.Remove()`	Deletes an item from the `Application` object's `Contents` collection.
	`Contents.RemoveAll()`	Deletes all items from the `Application` object's `Contents` collection.
	`Lock()`	Prevents other clients from modifying `Application` object properties.
	`Unlock()`	Allows other clients to modify `Application` object properties.

Example

Listing 9.4 shows how you could specify the version of your application that users are implementing, and then write it out.

Listing 9.4   Using the `Application` *Object*

```
<script runat="server" type="text/jscript" language="JScript">
Application("version") = "1.0"
var appVer = Application("version");
Response.Write(appVer);
</script>
```

Application.Application_OnEnd

ASP1+

Syntax

```
function Application_OnEnd(){
  code
}
```

Description

The `Application_OnEnd` event function of the `Application` object is called when the `Application_OnEnd` event is fired. This occurs when the application quits, which is after the `Session_OnEnd` event is fired.

Example

Listing 9.5 shows how you can append a string to the end of the log file of the last request of an application.

Listing 9.5 *Using the* Application_OnEnd *Event*

```
<script runat="server" type="text/jscript" language="JScript">
function Application_OnEnd(){
  Response.AppendToLog("Your application has ended");
}
</script>
```

Application.Application_OnStart

ASP1+

Syntax

```
function Application_OnStart(){
  code
}
```

Description

The Application_OnStart event function of the Application object is called when the Application_OnStart event is fired. This occurs when the application starts, which is before the Session_OnStart event is fired.

Example

In Listing 9.6 shows how you can append a string to the end of the log file on the first request of an application.

Listing 9.6 *Using the* Application_OnStart *Event*

```
<script runat="server" type="text/jscript" language="JScript">
function Application_OnStart(){
  Response.AppendToLog("Your application has started");
}
</script>
```

Application.Contents

ASP1+

Syntax

```
Application.Contents(name)
```

Description

The Contents collection of the Application object contains all the items that have been added to the application through script commands. You are able to access a specific item by specifying its *name*.

Example

Listing 9.7 shows how you can use the Remove() method of the Contents collection to remove *myItem*, which was added to the application.

Listing 9.7   Using the Contents Collection

```
<script runat="server" type="text/jscript" language="JScript">

// Add the item to the collection.
Application("myItem") = "My name is Allen";

// Remove the item.
Application.Contents.Remove("myItem");
</script>
```

Application.Contents.Remove()

ASP1+

Syntax

```
Application.Contents.Remove(name)
Application.Contents.Remove(num)
```

Description

The Remove() method of the Contents collection of the Application object is used to remove an item from the application's collection. This item can either be referenced by its *name* or its *num* index position.

Example

Listing 9.8 shows how you can use the Remove() method of the Contents collection to remove *myItem*, which was added to the application.

Listing 9.8   Using the Remove() Method

```
<script runat="server" type="text/jscript" language="JScript">

// Add the item to the collection.
Application("myItem") = "My name is Allen";

// Remove the item.
Application.Contents.Remove("myItem");
</script>
```

Application.Contents.RemoveAll()

ASP1+

Syntax

```
Application.Contents.RemoveAll()
```

Description

The RemoveAll() method of the Contents collection of the Application object is used to remove all items from the application's collection.

Example

Listing 9.9 shows how you can use the RemoveAll() method of the Contents collection to remove all items that have been added to the application.

Listing 9.9   *Using the* RemoveAll() *Method*

```
<script runat="server" type="text/jscript" language="JScript">

// Add two items to the collection.
Application("myItem") = "My name is Allen";
Application("yourItem") = "Your name is Reader";

// Remove all items.
Application.Contents.RemoveAll();
</script>
```

Application.Lock()

ASP1+

Syntax

```
Application.Lock()
```

Description

The Lock() method of the Application object prevents other clients from modifying any items stored in the Application object. To unlock the object, you must call the Unlock() method, or the server will unlock it either when the page has finished processing or times out.

Example

In Listing 9.10 we lock a counter item before updating it. This item could be used to count the number of users a given application has serviced.

Listing 9.10   *Using the* Lock() *Method*

```
<script runat="server" type="text/jscript" language="JScript">

// Initialize the counter, which should ONLY be done on the first page of
// the application.
Application("counter") = 0;

// Lock the application before incrementing the counter.
Application.Lock()
```

Listing 9.10 Continued

```
// Increment the counter.
Application("counter") += 1;

// Unlock the counter for others to modify.
Application.Unlock();
</script>
```

Application.StaticObjects

ASP1+

Syntax

```
Application.StaticObjects(name)
```

Description

The StaticObjects collection of the Application object stores all the objects created with <object> elements on a given ASP page. These are referenced by the *name* given to each instance of the elements.

Example

Listing 9.11 shows how you can grab the instance *myControl* from your current ASP page.

Listing 9.11 Using the StaticObjects Collection

```
<script runat="server" type="text/jscript" language="JScript">
Application.StaticObjects("myControl");
</script>
```

Application.Unlock()

ASP1+

Syntax

```
Application.Unlock()
```

Description

The Unlock() method of the Application object unlocks the previously locked Application object. To first lock the object, you must call the Lock() method. If you fail to call the Unlock() method, the server will unlock it when the page has finished processing or times out.

Example

In Listing 9.12 we lock a counter item before updating it. This item could be used to count the number of users a given application has serviced. After updating, we unlock it for others to access and modify.

Listing 9.12 **Using the** Unlock() *Method*

```
<script runat="server" type="text/jscript" language="JScript">

// Initialize the counter, which should ONLY be done on the first page of
// the application.
Application("counter") = 0;

// Lock the application before incrementing the counter.
Application.Lock()

// Increment the counter.
Application("counter") += 1;

// Unlock the counter for others to modify.
Application.Unlock();
</script>
```

ASPError

ASP3+

Syntax

Core ASP environment object

Description

The ASPError object is a core ASP environment object. Its properties and methods are used to retrieve information about errors that have occurred on a given page. This object is returned by the Server.GetLastError() method and exposes read-only properties. Table 9.2 contains a list of properties for this object.

Table 9.2 **Properties of the** ASPError *Object*

Property	Description
ASPCode	Returns the error code generated by the IIS Web server.
ASPDescription	Returns a detailed description of an ASP-related error.
Category	Indicates the source of the error, which can be internal to ASP, the scripting language, or an object.
Column	Indicates the .asp file column position that generated the error.
Description	Returns a short description of the error.
File	Indicates the name of the .asp file being processed when the error occurred.
Line	Indicates the line that generated the error.
Number	Returns the standard COM error code.
Source	Returns the actual source code, when available, of the line that caused the error.

Example

Listing 9.13 shows how you can write out a short description of an error that has been exposed to the ASPError object.

Listing 9.13   Using the ASPError Object

```
<script runat="server" type="text/jscript" language="JScript">
Response.Write(ASPError.Description);
</script>
```

ASPError.ASPCode

ASP3+

Syntax

```
ASPError.ASPCode
```

Description

The ASPCode property of the ASPError object contains error code generated by IIS.

Example

In Listing 9.14 we write out the value of the ASPCode property.

Listing 9.14   Using the ASPCode Property

```
<script runat="server" type="text/jscript" language="JScript">
Response.Write(ASPError.ASPCode);
</script>
```

ASPError.ASPDescription

ASP3+

Syntax

```
ASPError.ASPDescription
```

Description

The ASPDescription property of the ASPError object contains a more detailed description of the error returned.

Example

In Listing 9.15 we write out the value of the ASPDescription property.

Listing 9.15   Using the ASPDescription Property

```
<script runat="server" type="text/jscript" language="JScript">
Response.Write(ASPError.ASPDescription);
</script>
```

ASPError.Category

ASP3+

Syntax

```
ASPError.Category
```

Description

The `Category` property of the `ASPError` object indicates if the source of the error was internal to ASP, JScript, or an object.

Example

In Listing 9.16 we write out the value of the `Category` property.

Listing 9.16   Using the Category *Property*

```
<script runat="server" type="text/jscript" language="JScript">
Response.Write(ASPError.Category);
</script>
```

ASPError.Column

ASP3+

Syntax

```
ASPError.Column
```

Description

The `Column` property of the `ASPError` object contains the column position within the ASP file where the error occurred.

Example

In Listing 9.17 we write out the value of the `Column` property.

Listing 9.17   Using the Column *Property*

```
<script runat="server" type="text/jscript" language="JScript">
Response.Write(ASPError.Column);
</script>
```

ASPError.Description

ASP3+

Syntax

```
ASPError.Description
```

Description

The Description property of the ASPError object contains a short description of the error.

Example

In Listing 9.18 we write out the value of the Description property.

Listing 9.18   Using the Description *Property*

```
<script runat="server" type="text/jscript" language="JScript">
Response.Write(ASPError.Description);
</script>
```

ASPError.File

ASP3+

Syntax

```
ASPError.File
```

Description

The File property of the ASPError object contains the name of the ASP file being processed when the error occurred.

Example

In Listing 9.19 we write out the value of the File property.

Listing 9.19   Using the File *Property*

```
<script runat="server" type="text/jscript" language="JScript">
Response.Write(ASPError.File);
</script>
```

ASPError.Line

ASP3+

Syntax

```
ASPError.Line
```

Description

The Line property of the ASPError object contains the line number on which the error occurred.

Example

In Listing 9.20 we write out the value of the Line property.

Listing 9.20 **Using the** Line *Property*

```
<script runat="server" type="text/jscript" language="JScript">
Response.Write(ASPError.Line);
</script>
```

ASPError.Number

ASP3+

Syntax

```
ASPError.Number
```

Description

The Number property of the ASPError object contains the standard COM error code.

Example

In Listing 9.21 we write out the value of the Number property.

Listing 9.21 **Using the** Number *Property*

```
<script runat="server" type="text/jscript" language="JScript">
Response.Write(ASPError.Number);
</script>
```

ASPError.Source

ASP3+

Syntax

```
ASPError.Source
```

Description

The Source property of the ASPError object contains the actual source code, if available, that the error occurred in.

Example

In Listing 9.22 we write out the value of the Source property.

Listing 9.22 **Using the** Source *Property*

```
<script runat="server" type="text/jscript" language="JScript">
Response.Write(ASPError.Source);
</script>
```

blob() (Function)

ES2+

Syntax

blob(*path*)

Description

BLOB data represents *binary large objects* that can be stored in a database. This allows you to store various types of information, such as images, movie files, and sounds in the database.

> **NOTE**
>
> Be sure to consult the documentation on your specific database to see whether there are any limitations to BLOB data types.

The blob() function is used to store BLOB data in your database. This function takes the path to a BLOB file as its only parameter. Note that this path must be an absolute pathname and not a relative one.

Example

In Listing 9.23, a cursor instance has been created to perform a query on the database to find a specific row. Focus is then placed on that row and the blob() function is used to assign the data to a column. The final step in the process is to use the updateRow() method to commit the change.

Listing 9.23 Using the blob() Function to Insert BLOB Data into a Database

```
<server>

// SQL statement and instance of a cursor to execute it
var myStatement = 'SELECT * FROM family WHERE pic = null';
var myCursor = database.cursor(myStatement);

// Iterate through the returned rows.
while(myCursor.next()){

  // Assign 'blank.gif' in the PIC column of the returned rows.
  myCursor.pic = blob("/pictures/blank.gif");
  myCursor.updateRow("family");
}

// Close the cursor and write it to the page if there was an error.
var dbError = myCursor.close();

if(dbError) write(myCursor.close());
</server>
```

blob (Object)

ES2+

Syntax

Core object is created with the `blob.blobImage()` and `blob.blobLink()` methods.

Description

The top-level `blob` object contains methods that allow you to store and retrieve blob data in a database. *BLOB* data represents *binary large objects* that can be stored in a database. This allows you to store various types of information, such as images, movie files, and sounds in the database.

> **NOTE**
>
> Be sure to consult the documentation on your specific database to see whether there are any limitations to BLOB data types.

The core `blob` object is created when you use the methods of this object. Table 9.3 has the methods of the `blob` object and a description of what they do when invoked.

Table 9.3 *Methods of the* `blob` *Object*

Method	Description
`blobImage()`	Retrieves and displays a BLOB data instance stored in a database
`blobLink()`	Retrieves and displays a link that references a BLOB data instance stored in a database
`unwatch()`	Turns off the watch for a particular property.
`watch()`	Turns on the watch for a particular property.

Example

Listing 9.24 queries a database for a specific image, creating an instance of a `blob` object when retrieved. The image is then written to the page using the `write()` and `blobImage()` methods. The actual tag written will be as follows:

```
<IMG ALT="Click" ALIGN="left" WIDTH="468" HEIGHT="60" BORDER="0" ISMAP="false">
```

Listing 9.24 *Using the* `blobImage()` *Method to Format an* <img> *Tag*

```
<server>

// Find the image you want to display.
myCursor = myConn.cursor("SELECT path FROM images WHERE img = 1");

// Write the <img> tag to the page with the following attributes set.
write(myCursor.path.blobImage("gif", "Click", "left", 468, 60, 0, false));
```

Listing 9.24   Continued

```
// Close the cursor.
myCursor.close();
</server>
```

blob.blobImage()

ES2+

Syntax

cursor.column.blobImage(*fileType, altText, align, width, height, border, ismap*)

Description

The blobImage() method retrieves and displays a BLOB image stored in a database. The method actually returns the HTML for the <img> tag used to display the image. The href attribute of the <img> tag references the instance of this image in memory and does not have to contain a "normal" URL of the image itself.

This method can take up to seven parameters that set the various attributes of the <img> tag. These attributes are contained in Table 9.4. At a minimum, you must pass the *fileType* of the image.

Table 9.4   Properties That Can Be Set with the blobImage() ***Method***

Parameter	Attribute It Sets	Description
fileType	none	This parameter does not set an attribute. It specifies the type of file that is being displayed, such as gif or jpeg.
altText	alt	A string that is displayed when the browser has been set to not display images or when a mouse is over an image for a specified period of time.
align	align	This can be set to LEFT, RIGHT, or any other value your target browser supports.
width	width	The width in pixels of your image.
height	height	The height in pixels of your image.
border	border	An integer value that specifies the size of any border that might appear around the image if the image is surrounded by the <a> tag.
ismap	ismap	Specifies whether the image has a map file associated with it to handle any clicks that might occur within it. This parameter is set by specifying true if the image has a map file associated with it or false if not.

Example

Listing 9.25 queries a database for a specific image. The image is then written to the page using the `write()` and `blobImage()` methods. The actual tag written will be as follows:

```
<IMG ALT="Click" ALIGN="left" WIDTH="468" HEIGHT="60" BORDER="0"
 ➥ISMAP="false">
```

Listing 9.25   Using the `blobImage()` ***Method to Format an*** <img> ***Tag***

```
<server>

// Find the image you want to display.
myCursor = myConn.cursor("SELECT path FROM images WHERE img = 1");

// Write the <img> tag to the page with the following attributes set.
write(myCursor.path.blobImage("gif", "Click", "left", 468, 60, 0, false));

// Close the cursor.
myCursor.close();
</server>
```

blob.blobLink()

ES2+

Syntax

```
cursor.column.blobLink(mimeType, text)
```

Description

The `blobLink()` method retrieves BLOB data stored in a database, stores it in memory, and creates a temporary link to it. The method actually returns the HTML for the <a> tag used to display the link. The `href` attribute of the <a> tag references the BLOB data type, which has been stored in a temporary memory location, and does not contain a "normal" URL of this attribute. The data is stored in memory until the user clicks the link or until 60 seconds have elapsed.

The parameters this method takes are the MIME type of the file referenced, and the *text* that is displayed to the user as a link.

Example

Listing 9.26 queries a database for a specific image. A link referencing the image is then written to the page using the `write()` and `blobLink()` methods. The actual tag written will be as follows:

```
<a href="LIVEWIRE_TEMP1">Click Here!</a>
```

Listing 9.26 *Using the* `blobLink()` *Method to Format an* `<a>` *Tag*

```
<server>

// Find the image you want to display.
myCursor = myConn.cursor("SELECT path FROM images WHERE img = 1");

// Write the <a> tag to the page with the attributes set.
write(myCursor.path.blobLink("image/gif", "Click Here!"));

// Close the cursor.
myCursor.close();
</server>
```

callC()

ES2+

Syntax

`callC(JSFuncName, arg1, arg2, ..., argN)`

Description

The `callC()` function, which returns string values, is a top-level function that is not associated with any core object. `callC()` is used to call a JavaScript function that references a C function in a shared library. These libraries are the pre-built `.dll` files on Windows machine and `.so` files on Unix machines. `callC()` takes the JavaScript name you have assigned to the C function and any arguments the function needs as arguments.

Before you can call this function, you must register the C library using the server-side JavaScript `registerCFunction()`. `RegisterCFunction()` takes the JavaScript name with which you want to reference the function, the path to the library, and the C function name as parameters.

Example

Listing 9.27 registers an external C library, `extlib.dll`, that contains a function named `getMyDate`. The registration of this function assigns the name `JSExtLib` to be used within the script. If the function successfully registers, the `callC()` function is used to call the C function and pass it two parameters. The results are written to the user's page. If the function does not register properly, an error is written to the user's page.

Listing 9.27 *Using a C Function with* `callC` *That Has Been Registered*

```
<server>

// Register the library and function, assigning it a JavaScript
// function name.
```

```
var myExternalLib = registerCFunction("JSExtLib", "c:/winnt/extlib.dll",
➥"getMyDate")

// If the library registered without error, then call it using the
// callC function. If it failed, then write an error to the page.
if (myExternalLib) {
  write(callC("getMyDate", 1999, 2000));
}else{
  write("There was an error processing this external library function");
}

</server>
```

client

ES2+

Syntax

Core object is created with each connection of a client to your application.

Description

An instance of the `client` object is created with each connection of a user to your application. This object is used to maintain session variables for that user as she moves through your application's pages. Because the object is not created until a user connects to your application, you cannot use the object on the first page of your application.

> **NOTE**
>
> The `client` object is created for each user's connection to each application you have built using Server-side JavaScript, so a single user connected to two applications will have two `client` objects created.

The object itself is held until the user is inactive for a set period of time or the object is destroyed. At that time, the JavaScript runtime engine cleans up the object. The default timeout is ten minutes, but this can be changed by using the `expiration()` method or can be destroyed manually by using the `destroy()` method.

`client` objects do not have any default properties, but properties can be created for them. Do note that because of the method used to maintain user sessions, these properties are all converted to strings. If you have created a property that must be evaluated as a numeric value, use the `parseInt()` and `parseFloat()` methods for processing.

If you must store an object as a property, you will have to create an array of objects in the `project` or `server` objects. Then you can create a property to hold the index of your object in the `client` object.

Example

Listing 9.28 contains a form the user fills out with her name, e-mail address, and phone number. When the Submit button is clicked, the form is sent back to itself and the script sees information being passed in. This information is then assigned to three created properties of the client object and is then written to the user's page.

Listing 9.28   Assigning Properties to the client Object

```
<html>
<head>
  <title>Using the client object</title>
</head>
<body>
<server>

// See if they have submitted or just need the form.
if(request.method == "POST"){

  // Assign the client properties their values.
  client.name = request.name;
  client.email = request.email;
  client.phone = request.phone;

  // Write the user's information to the page.
  write('Hello ' + client.name + '!<br>');
  write('Please confirm your email, ' + client.email + ', and ');
  write('phone number, ' + client.phone);
  }else{

  // If this page was called and a form was not submitted
  write('<form name="myForm" method="post">');
  write('<table border="1"><tr><td>');
  write('<table border="0">');
  write('<tr align="left" valign="top">');
  write('<td><b>Name:</b></td>');
  write('<td><input type="text" name="name" size="30"></td>');
  write('</tr>');
  write('<tr align="left" valign="top">');
  write('<td><b>E-mail:</b></td>');
  write('<td><input type="text" name="email" size="30"></td>');
  write('</tr>');
  write('<tr align="left" valign="top">');
  write('<td><b>Phone:</b></td>');
  write('<td><input type="text" name="phone" size="30"></td>');
  write('</tr>');
  write('<tr align="left" valign="top">');
  write('<td colspan="2" align="right"><input type="submit"');
  write(' value="Submit"></td>');
  write('</tr>');
```

```
    write('</table>');
    write('</td></tr></table>');
    write('</form>');
}
</server>
</body>
</html>
```

client.destroy()

ES2+

Syntax

```
client.destroy()
```

Description

The destroy() method of the client object explicitly destroys that instance of the object and all its associated properties. If this method is not called, the JavaScript runtime will destroy the object after 10 minutes or after the time specified with the client.expiration() method.

If you are using cookies to maintain your client object, calling the destroy() method acts in the same manner but does not remove information stored in the browser's cookie file. To remove the cookie information, set the expiration to 0 seconds by using the client.expiration() method.

When using URL encoding to maintain the client object, the destroy() method will destroy all information with the exception that the links created before the method call will retain their properties. Because of this, good programming practice warrants calling the method at the top or bottom of a page.

Example

Listing 9.29 shows how to destroy the properties of your user's client object.

Listing 9.29   Using the destroy() **Method to Destroy the** client **Object Properties**

```
<server>

// Destroy the client properties.
client.destroy()

</server>
```

client.expiration()

ES2+

Syntax

`client.expiration(`*`seconds`*`)`

Description

The `expiration()` method of the `client` object sets the number of *seconds* of user inactivity before the JavaScript runtime destroys all properties associated with that session. The default timeout is 10 minutes if you do not explicitly set this property. Also, this method has no effect when using URL encoding to maintain your `client` objects.

> **NOTE**
>
> Setting this to **0** will remove any cookies associated with the `client` object when using client cookies to maintain sessions.

Example

Listing 9.30 sets the destruction of the `client` object to occur after five minutes of inactivity.

Listing 9.30   *Using the* `expiration()` *Method of the* `client` *Object*

```
<server>

// Set the expiration to 5 minutes.
client.expiration(300)

</server>
```

client.*property*

ES2+

Syntax

`client.`*`property`*

Description

When a *property* is created for an instance of the `client` object, it is accomplished by passing information from a form. When you pass a form element, designated by the name attribute, to the server, it is accessible through the `client.`*`property`* syntax, where *property* is the name passed.

Example

Listing 9.31 shows how the form value `zip` is accessible in a server-side JavaScript script by assigning it to an instance of the `client` object. Once assigned, the value stored in the property is written back out to the user's page.

Listing 9.31   Accessing a `Client` *Property*

```
<server>

// See if they have submitted.
if(request.method == "POST"){

  // Assign the client property its value.
  client.zip = request.zip;
}

// Write the value passed by the form to the page.
write(client.zip);
</server>
```

client.unwatch()

ES3+

Syntax

`client.unwatch(property)`

Description

The unwatch() method of the `client` object is used to turn off the watch for a particular *property*.

Example

Listing 9.32 shows how the unwatch() method is used to stop watching the user-defined property *p*.

Listing 9.32   Example of the `unwatch()` *Method*

```
<server>

// function that is called if property's value changes
function alertme(id, oldValue, newValue){
  write("ID (" + id + ") changed from " + oldValue + " to " + newValue);
  return newValue;
}

// See if they have submitted.
if(request.method == "POST"){

  // Assign the client property its value.
  client.zip = request.zip;
}

// watch property
client.watch("zip", alertme);
```

Listing 9.32   Continued

```
// change value
client.zip = null;

// turn off watch
client.unwatch("zip");

// change value again
client.zip = 3;

</server>
```

client.watch()

ES3+

Syntax

```
client.watch(property, function)
```

Description

The watch() method of the client object is used to turn on the watch for a particular property specified by *property*. Any time the specified *property* is changed after the watch() method has been called, the specified *function* is called.

Example

Listing 9.33 shows how the watch() method is used to start watching the user-defined property *p*.

Listing 9.33   Example of the watch() Method

```
<server>

// function that is called if property's value changes
function alertme(id, oldValue, newValue){
  write("ID (" + id + ") changed from " + oldValue + " to " + newValue);
  return newValue;
}

// See if they have submitted.
if(request.method == "POST"){

  // Assign the client property its value.
  client.zip = request.zip;
}

// watch property
client.watch("zip", alertme);
```

```
client.zip = null;

</server>
```

Connection

ES3+

Syntax

Core object is created when the `DbPool.connection()` method is called.

Description

The `Connection` object represents a given connection, pulled from a "*pool*", to a database. This object has only one property, the `prototype` property, which you can use to add properties to the object. Table 9.5 shows the methods associated with this object.

> **NOTE**
>
> If you only need a single connection to the database and do not need to create a pool, use the `database` object for your connection.

Table 9.5   Methods of the `Connection` *Object*

Method	Description
beginTransaction()	Begins a new SQL transaction
commitTransaction ()	Commits the current SQL transaction
connected()	Tests to see whether the pool connection is connected to the database
cursor()	Creates a `Cursor` object for the specified SQL SELECT statement
execute()	Performs the non-SELECT SQL statement passed
majorErrorCode()	Returns the major error code numeric value returned by the database or ODBC
majorErrorMessage()	Returns the major error message string value returned by the database or ODBC
minorErrorCode()	Returns the secondary error code numeric value returned by the database or ODBC
minorErrorMessage()	Returns the secondary error message string value returned by the database or ODBC
release()	Releases the specified connection back to the pool
rollbackTransaction()	Rolls back the specified transaction
SQLTable()	Formats the query results from a SELECT in HTML <table> format for easy writing to a client

Table 9.5   Continued

Method	Description
storedProc()	Creates a `Stproc` object and runs the specified stored procedure
toString()	Returns a string representing the specified object
unwatch()	Turns off the watch for a particular property
watch()	Turns on the watch for a particular property

Example

Listing 9.34 creates a pool of connections to an Oracle database and initializes a connection from that pool. It takes a user's UID and name that was passed in, runs a query (based on the UID) against the database to find that user's information, and updates the user's name. If a connection is not made, the error code and message is returned to the screen.

Listing 9.34   Creating and Using a `Connection` Object

```
<server>

// Assign the user submitted ID and name to the client object as properties.
client.uid = request.uid;
client.name = request.name;

// Create a pool of connections.
var myPool = new DbPool("ORACLE", "mySID", "myApp", "appsPWD", "myTNS");

// Open a connection from the pool. Give error if connection could
// not be made.
var myConn = myPool.connection('Employees', 15);
if(myConn.connected()){

  // Start a new SQL transaction to perform a SELECT.
  myConn.beginTransaction();
  var currRow = myConn.cursor('SELECT * FROM employees WHERE uid = ' +
➡ client.uid);

  // Focus on that line, change the name column for that user,
  // and update the row.
  currRow.next();
  currRow.name = client.name;
  currRow.updateRow("employees");

  // Close the cursor.
  currRow.close();

// If the connection fails, write an error message.
}else{
```

```
    write('Error ('+myConn.majorErrorCode()+'): '' + myConn.majorErrorMessage();
    }

</server>
```

Connection.beginTransaction()
ES3+

Syntax
connection.beginTransaction()

Description

The beginTransaction() method of the Connection object begins a new SQL transaction. This groups all the actions against the database together until the user exits the page or either the commitTransaction() or rollbackTransaction() methods are called. In the instance of the user exiting the page, the transaction is either committed or rolled back, depending on the setting of the commit flag when the DbPool object instance is created.

NOTE

You cannot have nested transactions.

Example

Listing 9.35 creates a pool of connections to an Oracle database and pulls one of the connections from the pool. After the connection has been verified, the beginTransaction() method is called and a SQL query is performed. The results are formatted in a table with the SQLTable() method and written to the user's page.

Listing 9.35 *Starting a New Transaction with the* beginTransaction() *Method*

```
<server>

// Assign the user submitted ID to the client object as properties.
client.uid = request.uid;

// Create a pool of connections.
var myPool = new DbPool("ORACLE", "mySID", "myApp", "appsPWD", "myTNS");

// Open a connection from the pool. Give error if connection could
// not be made.
var myConn = myPool.connection('Employees', 15);
if(myConn.connected()){
```

*Listing 9.35 **Continued***
```
    // Start a new transaction and write the results to a page, formatting
    // them with the SQLTable method.
    myConn.beginTransaction();
    write(myConn.SQLTable('SELECT * FROM employees WHERE uid >= '+client.uid));

    // Commit the transaction.
    myConn.commitTransaction();

// If the connection fails, write an error message
}else{
    write('Error ('+myConn.majorErrorCode()+'): '' + myConn.majorErrorMessage();
    }

</server>
```

Connection.commitTransaction()
ES3+

Syntax
```
connection.commitTransaction()
```

Description

The commitTransaction() method of the Connection object commits a new SQL transaction. This commits all the actions against the database since the last commit. If the commit is successful, 0 is returned. If a non-zero number is returned, an error is encountered. In this case, various methods of the Connection object can be used to retrieve the code and message of the error.

Example

Listing 9.36 creates a pool of connections to an Oracle database and pulls one of the connections from the pool. After the connection has been verified, the beginTransaction() method is called and a SQL query is performed. The results are formatted in a table with the SQLTable() method and written to the user's page.

*Listing 9.36 **Starting a New Transaction with the** commitTransaction()
Method*
```
<server>

// Assign the user submitted ID to the client object as properties.
client.uid = request.uid;

// Create a pool of connections.
var myPool = new DbPool("ORACLE", "mySID", "myApp", "appsPWD", "myTNS");
```

```
// Open a connection from the pool.  Give error if connection could
// not be made.
var myConn = myPool.connection('Employees', 15);
if(myConn.connected()){

  // Start a new transaction and write the results to a page, formatting
  // them with the SQLTable method.
  myConn.beginTransaction();
  write(myConn.SQLTable('SELECT * FROM employees WHERE uid >= '+client.uid));

  // Commit the transaction.
  myConn.commitTransaction();

// If the connection fails, write an error message.
}else{
  write('Error (' + myConn.majorErrorCode()+'): '' +
myConn.majorErrorMessage();
  }

</server>
```

Connection.connected()

ES3+

Syntax

connection.connected()

Description

The connected() method of the Connection object tells if the pool of connections to the database is still connected.

Example

Listing 9.37 creates a pool of connections and pulls a connection from the pool for processing. If the connection is made, any code within that section is executed. If the connection fails, the error is written to the page.

Listing 9.37   Testing a Connection with the connected() **Method**

```
<server>

// Create a pool of connections.
var myPool = new DbPool("ORACLE", "mySID", "myApp", "appsPWD", "myTNS");

// Open a connection from the pool.  Give error if connection could
// not be made.
var myConn = myPool.connection('Employees', 15);
```

Listing 9.37   Continued

```
if (myConn.connected()) {

  // You are connected, so perform any tasks here.

}else{

  // There was an error connecting to the database.
  write('Error ('+myConn.majorErrorCode()+'): '' + myConn.majorErrorMessage();
}

</server>
```

Connection.cursor()

ES3+

Syntax

```
connection.cursor(sql)
connection.cursor(sql, boolean)
```

Description

The cursor() method of the Connection object creates a Cursor object that can be used to run SQL queries against the database. The method takes the *sql* statement as a parameter, as well as an optional *boolean* value that specifies whether the cursor is updateable.

Example

Listing 9.38 shows how you would run a query against the database using the cursor() method. The while loop is used to write the results to the user's page.

Listing 9.38   Using the cursor() *Method to Run a Query Against the Database*

```
<server>

// Set the query to run.
var mySQL = myConn.cursor('SELECT name,title FROM employees');

// Iterate through the results and write them to the page.
while(mySQL.next()){
  write(mySQL.name + ': ' + mySQL.title + '<br>');
}

</server>
```

Connection.execute()

ES3+

Syntax

```
connection.execute(statement)
```

Description

The execute() method of the Connection object enables your application to execute a *DDL (Data Definition Language)* or *DML (Data Manipulation Language)* query, which does not return a Cursor, supported by your database. This includes statements such as CREATE, ALTER, and DROP.

NOTE

Be sure to use SQL that conforms to your database.

Example

Listing 9.39 deletes all rows with a UID less than the number passed to the script.

Listing 9.39   Using the execute() **Method to Run DML Queries**

```
<server>

// Assign the UID passed to the client object
client.uid = request.uid;

// Execute a DELETE based on the UID passed
myConn.execute('DELETE FROM employees WHERE uid < ' + client.uid);

</server>
```

Connection.majorErrorCode()

ES3+

Syntax

```
connection.majorErrorCode()
```

Description

The majorErrorMessage() method of the Connection object contains the ODBC or database numeric error code that is returned if an error occurs.

Example

Listing 9.40 shows how you would create a pool of connections, pull a connection from it, and test for the connection. If the test fails, the majorErrorCode() is used when writing the error to the page.

Listing 9.40   Using `majorErrorCode()` **to Retrieve a Database Connection Error**

```
<server>

// Create a pool of connections.
var myPool = new DbPool("ORACLE", "mySID", "myApp", "appsPWD", "myTNS");

// Open a connection from the pool. Give error if connection could
// not be made.
var myConn = myPool.connection('Employees', 15);

if (myConn.connected()) {

  // You are connected, so perform any tasks here.

}else{

  // There was an error connecting to the database.
  write('Error ('+myConn.majorErrorCode()+'): '' + myConn.majorErrorMessage();
}

</server>
```

Connection.majorErrorMessage()

ES3+

Syntax

`connection.majorErrorMessage()`

Description

The `majorErrorMessage()` method of the `Connection` object contains the ODBC or database string error message that is returned if an error occurs.

Example

Listing 9.41 shows how you would create a pool of connections, pull a connection from it, and test for the connection. If the test fails, the `majorErrorMessage()` is used when writing the error to the page.

Listing 9.41   Using `majorErrorMessage()` **to Retrieve a Database Connection Error**

```
<server>

// Create a pool of connections.
var myPool = new DbPool("ORACLE", "mySID", "myApp", "appsPWD", "myTNS");

// Open a connection from the pool. Give error if connection could
```

```
// not be made.
var myConn = myPool.connection('Employees', 15);

if (myConn.connected()) {

  // You are connected, so perform any tasks here.

}else{

  // There was an error connecting to the database
  write('Error ('+myConn.majorErrorCode()+'): '' + myConn.majorErrorMessage();
}

</server>
```

Connection.minorErrorCode()

ES3+

Syntax

connection.minorErrorCode()

Description

The `minorErrorMessage()` method of the `Connection` object contains the secondary ODBC or database numeric error code that is returned if an error occurs.

Example

Listing 9.42 shows how you would create a pool of connections, pull a connection from it, and test for the connection. If the test fails, the `minorErrorCode()` is used when writing the secondary error to the page.

Listing 9.42 *Using* `minorErrorCode()` *to Retrieve a Secondary Database Connection Error*

```
<server>

// Create a pool of connections.
var myPool = new DbPool("ORACLE", "mySID", "myApp", "appsPWD", "myTNS");

// Open a connection from the pool. Give error if connection could
// not be made.
var myConn = myPool.connection('Employees', 15);

if (myConn.connected()) {

  // You are connected, so perform any tasks here.
```

Listing 9.42 Continued

```
}else{

   // There was an error connecting to the database.
   write('Error ('+myConn.minorErrorCode()+'): '+myConn.minorErrorMessage);
}

</server>
```

Connection.minorErrorMessage()
ES3+

Syntax

`connection.minorErrorMessage()`

Description

The `minorErrorMessage()` method of the `Connection` object contains the secondary ODBC or the database string error message that is returned if an error occurs.

Example

Listing 9.43 shows how you would create a pool of connections, pull a connection from it, and test for the connection. If the test fails, the `minorErrorMessage()` is used when writing the secondary error to the page.

Listing 9.43 Using `minorErrorMessage()` to Retrieve a Secondary Database Connection Error

```
<server>

// Create a pool of connections.
var myPool = new DbPool("ORACLE", "mySID", "myApp", "appsPWD", "myTNS");

// Open a connection from the pool. Give error if connection could
// not be made.
var myConn = myPool.connection('Employees', 15);

if (myConn.connected()) {

   // You are connected, so perform any tasks here.

}else{

   // There was an error connecting to the database.
   write('Error ('+myConn.minorErrorCode()+'): '+myConn.minorErrorMessage);
}
```

Connection.prototype
ES3+

Syntax

```
connection.prototype.method = name
connection.prototype.property = value
```

Description

The prototype property of the Connection object allows you to add methods and properties to the Connection object. If you are adding a method, you set the instance equal to the *name* of the method you have defined.

Example

Listing 9.44 creates a new property and method of the Connection object. An instance is created and the new property is set. The new method is then called to verify the property and, if it is incorrect (which it is), an error message is written to the page.

Listing 9.44   Using the prototype **Property to Create a New Property and Method**

```
<server>

// Define the method that we prototyped.
function verifyODBC(){

  // Check to see if the type property we added is set to a valid value.
  if(this.type == "ODBC"){
    return true;
  }else{
    return false;
  }
}

// Create a new property and method of the Connection object.
Connection.prototype.type = null;
Connection.prototype.isODBC = verifyODBC;

// Create a pool of connections.
var myPool = new DbPool("ORACLE", "mySID", "myApp", "appsPWD", "myTNS");

// Open a connection from the pool.
var myConn = myPool.connection('Employees', 15);

// Using the prototype we defined, assign the type property.
myConn.type = "Oracle";
```

Listing 9.44 Continued

```
// Check the type of the connection to see if it is valid.
if(myConn.isODBC()){
  write(myConn + " has a valid type of " + myConn.type);
}else{
  write(myConn + " has an invalid type of " + myConn.type);
}

</server>
```

Connection.release()
ES3+

Syntax
`connection.release()`

Description
The `release()` method of the `Connection` object returns the connection to the `DbPool` instance after all cursors have been closed. If you do not close the cursor, the connection will remain until it times out or the variable holding your connection, assuming you assigned it to one, goes out of scope. Depending on how you have written your application, this can happen when the application is stopped, the Web server is stopped, or when control leaves the HTML page.

Example
Listing 9.45 shows a pool being created, a connection being pulled from the pool, and a query run against the database. When the cursor is closed, the connection is released.

Listing 9.45 Releasing a Connection Back to the Pool Using the
`release()` *Method*

```
<server>

// Assign the user submitted ID and name to the client object as properties.
client.uid = request.uid;
client.name = request.name;

// Create a pool of connections.
var myPool = new DbPool("ORACLE", "mySID", "myApp", "appsPWD", "myTNS");

// Open a connection from the pool. Give error if connection could
// not be made.
var myConn = myPool.connection('Employees', 15);
if(myConn.connected()){

  // Start a new SQL transaction to perform a SELECT.
  myConn.beginTransaction();
```

```
   var currRow = myConn.cursor('SELECT * FROM employees WHERE uid = ' +
➡ client.uid);

   // Focus on that line, change the name column for that user,
   // and update the row.
   currRow.next();
   currRow.name = client.name;
   currRow.updateRow("employees");

   // Close the cursor.
   currRow.close();

// If the connection fails, write an error message.
}else{
   write('Error ('+myConn.majorErrorCode()+'): '' + myConn.majorErrorMessage();
}

// Release the connection.
myConn.release();

</server>
```

Connection.rollbackTransaction()

ES3+

Syntax

connection.rollbackTransaction()

Description

The rollbackTransaction() method of the Connection object will undo all actions performed since the last beginTransaction() method call.

NOTE

You cannot have nested transactions.

Example

Listing 9.46 takes a *commit* field sent to the application from the user. If this evaluates to true, the transaction is committed. If not, it is rolled back.

Listing 9.46   Rolling Back a Transaction with the rollbackTransaction() **Method**

```
<server>

// See if the user wants to commit the last transaction.
client.commit = request.commit;
```

Listing 9.46   Continued

```
if(client.commit = "YES"){

  // Commit the transaction.
  myConn.commitTransaction();

}else{

  // Rollback the transaction.
  myConn.rollbackTransaction();
}

</server>
```

Connection.SQLTable()

ES3+

Syntax

```
connection.SQLTable(sql)
```

Description

The SQLTable() method of the Connection object takes a *sql* SELECT statement as a parameter and executes a query through the connection from which it was called. It returns the result formatted in an HTML table for easy writing to a client's page. This is a simple table in the following format:

```
<table border="1">
<tr>
<th>column 1</th>
<th>column 2</th>
...
<th>column N</th>
</tr>
<tr>
<td>value 1 of column 1</td>
<td>value 1 of column 2</td>
...
<td>value 1 of column N</td>
</tr>
<tr>
<td>value 2 of column 1</td>
<td>value 2 of column 2</td>
...
<td>value 2 of column N</td>
</tr>
...
</table>
```

Example

Listing 9.47 runs a user passed query and formats the result using the `SQLTable()` method. This information is then written to the user's page.

Listing 9.47   Using the `SQLTable()` Method to Format the Results of a SELECT Query

```
<server>

// Assign the user submitted query to the client object.
client.sql = request.sql;

// Create a pool of connections.
var myPool = new DbPool("ORACLE", "mySID", "myApp", "appsPWD", "myTNS");

// Open a connection from the pool. Give error if connection could
// not be made.
var myConn = myPool.connection('Employees', 15);
if(myConn.connected()){

  // Start a new transaction and write the results to a page, formatting
  // them with the SQLTable method.
  myConn.beginTransaction();
  write(myConn.SQLTable(client.sql));

  // Commit the transaction.
  myConn.commitTransaction();

// If the connection fails, write an error message.
}else{
  write('Error ('+myConn.majorErrorCode()+'): '' + myConn.majorErrorMessage();
}

// Release the connection.
myConn.release();

</server>
```

Connection.storedProc()
ES3+

Syntax

```
connection.storedProc(procName)
connection.storedProc(procName, arg1, arg2, ... , argN)
```

Description

The storedProc() method of the Connection object creates a Stproc object that allows you to execute a database-specific stored procedure using the connection from which it was invoked.

As shown in the syntactical definition, you can also pass any arguments needed to the method for processing. If you are using a stored procedure that requires arguments, or if you want to have the procedure run using default arguments, you must pass /Default/ as the argument. The following shows an example of passing a default value:

```
var myStproc = myConn.storedProc("sp_employees", "/Default/");
```

The scope of this procedure is restricted to the current page. Any methods of the Stproc object must be invoked on the current page. If this is not possible, a new object will have to be created on subsequent pages to access the properties needed.

Example

Listing 9.48 creates a pool of connections and pulls one of the connections. When the connection has been verified, the storedProc() method is used to invoke the fictitious sp_employees stored procedure.

Listing 9.48   Using the storedProc() **Method to Invoke a Stored Procedure on a Database**

```
<server>

// Create a pool of connections.
var myPool = new DbPool("ORACLE", "mySID", "myApp", "appsPWD", "myTNS");

// Open a connection from the pool.  Give error if connection could
// not be made.
var myConn = myPool.connection('Employees', 15);
if(myConn.connected()){

  myConn.beginTransaction();

  // Run the stored procedure.
  var myStproc = myConn.storedProc("sp_employees");

  // Commit the transaction.
  myConn.commitTransaction();

// If the connection fails, write an error message.
}else{
  write('Error ('+myConn.majorErrorCode()+'): '' + myConn.majorErrorMessage();
}
```

```
// Release the connection.
myConn.release();

</server> >
```

Connection.toString()
ES3+

Syntax

```
connection.toString()
```

Description

The `toString()` method of the `Connection` object returns a text value of the object. When invoked on an instance of a `Connection` object, the string is returned in the following format:

```
"dbName" "uid" "dbType" "dbInstance"
```

If the parameter is unknown, an empty string is returned. Table 9.6 contains the value of these returned values.

Table 9.6 Return Values of the `toString()` **Method**

Method	Description
dbName	The name of the database you want to log in to. For Oracle, DB2, and ODBC connections, this is a blank (`""`) string. In Oracle, the name of the database for these connections is set up in the `tnsnames.ora` file and is defined by the DSN for ODBC connections. DB2 does not have a database name and is referenced only by the `dbInstance`.
uid	The username or ID you want the connections to connect as.
dbType	The type of database it is. Possible values are ORACLE, SYBASE, INFORMIX, DB2, or ODBC.
dbInstance	This is the instance name of the database. For ODBC, it is the DSN entry name.

Example

Listing 9.49 creates an instance of the `Connection` object. Once created, the `write()` method is used to write its string value to the page.

Listing 9.49 Write the Results of Calling the toString() Method to a Page

```
<server>

// Create a pool of connections.
var myPool = new DbPool("ORACLE", "mySID", "myApp", "appsPWD", "myTNS");

// Open a connection from the pool. Give error if connection could
// not be made.
var myConn = myPool.connection('Employees', 15);
if(myConn.connected()){

  // Write the string value of the object to the page.
  write(myConn.toString());

// If the connection fails, write an error message.
}else{
  write('Error ('+myConn.majorErrorCode()+'): '' + myConn.majorErrorMessage();
}

// Release the connection.
myConn.release();

</server>
```

Connection.unwatch()

ES3+

Syntax

connection.unwatch(*property*)

Description

The unwatch() method of the Connection object is used to turn off the watch for a particular *property*.

Example

Listing 9.50 shows how the unwatch() method is used to stop watching the user-defined property *p*.

Listing 9.50 Example of the unwatch() Method

```
<server>

// Define the method that we prototyped.
function verifyODBC(){
```

```
  // Check to see if the type property we added is set to a valid value.
  if(this.type == "ODBC"){
    return true;
  }else{
    return false;
  }
}

// Function that is called if property's value changes.
function alertme(id, oldValue, newValue){
  write("ID (" + id + ") changed from " + oldValue + " to " + newValue);
  return newValue;
}

// Create a new property and method of the Connection object.
Connection.prototype.type = null;
Connection.prototype.isODBC = verifyODBC;

// Create a pool of connections.
var myPool = new DbPool("ORACLE", "mySID", "myApp", "appsPWD", "myTNS");

// Open a connection from the pool.
var myConn = myPool.connection('Employees', 15);

// Using the prototype we defined, assign the type property.
myConn.type = "Oracle";

// Watch the type property.
myConn.watch("type", alertme);

// Check the type of the connection to see if it is valid.
if(myConn.isODBC()){
  write(myConn + " has a valid type of " + myConn.type);
}else{
  write(myConn + " has an invalid type of " + myConn.type);
}

// change value
myConn.type = null;

// turn off watch
myConn.unwatch("type");

// change value again
myConn.type = "Sybase";

</server>
```

Connection.watch()

ES3+

Syntax

```
connection.watch(property, function)
```

Description

The watch() method of the Connection object is used to turn on the watch for a particular property specified by *property*. Any time the specified *property* is changed after the watch() method has been called, the specified *function* is called.

Example

Listing 9.51 shows how the watch() method is used to start watching the user-defined property *p*.

Listing 9.51   Example of the watch() **Method**

```
<server>

// Define the method that we prototyped.
function verifyODBC(){

  // Check to see if the type property we added is set to a valid value.
  if(this.type == "ODBC"){
    return true;
  }else{
    return false;
  }
}

// Function that is called if property's value changes.
function alertme(id, oldValue, newValue){
  write("ID (" + id + ") changed from " + oldValue + " to " + newValue);
  return newValue;
}

// Create a new property and method of the Connection object.
Connection.prototype.type = null;
Connection.prototype.isODBC = verifyODBC;

// Create a pool of connections.
var myPool = new DbPool("ORACLE", "mySID", "myApp", "appsPWD", "myTNS");

// Open a connection from the pool.
var myConn = myPool.connection('Employees', 15);

// Using the prototype we defined, assign the type property.
myConn.type = "Oracle";
```

```
// Watch the type property.
myConn.watch("type", alertme);

// Check the type of the connection to see if it is valid.
if(myConn.isODBC()){
  write(myConn + " has a valid type of " + myConn.type);
}else{
  write(myConn + " has an invalid type of " + myConn.type);
}

// change value
myConn.type = null;

</server>
```

Cursor

ES2+

Syntax

connection.cursor()
database.cursor()

Description

The Cursor object is a core object created when the cursor() method of the Connection or database object is called. A database query is said to return a cursor, so this object contains references to the rows returned from a query.

When working with cursor objects, you should explicitly close them using the close() method when you are finished. Not doing so will cause the JavaScript runtime to hold the cursor in memory until the connection or pool to which the cursor was tied goes out of scope.

The Cursor object has several methods and properties associated with it. These are listed in Table 9.7.

Table 9.7 Properties and Methods of the Cursor *Object*

Type	Item	Description
property	columnName	This property represents the column names that are returned from the SQL statement you passed to the cursor() method.
	prototype	This property allows you to add methods and properties to the Cursor object to be used when new instances are created.
method	close()	This method closes the cursor and frees any memory used by it.

Table 9.7 Continued

Type	Item	Description
	columnName()	This method takes an indexed numbered location and returns the column name of the column in that location.
	columns()	This method returns the number of columns in the cursor.
	deleteRow()	This method deletes the current row of the table passed to the method.
	insertRow()	This method inserts a new row in the table passed to the method.
	next()	This method moves from the current row in the Cursor object to the next row.
	unwatch()	This method is used to turn off the watch for a particular property.
	updateRow()	This method updates the current row in the table passed to the method.
	watch()	This method is used to turn on the watch for a particular property.

Example

Listing 9.52 takes a UID, passed as an area code, that is assigned to the client object. A pool of connections is then opened to the database, and one of the connections is pulled to run the query. The results of the query are stored in a Cursor object and are iterated through use of the next() method. After all rows have been updated with the new area code, the cursor is closed and the connection is released.

Listing 9.52   Using the Cursor Object

```
<server>

// Assign the user submitted ID and area code to the client object
// as properties.
client.uid = request.uid;
client.areacode = request.areacode;

// Create a pool of connections.
var myPool = new DbPool("ORACLE", "mySID", "myApp", "appsPWD", "myTNS");

// Open a connection from the pool. Give error if connection could
// not be made.
var myConn = myPool.connection('Employees', 15);
if(myConn.connected()){

  // Start a new SQL transaction to perform a SELECT.
  myConn.beginTransaction();
```

```
var currRow = myConn.cursor('SELECT areacode FROM employees WHERE uid >= '
➥ + client.uid);

  // For all the lines that matched, update the area code.
  while(currRow.next()){
    currRow.areacode = client.areacode;
    currRow.updateRow("employees");
  }

  // Close the cursor.
  currRow.close();

// If the connection fails, write an error message.
}else{
  write('Error ('+myConn.majorErrorCode()+'): '' + myConn.majorErrorMessage();
}

// Release the connection.
myConn.release();

</server>
```

Cursor.close()
ES2+

Syntax
cursor.close()

Description

The close() method of the Cursor object closes the cursor and frees all memory that had been used to store its information. If successful, the method returns 0, otherwise it returns an error code that can be obtained by using the majorErrorCode() and majorErrorMessage() methods of the Connection or database objects.

Example

Listing 9.53 creates a cursor and then closes it.

Listing 9.53   Closing a Cursor with the close() Method

```
<server>

// Create cursor
var currRow = myConn.cursor('SELECT areacode FROM employees WHERE uid >= '
➥ + client.uid);
```

Listing 9.53   Continued

```
// Close the cursor
currRow.close();

</server>
```

Cursor.*columnName*

ES2+

Syntax

cursor.columnName

Description

The *columnName* property of the Cursor object is an array of objects that corresponds to the name of the columns in the cursor.

Example

Listing 9.54 shows a cursor object being created. The various values are then written to the page using the *columnName* property as their reference.

Listing 9.54   Using the columnName **Property**

```
<server>

var currRow = myConn.cursor('SELECT areacode,phone,name FROM employees');

// Write each person's name and phone number to the page in the form:
// "<name>'s phone number is (<areacode>) <phone>"
while(currRow.next()){
  write(currRow.name + "'s phone number is (" + currRow.areacode + ") ");
  write(currRow.phone + "<br>");
}

// Close the cursor
currRow.close();

</server>
```

Cursor.columnName()

ES2+

Syntax

cursor.columnName(num)

Description

The `columnName()` method of the `Cursor` object takes the zero-based indexed number location, *num*, passed to the method and returns the name of the column in that location. Note that these names are not returned in any specific order unless you order them as such. Successive calls to the method, however, will return all the columns. See the example for more information on this.

Example

Listing 9.55 has two cursors. One of the cursors returns specific column names and the other returns all columns. See the comments in the code for the output.

Listing 9.55   Using the `columnName()` Method to Return the Names of the Columns in a Table

```
<server>

// Create a pool of connections.
var myPool = new DbPool("ORACLE", "mySID", "myApp", "appsPWD", "myTNS");

// Open a connection from the pool. Give error if connection could
// not be made.
var myConn = myPool.connection('Employees', 15);
if(myConn.connected()){

  // Start a new SQL transaction to perform a SELECT.
  myConn.beginTransaction();
  var currRow1 = myConn.cursor('SELECT areacode,phone FROM employees
➥WHERE uid >= 100');
  var currRow2 = myConn.cursor('SELECT * FROM employees WHERE uid >= 100');

  // Writes 'areacode', from the first cursor, to the page.
  write(currRow1.columnName(0));

  // Writes 'phone', from the first cursor, to the page.
  write(currRow1.columnName(1));

  // Writes all column names stored in the second cursor to the page.
  // This will include 'areacode' and 'phone' as well as any other
  // columns.
  for(var i = 0; i <= currRow2.columns(); i++){
    write(currRow2.columnName(i));
  }

  // Close the cursors.
  currRow1.close();
  currRow2.close();
```

Listing 9.55   *Continued*

```
// If the connection fails, write an error message.
}else{
  write('Error ('+myConn.majorErrorCode()+'): '' + myConn.majorErrorMessage();
}

// Release the connection.
myConn.release();

</server>
```

Cursor.columns()

ES2+

Syntax

```
cursor.columns()
```

Description

The `columns()` method of the `Cursor` object returns the number of columns in the cursor on which it is invoked. If the SQL string that was passed to create the cursor specified a set number of columns to return, this is the number returned by the method.

Example

Listing 9.56 shows how you can return all the column names of the columns in your cursor.

Listing 9.56   *Using the* `columns()` *Method to Determine How Many Columns Are in the Cursor Before Writing Them to the Page*

```
<server>

var currRow = myConn.cursor('SELECT * FROM employees');

// Writes all column names stored in the cursor to the page.
for(var i = 0; i <= currRow.columns(); i++){
  write(currRow.columnName(i));
}

// Close the cursors
currRow.close();

</server>
```

Cursor.deleteRow()

ES2+

Syntax

```
cursor.deleteRow(table)
```

Description

The `deleteRow()` method of the `Cursor` object uses an updateable cursor and deletes the current row in the specified *table* of the `Cursor` object. If the delete was successful, `0` is returned; otherwise it returns an error code that can be obtained by using the `majorErrorCode()` and `majorErrorMessage()` methods of the `Connection` or database objects.

Example

Listing 9.57 creates a `Cursor` object and selects all instances of a given *id*. The `deleteRow()` method is then used to delete each of these instances.

Listing 9.57   Deleting a Row from the Cursor Using the `deleteRow()` Method

```
<server>

// Assign the user submitted ID to the client object as properties.
client.uid = request.uid;

// Create a pool of connections.
var myPool = new DbPool("ORACLE", "mySID", "myApp", "appsPWD", "myTNS");

// Open a connection from the pool. Give error if connection could
// not be made.
var myConn = myPool.connection('Employees', 15);
if(myConn.connected()){

  // Start a new SQL transaction to perform a SELECT.
  myConn.beginTransaction();
var currRow = myConn.cursor('SELECT * FROM employees WHERE uid = '
➥ + client.uid, true);

  // Delete each row in the cursor.
  while(currRow.next(){
    currRow.delete("employees");
  }

  // Close the cursor.
  currRow.close();
```

Listing 9.57   Continued

```
// If the connection fails, write an error message.
}else{
  write('Error ('+myConn.majorErrorCode()+'): '' + myConn.majorErrorMessage();
}

</server>
```

Cursor.insertRow()

ES2+

Syntax

cursor.insertRow(*table*)

Description

The insertRow() method of the Cursor object uses an updateable cursor and inserts a new row in the specified *table* of the Cursor object. If the insert was successful, 0 is returned; otherwise, it returns an error code that can be obtained by using the majorErrorCode() and majorErrorMessage() methods of the Connection or data-base objects.

> **NOTE**
>
> Depending on your database, you might have to close the current cursor and reopen it if you want to access a newly inserted row. Also, if the next() method has been called on the cursor, any columns you do not specify values for will get the same values as the current row.

Example

Listing 9.58 creates a Cursor object and selects all rows. The insertRow() method is then used to insert a new row with three specified columns.

Listing 9.58   Inserting a Row from the Cursor Using the insertRow() Method

```
<server>

// Assign the user submitted ID to the client object as properties.
client.uid = request.uid;
client.name = request.name;
client.pwd = request.pwd;

// Create a pool of connections.
var myPool = new DbPool("ORACLE", "mySID", "myApp", "appsPWD", "myTNS");
```

```
// Open a connection from the pool. Give error if connection could
// not be made.
var myConn = myPool.connection('Employees', 15);
if(myConn.connected()){

  // Start a new SQL transaction to perform a SELECT. Notice the
  // cursor is updateable.
  myConn.beginTransaction();
  var currRow = myConn.cursor('SELECT uid,name,pwd FROM employees', true);

  // Assign values to the columns and insert a new row.
  currRow.uid = client.uid;
  currRow.name = client.name;
  currRow.pwd = client.pwd;
  currRow.insertRow("employees");
  myConn.commitTransaction();

  // Close the cursor and release the connection.
  currRow.close();
  myConn.release();

// If the connection fails, write an error message.
}else{
  write('Error ('+myConn.majorErrorCode()+'): '' + myConn.majorErrorMessage();
}

</server>
```

Cursor.next()

ES2+

Syntax

cursor.next()

Description

The next() method of the Cursor object moves the point in the current row to the next row in the cursor. This method is used to iterate through each of the rows returned by the cursor. This method returns true, unless it is the last row of the cursor, at which time it returns false.

Example

Listing 9.59 creates an instance of the Cursor object and iterates through its results, deleting each row. This is performed by using the next() method.

Listing 9.59   Using the `next()` *Method to Iterate Through the Rows in a Cursor*

```
<server>

var currRow = myConn.cursor('SELECT * FROM employees WHERE uid <= 200');

// Delete each row in the cursor.
while(currRow.next(){
  currRow.delete("employees");
}

// Close the cursor.
currRow.close();

</server>
```

Cursor.prototype
ES2+

Syntax
```
cursor.prototype.method = name
cursor.prototype.property = value
```

Description
The `prototype` property of the `Cursor` object allows you to create new properties and methods of the object. If you are adding a method, you set the instance equal to the *name* of the method you have defined.

Example
Listing 9.60 creates a new property and method of the `Cursor` object. An instance is created and the new property is set. The new method is then called to verify the property, and, if it is incorrect, an error message is written to the >page.

Listing 9.60   Using the `prototype` *Property to Create a New Property and Method*

```
<server>

// Define the method that we prototyped.
function verifySELECT(){

  // Check to see if the type property we added is set to a valid value.
  if(this.type == "SELECT"){
    return true;
  }else{
    return false;
```

```
    }
}

// Create a new property and method of the Cursor object.
Cursor.prototype.type = null;
Cursor.prototype.isSELECT = verifySELECT;

// Create a pool of connections, a connection, and a cursor.
var myPool = new DbPool("ORACLE", "mySID", "myApp", "appsPWD", "myTNS");
var myConn = myPool.connection('Employees', 15);
var currRow = myConn.cursor('SELECT * FROM employees');

// Using the prototype we defined, assign the type property.
currRow.type = "SELECT";

// Check the type of the connection to see if it is valid.
if(currRow.verifySELECT()){
  write(currRow + " has a valid type of " + currRow.type);
}else{
  write(currRow + " has an invalid type of " + currRow.type);
}

</server>
```

Cursor.unwatch()

ES3+

Syntax

cursor.unwatch(*property*)

Description

The unwatch() method of the Cursor object is used to turn off the watch for a particular *property*.

Example

Listing 9.61 shows how the unwatch() method is used to stop watching the user-defined property *p*.

Listing 9.61   Example of the unwatch() **Method**

```
<server>

// Define the method that we prototyped.
function verifySELECT(){
```

Listing 9.61 Continued

```
  // Check to see if the type property we added is set to a valid value.
  if(this.type == "SELECT"){
    return true;
  }else{
    return false;
  }
}

// Function that is called if property's value changes.
function alertme(id, oldValue, newValue){
  write("ID (" + id + ") changed from " + oldValue + " to " + newValue);
  return newValue;
}

// Create a new property and method of the Cursor object.
Cursor.prototype.type = null;
Cursor.prototype.isSELECT = verifySELECT;

// Create a pool of connections, a connection, and a cursor.
var myPool = new DbPool("ORACLE", "mySID", "myApp", "appsPWD", "myTNS");
var myConn = myPool.connection('Employees', 15);
var currRow = myConn.cursor('SELECT * FROM employees');

// Using the prototype we defined, assign the type property.
currRow.type = "SELECT";

// watch property
currRow.watch("type", alertme);

// Check the type of the connection to see if it is valid.
if(currRow.verifySELECT()){
  write(currRow + " has a valid type of " + currRow.type);
}else{
  write(currRow + " has an invalid type of " + currRow.type);
}

// change value
currRow.type = "DELETE";

// turn off watch
currRow.unwatch("type");

// change value again
currRow.type = "INSERT";

</server>
```

Cursor.updateRow()
ES2+

Syntax

```
cursor.updateRow(table)
```

Description

The `updateRow()` method of the `Cursor` object uses an updateable cursor and updates the current row in the specified *table* of the cursor object. If the insert was successful, 0 is returned; otherwise, it returns an error code that can be obtained by using the `majorErrorCode()` and `majorErrorMessage()` methods of the `Connection` or database objects.

Example

Listing 9.62 creates a `Cursor` object and selects all rows. The `updateRow()` method is then used to update the current row with three specified values.

Listing 9.62   Updating a Row from the Cursor Using the `updateRow()` ***Method***

```
<server>

// Assign the user submitted ID to the client object as properties.
client.uid = request.uid;
client.name = request.name;
client.pwd = request.pwd;

// Create a pool of connections.
var myPool = new DbPool("ORACLE", "mySID", "myApp", "appsPWD", "myTNS");

// Open a connection from the pool. Give error if connection could
// not be made.
var myConn = myPool.connection('Employees', 15);
if(myConn.connected()){

  // Start a new SQL transaction to perform a SELECT. Notice the
  // cursor is updateable.
  myConn.beginTransaction();
  var currRow = myConn.cursor('SELECT uid,name,pwd FROM employees WHERE uid = '
➥ + client.uid, true);

  // Select the row and assign values to the columns.
  currRow.next();
  currRow.uid = client.uid;
  currRow.name = client.name;
  currRow.pwd = client.pwd;
  currRow.updateRow("employees");
```

Listing 9.62 Continued

```
myConn.commitTransaction();

  // Close the cursor and release the connection.
  currRow.close();
  myConn.release();

// If the connection fails, write an error message.
}else{
  write('Error ('+myConn.majorErrorCode()+'): '' + myConn.majorErrorMessage();
}

</server>
```

Cursor.watch()

ES3+

Syntax

cursor.watch(*property, function*)

Description

The watch() method of the Cursor object is used to turn on the watch for a particular property specified by *property*. Any time the specified *property* is changed after the watch() method has been called, the specified *function* is called.

Example

Listing 9.63 shows how the watch() method is used to start watching the user-defined property *p*.

Listing 9.63 Example of the watch() **Method**

```
<server>

// Define the method that we prototyped.
function verifySELECT(){

  // Check to see if the type property we added is set to a valid value.
  if(this.type == "SELECT"){
    return true;
  }else{
    return false;
  }
}

// Function that is called if property's value changes.
function alertme(id, oldValue, newValue){
```

```
  write("ID (" + id + ") changed from " + oldValue + " to " + newValue);
  return newValue;
}

// Create a new property and method of the Cursor object.
Cursor.prototype.type = null;
Cursor.prototype.isSELECT = verifySELECT;

// Create a pool of connections, a connection, and a cursor.
var myPool = new DbPool("ORACLE", "mySID", "myApp", "appsPWD", "myTNS");
var myConn = myPool.connection('Employees', 15);
var currRow = myConn.cursor('SELECT * FROM employees');

// Using the prototype we defined, assign the type property.
currRow.type = "SELECT";

// watch property
currRow.watch("type", alertme);

// Check the type of the connection to see if it is valid.
if(currRow.verifySELECT()){
  write(currRow + " has a valid type of " + currRow.type);
}else{
  write(currRow + " has an invalid type of " + currRow.type);
}

// change value
currRow.type = "DELETE";

</server>
```

database

ES2+

Syntax

Core object is created when the `database.connect()` method is called.

Description

The `database` object represents a given connection to a database. This object has only one property, the `prototype` property, which you can use to add properties to the object. Table 9.8 lists the methods associated with this object.

NOTE

If you only need a pool of connections to the database, use the `DbPool` object for your connection to initialize a pool, and then use the `Connection.connection()` method to assign a connection.

Table 9.8 *Methods of the* database *Object*

Method	Description
`beginTransaction()`	Begins a new SQL transaction.
`commitTransaction ()`	Commits the current SQL transaction.
`connect()`	Connects to a particular database as a particular user.
`connected()`	Tests to see whether the connection is connected to the database.
`cursor()`	Creates a `Cursor` object for the specified SQL SELECT statement.
`disconnect()`	Disconnects a particular connection from the database.
`execute()`	Performs the non-SELECT SQL statement passed.
`majorErrorCode()`	Returns the major error code numeric value returned by the database or ODBC.
`majorErrorMessage()`	Returns the major error message string value returned by the database or ODBC.
`minorErrorCode()`	Returns the secondary error code numeric value returned by the database or ODBC.
`minorErrorMessage()`	Returns the secondary error message string value returned by the database or ODBC.
`rollbackTransaction()`	Rolls back the specified transaction.
`SQLTable()`	Formats the query results from a SELECT in HTML <table> format for easy writing to a client.
`storedProc()`	Creates a `Stproc` object and runs the specified stored procedure. This method was added in ES 3.0.
`storedProcArgs()`	Creates a prototype for DB2, ODBC, or Sybase stored procedures. This method was added in ES 3.0.
`toString()`	Returns a string representing the specified object.
`unwatch()`	Turns off the watch for a particular property.
`watch()`	Turns on the watch for a particular property.

Example

Listing 9.64 creates a connection to an Oracle database. It takes a user's UID and name that was passed in, runs a query (based on the UID) against the database to find that user's information, and updates her name. If a connection is not made, the error code and message are returned to the screen.

Listing 9.64   Creating and Using a database *Object*

```
<server>

// Assign the user submitted ID and name to the client object as properties.
client.uid = request.uid;
client.name = request.name;

// Open a connection.
var myConn = database.connect("ORACLE", "mySID", "myApp", "appsPWD", "myTNS");

if(myConn.connected()){

   // Start a new SQL transaction to perform a SELECT.
   myConn.beginTransaction();
   var currRow = myConn.cursor('SELECT * FROM employees WHERE uid = '
➥ + client.uid);

   // Focus on that line, change the name column for that user,
   // and update the row.
   currRow.next();
   currRow.name = client.name;
   currRow.updateRow("employees");
   myConn.commitTransaction();

   // Close the cursor and drop the connection.
   currRow.close();
   myConn.disconnect();

// If the connection fails, write an error message.
}else{
   write('Error ('+myConn.majorErrorCode()+'): '' + myConn.majorErrorMessage();
}

</server>
```

database.beginTransaction()

ES2+

Syntax

database.beginTransaction()

Description

The beginTransaction() method of the database object begins a new SQL transaction. This groups all the actions against the database together until the user exits the page or either the commitTransaction() or rollbackTransaction() methods are called. In the instance of the user exiting the page, the transaction is either committed or rolled back, depending on the setting of the commit flag when the database object instance is created.

> ## NOTE
>
> You cannot have nested transactions.

Example

Listing 9.65 creates a connection to an Oracle database. After the connection has been verified, the beginTransaction() method is called and a SQL query is performed. The results are formatted in a table with the SQLTable() method and written to the user's page.

Listing 9.65   Starting a New Transaction with the beginTransaction()
Method

```
<server>

// Assign the user submitted ID to the client object as properties.
client.uid = request.uid;

// Open a connection.
var myConn = database.connect("ORACLE", "mySID", "myApp", "appsPWD", "myTNS");

if(myConn.connected()){

  // Start a new transaction and write the results to a page, formatting
  // them with the SQLTable method.
  myConn.beginTransaction();
  write(myConn.SQLTable('SELECT * FROM employees WHERE uid >= ' + client.uid));

  // Commit the transaction.
  myConn.commitTransaction();

// If the connection fails, write an error message.
}else{
  write('Error ('+myConn.majorErrorCode()+'): '' + myConn.majorErrorMessage();
}

</server>
```

database.commitTransaction()
ES2+

Syntax

database.commitTransaction()

Description

The commitTransaction() method of the database object commits a new SQL transaction. This commits all the actions against the database since the last commit. If the commit is successful, 0 is returned. If a non-zero number is returned, an error was encountered. In this case, you can use the various methods of the database object to retrieve the code and message of the error.

Example

Listing 9.66 creates a connection to an Oracle database. After the connection has been verified, the beginTransaction() method is called and a SQL query is performed. The results are formatted in a table with the SQLTable() method and written to the user's page.

Listing 9.66 Starting a New Transaction with the commitTransaction() ***Method***

```
<server>

// Assign the user submitted ID to the client object as properties.
client.uid = request.uid;

// Open a connection.
var myConn = database.connect("ORACLE", "mySID", "myApp", "appsPWD", "myTNS");

if(myConn.connected()){

  // Start a new transaction and write the results to a page, formatting
  // them with the SQLTable method.
  myConn.beginTransaction();
  write(myConn.SQLTable('SELECT * FROM employees WHERE uid >= ' + client.uid));

  // Commit the transaction.
  myConn.commitTransaction();

// If the connection fails, write an error message.
}else{
  write('Error ('+myConn.majorErrorCode()+'): '' + myConn.majorErrorMessage();
}

</server>
```

database.connect()

ES2+

Syntax

database.connect(*dbType, dbInstance, uid, pwd, dbName*)

database.connect(*dbType, dbInstance, uid, pwd, dbName, maxConn*)

database.connect(*dbType, dbInstance, uid, pwd, dbName, maxConn, commitFlag*)

Description

The connect method of the database object is the actual method that connects to a database given the parameters passed. Before you open a connection to a database and have the ability to run queries against it, you should create an instance of this object. Each parameter is defined in Table 9.9.

Table 9.9 Parameters of the connect Method

Parameter	Description
dbType	The type of database it is. Possible values are ORACLE, SYBASE, INFORMIX, DB2, or ODBC.
dbInstance	This is the instance name of the database. For ODBC it is the DSN entry name.
uid	The username or ID you want the connection to connect as.
pwd	The password for the user you are connecting as.
dbName	The name of the database you want to log in to. For Oracle, DB2, and ODBC connections this should be a blank, "", string. In Oracle, the name of the database for these connections is set up in the tnsnames.ora file and is defined by the DSN for ODBC connections. DB2 does not have a database name and is referenced only by the dbInstance.
maxConn	The maximum number of connections to the pool. This is effectively the number of connections the pool will open to the database.
commitFlag	This flag determines whether a pending transaction is committed when connection is released. If it is set to false, the transaction is rolled back. If it is set to true, it is committed.

Depending on your database, it is possible to create an instance of this object by passing a limited set of these parameters. See your database documentation for this information.

Example

Listing 9.67 creates a connection to an Oracle database. It takes a user's UID and name that was passed in, runs a query (based on the UID) against the database to find that user's information, and updates her name. If a connection is not made, the error code and message are returned to the screen.

Listing 9.67 Connecting to a Database Using the connect() Method

```
<server>

// Assign the user submitted ID and name to the client object as properties.
client.uid = request.uid;
client.name = request.name;

// Open a connection.
```

```
var myConn = database.connect("ORACLE","mySID","myApp","appsPWD","myTNS",true);

if(myConn.connected()){

  // Start a new SQL transaction to perform a SELECT.
  myConn.beginTransaction();
  var currRow = myConn.cursor('SELECT * FROM employees WHERE uid = '
➥ + client.uid);

  // Focus on that line, change the name column for that user,
  // and update the row.
  currRow.next();
  currRow.name = client.name;
  currRow.updateRow("employees");
  myConn.commitTransaction();

  // Close the cursor and the connection.
  currRow.close();
  myConn.disconnect();

// If the connection fails, write an error message.
}else{
  write('Error ('+myConn.majorErrorCode()+'): '' + myConn.majorErrorMessage();
}

</server>
```

database.connected()

ES2+

Syntax

database.connected()

Description

The connected() method of the database object tells whether the connection to the database is still active.

Example

Listing 9.68 creates a connection to a database. If the connection is made, any code within that section is executed. If the connection fails, the error is written to the page.

Listing 9.68   Testing a Connection with the connected() Method

```
<server>

// Open a connection.
var myConn = database.connect("ORACLE", "mySID", "myApp", "appsPWD", "myTNS");
```

Listing 9.69   Continued

```
if (myConn.connected()) {

  // You are connected, so perform any tasks here.

}else{

  // There was an error connecting to the database.
  write('Error ('+myConn.majorErrorCode()+'): '' + myConn.majorErrorMessage();
}

</server>
```

database.cursor()

ES2+

Syntax

```
database.cursor(sql)
database.cursor(sql, boolean)
```

Description

The cursor() method of the database object creates a Cursor object that can be used to run SQL queries against the database. The method takes the sql statement as a parameter, as well as an optional boolean value that specifies whether the cursor is updateable.

Example

Listing 9.69 shows how you would run a query against the database using the cursor() method. The while loop is used to write the results to the user's page.

Listing 9.69   Using the cursor() Method to Run a Query Against the Database

```
<server>

// Set the query to run.
var mySQL = myConn.cursor('SELECT name,title FROM employees');

// Iterate through the results and write them to the page.
while(mySQL.next()){
  write(mySQL.name + ': ' + mySQL.title + '<br>');
}

</server>
```

database.disconnect()

ES2+

Syntax

database.disconnect()

Description

The disconnect method of the database object disconnects a connection to a database.

Example

Listing 9.70 creates a connection to an Oracle database. It takes a user's UID and name that was passed in, runs a query (based on the UID) against the database to find that user's information, and updates her name. If a connection is not made, the error code and message are returned to the screen. After the processing has been completed, the connection is dropped using the disconnect() method.

Listing 9.70   Disconnecting from a Database Using the disconnect() **Method**

```
<server>

// Assign the user submitted ID and name to the client object as properties.
client.uid = request.uid;
client.name = request.name;

// Open a connection.
var myConn = database.connect("ORACLE","mySID","myApp","appsPWD","myTNS",true);

if(myConn.connected()){

  // Start a new SQL transaction to perform a SELECT.
  myConn.beginTransaction();
  var currRow = myConn.cursor('SELECT * FROM employees WHERE uid = '
➡ + client.uid);

  // Focus on that line, change the name column for that user,
  // and update the row.
  currRow.next();
  currRow.name = client.name;
  currRow.updateRow("employees");
  myConn.commitTransaction();

  // Close the cursor and the connection.
  currRow.close();
  myConn.disconnect();
```

Listing 9.70   Continued

```
// If the connection fails, write an error message.
}else{
  write('Error ('+myConn.majorErrorCode()+'): '' + myConn.majorErrorMessage();
}

</server>
```

database.execute()

ES2+

Syntax

```
database.execute(statement)
```

Description

The execute() method of the database object enables your application to execute a *DDL (Data Definition Language)* or *DML (Data Manipulation Language)* query, which does not return a Cursor, supported by your database. This includes statements such as CREATE, ALTER, and DROP.

> **NOTE**
>
> Be sure to use SQL that conforms to your database.

Example

Listing 9.71 deletes all rows with a UID less than the number passed to the script.

Listing 9.71   Using the execute() *Method to Run DML Queries*

```
<server>

// Assign the UID passed to the client object.
client.uid = request.uid;

// Execute a DELETE based on the UID passed.
myConn.execute('DELETE FROM employees WHERE uid < ' + client.uid);

</server>
```

database.majorErrorCode()

ES2+

Syntax

```
database.majorErrorCode()
```

Description

The majorErrorCode() method of the database object contains the ODBC or database numeric error code that is returned if an error occurs.

Example

Listing 9.72 shows how you would create a connection and test for a successful connection. If the test fails, the majorErrorCode() is used when writing the error to the page.

Listing 9.72   Using majorErrorCode() ***to Retrieve a Database Connection Error***

```
<server>

// Open a connection.
var myConn = database.connect("ORACLE", "mySID", "myApp", "appsPWD", "myTNS");

if (myConn.connected()) {

  // You are connected, so perform any tasks here.

}else{

  // There was an error connecting to the database.
  write('Error ('+myConn.majorErrorCode()+'): '' + myConn.majorErrorMessage();
}

</server>
```

database.majorErrorMessage()
ES2+

Syntax

database.majorErrorMessage()

Description

The majorErrorMessage() method of the database object contains the ODBC or database string error message that is returned if an error occurs.

Example

Listing 9.73 shows how you would create a connection and test for a successful connection. If the test fails, the majorErrorMessage() is used when writing the error to the page.

Listing 9.73   Using `majorErrorMessage()` *to Retrieve a Database Connection Error*

```
<server>

// Open a connection.
var myConn = database.connect("ORACLE", "mySID", "myApp", "appsPWD", "myTNS");

if (myConn.connected()) {

  // You are connected, so perform any tasks here.

}else{

  // There was an error connecting to the database.
  write('Error ('+myConn.majorErrorCode()+'): '' + myConn.majorErrorMessage();
}

</server>
```

database.minorErrorCode()

ES2+

Syntax

`database.minorErrorCode()`

Description

The `minorErrorCode()` method of the `database` object contains the secondary ODBC or database numeric error code that is returned if an error occurs.

Example

Listing 9.74 shows how you would create a connection and test for a successful connection. If the test fails, the `minorErrorCode()` is used when writing the secondary error to the page.

Listing 9.74   Using `minorErrorCode()` *to Retrieve a Secondary Database Connection Error*

```
<server>

// Open a connection.
var myConn = database.connect("ORACLE", "mySID", "myApp", "appsPWD", "myTNS");

if (myConn.connected()) {
```

```
  // You are connected, so perform any tasks here.

}else{

  // There was an error connecting to the database.
  write('Error ('+myConn.minorErrorCode()+'): '+myConn.minorErrorMessage);
}

</server>
```

database.minorErrorMessage()

ES2+

Syntax

database.minorErrorMessage()

Description

The minorErrorMessage() method of the database object contains the secondary ODBC or database string error message that is returned if an error occurs.

Example

Listing 9.75 shows how you would create a connection and test for a successful connection. If the test fails, the minorErrorMessage() is used when writing the secondary error to the page.

Listing 9.75   Using minorErrorMessage() **to Retrieve a Secondary Database Connection Error**

```
<server>

// Open a connection.
var myConn = database.connect("ORACLE", "mySID", "myApp", "appsPWD", "myTNS");

if (myConn.connected()) {

  // You are connected, so perform any tasks here.

}else{

  // There was an error connecting to the database.
  write('Error ('+myConn.minorErrorCode()+'): '+myConn.minorErrorMessage);
}

</server>
```

database.prototype
ES2+

Syntax

```
database.prototype.method = name
database.prototype.property = value
```

Description

The `prototype` property of the `database` object allows you to add methods and properties to the `database` object. If you are adding a method, you set the instance equal to the *name* of the method you have defined.

Example

Listing 9.76 creates a new property and method of the `database` object. An instance is created and the new property is set. The new method is then called to verify the property, and, if it is incorrect (which it is), an error message is written to the page.

Listing 9.76   Using the `prototype` **Property to Create a New Property and Method**

```
<server>

// Define the method that we prototyped.
function verifyODBC(){

  // Check to see if the type property we added is set to a valid value.
  if(this.type == "ODBC"){
    return true;
  }else{
    return false;
  }
}

// Create a new property and method of the database object.
database.prototype.type = null;
database.prototype.isODBC = verifyODBC;

// Open a connection.
var myConn = database.connect("ORACLE", "mySID", "myApp", "appsPWD", "myTNS");

// Using the prototype we defined, assign the type property.
myConn.type = "Oracle";

// Check the type of the connection to see if it is valid.
if(myConn.isODBC()){
  write(myConn + " has a valid type of " + myConn.type);
}else{
```

```
  write(myConn + " has an invalid type of " + myConn.type);
}

</server>
```

database.rollbackTransaction()

ES2+

Syntax

database.rollbackTransaction()

Description

The rollbackTransaction() method of the database object will undo all actions performed since the last beginTransaction() method call.

> **NOTE**
>
> You cannot have nested transactions.

Example

Listing 9.77 takes a *commit* field sent to the application from the user. If this evaluates
to true, the transaction is committed. If not, it is rolled back.

Listing 9.77   Rolling Back a Transaction with the rollbackTransaction()
Method

```
<server>

// See if the user wants to commit the last transaction.
client.commit = request.commit;

if(client.commit = "YES"){

  // Commit the transaction.
  myConn.commitTransaction();

}else{

  // Rollback the transaction.
  myConn.rollbackTransaction();
}

</server>
```

database.SQLTable()

ES2+

Syntax

database.SQLTable(*sql*)

Description

The SQLTable() method of the database object takes a *sql* SELECT statement as a parameter and executes this query through the connection from which it was called. It returns the results formatted in an HTML table for easy writing to a client's page. This is a simple table in the following format:

```
<table border="1">
<tr>
<th>column 1</th>
<th>column 2</th>
...
<th>column N</th>
</tr>
<tr>
<td>value 1 of column 1</td>
<td>value 1 of column 2</td>
...
<td>value 1 of column N</td>
</tr>
<tr>
<td>value 2 of column 1</td>
<td>value 2 of column 2</td>
...
<td>value 2 of column N</td>
</tr>
...
</table>
```

Example

Listing 9.78 runs a user passed query and formats the result using the SQLTable() method. This information is then written to the user's page.

Listing 9.78   Using the SQLTable() Method to Format the Result of a SELECT Query

```
<server>

// Assign the user submitted query to the client object.
client.sql = request.sql;

// Open a connection.
```

```
var myConn = database.connect("ORACLE", "mySID", "myApp", "appsPWD", "myTNS");

if(myConn.connected()){

  // Start a new transaction and write the results to a page, formatting
  // them with the SQLTable method.
  myConn.beginTransaction();
  write(myConn.SQLTable(client.sql));

  // Commit the transaction.
  myConn.commitTransaction();

// If the connection fails, write an error message.
}else{
  write('Error ('+myConn.majorErrorCode()+'): '' + myConn.majorErrorMessage();
}

// Release the connection.
myConn.release();

</server>
```

database.storedProc()

ES3+

Syntax

```
database.storedProc(procName)
database.storedProc(procName, arg1, arg2, ... , argN)
```

Description

The storedProc() method of the database object creates a Stproc object that allows you to execute a database-specific stored procedure using the connection from which it was invoked.

As shown in the syntactical definition, you can also pass any arguments needed to the method for processing. If you are using a stored procedure that requires arguments, or if you want to have the procedure run using default arguments, you must pass /Default/ as the argument. The following shows an example of passing a default value:

```
var myStproc = myConn.storedProc("sp_employees", "/Default/");
```

The scope of this procedure is restricted to the current page. Any methods of the Stproc object must be invoked on the current page. If this is not possible, a new object will have to be created on subsequent pages to access the properties needed.

Example

Listing 9.79 creates a connection to a database. When the connection has been verified, the storedProc() method is used to invoke the fictitious *sp_employees* stored procedure.

Listing 9.79   Using the storedProc() **Method to Invoke a Stored Procedure on a Database**

```
<server>

// Open a connection.
var myConn = database.connect("ORACLE", "mySID", "myApp", "appsPWD", "myTNS");

if(myConn.connected()){

  myConn.beginTransaction();

  // Run the stored procedure.
  var myStproc = myConn.storedProc("sp_employees");

  // Commit the transaction.
  myConn.commitTransaction();

// If the connection fails, write an error message.
}else{
  write('Error ('+myConn.majorErrorCode()+'): '' + myConn.majorErrorMessage();
}

// Release the connection.
myConn.release();

</server> >
```

database.storedProcArgs()

ES3+

Syntax

```
database.storedProcArgs(procName)
database.storedProcArgs(procName, type1, type2, ... , typeN)
```

Description

The storedProcArgs() method of the database object creates a Stproc object that allows you to execute a database-specific stored procedure using the connection from which it was invoked on DB2, ODBC, and Sybase databases. If this method is invoked on Informix or Oracle databases, it has no effect. The difference between this method and the storedProc() method is that this method takes a type as a parameter for the arguments passed. These types can be IN, OUT, or INOUT. The following shows an example of passing these types:

```
var myStproc = myConn.storedProc("sp_employees", "INOUT", "OUT");
```

The scope of this procedure is restricted to the current page. Any methods of the Stproc object must be invoked on the current page. If this is not possible, a new object will have to be created on subsequent pages to access the properties needed.

Example

Listing 9.80 creates a connection to a database. After the connection has been verified, the storedProc() method is used to invoke the fictitious *sp_employees* stored procedure, and the storedProcArgs() method is used to specify the argument types.

Listing 9.80 Using the storedProcArgs() **Method to Set the Argument Types of a Stored Procedure**

```
<server>

// Open a connection.
var myConn = database.connect("ORACLE", "mySID", "myApp", "appsPWD", "myTNS");

if(myConn.connected()){

  myConn.beginTransaction();

  // Run the stored procedure.
  var myStprocArgs = myConn.storedProcArgs("sp_employees", "IN", "INOUT");
  var myStproc = myConn.storedProc("sp_employees", 3, "%John%");

  // Commit the transaction.
  myConn.commitTransaction();

// If the connection fails, write an error message.
}else{
  write('Error ('+myConn.majorErrorCode()+'): '' + myConn.majorErrorMessage();
}

// Release the connection.
myConn.release();

</server>
```

database.toString()

ES2+

Syntax

```
database.toString()
```

Description

The toString() method of the database object returns a text value of the object. When invoked on an instance of a database object, the string is returned in the following format:

```
"dbName" "uid" "dbType" "dbInstance"
```

If the parameter is unknown, an empty string is returned. Table 9.10 contains the value of these returned values.

Table 9.10   Return Values of the toString() **Method**

Method	Description
dbName	The name of the database you want to log in to. For Oracle, DB2, and ODBC connections, this is a blank, "", string. In Oracle, the name of the database for these connections are set up in the tnsnames.ora file and are defined by the DSN for ODBC connections. DB2 does not have a database name and is referenced only by the dbInstance.
uid	The username or ID you want the connections to connect as.
dbType	The type of database it is. Possible values are ORACLE, SYBASE, INFORMIX, DB2, or ODBC.
dbInstance	This is the instance name of the database. For ODBC, it is the DSN entry name.

Example

Listing 9.81 creates an instance of the database object. Once created, the write() method is used to write its string value to the page.

Listing 9.81   Write the Results of Calling the toString() **Method to a Page**

```
<server>

// Open a connection.
var myConn = database.connect("ORACLE", "mySID", "myApp", "appsPWD", "myTNS");

if(myConn.connected()){

  // Write the string value of the object to the page.
  write(myConn.toString());

// If the connection fails, write an error message.
}else{
  write('Error ('+myConn.majorErrorCode()+'): '' + myConn.majorErrorMessage());
}
```

```
// Release the connection.
myConn.release();

</server>
```

database.unwatch()
ES3+

Syntax

database.unwatch(*property*)

Description

The unwatch() method of the database object is used to turn off the watch for a particular *property*.

Example

Listing 9.82 shows how the unwatch() method is used to stop watching the user-defined property *p*.

Listing 9.82   Example of the unwatch() **Method**

```
<server>

// Define the method that we prototyped.
function verifyODBC(){

  // Check to see if the type property we added is set to a valid value.
  if(this.type == "ODBC"){
    return true;
  }else{
    return false;
  }
}

// function that is called if property's value changes
function alertme(id, oldValue, newValue){
  write("ID (" + id + ") changed from " + oldValue + " to " + newValue);
  return newValue;
}

// Create a new property and method of the database object.
database.prototype.type = null;
database.prototype.isODBC = verifyODBC;

// Open a connection.
var myConn = database.connect("ORACLE", "mySID", "myApp", "appsPWD", "myTNS");
```

Listing 9.82   Continued

```
// Using the prototype we defined, assign the type property.
myConn.type = "Oracle";

// Check the type of the connection to see if it is valid.
if(myConn.isODBC()){
  write(myConn + " has a valid type of " + myConn.type);
}else{
  write(myConn + " has an invalid type of " + myConn.type);
}

// watch property
myConn.watch("type", alertme);

// change value
myConn.type = null;

// turn off watch
myConn.unwatch("type");

// change value again
myConn.type = "Sybase";

</server>
```

database.watch()

ES3+

Syntax

database.watch(*property, function*)

Description

The watch() method of the database object is used to turn on the watch for a particular property specified by *property*. Any time the specified *property* is changed after
the watch() method has been called, the specified *function* is called.

Example

Listing 9.83 shows how the watch() method is used to start watching the user-defined
property *p*.

Listing 9.83   Example of the watch() ***Method***

```
<server>

// Define the method that we prototyped.
function verifyODBC(){
```

```
  // Check to see if the type property we added is set to a valid value.
  if(this.type == "ODBC"){
    return true;
  }else{
    return false;
  }
}

// function that is called if property's value changes
function alertme(id, oldValue, newValue){
  write("ID (" + id + ") changed from " + oldValue + " to " + newValue);
  return newValue;
}

// Create a new property and method of the database object.
database.prototype.type = null;
database.prototype.isODBC = verifyODBC;

// Open a connection.
var myConn = database.connect("ORACLE", "mySID", "myApp", "appsPWD", "myTNS");

// Using the prototype we defined, assign the type property.
myConn.type = "Oracle";

// Check the type of the connection to see if it is valid.
if(myConn.isODBC()){
  write(myConn + " has a valid type of " + myConn.type);
}else{
  write(myConn + " has an invalid type of " + myConn.type);
}

// watch property
myConn.watch("type", alertme);

// change value
myConn.type = null;



</server>
```

DbPool

ES3+

Syntax

```
new DbPool()

new DbPool(dbType, dbInstance, uid, pwd, dbName)
```

```
new DbPool(dbType, dbInstance, uid, pwd, dbName, maxConn)

new DbPool(dbType, dbInstance, uid, pwd, dbName, maxConn, commitFlag)
```

Description

The DbPool object is an object that holds a "*pool*" of connections to a database. Before you open a connection to a database and have the ability to run queries against it, you should create an instance of this object. After the instance is created, connections can be obtained from the pool as needed. The pool object itself takes all the parameters necessary to make the connection. It is possible to create a pool without specifying any parameters; however, you must pass the parameters when the first connection is attempted.

The creation of a DbPool object is done using the format defined in the syntax definition. Each parameter is defined in Table 9.11.

Table 9.11 *Parameters of the* DbPool *Object*

Parameter	Description
dbType	The type of database it is. Possible values are ORACLE, SYBASE, INFORMIX, DB2, or ODBC.
dbInstance	This is the instance name of the database. For ODBC, it is the DSN entry name.
uid	The username or ID you want the connections to connect as.
pwd	The password for the user you are connecting as.
dbName	The name of the database you want to log in to. For Oracle, DB2, and ODBC connections this should be a blank, "", string. In Oracle, the name of the database for these connections is set up in the tnsnames.ora file and is defined by the DSN for ODBC connections. DB2 does not have a database name and is referenced only by the dbInstance.
maxConn	The maximum number of connections to the pool. This is effectively the number of connections the pool will open to the database.
commitFlag	This flag determines whether a pending transaction is committed when connection is released. If it is set to false, the transaction is rolled back. If it is set to true, it is committed.

Depending on your database, it is possible to create an instance of this object by passing a limited set of these parameters, as well as passing none. The object itself has the methods listed in Table 9.12.

Table 9.12   *Methods of the* DbPool *Object*

Method	Description
connect()	Connects to a particular pool of database connections
connected()	Tests to see whether the pool is still connected to the database
connection()	Obtains an available connection from the pool
DbPool()	Creates the pool of connections to a database
disconnect()	Disconnects all connections in the pool from the database
majorErrorCode()	Returns the major error code numeric value returned by the database or ODBC
majorErrorMessage()	Returns the major error message string value returned by the database or ODBC
minorErrorCode()	Returns the secondary error code numeric value returned by the database or ODBC
minorErrorMessage()	Returns the secondary error message string value returned by the database or ODBC
storedProcArgs()	Creates a prototype for DB2, ODBC, or Sybase stored procedures
toString()	Returns a string representing the specified object
unwatch()	Turns off the watch for a particular property
watch()	Turns on the watch for a particular property

Example

Listing 9.84 creates a pool of connections to an Oracle database and initializes a connection from that pool. It takes a user's UID and name that was passed in, runs a query (based on the UID) against the database to find that user's information, and updates her name. If a connection is not made, the error code and message are returned to the screen.

Listing 9.84   *Creating and Using a* DbPool *Object*

```
<server>

// Assign the user submitted ID and name to the client object as properties.
client.uid = request.uid;
client.name = request.name;

// Create a pool of connections.
var myPool = new DbPool("ORACLE", "mySID", "myApp", "appsPWD", "myTNS");

// Open a connection from the pool. Give error if connection could
// not be made.
var myConn = myPool.connection('Employees', 15);
if(myConn){
```

Listing 9.84 *Continued*

```
// Start a new SQL transaction to perform a SELECT.
myConn.beginTransaction();
var currRow = myConn.cursor('SELECT * FROM employees WHERE uid = '
➥ + client.uid);

// Focus on that line, change the name column for that user,
// and update the row.
currRow.next();
currRow.name = client.name;
currRow.updateRow("employees");

// Close the cursor.
currRow.close();

// If the connection fails, write an error message.
}else{
  write('Error ('+myConn.majorErrorCode()+'): '' + myConn.majorErrorMessage();
}

</server>
```

DbPool.connect()

ES3+

Syntax

dbpool.connect(*dbType, dbInstance, uid, pwd, dbName*)

dbpool.connect(*dbType, dbInstance, uid, pwd, dbName, maxConn*)

dbpool.connect(*dbType, dbInstance, uid, pwd, dbName, maxConn, commitFlag*)

Description

The connect method of the DbPool object is used to connect to a database when the connection was not made with the initialization of the original DbPool object. The method takes all the parameters necessary to connect to the database. Each parameter is defined in Table 9.9.

Table 9.13 *Parameters of the* connect() *Method*

Parameter	Description
dbType	The type of database it is. Possible values are ORACLE, SYBASE, INFORMIX, DB2, or ODBC.
dbInstance	This is the instance name of the database. For ODBC it is the DSN entry name.
uid	The username or ID you want the connections to connect as.
pwd	The password for the user you are connecting as.

Parameter	Description
dbName	The name of the database you want to log into. For Oracle, DB2, and ODBC connections this should be a blank, "", string. In Oracle, the name of the database for these connections is set up in the `tnsnames.ora` file and is defined by the DSN for ODBC connections. DB2 does not have a database name and is referenced only by the `dbInstance`.
maxConn	The maximum number of connections to the pool. This is effectively the number of connections the pool will open to the database.
commitFlag	This flag determines whether a pending transaction is committed when connection is released. If it is set to `false`, the transaction is rolled back. If it is set to `true`, it is committed.

Depending on your database, it is possible to create an instance of this object by passing a limited set of these parameters. See your database documentation for this information.

Example

Listing 9.85 creates a connection pool. The `connect()` method is then called to open the pool to an Oracle database. If a connection is not made, the error code and message are returned to the screen.

Listing 9.85   Connecting to a Database Using the `connect()` Method

```
<server>

// Assign the user submitted ID and name to the client object as properties.
client.uid = request.uid;
client.name = request.name;

// Create a pool of connections.
var myPool = new DbPool();

// Create a connection for the pool.
myPool.connect("ORACLE", "mySID", "myApp", "appsPWD", "myTNS");

// Open a connection from the pool. Give error if connection could
// not be made.
var myConn = myPool.connection('Employees', 15);

if(myConn.connected()){

  // Do any database stuff here.
```

Listing 9.85   Continued

```
// If the connection fails, write an error message.
}else{
  write('Error ('+myConn.majorErrorCode()+'): '' + myConn.majorErrorMessage();
}

</server>
```

DbPool.connected()

ES3+

Syntax

```
dbpool.connected()
```

Description

The `connected()` method of the `DbPool` object tells whether the pool of connections to the database is still connected.

Example

Listing 9.86 creates a pool of connections and pulls a connection from the pool for processing. If the connection is made, any code within that section is executed. If the connection fails, the error is written to the page.

Listing 9.86   Testing a Connection with the `connected()` Method

```
<server>

// Create a pool of connections.
var myPool = new DbPool("ORACLE", "mySID", "myApp", "appsPWD", "myTNS");

// Open a connection from the pool. Give error if connection could
// not be made.
var myConn = myPool.connection('Employees', 15);

if (myConn.connected()) {

  // You are connected, so perform any tasks here.

}else{

  // There was an error connecting to the database.
  write('Error ('+myConn.majorErrorCode()+'): '' + myConn.majorErrorMessage();
}

</server>
```

DbPool.connection()

ES3+

Syntax

dbpool.connection(*name*, *seconds*);

Description

The connection() method of the DbPool object pulls a connection from the pool. The connection is returned from the method and can be stored in a variable to be used for processing.

The method takes two parameters. The first parameter is a *name*, which is a name you can give your connection. Because you actually store the connection in a variable, this name's primary function becomes one for debugging purposes. The second parameter is a *seconds* value for the number of seconds you give the instance to connect.

Example

Listing 9.87 creates a pool of connections to an Oracle database and initializes a connection from that pool. It takes a user's UID and name that was passed in, runs a query (based on the UID) against the database to find that user's information, and updates her name. If a connection is not made, the error code and message are returned to the screen.

Listing 9.87   Creating and Using a* connection() *Method

```
<server>

// Create a pool of connections.
var myPool = new DbPool("ORACLE", "mySID", "myApp", "appsPWD", "myTNS");

// Open a connection from the pool. Give error if connection could
// not be made.
var myConn = myPool.connection('Employees', 15);

if (myConn.connected()) {

  // You are connected, so perform any tasks here.

}else{

  // There was an error connecting to the database.
  write('Error ('+myConn.majorErrorCode()+'): '' + myConn.majorErrorMessage();
}

</server>
```

DbPool.DbPool()

ES3+

Syntax

```
new DbPool()

new DbPool(dbType, dbInstance, uid, pwd, dbName)

new DbPool(dbType, dbInstance, uid, pwd, dbName, maxConn)

new DbPool(dbType, dbInstance, uid, pwd, dbName, maxConn, commitFlag)
```

Description

The DbPool() method of the DbPool object is the underlying method that creates a "*pool*" of connections to a database. The creation of a DbPool object is done using the format defined in the syntax definition. Each parameter is defined in Table 9.14.

Table 9.14 Parameters of the DbPool() Method

Parameter	Description
dbType	The type of database it is. Possible values are ORACLE, SYBASE, INFORMIX, DB2, or ODBC.
dbInstance	This is the instance name of the database. For ODBC it is the DSN entry name.
uid	The username or ID you want the connections to connect as.
pwd	The password for the user you are connecting as.
dbName	The name of the database you want to log in to. For Oracle, DB2, and ODBC connections this should be a blank, "", string. In Oracle, the name of the database for these connections is set up in the tnsnames.ora file and is defined by the DSN for ODBC connections. DB2 does not have a database name and is referenced only by the dbInstance.
maxConn	The maximum number of connections to the pool. This is effectively the number of connections the pool will open to the database.
commitFlag	This flag determines whether a pending transaction is committed when connection is released. If it is set to false, the transaction is rolled back. If it is set to true, it is committed.

Depending on your database, it is possible to create an instance of this object by passing a limited set of these parameters.

Example

Listing 9.88 creates a pool of connections and pulls a connection from the pool for processing. If the connection is made, any code within that section is executed. If the connection fails, the error is written to the page.

Listing 9.88 *The* `DbPool()` *Method is the Underlying Method Used When a* `DbPool` *Object Instance Is Created*

```
<server>

// Create a pool of connections.
var myPool = new DbPool("ORACLE", "mySID", "myApp", "appsPWD", "myTNS");

// Open a connection from the pool. Give error if connection could
// not be made.
var myConn = myPool.connection('Employees', 15);

if (myConn.connected()) {

  // You are connected, so perform any tasks here.

}else{

  // There was an error connecting to the database.
  write('Error ('+myConn.majorErrorCode()+'): '' + myConn.majorErrorMessage();
}

</server>
```

DbPool.disconnect()

ES3+

Syntax

`dbpool.disconnect()`

Description

The `disconnect()` method of the `DbPool` object disconnects all connections to a database within that pool.

Example

Listing 9.89 creates a connection to an Oracle database. The next line drops the connection by using the `disconnect()` method.

Listing 9.89 *Disconnecting from a Database Using the* `disconnect()` *Method*

```
<server>

// Create a pool of connections.
var myPool = new DbPool("ORACLE", "mySID", "myApp", "appsPWD", "myTNS");
```

Listing 9.89 Continued

```
// Drop the connections.
myPool.disconnect();

</server>
```

DbPool.majorErrorCode()

ES3+

Syntax

```
dbpool.majorErrorCode()
```

Description

The `majorErrorCode()` method of the `DbPool` object contains the ODBC or database numeric error code that is returned if an error occurs.

Example

Listing 9.90 shows how you would create a pool of connections and test for the connection. If the test fails, the `majorErrorCode()` is used when writing the error to the page.

Listing 9.90 Using `majorErrorCode()` to Retrieve a Database Connection Error

```
<server>

// Create a pool of connections.
var myPool = new DbPool("ORACLE", "mySID", "myApp", "appsPWD", "myTNS");

if (myPool.connected()) {

  // You are connected, so perform any tasks here.

}else{

  // There was an error connecting to the database.
  write('Error ('+myPool.majorErrorCode()+'): '+myPool.majorErrorMessage);
}

</server>
```

DbPool.majorErrorMessage()

ES3+

Syntax

```
dbpool.majorErrorMessage()
```

Description

The `majorErrorMessage()` method of the `DbPool` object contains the ODBC or database string error message that is returned if an error occurs.

Example

Listing 9.91 shows how you would create a pool of connections and test for the connection. If the test fails, the `majorErrorMessage()` method is used to write the error to the page.

Listing 9.91   *Using* `majorErrorMessage()` *to Retrieve a Database Connection Error*

```
<server>

// Create a pool of connections.
var myPool = new DbPool("ORACLE", "mySID", "myApp", "appsPWD", "myTNS");

if (myPool.connected()) {

  // You are connected, so perform any tasks here.

}else{

  // There was an error connecting to the database.
  write('Error ('+myPool.majorErrorCode()+'): '+myPool.majorErrorMessage);
}

</server>
```

DbPool.minorErrorCode()

ES3+

Syntax

dbpool`.minorErrorCode()`

Description

The `minorErrorCode()` method of the `DbPool` object contains the secondary ODBC or database numeric error code that is returned if an error occurs.

Example

Listing 9.92 shows how to create a pool of connections and test for the connection. If the test fails, the `minorErrorCode()` method is used to write the secondary error to the page.

Listing 9.92   Using `minorErrorCode()` to Retrieve a Secondary Database Connection Error

```
<server>

// Create a pool of connections.
var myPool = new DbPool("ORACLE", "mySID", "myApp", "appsPWD", "myTNS");

if (myPool.connected()) {

  // You are connected, so perform any tasks here.

}else{

  // There was an error connecting to the database.
  write('Error ('+myPool.minorErrorCode()+'): '+myPool.minorErrorMessage);
}

</server>
```

DbPool.minorErrorMessage()

ES3+

Syntax

dbpool`.minorErrorMessage()`

Description

The `minorErrorMessage()` method of the `DbPool` object contains the secondary ODBC or database string error message that is returned if an error occurs.

Example

Listing 9.93 shows how to create a pool of connections and test for the connection. If the test fails, the `minorErrorMessage()` method is used to write the secondary error to the page.

Listing 9.93   Using `minorErrorMessage()` to Retrieve a Secondary Database Connection Error

```
<server>

// Create a pool of connections.
var myPool = new DbPool("ORACLE", "mySID", "myApp", "appsPWD", "myTNS");

if (myPool.connected()) {

  // You are connected, so perform any tasks here.

}else{
```

```
  // There was an error connecting to the database.
  write('Error ('+myPool.minorErrorCode()+'): '+myPool.minorErrorMessage);
}

</server>
```

DbPool.prototype
ES3+

Syntax
```
dbpool.prototype.method = name
dbpool.prototype.property = value
```

Description
The prototype property of the DbPool object allows you to add methods and properties to the DbPool object. If you are adding a method, you set the instance equal to the *name* of the method you have defined.

Example
Listing 9.94 creates a new property and method of the DbPool object. An instance is created and the new property is set. The new method is then called to verify the property, and, if it is incorrect, an error message is written to the page.

Listing 9.94   *Using the* prototype *Property to Create a New Property and Method*

```
<server>

// Define the method that we prototyped.
function verifyOracle(){

  // Check to see if the type property we added is set to a valid value.
  if(this.type == "Oracle"){
    return true;
  }else{
    return false;
  }
}

// Create a new property and method of the DbPool object.
DbPool.prototype.type = null;
DbPool.prototype.isOracle = verifyOracle;

// Create a pool of connections.
var myPool = new DbPool("ORACLE", "mySID", "myApp", "appsPWD", "myTNS");
```

Listing 9.94   Continued

```
// Using the prototype we defined, assign the type property.
myPool.type = "Oracle";

// Check the type of the connection to see if it is valid.
if(myPool.isOracle()){
  write(myPool + " has a valid type of " + myPool.type);
}else{
  write(myPool + " has an invalid type of " + myPool.type);
}

</server>
```

DbPool.storedProcArgs()

ES3+

Syntax

```
database.storedProcArgs(procName)
database.storedProcArgs(procName, type1, type2, ... , typeN)
```

Description

The storedProcArgs() method of the database object creates a Stproc object that allows you to execute a database-specific stored procedure using the connection from which it was invoked on DB2, ODBC, and Sybase databases. If this method is invoked on Informix or Oracle databases, it has no affect. The difference between this method and the storedProc() method is that this method takes a type as a parameter for the arguments passed. These types can be IN, OUT, or INOUT. The following shows an example of passing these types:

```
var myStproc = myConn.storedProc("sp_employees", "INOUT", "OUT");
```

The scope of this procedure is restricted to the current page. Any methods of the Stproc object must be invoked on the current page. If this is not possible, a new object will have to be created on subsequent pages to access the properties needed.

Example

Listing 9.95 creates a pool of connections to a database. The storedProc() method is used to invoke the fictitious *sp_employees* stored procedure, and the storedProcArgs() method is used to specify the argument types.

Listing 9.95   Using the storedProcArgs() *Method to Set the Argument Types of a Stored Procedure*

```
<server>

// Create a pool of connections.
var myPool = new DbPool("ORACLE", "mySID", "myApp", "appsPWD", "myTNS");
```

```
// Set the stored procedure arguments.
var myStprocArgs = myPool.storedProcArgs("sp_employees", "IN", "INOUT");
var myStproc = myPool.storedProc("sp_employees", 3, "%John%");

</server>
```

DbPool.toString()
ES3+

Syntax

dbpool.toString()

Description

The toString() method of the DbPool object returns a text value of the object. When invoked on an instance of a DbPool object, the string is returned in the following format:

"dbName" "uid" "dbType" "dbInstance"

If the parameter is unknown, an empty string is returned. Table 9.15 contains the value of these returned values.

Table 9.15 *Return Values of the* toString() *Method*

Method	Description
dbName	The name of the database you want to log in to. For Oracle, DB2, and ODBC connections this is a blank, "", string. In Oracle, the name of the database for these connections is set up in the tnsnames.ora file and is defined by the DSN for ODBC connections. DB2 does not have a database name and is referenced only by the dbInstance.
uid	The username or ID you want the connections to connect as.
dbType	The type of database it is. Possible values are ORACLE, SYBASE, INFORMIX, DB2, or ODBC.
dbInstance	This is the instance name of the database. For ODBC, it is the DSN entry name.

Example

Listing 9.96 creates an instance of the DbPool object. Once created, the write() method is used to write its string value to the page.

Listing 9.96   Write the Results of Calling the `toString()` **Method to a Page**

```
<server>

// Create a pool of connections.
var myPool = new DbPool("ORACLE", "mySID", "myApp", "appsPWD", "myTNS");

// Open a connection from the pool. Give error if connection could
// not be made.
var myConn = myPool.connection('Employees', 15);
if(myConn.connected()){

  // Write the string value of the object to the page.
  write(myPool.toString());

// If the connection fails, write an error message.
}else{
  write('Error ('+myConn.majorErrorCode()+'): '' + myConn.majorErrorMessage();
}

// Release the connection.
myConn.release();

</server>
```

DBPool.unwatch()

ES3+

Syntax

dbpool`.unwatch(`*property*`)`

Description

The `unwatch()` method of the `DbPool` object is used to turn off the watch for a particular *property*.

Example

Listing 9.97 shows how the `unwatch()` method is used to stop watching the user-defined property *p*.

Listing 9.97   Example of the `unwatch()` **Method**

```
<server>

// Define the method that we prototyped.
function verifyOracle(){
```

```
  // Check to see if the type property we added is set to a valid value.
  if(this.type == "Oracle"){
    return true;
  }else{
    return false;
  }
}

// function that is called if property's value changes
function alertme(id, oldValue, newValue){
  write("ID (" + id + ") changed from " + oldValue + " to " + newValue);
  return newValue;
}

// Create a new property and method of the DbPool object.
DbPool.prototype.type = null;
DbPool.prototype.isOracle = verifyOracle;

// Create a pool of connections.
var myPool = new DbPool("ORACLE", "mySID", "myApp", "appsPWD", "myTNS");

// Using the prototype we defined, assign the type property.
myPool.type = "Oracle";

// watch property
myPool.watch("type", alertme);

// Check the type of the connection to see if it is valid.
if(myPool.isOracle()){
  write(myPool + " has a valid type of " + myPool.type);
}else{
  write(myPool + " has an invalid type of " + myPool.type);
}

// change value
myPool.type = null;

// turn off watch
myPool.unwatch("type");

// change value again
myPool.type = "Sybase";

</server>
```

DBPool.watch()

ES3+

Syntax

dbpool.watch(*property, function*)

Description

The watch() method of the DBPool object is used to turn on the watch for a particular property specified by *property*. Any time the specified *property* is changed after the watch() method has been called, the specified *function* is called.

Example

Listing 9.98 shows how the watch() method is used to start watching the user-defined property *p*.

Listing 9.98   Example of the watch() **Method**

```
<server>

// Define the method that we prototyped.
function verifyOracle(){

  // Check to see if the type property we added is set to a valid value.
  if(this.type == "Oracle"){
    return true;
  }else{
    return false;
  }
}

// function that is called if property's value changes
function alertme(id, oldValue, newValue){
  write("ID (" + id + ") changed from " + oldValue + " to " + newValue);
  return newValue;
}

// Create a new property and method of the DbPool object.
DbPool.prototype.type = null;
DbPool.prototype.isOracle = verifyOracle;

// Create a pool of connections.
var myPool = new DbPool("ORACLE", "mySID", "myApp", "appsPWD", "myTNS");

// Using the prototype we defined, assign the type property.
myPool.type = "Oracle";
```

```
// watch property
myPool.watch("type", alertme);

// Check the type of the connection to see if it is valid.
if(myPool.isOracle()){
  write(myPool + " has a valid type of " + myPool.type);
}else{
  write(myPool + " has an invalid type of " + myPool.type);
}

// change value
myPool.type = null;

</server>
```

debug()

ES2+

Syntax

```
debug(expression)
debug(variable)
```

Description

The debug function is a top-level function that is not associated with any core object. This function is used to display the value of an expression or variable in the Trace Information window when running the application in the JavaScript Application Manager's debug window.

Example

Listing 9.99, when run in the JavaScript Application Manager's debugger, will display the value of the *request.name* when encountered.

Listing 9.99   Using the debug() **Function to Write Information to the Trace Information Window**

```
<server>

// Display the value of the name passed in the request
// to the application.
debug(request.name);

</server>
```

deleteResponseHeader()

ES3+

Syntax

deleteResponseHeader(*key*)

Description

The `deleteResponseHeader()` function is a top-level function and is not associated with any core object. This function is used to delete fields in the HTTP header before it is sent back to the client. Because of when the actual header is sent in relation to the body of the data, you should be sure to delete these fields before you call the `flush()` or `redirect()` functions.

> **NOTE**
>
> The JavaScript runtime engine flushes the output buffer after 64KB of content has been generated. You should be sure to call the `deleteResponseHeader()` function before this time.

Example

Listing 9.100 shows how you can delete the content-type header field before it is sent back to the browser.

Listing 9.100   Using the `deleteResponseHeader()` **Function to Delete the** `content.type` **of a File Being Sent to a Browser**

```
<server>

// Delete a field to the header.
deleteResponseHeader("content-type");

</server>
```

File()

ES2+

Syntax

new File(*path*)

Description

The `File` object allows you to perform various tasks such as reading and writing to a file on your disk. The object itself has many methods to use and a `prototype` property that allows a programmer to create new properties and methods of the object. Table 9.16 lists the methods accessible and a brief description of each. An instance of this object is created by simply passing the *path* of the file you want to create or read.

Table 9.16 **Methods of the** `File` **Object**

Method	Description
`byteToString()`	Converts the byte number passed into its string equivalent
`clearError()`	Clears the `File.eof()` and `File.error()` error status
`close()`	Closes the file you opened
`eof()`	Returns `true` if you are at the end of the file you have opened
`error()`	Returns the current error
`exists()`	Checks to see whether the file you want to process exists
`flush()`	Writes the contents of the current buffer to the file
`getLength()`	Returns the length of the file
`getPosition()`	Returns your current position within a file
`open()`	Opens the file
`read()`	Reads the specified number of characters into a string
`readByte()`	Reads the next byte, or character, in the file
`readln()`	Reads the current line, starting at your current position, into a string
`setPosition()`	Sets your position in a file
`stringToByte()`	Converts the string passed into its byte number equivalent
`unwatch()`	Turns off the watch for a particular property
`watch()`	Turns on the watch for a particular property
`write()`	Writes a string to the file you opened
`writeByte()`	Writes a byte of data to a binary file you opened
`writeln()`	Writes a string and a carriage return to the file you opened

The usage of the `File` object is very straightforward. The methods provided allow you to perform the various tasks needed on the files on your file system. Part of this functionality of working with these files is to allow programmers to specify how they want to open the files. A file can be opened to read, write, append, or open in binary mode. These options are specified in the `open()` method in the following form:

```
myFile.open("option");
```

Table 9.17 gives a list and description of these options.

Table 9.17 **Options of the** `open()` **Method**

Option	Description
a	This option opens a file for appending. If the file does not exist, it is created. This method always returns `true`.
a+	This option opens a file for reading and appending. If the file does not exist, it is created. This method always returns `true`.
r	This option opens a file for reading. If the file exists, the method returns `true`; otherwise, it returns `false`.
r+	This option opens a file for reading and writing. If the file exists, the method returns `true`; otherwise, it returns `false`. Reading and writing start at the beginning of the file.

Table 9.17   Continued

Option	Description
w	This option opens a file for writing. If the file does not exist, it is created. If it does exist, it is overwritten. This method always returns `true`.
w+	This option opens a file for reading and writing. If the file does not exist, it is created. If it does exist, it is overwritten. This method always returns `true`.
optionb	Appending `b` to the end of any of these options specifies that you want to perform the operation in binary mode.

Example

Listing 9.101 displays an option menu that allows a user to select a file to read. When the form is submitted, the script reads the file and displays its contents on a page.

Listing 9.101   Using the `File` Object

```
<html>
<head>
  <title> Using the File object</title>
</head>
<body>
<server>

// See if they have submitted or just need the forml
if(request.method == "POST"){

  // Create an instance of the File object and pass it the file
  // the user specified they wanted to view.
  var myLog = new File(request.file);

  // Try to open the file.
  if(!myLog.open("r")){

    // If there was an error, tell the user.
    write("There was an error opening the file: " + request.file);
  }else{

    // If there was not an error, then open the file and display it.
    write('<h3>The contents of ' + request.file + ' are as follows:</h3>');
    while(!myLog.eof()){
    write(myLog.readln());
    }
  }
}else{
```

```
// If this page was called then write the select box to the page for
// the user to use to select which log they want to see.

write('<form name="myForm" method="post">');
write('<select name="file">');
write('<option value="/logs/admin.log">Admin Log</option>');
write('<option value="/logs/user.log">User Log</option>');
write('<option value="/logs/error.log">Error Log</option>');
write('</select>');
write('<input type="submit" value="View Log">');
write('</form>');
}

</server>
</body>
</html>
```

File.byteToString()

ES2+

Syntax

`File.byteToString(num)`

Description

The `byteToString()` method of the `File` object is used to convert the numeric value passed to its ASCII equivalent. If the method is not passed a number, an empty string is returned.

Example

Listing 9.102 opens two files, one for reading and the other for appending. Bytes are then read using the `readByte()` method from the first file, converted back to string characters using the `byteToString()` method, and written to the second file. Both files are closed when the process has completed.

Listing 9.102   Using the `byteToString()` **Method to Convert the Bytes Read into Strings**

```
<server>

// Open a log file and a summary file.
var myLog = new File("/data/logs/today.log");
var mySummary = new File("/data/logs/summary.log");

// Open the log file for reading and the summary file for
// appending.
myLog.open("r");
```

Listing 9.102   Continued

```
mySummary.open("a");

// Append the contents of the log file to the summary file.
while (!myLog.eof()){
  myBytes = File.byteToString(myLog.readByte());
  mySummary.write(myBytes);
}

// Close the files.
myLog.close();
mySummary.close();

</server>
```

File.clearError()

ES2+

Syntax

```
file.clearError()
```

Description

The clearError() method of the File object clears the file error status and the value returned by the eof() method.

Example

Listing 9.103 opens a file for reading. If the operation returned an error, the error is written to the page. If there was an error, it is cleared after writing it.

Listing 9.103   Using the clearError() Method to Clear File Errors

```
<server>

// Open a log file.
var myLog = new File("/data/logs/today.log");

// Open the log file for reading.
myLog.open("r");

if (myLog.error() == 0) {

  // Perform actions on file.

}else{
```

```
  // Write out the error.
  write('Error: ' + myLog.error());

  // Clear the error.
  myLog.clearError()
}

// Close the file.
myLog.close();

</server>
```

File.close()
ES2+

Syntax
`file.close()`

Description

The `close()` method of the `File` object closes the file on which it has been invoked. This method returns `true` if it was successful and `false` if it was unsuccessful.

Example

Listing 9.104 shows how to open a file and then close it.

Listing 9.104   Closing a File with the `close()` Method

```
<server>

// Open a log file.
var myLog = new File("/data/logs/today.log");

// Open the log file for reading.
myLog.open("r");

// Close the file.
myLog.close();

</server>
```

File.constructor
ES2+

Syntax
`file.constructor`

Description

The `constructor` property of the `File` object specifies the function that creates the object.

Example

Listing 9.2105 shows an example of the `constructor` property.

Listing 9.105 ***Example of the*** `constructor` ***Property***

```
<server>

// Open a log file.
var myLog = new File("/data/logs/today.log");

// Open the log file for reading.
myLog.open("r");

if(myLog.constructor == File){
    write("Object created");
}



// Close the file.
myLog.close();

</server>
```

File.eof()

ES2+

Syntax

`file.eof()`

Description

The `eof()` method of the `File` object returns `true` if the position of the pointer within the file is past the end of the file. It returns `false` otherwise.

Example

Listing 9.106 reads a file and writes its contents to the page until the end of the file is found with the `eof()` method.

Listing 9.106   Reading a File Until You Come to the End of It, Which Can Be Evaluated Using the `eof()` *Method*

```
<server>

// Open a log file for reading.
var myLog = new File("/data/logs/today.log");
myLog.open("r");

// Write the contents of the log file to the page.
while (!myLog.eof()){
  myBytes = File.byteToString(myLog.readByte());
  write(myBytes);
}

// Close the file.
myLog.close();

</server>
```

File.error()

ES2+

Syntax

`file.error()`

Description

The `error()` method of the `File` object returns the operating system error code when an error occurs opening a file. This method returns 0 if there is no error, and -1 if the file you invoke the method on is unable to be opened.

Example

Listing 9.107 opens a file for reading. If there was a problem during this operation, the error is written to the user's page.

Listing 9.107   Using the `error()` *Method to Access an Error to Write to the User's Page*

```
<server>

// Open a log file.
var myLog = new File("/data/logs/today.log");

// Open the log file for reading.
myLog.open("r");
```

Listing 9.107 *Continued*

```
if (myLog.error() == 0) {

  // Perform actions on file.

}else{

  // Write out the error.
  write('Error: ' + myLog.error());

  // Clear the error.
  myLog.clearError()
}

// Close the file.
myLog.close();

</server>
```

File.exists()

ES2+

Syntax

`file.exists()`

Description

The exists() method of the File object returns a boolean value based on the existence of the file in which it was invoked. If the file exists, the method returns true. It returns false if the file does not exist.

Example

Listing 9.108 opens a file and then checks to see whether it exists.

Listing 9.108 *Using the* exists() *Method to See Whether a File Exists*

```
<server>

// Open a log file.
var myLog = new File("/data/logs/today.log");

// See if the file exists.
if(myLog.exists()){
  write('The file exists');
}else{
  write('The file does not exist');
}

</server>
```

File.flush()

ES2+

Syntax

`file.flush()`

Description

The `flush()` method of the `File` object is used to write buffered information to a file. This information is placed in a buffer when the `write()`, `writeln()`, and `writeByte()` methods are used. Note that this is not the same as the top-level `flush` function.

Example

Listing 9.109 opens a file for reading and another file for writing. If the file for reading exists, a string is written to the other file. The `flush()` method is used to write the buffered information to the file.

Listing 9.109   Using the `flush()` *Method*

```
<server>

// Open a log file.
var myLog = new File("/data/logs/today.log");
var mySummary = new File("/data/logs/summary.log");

myLog.open("r");
mySummary.open("w");

// See if the file exists.
if(myLog.exists()){
  mySummary.write('The file exists');
}else{
  mySummary.write('The file does not exist');
}

// Write the data in the buffer to the file.
mySummary.flush();

// Close the file.
myLog.close();
mySummary.close();

</server>
```

File.getLength()

ES2+

Syntax

file.getLength()

Description

The getLength() method of the File object returns the number of characters in a text file or the number of bytes in a binary file. If the method is unsuccessful, –1 is returned.

Example

Listing 9.110 opens a file for reading and another file for writing. The getLength() method is used in a for loop to determine when to stop reading from the file.

Listing 9.110   Using the getLength() Method

```
<server>

// Open the files.
var myLog = new File("/data/logs/today.log");
var mySummary = new File("/data/logs/summary.log");
myLog.open("r");
mySummary.open("w");

// Write the contents of the log file to the page.
for(var i = 0; i <= myLog.getLength(); i++){
  myBytes = File.byteToString(myLog.readByte());
  mySummary.write(myBytes);
}

mySummary.flush();

// Close the files.
myLog.close();
mySummary.close();

</server>
```

File.getPosition()

ES2+

Syntax

file.getPosition()

Description

The getPosition() method of the File object returns the zero-based index position of the current pointer in the file. If the pointer is on the first character, 0 is returned. If there is an error, -1 is returned.

Example

Listing 9.111 loops through each character, printing it on a new line next to its indexed location.

Listing 9.111 **Using the** getPosition() **Method**

```
<server>

// Open the files.
var myLog = new File("/data/logs/today.log");
var mySummary = new File("/data/logs/summary.log");
myLog.open("r");
mySummary.open("w");

// Write the contents of the log file to the page.
for(var i = 0; i <= myLog.getLength(); i++){
  myBytes = File.byteToString(myLog.readByte());
  mySummary.write('Character '+mySummary.getPosition()+' is '+myBytes+'<br>');
}

mySummary.flush();

// Close the files.
myLog.close();
mySummary.close();

</server>
```

File.open()

ES2+

Syntax

file.open(*option*)

Description

The open() method of the File object is used to open a file to read, write, and/or append to. The method returns true if it is successful and false otherwise. The options passed determine the mode in which the file is opened. The options are specified in Table 9.18.

Table 9.18   Options of the open() Method

Option	Description
a	This option opens a file for appending. If the file does not exist, it is created. This method always returns `true`.
a+	This option opens a file for reading and appending. If the file does not exist, it is created. This method always returns `true`.
r	This option opens a file for reading. If the file exists, the method returns `true`; otherwise, it returns `false`.
r+	This option opens a file for reading and writing. If the file exists, the method returns `true`; otherwise, it returns `false`. Reading and writing start at the beginning of the file.
w	This option opens a file for writing. If the file does not exist, it is created. If it does exist, it is overwritten. This method always returns `true`.
w+	Thisoption opens a file for reading and writing. If the file does not exist, it is created. If it does exist, it is overwritten. This method always returns `true`.
optionb	Appending b to the end of any of these options specifies that you want to perform the operation in binary mode.

Example

Listing 9.112 shows how to open a file in `read` mode.

Listing 9.112   Using the open() Method to Open a File

```
<server>

// Initialize a file
var myLog = new File("/data/logs/today.log");

// Open the file in read mode
myLog.open("r");

// Close the file
myLog.close();

</server>
```

File.prototype

ES3+

Syntax

```
file.prototype.method = name
file.prototype.property = value
```

Description

The `prototype` property of the `File` object allows you to add methods and properties to the `File` object. If you are adding a method, you set the instance equal to the *name* of the method you have defined.

Example

Listing 9.113 creates a new property and method of the `File` object. An instance is created and the new property is set. The new method is then called to verify the property, and, if it is incorrect (which it is), an error message is written to the page.

Listing 9.113 **Using the** `prototype` **Property to Create a New Property and Method**

```
<server>

// Define the method that we prototyped.
function verifyTEXT(){

  // Check to see if the type property we added is set to a valid value.
  if(this.type == "text"){
    return true;
  }else{
    return false;
  }
}

// Create a new property and method of the connection object.
File.prototype.type = null;
File.prototype.isText = verifyTEXT;

// Initialize a file
var myLog = new File("/data/logs/today.log");

// Open the file in read mode
myLog.open("r");

// Using the prototype we defined, assign the type property.
myLog.type = "text";

// Check the type of the connection to see if it is valid
if(myLog.isText()){
  write(myLog + " has a valid type of " + myLog.type);
}else{
  write(myLog + " has an invalid type of " + myLog.type);
}

</server>
```

File.read()

ES2+

Syntax

`file.read(num)`

Description

The `read()` method of the `File` object starts at the current pointer in the file and reads *num* characters in the file. If you try to read characters past the end of the file, the method will read all the characters and stop. Use the `readByte()` method if you are trying to read the byte data.

Example

Listing 9.114 reads information from a text file and writes every other character to the user's page. The `setPosition()` method is used to move the pointer correctly, and the `read()` method is used to read the data.

Listing 9.114   Using the `read()` *Method*

```
<server>

// Open the files.
var myLog = new File("/data/logs/today.log");
myLog.open("r");

// Write some characters to the page.
for(var i = 1; i <= myLog.getLength(); i + 2){

  // Set the position of the pointer.
  myLog.setPosition(i);

  // Write every other character to the page.
  write(myLog.read(1));
}

// Close the file.
myLog.close();

</server>
```

File.readByte()

ES2+

Syntax

`file.readByte(num)`

Description

The readByte() method of the File object starts at the current pointer in the file and reads *num* bytes in the file. If you try to read bytes past the end of the file, the method will read all the bytes and stop. Use the read() method if you are trying to read the characters in text data.

Example

Listing 9.115 reads information from a text file and writes every other byte to the user's page. The setPosition() method is used to move the pointer correctly, and the readByte() method is used to read the data.

Listing 9.115   *Using the* readByte() *Method*

```
<server>

// Open the files.
var myLog = new File("/data/logs/today.dat");
myLog.open("rb");

// Write some characters to the page.
for(var i = 1; i <= myLog.getLength(); i + 2){

  // Set the position of the pointer.
  myLog.setPosition(i);

  // Write every other byte to the page.
  write(myLog.readByte(1));
}

// Close the file.
myLog.close();

</server>
```

File.readln()

ES2+

Syntax

file.readln()

Description

The readln() method of the File object starts at the current pointer position and reads the rest of the line. When the method is complete, it will return the pointer to the first character on the next line.

NOTE

The return (\r) and newline (\n))characters are not contained in the string this method returns. However, the newline character determines when the end of the line is reached.

Example

Listing 9.116 reads in the first line of a file and writes it to the user's page.

Listing 9.116   Using the `readln()` **Method**

```
<server>

// Open the files.
var myLog = new File("/data/logs/today.log");
myLog.open("r");

// Write the first line.
write(myLog.readln());

// Close the file.
myLog.close();

</server> >
```

File.setPosition()

ES2+

Syntax

```
file.setPosition(num)
file.setPosition(num, refPoint)
```

Description

The `setPosition()` method of the `File` object sets the pointer's position to a relative *num* location in the file. By default, this is relative to the beginning of the file, but you can pass a reference point to determine where this relative location is located. The possible values of this reference point are listed in Table 9.19.

Table 9.19   Possible Values of the Reference Point

Value	Description
0	Sets the pointer relative to the beginning of the file
1	Sets the pointer relative to the current pointer position
2	Sets the pointer relative to the end of the file

Example

Listing 9.117 uses the `setPosition()` method to access every other character in the file.

Listing 9.117   *Using the* `setPosition()` *Method*

```
<server>

// Open the files.
var myLog = new File("/data/logs/today.log");
myLog.open("r");

// Write some characters to the page.
for(var i = 1; i <= myLog.getLength(); i + 2){

  // Set the position of the pointer.
  myLog.setPosition(i);

  // Write every other character to the page.
  write(myLog.read(1));
}

// Close the file.
myLog.close();

</server>
```

File.stringToByte()

ES2+

Syntax

`File.stringToByte(string)`

Description

The `stringToByte()` method of the `File` object is used to convert the first character of the string passed to its binary equivalent.

Example

Listing 9.118 opens two files, one for reading and the other for appending. Strings are then read using the `read()` method from the first file, converted back to byte characters using the `stringToByte()` method, and then written to the second file. Both files are closed when the process has after completed.

Listing 9.118   Using the `stringToByte()` *Method to Convert the Strings Read into Bytes*

```
<server>

// Open a log file and a summary file.
var myLog = new File("/data/logs/today.dat");
var mySummary = new File("/data/logs/summary.dat");

// Open the log file for reading and the summary file for
// appending.
myLog.open("rb");
mySummary.open("ab");

// Append the contents of the log file to the summary file.
for(var i = 0; i <= myLog.getLength(); i++){
  myLog.setPosition(i);
  myByte = File.stringToBytes(myLog.read(1));
  mySummary.writeByte(myByte);
}

// Flush the buffer to the file.
mySummary.flush();

// Close the files.
myLog.close();
mySummary.close();

</server>
```

File.unwatch()

ES3+

Syntax

`file.unwatch(property)`

Description

The unwatch() method of the `File` object is used to turn off the watch for a particular *property*.

Example

Listing 9.119 shows how the unwatch() method is used to stop watching the user-defined property *p*.

Listing 9.119 *Example of the* unwatch() *Method*

```
<server>

// Define the method that we prototyped.
function verifyTEXT(){

  // Check to see if the type property we added is set to a valid value.
  if(this.type == "text"){
    return true;
  }else{
    return false;
  }
}

// function that is called if property's value changes
function alertme(id, oldValue, newValue){
  write("ID (" + id + ") changed from " + oldValue + " to " + newValue);
  return newValue;
}

// Create a new property and method of the connection object.
File.prototype.type = null;
File.prototype.isText = verifyTEXT;

// Initialize a file.
var myLog = new File("/data/logs/today.log");

// Open the file in read mode.
myLog.open("r");

// Using the prototype we defined, assign the type property.
myLog.type = "text";

// watch property
myLog.watch("type", alertme);

// Check the type of the connection to see if it is valid.
if(myLog.isText()){
  write(myLog + " has a valid type of " + myLog.type);
}else{
  write(myLog + " has an invalid type of " + myLog.type);
}

// change value
myLog.type = null;

// turn off watch
myLog.unwatch("type");
```

Listing 9.119   Continued

```
// change value again
myLog.type = "ASCII";

</server>
```

File.watch()

ES3+

Syntax

```
file.watch(property, function)
```

Description

The watch() method of the File object is used to turn on the watch for a particular property specified by *property*. Any time the specified *property* is changed after the watch() method has been called, the specified *function* is called.

Example

Listing 9.120 shows how the watch() method is used to start watching the user-defined property *p*.

Listing 9.120   Example of the watch() Method

```
<server>

// Define the method that we prototyped.
function verifyTEXT(){

  // Check to see if the type property we added is set to a valid value.
  if(this.type == "text"){
    return true;
  }else{
    return false;
  }
}

// function that is called if property's value changes
function alertme(id, oldValue, newValue){
  write("ID (" + id + ") changed from " + oldValue + " to " + newValue);
  return newValue;
}

// Create a new property and method of the connection object.
File.prototype.type = null;
File.prototype.isText = verifyTEXT;
```

```
// Initialize a file.
var myLog = new File("/data/logs/today.log");

// Open the file in read mode.
myLog.open("r");

// Using the prototype we defined, assign the type property.
myLog.type = "text";

// watch property
myLog.watch("type", alertme);

// Check the type of the connection to see if it is valid.
if(myLog.isText()){
  write(myLog + " has a valid type of " + myLog.type);
}else{
  write(myLog + " has an invalid type of " + myLog.type);
}

// change value
myLog.type = null;

</server>
```

File.write()

ES2+

Syntax

file.write(*string*)

Description

The write() method of the File object writes the string passed to the method to the file on which it was invoked. The method returns true if it was successful and false otherwise. You should use the read() or readln() methods to read any string information from other files that you want to write. If you need to write binary information, use the writeByte() method.

Example

Listing 9.121 writes "Hello, World!" to the summary file opened.

Listing 9.121   Using write() to Write a String to a File

```
<server>

// Set an instance of a File.
var mySummary = new File("/data/logs/summary.log");
```

Listing 9.121   Continued

```
// Open the log file for writing.
mySummary.open("w");

// Write a string to the file.
mySummary.write('Hello, World!');

// Flush the buffer to the file.
mySummary.flush();

// Close the file.
mySummary.close();

</server>
```

File.writeByte()

ES2+

Syntax

`file.writeByte(byte)`

Description

The `writeByte()` method of the `File` object writes the byte passed to the method to the file on which it was invoked. The method returns `true` if it was successful and `false` otherwise. You should use the `readByte()` method to read any byte information from other files that you want to write. If you need to write text information, use the `write()` method.

Example

Listing 9.122 reads data from a binary file and writes it to another file.

Listing 9.122   Using `writeByte()` to Write Binary Data to a File

```
<server>

// Open a log file and a summary file.
var myLog = new File("/data/logs/today.dat");
var mySummary = new File("/data/logs/summary.dat");

// Open the log file for reading and the summary file for
// appending.
myLog.open("br");
mySummary.open("ba");

// Append the contents of the log file to the summary file.
for(var i = 0; i <= myLog.getLength(); i++){
  myLog.setPosition(i);
```

```
  myByte = myLog.readByte(1);
  mySummary.writeByte(myByte);
}

// Flush the buffer to the file.
mySummary.flush();

// Close the files.
myLog.close();
mySummary.close();

</server>
```

File.writeln()

ES2+

Syntax

file.writeln(*string*)

Description

The writeln() method of the File object writes the string passed to the method, followed by a carriage return to the file on which it was invoked. The method returns true if it was successful and false otherwise. You should use the read() or readln() methods to read any string information from other files you want to write. If you need to write binary information, use the writeByte() method.

Example

Listing 9.123 writes the line "Hello, World!" to the summary file opened.

Listing 9.123   Using writeln() *to Write a String and Carriage Return to a File*

```
<server>

// Set an instance of a File.
var mySummary = new File("/data/logs/summary.log");

// Open the log file for writing.
mySummary.open("w");

// Write a string to the file.
mySummary.writeln('Hello, World!');

// Flush the buffer to the file.
mySummary.flush();
```

Listing 9.123   Continued

```
// Close the file.
mySummary.close();

</server>
```

flush()

ES2+

Syntax

```
flush()
```

Description

The `flush()` function is a top-level function that is not associated with any object. The JavaScript runtime buffers the HTML page it is constructing in memory, and then sends it to the client after 64KB has been obtained. This function can be used to send this data on demand, which is useful when done before large database queries. Note this is not the same flush as the `File.flush()` method.

NOTE

The `flush()` function updates the cookie file as part of the HTTP header. If you are using a client cookie to maintain the `client` object, you should make any changes to this object before calling the `flush()` function.

Example

Listing 9.124 uses the `flush()` function to flush the buffer to the page after the initial write.

Listing 9.124   Using the `flush()` Function to Flush the Buffer to the Page

```
<server>

// Write a string to the page.
write('Hello, World!');

// Flush the buffer to the client.
flush();

</server>
```

getOptionValue()
Nes2+

Syntax

getOptionValue(*key*, *num*)

Description

The getOptionValue() function is a top-level function that is not associated with any object. This function returns the same value as the client-side Option.text property. The *key* passed in as an argument represents the name attribute of the <select> tag, whereas the *num* parameter is the indexed position of the selected option. Specifying *num* to 0 can reference the first selected option, which might not be the first option.

Example

Listing 9.125 displays a multi-select option box that allows a user to select different sports. When the Submit button is clicked, the form is sent back to itself and the script then uses a for loop and the getOptionValue() function to write the submitted selections to the user's page.

Listing 9.125   Using the getOptionValue() *Function*

```
<html>
<head>
  <title> Using the getOptionValue Function</title>
</head>
<body>
<server>

// See if they have submitted or just need the form.
if(request.method == "POST"){

  // Store the number of selected options in a variable.
  var counter = getOptionValueCount("sports");

  // Write the title.
  write('<b>You selected the following options</b><hr size=1>');

  // Iterate through the options and write which ones were selected.
  for(var i = 0; i < counter; i++){

    // Get the Option.text values of the selected options.
    var optionValue = getOptionValue("sports", i)
    write('Option ' + i + ': ' + optionValue + '<br>')
  }
}else{
  // If this page was called and a form was not submitted, then write the
  // form to the page for the user to use.
```

Listing 9.125   *Continued*

```
  write('<form name="myForm" method="post">');
  write('<select name="sports" multiple size="4">');
  write('<option>Baseball</option>');
  write('<option>Football</option>');
  write('<option>Basketball</option>');
  write('<option selected>Soccer</option>');
  write('<option>Rugby</option>');
  write('</select>');
  write('<input type="submit" value="Submit">');
  write('</form>');
}

</server>
</body>
</html>
```

getOptionValueCount()

ES2+

Syntax

```
getOptionValueCount(key)
```

Description

The getOptionValueCount() function is a top-level function that is not associated with any object. This function returns the number of selected options passed to the function. The *key* parameter represents the name attribute of the <select> tag on which you want to invoke the function.

Example

Listing 9.126 shows how to use the getOptionValueCount() function to determine how many options were selected in a "sports" select box.

Listing 9.126   *Using the* getOptionValueCount() *Function*

```
<server>

// Store the number of selected options in a variable.
var counter = getOptionValueCount("sports");

</server>
```

Lock()

ES3+

Syntax

```
new Lock()
```

Description

A `Lock()` object is used when you enter a section of code that can only be accessed from a single user at a time. Not implementing an instance of this object when needed can cause you to run out of system resources and will generate a runtime error. This object has only one property, which is the `prototype` property.

This property can be used to create new methods and properties for the `Lock()` object. Table 9.20 contains the methods accessible from this object.

Table 9.20   Methods of the `Lock()` Object

Method	Description
isValid()	Verifies the construction of the `Lock()`object instance
lock()	Locks the code
unlock()	Unlocks the code
unwatch()	Turns off the watch for a particular property
watch()	Turns on the watch for a particular property

Example

Listing 9.127 shows how you would create a new `Lock()` object instance. See the examples for `Lock.lock()` and `Lock.unlock()` for examples on locking and unlocking your code segments.

Listing 9.127   Creating a New `Lock()` Object

```
<server>

// Create a new Lock object.
var myLock = new Lock();

</server>
```

Lock.constructor

ES2+

Syntax

`lock.constructor`

Description

The `constructor` property of the `Lock` object specifies the function that creates the object.

Example

Listing 9.128 shows an example of the `constructor` property.

*Listing 9.128   **The** constructor **Property***

```
<server>

// Create a new Lock object.
var myLock = new Lock();

if(myLock.constructor == Lock){
    write("Object created");
}

</server>
```

Lock.isValid()

ES3+

Syntax

```
lock.isValid()
```

Description

The isValid() method of the Lock object verifies whether the lock was properly constructed. The method returns true if the lock was constructed successfully and false otherwise.

Example

Listing 9.129 shows how you can check whether a lock was properly constructed with an if statement.

*Listing 9.129   **Verifying a Lock with the** isValid() **Method***

```
<server>

// Create a new Lock object.
var myLock = new Lock();

// Verify the lock.
if(!myLock.isValid()){
  write('There has been an error constructing your lock');
}else{

  // Success: perform operations here.

}

</server>
```

Lock.lock()

ES3+

Syntax

```
lock.lock()
```

Description

The `lock()` method of the `Lock` object locks the code in which you are working until you perform an unlock. If the code is already locked, this method will wait until it can get the lock, a timeout occurs, or an error occurs.

Example

Listing 9.130 assumes that there is a `project` object with a counter property, *num*. Because you only want to increment the counter with each new user request, it must be locked.

Listing 9.130   Using the `lock()` *Method to Lock Your Code*

```
<server>

// Create a new Lock object under the project object.
var project.myLock = new Lock();

// Verify the lock.
if(!project.myLock.isValid()){
  write('There has been an error constructing your lock');
}else{

  // Lock the code and increment a project counter.
  project.myLock.lock();
  project.hitCount.num += 1;

  // Unlock the code.
  project.myLock.unlock();

}

</server>
```

Lock.prototype

ES3+

Syntax

```
lock.prototype.method = name
lock.prototype.property = value
```

Description

The prototype property of the Lock object allows you to add methods and properties to the Lock object. If you are adding a method, you set the instance equal to the *name* of the method you have defined.

Example

Listing 9.131 creates a new property and method of the Lock object. An instance is created and the new property is set. The new method is then called to verify the property, and, if it is incorrect, an error message is written to of the page.

Listing 9.131   Using the prototype *Property to Create a New Property and Method*

```
<server>

// Define the method that we prototyped.
function verifyProject(){

  // Check to see if the type property we added is set to a valid value.
  if(this.type == "project"){
    return true;
  }else{
    return false;
  }
}

// Create a new property and method of the Lock object.
Lock.prototype.type = null;
Lock.prototype.isProject = verifyProject;

// Create a new Lock object under the project object.
var project.myLock = new Lock();

// Using the prototype we defined, assign the type property.
project.myLock.type = "project";

// Check the type of the lock to see if it is valid.
if(project.myLock.isProject()){
  write(project.myLock + " has a valid type of " + project.myLock.type);
}else{
  write(project.myLock + " has an invalid type of " + project.myLock.type);
}

</server>
```

Lock.unlock()
ES3+

Syntax
```
lock.unlock()
```

Description
The unlock() method of the Lock object unlocks the code you have locked. This method returns true if the unlocking was successful and false otherwise.

Example
Listing 9.132 assumes that there is a project object with a counter property, *num*. Because you only want to increment the counter with each new user request, it must be locked. After the counter has been incremented, the project is unlocked.

Listing 9.132 *Using the* unlock() *Method to Lock Your application*

```
<server>

// Create a new Lock object under the project object.
var project.myLock = new Lock();

// Verify the lock.
if(!project.myLock.isValid()){
  write('There has been an error constructing your lock');
}else{

  // Lock the code and increment a project counter.
  project.myLock.lock();
  project.hitCount.num += 1;

  // Unlock the code.
  project.myLock.unlock();

}

</server>
```

Lock.unwatch()
ES3+

Syntax
```
lock.unwatch(property)
```

Description
The unwatch() method of the Lock object is used to turn off the watch for a particular *property*.

Example

Listing 9.133 shows how the `unwatch()` method is used to stop watching the user-defined property *p*.

Listing 9.133   Example of the `unwatch()` *Method*

```
<server>

// Define the method that we prototyped.
function verifyProject(){

  // Check to see if the type property we added is set to a valid value.
  if(this.type == "project"){
    return true;
  }else{
    return false;
  }
}

// function that is called if property's value changes
function alertme(id, oldValue, newValue){
  write("ID (" + id + ") changed from " + oldValue + " to " + newValue);
  return newValue;
}

// Create a new property and method of the Lock object.
Lock.prototype.type = null;
Lock.prototype.isProject = verifyProject;

// Create a new Lock object under the project object.
var project.myLock = new Lock();

// Using the prototype we defined, assign the type property.
project.myLock.type = "project";

// watch property
project.myLock.watch("type", alertme);

// Check the type of the lock to see if it is valid.
if(project.myLock.isProject()){
  write(project.myLock + " has a valid type of " + project.myLock.type);
}else{
  write(project.myLock + " has an invalid type of " + project.myLock.type);
}

// change value
project.myLock.type = null;
```

```
// turn off watch
project.myLock.unwatch("type");

// change value again
project.myLock.type = null;

</server>
```

Lock.watch()

ES3+

Syntax

`lock.watch(property, function)`

Description

The watch() method of the Lock object is used to turn on the watch for a particular property specified by *property*. Any time the specified *property* is changed after the watch() method has been called, the specified *function* is called.

Example

Listing 9.134 shows how the watch() method is used to start watching the user-defined property *p*.

Listing 9.134   Example of the watch() **Method**

```
<server>

// Define the method that we prototyped.
function verifyProject(){

  // Check to see if the type property we added is set to a valid value.
  if(this.type == "project"){
    return true;
  }else{
    return false;
  }
}

// function that is called if property's value changes
function alertme(id, oldValue, newValue){
  write("ID (" + id + ") changed from " + oldValue + " to " + newValue);
  return newValue;
}
```

Listing 9.134   Continued

```
// Create a new property and method of the Lock object.
Lock.prototype.type = null;
Lock.prototype.isProject = verifyProject;

// Create a new Lock object under the project object.
var project.myLock = new Lock();

// Using the prototype we defined, assign the type property.
project.myLock.type = "project";

// watch property
project.myLock.watch("type", alertme);

// Check the type of the lock to see if it is valid.
if(project.myLock.isProject()){
  write(project.myLock + " has a valid type of " + project.myLock.type);
}else{
  write(project.myLock + " has an invalid type of " + project.myLock.type);
}

// change value
project.myLock.type = null;

</server>
```

ObjectContext

ASP1+

Syntax

Core ASP environment object

Description

The `ObjectContext` object is a core ASP environment object. The events and methods of this object are used to commit or abort a transaction that has been initiated by a script. This object requires the `<%@ Transaction = Required %>` directive to execute properly within your scripts. Table 9.21 contains the events and methods of this object.

Table 9.21   Methods and events of the `ObjectContext` *Object*

Type	Item	Description
Event	`OnTransactionAbort`	Occurs if the transaction is aborted.
	`OnTransactionCommit`	Occurs after a transactional script's transaction commits.

Type	Item	Description
Method	SetAbort()	Declares that the transaction did not complete and the resources should not be updated.
	SetComplete()	Declares that the script is not aware of any reasons for the transaction to not complete. If all components participating in the transaction also call SetComplete(), the transaction will complete.

Example

Listing 9.135 assumes that the variable *processData* has been set to true or false previously and, based on its value, either processes the transaction or aborts it.

Listing 9.135   Using the ObjectContext Object

```
<%@ Transaction = Required %>
<script runat="server" type="text/jscript" language="JScript">

// Assume processData is a boolean variable defined previously.
if(processData){
  ObjectContext.SetComplete
  Response.Write("Processing data...");
}else{
  ObjectContext.SetAbort
  Response.Write("Error: ending transaction");
}
</script>
```

ObjectContext.OnTransactionAbort

ASP1+

Syntax

```
function onTransactionAbort(){
  code
}
```

Description

The onTransactionAbort event of the ObjectContext object occurs when a transaction is aborted. When this happens, IIS calls the onTransactionAbort() function, if one is defined, and executes *code*.

Example

In Listing 9.136 we have defined the `onTransactionAbort` function that will be executed if a transaction is aborted. In the case this event is fired, a message will be written to output.

Listing 9.136 **Using the** `onTransactionAbort` **Event**

```
<%@ Transaction = Required %>
<script runat="server" type="text/jscript" language="JScript">
function onTransactionAbort(){
  Response.Write("Transaction has been aborted");
}
</script>
```

ObjectContext.OnTransactionCommit

ASP1+

Syntax

```
function onTransactionCommit(){
  code
}
```

Description

The `onTransactionCommit` event of the `ObjectContext` object occurs when a transaction has completed. When this happens, IIS calls the `onTransactionCommit()` function, if one is defined, and executes *code*.

Example

In Listing 9.137 we have defined the `onTransactionCommit()` function that will be executed if a transaction is committed. In the case this event is fired, a message will be written to output.

Listing 9.137 **Using the** `onTransactionCommit` **Event**

```
<%@ Transaction = Required %>
<script runat="server" type="text/jscript" language="JScript">
function onTransactionCommit(){
  Response.Write("Transaction has completed");
}
</script>
```

ObjectContext.SetAbort()

ASP1+

Syntax

```
ObjectContext.SetAbort()
```

Description

The SetAbort() method of the ObjectContext object aborts a transaction.

Example

In Listing 9.138 we have defined the onTransactionAbort() function that will be executed when the transaction is aborted, which we will induce with the SetAbort() method. When fired, a message will be written to be output.

Listing 9.138   *Using the* SetAbort() *Method*

```
<%@ Transaction = Required %>
<script runat="server" type="text/jscript" language="JScript">

// Define the function.
function onTransactionAbort(){
  Response.Write("Transaction has completed");
}

// Create an abort, which will call the function.
ObjectContext.SetAbort();

</script>
```

ObjectContext.SetComplete()

ASP1+

Syntax

ObjectContext.SetComplete()

Description

The SetComplete() method of the ObjectContext object overrides any previous calls to the SetAbort() method.

Example

In Listing 9.139 we have defined the onTransactionAbort() function that will be executed when the transaction is aborted, which we will induce with the SetAbort() method. When fired, we will stop the abort before the message is written to output.

Listing 9.139   *Using the* SetComplete() *Method*

```
<%@ Transaction = Required %>
<script runat="server" type="text/jscript" language="JScript">

// Define the function.
function onTransactionAbort(){
  Response.Write("Transaction has be aborted");
}
```

Listing 9.139   Continued

```
// Create an abort, which will call the function.
ObjectContext.SetAbort();

// Override the abort.
ObjectContext.SetComplete();

</script>
```

project

ES2+

Syntax

Created by the server-side JavaScript runtime when the application starts.

Description

The project object is shared by all users accessing the application. This object is created when the application is started, and destroyed when it is stopped. The project object is often used to store global properties that need to be accessed or modified by all user sessions. A common use of this object might be a counter holding the number of users who have accessed your application.

The object itself has no default properties, but properties can be created simply by specifying a name and value for the property. The following is an example of how to create a property and assign it a value, which is the IP address of the client requesting the application.

```
var project.lastIP = request.ip;
```

Table 9.22 contains a list and a description of the methods of the project object.

Table 9.22   Methods of the project *Object*

Method	Description
lock()	Locks the code
unlock()	Unlocks the code
unwatch()	Turns off the watch for a particular property
watch()	Turns on the watch for a particular property

Example

Listing 9.140 shows how you can create and increment a counter property of the project object. Before this counter is incremented, the project is locked and then is unlocked afterward.

Listing 9.140 **Using the** project *Object*

```
<server>

// Lock the code and increment a project counter.
project.lock();
project.hitCount += 1;

// Unlock the code.
project.unlock();

</server>
```

project.lock()

ES2+

Syntax

```
project.lock()
```

Description

The lock() method of the project object locks the code in which you are working until you perform an unlock. If the code is already locked, this method will wait until it can get the lock, a timeout occurs, or an error occurs.

Example

Listing 9.141 sets a project object with a counter property, *hitCount*. Because you only want to increment the counter with each new user request, it must be locked.

Listing 9.141 **Using the** lock() *Method to Lock Your Code*

```
<server>

// Lock the code and increment a project counter.
project.lock();
project.hitCount += 1;

// Unlock the application.
project.unlock();

</server>
```

project.unlock()

ES2+

Syntax

```
project.unlock()
```

Description

The unlock() method of the project object unlocks the code that you have locked. This method returns true if the unlocking was successful and false otherwise.

Example

Listing 9.142 sets a project object with a counter property, *hitCount*. Because you only want to increment the counter with each new user request, it must be locked. After the counter has been incremented, the project is unlocked.

Listing 9.142   Using the unlock() Method to Unlock Your Code

```
<server>

// Lock the code and increment a project counter.
project.lock();
project.hitCount += 1;

// Unlock the code.
project.unlock();

</server>
```

project.unwatch()

ES3+

Syntax

```
project.unwatch(property)
```

Description

The unwatch() method of the project object is used to turn off the watch for a particular *property*.

Example

Listing 9.143 shows how the unwatch() method is used to stop watching the user-defined property *p*.

Listing 9.143   Example of the unwatch() Method

```
<server>

// function that is called if property's value changes
function alertme(id, oldValue, newValue){
  write("ID (" + id + ") changed from " + oldValue + " to " + newValue);
  return newValue;
}
```

```
project.type = "work";

// watch property
project.watch("type", alertme);

// change value
project.type = null;

// turn off watch
project.unwatch("type");

// change value again
project.type = null;

</server>
```

project.watch()

ES3+

Syntax

```
project.watch(property, function)
```

Description

The watch() method of the project object is used to turn on the watch for a particu-lar property specified by *property*. Any time the specified *property* is changed after the watch() method has been called, the specified *function* is called.

Example

Listing 9.144 shows how the watch() method is used to start watching the user-defined property *p*.

Listing 9.144   Example of the watch() Method

```
<server>

// function that is called if property's value changes
function alertme(id, oldValue, newValue){
  write("ID (" + id + ") changed from " + oldValue + " to " + newValue);
  return newValue;
}

project.type = "work";

// watch property
project.watch("type", alertme);
```

Listing 9.144   Continued

```
// change value
project.type = null;

</server>
```

redirect()

ES2+

Syntax

```
redirect(URL)
```

Description

The `redirect()` function is a top-level function that is not associated with any core object. This function is used to redirect the requesting browser to the URL it was passed as a parameter.

> **NOTE**
>
> Use the `addClient()` function to preserve `client` object properties and their values.

Example

Listing 9.145 checks whether the browser asking for the page is Internet Explorer. The `redirect()` function is then used to redirect the browser accordingly.

Listing 9.145   Using the `redirect()` ***Function to Redirect a User's Browser***

```
<server>

// Check to see if the browser is Internet Explorer.
if(request.agent.indexOf('MSIE') != -1){
  redirect(addClient("/iepages/index.html"));

// Redirect to another page if it is not IE.
}else{
  redirect(addClient("/defaultpages/index.html"));
}

</server>
```

registerCFunction()

ES2+

Syntax

registerCFunction(*JSFuncName*, *libPath*, *CFunc*)

Description

registerCFunction()is a top-level function that is not associated with any core object. RegisterCFunction() is used to register a C function in a shared library as a JavaScript function so it can be used in your scripts. These libraries are the pre-built .dll files on Windows machines and .so files on Unix machines. RegisterCFunction() takes the JavaScript name you want to assign the C function, the path to the library, and the actual name of the C function you want to register in the library. The function returns a boolean value based on the success of the registration.

After you call this function, you can use the C library with the server-side JavaScript callC() function. callC() takes the JavaScript name you assigned and any parameters that need to be passed to the function.

Example

Listing 9.146 registers an external C library, extlib.dll that contains a function named getMyDate. The registration of this function assigns the name JSExtLib to be used within the script. If the function successfully registers, the callC function is used to call the C function and pass it two parameters. The results are written to the user's page. If the function does not register properly, an error is written to the user's page.

Listing 9.146   Registering a C Function in a Shared Library with
registerCFunction()

```
<server>

// Register the library and function, assigning it a JavaScript
// function name.
var myExternalLib = registerCFunction("JSExtLib", "c:/winnt/extlib.dll",
➡"getMyDate")

// If the library registered without error, then call it using the
// callC function. If it failed, then write an error to the page.
if (myExternalLib) {
  write(callC("getMyDate", 1999, 2000));
}else{
  write("There was an error processing this external library function");
}

</server>
```

Request

ASP1+

Syntax

Core ASP environment object

Description

The Request object is a core ASP environment object. This object provides a means to retrieve HTTP information passed to the server from the user agent during a request. Table 9.23 contains the collections, methods, and a property of this object.

Table 9.23 Collections, Method, and a Property of the Request **Object**

Type	Item	Description
Collection	ClientCertificate	Values of fields stored in the client certificate.
	Cookies	Values of cookies.
	Form	Values of form elements.
	QueryString	Values of variables in the HTTP query string.
	ServerVariables	Values of predetermined environment variables.
Method	BinaryRead()	Retrieves POST data sent to the server from the client.
Property	TotalBytes	Read-only property that specifies the total number of bytes the client is sending in the body of the request.

Example

Listing 9.147 shows how you can use the Request object to access a specific querystring key, and then write out its value.

Listing 9.147 Using the Request **Object**

```
<script runat="server" type="text/jscript" language="JScript">

// Write out the value of the "name" querystring entry.
Response.Write(Request.QueryString("name"));
</script>
```

Request.BinaryRead()

ASP1+

Syntax

Request.BinaryRead(*num*)

Description

The BinaryRead() method of the Request object retrieves data sent to the server in a POST request, and stores the information in an array of unsigned bytes, called a *SafeArray*. The *num* represents the number of bytes to be read into the array.

Example

Listing 9.148 shows how you can check the length of a POST, and then read the data into a *SafeArray*.

Listing 9.148   *Using the* BinaryRead() *Method*

```
<script runat="server" type="text/jscript" language="JScript">

// Check the length of the POST.
var myLen = Request.TotalBytes;

// Read the data in.
var mySafeArray = Request.BinaryRead(myLen);

</script>
```

Request.ClientCertificate
ASP1+

Syntax

```
Request.ClientCertificate(field)
Request.ClientCertificate(subfield)
```

Description

The ClientCertificate collection of the Request object retrieves the certification fields from a request. If the request uses the SSL3.0/PCT1 protocol (also referred to as HTTPS) to connect to a server, the server will request certification at which time the browser sends the certification fields. If no certificate is sent, the ClientCertificate collection returns EMPTY.

Table 9.24 contains a list of *field*s that can be passed to this collection, whereas Table 9.25 contains a list of possible *subfield*s.

Table 9.24   *Fields of the* ClientCertificate *Collection*

Field	Description
Certificate	String containing the binary stream of the entire certificate in ASN.1 format.
Flags	Set of flags providing additional client certificate information. These flags can be ceCertPresent (client certificate is present) or ceUnrecognizedIssuer (last certification in this chain is from an unknown issuer).

Table 9.24   Continued

Field	Description
Issuer	String containing a list of *subfield* values containing information about the issuer of the certificate. If this value is specified without a *subfield*, the collection returns a comma-separated list of *subfields* (that is, C=US, O=Verisign, and so on).
SerialNumber	String containing the certification serial number as an ASCII representation of hexadecimal bytes separated by hyphens (-).
Subject	String containing a list of *subfield* values. If this value is specified without a *subfield*, the collection returns a comma-separated list of *subfields* (that is, C=US, O=Verisign, and so on).
ValidFrom	Date specifying when the certificate becomes valid.
ValidUntil	Date specifying when the certificate expires. The year value is displayed as a four-digit number.

NOTE

To use the Flags, you must include the client-certificate include file (cerjavas.inc) in your ASP page. These files are installed in the \Inetpub\ASPSamp\Samples directory.

Table 9.25   Subfields of the ClientCertificate *Collection*

Subfield	Description
C	Specifies the name of the country/region of origin.
CN	Specifies the common name of the user. (This is only used with the Subject field.)
GN	Specifies a given name.
I	Specifies a set of initials.
L	Specifies a locality.
O	Specifies the company or organization name.
OU	Specifies the name of the organizational unit.
S	Specifies a state or province.
T	Specifies the title of the person or organization.

The syntax for the use of *subfields* can be a bit strange looking, so here is a quick example. Notice that the *subfield* is actually the result of concatenating the field in our previous table with the *subfield* identifier.

```
Request.ClientCertificate("SubjectCN");
```

Example

In Listing 9.149 we write out the Subject field of a client certificate present in a request.

Listing 9.149   *Using the* ClientCertificate *Collection*

```
<script runat="server" type="text/jscript" language="JScript">
Response.Write(Request.ClientCertificate("Subject");)
</script>
```

Request.Cookies

ASP1+

Syntax

```
Request.Cookies(name)
Request.Cookies(name).HasKeys
Request.Cookies(name)(subkey)
```

Description

The Cookies collection of the Request object provides access to any cookies passed to the server. You can retrieve the value of the cookie by passing the *name* of the cookie. Additionally, you can pass the HasKeys attribute to check if the collection is a cookie dictionary. If so, you can pass the *subkey* property to retrieve any subkey values from cookie dictionaries.

Example

Listing 9.150 shows how you can use the AppendToLog() method in conjunction with the Request.Cookies collection to access and write the value of a cookie named ID to the end of the log file.

Listing 9.150   *Using the* Cookies *Collection*

```
<script runat="server" type="text/jscript" language="JScript">
Response.Write(Request.Cookies("ID");
Response.Flush();
</script>
```

Request.Form

ASP1+

Syntax

```
Request.Form(name)
Request.Form(name)(num)
```

Description

The Form collection of the Request object retrieves the values of form elements that have been POSTed to the server. This collection is used by passing the *name* of the element you want to retrieve. If multiple values are passed for a given *name*, you can specify the *num* location of the value you want to retrieve.

> **NOTE**
>
> This collection can only hold 100KB of information. If your POST is larger than that, you should use the `Request.ReadBinary()` method.

Example

Listing 9.151 shows how you can check the number of values for a given form name, and then write the last value to the page.

Listing 9.151   Using the Form *Collection*

```
<script runat="server" type="text/jscript" language="JScript">

// See how many values are in the "interest" element.
myElementLen = Request.Form("interest").Count;

// Write out the last value.
Response.Write(Request.Form("interest")(myElementLen));
</script>
```

Request.Form.Form.Count

ASP1+

Syntax

```
Request.Form(name).Count
```

Description

The `Count` property of the `Form` collection of the `Request` object contains the total number of values for a given form element that has been POSTed to the server. This collection is used by passing the *name* of the element you want to retrieve a count for.

Example

Listing 9.152 shows how you can check the number of values for a given form name, and then write the last value to the page.

Listing 9.152   Using the Count *Property of the* Form *Collection*

```
<script runat="server" type="text/jscript" language="JScript">

// See how many values are in the "interest" element.
myElementLen = Request.Form("interest").Count;

// Write out the last value.
Response.Write(Request.Form("interest")(myElementLen));
</script>
```

Request.QueryString

ASP1+

Syntax

```
Request.QueryString(name)
Request.QueryString(name)(num)
```

Description

The QueryString collection of the Request object retrieves the values of form elements that have been passed to the server using the GET method. This collection is used by passing the *name* of the element you want to retrieve. If multiple values are passed for a given *name*, you can specify the *num* location of the value you want to retrieve.

NOTE

A QueryString is signified as all characters after the first occurrence of the "?" character.

Example

Listing 9.153 shows how you can check the number of values for a given querystring name, and then write the last value to the page.

Listing 9.153   Using the QueryString Collection

```
<script runat="server" type="text/jscript" language="JScript">

// See how many values are in the "interest" element.
myElementLen = Request.QueryString("interest").Count;

// Write out the last value.
Response.Write(Request.QueryString("interest")(myElementLen));
</script>
```

Request.QueryString.Count

ASP1+

Syntax

```
Request.QueryString(name).Count
```

Description

The Count property of the QueryString collection of the Request object contains the total number of values for a given form element that has been sent to the server in a GET request. This collection is used by passing the *name* of the element you want to retrieve a count for.

Example

Listing 9.154 shows how you can check the number of values for a given form element, and then write the last value to the page.

Listing 9.154   Using the `Count` Property of the `QueryString` Collection

```jscript
<script runat="server" type="text/jscript" language="JScript">

// See how many values are in the "interest" element.
myElementLen = Request.QueryString("interest").Count;

// Write out the last value.
Response.Write(Request.QueryString("interest")(myElementLen));
</script>
```

Request.ServerVariables

ASP1+

Syntax

```
Request.ServerVariables(name)
```

Description

The `ServerVariables` collection of the `Request` object retrieves a list of predefined server environment variables. You can access the value of a given variable by passing the variable's *name*. Table 9.26 contains a list of possible values for *name*.

Table 9.26   Possible `ServerVariables` for Which Information Can Be Obtained

Variable	Description
ALL_HTTP	All HTTP headers sent by the client. Note that this method places an HTTP_ prefix before the header name, and the header name is always capitalized.
ALL_RAW	Retrieves all headers in raw form.
APPL_MD_PATH	Retrieves the metabase path for the ISAPI application .dll.
APPL_PHYSICAL_PATH	Retrieves the physical path corresponding to the metabase path.
AUTH_PASSWORD	Value entered in the client's authentication dialog.
AUTH_TYPE	Authentication method used to validate users when they attempt to access a protected script.
AUTH_USER	Raw authenticated username.
CERT_COOKIE	Unique ID for client certificate.
CERT_FLAGS	bit0 is set to 1 if the client certificate is present. bit1 is set to 1 if the cCertification authority of the client certificate is invalid.

Variable	Description
CERT_ISSUER	Issuer field of the client certificate (O=MS, OU=IAS, CN=user name, C=USA).
CERT_KEYSIZE	Number of bits in Secure Sockets Layer connection key size.
CERT_SECRETKEYSIZE	Number of bits in server certificate private key.
CERT_SERIALNUMBER	Serial number field of the client certificate.
CERT_SERVER_ISSUER	Issuer field of the server certificate.
CERT_SERVER_SUBJECT	Subject field of the server certificate.
CERT_SUBJECT	Subject field of the client certificate.
CONTENT_LENGTH	Length of the content as given by the client.
CONTENT_TYPE	Data type of the content.
GATEWAY_INTERFACE	Revision of the CGI specification used by the server.
HTTP_<HeaderName>	Value stored in the header HeaderName.
HTTP_ACCEPT	Returns the value of the Accept header.
HTTP_ACCEPT_LANGUAGE	Returns a string describing the language to use for displaying content.
HTTP_USER_AGENT	Returns a string describing the browser that sent the request.
HTTP_COOKIE	Returns the cookie string that was included with the request.
HTTP_REFERER	Returns a string containing the URL of the page that referred the request, but does not include redirect requests.
HTTPS	Returns ON if request came in through SSL or returns OFF if the request is for a non-secure channel.
HTTPS_KEYSIZE	Number of bits in the Secure Sockets Layer connection key size.
HTTPS_SECRETKEYSIZE	Number of bits in the server certificate private key.
HTTPS_SERVER_ISSUER	Issuer field of the server certificate.
HTTPS_SERVER_SUBJECT	Subject field of the server certificate.
INSTANCE_ID	Textual format ID for the IIS instance.
INSTANCE_META_PATH	Metabase path for the instance of IIS.
LOCAL_ADDR	Returns the Server Address on which the request came in. This is important on multihomed machines where multiple IP addresses can be bound to the machine.
LOGON_USER	Windows account the user is logged into.
PATH_INFO	Extra path information as given by the client.
PATH_TRANSLATED	Translated version that takes the path and performs any necessary virtual-to-physical mapping.
QUERY_STRING	Query information stored in the string following the question mark (?).
REMOTE_ADDR	IP address of the remote host.

Table 9.26 Continued

Variable	Description
REMOTE_HOST	Name of the host making the request.
REMOTE_USER	Unmapped username string sent in by the user.
REQUEST_METHOD	Method used to make the request.
SCRIPT_NAME	Virtual path to the script being executed.
SERVER_NAME	Server's hostname, DNS alias, or IP address.
SERVER_PORT	Port number.
SERVER_PORT_SECURE	String containing 1 if the request is handled on the secure port; otherwise it will be 0.
SERVER_PROTOCOL	Name and revision of the request information protocol.
SERVER_SOFTWARE	Name and version of the server software that answers the request and runs the gateway.
URL	Gives the base portion of the URL.

Example

Listing 9.155 shows how you can write out the user agent string of the browser making the request.

Listing 9.155   Using the ServerVariables **Collection**

```
<script runat="server" type="text/jscript" language="JScript">
Response.Write(Request.ServerVariables("HTTP_USER_AGENT");
</script>
```

Request.TotalBytes

ASP1+

Syntax

```
Request.TotalBytes
```

Description

The TotalBytes property of the Request object is a read-only property that contains the total number of bytes the user agent sent in the body of the request.

Example

Listing 9.156 shows how you can check the length of a POST, and then read the data into a *SafeArray*.

Listing 9.156 **Using the** TotalBytes *Property*

```
<script runat="server" type="text/jscript" language="JScript">

// Check the length of the POST.
var myLen = Request.TotalBytes;

// Read the data in.
var mySafeArray = Request.BinaryRead(myLen);

</script>
```

request
ES2+

Syntax

Core object created by JavaScript runtime for each client request.

Description

The request object contains specific information about the client's request. The object itself has several properties, as well as any properties that you might be passing from a form. This object also inherits Object.watch() and Object.unwatch(), which are defined in Chapter 7, "Core Language." The properties of this object are listed in Table 9.27.

Table 9.27 **Properties of the** request *Object*

Property	Description
agent	Contains the user-agent string sent in the HTTP request.
imageX	The x coordinate of an imagemap request.
imageY	The y coordinate of an imagemap request.
formKey	This could be any key, of a *key=value* pair, passed from within a <form> tag on a page.
ip	The IP address of the user request.
method	The HTTP method used in the request.
protocol	The protocol level the requesting agent supports.

Example

Listing 9.157 writes the various properties of a request to the page.

Listing 9.157 **Using the** request *Object to See Properties of the Requesting Agent*

```
<server>

// Write each of the properties of the request to the page.
write('User Agent: ' + request.agent + '<br>');
write('Y-coordinate of ISMAP: ' + request.imageY + '<br>');
```

Listing 9.157 Continued

```
write('X-coordinate of ISMAP: ' + request.imageX + '<br>');
write('IP Address: ' + request.ip + '<br>');
write('HTTP Method: ' + request.method + '<br>');
write('Protocol Version: ' + request.protocol);

</server>
```

request.agent

ES2+

Syntax

```
request.agent
```

Description

The agent property of the request object contains the user agent string of the requesting application. The following is an example of a user agent string for Navigator 4.5 on Windows 98.

```
Mozilla/4.5   (Win98; U)
```

You can use several methods of the String object in conjunction with this property to determine the type and version of the browser requesting the page.

Example

Listing 9.158 examines the requesting browser's agent string and redirects Internet Explorer browsers to an alternative page.

Listing 9.158 Accessing the agent Property of the request Object

```
<server>

// Check to see if the browser is Internet Explorer.
if(request.agent.indexOf('MSIE') != -1){
  redirect(addClient("/iepages/index.html"));
}

</server>
```

request.*formKey*

ES2+

Syntax

```
request.formKey
```

Description

The *formKey* property of the `request` object represents any form key that is sent. A key is specified by the `name` attribute in any element of an HTML `<form>`.

Example

Listing 9.159 shows how you can have a form with a "sports" key and use the `request.formKey` property to read the value.

Listing 9.159   Reading a `formKey` Property

```
<html>
<head>
  <title>Using the formKey Property</title>
</head>
<body>
<server>

// See if they have submitted or just need the form.
if(request.method == "POST"){

  // Print the selected option to the user's page.
  write('You selected ' + request.sports);

}else{
  // If this page was called and a form was not submitted, then write the
  // form to the page for the user to use.

  write('<form name="myForm" method="post">');
  write('<select name="sports">');
  write('<option>Baseball</option>');
  write('<option>Football</option>');
  write('<option>Basketball</option>');
  write('<option>Soccer</option>');
  write('<option>Rugby</option>');
  write('</select>');
  write('<input type="submit" value="Submit">');
  write('</form>');
}

</server>
</body>
</html>
```

request.imageX

ES2+

Syntax

`request.imageX`

Description

The `imageX` property of the `request` object contains the x coordinate of the imagemap request sent from the browser. These requests come in the following form, where *x* is the numeric x-coordinate and *y* is the numeric y coordinate:

```
http://www.purejavascript.com/clickthru.html?x,y
```

Example

Listing 9.160 pulls out the x and y coordinates passed in the request and writes them to the user's page.

Listing 9.160   Accessing the `imageX` *Property*

```
<server>

// Write the imageX and imageY properties to the page.
write('Y-coordinate of ISMAP: ' + request.imageY + '<br>');
write('X-coordinate of ISMAP: ' + request.imageX);

</server>
```

request.imageY

ES2+

Syntax

```
request.imageY
```

Description

The `imageY` property of the `request` object contains the y coordinate of the imagemap request sent from the browser. These requests come in the following form, where *x* is the numeric x coordinate and *y* is the numeric y coordinate:

```
http://www.purejavascript.com/clickthru.html?x,y
```

Example

Listing 9.161 pulls out the x and y coordinates passed in the request and writes them to the user's page.

Listing 9.161   Accessing the `imageY` *Property*

```
<server>

// Write the imageX and imageY properties to the page.
write('Y-coordinate of ISMAP: ' + request.imageY + '<br>');
write('X-coordinate of ISMAP: ' + request.imageX);

</server>
```

request.ip

ES2+

Syntax

```
request.ip
```

Description

The ip property of the request object specifies the IP address of the requesting client.

Example

Listing 9.162 checks the IP address of the requesting client. If the IP address is not within the correct domain, the browser is redirected to an "unauthorized IP" page.

Listing 9.162   Using the ip Property to Verify Authorization

```
<server>

// See if the IP address is ok.
if(request.ip.indexOf("207.200.75.") != -1){

  // Send them to an authorized page.
  redirect(addClient("/authorized.html"));

}else{

  // Send them to an error page.
  redirect(addClient("/unauthorized.html"));
}

</server>
```

request.method

ES2+

Syntax

```
request.method
```

Description

The method property of the request object specifies the HTTP method used in the request. This can either be PUT or GET, depending on the submission type.

Example

Listing 9.163 shows how you can use the same page to display a form and interpret it. If the method is POST, you know it was a form submission. If it was GET, you display the form.

Listing 9.163   Evaluating the method Property

```
<server>

// See if they have submitted or just need the form.
if(request.method == "POST"){

  // Perform your processing of the form here.

}else{

  //  Write the actual HTML form here.

}

</server>
```

request.protocol

ES2+

Syntax

```
request.protocol
```

Description

The protocol property of the request object specifies the version of the HTTP protocol used in the request. This version is conveyed in the following format:

```
HTTP/1.0
```

Example

Listing 9.164 takes a look at the protocol property to see whether the request is HTTP 1.1. You can then insert any processing code needed, based on the protocol version supported by the client.

Listing 9.164   Accessing the protocol Property

```
<server>

// Check the protocol version.
if(request.protocol.indexOf("1.1") != -1){

  // Perform your HTTP 1.1 processing of the form here.

}else{

  // Perform non-HTTP 1.1 processing here.
```

```
}
```

```
</server>
```

request.unwatch()

ES3+

Syntax

```
request.unwatch(property)
```

Description

The unwatch() method of the request object is used to turn off the watch for a particular *property*.

Example

Listing 9.165 shows how the unwatch() method is used to stop watching the user-defined property *p*.

Listing 9.165   Example of the unwatch() **Method**

```
<server>

// function that is called if property's value changes
function alertme(id, oldValue, newValue){
  write("ID (" + id + ") changed from " + oldValue + " to " + newValue);
  return newValue;
}

// watch property
request.watch("agent", alertme);

// change value
request.agent = null;

// turn off watch
request.unwatch("agent");

// change value again
request.agent = null;

</server>
```

request.watch()

ES3+

Syntax

```
request.watch(property, function)
```

Description

The watch() method of the request object is used to turn on the watch for a particular property specified by *property*. Any time the specified *property* is changed after the watch() method has been called, the specified *function* is called.

Example

Listing 9.166 shows how the watch() method is used to start watching the user-defined property *p*.

Listing 9.166   Example of the watch() **Method**

```
<server>

// function that is called if property's value changes
function alertme(id, oldValue, newValue){
  write("ID (" + id + ") changed from " + oldValue + " to " + newValue);
  return newValue;
}

// watch property
request.watch("agent", alertme);

// change value
request.agent = null;

</server>
```

Response

ASP1+

Syntax

Core ASP environment object

Description

The Response object is a core ASP environment object. This object is used to send data back to the user agent making the request. Table 9.28 contains the list of collections, methods, and properties in this object.

Table 9.28   Collections and Methods in the Response *Object*

Type	Item	Description
Collection	`Cookies`	Specifies and sets cookie values.
Method	`AddHeader()`	Sets an HTML header name to a value.
	`AppendToLog()`	Adds a string to the end of the server log entry for this request.
	`BinaryWrite()`	Writes information without any character-set conversion.
	`Clear()`	Erases any buffered output.
	`End()`	Stops processing the .asp file and returns the current result.
	`Flush()`	Sends buffered output immediately.
	`Redirect()`	Sends a redirect message to the browser.
	`Write()`	Writes a variable to the current HTTP output as a string.

Example

In Listing 9.167 we use the `Write()` method of the `Response` object to write `"Hello World"` to the page.

Listing 9.167   Using the `Write()` *Method of the* Response *Object*

```
<script runat="server" type="text/jscript" language="JScript">
Response.Write("Hello World");
</script>
```

Response.AddHeader()

ASP1+

Syntax

```
Response.AddHeader(name, value)
```

Description

The `AddHeader()` method of the `Response` object is used to add the *name* header, which is assigned *value*, to the HTTP header.

Example

In Listing 9.168 we show how you can add a P3P header pointing to your privacy policy reference file.

Listing 9.168   *Using the* AddHeader() *Method*

```
<script runat="server" type="text/jscript" language="JScript">
Response.AddHeader('P3P', 'policyref="http://www.purejavascript.com/p3p.xml"')
Response.Flush()
</script>
```

Response.AppendToLog()

ASP1+

Syntax

```
Response.AppendToLog(string)
```

Description

The AppendToLog() method/property of the Response object appends *string* to the end of the log entry for the given request. If called multiple times for a given request, it will continue appending to the end of that log entry.

Example

Listing 9.169 shows how you can use the AppendToLog() method in conjunction with the Request.Cookies collection to access and write the value of a cookie named ID to the end of the log file.

Listing 9.169   *Using the* AppendToLog() *Method*

```
<script runat="server" type="text/jscript" language="JScript">
Response.AppendToLog(Request.Cookies("ID");
Response.Flush();
</script>
```

Response.BinaryWrite()

ASP1+

Syntax

```
Response.BirnaryWrite(data)
```

Description

The BinaryWrite() method of the Response object is used to write non-string *data* back to the user agent. This parameter should be of type VT_ARRAY or VT_UI1, which is a variant array of unsigned one-byte characters.

Example

In Listing 9.170 we assume that you have an object that will create binary data, and then we use the BinaryWrite() method to write out the data.

Listing 9.170   Using the `BinaryWrite()` **Method**

```
<script runat="server" type="text/jscript" language="JScript">

// Assumes you have an object that will create binary data.
Set myBin = Server.CreateObject"myApp.createBin");
myResult = myBin.createGif;

// Send the data out.
Response.BinaryWrite(myResult);
</script>
```

Response.Buffer

ASP1+

Syntax

```
Response.Buffer = boolean
```

Description

The `Buffer` property of the `Response` object specifies whether the server should buffer page output or not. When *boolean* is TRUE, all data is buffered and is not sent to the user agent until the page has finished processing, or the `Response.End()` or `Response.Flush()` methods are called. Because this property cannot be set after data has been sent to the agent, this needs to be set in the first line of your file.

Example

Listing 9.171 shows how to tell the server to buffer the content, and then send it when the `Response.Flush()` method is called.

Listing 9.171   Using the `Buffer` **Property**

```
<script runat="server" type="text/jscript" language="JScript">
Response.Buffer = TRUE;
Response.Write("Hello World");
Response.Flush();
</script>
```

Response.CacheControl

ASP1+

Syntax

```
Response.CacheControl = string
```

Description

The `CacheControl` property of the `Response` object is used to override the `Private` default *string* by setting it to `Public`. The default setting states that only private caches can cache the content generated by this page, whereas a `Public` setting informs proxies and other servers that they can cache the content.

Example

Listing 9.172 shows how you can use the `CacheControl` property to allow proxies to cache ASP content.

Listing 9.172   Using the `CacheControl` *Property*

```
<script runat="server" type="text/jscript" language="JScript">
Response.CacheControl = Public;
</script>
```

Response.Charset

ASP1+

Syntax

```
Response.Charset = charset
```

Description

The `Charset` property of the `Response` object appends the *charset* to the end of the content-type HTTP header directive.

Example

Listing 9.173 shows how you can append ISO-LATIN-7 to the end of the content-type is header.

Listing 9.173   Using the `Charset` *Property*

```
<script runat="server" type="text/jscript" language="JScript">

// Generates content-type:text/html; charset=ISO-LATIN-7.
Response.Charset = "ISO-LATIN-7";
</script>
```

Response.Clear()

ASP1+

Syntax

```
Response.Clear()
```

Description

The `Clear()` method of the `Response` object is used to erase any buffered HTTP response body output, but not HTTP response header output. For this method to work, you must first set `Response.Buffer = TRUE`.

Example

Listing 9.174 shows how you can use the Clear() method to clear any buffered HTTP response body data.

Listing 9.174 *Using the* Clear() *Method*

```
<script runat="server" type="text/jscript" language="JScript">

// Turn on buffering.
Response.Buffer = TRUE;

// Write data to buffer then flush it.
Response.Write("Hello World");
Response.Flush();

// Clear response body.
Response.Clear()
</script>
```

Response.ContentType
ASP1+

Syntax

```
Response.ContentType = contentType
```

Description

The ContentType property of the Response object sets the content-type header directive. If no value is passed, text/html is assumed.

Example

Listing 9.175 shows how you can pass back your content as plain ASCII text, rather than HTML.

Listing 9.175 *Using the* ContentType *Property*

```
<script runat="server" type="text/jscript" language="JScript">
Response.ContentType = "text/plain"
Response.Write('<b>You will see the tags, and not bold text</b>');
</script>
```

Response.Cookies
ASP1+

Syntax

```
Response.Cookies(name) = value
Response.Cookies(name).attribute = value
Response.Cookies(name)(subkey) = value
```

Description

The Cookies collection of the Response object creates and stores any cookies to pass to the user agent. You can create a cookie called *name* of *value* using the first syntactical method. It is also possible to pass a *subkey*, which creates a cookie dictionary and inserts *value* as a key in that dictionary. Additionally, you can pass a specific *attribute* to just set or change part of the cookie.

Example

Listing 9.176 shows how you can use the Response.Cookie() collection to create, collect, and pass back a cookie with two subkeys.

Listing 9.176 Using the Cookies Collection

```
<script runat="server" type="text/jscript" language="JScript">

// Sends out Set-Cookie:ID=site=abc&network=123
Response.Cookies("ID")("site") = "abc"
Response.Cookies("ID")("network") = "123"
</script>
```

Response.End()

ASP1+

Syntax

```
Response.End()
```

Description

The End() method of the Response object tells the server to stop processing the script and return the current results.

Example

Listing 9.177 shows how you can call this method to stop execution of the current page.

Listing 9.177 Using the End() Method

```
<script runat="server" type="text/jscript" language="JScript">
Response.Write("this will be written");
Response.End();
Response.Write("this will not be written);
</script>
```

Response.Expires

ASP1+

Syntax

```
Response.Expires = num
```

Description

The Expires property of the Response object sets the expiration header for the returned document by specifying the *num* of minutes before the document expires. Browsers use this to measure the amount of time they should cache the document.

Example

Listing 9.178 shows how you can set an expiration of only five minutes for the given page.

Listing 9.178   Using the Expires *Property*

```
<script runat="server" type="text/jscript" language="JScript">
Response.Expires = 5;
Response.Write("Hello World");
</script>
```

Response.ExpiresAbsolute

ASP1+

Syntax

```
Response.ExpiresAbsolute = datetime
```

Description

The ExpiresAbsolute property of the Response object sets the absolute expiration date for the returned document by specifying the *datetime* the document expires. Browsers use this to measure the amount of time they should cache the document.

Example

Listing 9.179 shows how you can set the expiration to October 31st, 2001 at 8:00 a.m. for the given page.

Listing 9.179   Using the ExpiresAbsolute *Property*

```
<script runat="server" type="text/jscript" language="JScript">
Response.ExpiresAbsolute = 'October 31,2001 08:00:00';
Response.Write("Hello World");
</script>
```

Response.Flush()

ASP1+

Syntax

```
Response.Flush()
```

Description

The `Flush()` method of the `Response` object is used to send the currently buffered content to the user agent. For this method to work properly, the `Response.Buffer` property must be set to TRUE.

Example

Listing 9.180 shows how to tell the server to buffer the content, and then send it when the `Response.Flush()` method is called.

Listing 9.180   Using the `Flush()` *Method*

```
<script runat="server" type="text/jscript" language="JScript">
Response.Buffer = TRUE;
Response.Write("Hello World");
Response.Flush();
</script>
```

Response.IsClientConnected

ASP1+

Syntax

```
Response.IsClientConnected
```

Description

The `IsClientConnected` property of the `Response` object is a boolean value that lets you see whether a client is still connected.

Example

Listing 9.181 shows how you can evaluate the `IsClientConnected` property within an `if` statement before writing out your content. If the client is not connected, it writes an error to the Web log file.

Listing 9.181   Using the `IsClientConnected` *Property*

```
<script runat="server" type="text/jscript" language="JScript">
if(Response.IsClientConnected){
  Response.Write("Client is connected");
}else{
  Response.AppendToLog("Error: client disconnected");
}
</script>
```

Response.PICS

ASP1+

Syntax

```
Response.PICS(label)
```

Description

The `PICS` property of the `Response` object adds the PICS-label HTTP header directive to the current output. The `label` property contains a properly formatted PICS label.

Example

Listing 9.182 shows how you can use the `PICS` property to add the PICS-label HTTP header directive to the current output.

Listing 9.182 Using the `PICS` Property

```
<script runat="server" type="text/jscript" language="JScript">
Response.PICS("(PICS-1.1 <http://www.rsac.org/ratingv01.html> labels on "
             & chr(34) & "2001.01.05T08:15-0500" & chr(34) & " until"
             & chr(34) & "2002.12.31T23:59-0000" & chr(34)
             & " ratings (v 0 s 0 l 0 n 0))");
</script>
```

Response.Redirect()

ASP1+

Syntax

```
Response.Redirect(url)
```

Description

The `Redirect()` method of the `Response` object sends back an appropriate 302 HTTP header directive instructing the browser to request and load the `url` passed.

Example

Listing 9.183 shows how you can redirect the browser to a new page if a user accesses your root directory page (for example, www.purejavascript.com).

Listing 9.183 Using the `Redirect()` Method

```
<script runat="server" type="text/jscript" language="JScript">
Response.Redirect("/welcome.asp");
</script>
```

Response.Status

ASP1+

Syntax

```
Response.Status = string
```

Description

The `Status` property of the `Response` object specifies the HTTP status of the response.

Example

Listing 9.184 shows how you can return an error to the user if she has made an illegal request.

Listing 9.184   Using the `Status` **Property**

```
<script runat="server" type="text/jscript" language="JScript">
Response.Status = "404 Document Not Found";
</script>
```

Response.Write()

ASP1+

Syntax

```
Response.Write(string)
```

Description

The `Write()` method of the `Response` object is used to write an ASCII *string* to the output.

Example

Listing 9.185 shows how you can write `"Hello World"` to output.

Listing 9.185   Using the `Write()` **Method**

```
<script runat="server" type="text/jscript" language="JScript">
Response.Write("Hello World");
</script>
```

Resultset

ES3+

Syntax

Core object created by the `Stproc.resultSet()`.

Description

The `Resultset` object is one of the core server-side JavaScript objects. This object is created by the `resultSet()` method of the `Stproc` object. For stored procedures run against DB2, Oracle, Sybase, and ODBC databases, the stored procedure object has one `Resultset` object for each SQL `SELECT` statement executed by the procedure. An Informix stored procedure, on the other hand, has one `Resultset` object.

Each instance of this object has a property for each column in the resultset. For Oracle, Sybase, and ODBC stored procedures, these properties can be referred to by the column name. Informix and DB2 stored procedures do not have named columns, so you must use a zero-based numeric index to refer to the column.

You should always call the `close()` method of the `Resultset` object after you have finished. The JavaScript runtime will attempt to close the object when the associate `DbPool` or `database` object goes out of scope.

NOTE

> After creating a resultset, you must perform all operations on the set before calling the `commitTransaction()`, `returnValue()`, `outParameters()`, `Connection.cursor()`, or `Connection.SQLTable()` method.

This object has only one property—`prototype`. This property can be used to create new methods and properties for the `Resultset` object. Table 9.29 contains the methods accessible from this object.

Table 9.29 Methods of the `Resultset` Object

Method	Description
`close()`	Closes the `Resultset` object and frees any memory used
`columnName()`	Takes an indexed numbered location and returns the column name of the column in that location
`columns()`	Returns the number of columns in the `Resultset`
`next()`	Moves from the current row in the `Resultset` object to the next row
`unwatch()`	Turns off the watch for a particular property
`watch()`	Turns on the watch for a particular property

Example

Listing 9.186 creates a connection to a database. After the connection has been verified, the `storedProc()` method is used to invoke the fictitious *sp_employees* stored procedure. The resultsets for this stored procedure are then held in an instance of the `Resultset` object.

Listing 9.186 The `Resultset` Object

```
<server>

// Open a connection.
var myConn = database.connect("ORACLE", "mySID", "myApp", "appsPWD", "myTNS");

if(myConn.connected()){

  myConn.beginTransaction();

  // Run the stored procedure.
  var myStproc = myConn.storedProc("sp_employees");

  var myResultSet = myStproc.resultSet();
```

Listing 9.186 Continued

```
  // Commit the transaction.
  myConn.commitTransaction();

  // Close the result set.
  myResultSet.close();

  // Release the connection.
  myConn.release();

// If the connection fails, write an error message.
}else{
  write('Error ('+myConn.majorErrorCode()+'): '' + myConn.majorErrorMessage();
}

</server>
```

Resultset.close()

ES3+

Syntax

resultset.close()

Description

The close() method of the Resultset object closes the resultset and frees all memory used to store its information. If successful, the method returns 0; otherwise, it returns an error code that can be obtained by using the majorErrorCode() and majorErrorMessage() methods of the Connection or database objects.

Example

Listing 9.187 creates a resultset and then closes it.

Listing 9.187 Closing a Resultset with the close() Method

```
<server>

// Open a connection.
var myConn = database.connect("ORACLE", "mySID", "myApp", "appsPWD", "myTNS");

myConn.beginTransaction();

// Run the stored procedure.
var myStproc = myConn.storedProc("sp_employees");

// Store the resultset.
myResultSet = myStproc.resultSet();
```

```
// Commit the transaction.
myConn.commitTransaction();

// Close the resultset.
myResultSet.close();

</server>
```

Resultset.columnName()

ES3+

Syntax

resultset.columnName(*num*)

Description

The columnName() method of the Resultset object takes the zero-based indexed number location, *num*, passed to the method and returns the name of the column in that location. Note that these names are not returned in any specific order unless you order them as such. Successive calls to the method, however, will return all the columns. See the example for more information.

Example

Listing 9.188 has two resultsets. One of the sets returns specific column names and the other returns all columns. See the comments in the code for the output.

Listing 9.188   Using the columnName() *Method to Return the Names of the Columns in a Table*

```
<server>

// Create a pool of connections.
var myPool = new DbPool("ORACLE", "mySID", "myApp", "appsPWD", "myTNS");

// Open a connection from the pool. Give error if connection could
// not be made.
var myConn = myPool.connection('Employees', 15);

if(myConn.connected()){

  // Start a new SQL transaction.
  myConn.beginTransaction();

  // Run the stored procedure.
  var myStproc = myConn.storedProc("sp_employees");
```

Listing 9.188   Continued

```
// Store the resultsets.
var myResultSet1 = myStproc.resultSet();
var myResultSet2 = myStproc.resultSet();

// Writes column #1, from the first resultset, to the page.
write(myResultSet1.columnName(0));

// Writes column #2, from the first resultset, to the page.
write(myResultSet1.columnName(1));

// Writes all column names stored in the second resultset to the page.
for(var i = 0; i <= myResultSet2.columns(); i++){
  write(myResultSet2.columnName(i));
}

// Close the resultsets.
myResultSet1.close();
myResultSet2.close();

// End SQL transaction.
myConn.commitTransaction();

// If the connection fails, write an error message.
}else{
  write('Error ('+myConn.majorErrorCode()+'): '' + myConn.majorErrorMessage());
}

// Release the connection
myConn.release();

</server>
```

Resultset.columns()

ES3+

Syntax

resultset.columns()

Description

The columns() method of the Resultset object returns the number of columns in the resultset on which it is invoked. If the SQL used to create the resultset specifies a set number of columns to return, that is the number returned by this method.

Example

Listing 9.189 shows how you can return all the column names of the columns in your resultset.

Listing 9.189 *Using the* `columns()` *Method to Determine How Many Columns Are in the Resultset Before Writing Them to the Page*

```
<server>

// Run the stored procedure.
var myStproc = myConn.storedProc("sp_employees");

// Store the resultset.
var myResultSet = myStproc.resultSet();

// Writes all column names stored in the resultset to the page.
for(var i = 0; i < myResultSet.columns(); i++){
  write(myResultSet.columnName(i));
}

// Close the resultset.
myResultSet.close();

</server>
```

Resultset.next()

ES3+

Syntax

resultset.next()

Description

The `next()` method of the `Resultset` object moves the pointer in the current row to the next row in the resultset. This method is used to iterate through each of the rows returned by the resultset. This method returns `true`, unless it is the last row of the resultset; at which time it returns `false`.

Example

Listing 9.190 creates an instance of the `Resultset` object and iterates through its results. This is performed by using the `next()` method.

Listing 9.190 *Using the* `next()` *Method to Iterate Through the Rows in a Resultset*

```
<server>

// Run the stored procedure.
var myStproc = myConn.storedProc("sp_employees");

// Store the resultset.
var myResultSet = myStproc.resultSet();
```

Listing 9.190   Continued

```
// Iterate through each return of the resultset.
while(myResultSet.next()){

  // Perform processing here.

}

// Close the resultset.
myResultSet.close();

</server>
```

Resultset.prototype

ES3+

Syntax

```
resultset.prototype.method = name
resultset.prototype.property = value
```

Description

The prototype property of the Resultset object allows you to create new properties and methods of the object. If you are adding a method, set the instance equal to the *name* of the method you have defined.

Example

Listing 9.191 creates a new property and method of the Resultset object. An instance is created and the new property is set. The new method is then called to verify the property, and, if it is incorrect, an error message is written to the page.

Listing 9.191   Using the prototype **Property to Create a New Property and Method**

```
<server>

// Define the method that we prototyped.
function verifyWork(){

  // Check to see if the type property we added is set to a valid value.
  if(this.type == "work"){
    return true;
  }else{
    return false;
  }
}
```

```
// Create a new property and method of the Resultset object.
Resultset.prototype.type = null;
Resultset.prototype.isWORK = verifyWork;

// Create a pool of connections, a connection, a stored procedure,
// and a resultset.
var myPool = new DbPool("ORACLE", "mySID", "myApp", "appsPWD", "myTNS");
var myConn = myPool.connection('Employees', 15);
var myStproc = myConn.storedProc("sp_employees");
var myResultSet = myStproc.resultSet();

// Using the prototype we defined, assign the type property.
myResultSet.type = "work";

// Check the type of the resultset to see if it is valid.
if(myResultSet.isWORK()){
  write(myResultSet + " has a valid type of " + myResultSet.type);
}else{
  write(myResultSet + " has an invalid type of " + myResultSet.type);
}

</server> >
```

Resultset.unwatch()
ES3+

Syntax
resultset.unwatch(*property*)

Description
The unwatch() method of the Resultset object is used to turn off the watch for a particular *property*.

Example
Listing 9.192 shows how the unwatch() method is used to stop watching the user-defined property *p*.

Listing 9.192   Example of the unwatch() Method
```
<server>

// Define the method that we prototyped.
function verifyWork(){

  // Check to see if the type property we added is set to a valid value.
  if(this.type == "work"){
    return true;
```

Listing 9.192   Continued

```
  }else{
    return false;
  }
}

// function that is called if property's value changes
function alertme(id, oldValue, newValue){
  write("ID (" + id + ") changed from " + oldValue + " to " + newValue);
  return newValue;
}

// Create a new property and method of the Resultset object.
Resultset.prototype.type = null;
Resultset.prototype.isWORK = verifyWork;

// Create a pool of connections, a connection, a stored procedure,
// and a resultset.
var myPool = new DbPool("ORACLE", "mySID", "myApp", "appsPWD", "myTNS");
var myConn = myPool.connection('Employees', 15);
var myStproc = myConn.storedProc("sp_employees");
var myResultSet = myStproc.resultSet();

// Using the prototype we defined, assign the type property.
myResultSet.type = "work";

// watch property
myResultSet.watch("type", alertme);

// Check the type of the resultset to see if it is valid.
if(myResultSet.isWORK()){
  write(myResultSet + " has a valid type of " + myResultSet.type);
}else{
  write(myResultSet + " has an invalid type of " + myResultSet.type);
}

// change value
myResultSet.type = null;

// turn off watch
myResultSet.unwatch("type");

// change value again
myResultSet.type = "home";

</server>
```

Resultset.watch()

ES3+

Syntax

```
resultset.watch(property, function)
```

Description

The watch() method of the Resultset object is used to turn on the watch for a particular property specified by *property*. Any time the specified *property* is changed after the watch() method has been called, the specified *function* is called.

Example

Listing 9.193 shows how the watch() method is used to start watching the user-defined property *p*.

Listing 9.193   Example of the watch() **Method**

```
<server>

// Define the method that we prototyped.
function verifyWork(){

  // Check to see if the type property we added is set to a valid value.
  if(this.type == "work"){
    return true;
  }else{
    return false;
  }
}

// function that is called if property's value changes
function alertme(id, oldValue, newValue){
  write("ID (" + id + ") changed from " + oldValue + " to " + newValue);
  return newValue;
}

// Create a new property and method of the Resultset object.
Resultset.prototype.type = null;
Resultset.prototype.isWORK = verifyWork;

// Create a pool of connections, a connection, a stored procedure,
// and a resultset.
var myPool = new DbPool("ORACLE", "mySID", "myApp", "appsPWD", "myTNS");
var myConn = myPool.connection('Employees', 15);
var myStproc = myConn.storedProc("sp_employees");
var myResultSet = myStproc.resultSet();
```

Listing 9.193   Continued

```
// Using the prototype we defined, assign the type property.
myResultSet.type = "work";

// watch property
myResultSet.watch("type", alertme);

// Check the type of the resultset to see if it is valid.
if(myResultSet.isWORK()){
  write(myResultSet + " has a valid type of " + myResultSet.type);
}else{
  write(myResultSet + " has an invalid type of " + myResultSet.type);
}

// change value
myResultSet.type = null;

</server>
```

ScriptingContext
ASP1+

Syntax
Core ASP environment object

Description
The ScriptingContext object is a core, but obsolete, ASP environment object. It will return the Application, Request, Response, Server, or Session built-in objects. Rather than using this object, you should use ObjectContext instead.

Example
Please see the examples under the ObjectContext object for methods of accomplishing the same thing as this obsolete object.

SendMail
ES3+

Syntax
```
new SendMail()
```

Description
The SendMail object is a core server-side object that is created using the new keyword. This object provides the properties and methods necessary to send e-mail with your JavaScript applications. Table 9.30 lists the properties and methods of this object.

Table 9.30 `SendMail` *Methods and Properties*

Type	Item	Description
Property	Bcc	Property that contains the e-mail addresses of those users you want to blind carbon copy (Bcc)
	Body	Property that contains the actual body of the message
	Cc	Property that contains the e-mail addresses of those users you want to carbon copy
	Errorsto	Property that contains the e-mail address to which to send error messages
	From	Property that contains the sender's e-mail address
	Organization	Property that contains the sender's organization
	Replyto	Property that contains the sender's reply to e-mail address
	Smtpserver	Property that specifies the IP address or hostname of the mail server to send the message
	Subject	Property that contains the subject of the e-mail
	To	Property that contains the e-mail address of the recipient
Method	errorCode()	Method that returns an integer error code that might be incurred when sending e-mail
	errorMessage()	Method that returns a string related to any error messages that might be incurred when sending e-mail
	send()	Method that sends the e-mail
	unwatch()	Method that is used to turn off the watch for a particular property
	watch()	Method that is used to turn on the watch for a particular property

Using the `SendMail` object is very straightforward. Simply set the same properties contained in the everyday e-mail you send and invoke the `send()` method. If an error is encountered, it can be analyzed by using the error methods supplied.

Example

Listing 9.194 shows the use of the `SendMail` object to create a page for users to send e-mail.

Listing 9.194   *Example of Using the* `SendMail` *Object*

```
<html>
<head>
  <title>Using the SendMail object</title>
</head>
<body>
<server>
```

Listing 9.194   Continued

```
// See if they have submitted or just need the form.
if(request.method == "POST"){

  // Create an instance of the SendMail object.
  var myMail = new SendMail();

  // Assign the properties their values.
  myMail.To = request.toAddress;
  myMail.From = request.fromAddress;
  myMail.Subject = request.subject;
  myMail.Body = request.body;
  myMail.Smtpserver = "mail.purejavascript.com";
  myMail.Errorsto = "errors@purejavascript.com"

  // Try to send the mail.
  if(!myMail.send()){

    // If there was an error, give the user the email address of who they
    // should contact about the error, as well as the error code and message.
    write("There was an error sending your message. Please send email to ");
    write(myMail.Errorsto + " with the following error message");
    write("Error " + myMail.errorCode() + ": " + myMail.errorMessage());
  }else{

    // If there was not an error, tell the user they were successful.
    write("Your message was sent successfully!");
  }
}else{

  // If this page was called and a form was not submitted, then write the
  // email form to the page for the user to use.

  write('<form name="myForm" method="post">');
  write('<table border="1"><tr><td>');
  write('<table border="0">');
  write('<tr align="left" valign="top">');
  write('<td><b>To:</b></td>');
  write('<td><input type="text" name="toAddress" size="30"></td>');
  write('</tr>');
  write('<tr align="left" valign="top">');
  write('<td><b>From:</b></td>');
  write('<td><input type="text" name="fromAddress" size="30"></td>');
  write('</tr>');
  write('<tr align="left" valign="top">');
  write('<td><b>Subject:</b></td>');
  write('<td><input type="text" name="subject" size="30"></td>');
  write('</tr>');
```

```
  write('<tr align="left" valign="top">');
  write('<td><b>Body:</b></td>');
  write('<td><textarea name="body" cols="60" rows="10" wrap="soft">');
  write('</textarea></td>');
  write('</tr>');
  write('<tr align="left" valign="top">');
  write('<td colspan=2 align="right">');
  write('<input type="submit" value="Send Mail"></td>');
  write('</tr>');
  write('</table>');
  write('</td></tr></table>');
  write('</form>');
}
</server>
</body>
</html>
```

SendMail.Bcc

ES3+

Syntax

sendmail.Bcc

Description

The Bcc property of the SendMail object specifies the e-mail addresses of those recipients you want to blind carbon copy. If you want to specify more than one recipient, separate their e-mail addresses with commas.

Example

Listing 9.195 shows you how to set the Bcc property of an instance of the SendMail object.

Listing 9.195   Setting the Bcc *Property*

```
<server>

// Set the Bcc property.
myMail.Bcc = "publisher@purejavascript.com";

</server>
```

SendMail.Body

ES3+

Syntax

sendmail.Body

Description

The `Body` property of the `SendMail` object specifies the body of the e-mail you want to send.

Example

Listing 9.196 shows you how to set the `Body` property of an instance of the `SendMail` object.

Listing 9.196   Setting the Body *Property*

```
<server>

// Set the Body property.
myMail.Body = "Here is the text of the message";

</server>
```

SendMail.Cc
ES3+

Syntax

sendmail.Cc

Description

The `Cc` property of the `SendMail` object specifies the e-mail addresses of those recipients you want to carbon copy. If you want to specify more than one recipient, separate their e-mail addresses with commas.

Example

Listing 9.197 shows you how to set the `Cc` property of an instance of the `SendMail` object.

Listing 9.197   Setting the Cc *Property*

```
<server>

// Set the Cc property.
myMail.Cc = "techedit@purejavascript.com";

</server>
```

SendMail.constructor
ES2+

Syntax

sendmail.constructor

Description

The constructor property of the SendMail object specifies the function that creates the object.

Example

Listing 9.2198 shows an example of the constructor property.

Listing 9.198   Example of the constructor *Property*

```
<server>

// Create an instance of the SendMail object.
var myMail = new SendMail();

if(myMail.constructor == SendMail){
    write("Object created");
}

</server>
```

SendMail.errorCode()
ES3+

Syntax

```
sendmail.errorCode()
```

Description

The errorCode() method of the SendMail object returns one of six error codes after attempting to send an e-mail. These codes are described in Table 9.31.

Table 9.31   Error Codes Generated from Sending E-mail with the SendMail.send() *Method*

Code	Description
0	The e-mail was sent successfully.
1	The SMTP sending mail server was not specified.
2	The SMTP sending mail server was down or does not exist.
3	No recipient e-mail address was specified.
4	No sender's e-mail address was specified.
5	Connection problems and data not sent.

Example

Listing 9.199 tries to send an instance of the SendMail object. If the send() method fails, the error it encounters is written to the page.

Listing 9.199   Displaying the Error Code on a Failed E-mail Delivery Using the errorCode() *Method.*

```
<server>

// Try to send an instance of the mail.
if(!myMail.send()){

    // If there was an error, give the user the email address of who they
    // should contact about the error, as well as the error code and message.
    write("There was an error sending your message. Please send email to ");
    write(myMail.Errorsto + " with the following error message");
    write("Error " + myMail.errorCode() + ": " + myMail.errorMessage());

}else{

  // If there was not an error, tell the user they were successful.
  write("Your message was sent successfully!");
}

</server>
```

SendMail.errorMessage()

ES3+

Syntax

```
sendmail.errorMessage()
```

Description

The errorMessage() method of the SendMail object returns the string error message generated after attempting to send an e-mail.

Example

Listing 9.200 tries to send an instance of the SendMail object. If the send() method fails, the error it encounters is written to the page.

Listing 9.200   Displaying the Error Message on a Failed E-mail Delivery Using the errorMessage() *Method.*

```
<server>

// Try to send an instance of the mail.
if(!myMail.send()){

    // If there was an error, give the user the email address of who they
    // should contact about the error, as well as the error code and message.
    write("There was an error sending your message. Please send email to ");
```

```
   write(myMail.Errorsto + " with the following error message");
   write("Error " + myMail.errorCode() + ": " + myMail.errorMessage());

}else{

   // If there was not an error, tell the user they were successful.
   write("Your message was sent successfully!");
}

</server>
```

SendMail.Errorsto

ES3+

Syntax

sendmail.Errorsto

Description

The Errorsto property of the SendMail object specifies the e-mail address of a recipient that should receive the error message. The default value of this error is the sender's address. If you want to specify more than one recipient, separate their e-mail addresses with commas.

Example

Listing 9.201 shows you how to set the Errorsto property of an instance of the SendMail object.

Listing 9.201   Setting the Errorsto *Property*

```
<server>

// Set the Errorsto property.
myMail.Errorsto = "authors@purejavascript.com";

</server>
```

SendMail.From

ES3+

Syntax

sendmail.From

Description

The From property of the SendMail object specifies the e-mail address of the sender of the message.

Example

Listing 9.202 shows you how to set the From property of an instance of the SendMail object.

Listing 9.202   Setting the From *Property*

```
<server>

// Set the From property using the email key in a form sent by the client.
myMail.From = request.email;

</server>
```

SendMail.Organization

ES3+

Syntax

```
sendmail.Organization
```

Description

The Organization property of the SendMail object specifies the organization of the sender.

Example

Listing 9.203 shows you how to set the Organization property of an instance of the SendMail object.

Listing 9.203   Setting the Organization *Property*

```
<server>

// Set the Organization property.
myMail.Organization = "TIPs Technical Publishing";

</server>
```

SendMail.prototype

ES3+

Syntax

```
sendmail.prototype.method = name
sendmail.prototype.property = value
```

Description

The prototype property of the SendMail object allows you to create new properties and methods of the object. If you are adding a method, set the instance equal to the *name* of the method you have defined.

Example

Listing 9.204 creates a new property and method of the `SendMail` object. An instance is created and the new property is set. The new method is then called to verify the property, and, if it is incorrect, an error message is written to the page.

Listing 9.204   Using the `prototype` *Property to Create a New Property and Method*

```
<server>

// Define the method that we prototyped.
function verifyAttach(){

  // Check to see if the type property we added is set to a valid value.
  if(this.type){
    return true;
  }else{
    return false;
  }
}

// Create a new property and method of the SendMail object.
SendMail.prototype.attachment = null;
SendMail.prototype.hasAttach = verifyAttach;

// Create a SendMail object.
var myMail = new SendMail();

// Using the prototype we defined, assign the type property.
myMail.type = false;

// Check to see if there is an attachment.
if(myMail.hasAttach()){
  write(myMail + " has a valid type of " + myMail.type);
}else{
  write(myMail + " has an invalid type of " + myMail.type);
}

</server>
```

SendMail.Replyto

ES3+

Syntax

sendmail.ReplyTo

Description

The `ReplyTo` property of the `SendMail` object specifies the e-mail addresses to which the sender wants any replies to be routed.

Example

Listing 9.205 shows you how to set the `ReplyTo` property of an instance of the `SendMail` object.

Listing 9.205   Setting the `ReplyTo` _Property_

```
<server>

// Set the ReplyTo property using the email key in a form sent by the client.
myMail.ReplyTo = request.replyto;

</server>
```

SendMail.send()

> ES3+

Syntax

```
sendmail.send()
```

Description

The `send()` method of the `SendMail` object attempts to send the e-mail from the value specified in the `From` property to those specified in the `To`, `Cc`, and `Bcc` properties through the e-mail server specified in the `Smtpserver` property. This method returns `true` if successful and `false` otherwise.

Example

Listing 9.206 tries to send a message. If an error occurs when trying to send the message, an error message is written to the user's page.

Listing 9.206   Sending a Message with the `send()` _Method_

```
<server>

// Try to send an instance of the mail.
if(!myMail.send()){

    // If there was an error, give the user the email address of whom they
    // should contact about the error, as well as the error code and message.
    write("There was an error sending your message. Please send email to ");
    write(myMail.Errorsto + " with the following error message");
    write("Error " + myMail.errorCode() + ": " + myMail.errorMessage());
```

```
}else{

  // If there was not an error, tell the user they were successful.
  write("Your message was sent successfully!");
}

</server>
```

SendMail.Smtpserver

ES3+

Syntax

```
sendmail.Smtpserver
```

Description

The Smtpserver property of the SendMail object specifies the SMTP sending email IP address or server name. This value defaults to the value set in the Administration Server settings for the instance of the Enterprise Server under which your application is running.

Example

Listing 9.207 shows you how to set the Smtpserver property of an instance of the SendMail object.

Listing 9.207   Setting the Smtpserver *Property*

```
<server>

// Set the Smtpserver property using the email key in a form
// sent by the client.
myMail.Smtpserver = request.smtp;

</server>
```

SendMail.Subject

ES3+

Syntax

```
sendmail.Subject
```

Description

The Subject property of the SendMail object specifies the subject of the e-mail you want to send.

Example

Listing 9.208 shows you how to set the Subject property of an instance of the SendMail object.

Listing 9.208   Setting the Subject *Property*

```
<server>

// Set the Subject property.
myMail.Subject = "I really liked your book!";

</server>
```

SendMail.To

ES3+

Syntax

```
sendmail.To
```

Description

The To property of the SendMail object specifies the e-mail addresses of the recipients of the message. If you want to specify more than one recipient, separate their e-mail addresses with commas.

Example

Listing 9.209 shows you how to set the To property of an instance of the SendMail object.

Listing 9.209   Setting the To *Property*

```
<server>

// Set the To property.
myMail.To = "authors@purejavascript.com";

</server>
```

SendMail.unwatch()

ES3+

Syntax

```
sendmail.unwatch(property)
```

Description

The unwatch() method of the SendMail object is used to turn off the watch for a particular *property*.

Example

Listing 9.210 shows how the unwatch() method is used to stop watching the user-defined property *p*.

Listing 9.210   *Example of the* unwatch() *Method*

```
<server>

// function that is called if property's value changes
function alertme(id, oldValue, newValue){
  write("ID (" + id + ") changed from " + oldValue + " to " + newValue);
  return newValue;
}

// Create a SendMail object.
var myMail = new SendMail();

myMail.To = "allen@purejavascript.com";

// watch property
myMail.watch("To", alertme);

// change value
myMail.To = "jason@purejavascript.com";

// turn off watch
myMail.unwatch("To");

// change value again
myMail.To = "chuck@purejavascript.com";

</server>
```

SendMail.watch()

ES3+

Syntax

sendmail.watch(*property, function*)

Description

The watch() method of the SendMail object is used to turn on the watch for a particular property specified by *property*. Any time the specified *property* is changed after the watch() method has been called, the specified *function* is called.

Example

Listing 9.211 shows how the watch() method is used to start watching the user-defined property *p*.

Listing 9.211   Example of the watch() **Method**

```
<server>

// function that is called if property's value changes
function alertme(id, oldValue, newValue){
  write("ID (" + id + ") changed from " + oldValue + " to " + newValue);
  return newValue;
}

// Create a SendMail object.
var myMail = new SendMail();

myMail.To = "allen@purejavascript.com";

// watch property
myMail.watch("To", alertme);

// change value
myMail.To = "jason@purejavascript.com";

</server>
```

Server

ASP1+

Syntax

Core ASP environment object

Description

The Server object is a core ASP environment object. This object provides access to the server's utility functions. Table 9.32 contains the list of a property and methods of this object.

Table 9.32   A Property and Methods of the Server **Object**

Type	Item	Description
Methods	CreateObject()	Creates an instance of a server component.
	Execute()	Executes an .asp file.
	GetLastError()	Returns an ASPError object with the error condition.
	HTMLEncode()	Applies HTML encoding to the specified string.
	MapPath()	Maps either an absolute path on the server or the path relative to the current page, into a physical path.

Type	Item	Description
	`Transfer()`	Sends all the current state information to another .asp file for processing.
	`URLEncode()`	Applies URL encoding rules and escape characters to the string.
Property	`ScriptTimeout`	Amount of time a script can run before it times out.

Example

Listing 9.212 shows how you can use the `ScriptTimeout` property of the `Server` object to specify the number of seconds before a script stops processing.

Listing 9.212 *Using the* `Server` *Object*

```
<script runat="server" type="text/jscript" language="JScript">
Server.ScriptTimeout = 60;
</script>
```

Server.CreateObject()

ASP1+

Syntax

```
Server.CreateObject(objID)
```

Description

The `CreateObject()` method of the `Server` object creates an instance of the server component referenced by *objID*. This *objID* is usually in the following format:

Vendor.Component.Version

Example

Listing 9.213 creates an instance of a fictitious *Marketing* component from the *MyCo* company.

Listing 9.213 *Using the* `CreateObject()` *Method*

```
<script runat="server" type="text/jscript" language="JScript">
Server.CreateObject(MyCo.Marketing);
</script>
```

Server.Execute()

ASP3+

Syntax

```
Server.Execute(path)
```

Description

The Execute() method of the Server object executes the ASP file located at *path*, processing it as if it were part of the current page.

Example

Listing 9.214 executes the *gettime.asp* page while being processed.

Listing 9.214   Using the Execute() Method

```
<script runat="server" type="text/jscript" language="JScript">
Server.Execute("/tools/gettime.asp");
</script>
```

Server.GetLastError()

ASP3+

Syntax

```
Server.GetLastError()
```

Description

The GetLastError() method of the Server object creates an instance of the ASPError object that contains a description of the last error that occurred.

Example

Listing 9.215 writes out the last error that has occurred on a page.

Listing 9.215   Using the GetLastError() Method

```
<script runat="server" type="text/jscript" language="JScript">
Response.Write(Server.GetLastError().Description);
</script>
```

Server.HTMLEncode()

ASP1+

Syntax

```
Server.HTMLEncode(string)
```

Description

The HTMLEncode() method of the Server object applies HTML encoding to a specified *string*.

Example

Listing 9.216 creates a string that includes two HTML tags, and before it is written to the page, HTML encoding is applied.

Listing 9.216 *Using the* HTMLEncode() *Method*

```
<script runat="server" type="text/jscript" language="JScript">
var myString = new String();
myString = "View the source to see no <b> tag in this <p>";
Response.Write(Server.HTMLEncode(myString));
</script>
```

Server.MapPath()

ASP1+

Syntax

```
Server.MapPath(path)
```

Description

The MapPath() method of the Server object maps the relative or virtual *path* to a physical directory on the file system.

Example

Listing 9.217 will write out the file system path for the requested URL.

Listing 9.217 *Using the* MapPath() *Method*

```
<script runat="server" type="text/jscript" language="JScript">
Response.Write(Server.MapPath(Request.ServerVariables("PATH_INFO")));
</script>
```

Server.ScriptTimeout

ASP1+

Syntax

```
Server.ScriptTimeout
```

Description

The ScriptTimeout property of the Server object specifies the number of seconds that should elapse before the currently executing script times out.

Example

Listing 9.218 shows how you can use the ScriptTimeout property of the Server object to specify the number of seconds before a script stops processing.

Listing 9.218 *Using the* ScriptTimeout *Property*

```
<script runat="server" type="text/jscript" language="JScript">
Server.ScriptTimeout = 60;
</script>
```

Server.Transfer()

ASP3+

Syntax

```
Server.Transfer(path)
```

Description

The Transfer() method of the Server object sends all the processed information available for the current page to the ASP file located at *path*.

Example

Listing 9.219 shows how the current script passes its data on to another script.

Listing 9.219 Using the Transfer() Method

```
<script runat="server" type="text/jscript" language="JScript">

// Define item to transfer.
var version = "1.0";

Server.Transfer("/scripts/logversion.asp");
</script>
```

Server.URLEncode()

ASP1+

Syntax

```
Server.URLEncode(string)
```

Description

The URLEncode() method of the Server object applies URL encoding to a specified *string*.

Example

Listing 9.220 creates a string that includes two HTML tags and some whitespace. Before it is written to the page, URL encoding is applied.

Listing 9.220 Using the URLEncode() Method

```
<script runat="server" type="text/jscript" language="JScript">
var myString = new String();
myString = "View the source to see no <b> tag in this <p>";
Response.Write(Server.URLEncode(myString));
</script>
```

server

ES2+

Syntax

Core object created when the instance of Enterprise Server is started.

Description

The server object is one of the core server-side objects. An instance of this object is created for each instance of the Enterprise server you have running. This object is destroyed when the server process is stopped.

This object should be used to store global data you want to share and manage across your applications. Because of this, you will need to lock and unlock your code if you are changing any properties you have defined in your applications. The server object has the properties and methods listed in Table 9.33. Note that the properties are all read-only.

Table 9.33   *Properties and Methods of the* server *Object*

Type	Item	Description
Method	lock()	Locks your code while you perform data manipulation that should only have a single thread connected to it.
	unlock()	Unlocks previously locked code.
	unwatch()	Turns off the watch for a particular property.
	watch()	Turns on the watch for a particular property.
Property	host	Specifies the server name, sub-domain, and domain name of the Web server.
	hostname	Contains the same information as concatenating the host property with the port property and separating them with a colon.
	port	Specifies the port number on which the server is running.
	protocol	Contains the protocol portion of the URL. This includes the information up to the first colon, as in http:.

Example

Listing 9.221 uses the lock() and unlock() methods of the server object to lock the working code while the property, totalHits, is modified.

Listing 9.221   *Accessing Properties of the* server *Object*

```
<server>

// Lock the code and increment a server counter.
server.lock();
server.totalHits += 1;

// Unlock the code.
server.unlock();

</server>
```

server.host

ES2+

Syntax

```
server.host
```

Description

The host property of the server object contains the server name, any sub-domain, and domain name of the Web server.

Example

Listing 9.222 writes the host of the server to the user's page.

Listing 9.222   *Accessing the* host *Property*

```
<server>

// Write the host property to the user's page.
write(server.host);

</server>
```

server.hostname

ES2+

Syntax

```
server.hostname
```

Description

The hostname property of the server object contains the server name, any sub-domain, domain name, and port of the Web server. This property is the same as concatenating the host property with the port property and separating them with a colon.

Example

Listing 9.223 writes the hostname of the server to the user's page.

Listing 9.223   Accessing the hostname *Property*

```
<server>

// Write the hostname property to the user's page.
write(server.hostname);

</server>
```

server.lock()

ES2+

Syntax

```
server.lock()
```

Description

The lock() method of the server object locks the code in which you are working until you perform an unlock. If the code is already locked, this method will wait until it can get the lock, a timeout occurs, or an error occurs.

Example

Listing 9.224 sets a server object with a counter property, *totalHits*. Because you only want to increment the counter with each new user request on each application, it must be locked.

Listing 9.224   Using the lock() *Method to Lock Your Code*

```
<server>

// Lock the code and increment a server counter
server.lock();
server.totalHits += 1;

// Unlock the application
server.unlock();

</server>
```

server.port

ES2+

Syntax

```
server.port
```

Description

The port property of the server object contains the port number to which the Web server is responding.

Example

Listing 9.225 writes the port of the server to the user's page.

Listing 9.225   Accessing the port *Property*

```
<server>

// Write the port property to the user's page.
write(server.port);

</server>
```

server.protocol

ES2+

Syntax

```
server.protocol
```

Description

The protocol property of the server object contains the protocol to which the server is responding. This includes the information up to the first colon, as in http:.

Example

Listing 9.226 writes the protocol of the server to the user's page.

Listing 9.226   Accessing the protocol *Property*

```
<server>

// Write the protocol property to the user's page.
write(server.protocol);

</server>
```

server.unlock()

ES2+

Syntax

```
server.unlock()
```

Description

The unlock() method of the server object unlocks the code that you have locked. This method returns true if the unlocking was successful and false otherwise.

Example

Listing 9.227 sets a server object with a counter property, *hitCount*. Because you only want to increment the counter with each new user request, it must be locked. When the counter has been incremented, the project is unlocked.

Listing 9.227 *Using the* unlock() *Method to Unlock Your Code*

```
<server>

// Lock the code and increment a server counter.
server.lock();
server.hitCount += 1;

// Unlock the code.
server.unlock();

</server>
```

server.unwatch()

ES3+

Syntax

```
server.unwatch(property)
```

Description

The unwatch() method of the server object is used to turn off the watch for a particular *property*.

Example

Listing 9.228 shows how the unwatch() method is used to stop watching the user-defined property *p*.

Listing 9.228 *Example of the* unwatch() *Method*

```
<server>

// function that is called if property's value changes
function alertme(id, oldValue, newValue){
  write("ID (" + id + ") changed from " + oldValue + " to " + newValue);
  return newValue;
}

// watch property incase it changes
server.watch("hostname", alertme);

// turn off watch
server.unwatch("hostname");

</server>
```

server.watch()

ES3+

Syntax

```
server.watch(property, function)
```

Description

The watch() method of the server object is used to turn on the watch for a particular property specified by *property*. Any time the specified *property* is changed after the watch() method has been called, the specified *function* is called.

Example

Listing 9.229 shows how the watch() method is used to start watching the user-defined property *p*.

Listing 9.229   *Example of* watch() *method*

```
<server>

// function that is called if property's value changes
function alertme(id, oldValue, newValue){
  write("ID (" + id + ") changed from " + oldValue + " to " + newValue);
  return newValue;
}

// watch property in case it changes
server.watch("hostname", alertme);

</server>
```

Session

ASP1+

Syntax

Core ASP environment object

Description

The Session object is a core ASP environment object. This object is used to store information about a particular user in a session. This information will last for the user's entire session, not just the current page she is on. The server automatically creates this object when a user without a session makes a request. Table 9.34 contains the list of collections, events, methods, and properties available from this object.

Table 9.34   Contains the Collections, Events, Methods, and Properties Available from the Session *Object*

Type	Item	Description
Collection	Contents	Contains items added to the session with script commands.
	StaticObjects	Contains objects created with the <object> tag and given session scope.
Event	Session_OnEnd	Declared in the Global.asa file.
	Session_OnStart	Declared in the Global.asa file.
Method	Abandon()	Destroys a Session object and releases its resources.
	Contents.Remove()	Deletes an item from the Contents collection.
	Contents.RemoveAll()	Deletes all items from the Contents collection.
Property	CodePage	Sets the code page that will be used for symbol mapping.
	LCID	Identifies Locale.
	SessionID	Returns the session identification for this user.
	Timeout	Specifies the timeout period for the session state.

Example

Listing 9.230 shows how you can use the Timeout property of the Session object to specify the number of minutes before a script session ends.

Listing 9.230   Using the Session *Object*

```
<script runat="server" type="text/jscript" language="JScript">
Session.Timeout = 15;
</script>
```

Session.Abandon()

ASP1+

Syntax

```
Session.Abandon()
```

Description

The Abandon() method of the Session object destroys all items that have been added to a given Session instance, and frees all resources they were consuming. If this method is not called explicitly, the server invokes it when a session has ended.

> **NOTE**
>
> When this method is called, the resources and items are not cleared until the page finishes processing. So, it is possible to use items that have been *marked* for abandonment on the current page, but not on subsequent pages.

Example

Listing 9.231 creates an item for the session, destroys all items in the session, and then creates a new item. After this has completed, the script attempts to write both items to the page. Because these are both on the same page as the Abandon() method call, both will be written. However, the *version* item will not be accessible on subsequent pages in the same session.

Listing 9.231   *Using the* Abandon() *Method*

```
<script runat="server" type="text/jscript" language="JScript">

// Create a "version" item that will only last for this page.
Session("version") = "1.0";

// Destroy session.
Session.Abandon();

// Create a new item that will last until another Abandon()
// is called, or session ends.
Session("name") = "Allen";

// Try writing both to the page.
Response.Write(Session("version"));
Response.Write(Session("name"));
</script>
```

Session.CodePage

ASP1+

Syntax

```
Session.CodePage(codepage)
```

Description

The CodePage property of the Session object determines the code page that will be used for displaying dynamic content. Code page is a numeric value for the character set that is used to identify different languages and locales.

Example

Listing 9.232 sets the CodePage property to represent American English ANSI content.

Listing 9.232   Using the CodePage **Property**

```
<script runat="server" type="text/jscript" language="JScript">
Session.CodePage(1252);
</script>
```

Session.Contents

ASP1+

Syntax

```
Session.Contents(name)
```

Description

The Contents collection of the Session object contains a collection of items that have been created for the session instance without the use of the <object> element. You can access specific items by their *name*. This collection also has Remove() and RemoveAll() methods.

Example

Listing 9.233 shows how you can add items to a Session object instance, access specific items through the Contents collection, and then clear all the items using the RemoveAll() method.

Listing 9.233   Using the Contents **Collection**

```
<script runat="server" type="text/jscript" language="JScript">

// Add some items to the session.
Session("version") = "1.0";
Session("author") = "R. Allen Wyke";

// Access the "author" item.
Response.Write(Session.Contents("author"));

// Now remove all the items in the Session object.
Session.Contents.RemoveAll();
</script>
```

Session.Contents.Remove()

ASP1+

Syntax

```
Session.Contents.Remove(name)
Session.Contents.Remove(num)
```

Description

The Remove() method of the Contents collection of the Session object can be used to remove the *name* item from the collection. Additionally, you can specify the *num* index location and remove the items using this method as well.

Example

Listing 9.234 shows how you can add items to a Session object instance, access specific items through the Contents collection, and then clear the item using the Remove() method.

Listing 9.234   *Using the* Remove() *Method*

```
<script runat="server" type="text/jscript" language="JScript">

// Add some items to the session.
Session("version") = "1.0";
Session("author") = "R. Allen Wyke";

// Access the "author" item.
Response.Write(Session.Contents("author"));

// Now remove the "author" item from the Session object.
Session.Contents.Remove("author");
</script>
```

Session.Contents.RemoveAll()

ASP1+

Syntax

```
Session.Contents.RemoveAll()
```

Description

The RemoveAll() method of the Contents collection of the Session object removes all items that have been added to the session.

Example

Listing 9.235 shows how you can add items to a Session object instance, access specific items through the Contents collection, and then clear all the items using the RemoveAll() method.

Listing 9.235   *Using the* RemoveAll() *Method*

```
<script runat="server" type="text/jscript" language="JScript">

// Add some items to the session.
Session("version") = "1.0";
Session("author") = "R. Allen Wyke";
```

```
// Access the "author" item.
Response.Write(Session.Contents("author"));

// Now remove all the items in the Session object.
Session.Contents.RemoveAll();
</script>
```

Session.LCID

ASP1+

Syntax

```
Session.LCID
```

Description

The LCID property of the Session object sets the locale identifier to display dynamic content. This explicit setting will override any @LCID directives you might have set in your file.

Example

Listing 9.236 shows how you can set the locale identifier to British English.

Listing 9.236   Using the LCID *Property*

```
<script runat="server" type="text/jscript" language="JScript">
Session.LCID = 2057;
</script>
```

Session.SessionID

ASP1+

Syntax

```
Session.SessionID
```

Description

The SessionID property of the Session object contains the unique identifier generated by the server for the current Session object instance.

Example

Listing 9.237 writes out the value of the current SessionID property.

Listing 9.237   Using the SessionID *Property*

```
<script runat="server" type="text/jscript" language="JScript">
Response.Write(Session.SessionID);
</script>
```

Session.Session_OnEnd
ASP1+

Syntax
```
function Session_OnEnd(){
  code
}
```

Description
The Session_OnEnd event function of the Session object is called when the Session_OnEnd event is fired. This occurs when a session ends or times out.

Example
Listing 9.238 shows how you can append a string to the end of the log file of the last request of a session.

Listing 9.238 Using the Session_OnEnd Event
```
<script runat="server" type="text/jscript" language="JScript">
function Session_OnEnd(){
  Response.AppendToLog("Your session has ended");
}
</script>
```

Session.Session_OnStart
ASP1+

Syntax
```
function Session_OnStart(){
  code
}
```

Description
The Session_OnStart event function of the Session object is called when the Session_OnStart event is fired. This occurs when the session starts.

Example
Listing 9.239 shows how you can append a string to the end of the log file on the first request of a session.

Listing 9.239 Using the Session_OnStart Event
```
<script runat="server" type="text/jscript" language="JScript">
function Session_OnStart(){
  Response.AppendToLog("Your application has started");
}
</script>
```

Session.StaticObjects

ASP1+

Syntax

```
Session.StaticObjects(name)
```

Description

The StaticObjects collection of the Session object stores all the objects created with <object> elements within the scope of a given session. These are referenced by the name given to each instance of the elements.

Example

Listing 9.240 shows how you can grab the instance *myControl* from your current ASP page.

Listing 9.240 ***Using the*** StaticObjects ***Collection***

```
<script runat="server" type="text/jscript" language="JScript">
Session.StaticObjects("myControl");
</script>
```

Session.Timeout

ASP1+

Syntax

```
Session.Timeout
```

Description

The Timeout property of the Session object specifies the number of minutes that should elapse before the current session times out.

Example

Listing 9.241 shows how you can use the Timeout property of the Session object to specify the number of minutes before a session ends.

Listing 9.241 ***Using the*** Timeout ***Property***

```
<script runat="server" type="text/jscript" language="JScript">
Session.Timeout = 15;
</script>
```

ssjs_generateClientID()

ES3+

Syntax

```
ssjs_generateClientID()
```

Description

The ssjs_generateClientID() function is a top-level function that is not associated with any core server-side object. This function returns a unique identifier from the run-time engine. This allows you to track a user's session across several pages when using client-side maintenance. You might want to store the identifier as a property of the client object, but be careful to keep it from being accessed by other clients.

Example

Listing 9.242 shows how you can assign a property of the client object an identifier to track a user.

Listing 9.242   Using the ssjs_generateClientID() Function

```
<server>

// Store the identifier in a client property.
client.sessionID = ssjs_generateClientID();

</server>
```

ssjs_getCGIVariable()

ES3+

Syntax

```
_ssjs_getCGIVariable(envVariable)
```

Description

The ssjs_getCGIVariable() function is a top-level function that is not associated with any core server-side object. This function allows you to retrieve environment variables that are available to your CGI processes. When a variable cannot be found, the function returns null. Table 9.35 contains the default list of variables you can access.

Table 9.35   Environment Variables Accessible by the ssjs_getCGIVariable() Function

Variable	Description
AUTH_TYPE	The authorization type if the request is protected by a type of authorization. This returns values such as basic.
HTTPS	This shows if security is active on the server. This returns values of ON or OFF.
HTTPS_KEYSIZE	The number of bits in the key used to encrypt the session.
HTTPS_SECRETKEYSIZE	The number of bits used to generate the server's private key.
PATH_INFO	Path information to the file you want to retrieve. This would be something similar to /sports/baseball.html.

Variable	Description
PATH_TRANSLATED	The actual path to the file you want to retrieve. This would be something similar to */netscape/suitespot/docs/sports/baseball.html*.
QUERY_STRING	Any information after a ? character in the URL.
REMOTE_ADDR	The IP address of the host submitting the request.
REMOTE_HOST	The hostname address of the host submitting the request. DNS must be turned on for this feature.
REMOTE_USER	The name of the local HTTP user of the Web browser, if access authorization is turned on for this URL.
REQUEST_METHOD	The type of request that is being made, such as GET or POST.
SCRIPT_NAME	The filename you are trying to retrieve, such as *index.html*.
SERVER_NAME	The hostname or IP under which the server is running.
SERVER_PORT	The port number to which the server is responding.
SERVER_PROTOCOL	The protocol version supported by the requesting client, such as HTTP/1.0.
SERVER_URL	The URL a user would have to enter to access the server, such as *http://www.purejavascript.com:6969*.

Example

Listing 9.243 returns the SERVER_URL variable to a property of the server object.

Listing 9.243   *Retrieving an Environment Variable*

```
<server>

// Store the identifier in a server property.
server.serverURL = ssjs_getCGIVariable(SERVER_URL);

</server>
```

ssjs_getClientID()
ES3+

Syntax

```
ssjs_getClientID()
```

Description

The ssjs_getClientID() function is a top-level function that is not associated with any core server-side object. This function returns a unique identifier from the runtime engine. This allows you to track a user's session across several pages when using server-side maintenance. When using this function, there is no need to store the identifier as a property of the client object.

Example

Listing 9.244 writes the identifier generated by the `ssjs_getClientID()` function to the page.

Listing 9.244   Seeing the `ssjs_getClientID` ***Function***

```
<server>

// Store the identifier in a variable.
var myIdentifier = ssjs_getClientID();

// Write the ID to the page.
write(myIdentifier);

</server>
```

Stproc

ES3+

Syntax

Core object created by the `storedProc()` method of the database or `Connection` objects.

Description

The `Stproc` object is a core server-side object that is created by the `storedProc()` method of the `database` or `Connection` objects. Because of the nature of connections to a database, you should call the `close()` method of this object when you have completed your processing. This will free any and all memory used by the stored procedure. Otherwise, the object will be destroyed when the `database` or `Connection` objects go out of scope.

The object itself has only one property—`prototype`. This property can be used to add methods and properties to the object as needed. Table 9.36 lists the methods of the `Stproc` object.

Table 9.36   Methods of the `Stproc` ***Object***

Method	Description
`close()`	Closes a stored procedure instance
`outParamCount()`	Returns the number of output parameters from the stored procedure
`outParameters()`	Returns the value of the output parameter passed to the method
`resultSet()`	Creates a new `Resultset` object
`returnValue()`	Returns the return value for the stored procedure
`unwatch()`	Turns off the watch for a particular property
`watch()`	Turns on the watch for a particular property

Example

Listing 9.245 creates an instance of the Stproc object, via a Connection. storedProc() method call, and then closes it.

Listing 9.245 *Creating an Instance of the* Stproc *Object*

```
<server>

// Open a connection.
var myConn = database.connect("ORACLE", "mySID", "myApp", "appsPWD", "myTNS");

myConn.beginTransaction();

// Run the stored procedure.
var myStproc = myConn.storedProc("sp_employees");

// Commit the transaction.
myConn.commitTransaction();

// Close the resultset.
myConn.close();

</server>
```

Stproc.close()

ES3+

Syntax

```
stproc.close()
```

Description

The close() method of the Stproc object closes the stored procedure and frees all memory used to store its information. If successful, the method returns 0; otherwise, it returns an error code that can be obtained by using the majorErrorCode() and majorErrorMessage() methods of the Connection or database objects.

Example

Listing 9.246 creates a stored procedure and then closes it.

Listing 9.246 *Closing a Cursor with the* close() *Method*

```
<server>

// Open a connection.
var myConn = database.connect("ORACLE", "mySID", "myApp", "appsPWD", "myTNS");

myConn.beginTransaction();
```

Listing 9.246   Continued

```
// Run the stored procedure.
var myStproc = myConn.storedProc("sp_employees");

// Store the resultset.
var myResultSet = myStproc.resultSet();

// Commit the transaction.
myConn.commitTransaction();

// Close the resultset.
myResultSet.close();

</server>
```

Stproc.outParamCount()

ES3+

Syntax

stproc.outParamCount()

Description

The outParamCount() method of the Stproc object returns the number of output para-meters from the stored procedure. Be sure to call this method before calling the outParameters() method to make sure that parameters have been returned.

NOTE

Informix stored procedures do not have output parameters, so this method always returns 0 when run against an Informix database.

Example

Listing 9.247 opens a connection to the database and runs a stored procedure. Based on the number of output parameters, the script writes the parameters to the user's screen.

Listing 9.247   Using the outParamCount() **Method**

```
<server>

// Open a connection.
var myConn = database.connect("ORACLE", "mySID", "myApp", "appsPWD", "myTNS");

myConn.beginTransaction();

// Run the stored procedure.
var myStproc = myConn.storedProc("sp_employees");
```

```
// Write the output parameters of this stored procedure to the
// user's page.
for(var i = 0; i < myStproc.outParamCount(); i++){
  write(myStproc.outParameters(i) + '<br>');
}

// Close the resultset.
myStproc.close();

// Commit the transaction.
myConn.commitTransaction();

</server>
```

Stproc.outParameters()
ES3+

Syntax
stproc.outParameters(*num*)

Description
The outParameters() method of the Stproc object returns the output parameter from the stored procedure that is indexed at the *num* location. The return value of this method can be a string, number, double, or object. Be sure to call the outParamCount() method before calling this method to make sure that parameters have been returned.

> **NOTE**
>
> Informix stored procedures do not have output parameters, so there is no need to run this method.

Example
Listing 9.248 opens a connection to the database and runs a stored procedure. Based on the number of output parameters, the script writes the parameters to the user's screen.

Listing 9.248   Using the outParameters() **Method**

```
<server>

// Open a connection.
var myConn = database.connect("ORACLE", "mySID", "myApp", "appsPWD", "myTNS");

myConn.beginTransaction();
```

Listing 9.248   Continued

```
// Run the stored procedure.
var myStproc = myConn.storedProc("sp_employees");

// Write the output parameters of this stored procedure to the
// user's page.
for(var i = 0; i < myStproc.outParamCount(); i++){
  write(myStproc.outParameters(i) + '<br>');
}

// Close the resultset.
myStproc.close();

// Commit the transaction.
myConn.commitTransaction();

</server>
```

Stproc.prototype

ES2+

Syntax

```
stproc.prototype.method = name
stproc.prototype.property = value
```

Description

The `prototype` property of the `Stproc` object allows you to create new properties and methods of the object. If you are adding a method, set the instance equal to the *name* of the method you have defined.

Example

Listing 9.249 creates a new property and method of the `Stproc` object. An instance is created and the new property is set. The new method is then called to verify the property, and, if it is incorrect, an error message is written to the page.

Listing 9.249   Using the `prototype` **Property to Create a New Property and Method**

```
<server>

// Define the method that we prototyped.
function verifyWork(){

  // Check to see if the type property we added is set to a valid value.
  if(this.type == "work"){
    return true;
```

```
  }else{
    return false;
  }
}

// Create a new property and method of the Stproc object.
Stproc.prototype.type = null;
Stproc.prototype.isWORK = verifyWork;

// Create a pool of connections, a connection, a stored procedure,
// and a resultset.
var myPool = new DbPool("ORACLE", "mySID", "myApp", "appsPWD", "myTNS");
var myConn = myPool.connection('Employees', 15);
var myStproc = myConn.storedProc("sp_employees");

// Using the prototype we defined, assign the type property.
myStproc.type = "work";

// Check the type of the stored procedure to see if it is valid.
if(myStproc.isWORK()){
  write(myStproc + " has a valid type of " + myStproc.type);
}else{
  write(myStproc + " has an invalid type of " + myStproc.type);
}

</server>
```

Stproc.resultSet()

ES3+

Syntax

`stproc.resultSet()`

Description

The resultSet() method of the Stproc object creates a Resultset object for storing the results of running a stored procedure. For stored procedures run against DB2, Oracle, Sybase, and ODBC databases, the stored procedure object has one Resultset object for each SQL SELECT statement executed by the procedure. An Informix stored procedure, on the other hand, has one Resultset object.

Each instance of this object has a property for each column in the result set. For Oracle, Sybase, and ODBC stored procedures, these properties can be referred to by the column name. Informix and DB2 stored procedures do not have named columns, so you must use a zero-based numeric index to refer to the column.

You should always call the `close()` method of the `Stproc` object after you have finished. The JavaScript runtime will attempt to close the object when the associated
`DbPool` or database object goes out of scope.

NOTE

After creating a resultset, you must perform all operations on the set before calling
the `commitTransaction()`, `returnValue()`, `outParameters()`,
`Connection.cursor()`, or `Connection.SQLTable()` method.

Example

Listing 9.250 creates a connection to a database. After the connection has been verified, the `storedProc()` method is used to invoke the fictitious *sp_employees* stored
procedure. The resultsets for this stored procedure are then held in an instance of the
`Resultset` object that was created with the `resultSet()` method.

Listing 9.250   Calling the *resultSet()* Method

```
<server>

// Open a connection.
var myConn = database.connect("ORACLE", "mySID", "myApp", "appsPWD", "myTNS");

if(myConn.connected()){

  myConn.beginTransaction();

  // Run the stored procedure.
  var myStproc = myConn.storedProc("sp_employees");

  myResultSet = myStproc.resultSet();

  // Commit the transaction.
  myConn.commitTransaction();

  // Close the resultset.
  myResultSet.close();

  // Release the connection.
  myConn.release();

// If the connection fails, write an error message.
}else{
  write('Error ('+myConn.majorErrorCode()+'): '' + myConn.majorErrorMessage();
}

</server>
```

Stproc.returnValue()

ES3+

Syntax

`stproc.returnValue()`

Description

The `returnValue()` method of the `Stproc` object returns the return value of the stored procedure. For DB2, Informix, and ODBC, this method always returns `null`. Oracle only returns `null` if the stored procedure did not return a value. Sybase always returns a value.

> **NOTE**
>
> Before you call this method, you must retrieve any `Resultset` objects. When this method is called, no more data can be obtained from the current resultset and no more resultsets can be created.

Example

Listing 9.251 calls a stored procedure, creates a resultset, and obtains the result value. This value is then written to the user's page.

Listing 9.251   Accessing a Stored Procedure's Return Value Using the `returnValue()` **Method**

```
<server>

// Call the stored procedure.
var myStproc = database.storedProc("sp_employees");

// Generate a resultset.
var myResultset = myStproc.resultSet();

// Get the return value. Note that you can no longer
// reference the myResultset variable.
var myReturnValue = myStproc.returnValue();

// Write the resultset to the page.
write(myReturnValue);

</server>
```

Stproc.unwatch()

ES3+

Syntax

`stproc.unwatch(property)`

Description

The unwatch() method of the Stproc object is used to turn off the watch for a particular *property*.

Example

Listing 9.252 shows how the unwatch() method is used to stop watching the user-defined property *p*.

Listing 9.252   Example of the unwatch() **Method**

```
<server>

// Define the method that we prototyped.
function verifyWork(){

  // Check to see if the type property we added is set to a valid value.
  if(this.type == "work"){
    return true;
  }else{
    return false;
  }
}

// Create a new property and method of the Stproc object.
Stproc.prototype.type = null;
Stproc.prototype.isWORK = verifyWork;

// Create a pool of connections, a connection, a stored procedure,
// and a resultset.
var myPool = new DbPool("ORACLE", "mySID", "myApp", "appsPWD", "myTNS");
var myConn = myPool.connection('Employees', 15);
var myStproc = myConn.storedProc("sp_employees");

// Using the prototype we defined, assign the type property.
myStproc.type = "work";

// Check the type of the stored procedure to see if it is valid.
if(myStproc.isWORK()){
  write(myStproc + " has a valid type of " + myStproc.type);
}else{
  write(myStproc + " has an invalid type of " + myStproc.type);
}

// watch property
myStproc.watch("type", alertme);

// change value
myStproc.type = null;
```

```
// turn off watch
myStproc.unwatch("type");

// change value again
myStproc.type = "home";

</server>
```

Stproc.watch()
ES3+

Syntax
stproc.watch(property, function)

Description
The watch() method of the stproc object is used to turn on the watch for a particular property specified by *property*. Any time the specified *property* is changed after the watch() method has been called, the specified *function* is called.

Example
Listing 9.253 shows how the watch() method is used to start watching the user defined property *p*.

Listing 9.253 Example of the watch() Method

```
<server>

// Define the method that we prototyped.
function verifyWork(){

  // Check to see if the type property we added is set to a valid value.
  if(this.type == "work"){
    return true;
  }else{
    return false;
  }
}

// Create a new property and method of the Stproc object.
Stproc.prototype.type = null;
Stproc.prototype.isWORK = verifyWork;

// Create a pool of connections, a connection, a stored procedure,
// and a resultset.
var myPool = new DbPool("ORACLE", "mySID", "myApp", "appsPWD", "myTNS");
var myConn = myPool.connection('Employees', 15);
var myStproc = myConn.storedProc("sp_employees");
```

Listing 9.253   Continued

```
// Using the prototype we defined, assign the type property.
myStproc.type = "work";

// Check the type of the stored procedure to see if it is valid.
if(myStproc.isWORK()){
  write(myStproc + " has a valid type of " + myStproc.type);
}else{
  write(myStproc + " has an invalid type of " + myStproc.type);
}

// watch property
myStproc.watch("type", alertme);

// change value
myStproc.type = null;

</server>
```

write()
ES2+

Syntax

```
write(string)
```

```
write(num)
```

```
write(expression)
```

Description

The write function is a top-level function that is not associated with any object. This function writes information to the HTML page the script is generating to send back to the client. This function can take and write a string, numeric value, or an expression that returns an alphanumeric result. To write data to a file, see the entry for File.write() and File.writeln().

> **TIP**
>
> The JavaScript runtime buffers all write data until 64KB have been collected. Then the buffer is flushed to the file. You can manually call the top-level flush function to improve performance of your pages, if they are waiting on database query results, by calling the function before you run the query.

Example

Listing 9.254 writes a string "Hello, World!" to the user's page.

Listing 9.254   Using the `write` *Function*

```
<server>

// Write a string to the page
write('Hello, World!');

</server>
```

INDEX

Special Note to Readers

*Chapters 1-9 are located in the book.
Chapters 10-15 appear on the CD. The
indexes found in both the book and the
CD are identical.*

*When you look up information in either
index, you will notice that some page
numbers have* **CD:** *before them. These
refer to pages found only on the CD. For
example, the following listing lets you know
whether information is located in the book
or on the CD:*

checked property, 615, CD:1585, CD:1590

Symbols

F

I

N

X-Y-Z